Lonely Planet Publications
Melbourne | Oakland | London | Paris

W9-BTJ-383

Steve Fallon

Hong Kong
& Macau

The Top Five

1 Peak Tram
The scarier-than-it-looks funicular up the Peak (p350)

2 Temple St night market
Nosh, live opera, fortune tellers and lots of cheap clothes (p106)

3 Tian Tan Buddha statue
Lantau's massive and much-hyped religious icon, which somehow retains its spirituality (p148)

4 Star Ferry
A memory-making way to cross Victoria Harbour, especially at night (p339)

5 Hong Kong Heritage Museum
A journey through Hong Kong history and culture, Cantonese opera and Chinese fine art (p133)

Contents

Published by Lonely Planet Publications Pty Ltd
ABN 36 005 607 983

Australia Head Office, Locked Bag1, Footscray
Victoria 3001, ☎ 03 8379 8000, fax 03 8379 8111
talk2us@lonelyplanet.com.au

USA 150 Linden St, Oakland, CA 94607
☎ 510 893 8555, toll free 800 275 8555
fax 510 893 8572, info@lonelyplanet.com

UK 72–82 Rosebery Ave, Clerkenwell, London,
EC1R 4RW ☎ 020 7841 9000, fax 020 7841 9001
go@lonelyplanet.co.uk

France 1 rue du Dahomey, 75011 Paris
☎ 01 55 25 33 00, fax 01 55 25 33 01
bip@lonelyplanet.fr, www.lonelyplanet.fr

© Lonely Planet 2004
Photographs © Phil Weymouth and as listed on p383,
2004

All rights reserved. No part of this publication may be
copied, stored in a retrieval system, or transmitted in any
form by any means, electronic, mechanical, recording
or otherwise, except brief extracts for the purpose of
review, and no part of this publication may be sold or
hired, without the written permission of the publisher.

Printed through The Bookmaker International Ltd.
Printed in China

Lonely Planet and the Lonely Planet logo are trade-
marks of Lonely Planet and are registered in the US
Patent and Trademark Office and in other countries.

Lonely Planet does not allow its name or logo to be
appropriated by commercial establishments, such as
retailers, restaurants or hotels. Please let us know of any
misuses: www.lonelyplanet.com/ip.

Although the authors and Lonely Planet have taken
all reasonable care in preparing this book, we make
no warranty about the accuracy or completeness of
its content and, to the maximum extent permitted,
disclaim all liability arising from its use.

The Authors

STEVE FALLON

 A native of Boston, Massachusetts, Steve graduated from Georgetown University with a Bachelor of Science in modern languages and then taught English at the University of Silesia near Katowice in Poland. After working for several years for an American daily newspaper and earning a master's degree in journalism, his fascination with the 'new' Asia led him to Hong Kong, where he lived for over a dozen years, working for a variety of media organisations and running a travel bookshop. Steve lived in Budapest for 2½ years before moving to London in 1994, and returns to his 'hometown' of Hong Kong regularly. He has written or contributed to more than two dozen Lonely Planet titles, including the Lonely Planet Journeys title *Home with Alice: A Journey in Gaelic Ireland*.

CONTRIBUTING AUTHOR
VICTORIA BUNTINE
Dr Buntine wrote the Health section for this guide. She worked as a general practitioner in Hong Kong for 10 years, dealing almost exclusively with expatriate workers and their families, as well as Western tourists visiting the region. She has been a regular contributor to the *Australian Association of Hong Kong* magazine since 1997, and in 1999 created a website (www.healthinasia.com) to store her articles.

PHOTOGRAPHER
PHIL WEYMOUTH
Phil's family moved from Australia to Iran in the late 1960s and called Tehran home until the revolution in 1979. Phil studied photography in Melbourne and returned to the Middle East to work as a photographer in Bahrain for several years. He then spent a decade working with an Australian rural media company. Currently he runs a freelance photojournalism business based in Melbourne, working for a variety of Australian and international media and publishing companies.

Past commissions for Lonely Planet include the guides to Hong Kong, Beijing and Shanghai. Phil continues to travel extensively, supplying images to Lonely Planet Images, writing stories and avoiding his office.

Lonely Planet books provide independent advice. Lonely Planet does not accept advertising in guidebooks, nor do we accept payment in exchange for listing or endorsing any place or business. Lonely Planet writers do not accept discounts or payments in exchange for positive coverage of any sort.

Introducing Hong Kong

Hong Kong is a pulsating, superlative-ridden fusion of West and East, an exercise in controlled chaos, a densely populated place that simply 'shouldn't be, but is'. Hong Kong is like no other city on earth.

The vast majority of the people of Hong Kong are Chinese; their customs, folklore and dreams are in Cantonese. The Chinese world, with its noise, activity, unusual dishes and language, is everywhere, but intruding into this sphere are familiar icons of the West – sparkling skyscrapers wedged between squatter huts, Christian churches next to Taoist and Buddhist temples, minimalist fusion restaurants beside noodle shops and *dai pai dong* (open-air street stalls). The meeting of these two worlds shakes and stirs into an invigorating cocktail of colour and aroma, taste and sensation.

Hong Kong has something for everyone. Shoppers will trip over themselves trying to reach the huge malls of Central, Admiralty and Kowloon, and the street-fashion factory outlets in Causeway Bay and Tsim Sha Tsui. Travellers with a sense of romance will gaze by night at the lights across Victoria Harbour or down from the Peak. Aficionados of modern architecture will appreciate Hong Kong's arresting Central district, and world-class museums abound for those who wish to dig deeper into local history and culture. For those who yearn for the great outdoors (or at least a bit more space), sandy beaches and secluded walks await.

Hong Kong has a surprising number of natural retreats. Much of Lantau Island, a short ferry ride away, is designated parkland. The New Territories cuts a huge swathe to the north and, while it is becoming increasingly urbanised, it still offers dramatic scenery, challenging hikes and one of the region's most important wetlands for birds.

Gastronomes will be spoiled for choice in the city's eclectic eateries, and not just when selecting Chinese and other Asian dishes; Hong Kong today is a veritable atlas of world food. Hong Kong's bars, pubs and clubs colour the spectrum, from the alternative and the chic to the oh-so-refined.

Just an hour by ferry to the west is charming, less-frenetic Macau, which returned to Chinese sovereignty in 1999 after some 450 years under Portuguese rule. Here, Portuguese and Chinese influences have combined to form a unique 'Macanese' culture, and the pastel-coloured Catholic churches and civic buildings, narrow streets, traditional shops and splendid Portuguese and Macanese food give Macau more a Mediterranean than southern Chinese feel. Macau brims not just with atmosphere but sights, including a host of superb museums.

My partner and I arrived in Hong Kong in late 1979, planning to spend a year or two in what was then a 'British-administered territory'. We left some 12½ years later, and for us Hong Kong remains every bit the 'moveable feast' that was Paris to Hemingway. Arrive with your eyes and ears open, your taste buds and olfactory senses primed and your fingers at the ready to see and hear, touch, smell and taste the essence of Hong Kong and its little neighbour across the Pearl River estuary. It may not last a dozen years, but your ride will be every bit as memorable as ours was.

STEVE'S TOP DAY

I awake early in a leafy section of the Mid-Levels and hop on the Central Escalator to Sheung Wan for a raucous dim sum breakfast. The MTR whisks me *sans correspondence* to Prince Edward station and the Yuen Po St Bird Garden and Flower Market for some quality time with favourite fronds and feathered friends. Feeling ambitious, I walk south through the shopping chaos of Nathan Rd, stopping to check out the colourful arcades of Chungking Mansions and perhaps have a quick Indian curry. Just over Salisbury Rd, the Hong Kong Museum of History is a peaceful (and highly instructive) oasis in which to spend an hour or two. On the Star Ferry towards Central I decide I haven't had enough of Hong Kong's mountains and water, and catch the boat to Yung Shue Wan to walk for an hour over the Lamma hills to Sok Kwu Wan. I may have some steamed prawns (and certainly a Tsingtao beer or two) at one of the waterfront restaurants before catching the ferry back to Central. Depending on my mood, I'll meet friends at the Foreign Correspondents' Club or Lan Kwai Fong in Central, or jump on the tram to Wan Chai for a pub crawl.

City Life

City Life

HONG KONG TODAY

'Hong Kong spins clichés and superlatives as furiously as it does garments,' I once wrote in the introduction of a series of articles for a Hong Kong–based travel magazine. And while the latter is history, with all the mills and factories having moved to the Shenzhen Special Economic Zone (SEZ) long ago, the former is as true as it was almost 20 years ago when the articles first appeared. 'Hong Kong is like no other place in the world, where the East collides head on with the West' was from an article that dealt with the territory as an exotic destination, while 'Hong Kong is a capitalist mouse at the foot of a communist giant (or, alternatively, the pimple on Goliath's bottom)' spoke about the political realities of the time. And its people – both local and foreign? 'Hong Kong is ostensibly cosmopolitan, yet has all the gossip and scandal-mongering of a village' and 'Hong Kong people are overly materialistic, unfriendly and rude' said it all.

But clichés and superlatives have always been acceptable to most people in the world's largest Cantonese city. How else is one to describe a place that shouldn't be, but is?

Hong Kong is, for certain, like no other place on earth. Almost 7 million people call a territory of just 1100 sq km home, but are squeezed on to about 10% of the available land space. That means 14 million elbows all seeking room, along with the usual problems inherent to any big city: smog, odour, clutter and clatter.

The long-anticipated handover of the territory from the UK to the People's Republic of China (PRC) brought to an end Hong Kong's 150-odd years as a borrowed place on borrowed time. Prophets of doom and gloom had much to say about how things would turn out after 30 June 1997, but the new Special Administrative Region (SAR) of Hong Kong woke up the next morning and did what it has always done best: it went back to work.

Unfortunately, the timing was all wrong. The financial crisis that had rocked Southeast Asia began to be felt in Hong Kong at the end of that year. It has since worsened (with deflation making itself at home here) and this, combined with both terrorist activities worldwide and Severe Acute Respiratory Syndrome (SARS; see p362), has decimated tourist numbers and forced tens of thousands of companies out of business. In a city where 'just yesterday' someone's amah (maid) could make HK$1 million overnight on a good stock market tip, many homeowners today are unable to meet their mortgage payments and many more are losing their jobs. Another cliché has been born: the early years of the 21st century have not been Hong Kong's glory days.

It would be easy (and tempting) to lay all the blame at the feet of Chief Executive Tung Chee Hwa, now in his second five-year term and viewed by many as weak, indecisive and lacking the gumption to confront the problem head on. But there are far too many other factors for such a facile analysis, including the ongoing economic crisis in Japan, the loss of Hong Kong markets in the USA, the downturn in tourism worldwide and the ascendancy of Shanghai.

Pedestrians, Soho.

Did You Know...

- That Kwun Tong District in New Kowloon is the most densely populated place on earth, with 50,080 people per sq km?
- That Hong Kong is the world's leading exporter of garments, imitation jewellery, travel goods, handbags, umbrellas, artificial flowers, toys and clocks (most of it actually made in China)?
- That the world's tallest (outdoor, seated and bronze) Buddha statue is on Lantau?
- That Hong Kong consumes more oranges than any other place on earth?
- That the territory has the world's highest per-capita consumption of cognac, accounting for more than 10% of the worldwide market?
- That British writer and humorist PG Wodehouse was the son of a Hong Kong police superintendent or that US actor Clark Gable supposedly introduced a drink called the Screwdriver to the Peninsula Hotel bar?

Yet despite all its recent setbacks, Hong Kong remains a vibrant and exciting place in which to live and work. On the surface, at least, Hong Kong looks cleaner and, judging from the plethora of 'green' posters in the MTR, the newspaper articles about pollution in the territory and the letters to the editor, improving the environment appears to be a major concern among Hong Kong people. At the same time, the local film and music industries continue to thrive, the home-grown 'rag trade' appears to have found a new voice both in high-class threads and street fashion, and the restaurants and bars continue to do a brisk trade. Every year new skyscrapers enhance the skyline of Central and elsewhere in the territory.

It remains to be seen where Hong Kong will be in 50 years' time; whether it will retain its position as Asia's top financial centre and port or return to being the sleepy backwater it was before WWII and the formation of the PRC. But Hong Kong has always been adept at reinventing itself – changing chameleon-like from treaty port to manufacturing base to high-tech financial centre – and there's no reason to doubt that it won't do so again.

Not everyone is so optimistic, however. In her *Hong Kong: Epilogue to an Empire*, published just before the handover, Jan Morris wondered whether 'the story of Hong Kong, its brilliant rise to glory, its precipitous end, is likely to leave profounder messages behind'. In a subsequent edition published three years later she believed she had found the answer: 'No messages…no useful examples, no parables: only the pang of melancholy we must all feel when something strange and wonderful recedes into history.'

We respectfully disagree.

CITY CALENDAR

No matter what the time of year, you're almost certain to find some colourful festival or event occurring in Hong Kong. Exact dates vary from year to year, so if you want to time your visit to coincide with a particular event, it would be wise to check the website of the Hong Kong Tourism Board (www.discoverhongkong.com).

Many Chinese red-letter days, both public holidays and privately observed affairs, go back hundreds, even thousands, of years, and the true origins of some are often lost in the mists of time. Most (but not all) are celebrated in both Hong Kong and Macau. For festivals and events specific to Macau, see p292. For dates of public holidays, see p362.

January

CHINESE NEW YEAR

Southern China's most important public holiday period; takes place in late January/early February (see 'Kung Hei Fat Choi!' p10).

HONG KONG FRINGE CLUB CITY FESTIVAL

The alternative Fringe Club sponsors three weeks of performances between late January and early February by an eclectic mix of up-and-coming local and overseas artists and performers.

INTERNATIONAL CHINESE NEW YEAR PARADE

This relatively new annual event, which began in 2001, takes place between late January

Kung Hei Fat Choi!

The Lunar New Year is the most important holiday of the Chinese year. Expect a lot of colourful decorations but not much public merrymaking; for the most part, this is a festival for the family, though there is a parade on the first day, a fantastic fireworks display over Victoria Harbour on the evening of the second day, and one of the largest horse races is held at Sha Tin on day three.

Chinese New Year, which is called Spring Festival on the mainland, begins on the first new moon after the sun enters Aquarius (any time between 21 January and 19 February) and ends, at least officially, 15 days later. In Hong Kong it is a three-day public holiday and celebrated for four days.

The build-up to the holiday – the end of the month known as the 'Bitter Moon' since it's the coldest part of the year in Hong Kong – is very busy as family members clean house, get haircuts and cook, all of which are activities prohibited during the holiday. Debts and feuds are settled and all employees get a one-month New Year bonus.

You'll see many symbols in Hong Kong at this time of year, all of which have special meaning for people here. Chinese use a lot of indirect speak, and 'punning' is very important in the use of symbols. A picture of a boy holding a *gamyu* (goldfish) and a *he* (lotus) is wishing you 'abundant gold and harmony' since that's what the words can also mean when a different tone is used to say them. Symbols of bats are everywhere; its name in Chinese *(fu)* also means 'good luck'. The peach and plum blossoms decorating restaurants and public spaces symbolise both the arrival of spring and 'immortality', while the golden fruit of the kumquat tree is associated with good fortune. The red and gold banners you'll see in doorways are wishing all and sundry 'prosperity', 'peace' or just 'spring'.

Of course, much of the symbolism and well-wishing has to do with wealth and prosperity. Indeed, 'kung hei fat choi', the most common New Year greeting in southern China, literally means 'respectful wishes, get rich'. The *laisee* packet is very important. It's a small red and gold envelope in which bills in pairs or sums of eight (*bat*, which also means 'prosper') are enclosed and given as gifts.

The first day of Chinese New Year will fall on 9 February in 2005 and 29 January in 2006.

and early February at the Tamar (now the PLA Central Barracks) site and along the waterfront between Central and Wan Chai.

February

SPRING LANTERN FESTIVAL
A colourful on the 15th day of the first moon (mid- to late February) marking the end of the New Year period and the day for lovers.

HONG KONG MARATHON
This major sporting event also includes a half-marathon and 10km race.

HONG KONG ARTS FESTIVAL
Hong Kong's most important cultural event is a month-long extravaganza of music, performing arts and exhibitions by hundreds of local and international artists. It takes place between February and March.

March

HONG KONG INVITATIONAL SEVEN-A-SIDE RUGBY TOURNAMENT
The 'Rugby Sevens', Hong Kong's premier sporting event, is held over three days around late March/early April at Hong Kong Stadium and attracts teams from all over the world.

April

CHING MING
A family celebration, held in early April, when people visit and clean the graves of ancestors.

HONG KONG INTERNATIONAL FILM FESTIVAL
This is a 16-day extravaganza with screenings of more than 200 films from around the world.

BIRTHDAY OF TIN HAU
A festival in honour of the patroness of fisherfolk and one of the territory's most popular goddesses; in Macau it is known as the A-Ma Festival. It is held around late April/early May.

CHEUNG CHAU BUN FESTIVAL
Taking place around late April/early May, this is an unusual festival that is observed uniquely on Cheung Chau (see 'Going for the Buns' p143).

May

BIRTHDAY OF LORD BUDDHA
A public holiday during which Buddha's statue is taken from monasteries and temples and ceremoniously bathed in scented water.

June

DRAGON BOAT FESTIVAL

Also known as Tuen Ng (Double Fifth) as it falls on the fifth day of the fifth moon. It commemorates the death of Qu Yuan, a poet-statesman of the 3rd century BC who hurled himself into the Mi Lo River in Hunan province to protest against a corrupt government; traditional rice dumplings are eaten in memory of the event, and dragon-boat races are held in at Shau Kei Wan, Aberdeen, Yau Ma Tei and Tai Po, as well as on Lantau, Cheung Chau and in Macau, but the most famous is at Stanley.

HONG KONG INTERNATIONAL DRAGON BOAT RACES

This event takes place a week after the local dragon boat races (between June and early July).

August

MAIDENS' FESTIVAL

A minor holiday, also known as Seven Sisters Day, that's held on the seventh day of the seventh moon and reserved for girls and young lovers.

HUNGRY GHOSTS FESTIVAL

Celebrated on the first day of the seventh moon (between August and September), when the gates of hell are opened and 'hungry ghosts' (restless spirits) are freed for two weeks to walk the earth. On the 14th day, paper 'hell' money and votives in the shape of cars, houses and clothing are burned for the ghosts, and food is offered.

HONG KONG INTERNATIONAL ARTS CARNIVAL

This unusual festival promotes performances by and for children.

September

MID-AUTUMN FESTIVAL

A colourful festival held on the 15th night of the eighth moon (sometime in September or October). It marks an uprising against the Mongols in the 14th century when plans for a revolution were passed around in little round cakes known as moon cakes, which are still eaten on this day.

October

CHEUNG YEUNG

Celebrated on the ninth day of the ninth month (mid- to late October), and based on a story from the Han dynasty (206 BC–AD 220), where an oracle advised a man to take his family to a high place to escape a plague. When he returned the man found every living thing had died. Many people still head for the hills on this day and also visit the graves of ancestors.

November

HONG KONG OPEN GOLF CHAMPIONSHIPS

Hong Kong's premier golfing event, also part of the Asian PGA Tour, is held at the Fanling Golf Course in late November.

CULTURE

THE PSYCHE OF THE SAR

It *is* easy to describe the Hong Kong Special Administrative Region as the place where 'East meets West', but the cliché reduces Hong Kong to a mere gateway or bridge through or over which Chinese and Western influences pass, denying it any separate identity. This is far from the truth.

It's difficult – and dangerous – to generalise about a city and a society of almost 7 million people, but we'll give it a go anyway. The most common preconceptions about Hong Kong people in the past were that they were racist and greedy and, in the case of service staff, discourteous to the point of being rude.

The word *gwailo*, meaning 'ghost person' (*gwaipo* is used for white women, *hakgwai* for a 'black ghost'), was used regularly and often contemptuously. And although Caucasians have 'possessed' this word and use it jocularly among themselves, it was – and remains – a deeply pejorative word in Hong Kong; ask any Chinese. Now there's even a **Race Relations Unit** (☎ 2835 1579) within the Home Affairs Bureau to deal with complaints against racial discrimination.

It's true that some travellers may find the consumerism here almost offensive. But as the award-winning 1985 documentary series on China, *Heart of the Dragon*, pointed out: 'To understand a nation, you must know its memories.' For many middle-aged and older people in Hong Kong, these are memories of economic oppression, war and hunger. Hong Kong Chinese revel in the ability to make a buck – and spend it as they choose.

The rudeness seems to have all but disappeared, and everyone remarks on it. Some people say it's because the economic crisis had Hong Kong people eating humble pie for the first time in decades. Others say that when many Hong Kong Chinese people awoke on 1 July 1997 they realised something for the first time: they were different from their cousins on the mainland. Chinese, yes, through and through, but somehow different…

Not only could the foreigners stay, they were encouraged to do so (legally, of course). Otherwise, Hong Kong would just become another spot on the backside

of China, not the cosmopolitan place it was and, hopefully, will remain. It should be noted that, according to Hong Kong's Basic Law (effectively its constitution), Hong Kong SAR passports can only be issued to 'Chinese citizens who are Hong Kong permanent residents'. So race is the deciding factor – not place of birth. This also poses a problem for other nationalities, such as Hong Kong's centuries-old Indian community, whose numbers now stand at just under 22,000. They are issued Documents of Identity for Visa Purposes (or DIs) and are in effect stateless.

All this is not to make excuses for the colonial government or to suggest many people would like to see its return. On the contrary; until the arrival of the all-but-canonised Chris Patten as Hong Kong's last governor, the colonial government was an arrogant and patronising pseudo-democracy that at times could be as despotic, arbitrary and archaic as any tinpot dictatorship. Most Britons would be shocked if they understood fully just how

Population & People

Hong Kong's population is 6.787 million, with an annual growth rate of about 1.25%. Each year an estimated 55,000 legal immigrants from China move into the territory; there is estimated to be over 200,000 illegal immigrants from China here already. Hong Kong, once a very young society, is ageing; the median age rose from 30 in 1989 to 37 in 2001.

Almost half the population (48.1%) lives in the New Territories, followed by Kowloon (30.1%), Hong Kong Island (19.7%) and the Outlying Islands (2%). A tiny percentage (0.1%, or just under 6800 people) live at sea. The overall population density is 6250 people per sq km, but this figure is deceiving as the density varies greatly from district to district.

About 94% of Hong Kong's population is ethnic Chinese, most of whom can trace their origins to Guangdong province in southern China. Only about 57% of Hong Kong Chinese were actually born in the territory.

Hong Kong has a community of foreigners, but this figure is deceiving as well since many 'foreign passport holders' are Hong Kong Chinese. In any case, of the 410,680 people so described, the three largest groups are Filipinos at 147,310, Indonesians at 75,330 and Canadians at 31,930, closely followed by Americans at 31,180. Australians and Britons fall well behind at 21,020 and 20,610 respectively.

unenlightened *their* colonial government actually was. Homosexuality, for example, was outlawed (even between consenting adults) until – wait for it – 1991.

Hong Kong is Chinese, and an essential part of China. Everyone has known that since 1841; it just took a while to settle the matter. But it is now Chinese with an international flavour. This was thanks, to some degree, to more than 150 years under the *ying gwok yahn* (British). Was that too high a price to pay to produce one of the most dynamic and vibrant societies on earth? We humbly submit that it was not.

By Asian standards, Hong Kong is a highly educated society, with a literacy rate of about 93%. The education system is based on the British model. Education is free and compulsory for nine years (generally from ages six to 15). At secondary level, students begin to specialise; some go on to university or college preparatory programs, while others select vocational education combined with apprenticeships.

An ongoing debate in Hong Kong concerns the linguistic medium of instruction at secondary level. While primary school classes are taught almost exclusively in Cantonese (with the exception of international schools), about a quarter of secondary schools use English, with the rest – about 300 schools in total – teaching in the vernacular.

The official reason has always been that the schools considered English a useful language for success in life, with the goal being the creation of a biliterate (written Chinese and English) and trilingual (Cantonese, Mandarin and English) society. Most parents, however, sent their children to so-called Anglo-Chinese schools in order for them to secure a place at Hong Kong University – the most prestigious tertiary institution in the territory – where lectures are in English. When the post-handover government insisted that government-assisted schools make the switch to tuition in Cantonese, all hell broke loose. Eventually a compromise was reached and those schools fulfilling certain requirements (some 112 of them) are allowed to teach in English. The independent and mostly self-funding English Schools Foundation, which runs 18 English-language institutions, receives a government grant though this could disappear as Hong Kong's economic situation worsens.

At the tertiary level, education is competitive but, with the advent of so many new universities (see Universities p371), not as fierce as it once was. Just over 20% of the eligible age group now has the chance to secure a university placement in degree or non-degree courses – more than double the figure in 1990.

TRADITIONAL CULTURE

While Hong Kong may appear to be as Western as a Big Mac on the surface, many old Chinese traditions persist. Whether people still believe in all of them or just go through the motions to please parents, neighbours or co-workers is hard to say. But during your visit you'll encounter many examples of the following.

Superstitions

One of the most important words in traditional Hong Kong Chinese culture is joss, an Anglo-Chinese pidgin word meaning 'luck' and borrowed from the Portuguese *deus*, or 'god'. But the Hong Kong Chinese are too astute to leave something as important as luck to chance. Gods have to be appeased, bad spirits blown away and sleeping dragons soothed to keep joss on their side. No house, wall or shrine is built until an auspicious date for the start of construction is chosen and the most favourable location is selected.

Worshippers, Man Mo Temple (p85), Sheung Wan

NUMBERS

In the Cantonese language, many words share the same pronunciation: their difference is marked by one of six tones. This gives rise to numerous homonyms. For example, the word for 'three' sounds similar to 'life', 'nine' like 'eternity' and the ever-popular number 'eight' like 'prosperity'. Lowest on the list is 'four', which shares the same pronunciation with the word for 'death'.

Companies or homebuyers will shell out extra money for an address that contains one or more number eights. Each year the Hong Kong government draws in millions of dollars for charity by auctioning off automobile licence plates that feature lucky numbers. Dates and prices are affected too. The Bank of China Tower was officially opened on 8 August 1988 (8/8/88), a rare union of the prosperous numbers. August is always a busy month for weddings.

FOODS

Some foods are considered lucky. Birthday celebrants eat noodles, as the long strands symbolise longevity. Sea moss, which in Cantonese has the same sound as 'prosperity', is always an auspicious ingredient at Chinese New Year, as are oysters ('good business'), chicken ('luck') and prawns ('laughter'). Peach juice is believed to be an elixir, while garlic and ginger can protect babies against evil.

Other foods are unlucky. A Chinese bride avoids eggplant, as it is believed to cause sterility. The groom shuns pig's brains as they can bring on impotence.

As the god of longevity rides on the back of the deer (just as Jesus rode the ass into Jerusalem) parts of the unfortunate creature are used in Chinese medicine to cure ailments and prolong life. Similarly, the long life of the tortoise can be absorbed through a soup made from its flesh. The carp, which can live for up to 40 years, is among the most prized possessions in a wealthy household's fishpond.

Feng Shui

Feng shui literally means 'wind water'. Westerners call it geomancy, the art (or science if you prefer) of manipulating or judging the environment to produce good fortune. If you want to build a house or find a suitable site for a grave, you call in a geomancer. The Chinese warn that violating the principles of good feng shui can have dire consequences. Therefore, feng shui masters are consulted before an apartment block is built, a highway laid down, telephone poles erected or trees chopped down.

Trees may have a spirit living inside, and for this reason some villages and temples in the New Territories still have feng shui woods or groves for the good spirits to live in. Attempts to cut down feng shui groves to construct new buildings have sometimes led to massive protests and even violent confrontations.

Businesses that are failing may call in a geomancer. Sometimes the solution is to move a door or window or place an aquarium with goldfish near the entrance. If this doesn't do the trick, it might be necessary to move an ancestor's grave. If it's in a bad spot or facing the wrong way, there is no telling what trouble the spirit might cause.

Zodiac

Astrology has a long history in China and is integrated with religious beliefs. As in the Western system of astrology there are 12 zodiac signs, but their representations are all animals. Your sign is based on the year of your birth (according to the lunar calendar) rather than the time of year you were born, though the exact day and time of birth is also carefully considered in charting an astrological path.

It is said that the animal year chart originated from when Buddha commanded all the beasts of the earth to assemble before him. Only 12 animals bothered to show up and they were rewarded by having their names given to a specific year. Buddha also decided to name each year in the order in which the animals arrived – the first was the rat, then the ox, tiger, rabbit and so on.

Being born or married in a particular year is believed to determine one's fortune. The year of the dragon sees the biggest jump in the birth rate, closely followed by the year of the tiger. A girl born in the year of the pig could have trouble later in life.

Fortune Telling

If you're interested in having your destiny laid out before you, you'll be spoiled for choice in Hong Kong. You can go to a temple and consult the gods and spirits or have your palm or face read. At Sik Sik Yuen Wong Tai Sin Temple in Kowloon (see p118) some of the fortune-tellers speak English.

The most common method of divination in Hong Kong is using so-called fortune sticks. The altar of a temple, be it Buddhist or Taoist, is usually flanked by stacks of bamboo canisters containing narrow wooden sticks called *chim*. The routine is to ask the spirits or gods a question and shake the canister until one stick falls out. Each stick bears a numeral, which corresponds to a printed slip of paper in a set held by the temple guardian. That slip of paper should be taken to the temple's fortune-teller, who can interpret its particular meaning for you. The fortune-teller will also study your face and ask your date and time of birth.

If you are asking a simple 'yes' or 'no' question (eg 'will I ever be happy in this mortal life?') you can turn to two clam-shaped pieces of wood called *bui* (shell). The way they fall when thrown in the air in front of the altar indicates the gods' answer to your query. One

Herbs & Needles: Chinese Medicine Unmasked

Chinese herbal medicine is holistic and seems to work best for the relief of unpleasant symptoms (stomach ache, sore throat etc), common colds, flu and for chronic conditions that resist Western medicine, such as migraine headaches, asthma and chronic backache. For most acute life-threatening conditions, such as heart problems or appendicitis, however, it is still wise to see a Western-style doctor.

In Chinese medicine, a broad-spectrum remedy such as snake gall bladder may be good for treating colds, flatulence and poor blood circulation, but there are many different aspects of these conditions. The best way to treat anything with herbal medicine is to see a Chinese herbalist first and get a specific prescription. The pills on sale in herbal medicine shops are generally broad-spectrum, while a prescription remedy will usually require that you take home bags full of specific herbs and cook them into a thick broth.

When you visit a Chinese doctor, you might be surprised by what he or she discovers about your body. For example, the doctor will almost certainly take your pulse and may tell you that you have a 'slippery' or 'thready' pulse. A pulse can be 'empty', 'leisurely', 'bowstring' or even 'regularly irregular'. The doctor may then examine your tongue and pronounce that you have 'wet heat', as evidenced by a slippery pulse and a red, greasy tongue.

Many Chinese medicines are powders that come in vials. Typically, you take one or two vials a day. Some of these powders are relatively neutral-tasting while others are very bitter and difficult to swallow. If you can't tolerate the taste, you may want to buy some empty gelatine capsules and fill them with the powder.

The Chinese notion of health food differs somewhat from that of the West. While the Western variety emphasises low-fat, high-fibre and a lack of chemical additives, the Chinese version puts its main emphasis on the use of traditional ingredients and herbs.

It is a widely held belief in China that overwork and sex wears down the body and that such 'exercise' will result in a short life. To counter the wear and tear, some Chinese practice *jinbu* (the consumption of tonic food and herbs). This can include, for example, drinking raw snake's blood or bear's bile, or eating deer antlers, all of which are claimed to improve vision, strength and sexual potency.

Like herbal medicine, Chinese acupuncture tends to be more helpful in treating long-term complaints than acute conditions and emergencies. Surgical operations are sometimes performed using acupuncture as the only anaesthetic, however. In this case, a small electric current is passed through the needles, which are usually inserted in the scalp.

The exact mechanism by which acupuncture works is not fully understood. The Chinese talk of energy channels or meridians, which connect the needle insertion point to the particular organ, gland or joint being treated. The acupuncture point is sometimes quite far from the area of the body being treated.

Having needles stuck into you might not sound pleasant, but if done properly it doesn't hurt. Knowing just where to insert the needle is crucial. Acupuncturists have identified more than 2000 insertion points, but only about 150 are commonly used.

There's a plethora of books on the subject, including *Chinese Medicine: The Web that Has No Weaver* by Ted J Kaptchuk and *The Streetwise Guide to Chinese Herbal Medicine* by Wong Kang Ying and Martha Dahlen. Daniel Reid's *A Handbook of Chinese Healing Herbs* is a much more advanced text and introduces the reader to more than 100 Chinese herbs and herbal formulas. *The Ancient Healing Art of Chinese Herbalism* by Anna Selby is richly illustrated.

side of each piece of wood is *yeung* (*yin* in Mandarin), or male; the other side is *yam* (*yang*), which is female. If both pieces land with the same side up, the answer is negative. But if they fall with different sides up, it indicates a balance of yin and yang, denoting an affirmative answer.

Palm-readers usually examine both the lines and features of the hand. Palms are thought to be emotional; their lines change according to your life experiences and can reveal the past and what the future may hold. Readings for men are taken from the left palm, those for women from the right.

Palmists will sometimes examine your facial features. There are eight basic shapes, but 48 recognised eye patterns that reveal character and fortune. Clues are also provided by the shape of your ears, nose, mouth, lips and eyebrows. For example, people with small earlobes are less likely to become wealthy. Palmists can be found near street markets and in temple compounds.

Fortune teller

At Temple St you'll also find fortune-tellers with birds who will pick the answer to your question from a stack of papers. The dumb clucks don't speak English.

DOS & DON'TS

There aren't many unusual rules of etiquette or codes of conduct to follow in Hong Kong; in general, commonsense will take you as far as you'll need to go. But on matters of identity, appearance, gift-giving and the big neighbour to the north, local people might see things a little differently than you do. For pointers on how to conduct yourself at the table, see Etiquette (p47).

Clothing

Hong Kong is a very fashion-conscious city. Still, it's also very cosmopolitan so you can really get away with wearing just about anything. Revealing clothing – short shorts, mini-skirts and low-cut tops – is OK, but save the bikini top and the flip-flops (thongs) for the beach. Nude bathing is a definite no-no.

Colours

Most colours are symbolic to the Chinese, and they often convey a message. Red is normally a happy colour – it symbolises good luck, virtue and wealth – and brides wear red. Messages written in red ink, however, convey anger, hostility or unfriendliness. White – or anything not dyed – is the colour of death and it is appropriate to give white flowers only at funerals.

Gifts

If invited to someone's home – a rare privilege among the Hong Kong Chinese, who live in small flats and prefer to entertain at restaurants – it's a good idea to bring some sort of gift, such as flowers or chocolates. More and more Hong Kong Chinese are drinking wine, and a bottle of brandy always goes down a treat.

Money is given at weddings and in the form of *laisee* (see 'Kung Hei Fat Choi!' p10) to children and the unmarried at Chinese New Year. The money should be placed in one of the little red envelopes sold in stationery shops all over Hong Kong.

ace

Much is made of the Chinese concept of 'face', which is roughly equivalent to status or respect. Owning nice clothes, a big house or flat in a prime location, or an expensive car all help to 'gain face'. On the other hand, getting into a loud argument in front of others with, say, a shopkeeper is not the way to gain face; they will do their utmost not to knuckle under and lose face themselves. If you want to help people gain face – and get some in return – treat them with respect and show consideration for their culture.

Identity

City Life – Culture

Hong Kong is name-card crazy, and cards make a good impression. If you don't have any of your own, they can be printed cheaply at print shops throughout the territory (Sheung Wan is a good place to start); expect to pay about HK$200 for 100 cards.

You will notice that Hong Kong Chinese always distribute their business cards with two hands, sometimes accompanied by a slight lowering of the head. Using just one hand may be interpreted as rudeness. Cards signify a person's status (see Face above) and should be studied carefully for a few moments. Never put cards immediately into your pocket or wallet, as this may be interpreted as a lack of interest or, worse, disrespect.

The Mainland

Please, do us all a favour and don't rag on about China. Very few Hong Kong Chinese people have the attitude of 'my country, right or wrong' and do not always support what the mainland announces, denounces or legislates. Nevertheless, remember that you are in China while in the Hong Kong SAR and, despite their problems with some aspects of the motherland, most Hong Kong people are proud of China's successes since the birth of the republic in 1912. Don't dwell on its failures – everyone here knows all about those already. That's why they (or their parents or their grandparents) 'voted with their feet' and found their way to Hong Kong.

RELIGION
Traditional Chinese Beliefs

Buddhism and Taoism – entwined with elements of Confucianism, ancient animist beliefs and ancestor worship – are the dominant religions in Hong Kong. The number of active Buddhists in Hong Kong is estimated at around 700,000, though the figure probably includes a good number of Taoists as well.

On a daily level the Chinese are much less concerned with the high-minded philosophies and asceticism of Buddha, Confucius or Laozi (the founder of Taoism) than they are with the pursuit of worldly success, the appeasement of the dead and spirits, and the seeking of knowledge about the future.

Visits to temples are usually made to ask the gods' blessings or favours for specific things: a relative's health, the birth of a son, the success of a business, or even a lucky day at the racetrack. Feng shui and the Chinese zodiac also play key roles in choosing dates for funerals and sites for graves and ancestral shrines. Integral parts of Chinese religion are death, the afterlife and ancestor worship.

Hong Kong has about 600 temples, monasteries and shrines, most of which are Buddhist or Taoist. More than 40 of the temples are public ones maintained by the Chinese Temples Committee of the Home Affairs Bureau, which derives some of its income from donations by worshippers. Temples are usually dedicated to one or two deities, whose images can be found in the main hall. Side halls house images of subsidiary gods or *Bodhisattvas* (Buddhist saints). Since Buddhism and Taoism are both accepted as traditional Chinese religions, deities from each faith are often honoured within the same temple. The majority of temples are tiny, but there are some enormous ones such as the Po Lin Monastery (p148) on Lantau Island, the 10,000 Buddhas Monastery (p132) at Sha Tin, and the Sik Sik Yuen Wong Tai Sin Temple (p118) in New Kowloon.

17

Other Religions

Many other faiths are practised in Hong Kong apart from traditional Chinese ones. There are an estimated 536,000 Christians, about 55% of whom are Protestant and 45% Catholic. Due to the zeal of lay Christians and missionaries, the number of independent Protestant churches has steadily risen since the 1970s and now includes around 1300 congregations in more than 50 denominations.

The Roman Catholic Church established its first mission in Hong Kong in 1841. The present bishop, Joseph Zen, succeeded the late and much-loved Cardinal John Baptist Wu in 2002. The majority of services at the 55 parishes are conducted in Cantonese, though a few churches provide services in English.

Hong Kong is also home to approximately 80,000 Muslims. More than half are Chinese, with the rest either locally born non-Chinese or believers from Pakistan, India, Malaysia, Indonesia, the Middle East or Africa. There are four principal mosques that are used daily for prayers. The oldest is the Jamia Masjid on Shelley St in the Mid-Levels, which was established in 1849 and rebuilt in 1915. Over in Kowloon stands the Kowloon Mosque and Islamic Centre, a white marble structure that has become a Tsim Sha Tsui landmark since opening in 1984.

There are approximately 15,000 Hindus and 8000 Sikhs in Hong Kong. The Jewish community, which can trace its roots back to the time of the British arrival, numbers about 1500.

For a list of churches, temples and mosques open to the visiting faithful, see p368.

(Continued on page 27)

The Gods & Goddesses of South China

Chinese religion is polytheistic, meaning it worships many divinities. Almost every household has its house, kitchen and/or door gods; trades and businesses have their own deities too. Pawnshop owners pray to Kwan Yu, for example, while students worship Man Cheung.

The following are profiles of some of the most important ones.

Kwan Yu A real-life Han dynasty soldier born in the 2nd century AD and sometimes referred to as Kwan Tai, Kwan Yu (Guanyu in Mandarin) is the red-cheeked god of war. Kwan Yu is worshipped not just for his prowess in battle but for his righteousness, integrity and loyalty too. In addition to soldiers, he is the patron of restaurateurs, the police force and members of secret societies, including the Triads. There's a temple dedicated to Kwan Yu in Tai O on Lantau Island (see p149), and he shares the Man Mo Temple (p85) in Sheung Wan with Man Cheung (see below) and the temple on Tap Mun Chau (p138) with Tin Hau.

Kwun Yam The goddess of mercy, Kwun Yam (Guanyin in Mandarin) is the Buddhist equivalent of Tin Hau (see below) and she exudes tenderness and compassion for the unhappy lot of mortals. You'll find Kwun Yum temples at Repulse Bay and Stanley on Hong Kong Island and on Cheung Chau. There are a couple of important temples dedicated to Kwun Yum in Macau (where her name is spelled Kun Iam) as well as a 20m statue atop an ecumenical centre (see Macau Peninsula p304).

Man Cheung This civil deity (Wen Chang in Mandarin) was a Chinese statesman and scholar of the 3rd century BC, and today is worshipped as the god of literature and is represented dressed in green holding a writing brush. He shares the Man Mo Temple (p138), in Sheung Wan, with Kwan Yu.

Tin Hau The queen of heaven, whose duties include protecting seafarers, is one of the most popular gods in coastal Hong Kong and in Macau, where she goes under the name A-Ma. Followers of Tin Hau (Tianhou in Mandarin) number some 250,000 fisherfolk in Hong Kong, and there are almost 60 temples dedicated to her. The most famous of these is Tai Miu ('great temple'; p139) at Joss House Bay in the New Territories. Other important temples dedicated to Tin Hau include those on Cheung Chau, Lamma and Tap Mun Islands, in Yau Ma Tei in Kowloon and in Causeway Bay and Stanley on Hong Kong Island.

Tou Tei Known as Toudei in Mandarin, Tou Tei is the earth god who rules over anything and everything from a one-room flat or shop to a section of a village or town. Shrines to Tou Tei are usually small and inconspicuous but always a delight. There's a very good example of one on Cheung Chau (see p160).

1 Queen's Rd Central (p79)
2 Groovy Mule (p223) 3 Double-
decker tram, Central (p349)
4 Commuters, Soho (p83)

1 Vendor, Yuen Po Street Bird Garden & Flower Market (p116)
2 Playing basketball near the King's Park sports ground (p243)
3 Roller skating, Hong Kong Park (p90) 4 Double-decker tram (p349)

您已賺取到「亞

小心摺門 請勿接近

FOLDING KEEP
DOOR CLEAR

1 Pushing a trolley past a fire station 2 Rickshaw driver (p350) 3 Construction site 4 Bamboo scaffolding (p38)

1 Kowloon Walled City Park (p118)
2 Parrot, Yuen Po Street Bird Garden & Flower Market (p116)
3 Hong Kong Zoological & Botanical Gardens (p83)
4 Sai Kung Peninsula (p134)

1 Hong Kong, from Victoria Peak (p89) 2 Relaxing at Victoria Harbour 3 Water traffic, Victoria Harbour 4 Hong Kong Island (p78)

1 *View from Peak Tower (p88)*
2 *Hong Kong Space Museum (p103)* 3 *Bank of China Tower (p81)* 4 *Hong Kong Convention & Exhibition Centre, with Central Plaza in background (p91)*

1 Two IFC (p82) **2** Lippo Centre (p38) **3** View from Hong Kong Convention & Exhibition Centre (p91) **4** Hong Kong Convention & Exhibition Centre (p91)

1 Chi Lin Nunnery (p119) **2** Jade Market (p106) **3** Murray House (p98) **4** 10,000 Buddhas Monastery (p132)

(Continued from page 18)

HONG KONG & YOU

For its size, Hong Kong is a very safe city and most people will feel quite at home. It is safe to walk around just about anywhere in the territory after dark, though it's best to stick to well-lit areas. Tourist districts like Tsim Sha Tsui are heavily patrolled by the police.

Hong Kong Chinese adore (and spoil) children, respect older people and pamper women. There's still a lot of room for improvement in the welcomes extended to gay, lesbian and disabled visitors, but things are getting better.

For information on crime and emergencies, legal matters, and services and facilities for a range of travellers including children and the disabled, consult the following sections in the Directory (p353): Children, Disabled Travellers, Emergencies, Gay & Lesbian Travellers, Legal Matters, Senior Travellers, and Women Travellers.

LIFESTYLE

LEISURE

Hong Kong people make great use of what little free time their hectic schedules allow. Favourite pursuits include dining together (be it yum cha, a 12-course banquet or a huge bowl of *wonton mien* at a *dai pai dong* with friends); gambling at the Mark Six lottery, the new football pools or (and most importantly) a day of fluttering at the races in Sha Tin or Happy Valley; and watching or participating in organised sport – from cricket and tennis to football and rugby (see Sport p30).

Sir Murray MacLehose, Hong Kong governor from 1971 to 1982 and a keen walker himself, is credited with opening up large tracts of Hong Kong's countryside to hikers and trekkers; hiking is today one of the most popular outdoor activities in Hong Kong (see p162). Many of Hong Kong's beaches opened during Sir Murray's term and local Chinese, apathetic to swimming and other water sports just a generation ago, now take to the water like ducks (see Swimming p242). Windsurfing and wakeboarding are also popular; indeed, Hong Kong's only Olympic gold medallist so far is a windsurfer from Cheung Chau.

Kung Fu & You

Chinese *gongfu* (kung fu) is the basis for many Asian martial arts. There are hundreds of styles of martial arts that have evolved since about AD 500, including *wushu*, which is full of expansive strides and strokes and great to watch in competition; *wing chun*, Bruce Lee's original style and indigenous to Hong Kong, which combines blocks, punches and low kicks; and the ever-popular t'ai chi *(taijiquan)*, or 'shadow boxing'.

Seen every morning in parks throughout Hong Kong, t'ai chi is the most visible and commonly practiced form of kung fu today. Not only is it a terrific form of exercise, promoting health and well-being, but it can also form a solid foundation for any other martial arts practice. Its various forms are characterised by deep, powerful stances, soft and flowing hand techniques and relaxed breathing. During the Cultural Revolution in China, where all teachings outside Maoist philosophy were suppressed, the practice of innocuous-looking t'ai chi forms were allowed, helping kung fu to live on.

The visibility of this ancient art on the ground can be elusive in Hong Kong, though you might make your way over to Kung Fu Corner in Kowloon Park (see p104) on Sunday afternoon. In China, martial arts were traditionally passed down through patriarchal family lines and seldom taught to outsiders; in ancient times these skills were far too valuable to spread indiscriminately.

If you are interested in learning the techniques yourself, contact any of the outfits listed under Martial Arts in the Entertainment chapter (p240). Otherwise an early-morning + constitutional may be just the thing. The Hong Kong Tourism Board (HKTB) organises free t'ai chi lessons lasting an hour four times a week; see p240 for details. Bruce Lee fans should contact the **Bruce Lee Fans Society** (Map p415; 2771 7093; fax 2771 7269; Shop 160-161, In's Point Shopping Mall, 530 Nathan Rd, Ya Ma Tei; 1-9pm Mon-Sat), which has videos of his films, a mini-library and items for sale.

Although lots of Hong Kong Chinese drink alcohol (and some problematically), for the vast majority of the population a night spent in a pub or a bar carousing with friends doesn't even place.

FASHION

In the not-so-distant past, the strength of the Hong Kong fashion industry lay in its ability to duplicate designs, and copies of top-end luxury brands proliferated. Indeed, for many travellers a shopping trip to Hong Kong meant amassing *faux* but authentic-looking Chanel purses, Louis Vuitton bags and Cartier wrist watches – a pursuit that lives on over the border in the Special Economic Zone of Shenzhen.

With the crackdown by the Hong Kong government on such activities and a maturing of the market, the industry has taken on a much more creative role, finding a new voice in everything from haute couture and casual wear to hip street fashion.

The fashion industry here includes: established designers who, for the most part, are couturiers and create one-off made-to-measure outfits; younger 'name' designers who have popular collections and sell both in Hong Kong and for export; and local brands, covering the spectrum from evening and party wear to casual and street wear.

Of the established designers a few names stand out, including the New York–based Vivienne Tam, who was trained here, and Walter Ma, often cited as the voice of Hong Kong fashion, whose women's wear is both sophisticated and adventurous. Barney Cheng's designs are very luxurious, often embellished with beads and sequins; actresses Michelle Yeoh *(Crouching Tiger, Hidden Dragon)* and Maggie Cheung *(In the Mood for Love)* wore his frocks to the Oscars and Cannes. Other names to watch out for include Lu Lu Cheung, especially her Terra Rosalis line, with subtle, Japanese-influenced pieces; Cecilia Yau (gowns); Joanna Chiu-Liao, with simple but chic fashion for women in their 20s to 40s in her Flair by Joc collection; and Silvio Chan, one of the biggest risk takers in the industry, with very evocative, almost steamy designs. Blanc de Chine does mostly tailored outfits (it created a few gems for the former governor's wife, Lavender Patten), which are quietly elegant and distinctively Oriental.

Shanghai Tang (p259), Central

The Wardrobe of Suzie Wong

Neon-coloured Indian saris are beautiful things when fastidiously wrapped and tucked, and Japanese kimonos can be like bright cocoons from which a chrysalis coyly peaks. And what's so wrong with a sarong with a blue lagoon as backdrop?

But there's nothing quite like a cheongsam, the close-fitting sheath that is as Chinese as a bowl of wonton noodle soup. It lifts where it should and never pulls where it shouldn't. And those thigh-high side slits – well, they're enough to give any man apoplexy. It's sensuous but never lewd; it reveals without showing too much.

Reach into any Hong Kong Chinese woman's closet and you're bound to find at least one cheongsam (*qipao* in Mandarin), the closest thing the territory has to national dress. It's there for formal occasions like Chinese New Year gatherings, work (most receptionists at Hong Kong's hangar-sized dim sum restaurants wear them, as do many nightclub hostesses), school (cotton cheongsam are still the uniform at several colleges and secondary schools) or for the 'big day'. Modern Hong Kong brides may take their vows in white just as their sisters around the world do, but when they're slipping off for the honeymoon, they slip on a red cheongsam.

It's difficult to imagine that this bedazzling dress started life as a man's garment. During the Qing dynasty, the Manchus ordered Han Chinese to emulate their way of dress – elite men wore a loose 'long robe' (*changpao*) with a 'riding jacket' (*makwa*) while women wore trousers under a long garment. By the 1920s, modern women in the international port of Shanghai had taken to wearing the androgynous *changpao*, which released them from layers of confining clothing. From this evolved the cheongsam as we know it today.

The 'bourgeois' cheongsam dropped out of favour in China when the Communists came to power in 1949 and was banned outright during the Cultural Revolution, but the 1950s and '60s was the outfit's heyday in Hong Kong. This was the era of Suzie Wong (the cheongsam is still called a 'Suzie Wong dress' in London) and, although hemlines rose and dropped, collars stiffened and more darts were added to give it more of a Marilyn Monroe–style fit, the cheongsam remained essentially the same: elegant, sexy and very Chinese.

The place to have a cheongsam made to order is Linva (p258).

Among the younger designers, Benjamin Lau produces innovative but very wearable pieces noted for their fine cutting. His Madame Benjie line of contemporary ready-to-wear for young women is one of the few in Hong Kong not influenced by trends. Johanna Ho's clothing is low-key and characterised by elegant straight lines and stylish but classic design. The signature pieces of one of the most amusing designers in the game, Pacino Wan, are T-shirts with kooky stencilling (the Queen, Cup o' Noodles packets) and denim (jackets and skirts). Ruby Lee is another young designer producing fun to wear pieces for the young and trendy; Virginia Lai concentrates on evening wear in her Virginia L line.

Arguably the most exciting aspect of the Hong Kong fashion industry at the moment is the meteoric rise in recent years of local brands. In the late 1980s and early '90s, established smart casual brands such as Esprit, Michel Renés and Giordano made room for much more edgy lines: Kitterick, set up by three Hong Kong Polytechnic students in 1988 and Blues Heroes (of the D-mop house). Young people flocked to 'micro malls' such as Island Beverley, Fashion Island and The Goldmark in Causeway Bay and the Beverley Commercial Centre and Rise Commercial Centre in Tsim Sha Tsui (see Micro Malls on p251). These places remain popular and it's not uncommon for some designers to do as few as 10 pieces for an outlet.

Today some of the more popular brands are the i.t group (www.izzue.com), with a hip casual-wear line and its 5cm line of easy coordinates and trendy street-wear, and Fait a Main, women's contemporary lines designed by John Cheng. Spy is funky and provocative, while Moiselle, with more than 40 shops in the territory, stocks embroidered and beaded tops, dresses and footwear. Modèle de Prudence does creative but wearable coordinates for both men and women and now counts four outlets in Hong Kong. Shanghai Tang has modern off-the-rack designs with traditional Chinese motifs, often dyed in neon-like colours.

Hong Kong Fashion Week in mid-July is the industry's most important annual event. The main parades and events, including the announcement of the Hong Kong New Fashion Collection Award winner, take place at the Hong Kong Convention and Exhibition Centre in Wan Chai (Map pp406–8), but keep an eye out for well-dressed shindigs in shopping centres around the territory.

SPORT

Sporting events are well covered in the sports section of Hong Kong's English-language newspapers. Many of the annual sporting events don't fall on the same day or even month every year, so contact the HKTB for further information.

Cricket

The Hong Kong International Cricket Sixes is held in late September/early October. This two-day event at Hong Kong Stadium sees teams from England, Australia, New Zealand, India, Pakistan, Sri Lanka, South Africa, the Caribbean and more battle it out in a speedy version of the game sponsored by the Hong Kong Cricket Club (see Cricket p238).

Football

Hong Kong has a lively amateur soccer league. Games are played on the fields inside the **Happy Valley Sports Ground** (Map pp406-8; ☎ 2895 1523; Sports Rd, Happy Valley) and at **Mong Kok Stadium** (Map p415; ☎ 2380 0188; 37 Flower Market Rd, Mong Kok). The sports section of the English-language papers carries information on when and where matches are held (also see Football & Rugby on p239). The big event of the year is the Carlsberg Cup on the first and fourth days of Chinese New Year (late January/early February).

Horse Racing

Without a doubt, horse racing is Hong Kong's biggest spectator sport, probably because until recently it was the only form of legalised gambling in the territory apart from the Mark Six Lottery, and no people like to wager like the Hong Kong Chinese. There are about 80 meetings a year at two racecourses: one in Happy Valley on Hong Kong Island (see p94) with a capacity for 55,000 punters and the other at Sha Tin in the New Territories (see p133) accommodating 80,000.

The racing season is from September to late June with most race meetings in Happy Valley taking place on Wednesday at 7pm or 7.30pm and at Sha Tin on Saturday afternoon. This schedule is not etched in stone, however, and sometimes extra races are held at Sha Tin on Sunday and public holidays. Check the Hong Kong Jockey Club (HKJC) website (www.hongkongjockeyclub.com) for details or pick up a list of race meetings from any HKTB centre.

If you've been in Hong Kong for less than 21 days you can get a tourist ticket to attend the races, despite the crowds, and can also walk around next to the finish area. A seat in the public stands costs HK$10 while a visitor's badge to sit in the members' box costs HK$50. These can be purchased at the gate on the day of the race, or up to two days in advance at any branch of the HKJC. Make sure to bring along your passport as proof. You might also consider joining one of the racing tours sponsored by the HKTB (see Happy Valley p94).

Betting is organised by the HKJC, and many combinations are available, including the quinella (picking the first and second place-getters in a race), double quinella (picking the first and second from two races), the treble (picking the winner from three specific races) and the six-up (picking the first or second from all six of the day's races). The **HKJC** (☎ 2966 8111, information hotline ☎ 1817; www.hongkongjockeyclub.com) maintains off-track betting centres around the territory, including one in **Central** (Map pp400-3; Unit A1, Ground fl, CMA Bldg, 64 Connaught Rd Central), **Wan Chai** (Map pp406-8; Shop A, Ground fl, Allied Kajima Bldg, 134-145 Gloucester Rd) and **Tsim Sha Tsui** (Map pp412-14; Ground fl, Eader Centre, 39-41 Hankow Rd).

Red-letter days at the races include the Chinese New Year races in late January or early February, the Hong Derby in March, the Queen Elizabeth II Cup in April, and the Hong Kong International Races in December.

Rugby

The Seven-A-Side Invitational Rugby Tournament, popularly known as the Rugby Sevens or just 'the Sevens', sees teams from all over the world come together in Hong Kong in late March/early April for three days of lightning fast (15-minute) matches at 40,000-seat **Hong Kong Stadium** (Map pp406-8; ☎ 2895 7895; www.hksevens.com.hk). Even non-rugby fans scramble to get tickets (HK$750/250 adults/children under 12) because the Sevens is a giant, international, three-day party. For inquiries and tickets, contact **Hong Kong Rugby Football Union** (☎ 2504 8311; www.hkrugby.com; Room 2001, Sports House, 1 Stadium Path, So Kon Po).

Tennis

Several international tennis tournaments are held each year in Victoria Park in Causeway Bay. The largest is the Salem Open in September, Hong Kong's only official ATP tennis tournament. Check the local English-language newspapers for information on times and ticket availability.

ECONOMY

Although Hong Kong presents its much vaunted laissez faire economic policies as a capitalist's dream, considerable sections of the economy, including transport and power generation, are dominated by a handful of cartels and monopolistic franchises. Nonetheless, Hong Kong's economy is by far the freest in Asia, enjoying low taxes, a modern and efficient port and airport, excellent worldwide communications and strict anti-corruption laws.

Hong Kong has moved from labour- to capital-intensive industries in recent decades. Telecommunications, banking, insurance, tourism and retail sales have pushed manufacturing into the background, and almost all manual labour is now performed across the border in southern China. The shift from manufacturing to services has not been without problems. The change may have seen a dramatic increase in wages, but there has not been a corresponding expansion of the welfare state and unemployment has reached new heights.

Hong Kong has a very small agricultural base. Only 2.3% of the total land area is under cultivation and just over 20,400 people – a mere 0.3% of the population – is engaged in agriculture or fishing. Most food is imported from the mainland.

Indeed, Hong Kong depends on imports for virtually all its requirements; it buys half of its water supplies from China. To pay for these imports Hong Kong has to generate foreign exchange through exports, tourism and overseas investments, which has not been easy over the past few years.

The early 21st century has been a trying time for the Hong Kong economy overall. Hong Kong's gross domestic product grew an average 5% per annum between 1989 and 1997, putting its GDP on a par with the four leading economies of Western Europe. The Asia-wide economic crisis of 1997–98 pushed it into recession, but a recovery became apparent in 1999 when GDP grew by 1.9%. It achieved phenomenal growth of over 10% in 2000, but since then things have gone from bad to worse. Growth for 2001 was 0.6% and for 2002 it was just over 2%.

In 2003, on the heels of the SARS epidemic, the government halved its estimate for growth from 3% to 1.5%. By mid-2003, Hong Kong had entered its fourth year of deflation – a generalised fall in prices that pushes borrowers further into debt – and tens of thousands of homeowners (more than 50% of homes are owner-occupied in Hong Kong) were in negative equity and unable to pay their mortgages. In terms of purchasing power, however, Hong Kong's annual per capita GDP of US$25,000 ranks second in Asia after Japan. By comparison China's amounts to just $4300.

Bank of China Tower (p81), Central

Hong Kong people get to keep most of their earnings. The maximum personal income tax is 16%, company profits tax is 17.5% and there are no capital gains or transfer taxes. In the past, these attractive tax conditions attracted dynamic businesses and professionals to Hong Kong. But a 60% slump in property values since 1997 forced the government to halt land sales in order to save the market in 2003, thereby slashing government income and raising concern about the narrowness of the tax base. Generous personal tax allowances mean only a little more than 40% of the working population of 3.2 million pays any salaries tax at all and a mere 0.3% pays the full 16%.

Although unemployment in Hong Kong rose during the Asian crisis and remains high – it was predicted to exceed 8% in 2003, a record for Hong Kong – the territory has traditionally suffered from a labour shortage. Most of the menial work (domestic, construction etc) is performed by imported labour, chiefly from the Philippines. The labour shortage is most acute in the hi-tech and financial fields, prompting the government to consider further relaxing restrictions on importing talent from the mainland, a move deeply unpopular with Hong Kong's working class.

GOVERNMENT & POLITICS

The government of the Hong Kong SAR is a complicated hybrid of a quasi-presidential system glued awkwardly onto a quasi-parliamentary model. It is not what could be called a democratic system, although democratic elements exist within its structure.

The executive branch of government is led by the chief executive, currently Shanghai business tycoon Tung Chee Hwa, who retained office for a second five-year term in 2002. The chief executive selects members (which number 16 at present) of the Executive Council, which serves effectively as the cabinet and advises on policy matters. The top three policy secretaries are the chief secretary for the administration of government, the financial secretary and the secretary for justice. Council members are usually civil servants or from the private sector.

The Legislative Council is responsible for passing legislation proposed by the Executive Council. It also approves public expenditure and, in theory, monitors the administration. The pre-handover Legislative Council was shadowed by a Beijing-appointed Provisional Legislature, which was installed on 1 July 1997. This provisional body served until May 1998, when a new Legislative Council was elected partially by the people of Hong Kong, partially by the business constituencies and partially by powerbrokers in Beijing.

The pro-democracy camp won two-thirds of the popular vote, but due to the rules of appointment they took only one-third of the seats. In subsequent elections they again dominated the popular vote, but remained a minority in the house.

This is because only 20 of the total 60 seats in the Legislative Council are returned through direct election. Ten are returned by a Selection Committee dominated by pro-Beijing functionaries and institutions, and the other 30 by narrowly defined, occupationally based 'functional constituencies'. With a few exceptions, 'corporate voting' is the rule, enfranchising only a few powerful and conservative members of each functional constituency.

The judiciary is headed by the chief justice and is, according to the Basic Law, independent of the executive and the legislative branches. The most significant change to the legal system after the handover was the replacement of the Privy Council with a Court of Final Appeal, which is now the highest court in the land and has the power of final adjudication.

The 18 District Boards, created in 1982 and restructured in 1997, are meant to give Hong Kong residents a degree of control in their local areas. These boards consist of government officials and elected representatives, but they have little power.

Although the stated aim of the Basic Law is 'full democracy', it supplies no definition for this. Furthermore, the law requires a political review of all democratic reforms in 2007. Changes to the system can only be made with the agreement of the chief executive and a two-thirds majority of the legislature. With the democratic camp in the minority in the Legislative Council, many are pessimistic about the prospects of installing genuine democracy in Hong Kong.

ENVIRONMENT

Hong Kong measures 1100 sq km, an increase of 3% of the total surface in the past decade or so due to land reclamation. The territory is divided into four main areas: Hong Kong Island, Kowloon, the New Territories and the Outlying Islands.

Hong Kong Island covers 80 sq km, or just over 7% of the total land area. It lies on the southern side of Victoria Harbour, and contains the main business district. Kowloon is a peninsula on the northern side of the harbour. The southern tip, an area called Tsim Sha Tsui (pronounced 'chim sha choy'), is a major tourist area. Kowloon only includes the land south of Boundary St, but land reclamation and encroachment into the New Territories gives it an area of about 47 sq km, or just over 4% of the total. The New Territories occupies 796 sq km, or more than 72% of Hong Kong's land area, and spreads out like a fan between Kowloon and the mainland Chinese border. What was once the territory's rural hinterland has become in large part a network of 'New Towns'. The Outlying Islands refer to the territory's 234 islands, but doesn't include Hong Kong Island or Stonecutters Island, which is off the western shore of the Kowloon Peninsula and has been absorbed by land reclamation. Officially, they are part of the New Territories and their 177 sq km make up just over 16% of Hong Kong's total land area.

The Hong Kong countryside is very lush though only 12% of the land area is forested. Take a close look and you'll see many of the estimated 2900 species of indigenous and introduced plants, flowers and trees, including Hong Kong's own flower, the bauhinia *(Bauhinia blakeana)*. Hong Kong's beaches and coastal areas are also home to a wide variety of plant life, including creeping beach vitex *(Vitex trifolia)*, rattlebox *(Croatalaria retusa)*, beach naupaka *(Scaevola sericea)* and screw pine *(Pandanus tectorius)*.

Hong Kong is home to a wide variety of animal life. While the constant creation and expansion of New Towns has decreased the number of larger animals, there are smaller mammals, amphibians, reptiles, birds and insects in large numbers.

One of the largest natural habitats for wildlife in Hong Kong is the Mai Po Marsh (p126). There are also sanctuaries in the wetland areas of Tin Shui Wai, Kam Tin and Kwu Yung around Mai Po.

Wooded areas throughout Hong Kong are habitats for warblers, flycatchers, robins, bulbuls and tits. Occasionally you'll see sulphur-crested cockatoos, even on Hong Kong Island, and flocks of domestic budgerigars (parakeets) – domestic pets that have managed to fly the coop.

The areas around some of Hong Kong's reservoirs shelter a large number of long-tailed macaques and rhesus monkeys, both of which are non-native species. Common smaller mammals include woodland and house shrews and bats. Occasionally spotted are leopard and civet cats, the black and white Chinese porcupine, masked palm civets, ferret badgers and barking deer. An interesting creature is the Chinese pangolin, a scaly mammal resembling an armadillo that rolls itself up into an impenetrable ball when threatened.

Frogs, lizards and snakes – including the deadly red-necked keelback, which has not one but *two* sets of fangs – can be seen in the New Territories and the Outlying Islands. Hong Kong is also home to an incredible variety of insects. There are some 200 species of butterflies and moths alone, including the giant silkworm moth with a wingspan of over 20cm. One favourite arachnid is the enormous woodland spider.

Hong Kong waters are rich in sea life, including sharks; most gazetted beaches are equipped with shark nets. Hong Kong is also visited by four species of whale and 11 species of dolphin, including Chinese white dolphins, which are actually pink in colour (see 'Seeing Pink Dolphins' on p150), and the finless porpoise. Endangered green turtles call on Sham Wan beach on Lamma to lay eggs; see 'Green Turtles & Eggs' (p142). Hong Kong waters also support some 50 species of coral.

About 38% of the territory's total land area has been designated as protected country parks. These 23 parks – for the most part in the New Territories and Outlying Islands, but encompassing the slopes of Hong Kong Island too – comprise uplands, woodlands, coastlines, marshes and all of Hong Kong's 17 freshwater reservoirs. In addition, there are four protected marine parks and one marine reserve.

Pollution of all types has been and remains a problem. The first major step taken to deal with the causes rather than just treat the symptoms of Hong Kong's environmental problems came in 1989 with the formation of the Environmental Protection Department. The EPD was set up as an advisory and regulatory body to deal with the 18,000 tonnes of domestic, industrial and construction waste generated daily in Hong Kong. Three large landfills in the New Territories now absorb all Hong Kong municipal solid waste. This, as well as the increased use of private garbage collectors and more recycling, which amounted to 35% of total municipal waste in 1999 (though only 8% in the domestic sector), appears to be having some effect.

Water pollution has been one of Hong Kong's most serious ecological problems over the years. Victoria Harbour remains in a pitiful state, suffering from the effects of years of industrial and sewage pollution, though a new disposal system called the Harbour Area Treatment Scheme is now collecting up to 70% of the sewage entering the harbour and the *E.coli* count (the bacteria that can indicate the presence of sewage) has stabilised. By law, farms in the New Territories must now have their own sewage disposal systems and are fined heavily for dumping untreated industrial or animal waste into freshwater rivers or streams. A great deal of damage has already been done, of course. But the percentage of rivers in the 'good' and 'excellent' categories increased from 27% in 1986 to 65% in 2000.

The quality of the water at Hong Kong's 34 gazetted beaches must be rated 'fair' or 'good' to allow public use, but many beaches here fall below the World Health Organization's levels for safe swimming due to pollution. Since 1998 water has been tested at each beach every two weeks during the swimming season (April to October) and judgements made based upon the level of *E. coli* bacteria present in the sample. The list of beaches deemed safe enough for swimming is printed in the newspapers and on the EPD's website (www.info.gov.hk/epd).

Another of Hong Kong's most serious problems is air pollution. Ceaseless construction, a high proportion of diesel vehicles and industrial pollution from Shenzhen have made for dangerous levels of particulate matter and nitrogen dioxide, especially in Central, Causeway Bay and Mong Kok. Case numbers of asthma and bronchial infection have soared in recent years, and doctors blame it on poor air quality; in September 2002 Hong Kong air pollution hit a record high of 185 – just 15 points short of 'severe'. An hourly update of Hong Kong's air pollution index can be found on the EPD's website. In April 2002, the Hong Kong and Guangdong provincial governments jointly announced a consensus on reducing by 20% the regional emissions of sulphur dioxide, nitrogen oxides, breathable suspended particulates and volatile organic compounds to 55% by 2010.

Arguably the most annoying form of pollution in Hong Kong is the noise created by traffic, industry and commerce. Laws governing the use of construction machinery appear strict on paper, but this being Hong Kong, there's usually a way around things. General construction is allowed to continue between the hours of 7pm and 7am as long as builders secure a permit.

Arts & Architecture

Arts & Architecture

The epithet 'cultural desert' can no longer be used to describe Hong Kong. There are both philharmonic and Chinese orchestras, Chinese and modern dance troupes, a ballet company, several theatre groups and numerous art schools and organisations. Government funds also allow local venues to bring in top international performers, and the number of international arts festivals hosted here seems to grow each year. Local street-opera troupes occasionally pop up around the city. Both local and mainland Chinese opera troupes can also sometimes be seen in more formal settings.

DANCE

Hong Kong has three professional dance companies. The Hong Kong Dance Company, founded in 1981, focuses on Chinese traditional and folk dancing, as well as full-length dance dramas based on local and Chinese themes. The City Contemporary Dance Company stages modern dance performances that include new commissions and past works, often choreographed by local people. Both companies frequently work with artists from China, and sometimes with those from other Asian countries. Founded in 1979, the Hong Kong Ballet regularly performs both classical and modern pieces, and tours overseas each year.

The lion dance is one Chinese tradition that lives on in Hong Kong. Dancers and martial artists take position under an elaborately painted costume of a mythical Chinese lion. To the accompaniment of banging cymbals and, if in a remote location like one of the Outlying Islands, sometimes exploding firecrackers (which are illegal in Hong Kong), the lion leaps its way around the crowd, giving the dancers a chance to demonstrate their acrobatic skills. The lion's mouth and eyes open and close and a beard hangs down from the lion's lower jaw; the longer the beard, the more venerable the school that performs the dance. Lion dances are most commonly seen during the Lunar New Year in late January or February.

MUSIC
TRADITIONAL MUSIC

Whereas Western music employs a seven-tone diatonic scale, traditional Chinese music uses just five tones. Think of it as playing just the black keys on a piano and you'll get the idea. For a good many Westerners it is *not* an acquired taste.

Chinese music theory distinguishes between eight different types of instruments. These are classified not according to how they are played, but by the material with which they are made: metal, stone, silk, bamboo, gourd, clay, hide and wood.

Unfortunately, you won't hear traditional Chinese music on the streets of Hong Kong, except perhaps the doleful *dida*, a clarinet-like instrument played in a funeral procession; the hollow-sounding *goo* (drums) and

Chinese Opera display, Museum of History (p255)

crashing *loh* (gongs) and *bat* (cymbals) at temple ceremonies; and lion dances or the *yi woo* (*erhu* in Mandarin), a two-stringed fiddle favoured by beggars for its plaintive sound. The best place to hear this kind of music in full orchestration is by attending a Chinese opera (see Theatre p42) or a concert given by the Hong Kong Chinese Orchestra, which is the territory's only ensemble devoted to traditional music.

CLASSICAL MUSIC

Western classical music is very popular among Hong Kong Chinese. The territory boasts the Hong Kong Philharmonic Orchestra and Hong Kong Sinfonietta as well as chamber orchestras, while the Hong Kong Chinese Orchestra often combines Western orchestration with traditional Chinese instruments. Overseas performers of world repute frequently make it to Hong Kong, and the number of foreign performances soars during the territory's most important cultural event, the Hong Kong Arts Festival, held in late February and March each year.

POPULAR MUSIC

Hong Kong's home-grown music scene is dominated by'Cantopop' – original compositions that often blend Western rock or pop with traditional Chinese melodies or rhythms. There is an entire constellation of local stars that, while well known among Chinese-speaking communities throughout Asia, are all but unheard of in the West. Many younger Hong Kong people pay homage to their favourite stars by crooning their tunes at karaoke bars, which are among Hong Kong's most popular music venues.

Big names in the music industry are the thespian/crooner Andy Lau, Mr Nice Guy Jackie Cheung, ex-Beijing waif Faye Wong, the immortal Sally Yip and more recent arrivals like Sammi Cheung, Candy Lo, Grace Ip and bad boy Nicholas Tse.

ARCHITECTURE

Over the years Hong Kong has played host to scores of Chinese temples, walled villages, Qing dynasty forts, Victorian mansions and Edwardian hotels. But Hong Kong's ceaseless cycle of deconstruction and rebuilding means that few structures have survived the wrecking ball. Enthusiasts of modern architecture, on the other hand, will have a field day.

CHINESE & COLONIAL ARCHITECTURE

About the only examples of pre-colonial Chinese architecture left in urban Hong Kong are Tin Hau temples dating from the early to mid-19th century, including those at Tin Hau near Causeway Bay, Shau Kei Wan and Aberdeen. Museums in Chai Wan and Tsuen Wan have preserved a few buildings left over from Hakka villages that predate the arrival of the British. For anything more substantial, however, you have to go to the New Territories or the Outlying Islands, where walled villages, fortresses and 18th-century temples can be found.

Colonial architecture is also in fairly short supply. Most of what is left can be seen on Hong Kong Island, especially in Central, such as the Legislative Council building (formerly the Supreme Court; p82), built in 1912, and Government House (p84), the residence of British governors from 1856 till 1997. In Sheung Wan there's the Western Market (p85), built in 1906, and in the Mid-Levels the Edwardian-style Old Pathological Institute, now the Hong Kong Museum of Medical Sciences (p87) and dating from 1905. The Old Stanley Police Station (1859; p98) and nearby Murray House (1848; p98) are important colonial structures in Island South. The **Hong Kong Antiquities & Monuments Office** (Map pp412-14; ☎ 2721 2326; www.amo.gov.hk; 136 Nathan Rd, Tsim Sha Tsui; ☯ 9am-5pm Mon-Sat, 1-5pm Sun), itself housed in a British schoolhouse dating from 1902, has information and exhibits on current preservation efforts.

CONTEMPORARY ARCHITECTURE

Manhattan it may not be, but Hong Kong has an increasingly attractive skyline (it was always dramatic) that is further enhanced by the surrounding water and mountains, the *sine qua non* of traditional Chinese painting.

Hong Kong's verticality was born out of necessity – the scarcity of land and the sloping terrain has always put property at a premium in this densely populated city. While reclaiming land has been a solution since as early as 1851, going upwards offers a viable, less costly alternative.

Some buildings, such as Central Plaza (p91) and the new Two International Finance Centre (p82), seize height at all costs; others are smaller but revel in elaborate detail, such as the Hongkong and Shanghai Bank building (p81). A privileged few, such as the Hong Kong Convention and Exhibition Centre (p234), are even able to make the audacious move to go horizontal. Other prominent buildings include the Bank of China Tower (p81), the Hong Kong Cultural Centre (p102), the Lippo Centre, and the Center (p82).

It's not unfair to say that truly inspired modern architecture only reached Hong Kong when Sir Norman Foster's award-winning Hongkong and Shanghai Bank building opened in Central in 1985. For the first time the territory was seeing what modern architecture can and should be: innovative, functional and startlingly beautiful.

Hong Kong has more than its fair share of booby-prize winners, but before anyone gets too judgmental about the territory's New Towns and their less-than-inspired housing estates, they really should spare a thought for the thousands of refugees and illegal immigrants who were swamping the territory every day following the end of WWII, during the Cultural Revolution and in the late 1970s and early '80s. The government had to move them from squatter settlements and shoehorn them into housing blocks quickly; aesthetics took a back seat to four walls and a roof over their heads.

Lippo Centre, from Hong Kong Park (p90)

Bamboo Scaffolding

Hong Kong may be among the most high-tech places on earth – boasting everything from a cutting-edge airport and an escalator that whisks commuters up a hillside to universal broadband. But when it comes to one aspect of the building trade, it is lower than a well-digger's bottom.

A sure sign that a building is going up (or coming down, for that matter) in Hong Kong – the equivalent of a 'watch this space' advertisement – is the arrival of the bamboo polls. First a base tier of very thick poles is set up, followed by two more levels of lighter bamboo polls lashed together with plastic bindings to form a grid. The whole structure is then covered in green netting and that white, red and blue plastic material used to make the cheap holdalls that you'll see everywhere in Hong Kong.

Bamboo (a grass not a tree) is lighter, cheaper and more flexible than the bolted steel tubing used by scaffolders in the West. It also copes much better with tensile stress as you'll see if you watch builders scuttle by in their thin-soled slippers, barely causing a ripple.

Hong Kong tradition dictates that those who erected the scaffolding must also dismantle it, which probably has as much to do with keeping 'jobs for the boys' as it does superstition. Chinese scaffolders share their deity, Wah Gong (Huaguang in Mandarin), with Chinese opera troupes, who traditionally used bamboo to erect their stages.

Those wanting to learn more about Hong Kong's contemporary architecture should pick up a copy of the illustrated vest-pocket guide *Skylines Hong Kong* by Peter Moss or the more academic *Hong Kong: A Guide to Recent Architecture* by Andrew Yeoh and Juanita Cheung.

PAINTING

Painting in Hong Kong falls into three broad categories: classical Chinese, Western and modern local. Local artists dedicated to preserving such classical Chinese disciplines as calligraphy and Chinese landscape painting have usually spent years studying in China, and their work tends to reflect current trends in classical painting there. While Hong Kong does not have a great deal of home-grown Western art, the Hong Kong Museum of Art in Tsim Sha Tsui has both a permanent collection and temporary exhibits from abroad. Hong Kong modern art has gone through many phases – from the dynamic to the moribund – since it first arrived on the scene after WWII.

CONTEMPORARY ART

Contemporary Hong Kong art differs enormously from that produced in mainland China, and for good reason. Those artists coming of age in Hong Kong after WWII were largely (though not entirely) the offspring of refugees, distanced from the memories of economic deprivation, war and hunger. They were the products of a cultural fusion and sought new ways to reflect a culture that blended two worlds – the East and the West.

In general, Chinese are interested in traditional forms and painting processes – not necessarily composition and colour. Brush strokes and the utensils used to produce them are of vital importance and interest. In traditional Chinese art, change for the sake of change was never the philosophy or the trend; Chinese artists would compare their work with that of the master and judge it accordingly.

The influential Lingnan School of Painting, founded by the watercolourist Chao Shao-an (1905–98) in the 1930s and moved to Hong Kong in 1948, attempted to redress the situation. It combined traditional Chinese, Japanese and Western artistic traditions to produce a unique and rather decorative style, and basically dominated what art market there was in Hong Kong for the next two decades.

WWII brought great changes not only to China but to Hong Kong, and the post-war generation of artists was characterised by an intense search for identity – Hong Kong rather than Chinese. It also set the stage for the golden age of modern Hong Kong art to come.

The late 1950s and early '60s saw the formation of several avant-garde groups, including the influential Modern Literature and Art Association, which counted Lui Shou-kwan, Wucius Wong, Jackson Yu and Irene Chou among its members. Very structural, but at the same time inspired, the association spawned a whole generation of new talent obsessed with romanticism and naturalism. The Circle Art Group, founded by Hon Chee Fun in 1963, was influenced by Abstract Expressionism and characterised by its spontaneous brush work.

Like young artists in urban centres everywhere, Hong Kong painters today are concerned with finding their orientation in a great metropolis through personal statement. They are overwhelmingly unfussed with orthodox Chinese culture and, judging from their work, not overly concerned with their Hong Kong identity.

Of course, Hong Kong's artists form a society that is hardly typical of society as a whole. Artists here have always fought against a deep-seated apathy to art in a community that makes business and financial success the ultimate achievement. Even the most successful artists were 'Sunday painters' – Wucius Wong taught at what was then the Hong Kong Polytechnic, Chu Hung-Wah worked in a psychiatric hospital.

The best place to view the works of modern Hong Kong painters is the Contemporary Hong Kong Art Gallery in the Hong Kong Museum of Art (p103) in Tsim Sha Tsui. There are no galleries specialising exclusively in local art, though the galleries Hanart TZ Gallery (p261) and Plum Blossom in Central (p261) stage exhibits from time to time as does the Hong Kong Visual Arts Centre (p90). **Para/Site Artspace** (Map pp400-3; ☎ 2517 4620; www.para-site.org.hk; 3 Po Yan St, Sheung Wan; ☿ noon-7pm Wed-Sun & noon-8pm Thu) is one of the most important artists' cooperatives in Hong Kong and exhibits the cream of local talent.

Hong Kong's Finest Fine Artists

While visiting the Contemporary Hong Kong Art Gallery in the Hong Kong Museum of Art (p103), keep an eye out for works by the following painters. They represent *la crème de la crème* of modern Hong Kong art.

Gaylord Chan (1925–) Chan's work is characterised by highly enigmatic and haunting shapes in bold primary colours (eg *The Story of Eyes* and the anthropomorphic *Yellow Ribbons*).

Luis Chan (1905–95) The first Hong Kong Chinese artist to paint in the Western style, Chan produced everything from psychedelic landscapes *(New Territories)* to colourful naive forms epitomised in *Reptiles* and the amusing *Conversation in Two Parts*.

Irene Chou (1924–) A student of Lui Shou-kwan, Chou's intensely personal landscapes take on long, geodesic lines that appear like biomorphic nerves or hair, and somewhere in her work (eg *The Fire, Internal Landscapes*) is at least one curious sphere that suggests a seed or catalyst of some sort.

Lui Shou-kwan (1919–75) The most influential of all Hong Kong painters, Lui abandoned landscapes early on for abstract forms, employing mostly Chinese black ink and red paste (eg *Painting #0-64*).

Wucius Wong (1936–) This elder statesman of contemporary Hong Kong art was originally inspired by traditional Chinese landscape painting, which led to his characteristic 'grids' laid over water (*River Thoughts*), mountains (*Beyond Solitude #1*) and sky (*Soaring Clouds #3*).

The best sources of up-to-date information on contemporary Hong Kong and other Asian art is the bimonthly *Asian Art News* (www.asianartnews.com). The two-volume *Hong Kong Artists* is a hefty and substantial reference work and can be bought at the Hong Kong Museum of Art bookshop. Also see the Fine Art entry in the Shopping chapter (p261).

SCULPTURE

Hong Kong's most celebrated sculptor of recent years was Antonio Mak, who died tragically at the age of 41 in 1994. Working primarily in bronze, Mak focused on the human figure as well as on animals important in Chinese legend and mythology (eg horses and tigers) and was greatly influenced by Rodin. His work employs much visual 'punning'; for example, in his *Mak's Bible from Happy Valley*, a racing horse is portrayed with a wing-like book made of lead across its back. The word 'book' in Cantonese has the same sound as to 'to lose (at gambling)'.

Salisbury Gardens, leading to the entrance of the Hong Kong Museum of Art in Tsim Sha Tsui (p103), is lined with modern sculptures by contemporary Hong Kong sculptors. Dotted among the greenery of Kowloon Park (p104) is Sculpture Walk, with about 30 marble, bronze and other weather-resistant works by both local and overseas artists, including a magnificent bronze by Scotland's Sir Eduardo Paolozzi. *The Flying Frenchman* at the Hong Kong Cultural Centre (p102) in Tsim Sha Tsui is the work of the French sculptor César Baldaccini (known to the world simply as César). In Central you'll find sculptures by Britons Henry Moore and Dame Elizabeth Frink and the Taiwanese sculptor Ju Ming. Local boy Cheung Yee has copper reliefs on display in the Mandarin Oriental Hotel.

The quarterly *World Sculpture News* (www.worldsculpturenews.com) is a good start for those interested in contemporary Hong Kong and other Asian sculptors.

CINEMA

Hong Kong is something of an Eastern Hollywood, churning out about 125 films each year, the third highest after Hollywood and Mumbai. The figures are deceiving, however: up to 50% of the films produced here go directly into video format, to be pirated and sold as VCDs or DVDs in the markets of Mong Kok and Shenzhen.

Modern Hong Kong cinema arrived with the films of Bruce Lee, who first appeared in *The Big Boss* (1971), and the emergence of kung fu as a film genre. The 'chop sockey' trend continued through the 1970s and into the early '80s, when bullet-riddled action films took over.

Two directors of this period stand out. King Hu directed several stylish Mandarin kung fu films in the early 1970s, and the films of today still take his work as a reference point for action design. Michael Hui, along with his brother Sam, produced many popular social comedies, including *Private Eyes* (1976) and *The Pilferers' Progress* (1977; directed by John Woo). In terms of actors, Jackie Chan was making his mark during this period, with kung fu movies such as *Snake in the Eagle's Shadow* (1978) and *Drunken Master* (1978) – both directed by Yuen Wo Ping – but he later moved on to police-related stories such as *The Protector* in 1985 and the highly popular *Police Story* series.

Overall, however, it was an uphill battle for the local product at this time, with market share declining in the face of foreign competition. The upturn came in the mid-1980s, with John Woo's *A Better Tomorrow* series. Also prominent were the historical action films by Tsui Hark, including the *Once Upon a Time in China* series based on the exploits of the hero Wong Fei Hung, and featuring great action design and a stirring score.

The new wave of Hong Kong films in the 1990s attracted fans worldwide, particularly John Woo's blood-soaked epics *Hardboiled* and *The Killer*. Woo was courted by Hollywood and achieved international success directing films such as *Face/Off* and *Mission Impossible 2*.

Jackie Chan, whose blend of kung fu and self-effacing comedy is beloved the world over, is one of several local stars to make it in Hollywood. He starred in *Crime Story*, Stanley Tong's *Rumble in the Bronx* (a better-than-average action flick) and teamed up with Owen Wilson in *Shanghai Noon* and *Shanghai Knights*. Lamma native Chow Yun Fat featured in *The Replacement Killers* and *Anna & the King*. Jet Li, star of *Lethal Weapon 4* and *Romeo Must Die*, is another Hong Kong boy who has made a splash overseas. Wong Kar Wai, director of the cult favourite *Chung King Express*, received the Palme d'Or at the Cannes Film Festival in 1997 for his film *Happy Together*.

By the time of the handover, however, all was not well with the Hong Kong film industry; only 92 films were made in 1998 against some 200 a year during the early '90s. The economic downturn was partly to blame but, more importantly, local box offices were taking a beating from the proliferation of pirated VCDs and DVDs. With the price of a pirated version half that of a normal cinema ticket, moviegoers were staying home.

In just a few short years, however, the industry has rebounded and seems to have entered a new, more mature phase. Wong Kar Wai's sublime *In the Mood For Love* (2000), a complicated tale of infidelity and obsession, raised Hong Kong film to a new level and earned its star, Tony Leung, the Best Actor award at Cannes. A film that took the world by storm, the Oscar 2001 award-winning martial arts epic *Crouching Tiger, Hidden Dragon* (2000) may have been shot by a Taiwanese director (Ang Lee), but most of the cast were Hong Kong talent.

Directors to watch out for include Peter Chan Ho-sun (*Comrades, Almost a Love Story, The Love Letter*, and *He's a Woman, She's a Man*); Fruit Chan *(Made in Hong Kong)*; Andy Lau *(Young and Dangerous* and *A Man Called Hero)*; Chan Muk Sing (the *Gen-Y Cops* series); and Stanley Kwan *(New York Stories)*. Yau Ching's *Ho Yuk – Let's Love Hong Kong* (2002), one of the territory's more unusual (and courageous) films in recent years, is the story of three alienated women pursuing or being pursued or not being pursued by each other.

Along with producing its own films, Hong Kong actively promotes itself as a location for foreign films, and the **Film Services Office** (FSO; ☎ 2594 5758;

Film posters at the entrance to Silvercord Cinema (p236)

www.fso-tela.gov.hk) publishes a chunky and useful *Guide to Filming in Hong Kong* each year. The territory has been the setting of many Western-made films (memorable or other wise), including: *Love is a Many-Splendored Thing* (1955), starring William Holden, and Jennifer Jones as his Eurasian doctor paramour, with great shots on and from Victoria Peak *The World of Suzie Wong* (1960), with Holden again and Nancy Kwan as the pouting Wan Chai bar girl; *Lord Jim* (1965), parts of which were also shot at Angkor Wat, starring Peter O'Toole; *Enter the Dragon* (1973), Bruce Lee's first Western-made kung fu vehicle; *The Man with the Golden Gun* (1974), with Roger Moore as James Bond and filmed partly at Tsim Sha Tsui's Bottoms Up nightclub (p228); *Year of the Dragon* (1985), with Micky Rourke and *Tai-Pan* (1986), the less-than-successful film version of James Clavell's doorstop novel (don't miss the bogus typhoon footage).

More recent foreign films shot partly or in full here include *Double Impact* (1991), *Mortal Kombat* (1995), *Rush Hour* (1998) and *Tomb Raider 2* (2003).

Excellence in Hong Kong films is recognised each April with the presentation of the Hong Kong Film Awards, the territory's own 'Oscars'. The annual 16-day Hong Kong International Film Festival held in April brings in more than 200 films and is now one of the world's major film festivals.

One of the best sources for information on Hong Kong movies is *Hong Kong Babylon: An Insiders Guide to the Hollywood of the East* by Frederic Dannen and Barry Long, a rollicking ride through the Byzantine world of the local film industry. For information about the Hong Kong Film Archive in Sai Wan Ho, see p95.

THEATRE

Nearly all theatre in Hong Kong is Western in form, if not content. Most productions are staged in Cantonese, and a large number are new plays by Hong Kong writers. The plays often provide an insightful and sometimes humorous look at contemporary Hong Kong life. The independent Hong Kong Repertory Theatre, formed in 1977, tends to stage larger-scale productions of both original works on Chinese themes or translated Western plays. More experimental troupes are the Chung Ying Theatre Company and the multimedia Zuni Icosahedron.

English-language theatre in Hong Kong is mostly the domain of expatriate amateurs, and plays are more often than not scripted by local writers. Among the more popular venues are the two theatres at the Fringe Club in Central (see p237). The Hong Kong Cultural Centre (p102), the Hong Kong Academy for the Performing Arts (p91) and the Shouson Theatre at the nearby Hong Kong Arts Centre (p91) all host foreign productions, ranging from grandiose Western musicals to minimalist Japanese theatre.

CHINESE OPERA

Kek (Chinese opera) is a world away from its Western counterpart, but the themes are pretty much the same: mortal heroes battle overwhelmingly powerful supernatural foes; legendary spirits defend the world against evil; lovers seek escape from domineering and disapproving parents.

Foreigners will find that Chinese opera performances take some getting used to. Both male and female performers sing in an almost reedy falsetto designed to pierce through crowd noise, and the instrumental accompaniment often takes the form of drumming, gonging and other nonmelodic punctuation. Performances can last as long as five or six hours, and the audience makes an evening of it – eating, chatting among themselves and changing seats when bored, laughing at the funny parts, crying at the sad bits.

There are three types of Chinese opera performed in Hong Kong. The Beijing opera *(ging kek)* is a highly refined style that uses almost no scenery but a variety of traditional props. This is where you'll find the most acrobatics and swordplay. The Cantonese variety *(yuet kek)* is more a 'music hall' style, usually with a 'boy meets girl' theme, and often incorporating modern and foreign references. The most traditional is Chiu Chow opera *(chiu kek)*. It is staged almost as it was during the Ming dynasty, with stories from the legends and folklore of the Chiu Chow (Chaozhou in Mandarin), an ethnic group from the easternmost region of Guangdong province.

Much of the meaning in a Chinese opera is derived from costumes, props and body language, so a little homework beforehand may make things easier to understand and enjoy. the Hong Kong Heritage Museum (p133) has an entire hall dedicated to Cantonese opera, including costumes, make-up, sets and videos of classic performances.

The best time to see Cantonese opera is during the Hong Kong Arts Festival (February–March). Outdoor performances also are staged in Victoria Park on Hong Kong Island during the Mid-Autumn Festival. At other times, you might take your chances at catching a performance at the Temple St night market in Yau Ma Tei (p106), but the most reliable venue for opera performances year round is the Sunbeam Theatre in North Point (p237).

PUPPET THEATRE

Puppetry is the oldest of the Chinese theatre arts. Styles include rod, shadow and glove puppets. The rod puppets, visible only from waist up, are fixed to a long pole with short sticks for hand movements. The puppets are made from camphor wood and the main characters have larger heads than the rest of the cast. Shadow puppets are made from leather and perform from behind a silken screen. Shadow and glove puppet performances are accompanied by the two-stringed *yi woo* (*erhu* in Mandarin) and zither-like *jang*. Most performances relate tales of past dynasties. Live puppet shows are somewhat rare these days, but they are sometimes broadcast on television. The Law Uk Folk Museum in Chai Wan (p96) has a large collection of rod puppets, props and sets.

Food

Food

If the pursuit of wealth is the engine that drives Hong Kong, its fuel is food. Noodles are slurped, succulent seafood savoured and dishes at banquets praised for their presentation, freshness and texture, as well as taste. A housewife selects a fish for her family's dinner as a gem-cutter chooses a rough diamond; certain chefs enjoy celebrity status and are followed from restaurant to restaurant by gourmets as groupies pursue rock stars. Food – and the business of eating it – is taken *very* seriously in Hong Kong.

Chinese food – be it Cantonese, Chiu Chow, Northern, Shanghainese or Sichuan – is not the only cuisine local people enjoy here. The territory also counts some of the world's top international eateries, ranging from trendy Italian to basic Thai; see the Eating chapter (p167) for some idea of the other types of nosh they tuck into and the enormous range of options available in the territory. But 'Hong Kong food' really means Chinese food – in all its incarnations and variations.

While eating well in Hong Kong does not have to be expensive, nor is it especially cheap. Budget eating will leave a fair bit of change in your pocket if you're willing to eat from pushcarts and Styrofoam boxes while sitting on wobbly, plastic stools or standing, but the fare will be pretty standard. Finding a top-notch Chinese restaurant is easy, but locating one that's both good and cheap can take some perseverance.

Depending on the district, it can be especially hard to find a good-quality, inexpensive restaurant that has a menu in English. If you don't read or speak Cantonese, the problem can be lessened by eating dim sum in a Chinese restaurant. The dishes are usually wheeled around on trolleys, so it's just matter of pointing at what catches your eye. In many restaurants you can also just point at what your neighbour is eating – people won't be offended but delighted.

Even those who are literate in Chinese or know some key characters may be stumped by the names of some dishes appearing on Chinese menus. As Westerners name dishes things like 'beef Wellington' and 'baked Alaska', the Chinese are fond of giving dishes fanciful appellations. You'll almost certainly need help with things like 'Buddha Jumped over the Fence', 'Ants Climbing Trees' and 'Coral and Jade'. Be warned: dishes prefaced with 'White Flower' may contain tripe.

The best source for travellers exploring the culinary world of Hong Kong is the annual *HK Magazine Restaurant Guide* (HK$50), which reviews 600 eateries, including some in Macau as well. For details and other food guide recommendations, see p355.

HISTORY & CULTURE

The story of Hong Kong cuisine begins with the collision of two empires. Before that seismic event Hong Kong was a backwater in every sense. It had been long inhabited by humble fisherfolk, farmers and a lesser breed of pirate. They had eked out a living for centuries – all but unnoticed. In the 16th century, across the mouth of the Pearl River, the Portuguese established themselves in what is now Macau, and whatever attention the world focused on the region went there. But then came the First Opium War (see p64) and almost overnight the world turned its eyes to Hong Kong.

This did not bring good dining instantly. The British brought their own provisions, and in this far corner continued to eat their gammon and sausage, pies and kippers, and wash it all down with milky tea and warm beer. The Chinese opportunity seekers who flowed in with the British brought their traditions, for the most part Cantonese, which is considered by many to be the acme of Chinese cookery. There was no Promethean spark in the Hong Kong kitchen, but there began a slow building of the foundation of Hong Kong's culinary culture.

It was fortunate, for diners, that the Crown Colony had come to rely on the mainland city of Guangzhou (Canton) for its survival, as it provided food, labour, building materials, water, cooks and inspiration. For mainland cooks, pay was always better in Hong Kong, as it is today. People say that the best cooks in China go to Guangzhou and the best of Guangzhou comes to Hong Kong. And so for many decades Hong Kong was 'the real Guangzhou', because there was the money and the acumen to always strive for the best, the most exotic, the new. There were other Chinese people in Hong Kong, such as the Hakka, but their culinary contribution would have to wait to be noticed.

With the declaration of the People's Republic of China in 1949, floods of immigrants, including many chefs and cooks, came to Hong Kong from all over the mainland. From Shanghai, Sichuan, Hunan and Beijing (Peking) they came, looking for safety, jobs and a new life. Though they might never see their homelands again, they could at least nourish themselves on the memories. They could keep their birthplaces alive in the hearth and at the table. And they thrive there to this day. Though they eat each other's fare, they do not blend them. They maintain their culinary identity. Hong Kong is not an amalgam of Chinese cookery, it is a focus.

HONG KONG–STYLE COOKING

There aren't many dishes or sauces unique to Hong Kong; even *hou yau* (oyster sauce), which is so strongly associated with the territory, is originally from Guangzhou. There is, however, Hong Kong style – the territory's way of preparing a dish – and it's often an improvement on the original. Hong Kong chefs pride themselves on innovation: experimenting, improvising and creating. They will instantly seize upon a new ingredient and find ways to use it. For example, asparagus is a vegetable little known in the rest of China, but Hong Kong chefs serve it every day, combining it with baby abalone and olive oil or with caviar and preserved eggs.

Even more than the willingness to try new ingredients is the willingness to practice new techniques. This is the crux of Hong Kong style: to refine and extract the maximum from a recipe. A Hong Kong technique known as 'velveting' is a good example. Meats are marinated in spices whipped into a froth of egg white, giving the meat a soft and pleasing texture. The use of yeast or baking powder in deep-fry batters produces a light crust.

Very high heat is an important factor in Hong Kong cooking. In most parts of China the claypot is used for slow cooking, but in Hong Kong it is placed over a blast of high heat to quickly infuse flavours into the dish. And even more importantly, Hong Kong chefs hew to the concept of *wok chi*. The term refers to what could be called a hot wind that roars off a super-heated wok. This can only be achieved with a powerful fire burner that covers the entire underside of the wok, not just the small ring of fire found on the common cooker. This produces a fire so hot that home kitchens cannot use it. This cooking technique sears and carbonises the outer surfaces of foods and seals in flavour. It also imparts natural iron to the food being cooked.

ETIQUETTE

The Chinese are, by and large, casual about etiquette at the table, and they don't expect foreigners to understand all of their dining customs. But there are a few unique ways of doing things here that are useful to know.

Chinese meals in Hong Kong are social and very noisy events. Westerners drink together to relax and let off steam; Chinese people eat. Typically, a group of people sits at a round table and orders dishes (at least one per person) from which everyone partakes. Ordering a dish just for yourself as some people still do in Chinese restaurants in Europe would be unthinkable here; everyone wants a piece – literally – of the action. It's also not unusual for one person at the table to take command and order on everyone's behalf.

If you are attending a formal affair or eating at someone's home, it's best to wait for some signal from the host before digging in. You will most likely be invited to take the first taste if you are the guest. Often your host will serve it to you, placing a piece of meat, chicken or fish in your bowl. If a whole fish is served, you might be offered the head, the cheeks of which are considered to be the tastiest part. It's all right to decline; someone else will gladly devour the delicacy.

The Chinese think nothing of sticking their chopsticks into a communal dish, which is one reason why hepatitis is still a problem in China and, less so, in Hong Kong and Macau. Better restaurants provide separate serving chopsticks or even spoons with each dish; use them if they do. Leaving chopsticks sticking vertically into the bowl – as unlikely as that sounds – is a bad omen as they resemble incense sticks in a bowl of ashes, a sign of death. And never, ever, flip a fish over to reach the flesh on the bottom. The next fishing boat you pass will capsize. Just use your chopsticks to break off pieces through the bones.

If you absolutely can't manage chopsticks, don't be afraid to ask for a fork; nearly all Chinese restaurants have these. It's better to swallow a little humble pie than miss out all those treats set before you.

At a Chinese meal, everyone gets an individual bowl of rice or a small soup bowl. It's quite acceptable to hold the bowl close to your lips and shovel the contents into your mouth with chopsticks. An alternative is to hold a spoon in one hand and use the chopsticks to push the food onto the spoon. Then use the spoon as you normally would.

If the food contains bones, just put them out on the tablecloth or, if you want to be extra polite, into a separate bowl. And you needn't use a napkin to hide what you're doing; except at very upmarket restaurants most Hong Kong people just spit them on the table.

As you'll discover, there's generally a big mess after a meal. Restaurants know this and are prepared – the staff change the tablecloth after each customer leaves.

Chinese make great use of toothpicks – foreign residents sometimes call them 'Chinese dessert' – after a meal and even occasionally between courses. The polite way to use them is to cover your mouth with one hand while using the toothpick with the other.

Beer, soft drinks or even brandy *may* be served with the meal, but tea most definitely will; for details see Tea p60. When your waiter or host pours your tea, thank them by tapping your middle and index fingers lightly on the table. When the teapot is empty and you want a refill or hot water, signal the waiter by taking the lid off the pot and resting it on the handle.

Toasts in Hong Kong are not usually accompanied by long-winded speeches and less-than-amusing anecdotes that usually befall Western banquets. Sometimes a toast is limited to the words *'yam seng'* (roughly, 'down the hatch').

HOW HONG KONG PEOPLE EAT

In a world where food is paramount, it should come as no surprise that Hong Kong people eat up to five times a day: breakfast, lunch, afternoon tea, dinner and a late-night snack. Afternoon tea and a late night snack are not considered meals, though; that's just filling up space. A proper meal must comprise rice and other dishes as garnishes.

In Hong Kong, workers might breakfast at home or in a small restaurant specialising in breakfast foods such as *juk* (congee or rice porridge), which is either eaten plain or with a multitude of garnishes and condiments. Secretaries and other office workers may grab a bowl of soup noodles and bring it to the work place, happily slurping away at their desks. At the weekend and on holidays everyone goes for dim sum. It might be an early breakfast, brunch or even lunch.

Lunch in the built-up areas during the week will often be a set lunch consisting of one or two dishes at a fixed price. However, lunch can also be a bowl of soup noodles with shrimp won tons or a plate of rice with roast pork, duck or goose. It might be something more elaborate at one of the hotel dining rooms or even a buffet.

Afternoon tea in Hong Kong is especially popular on weekends at the good hotels. This can be an elaborate affair, a traditional English high tea, or dim sum. It might be at the office and comprise little more than tea and biscuits or a steamed bun. At home a housewife might invite her neighbour over for tea and melon seeds or sesame crisps. Labourers will stop for just a few minutes to pour a cup of tea and eat a custard tart before going back to work.

Dinner is a big event every day, especially dinner in a restaurant. The majority of Hong Kong people live in very small flats with handkerchief-sized kitchens; dining out with friends and family solves the problem of space. This is one reason Hong Kong's restaurants are always so noisy; this is where people come to catch up on all the gossip, make plans, tell jokes and just enjoy life. Life does not happen in a pub or a bar in Hong Kong, but around the table.

Dishes at a Chinese meal are always served together. Tables, which are invariably round in Chinese restaurants, are often equipped with a turntable – a lazy Susan – on which the food is placed. It's not unusual for dishes to be served with tiny saucers filled with various sauces, with *see yau* (soy sauce), *bat gai* (hot mustard) and *lat jiu jeung* (chilli sauce) the most common ones. Feel free to stand up and lean over the table to dip if the sauce (or a particularly tasty morsel, for that matter) is on the other side.

Often you'll see several small bottles on the table, usually containing soy sauce and vinegar. The vinegar is usually a dark colour and is easily confused with soy sauce, so taste some first before pouring. Sauces aren't dumped on food – instead the food is dipped into a separate dish. Staff will usually let you know which sauce goes with which dish.

Hong Kong people also love to snack – favouring the savoury over the sweet in most cases. Apart from dim sum (see Cantonese p54), the more traditional Chinese snacks consumed are various seafood titbits, often served on a bamboo skewer. Squid or fish balls barbecued on a stick is one example. Fish-ball soup served in a Styrofoam cup is a modern variation of a traditional snack. A winter snack that has to be smelled to be believed is *chau doufu*, or 'stinky beancurd', which is fermented tofu deep-fried in oil.

STAPLES & SPECIALITIES

What are the staples and specialities of a people who are not only willing but eager to eat anything and everything so long as it has 'its back to the sky' (as they say in Cantonese)? Here you'll find the foods from every region of China and every other part of the world for that matter. The best we can do is tell you what you will find most of in Hong Kong, and advise you to keep an eye out for more. The vast majority of staples, of course, will be those used in cooking Chinese food.

EGGS

Eggs – all kinds of eggs – are consumed with relish in Hong Kong. Chicken, duck and goose eggs, fish, prawn and crab roe – Hong Kong people are over the moon for ova.

A taste sensation are 1000-year-old eggs (also known as 100-year-old eggs), which are actually just a month or two old, and are called *pei dan* (preserved egg) in Cantonese. They are duck eggs soaked in a lime solution, which turns the egg white green and the yolk a greenish-black. These are usually served as a starter or condiment.

Ham dan (salted duck eggs) are soaked in a saline solution for about 40 days. This process crystallises the yolk and turns it bright orange. Unlike preserved eggs, these must be cooked. They might be broken into a dish of stir-fried tofu or fried rice, or hardboiled and chopped up into a bowl of *juk*. Hard-boiled *ham dan* make a tasty, though filling, breakfast on their own. You can recognise salted eggs at the market because they are wrapped in what looks like cow manure, but is actually just packed earth.

Baskets of preserved and fresh eggs

FISH & SHELLFISH

Cantonese love freshly and simply prepared seafood and fish – and with China's long coastline and many rivers and lakes, it is no wonder that fish has always been important to their diet. In Chinese, the word for fish is *yu*. Pronounced with a different tone, the word can also mean 'plenty' or 'abundance'. So a traditional final dish at a formal dinner banquet is often a whole fish, signifying to the guests that although many courses have already been consumed, there is plenty more to eat if they so desire.

When the fish, crab, prawn or lobster is plucked from the sea (or river or pond), it must be cooked immediately. It is vital to capture the freshness of the fish in the wok – a maxim held by chefs in every Chinese kitchen. In fact Cantonese chefs have an insistence bordering on obsession for freshness, so it is common to see fish tanks in many restaurants in Hong Kong.

Popular fish and shellfish dishes:

bak cheuk ha – steamed fresh prawns

hai ji yue chi tong – shark's fin soup with crab roe

jin hou beng – oyster omelette

jing yue – steamed whole fish (usually grouper)

tim suen yue – sweet-and-sour fish (usually yellow croaker)

xi jap lung ha – lobster in black bean sauce

xiu yue chi – braised shark's fin

yue dan – fish balls, usually made from pike

MEAT

The people of Hong Kong consume more protein per capita than any other group in the world. Of course some of that is tofu, but this is far and away the most carnivorous city in China. Pork is the premier meat, as it is anywhere in China, but chicken, duck and beef are also relished and served braised, steamed or fried. Lamb and mutton are unknown outside northern Chinese restaurants. Southern Chinese cannot stand the smell.

Favoured pork, beef, chicken, duck and goose dishes:

bak ging ngaap – Peking duck

cha siu – roast pork

cha siu ngaap – roast duck

cha siu ngoh – roast goose

chiu jau lou sui ngoh – Chiu Chow soyed goose

hat yi gai – 'beggar's chicken' (whole, partially deboned chicken stuffed with pork, vegetables, mushrooms, ginger and other seasonings, wrapped in lotus leaves and wet clay or pastry and baked for several hours)

ho yau ngau yuk – sliced beef with oyster sauce

hung siu baat bou ap – 'eight-jewelled duck' (braised and stewed duck with ginger, abalone, black mushrooms, lotus seeds, bamboo shoots, dried scallops, prawns and Chinese greens)

hung siu pai gwat – braised pork spareribs

hung xu ju sau – red simmered pork knuckle

ja ji gai – crispy skin chicken

jeung cha ap – camphor tea-smoked duck

jui gai – 'drunken chicken' (poached chicken that's marinated in broth and rice wine and served cold as an appetiser)

ma ngei seung xu – 'ants climbing trees' (cellophane noodles braised with seasoned minced pork)

mui choi kau yuk – twice-cooked pork with pickled cabbage

ning mung gai – lemon chicken

siu yue jue – roast suckling pig

tim suen pai gwat – sweet-and-sour pork

xi ji tau – 'lion's heads' (large stewed and seasoned pork meatballs)

xi jui cao pai gwat – beef spareribs in black bean sauce

yim guk gai – salt-baked Hakka-style chicken

NOODLES

Noodles are thought to have originated in northern China during the Han dynasty (206 BC–AD 220) when the Chinese developed techniques for large-scale flour grinding. Not only were noodles nutritious, cheap and versatile, they were portable and could be stored for long periods. Legend credits Marco Polo with having brought noodles to Italy in 1295, where it developed into pasta.

Chinese like to eat noodles at all times, but especially at birthdays and the New Year since the shape symbolises longevity. That's why it's bad luck to break noodles before cooking them. You just might be shortening more than you think.

Various regions of China (and other parts of Asia too) claim different types of noodles as their own, but Hong Kong people don't care. They eat them all. Thin, translucent strands made from mung bean starch are called *fen xi* (cellophane noodles or bean threads). They are used most often in Southeast Asian dishes, and are usually cooked in soups or deep fried. Thin, translucent noodles made from rice flour are called *gon hoh fen* (rice sticks). Vietnamese cooks use these extensively in all kinds of dishes. *Haw fun* are wide, white, flat, slippery rice noodles, and are usually pan fried.

The Cantonese word for noodle is *min*, and *chau min* is arguable the most popular dish here. There are many variations, but most often the thin noodles are fried crisp.

Chef making noodles

The story goes that in the 19th century a certain Chinese cook was employed by the railroad. When frying noodles one day for the boss, the lazy fellow fell asleep and when he awoke the noodles were burnt to a crisp. As he had no more noodles he served them to the boss and hoped for leniency. But the boss, never having had chow mein before, pronounced them delicious and demanded that they be served every day.

Won ton are not exactly noodles, more noodle packets and not dissimilar to ravioli. Normally no wider than a watch face, they are filled with pounded prawns, pork or vegetables and can be fried, steamed or added to soup.

Restaurant windows fogged from the steam of vats bubbling with won ton noodle soup or congee are great places to sample Hong Kong's indigenous 'fast food'. You'll also see *cha siu* (roast pork) and *cha siu ngaap* (roast duck) hanging from hooks in windows, the fat dripping into pans below. Noodles come in a variety of colours, textures and cooking styles. Yellow balls of twine-like noodles are most common with won ton in soup, sometimes with a few pieces of green vegetable thrown in for extra crunch. If you think won ton noodles has the slight taste of ammonia, that's because alkali and duck egg is sometimes added when mixing the dough for the noodles.

Typical dishes at noodle shops:

cha siu fan – barbecued pork with rice

chaau fan – fried rice

gai juk – chicken congee

hainan gai – Hainanese chicken
(steamed chicken served with chicken-flavoured rice)

sin ha won ton – won tons made with prawns

singjau chaau min – Singapore noodles
(rice noodles stir-fried with curry powder)

won ton min – won ton noodle soup

yue dan – fish balls

yupin juk – congee with sliced fish

RICE

Rice is deeply, er, ingrained in Chinese culinary tradition and an inseparable part of virtually every meal. The Chinese don't ask 'Have you had your dinner/lunch yet?' but 'Have you eaten rice yet?' It's that central to the equation.

The Chinese revere rice not only as their staff of life but also for its aesthetic value. Its mellow aroma is not unlike bread. Its texture when properly done – soft yet offering some resistance, the grains detached – sets off the textures of the foods that surround it, their shimmering colours the more vivid for the rice's whiteness. Flavours are brought into better focus by its simplicity. Rice is the unifier of the table, bringing all the dishes into harmony.

Rice comes in lots of different preparations – as the rice porridge that's favoured at breakfast or fried with tiny shrimps, pork or vegetables and eaten at lunch or as a snack. Glutinous rice dumplings are made from sticky rice, to which pork, chicken or prawns have been added, which are wrapped in lotus leaves and steamed. But plain steamed white rice – fragrant yet neutral – is what you should order at dinner. It's the canvas on which to paint your own culinary masterpiece.

Congee

Hong Kong is famous for its *juk* and it is usually eaten outside the house. Unless you're prepared to accept rice powder as a rapid-cooking substitute (we're not), it demands standing and stirring for a couple of hours until the grains have engorged and exploded into a porridge-like consistency; few people have the time or inclination for that amount of work. You can eat congee plain with *yau ja gwai* ('devils' tails'), dough rolled and fried in hot oil, or dressed for the fair with salted pork, fish balls, condiments, toasted garlic and/or bean sprouts. It's comfort food at its best (and, by the way, an excellent hangover cure or easer).

SAUCES & FLAVOURINGS

Chinese cooking employs spices and flavourings that are not major components of a Western kitchen: five-spice powder (a blend of ground star anise, fennel or anise seed, cloves, cinnamon and Sichuan peppercorns that's used to flavour barbecued meats and stews); star anise (a clove-like spice that yields a strong liquorice flavour and is used to enhance soups and stews); and sesame oil (added to marinades or at the last moment of cooking to flavour certain dishes).

Sauces, both cooked with meat or fish or used for dipping:

black bean sauce – fermented black beans (a type of soybean) that are combined with soy sauce, ginger, rice wine, sugar and oil

hoisin sauce – sweet, slightly piquant brown paste made from soybeans, red beans, sugar, garlic, vinegar, chilli, sesame oil and flour (essential with Peking duck)

oyster sauce – thick dark sauce made from oysters, water, salt, soy sauce and cornstarch and often served over vegetables

soy sauce – The quintessential Chinese condiment and cooking ingredient made through a fermentation process involving soybeans and wheat flour or barley. There is a wide range of soy sauces available, all of which can be divided into light and dark soy. Light soy is used in things like soup, when the cook wants a delicate flavour of soy but not the colour, and as a condiment. Dark soy contains caramel and is thicker and richer and thicker. It's used in marinades and sometimes as a condiment.

XO sauce – very popular condiment made from crushed conpoy (dried scallops), chilli, garlic and oil

SOUP

In Hong Kong, a balanced meal simply must have soup. Traditionally it was the beverage component of the meal, and nowadays it shares that role with other liquids. It is also one of the chief means by which the Chinese maintain their health. Soup is the main vehicle for the delivery of medicinal and balance enhancing properties of foods. It gives you heat in winter and keeps you cool in summer.

Soups Hong Kong people love:

daan fa tong – egg flower soup (also called egg drop soup, it's a light stock into which a raw egg is dropped)

dung gua tong – winter melon soup

hai yuk suk mei gang – crab and sweet corn soup

lai tong – Chinese cabbage soup

won ton tong – won ton soup

yin woh geng – bird's nest soup

TOFU

The pressed curd of the soybean is sometimes called 'poor man's meat'. Tofu contains all the essential amino acids, is low in calories and is devoid of cholesterol. It is mainly used for its texture and goes well with any other ingredients. You can do absolutely anything with tofu: deep fry, sauté, steam, bake, simmer, broil or purée it. It comes in three textures: soft, which is added to soups or steamed dishes where cooking time is brief; semi-soft, which is used in stir-fry dishes; and firm, which is used for stuffing and deep frying.

Other tofu products include tofu skin, which is the skin that forms when the soybeans are being boiled. It is used to add texture to stir-fry dishes and to wrap up meat and fish. You will also find marinated tofu sold in jars, the taste of which can be extremely strong, but not as strong as *chau doufu* (stinky tofu).

Fresh produce for sale at a market stall

Tofu is also used to make *nam yu* (pressed tofu cubes fermented in salt, spices and rice wine until red in colour) and *ji juk* (cream-coloured sticks of dried tofu that have a nutty flavour).

VEGETABLES

Cantonese people are mad for vegetables, especially greens, and consume great quantities of *choisam* (rape or flowering cabbage), *tung choi* (water spinach), *bak choi* (Chinese white cabbage) and *gai lan* (Chinese broccoli). Other popular vegetables include: bamboo shoots; bean sprouts; bitter melon (or gourd); long beans; black, tree ear and straw mushrooms; lotus and taro root; and water chestnuts.

DESSERT

Dessert (at least as Westerners know it) is not a big-ticket item in Chinese homes or restaurants. Hong Kong Chinese will traditionally end a meal with a sweet soup – sometimes made of red bean or almonds – or fresh fruit (see p168), usually oranges since they symbolise wealth. At dim sum you may find egg custard tarts (best when served warm), steamed buns with sweet red bean paste, coconut snowballs (sweet rice-flour balls dressed with coconut slices), and various other sweets made with sesame seeds. You will never be served fortune cookies at the end of a meal at a Hong Kong Chinese restaurant. These are a foreign invention.

REGIONAL VARIATIONS

China can be divided into many geographical areas, and each area has a distinct style of cooking. The ingredients used in the food tend to reflect the agricultural produce available in a region. Northern China, for example, is suited to growing wheat, so noodles, dumplings and other gluten-based preparations are common. In the south, where the climate is warm and wet, rice is the staple. The Sichuan area, where spices grow well, is famous for its fiery hot dishes. Coastal areas, needless to say, excel in their preparations of seafood.

It is not only geography that determines the ingredients used – tradition and culture play a part as well. The Cantonese, the most adventurous among the Chinese when it comes to food, are known for their willingness to eat virtually anything. Consequently, animals with

53

physical and/or sexual prowess (real or imagined) are widely sought after; the Chinese are firm believers in the adage 'You are what you eat'. Snake meat, for example, is considered good for the health, especially in winter when snake soup stalls abound and restaurants put snake dishes on their menus. The more venomous the snake, the greater its reputation as a revitaliser. Older women drink snake blood because they believe it cures or alleviates arthritis. Some men are convinced the blood is an aphrodisiac, so it's often mixed with Chinese wine and drunk.

The most popular cuisines in Hong Kong are Cantonese, Chiu Chow, northern (ie the food of Beijing and Mongolia), Shanghainese, and Sichuan. Many restaurants that bill themselves as northern will include dishes from Sichuan and vice versa.

A difference between Chinese food in Hong Kong and that on the mainland is that local dishes tend to be more refined, influenced by international tastes and made with higher-quality ingredients. To some, this means less flavourful food.

CANTONESE

Originating in Guangdong province from where most Hong Kong Chinese people can trace their roots, Cantonese food is by far the most popular cuisine in Hong Kong. And when it's done well (as it so often is here), it is the best of the lot. The flavours are more subtle than other Chinese cooking styles and the sauces are rarely strong. It was from Guangdong too that the main bulk of Chinese emigrants went abroad. Consequently Cantonese cuisine established itself as 'Chinese cuisine' in the Western world.

Cantonese cuisine has the largest collection of specialised dishes in all of China and is characterised by elaborate preparation and the use of an infinite variety of ingredients. Subtle flavours are combined with a light touch of soy sauce and ginger, enhancing the freshness of the ingredients. Flavours are delicate and well balanced – neither salty nor greasy – and are obtained through cooking techniques such as quick stir-frying and steaming.

The Cantonese are almost religious about the importance of fresh ingredients. It is common to see tanks in seafood restaurants full of finned and shelled creatures enjoying their final moments on *terra infirma*. Housewives still prefer a live chicken or squab plucked from (and plucked in, come to think of it) a market for the evening meal, though the cost of fresh poultry makes the supermarket variety more popular.

The love of food and the increase in foreign travel by local people means there's a lot more experimentation with food these days. Macadamia nuts find their way into scallop dishes, XO brandy is the base for a sauce served with beef and you're just as likely to find sautéed cod slices with pine seeds and fresh fruit as you are traditional steamed grouper on a menu.

Seasonal foods still play a big role in what's on offer at restaurants. Hot pots of pork tripe and other innards can be found in winter, dried scallops with sea moss at Chinese New Year, and winter melon soup in August.

Expensive dishes – some of which are truly tasty, others that carry with them something of a 'face' status – include abalone, shark's fin and bird's nest. Pigeon is a tasty Cantonese speciality served in various ways but most commonly roasted.

Popular Cantonese dishes:

bak cheuk ha – poached fresh prawns served with dipping sauces

ching chau gai lan – stir-fried Chinese broccoli

ching jing sek ban yue – steamed grouper (or garoupa) fish with soy sauce

geung chung guk hai – baked crab with ginger and spring onions

hai yuk pa dau miu – sautéed pea shoots with crab meat

hai yuk suk mei gang – crab and sweet corn soup

hou hyau choi sam – choisum with oyster sauce

hou hyau ngau yuk – stir-fried sliced beef with oyster sauce

jiuyim pai gwat – deep-fried spareribs served with coarse salt and pepper

sailan fa dai ji – stir-fried broccoli with scallops

sang siu gap – roast pigeon

sijiu yau yu – stir-fried cuttlefish with black bean and chilli sauce

sin ning jin yuen gai – lemon chicken

she gang – snake soup

For the best of Cantonese food, try Yung Kee (p175) in Central; Che's Cantonese Restaurant (p182) in Wan Chai; Heichinrou (p189) in Causeway Bay; Aberdeen Ruby Chinese Restaurant (p195) in Aberdeen and Fook Lam Moon (p197) in Tsim Sha Tsui.

Dim Sum

Dim sum is a uniquely Cantonese 'meal' eaten as breakfast, brunch or lunch. The term literally means 'to touch the heart', but 'snack' is more accurate. The act of eating dim sum is usually referred to as *yum cha*, or 'to drink tea' as the beverage is always consumed in copious amounts with dim sum. The HKTB distributes a useful pamphlet called *Hong Kong Snacks Guide* with favourite dim sum dishes listed and recommended places to try them.

Eating dim sum is a social occasion and something you should do in a group. Of course you can eat dim sum alone, but it consists of many separate dishes, which are meant to be shared; you can't simply order a plate with a variety of dim sum dishes. Having several people to share with you means you can try many different dishes.

Dim sum delicacies are normally steamed in small bamboo baskets. Typically, each basket contains three or four identical pieces; you pay by the number of baskets you order. The baskets are stacked up on pushcarts and rolled around the dining room.

You don't need a menu (though these exist too but almost always in Chinese only); just stop the waiter or waitress and choose something from the cart. It will be marked down on a bill left on the table. Don't try to order everything at once. Each pushcart has a different selection, so take your time and order as they come. It's said that there are about 1000 dim sum dishes.

Dim sum restaurants are normally brightly lit and very large and noisy – it's rather like eating in an aircraft hangar. Nevertheless, it can get very crowded, especially at lunch time.

Favourite (and reliable) dim sum restaurants include Luk Yu Tea House (p173) in Central; Fung Shing Restaurant (p181) in Sheung Wan; Victoria City (p186) in Wan Chai; East Lake (p188) in Causeway Bay; Jade Garden (p198) in Tsim Sha Tsui and East Ocean (p183) in Tsim Sha Tsui East.

Popular dim sum dishes:

cha siu bau – steamed barbecued pork buns

cheung fan – steamed rice flour rolls with shrimp, beef or pork

ching chau sichoi – fried green vegetable of the day

chun guen – fried spring rolls

fan gwo – steamed dumplings with shrimp and bamboo shoots

fu pei gun – crispy beancurd rolls

fung jau – fried chicken's feet

gon siu yimin – dry-fried noodles

ha gau – steamed shrimp dumplings

ho yip fan – rice wrapped in lotus leaf

pai guat – braised spareribs (usually bite-sized with black beans)

san juk ngau yok – steamed minced beef balls

siu mai – steamed pork and shrimp dumplings

CHIU CHOW

The Chiu Chow (or Chaozhou in Mandarin) people hail from the area around the seaport of Shantou (formerly Swatow) in northeast Guangdong province. Although part of that province, Chiu Chow cuisine is distinctive enough to be identified as a regional form of cooking all its own. Birds' nests gathered on cliffs of Southeast Asia are a speciality. These are in fact nests made from the saliva of swiftlets, which contains semi-digested seaweed. Other Chiu Chow dishes reflect a love of seafood, including *dai yuechi tong* (shark's fin soup).

Chiu Chow cuisine puts more emphasis on accompanying sauces than Cantonese cooking does. Sauces can be on the sweet side and often use orange, tangerine or sweet bean as flavouring agents. There is a wonderful garlic and vinegar dip for the famous *chiu jau lou sui ngoh* (Chiu Chow soyed goose) and kumquat jam flatters *tim suen hung xiu ha (hai) kau* (deep-fried shrimp balls with honey sauce). A distinctive sauce known as *chin jiu* is made from a skilful blend of spices including wild peppercorn, pepper and chillies, and is an integral component of many Chiu Chow dishes. Duck and goose, cooked in an aromatic sauce that is used again and again and known as *lo sui*, or 'old water', are also popular.

Other Chiu Chow specialities include *chiu jau yi min* (pan-fried egg noodles served over chives) and *chiu jau yu tong* (aromatic fish soup). And no Chiu Chow meal is complete without thimble-size cups of strong and bitter *ti kwan yu* (iron buddha tea), a fermented oolong, at the end. Chiu Chow chefs are also known for their skill in carving raw vegetables into wonderful fancy floral designs.

Chiu Chow dishes to try:

bakgu sailanfa – stewed broccoli with black mushrooms

bingfa gong yin – cold sweet bird's nest soup (dessert)

chin jui gai – diced chicken fried in a light sauce

ching jiu ngau yoksi – fried shredded beef with green pepper

chiu jau lou sui ngoh – Chiu Chow goose

dai yuechi tong – shark's fin soup

fongyue gailan – fried kale with dried fish

jang heung ngap – deep-fried spiced duck

seklau gai – steamed egg-white pouches filled with minced chicken

tim suen hung xiu ha (hai) kau – prawn (crab) balls with sweet, sticky dipping sauce

tong jing hai – cold steamed crab

Chiu Chow places in which to try these dishes (and many more) include Leung Hing Seafood Restaurant (p181) in Sheung Wan; Carriana Chiu Chow Restaurant (p182) in Wan Chai; Eastern Palace Chiu Chow Restaurant (p197) in Tsim Sha Tsui and Chong Fat Chiu Chow Restaurant (p205) in Kowloon City.

NORTHERN CHINESE

Cuisine from Beijing and the north-central provinces hails from the wheat basket in the chilly north of China. Steamed bread, dumplings and noodles figure more frequently than rice. Lamb and mutton, seldom seen in the south, appear on menus thanks to the region's nomadic and Muslim populations.

The food of north China can be identified by the extensive use of oils, such as sesame oil and chilli oil, coupled with ingredients such as vinegar, garlic, spring onions, bean pastes and dark soy sauce. The better Beijing restaurants put on quite a show of noodle-making for tourists. The chef (or performance artist) adroitly twirls the dough, stretches it, splits it into two thick strands, stretches it again, divides it into four thinner ones and so on until the noodles are as thin as threads.

The most famous speciality of northern Chinese cuisine is Peking duck, served with pancakes, plum sauce and shreds of spring onion. Another Mongolian-influenced favourite is *da bin lou*, 'hotpot', 'fire kettle' or 'steamboat'. It's a bit like fondue. Picture a hollow metal cone about 30cm high and 7.5cm wide at the base. Fitted to the outside about halfway up is a metal moat, the shape of a bagel or donut split in half. Inside the cone is a fire, and in the moat is soup stock. Beside the hotpot are plates of raw meat, tofu, vegetables and noodles that you put into the bubbling broth and cook to taste and at your own pace. Hotpot is usually eaten during winter.

Beggar's chicken, another popular dish, was supposedly created by a pauper who stole a chook but had no pot to cook it in. Instead, he plucked it, covered it with clay and put it on the fire. And *voilà*, yet another dish had risen from the flames, phoenix-like, to join the panoply of culinary immortals. Nowadays, the bird is stuffed with mushrooms, pickled Chinese cabbage, herbs and onions, then wrapped in lotus leaves, sealed in clay and baked all day in hot ashes.

Favourite dishes from the north:

bakging fungchau laimin – noodles fried with shredded pork and bean sprouts

bakging tinngap – Peking duck

bakgupa junbakchoi – Tianjin cabbage and black mushrooms

chongyau beng – pan-fried spring onion cakes

congbao yangyok – sliced lamb with onions on sizzling platter

foogwai gai – beggar's chicken

gonchau ngauyoksi – dried shredded beef with chilli sauce

san yeung yug – Mongolian hotpot

sansin tong – clear soup with chicken, prawn and abalone

If you want to sample northern Chinese cuisine, try American Restaurant (p182) in Wan Chai; Spring Deer (p200) in Tsim Sha Tsui and Islam Food (p205) in Kowloon City.

SHANGHAINESE

The cuisine of the Shanghai area contains more oil and is generally richer, sweeter and more strongly flavoured than other Chinese styles of cooking. Stewing, frying and braising are the principal cooking techniques. Seafood, preserved vegetables, pickles and salted meats are widely used. A speciality are the dishes of cold meats served with various sauces.

Shanghai winters are cold and – as in northern China – bread, thick noodles and a wide range of dumplings are staples. During the hot and humid summers, people prefer cooling foods such as soybean products, fish, prawns and mushrooms.

A few dishes to get you started:

chung pei hai – hairy crabs (an autumn dish)

fotui siuchoi – Shanghai cabbage with ham

hongsiu ju sau – richly simmered pigs knuckle

ja jigai – deep-fried chicken

jui gai – 'drunken chicken' (chicken marinated in cold rice wine)

lungjin hajen – shrimps with 'dragon-well' tea leaves

ngheung ngauyok – cold spiced beef

seunghoi chochau – fried Shanghai-style (thick) noodles with pork and cabbage

sinyok siulong bau – steamed minced pork dumplings

sungsue wongyue – sweet-and-sour yellow croaker fish

There are a large number of Shanghai restaurants in Hong Kong – the cuisine seems to have enjoyed something of a renaissance in recent years – so you won't have to look far for a good one. Try Ning Po Residents Association (p173) and Yi Jiang Nan (p180) in Central; Liu Yuan Restaurant (p184) in Wan Chai; Hangzhou Restaurant (p189) in Causeway Bay; Hong Kong Old Restaurant (p192) in North Point and Wu Kong Shanghai Restaurant (p202) in Tsim Sha Tsui.

SICHUAN

China's west-central provinces of Sichuan and Hunan are known for their fiery food but, in reality, the heat is nothing compared with that of, say, Thai food. Chillies are widely used in this style of cooking, along with aniseed, coriander, fennel seed, garlic, peppercorns, broad-bean paste and vinegar. Dishes are simmered to give the chilli peppers time to work into the food. Not all dishes (eg camphor smoked duck) are hot. These provinces are a long way from the coast, so pork, chicken and beef are the staples – not seafood.

Sichuan food aims for a perfect blend of five key flavours: sweet, sour, salt, pepper and, of course, hot; a good example is *suen lat tong* (hot and sour soup). The food is highly fragrant, and the contrast in textures interesting. This is a result of intricate cooking methods. Stir-fried dishes, for instance, are first deep-fried, then returned to the wok and cooked to the point where juices are almost entirely reduced. The results are chewy yet tender, dry yet flavoursome.

The Sichuan speciality *jeung cha ap* (camphor smoked duck) is a serious contender to Peking duck as China's top fowl dish. The duck is seasoned with ginger, orange peel, cinnamon, peppercorns and coriander, then marinated in Chinese rice wine. After an initial steaming, the duck is smoked over a charcoal fire sprinkled with chips of camphorwood and red tea leaves. Served with fluffy white steamed buns, the final result is a heavenly blend of flavours.

Protein-rich tofu in all its forms is another of Sichuan's treasures. *Ma po doufu* ('grandmother's tofu'; with beef, garlic, chilli, soy sauce, rice wine, peppercorn and spring onion added to the beancurd) is a very Sichuanese dish but is cooked and eaten all over China.

Some favourites:

ching jiu ngau yoksi – sautéed shredded beef and green pepper

chuipei wongyuepin – fried fish in sweet-and-sour sauce

dan dan min – noodles in savoury sauce

gonbin seigwai dau – pan-fried spicy string beans

gongbau gaiding – sautéed diced chicken and peanuts in sweet chilli sauce

huiguo rou – slices of braised pork with chillies

jeungcha hau ngap – duck smoked in camphor wood

ma ngei seung xu – 'ants climbing trees' (bean-thread noodles braised with minced pork)

ma po daufoo – stewed beancurd with minced pork and chilli

sichuan mingha – Sichuan chilli prawns

suen la tong – hot and sour soup with shredded meat (and sometimes congealed pig's blood)

yue heung keiji – sautéed eggplant in a savoury, spicy sauce

For authentic Sichuanese/Hunanese food, try Hunan Garden (p172) in Central or Red Pepper (p190) in Causeway Bay.

VEGETARIANS

Chinese vegetarian food has undergone a renaissance in recent years and it is consumed by both strict Buddhists and the health-conscious. Out of Buddhist piety many Hong Kong people will go vegetarian on the first and 15th day of the lunar month. But many will still consume dishes made with chicken stock, which seems to be regarded as liquid vegetable substance.

Chinese chefs are masters at adding variety to vegetarian cooking and creating 'mock meat' dishes. Chinese Buddhist vegetarian food is based on tofu to which chefs do some miraculous things. Not only is it made to taste like any food you could possibly think of, it's also made to look like it as well. A dish that is sculptured to look like spareribs or a chicken can either be made from layered pieces of dried beancurd or fashioned from mashed taro root.

Large monasteries often have vegetarian restaurants, including Po Lin (p214) on Lantau, though you will also find many restaurants in Kowloon and on Hong Kong Island. For the most part they are Cantonese or Shanghainese and strictly vegetarian as they are owned and operated by Buddhists. You don't have to go to a vegetarian restaurant to find meatless dishes, though. Vegetarian congee is available in most noodle shops, and yum cha houses serve a number of vegetarian treats, including *chongyau beng* (onion cakes), *fu pei gun* (crispy tofu roll) and sweets.

Chinese vegetarian dishes:

bolo chaufan – fried rice with diced pineapple

chingdun bakgu tong – black mushroom soup

chun guen – vegetarian spring rolls

gamgu sunjim – braised bamboo shoots and black mushrooms

jailoumei – mock chicken, barbecued pork or roast duck

lohon choi – stewed mixed vegetables

lohon jai yimin – fried noodles with braised vegetables

yehchoi guen – cabbage rolls

Some of the best Chinese vegetarian restaurants in Hong Kong are Healthy Mess Vegetarian Restaurant (p184) in Wan Chai; Kung Tak Lam (p189) and Vegi Food Kitchen (p191) in Causeway Bay; Kung Tak Lam (p199) in Tsim Sha Tsui and Joyful Vegetarian (p204) in Yau Ma Tei.

COOKING COURSES

Hong Kong is a good place to learn about or hone you skills in the art of Chinese cookery.

CHINESE CUISINE TRAINING INSTITUTE Map pp398–9
☎ 2538 2382; www.ccti.vtc.edu.hk; 7th fl, Pokfulam Training Centre Complex, 145 Pok Fu Lam Rd, Pok Fu Lam
Four-hour courses from HK$620 per person, including lunch.

HOME MANAGEMENT CENTRE
Map pp398–9
☎ 2510 2828; www.hec.com.hk/hec; 10th fl, Electric Centre, 28 City Garden Road, North Point
You can learn three simple Chinese dishes in two hours at the HMC on Wednesday mornings for HK$100.

TOWNGAS COOKING CENTRE
Map pp406–8
☎ 2576 1535; www.towngas.com; Basement, Leighton Centre, 77 Leighton Rd, Causeway Bay
The centre has classes in a vast range of Chinese cooking styles (HK$60 to HK$370).

DRINKS
NONALCOHOLIC DRINKS
Coffee
The last few years have seen a miniature explosion of cafés in Hong Kong. In general they are expensive but serve a wide range of coffees. Local people enjoy chilled coffee *dong gafe*, a soft drink really, which can also be bought everywhere in cans.

Juices
Corner sundry shops and stalls in Hong Kong sell a whole range of made-on-the-spot fruit juices that cost from about HK$6, but avoid the ones where the blenders (liquidisers) are

Pouring tea, Lock Cha Tea Shop (p262)

already full and just spun around a couple of times for each customer. Orange, melon and sugarcane juices are the best.

Soft Drinks
Fleecy is a popular sweet and cold drink that contains some sort of lumpy mixture, usually red or green mung beans, pineapple or some other fruit, and black grass jelly. Condensed milk or ice cream is usually part of the mixture. You can sample these drinks almost anywhere, including Chinese fast-food joints.

Tea
In Chinese restaurants, tea is either offered free of charge or costs a couple of dollars for a large pot that is refilled indefinitely. There are three main types of tea: green or unfermented; *bolei*, which is fermented tea and is also known as black tea; and *oolong*, which is semi-fermented. In addition, there are other variations, including *heung ping* (jasmine), which is a blend of black tea and flower petals. Chinese tea is never served with milk or sugar.

ALCOHOLIC DRINKS
Beer
Lager is by far and away the most popular alcoholic beverage in Hong Kong, and there's a wide choice of the amber nectar in supermarkets, convenience stores and bars. Hong Kong brews two beers under license: Carlsberg (Denmark) and San Miguel (Philippines). Tsingtao, China's slightly fruity export beer, is sold everywhere.

The Hong Kong SAR Brewery Company (www.hongkongbrewery.com) makes several decent brews including German-style Hong Kong Gold Premium lager and a hoppy lager called Red Dawn. The company's Dragon's Back India Pale is a fruity ale, while Aldrich Bay is more akin to an English ale. It also produces beers for local bars, including Delaney's Lager, Delaney's Ale and Caledonia Brown Porter.

Brandy & Spirits
Among Hong Kong's wealthier drinkers, cognac is the tipple of choice. Indeed, the territory has the world's highest per capita consumption of the brandy. People here generally drink it neat, but rarely sip; sometimes you'll even see a group of enthusiastic diners shouting *gon bui!* (literally 'empty glass') and downing it like shots of whisky or tequila. Supermarkets, department stores, restaurants and bars usually have a decent selection of other spirits and wines.

Wine
Though the Chinese tend to refer to all their own alcohol as 'wine' in English, the majority are spirits distilled from grains like rice, sorghum or millet. Most are potent, colourless and extremely volatile. They are available in supermarkets, restaurants and a few bars.

The best known, and most expensive, Chinese 'wine' is *mao tai*, distilled from millet. Another delicacy is *goh leung* (*gao liang* in Mandarin), which is made from sorghum.

History

History

Strictly speaking, the story of Hong Kong as it exists today (a Special Administrative Region of the People's Republic of China) begins only on 1 July 1997, when the mainland resumed control of the territory after more than 150 years of British rule. But like everything else here, it's not that simple. A lot was going on in these parts before the 'handover' and even before that wintry morning in 1841 when a contingent of British marines clambered ashore and planted the Union flag on the western part of Hong Kong Island, claiming it for the crown.

EARLY INHABITANTS

Hong Kong has supported human life since at least the late Stone Age. Archaeological finds – tools, pottery and other artefacts – suggest that as far back as the Neolithic period (c. 4000–2500 BC) nomadic gatherers, hunters and fisherfolk lived along the coast, constantly shifting their settlements from bay to bay. They appear to have enjoyed a relatively nutritious diet of iron-rich vegetables, small mammals, shellfish and fish harvested far offshore.

Finds uncovered at some 94 archaeological sites in the territory, including a rich burial ground found on Ma Wan Island in 1997, suggest that the inhabitants of these settlements were warlike. The remnants of Bronze Age habitations unearthed on Lamma and Lantau islands and at some 20 other sites – as well as the eight geometric rock carvings that can still be seen at various locations along Hong Kong's coastline – also indicate that these early peoples practised some form of cosmology.

THE FIVE GREAT CLANS

Just when the area that is now Hong Kong became an integral part of the Chinese empire is difficult to say. What is certain, however, is that by the Eastern Han dynasty (206 BC–AD 220) imperial rule had been extended over the region that now incorporates the territory of Hong Kong. The discovery of a number of Han coins on Lantau and Kau Sai Chau and several important sites, including the tomb of a senior Han warrior at Lei Cheng Uk in central Kowloon, testifies to this.

By the Eastern Han dynasty (206 BC–AD 220) Chinese imperial rule had been extended over Hong Kong. The first of Hong Kong's mighty 'Five Clans' (Han Chinese whose descendants hold political and economic clout to this day) began settling in walled villages in the fertile plains and valleys of what are now the New Territories around the 12th century AD. The first and most powerful of the arrivals were the Tang, who initially settled around Kam Tin. The once-moated hamlet of Kat Hing Wai (*wai* means 'protective wall', *tin* means 'field'), which is probably the most visited of the remaining traditional walled villages in the New Territories, formed part of this cluster.

Over the next 500 years or so, the Tang were followed by the Hau, who spread around what is present-day Sheung Shui, and the Pang from central Jiangsu province, who settled in what is now the area around Fanling. These three clans were followed by the Liu in the 15th century and the Man a century later.

The Cantonese-speaking newcomers called themselves Punti, the English transliteration for *bun dei*, meaning 'indigenous' or 'local' – something they clearly were not. They looked

TIMELINE	4000–2500 BC	AD 25–220	12th–16th centuries
	Small groups of Neolithic hunter-gatherers and fisherfolk settle coastal areas.	Chinese imperial rule extends to Hong Kong during the late Han dynasty.	Hong Kong's Five Clans settle in what is now the New Territories.

down on the original inhabitants, many of whom had been shunted off the land and had begun living on boats. It is thought that today's fisherfolk called the Tanka, or 'egg people' (a derogatory term used in Cantonese for these people because of the egg-shaped awnings on their boats) emerged from this persecuted group. The Tanka in turn feuded with the Hoklo boat people, a rival fishing community originating from the coastal regions of present-day Fujian province which has retained its own language.

AN IMPERIAL OUTPOST

Clinging to the southern edge of the Chinese province of Canton (now Guangdong), the peninsula and islands that would become the territory of Hong Kong counted only as a remote pocket in a neglected corner of the Chinese empire. Among the scattered communities of farmers and fisherfolk were pirates who hid from the authorities among the rocky islands that afforded easy access to the nearby Pearl River.

Hong Kong's first recorded brush with imperial China was in the 13th century and was as brief as it was tragic. In 1276, a group of loyal retainers of the Song dynasty (AD 960–1279) smuggled the boy emperor, Duan Zong, south to the remote fringes of the empire after the Song capital, Hangzhou, had fallen to the Mongol hordes sweeping China. Thus the Song court reigned briefly and in name only from Hong Kong.

Nine-year-old Duan Zong drowned when Mongol ships defeated the tattered remnants of the imperial fleet in a battle on the Pearl River, but his legacy has endured in the name of Kowloon, the peninsula north of Hong Kong Island (see p101).

The Punti flourished until the struggle that saw the moribund Ming dynasty (1368–1644) overthrown. The victorious Qing (1644–1911), angered by the resistance put up by southerners loyal to the *ancien régime* and determined to solve the endemic problem of piracy, ordered a forced evacuation inland in the 1660s of all the inhabitants of Guangdong's San On district, including Hong Kong. All crops and properties were destroyed, and the resulting famine reduced a thriving coastal population of almost 20,000 to little more than 2000.

These turbulent times saw the birth of the Triads, which would degenerate over the centuries into Hong Kong's own version of the Mafia. They were originally founded as patriotic secret societies dedicated to overthrowing the Qing dynasty and restoring the Ming. Today's Triads still recite an oath of allegiance to the Ming, but their loyalty is to the dollar rather than the vanquished Son of Heaven.

More than four generations passed before the population was able to recover to its mid-17th-century levels, boosted in part by the influx of the Hakka (Cantonese for 'guest people'). These hardy migrants from northeastern China were resented by the southerners for their aggression, studiousness and self-sufficiency. Most are now assimilated into the Cantonese-speaking mainstream of Hong Kong, but some retain their own language, songs and folklore. Hakka women can be recognised in the New Territories by their distinctive spliced-bamboo hats with wide brims and black cloth fringes.

ARRIVAL OF THE 'OUTER BARBARIANS'

Regular trade between China and the West began in 1557 when Portuguese navigators were granted permission to set up a base within a walled enclave in Macau, 65km west of Hong Kong. Jesuit priests arrived in 1582, and their scientific and technical knowledge so aroused the interest of the imperial court that a few of the clerics were permitted to live in Peking (now Beijing).

For centuries, the Pearl River estuary had been an important trading artery centred on the port of Canton (now Guangzhou). Arab traders had entered – and sacked – the settlement as early as the 8th century AD. Guangzhou was 2500km south of Peking, and

1276	1660s	Mid-17th century	1757
Mongol ships defeat imperial fleet in the Pearl River; Song boy-emperor, Duan Zong, drowns in Hong Kong.	Forced evacuation of Guangdong coastal inhabitants inland devastates the local population.	Arrival of Hakka groups from northeastern China.	The *cohong* (local merchants' guild) awarded the monopoly on China's trade with foreigners in Guangdong.

the Cantonese view that the 'mountains are high and the emperor is far away' was not disputed in the imperial capital. The Ming emperors regarded their subjects to the south as akin to witches and sorcerers, their language unintelligible and their culinary predilections downright disgusting. It was therefore fitting that the Cantonese should trade with the 'outer barbarians', or foreign traders.

Dutch traders came in the wake of the Portuguese and were in turn followed by the French. British ships had begun arriving as early as 1685 from the East India Company concessions along the coast of India, and by 1714 the company had established 'factories', offices and warehouses with 'factors' (or managers), in Guangzhou to trade for tea, silk and porcelain. By the end of the 18th century, the flags of more than a dozen nations, including Britain, would be flying over the buildings along 13 Factories Street.

In 1757 an imperial edict awarded the *cohong*, a local merchants' guild, the monopoly on China's trade with foreigners. Numerous restrictions were placed on Western traders: it was illegal for them to learn the Chinese language or to deal with anyone except merchants of the cohong; they could not enter Guangzhou proper but were restricted to Shamian Island in the Pearl River; they were allowed to remain only for the trading season (November to May); and they had to leave their wives and families behind in Macau. The traders complained about the tight restrictions but, nevertheless, business flourished.

Statue of Sir Thomas Jackson, founder of the Hongkong & Shanghai Bank, outside the HSBC headquarters (p81)

'AS THE PORT OF CANTON IS THE ONLY ONE AT WHICH THE OUTER BARBARIANS ARE PERMITTED TO TRADE, ON NO ACCOUNT CAN THEY BE PERMITTED TO WANDER AND VISIT OTHER PLACES IN THE MIDDLE KINGDOM.'

From an Imperial Edict (1836)

OPIUM & WAR

While the West had developed a voracious demand for Chinese products, especially tea, the Chinese were largely self-sufficient, for the most part disdaining Western manufactured goods. The West's ensuing trade deficit was soon reversed, however, after the British discovered a commodity that the Chinese craved: opium. In 1773 they unloaded 1000 chests at Guangzhou, each containing almost 70kg of Indian opium.

Addiction swept China like wildfire, pulling mandarins and coolies alike into its narcotic embrace, and sales of what the Chinese called 'foreign mud' skyrocketed. The British, with a virtually inexhaustible supply of the drug from the poppy fields of India, developed the trade aggressively, and opium formed the basis of most of their transactions with China by the start of the 19th century.

1799	1834	1839	1840–42
Qing imperial court bans trade in opium.	British East India Company loses its monopoly on China trade.	Imperial emissary Lin Zexu attempts to stamp out the opium trade in southern China.	First Opium War.

Alarmed by the drain of silver out of the country to pay for the opium and the spread of addiction, Emperor Chia Ch'ing (Jiaqin) issued an edict in 1799 banning the trade in opium in China, while his son and successor, Tao Kuang (Daoguang), banned the drug from Whampoa and Macau in 1820. But in Guangzhou the *cohong* and corrupt officials helped ensure that the trade continued, and fortunes were amassed on both sides. Imports of the drug increased further after 1834, when the British East India Company lost its monopoly on China trade and other firms rushed in, delivering some 40,000 chests of opium to China each year, some from as far away as Turkey and the Levant.

This was all supposed to change in 1839 with the arrival of Lin Zexu, governor of Hunan and a mandarin of great integrity, with orders from Beijing to stamp out the opium trade altogether. It took Lin a week to surround the British in Guangzhou and cut off their food supplies and demand the surrender of all opium in their possession. The British held out for six weeks until they were ordered by Captain Charles Elliot, Britain's chief superintendent of trade, to turn over more than 20,000 chests of the drug. Lin then had the shipment publicly burned.

'IN HONG KONG FIX AND PASSEPARTOUT SAW THAT THEY WERE IN A SMOKING-HOUSE HAUNTED BY THOSE WRETCHED, CADAVEROUS, IDIOTIC CREATURES TO WHOM THE ENGLISH MERCHANTS SELL EVERY YEAR THE MISERABLE DRUG CALLED OPIUM...THOUSANDS DEVOTED TO ONE OF THE MOST DESPICABLE VICES WHICH AFFLICT HUMANITY!'

Jules Verne, Around the World in 80 Days *(1873)*

Elliott suspended all trade with China while he awaited instructions from London. The British traders retreated to Macau, but the Portuguese, officially neutral, could not guarantee their safety and they took refuge on board ships anchored in Hong Kong harbour. This was a ruse for hawkish elements in the British government to win support for military action against China. The foreign secretary, Lord Palmerston, goaded on by prominent Scottish merchants in Guangzhou, William Jardine and James Matheson, ordered the Royal Navy in Guangzhou to force a settlement in Sino–British commercial relations. An expeditionary force of 4000 men under Rear Admiral George Elliot, a cousin of Captain Charles Elliot, was sent to extract reparations and secure favourable trade arrangements from the Chinese government.

What would become known as the First Opium War (or First Anglo–Chinese War) began in June 1840 when British forces besieged Guangzhou before sailing north and occupying or blockading a number of ports and cities along the Yangzi River and the coast as far as Shanghai. To the emperor's great alarm, the force threatened Beijing, and he sent his envoy (and Lin's successor) Qi Shan to negotiate with the Elliots. In exchange for the Britons' withdrawal from northern China, Qi agreed to the Convention of Chuenpi (now Chuanbi), which ceded Hong Kong Island to Britain.

Though neither side accepted the terms of the convention, a couple of subsequent events would see Hong Kong's fate signed and sealed. In January 1841 a naval landing party hoisted the British flag at Possession Point (now Possession Street). The following month Captain Elliot attacked the Bogue (Humen) forts, took control of the Pearl River and laid siege to Guangzhou, withdrawing only after having extracted considerable financial reparations and other concessions from the merchants there. Six months later a powerful British force led by Elliot's successor, Sir Henry Pottinger, sailed north and seized Amoy (Xiamen), Ningpo (Ningbo), Shanghai and other ports. With the strategic city of Nanking (Nanjing) under immediate threat, the Chinese were forced to accept Britain's terms.

1841	1842	1856–60	1857
British flag raised on Possession Point.	Treaty of Nanking cedes Hong Kong Island in perpetuity to Great Britain.	Second Opium War.	Poisoned Bread Case.

The Treaty of Nanking abolished the monopoly system of trade, opened five 'treaty ports' to British residents and foreign trade, exempted British nationals from all Chinese laws and, most important of all (in hindsight if not at the time), ceded the island of Hong Kong to the British 'in perpetuity'. The treaty, signed in August 1842 and ratified the following year, set the scope and character of the unequal relationship between China and the West.

BRITISH HONG KONG

'Albert is so amused at my having got the island of Hong Kong', wrote Queen Victoria to King Leopold of Belgium in 1841, and then wondered whether their daughter 'ought to be called Princess of Hong Kong in addition to Princess Royal'. While the queen's consort may have seen the funny side of her owning an apparently useless lump of rock off the southern coast of China, Lord Palmerston was less than amused and relieved Captain Charles Elliot of his post.

'A BARREN ISLAND WITH HARDLY A HOUSE UPON IT! IT WILL NEVER BE A MART FOR TRADE. YOU HAVE TREATED MY INSTRUCTIONS AS IF THEY WERE WASTE PAPER.'

Lord Palmerston, British Foreign Secretary, to Captain Charles Elliot (1841)

Even in the early 1840s Hong Kong was not quite the backwater portrayed by the foreign secretary and the local press. At the time, Hong Kong contained about 20 villages and hamlets, with a population of some 3650 on land and another 2000 living on fishing boats in the harbour. While 80% of the terrain was too mountainous to farm and lacked water, it did offer one distinct advantage for the British trading fleet: a deep, well-sheltered harbour.

The place was familiar to British sailors, who had been using the fine harbour to anchor vessels carrying opium since the 1820s and knew of a waterfall on the island's southern shore as a source of fresh water. They called the island Hong Kong, after the Cantonese name *heung gong*, or 'fragrant harbour'.

As Captain Elliot saw it, from here the British Empire and its merchants could conduct all their trade with China and establish a permanent outpost, under British sovereignty, in the Far East. But the British merchants in Guangzhou and the Royal Navy sided with Lord Palmerston; a small barren island with nary a house on it was not the type of sweeping concession that a British victory was supposed to achieve.

'WE NOW ONLY REQUIRE HOUSES, INHABITANTS, AND COMMERCE TO MAKE THIS SETTLEMENT ONE OF THE MOST VALUABLE OF OUR POSSESSIONS.'

Canton Press (1841)

GROWING PAINS

What would later be called the Second Opium War (or Second Anglo–Chinese War) broke out in October 1856 when Chinese soldiers boarded the British merchant schooner *Arrow* to search for pirates. French troops supported the British in this war, while Russia and the USA lent naval support. The first stage of the war was brought to an end two years later by the Treaty of Tientsin (Tianjin), which gave foreigners the right to diplomatic representation in Beijing, but not without a rise of xenophobia (see the boxed text 'Arsenic on Toast').

1860	1865	1888	1894
First Convention of Peking cedes Kowloon and Stonecutters Island to Hong Kong.	Hongkong and Shanghai Bank founded.	Peak Tram opens.	Bubonic plague kills 2500 people.

Arsenic on Toast

Before the 1997 handover, people in Hong Kong used to joke rather darkly that if China wanted to rid the territory of all expatriates once and for all, it need only drop a bomb on Hong Kong Stadium on the second day – the Sunday – of the annual Rugby Sevens tournament, *the* most important and accessible social event of the year for foreigners. What most people didn't realise was that something similar had actually happened 150 years before.

Shortly after breakfast on the morning of 15 January 1857 a sizeable percentage of Europeans living in Hong Kong – some 400 in fact – began falling to the floor, retching uncontrollably and collapsing into convulsions. It didn't take long to sort out that the bread from the E-Sing Bakery in Wan Chai, a favourite of foreigners, had been poisoned – laced with so much arsenic that it had brought on acute vomiting, but not enough that it caused death, as was obviously intended. Not surprisingly all fingers pointed to one Cheong Ah Lum, rich merchant, moneylender and the owner of the bakery.

It had been a trying time for the fledgling colony. Bickering, lawsuits and official inquiries had weakened the administration of Governor Sir John Bowring. More worrying, just three months earlier Chinese officials had boarded the British schooner *Arrow* (see p66) in Guangzhou to which the British navy had responded by bombarding the port. Anti-foreigner sentiment was strong in Hong Kong, and posters had appeared all over Victoria calling for the Chinese to overthrow their foreign masters. Prosecutors assumed that Cheong was a fellow traveller and had taken matters into his own hands.

But when the baker was tried by judge and jury – all of whom had swallowed some of the arsenic – he was found not guilty and released. It turned out that although he had sailed to Macau the very morning of the dastardly deed, he too had been affected by the poison and had returned to Hong Kong voluntarily. Needless to say, with the colony gripped by fear and panic, the verdict was not a popular one, and Europeans demanded that Cheong be re-arrested and tried on some other charge. In the end the government proposed that Cheong go into voluntary exile for five years, which he promptly did.

The authorities never discovered who was behind what has become known as the Poisoned Bread Case though, with the motive clearly a political one, suspicions fell on the mandarins of Guangzhou. E-Sing Bakery ceased trading and Lane, Crawford and Company, a fancy-goods emporium established in the 1840s and still going strong as the Lane Crawford Department, set up its own bakery – staffed, of course, by Europeans.

Despite warnings from the Chinese, the British tried to capitalise on this agreement in 1859 by sending a flotilla carrying the first 'British envoy and minister plenipotentiary', Frederick Bruce, up the Pei Ho River to Beijing. The Chinese fired on the armada, which sustained heavy losses. Using this as an excuse, a combined British and French force invaded China and marched on Beijing. The victorious British forced the Chinese to the Convention of Peking in 1860, which ratified the Treaty of Tientsin and ceded the southern tip of the Kowloon Peninsula and Stonecutters Island to Britain. Britain was now in complete control of Victoria Harbour and its approaches.

Within 40 years, Hong Kong's population had almost tripled and the British army felt it needed more land to protect the colony. Hong Kong made its move when the Qing dynasty was at its nadir, fending off concession demands from France, Germany and Russia and losing a war with Japan (1894–95), in which the Chinese were forced to cede Formosa (Taiwan).

The government petitioned China for a land extension and in June 1898 the Second Convention of Peking presented Britain with a larger-than-expected slice of territory running north to the Shumchun (or Shenzhen) River and 235 islands, increasing the colony's size by 90 percent. But instead of annexing the 'New Territory' (later called the New Territories), the British agreed to sign a 99-year lease, beginning on 1 July 1898 and ending at midnight on 30 June 1997.

1898	1900	1904	1910
Second Convention of Peking leases the New Territories to Hong Kong for 99 years.	Population jumps to 265,000 from 33,000 in 1850.	Electrified tramlines begin operation.	Kowloon–Canton Railway completed.

A SLEEPY BACKWATER

While the *hongs* – Hong Kong's major trading houses such as Jardine, Matheson and Swire – prospered from the China trade, the colony hardly thrived in its early decades. Fever, bubonic plague, typhoons and at least one sinister plot to rid the colony of Europeans (see the boxed text 'Arsenic on Toast', p67) threatened life and property, and at first the colony attracted a fair number of criminals and vice merchants. Opium dens, gambling clubs and brothels proliferated; just a year after Britain took possession, an estimated 450 prostitutes worked out of two dozen houses. Australian 'actresses' were based in Lyndhurst Terrace – *bak fa gai*, or 'White Flower Street', in Chinese.

'VICE MUST BE PRETTY MUCH THE SAME ALL OVER THE WORLD, BUT IF A MAN WISHES TO GET OUT OF PLEASURE WITH IT, LET HIM GO TO HONG KONG.'

Rudyard Kipling, From Sea to Sea *(1889)*

Gradually, Hong Kong began to shape itself into a more substantial community. The territory's population leapt from 33,000 in 1850 to 265,000 in 1900. Gas and electrical power companies were set up, ferries, trams, the Kowloon-Canton Railway and the newfangled High Level Tramway (later known as the Peak Tram) provided a decent transport network, and land was reclaimed. The waterfront Praya in Victoria (today's Central) was flanked by handsome new buildings, the hillsides had been planted with trees, colonials flocked to the races at Happy Valley Certain and the prestigious Hong Kong Club opened. More than a few contemporary visitors were as impressed with the colony's social life as they were its development. Nonetheless, from the late-19th century right up to WWII, Hong Kong lived in the shadow of the treaty port of Shanghai, which had become Asia's premier trade and financial centre – not to mention its style capital.

Hong Kong also became a beacon for China's regular outflow of refugees. One of the earliest waves was sparked by the Chinese Revolution of 1911, which ousted the decaying Qing dynasty and ushered in several decades of strife, rampaging warlords and mass starvation. The civil war in China kept the numbers of refugees entering the colony high, but the stream became a flood after Japan invaded China in 1937. As many as 750,000 mainland Chinese sought shelter in Hong Kong over the next three years.

Hong Kong's status as a British colony would only offer the refugees a temporary haven, however. The day after its attack on the US naval base at Pearl Harbor on 7 December 1941, Japan's military machine swept down from Guangzhou and into Hong Kong. After just over two weeks of fierce but futile resistance, the British forces surrendered on Christmas Day, beginning nearly four years of Japanese occupation.

Conditions were harsh, with indiscriminate massacres of mostly Chinese civilians. European civilians were incarcerated at Stanley Prison on Hong Kong Island. Many Hong Kong Chinese fled to Macau, administered by neutral Portugal. In the latter years of the war Japan actually started deporting people from Hong Kong in a bid to ease the severe food shortages there. The population, numbering about 1.6 million in 1941, was reduced to some 610,000 by the end of the war.

THE ROAD TO BOOMTOWN

After Japan's withdrawal from Hong Kong, and subsequent surrender in August 1945, the colony looked set to resume its hibernation. But events both at home and on the mainland forced the colony in a new direction.

Just before WWII Hong Kong had begun to shift from entrepôt trade servicing China to home-grown manufacturing. The turmoil on the mainland, leading to the defeat of the

1911	1937	1941	1945
Chinese Revolution brings thousands of refugees to Hong Kong.	Japan invades China; 750,000 mainland Chinese flee to Hong Kong over the next three years.	Japan seizes Hong Kong.	Japan surrenders to the Allies; Hong Kong returns to British rule.

Nationalists by the victorious Communists in 1949, unleashed a torrent of refugees – both rich and poor – into Hong Kong. By 1947, the population had once again reached the level it had been at the start of the war and, by the end of 1950, it mushroomed to more than two million. When Beijing sided with North Korea that year and went to war against the forces of the USA and the United Nations, the UN embargo on all trade with China (1951) threatened to strangle the colony economically.

But on a paltry, war-torn foundation, both local and foreign businesses built an immense manufacturing (notably textiles and garments) and financial services centre that transformed Hong Kong into one of the world's great economic success stories.

Much of the success depended on the enormous pool of cheap labour from China. Working conditions in those early years of Hong Kong's economic revolution were often Dickensian: 16-hour days, unsafe working conditions, low wages and child labour were all common. Refugee workers endured, and some even earned their way out of poverty and into prosperity. The Hong Kong government, after coming under international pressure, eventually began to establish and enforce labour standards and the situation gradually improved.

Hong Kong was a haven in comparison with life on the mainland, but trouble flared up in the 1950s and '60s due to social discontent and poor working conditions. Feuding between Communist and Nationalist supporters in Hong Kong led to riots in 1957 and again in 1962. The 1966 riots, ostensibly over a 10-cent fare increase on the Star Ferry, demonstrated the frustration many local people had with the colonial government.

'BRITISH HONG KONG DANGLES FREAKISHLY FROM THE GREAT UNDERBELLY OF COMMUNIST CHINA LIKE SOME SMALL BUT SURPRISING ANATOMICAL MONSTER.'

Dennis Bloodworth, Chinese Looking Glass, 1976

When the Communists came to power in China in 1949, many people were sure that Hong Kong would be overrun. Even without force, the Chinese could simply have ripped down the fence on the border and sent the masses to settle on Hong Kong territory. In 1962 China actually staged what looked like a trial run for this, sending 70,000 people across the frontier in a couple of weeks. But though the Chinese continued to denounce the 'unequal treaties', they recognised Hong Kong's importance to the national economy.

At the height of the so-called Cultural Revolution in 1967, when the ultra-leftist Red Guards were in de facto control in China, Hong Kong's stability again looked precarious. Riots rocked the colony, bringing with them a wave of bombings, looting and arson attacks. A militia of 300 armed Chinese crossed the border, killing five policemen and penetrating 3km into the New Territories before pulling back.

'SINCE MAY 1967, COMMUNIST ORGANIZATIONS IN HONG KONG HAVE SOUGHT TO IMPOSE THEIR WILL ON THE GOVERNMENT AND THE PEOPLE BY INTIMIDATING WORKERS, FOMENTING WORK STOPPAGES...AND BY INDISCRIMINATE VIOLENCE. IT HAS BEEN A TESTING TIME FOR THE PEOPLE OF HONG KONG.'

Hong Kong Yearbook 1967

Property values in Hong Kong plunged, as did China's foreign exchange earnings, as trade and tourism ground to a halt. However the bulk of the population – and, importantly, the Hong Kong police – stood firm with the colonial authorities. By the end of the 1960s China, largely due to the intervention of Premier Chou Enlai, had come to its senses and order had been restored.

1949	1966–67	1972	1973
Communist forces are victorious in China; refugees flood into Hong Kong.	Pro-Communist riots.	Cross-Harbour Tunnel opens between Causeway Bay and Hung Hom.	Sha Tin, the first 'New Town', is completed.

A SOCIETY IN TRANSITION

After China had, in effect, retreated, Hong Kong got on with the business of making money, which included improving the territory's infrastructure. In 1972, the Cross-Harbour Tunnel between Causeway Bay and Hung Hom opened, ending the reliance on ferry transport between Hong Kong Island and Kowloon. The next year, the expansion of the first 'New Town' – Sha Tin – was completed, paving the way towards better housing for millions of Hong Kong people. By 1979 the colony had its own underground railway, with the opening of the first line of the Mass Transit Railway (MTR).

The stock market collapsed in 1973, but Hong Kong's economy resumed its upward trend later in the decade. At the same time, many of Hong Kong's neighbours, including Taiwan, South Korea and Singapore, began to mimic the colony's success. Just as their cheap labour was threatening to undermine the competitive edge of Hong Kong manufacturers, China began to emerge from its self-imposed isolation. Deng Xiaoping, who took control of China in the mayhem following Mao Zedong's death in 1976, opened up the country to tourism and foreign investment in 1978.

Deng's 'Open Door' policy, designed to pull China into the 20th century, revived Hong Kong's role as the gateway to the mainland. Local and foreign investment in China grew and trade in Hong Kong skyrocketed as it became the trans-shipment point for China's exports and, later on, imports. Underpinning the boom was the drive to rake in as much profit as possible ahead of 1997, when Hong Kong's unpredictable new master was due to take over.

'HONG KONG...WORKS SPLENDIDLY – ON BORROWED TIME IN A BORROWED PLACE.'

Han Suyin, 'Hong Kong's Ten-Year Miracle', Life, 1959

THE 1997 QUESTION

In reality, few people gave much thought to Hong Kong's future until the late 1970s, when the British and Chinese governments met for the first time to decide what would happen in (and after) 1997. Britain was legally bound to hand back only the New Territories – not Hong Kong Island and Kowloon. However, with nearly half of Hong Kong's population living in the New Territories by that time, it would have been an untenable division.

It was Deng Xiaoping who decided that the time was ripe to recover Hong Kong, forcing the British to the negotiating table. In December 1984, after more than two years of closed-door wrangling, the two parties announced that the UK had agreed to hand back the entire colony just after midnight on 30 June 1997. The decision laid to rest political jitters that had seen the Hong Kong dollar collapse – and subsequently be pegged to the US dollar – in 1983, but there was considerable resentment that the fate of 5.5 million people had been decided without their input and that Whitehall had chosen not to provide Hong Kong people with full British passports and the right of abode in the UK.

'INVESTORS IN HONG KONG SHOULD PUT THEIR HEARTS AT EASE [BUT ANY SETTLEMENT] SHOULD BE BASED ON THE PREMISE THAT THE TERRITORY IS PART OF CHINA.'

Deng Xiaoping quoted by Sir Murray MacLehose, Governor of Hong Kong (1979)

Despite soothing words from China, Britain and the Hong Kong government, over the next 13 years the population of Hong Kong suffered considerable anxiety at the possible political and economic consequences of the handover. Tens of thousands of people immigrated to Canada, the USA, Australia, the UK and New Zealand – or at least managed to secure a foreign passport and the right to live there.

1979	1983	1984	1989
First line of the Mass Transit Railway (MTR) opens.	Hong Kong dollar collapses and is pegged to the US dollar.	Anglo-Chinese agreement over the future of Hong Kong.	Tiananmen massacre propels dissidents to Hong Kong.

'ONE COUNTRY, TWO SYSTEMS'

The agreement signed by China and Britain, enshrined in a document known as *The Sino-British Joint Declaration on the Question of Hong Kong*, pledged to allow Hong Kong to retain its pre-handover social, economic and legal systems for 50 years after 1997. Hong Kong as a 'British-administered territory' would disappear and re-emerge as a Special Administrative Region (SAR) of China. The Hong Kong SAR would be permitted to retain its capitalist system after 1997, while across the border the Chinese would continue with a system that it labelled socialist. The Chinese catch phrase for this was 'One Country, Two Systems'.

In 1988, the details of this rather unorthodox system of government were spelled out in the Basic Law for Hong Kong, the SAR's future constitution. The Basic Law, ratified by the National People's Congress in Beijing in 1990, confirmed that Hong Kong people would govern Hong Kong. It preserved Hong Kong's English common law judicial system and guaranteed the right of property and ownership. It also included the rights of assembly, free speech, association, travel and movement, correspondence, choice of occupation, academic research, religious belief and the right to strike. The SAR would enjoy a high degree of autonomy except in foreign affairs and matters of defence.

As China's own constitution has lofty guarantees of individual freedoms and respect for human rights, few Hong Kong Chinese had faith in the Basic Law. The guarantees were seen as empty promises and many felt the Basic Law provided Beijing with the means to interfere in Hong Kong's internal affairs to preserve public order, public morals and national security. Hong Kong's fledgling democratic movement denounced the Joint Declaration as the new 'unequal treaty' and the Basic Law as a 'basic flaw'.

Although Hong Kong under the British had never been more than a benignly ruled oligarchy, Whitehall had nevertheless promised to introduce democratic reforms prior to the handover. But it soon became apparent that British and Chinese definitions of democracy differed considerably. Beijing made it abundantly clear that it also would not allow Hong Kong to establish its own democratically elected government. The chief executive was to be chosen by a Beijing-appointed panel of delegates; the people of Hong Kong would elect some lower officials. In the face of opposition from Beijing, planned elections for 1988 were postponed until 1991.

TIANANMEN & ITS AFTERMATH

The concern of many Hong Kong people over their future turned to outright fear on 4 June 1989, when Chinese troops used tanks and machine guns to mow down pro-democracy demonstrators in Beijing's Tiananmen Square. The massacre of students and their supporters horrified Hong Kong people, many of whom had donated funds and equipment to the demonstrators. Up to one million Hong Kong people – one in six of the population – braved a typhoon to march in sorrow and anger. As the Chinese authorities spread out to hunt down activists, an underground smuggling operation, code-named Yellow Bird, was set up in Hong Kong to spirit them to safety overseas.

The Tiananmen massacre, still marked every year on the evening of 4 June with a candlelight vigil in Victoria Park on Hong Kong Island, was a watershed for Hong Kong. Sino-British relations deteriorated, the stock market fell 22% in one day and a great deal of capital left the territory for destinations overseas.

The Hong Kong government sought to rebuild confidence by launching a new airport and shipping port; with an estimated price tag of HK$160 billion, this was the world's most expensive infrastructure project of the day, it was designed to lure foreign investors. But China had already signalled its intentions loud and clear.

1990	1991	1992	1995
The Basic Law for Hong Kong ratified; Bill of Rights introduced.	First direct Legislative Council elections.	Last British governor of Hong Kong, Chris Patten, arrives.	First totally elected Legislative Council.

Hong Kong–based Chinese officials who had spoken out against the Tiananmen killings were yanked from their posts or sought asylum in the USA and Europe. Local Hong Kong people with money and skills made a mad dash to emigrate to any country that would take them. At its height in 1990, more than 1000 people were emigrating each week, especially to Canada and Australia. Tiananmen hardened the resolve of those people who either could not leave or chose not to, giving rise to the territory's first official political parties. In a bid to restore credibility, a Bill or Rights was introduced in 1990 and the following year the government bestowed on Hong Kong citizens the right to choose 18 of the 60 members of the Legislative Council (Legco), until then essentially a rubber-stamp body chosen by the government and special-interest groups.

DEMOCRACY & THE LAST GOVERNOR

Hong Kong was never as politically apathetic as was generally thought in the 1970s and '80s. The word 'party' may have been anathema to the refugees who had fled from the Communists or Nationalists in the 1930s and '40s, but not necessarily to their sons and daughters.

Born and bred in the territory, these first-generation Hong Kong youths were entering the universities and colleges by the 1970s and becoming politically active. Like student activists everywhere they were idealistic and passionate, agitating successfully for Chinese to be recognised as an official language alongside English. They opposed colonialism, expressed pride in their Chinese heritage and railed against the benign dictatorship of the Hong Kong government. But they were split between those who supported China and the Chinese Communist Party at all costs and those who had reservations or mistrusted it.

This generation, the first to consider themselves 'Hong Kong people' rather than refugees from China, formed the pressure groups emerging in the 1980s to debate Hong Kong's future. By the end of the decade they were coalescing into nascent political parties and preparing for the 1991 Legco elections.

The first party to emerge was the United Democratic Party, led by outspoken democrats Martin Lee and Szeto Wah. The pair, initially courted by China for their anti-colonial positions and appointed to the committee that drafted the Basic Law, infuriated Beijing by publicly burning copies of the proto-constitution in protest over the Tiananmen massacre. Predictably, China denounced them as subversives.

Sino–British relations worsened with the arrival in 1992 of Chris Patten, Hong Kong's 28th – and last – British governor. Patten lost no time in putting the British plans for limited democracy back on track and even widened their scope.

His legislative reforms were not particularly radical – he lowered the voting age from 21 to 18 and broadened the franchise for the indirectly elected segment of Hong Kong's complicated electoral system. Hong Kong residents were largely sceptical at first, with many wondering why Britain had chosen to wait until this late date to start experiments in democracy.

China reacted badly, first levelling daily verbal attacks on the governor – at various times he was called a 'whore' and 'the sinner of a thousand generations' for his attempt at democratic reforms in the territory – then threatening the post-1997 careers of any pro-democracy politicians or officials. When these tactics failed, it targeted Hong Kong's economy. Negotiations on certain business contracts straddling 1997 suddenly came to a halt, and Beijing scared off foreign investors by boycotting all talks on the new airport program.

Sensing that it had alienated even its supporters in Hong Kong, China backed down and in 1994 gave its blessing to the new airport at Chek Lap Kok. It remained hostile to direct elections, however, and vowed to disband the democratically elected legislature after 1997.

1997	1998
Hong Kong returns to Chinese sovereignty; Tung Chee Hwa named Chief Executive; avian flu breaks out in Hong Kong.	Hong Kong International Airport opens at Chek Lap Kok.

In August 1994, China adopted a resolution to abolish the terms of office of Hong Kong's three tiers of elected bodies – the legislature, the municipal councils and the district boards. A Provisional Legislative Council was elected by Beijing, which included pro-Beijing councillors defeated by democratic ones in the existing Legco. The rival chamber met over the border in Shenzhen, as it had no authority in Hong Kong until the transfer of power.

As for the executive branch of power, no one was fooled by the pseudo-election choreographed by China in 1996 to select Hong Kong's first post-colonial leader. But Tung Chee Hwa (1937–), the Shanghai-born shipping magnate destined to become chief executive, won approval by retaining Patten's right-hand woman, Anson Chan, as his chief secretary and Sir Donald Tsang as financial secretary.

On the night of 30 June 1997 the handover celebrations held at the purpose-built Convention Centre in Wan Chai were watched by millions around the world. Prince Charles was stoic and Chris Patten shed a tear while Chinese Premier Jiang Zemin beamed. China had agreed to a low-key entry into Hong Kong and PLA troops were trucked straight to their barracks in Stanley, Kowloon Tong and Bonham Rd in the Mid-Levels.

'NOW WE ARE MASTERS OF OUR OWN HOUSE.'

Chief Executive Tung Chee Hwa at SAR inauguration ceremony

POST-1997 HONG KONG

The Hong Kong SAR started out on a positive footing. While the predicted political storm failed to appear, other slip-ups and disasters – economic recession, a plague and an ill-fated launch for the new airport – helped to sandbag the new SAR in its early years.

The financial crisis that rocked Thailand and then South Korea before spreading across Southeast Asia began to be felt in Hong Kong at the end of 1997. A strain of deadly avian flu, which many people feared would become a worldwide epidemic, saw Hong Kong slaughtering some 1.4 million chickens. Then came the Chek Lap Kok-up of 1998, when the much trumpeted new airport opened to a litany of disasters. Hong Kong was making world headlines again – but for all the wrong reasons.

Meanwhile, Chief Executive Tung Chee Hwa's popularity was declining. He was seen increasingly as Beijing's puppet, often dictatorial but strangely weak and indecisive in times of crisis. One often cited example of this was his handling of the Falun Gong, a New Age cult that had emerged in China in 1992.

The Falun Gong defined itself not as a religion at all but a system for 'improving and elevating the mind, body and spirit' through simple t'ai chi–style exercises and *qigong* breathing. Adherents on the mainland claimed that continued persecution by the Chinese authorities led to the public suicide of five Falun Gong members by self-immolation in Tiananmen Square in January 2001. Although the Basic Law guaranteed religious freedom in the Hong Kong SAR – and word on the street was that Beijing had given Tung carte blanche to make his own decision – in early 2001 the chief executive followed the lead of the mainland and branded the Falun Gong a 'vicious cult', a move that would limit the group's activities in Hong Kong.

Perhaps the greatest damage to the credibility of the SAR administration since the change in sovereignty came in 1999 when the government decided to challenge a high court ruling allowing residency rights for the China-born offspring of parents who became Hong Kong citizens after 1997. It appealed to the standing committee of the National People's Congress (NPC), China's rubber-stamp parliament, to 'reinterpret' the relevant clauses of the Basic Law, which the NPC dutifully did. When it discovered that 1.6 million people on the mainland would be eligible for right of abode according to the law, the NPC ruled according to what the law drafters 'meant' but had somehow failed to write into law.

2001	2002
Tung brands Falun Gong a 'vicious cult'.	Tung begins second term of office.

Opinion poll after opinion poll showed that, if given the choice, Hong Kong people would have preferred to see Chief Secretary Anson Chan, dubbed the 'conscience of Hong Kong' at the helm. Her departure in mid-2001 raised fears of an impending 'Singapore-isation' of Hong Kong, with a strongman in charge of a rubber-stamping legislature, and of the hardline 'one country' side of the equation coming to dominate the pluralistic 'two systems' side. Many saw Chan's departure as the last nail in the coffin.

THE RETURN OF TUNG

Tung was returned for a second five-year term in March 2002 and moved to reform the executive branch, instituting a cabinet-like system with secretaries to be held accountable for their portfolios. Hopes were raised but then dashed as the government bounced from controversy to scandal.

In July 2002, the Hong Kong Stock Exchange created a market panic by proposing to delist stocks that traded under HK$0.50, which accounted for one-third of all listed stocks. The subsequent sell-off wiped some HK$11 million off the market in an hour. In the enquiry that followed, no-one was held responsible.

In February 2003, the administration announced plans not only to lower the minimum wage of Hong Kong's foreign domestic workers by 11% per cent, but also to slap on a HK$400 monthly 'levy', even though their annual wage falls below the taxation cut-off point of about HK$100,000 a year. Observers saw the move both as both threatening and racist.

In March 2003 Financial Secretary Anthony Leung purchased a new Lexus 430 automobile six weeks before announcing a hefty rise in first-registration vehicle tax in his 2003 budget, saving himself some HK$50,000. Tung criticised Leung for showing 'gross negligence', but refused to accept his resignation. Leung eventually quit four months later.

In July 2003 the government was set to put into law a national security bill called Article 23, which Beijing had added to Hong Kong's Basic Law in the aftermath of the Tiananmen student movement of 1989. The bill dealt with acts 'endangering public security' such as treason, subversion and sedition. While some supporters argued that Article 23 was less severe than laws currently in place in the UK and USA, on Hong Kong Establishment Day (1 July), 500,000 people took to the streets to voice their opposition to the bill, in the city's biggest demonstration since a million people turned out to protest the Tiananmen Square massacre in 1989. The government subsequently deleted certain clauses in the bill and delayed its passage indefinitely in September.

2003

Outbreaks of Severe Acute Respiratory Viral Pneumonia (SARS) kill around 300 people; 500,000 people march in opposition to proposed anti-subversion legislation.

Districts & Islands

Districts & Islands

Although the Hong Kong Special Administrative Region (SAR) is divided politically into 18 districts of varying sizes, these political divisions are not of much interest or use to the traveller. For visitors, the territory can be divided into four main areas – Hong Kong Island, Kowloon, the New Territories and the Outlying Islands – each of which includes a number of districts and neighbourhoods.

This chapter begins on the north side of Hong Kong Island in Central, which, as its name implies, is where much of what happens or is decided in Hong Kong takes place; come here for business, sightseeing, umpteen transport options, and entertainment in the Lan Kwai Fong and Soho nightlife districts. Contiguous to Central to the west is more-traditional Sheung Wan, which manages to retain the feel of prewar Hong Kong, and rising above Central are the Mid-Levels residential area and the Peak, home to the rich, the famous and the indefatigable Peak Tram. To the east of Central are Admiralty, not much more than a cluster of office towers, hotels and shopping centres, but an important transport hub; Wan Chai, a seedy red-light district during the Vietnam War but now a popular entertainment area; and Causeway Bay, the most popular shopping area on the island.

Just south of Causeway Bay is Happy Valley, celebrated for its racecourse. Further east along the coast are the various districts of Island East – Quarry Bay, Sai Wan Ho, Shau Kei Wan and Chai Wan – offering shopping centres in spades, some choice venues for wining and dining, and a surprising number of excellent museums. Island South is made up of tranquil Shek O, which has become something of an activities centre; Stanley, with its fashionable restaurants, cafés and famous market; Repulse Bay and Deep Water Bay, where you'll find the two most popular beaches on the island; and Aberdeen, Hong Kong's original settlement, where you can ride in a sampan (motorised launch) around the harbour or visit nearby Ocean Park, Hong Kong's largest (for the moment) amusement and theme park.

North of Hong Kong Island and across Victoria Harbour is Kowloon, with its epicentre the shopping and entertainment district of Tsim Sha Tsui (sadly, about as far as residents of the island ever travel). To the east is the reclaimed area of Tsim Sha Tsui East, awash with top-end hotels and world-class museums, and Hung Hom, from where rail journeys into and out of mainland China and the New Territories begin and end. To the north of Tsim Sha Tsui are the working-class areas of Yau Ma Tei, where you'll stumble across pawnshops, outdoor markets, Chinese pharmacies, mahjong parlours and other retailers plying their time-honoured trades; and Mong Kok, a somewhat seedy district of street markets and brothels. Beyond are the districts of so-called New Kowloon – Sham Shui Po, Kowloon Tong, Kowloon City, Wang Tai Sin and Diamond Hill – which boast everything from the cheapest computers to the largest temple complex in Hong Kong.

The New Territories, once Hong Kong's country playground, is today a mixed bag of housing estates and some surprisingly unspoiled rural areas and country parks. We've divided what locals call 'the NT' into the New Towns of Tsuen Wan, Tuen Mun, Yuen Long, Fanling, Sheung Shui, Tai Po and Sha Tin, all of which are worth a visit for their temples, monasteries and/or museums hidden somewhere below all the skyscrapers, and its more tranquil areas: the Hakka walled villages of Kam Tin; Tai Mo Shan, Hong Kong's highest peak; Mai Po Marsh, an important wetland for wildlife; Tai Po Kau, with its thickly forested nature reserve; and the idyllic Sai Kung Peninsula and the remote islands of Tap Mun Chau and Ping Chau, which can be reached easily from points in the New Territories.

The Hong Kong archipelago counts hundreds of islands, but the vast majority are uninhabited, inaccessible or both. Among the so-called Outlying Islands that can be reached easily on a day trip from Hong Kong Island (or, in certain cases, Kowloon) are: Cheung Chau, with its traditional village and fishing fleet; Lamma, famed for its restaurants and easy country walks; Lantau, the largest island of all, with excellent beaches and country trails; little Peng Chau, fast becoming a shopping mecca; Ma Wan and Tsing Yi, the 'anchors' for two colossal bridges linking Lantau with the New Territories; Tung Lung Chau, with the remains of a 300-year-old fort; and Po Toi, a haven for seafood lovers.

In this chapter, the 'Transport' boxed texts provide quick reference for the location of Mass Transit Rail (MTR), Kowloon-Canton Railway (KCR), Light Rail Transit (LRT) and bus stations, ferry piers etc in each district. For more detailed information on how to get to, from and around Hong Kong Island, Kowloon, the New Territories and the Outlying Islands, including routes, schedules and fares, see the Transport chapter (p331). For suggestions on the best plans and hiking maps to buy, see Maps (p328).

Itineraries

One Day If you have only one day in Hong Kong, you can catch a tram up to **the Peak** (p87) for a good view of the city and stretch your legs on a summit circuit before lunching at the **Peak Lookout** (p182). Back down at sea level, you could do some shopping at the **Pacific Place** (p251) shopping centre in Admiralty and watch the sun go down from **Cyrano's** (p223), a bar on the 56th floor of the Island Shangri-La Hotel.

Two Days If you have two days to spare, you could also take the Star Ferry to **Tsim Sha Tsui** (p101) and visit the **Museum of Art** (p103), **Space Museum** (p103) **or Museum of History** (p105), have a yum cha brunch at **Wan Loong Court** (p201) in the Kowloon Hotel, then browse along **Nathan Rd** (p103) until you're hungry enough for afternoon tea at the **Peninsula Hotel** (p279). A wander up Temple St for the **night market** (p106), listening to some open-air Cantonese opera and sampling street food are also worthwhile.

Three Days With another day to look around the territory, you could wander around **Central** (p79) and **Sheung Wan** (p84), poking your head into traditional shops before lunching and gallery-hopping in **Soho** (p83). Take a tram to **Wan Chai** (p89) for a night of Chinese opera or theatre at the **Hong Kong Arts Centre** (p91) and strut your stuff at a Wan Chai bar before dining late at the **American Restaurant** (p182).

One Week If you have one week you can see many of the sights listed in the Hong Kong Island and Kowloon sections, visit an Outlying Island. Choose Lantau for the **Tian Tan Buddha** (p148), the fabulous walks and the beaches, or **Lamma** (p140) for the seafood restaurants, jump aboard a bus or the KCR for the New Territories; **Kam Tin** (p127) and surrounds, **Sai Kung Peninsula** (p134) and **Mai Po Marsh** (p126) are all sure bets, and take a day trip to or spend the night in **Macau** (see p291).

ORGANISED TOURS

Tourism is one of Hong Kong's main money-spinners, so it's not surprising that there is a mind-boggling number of tours available to just about anywhere in the territory. If you only have a short time in Hong Kong or don't want to deal with public transport, an organised tour may suit you. Some tours are standard excursions covering major sights on Hong Kong Island such as the Peak and Hollywood Rd, while other tours take you on harbour cruises, out to the islands or through the New Territories.

For walking and outdoor-adventure tours in Hong Kong, see the Walking Tours chapter (p153). For tours to Macau, see Organised Tours (p313).

Air

If you hanker to see Hong Kong from on high – whatever the expense – consider chartering a helicopter. **Heliservices** (☎ 2802 0200; www.heliservices.com.hk) has chartered Aerospatiale Squirrels for up to five passengers available for HK$1800/2500 for each 10-/15-minute period. **Heli Hong Kong** (☎ 2108 4838; www.helihongkong.com) charges just HK$800 per person for a 12-minute flight over Hong Kong. A half-hour flight in a six-seater costs HK$4900; count on HK$9800 for an hour's flight over and around most of the territory. **Hong Kong Heliport** (Map pp400–3) is just north of Citic Tower in Admiralty.

Boat

Many agents, including **Gray Line, Splendid Tours & Travel** and **Harbour Cruise Bauhinia** (☎ 2802 2886 www.cruise.com.hk), have tours of Victoria and Aberdeen Harbours, but the company with the longest experience in these is **Watertours** (Map pp412-14; ☎ 2926 3868, 2730 3031; www .watertourshk.com; Shop 5C, ground floor, Star House, 3 Salisbury Rd, Tsim Sha Tsui). Some eight different tours of the harbour and the Outlying Islands, as well as dinner and cocktail cruises, are available. Prices range from HK$220 (child two to 12 years HK$130) for the Morning Harbour & Noon Day Gun Firing Cruise, to HK$670 (child HK$620) for the Top of Town & Night Cruise. If you want to take in the enormity of the Tsing Ma Bridge, Watertours' Afternoon Western Shoreline Cruise (adult/child HK$220/130) can take you there.

Jubilee International Tour Centre (☎ 2530 0530; www.jubilee.com.hk) has a five-hour tour (HK$350) of the islands off Sai Kung, with pick-up at 9am on Tuesday, Thursday and Saturday from the Kowloon Hotel (19–21 Nathan Rd, Tsim Sha Tsui). For the Outlying Islands, **HKKF Travel** (☎ 2533 5339; info@hkkf.com.hk) has a five-hour Outlying Islands Escapade (HK$320) that takes in Cheung Chau and Lamma. Departure is from pier 5 at the Outlying Islands ferry terminal in Central.

Bus

For first-time visitors to Hong Kong trying to get their bearings, **Splendid Tours & Travel** (☎ 2316 2151; www.splendidtours.com) has some interesting 'orientation' tours of Hong Kong Island as well as Kowloon and the New Territories. The tours last four to five hours and cost HK$280/190 per adult/child three to 12 years. Another tour company to try is the old stalwart **Gray Line** (☎ 2368 7111; www.grayline.com.hk), which has a five-hour tour (HK$295/190) taking in Man Mo Temple, Victoria Peak, Aberdeen, Stanley and Repulse Bay.

Some of the most popular surface tours of the New Territories are offered by the **Hong Kong Tourism Board (HKTB)**. The ever-popular Land Between Tour takes in the Yuen Yuen Institute temple complex in Tsuen Wan, Tai Mo Shan lookout and the fishing village of Sam Mun Tsai, as well as several other sights. The full-day tour (adult/child under 16 or senior over 60 HK$385/335) takes 6½ hours and includes lunch; the half-day tour (HK$290/240) is five hours, without lunch. The five-hour Heritage Tour (HK$290/240), which does not include lunch, takes in such New Territories sights as Man Mo Temple in Tai Po, the Lam Tsuen Wishing Tree and the walled village of Lo Wai. Contact the **HKTB tour operations department** (☎ 2368 7112; ☿ 7am-9pm) for information and bookings.

HONG KONG ISLAND

Although Hong Kong Island makes up only about 7% of the territory's total land area (and its population less than 20% of the total), its importance as the historical, political and economic centre of Hong Kong far outweighs its size. For a start, it was here that the original settlement, Victoria, was founded.

Most of the major businesses, government offices, a good many top-end hotels and restaurants, nightlife areas and exclusive residential neighbourhoods are on Hong Kong Island. It is where you'll find the ex-governor's mansion, the stock exchange, the legislature and High Court, the territory's premier shopping districts, the original horse-racing track and a host of other places that define Hong Kong's character. Not surprisingly, many of Hong Kong's top sights are also on the island.

It may sound like a simplification, but Hong Kong is to Kowloon what north of the Thames is to south of the river in London, Manhattan to New Jersey, Pest to Buda. Virtually everything of importance in Hong Kong starts, finishes or takes place on Hong Kong Island.

The commercial heart of Hong Kong pumps away on the northern side of the island, where banks and businesses and a jungle of high-rise apartment blocks and hotels claim a good part of its 80 sq km. Since the handover in 1997, there have been a few visible changes – the occasional red-and-yellow flag of the People's Republic of China fluttering in the breeze, the name of the Prince of Wales (or Tamar) Building erased and changed to Central Barracks in Chinese – but generally the island remains as it was before: a metropolis of a few preserved monuments overwhelmed by a dazzling modernity.

Looking across from Tsim Sha Tsui on the Kowloon side will impress you with how unbelievably built-up and crowded the northern side of Hong Kong Island is; about the only bits of visible greenery are the steep hills rising behind the skyscrapers. And as well as moving up (in every sense of the word), Hong Kong continues to move out; reclamation along the harbour edge continues to add the odd quarter of a kilometre every so often, and buildings once on the waterfront are now several hundred metres back. The most recent round of reclamation has altered – and substantially added to – the shorelines of Sheung Wan, Central, Admiralty and Wan Chai.

One of the best ways to see the northern side of the island is to jump on one of the green double-decker trams that trundle between Kennedy Town in the west and Shau Kei Wan in the east. Try to board during mid-morning or mid-afternoon when there's a better chance of grabbing a front seat on the upper deck. The trams are slow, and while this may not be ideal for rushed commuters, if you want to sit back and get a feel for Hong Kong city life, this is the way to do it.

The southern side of Hong Kong Island is of a totally different character to the north. The coast is dotted with fine beaches, where the water is clean enough to swim in. The best beaches are at Big Wave Bay, Deep Water Bay, Shek O, Stanley and Repulse Bay. To get to the southern part of Hong Kong Island, the bus is the best way to go.

CENTRAL

Eating p169; Sleeping p270

Most visitors to Hong Kong pass through **Central** at some stage – for sightseeing, taking care of errands such as changing money or buying plane tickets, en route to the bars and restaurants of Lan Kwai Fong and Soho, or getting on or off the Airport Express to/from Hong Kong International Airport at Chek Lap Kok. In fact, many business travellers spend all their time in this district, where most of Hong Kong's larger international companies have their offices.

Not surprisingly, Central has some impressive architectural treasures (see Architecture p37) that can be quite magnificent, especially at night. Though Hong Kong has always been less than sentimental about its past (see the boxed text p98), there's an eclectic assortment of historical civic buildings and churches in the district. Parks, gardens and other green 'lungs' help to round out the picture.

The district was originally named Victoria after the British sovereign who had ascended to the throne just two years before a naval landing party hoisted the British flag at Possession Point west of here in 1841. But as the 'capital' of the territory, it has been called Central for nigh on half a century.

Orientation

Though they're open to interpretation, Central's limits are Garden Rd to the east, somewhere between Central Market and Wing On Department Store to the west, Caine Rd and the Hong Kong Zoological & Botanical Gardens to the south, and the harbour to the north.

Central's main thoroughfares going west to east are Connaught Rd Central, Des Voeux Rd Central and Queen's Rd Central; important streets running (roughly) south and uphill from the harbour are Ice House St, Pedder St and Pottinger St.

The best way to view Central is from a Star Ferry as it crosses the harbour from Kowloon. Conveniently, the best place from which to start exploring the district is the **Star Ferry pier** (Map pp400–3), from where the floating green workhorses (see the boxed text on p340) carry passengers to and from Tsim Sha Tsui.

Transport

MTR Central station (Map pp400–3) on Central and Tsuen Wan lines

Airport Express Hong Kong station below One IFC (Map pp400–3)

Bus Central bus terminus below Exchange Square (Map pp400–3) for No 6 to Stanley and Repulse Bay and No 15 to the Peak on Hong Kong Island, No 101 to Hung Hom in Kowloon, No 960 to Tuen Mun in the New Territories; Star Ferry pier (Map pp400–3) for No 15C to Peak Tram (lower terminus)

Tram Along Des Voeux Rd Central (Map pp400–3)

Star Ferry Terminal (Map pp400–3) at Edinburgh Pl to Tsim Sha Tsui, Tsim Sha Tsui East and Hung Hom in Kowloon

Central Escalator Lower terminus at Central Market (Map pp400–3) to Mid-Levels

Peak Tram Lower terminus at 33 Garden Rd (Map pp400–3) to the Peak

Outlying Islands Ferry Ferries (Map pp400–3) to Discovery Bay (pier 3), Lamma (pier 4), Cheung Chau (pier 5), Lantau and Peng Chau (pier 6)

JARDINE HOUSE Map pp400–3
1 Connaught Pl

A short distance southeast of Star Ferry pier, this 52-storey silver monolith punctured with 1750 porthole-like windows was Hong Kong's first true 'skyscraper' when it opened as the Connaught Centre in 1973. Hong Kong Chinese like giving nicknames to things (and people) and the centre has been dubbed the 'House of 1000 Arseholes'. To the east of Jardine House is **Connaught Garden**, a small plaza featuring the sculpture *Double Oval* by Henry Moore.

HONG KONG CITY HALL Map pp400–3
☎ 2921 2840; 1 Edinburgh Pl

Southwest of Star Ferry pier, City Hall was built in 1962 and is still a major cultural venue in Hong Kong, with concert and recital halls, a theatre and exhibition galleries. Within the lower block but entered to the east of City Hall's main entrance, the **Hong Kong Planning & Infrastructure Exhibition Gallery** (Map pp400–3; ☎ 3101 6516; 3 Edinburgh Pl; admission free; ⓨ 10am-6pm Wed-Mon, closed Tue & some public holidays) may not sound like a crowd pleaser but it will awaken the Meccano builder in more than a few visitors. The exhibition

follows an 18.5m 'walk' past recent, ongoing and future civil engineering, urban renewal and environment improvement projects.

STATUE SQUARE Map pp400–3

Statue Square, due south of Star Ferry pier, is divided roughly in half by Chater Rd. In the northern part, which can be accessed via a pedestrian underpass from the pier, is the **Cenotaph** (Greek for 'empty tomb'), a memorial to Hong Kong residents killed during the two world wars. Due west is the venerable **Mandarin Oriental Hotel** (5 Connaught Rd Central), which opened in 1963 and is consistently voted the best hotel in the world, and to the east the **Hong Kong Club Building** (1 Jackson Rd), which houses a prestigious club of that name that was still not accepting Chinese members until well after WWII. The original club building, a magnificent four-storey colonial structure, was torn down in 1981 despite public outcry, and was replaced with the modern bow-fronted monstrosity there now.

Statue Square, on the south side of Chater Rd, is notable for its collection of fountains and covered outside seating areas; it is best known in Hong Kong as the meeting place of choice for tens of thousands of Filipino migrant workers on the weekend, especially Sunday, when it becomes a cacophony of Manilans, Vizayans and Ilocans (see the boxed text 'Maid in Hong Kong' opposite).

Crowds, Statue Square

The square derives its name from the various effigies of British royalty once on display here which were spirited away by the Japanese during the occupation. Only one statue actually remains, a bronze likeness of Sir Thomas Jackson, a particularly successful Victorian chief manager of the Hongkong & Shanghai Bank.

HONGKONG AND SHANGHAI BANK BUILDING Map pp400–3
1 Queen's Rd Central

Fittingly, the statue of Sir Thomas Jackson in Statue Square is gazing at the stunning headquarters of what is now the **HSBC** (formerly the Hongkong & Shanghai Bank), designed by British architect Norman Foster in 1985. The two bronze lions guarding the bank's main entrance were designed by British sculptor WW Wagstaff to mark the opening of the bank's previous headquarters in 1935; the lions are known as Stephen and Stitt, after two bank employees of the time. The Japanese used the lions as target practice during the occupation, and you can still see bullet holes in the one to the right.

The Hongkong & Shanghai Bank Building is a masterpiece of precision, sophistication and innovation. The building reflects architect Sir Norman Foster's wish to create areas of public and private space and to break the mould of previous bank architecture. The ground floor is public space, which people can traverse without entering the building; from there, escalators rise to the main banking hall. The building is inviting to enter – not guarded or off limits.

It's worth taking the **escalator** (🕑 9am-4.30pm Mon-Fri, 9am-12.30pm Sat) to the 1st floor to gaze at the cathedral-like atrium and the natural light filtering through.

BANK OF CHINA BUILDINGS
Map pp400–3
1 Bank St

To the east of the HSBC building is the **old Bank of China (BOC) building**, built in 1950, which now houses the bank's Central branch and, on the top three floors, the exclusive China Club, which evokes the atmosphere of old Shanghai. The BOC is now headquartered in the awesome **Bank of China Tower** (1 Garden Rd), designed by Chinese-born American architect IM Pei and completed in 1990.

The 70-storey Bank of China Tower, designed by Pei, is Hong Kong's third-tallest structure after Two International Finance Centre and Central Plaza. The asymmetry of the building is puzzling at first glance, but is really a simple geometric exercise. Rising from the ground

Districts & Islands – Hong Kong Island

Maid in Hong Kong

A large number of households in Hong Kong have an amah, who is either a live-in maid who cooks, cleans, minds the children and/or feeds the dog, or someone who comes in once or twice a week. In the old days amahs were usually Chinese spinsters who wore starched white tunics and black trousers, put their hair in a long plait and had a mouthful of gold fillings. Their employers became their families. Today, however, those amahs are virtually extinct, and the work is now done by foreigners – young women (and increasingly men) from the Philippines, Indonesia, Nepal, Thailand and Sri Lanka on two-year renewable visas.

Filipinos are by far the largest group, accounting for some 60% of the territory's 250,000 foreign domestic workers. While the Indonesians prefer Victoria Park and the Nepalese Tsim Sha Tsui, on Sunday, Filipino amahs take over the pavements and public squares of Central. They come in their thousands to share food, gossip, play cards, read the Bible and do one another's hair. You can't miss them around Statue Square, Exchange Square and the plaza below the HSBC building.

A reader writes of her impressions of a Sunday spent with amahs in Central: 'I had read of these gatherings in *Hong Kong* by Jan Morris, but was unprepared for the scale and for the emotional impact. I had planned to spend my last day sunning myself on a beach but instead was infected by the joy these women had in each others' company and stayed among them for some hours. They chatted ceaselessly, the noise of the chatter giving a strangely fascinating, almost musical, loud hum to the area. There were so many of them, yet the experience was so peaceful, so energising. They were like birds released from cages for a time'.

In many ways, that's exactly what they are like. For young Filipinos, a contract to work in Hong Kong is a dream come true, an escape from the dust and poverty of the provincial Philippines, even if the minimum monthly salary is a paltry HK$3670 – or HK$3270 if the 11% reduction kicks in (see The Return of Tung p74). But such 'freedom' doesn't come without a heavy price. According to Hong Kong–based Asian Migrant Centre (www.asian-migrants.org), as much as 25% of foreign domestic helpers in Hong Kong suffer physical and/or sexual abuse from their employers.

like a cube, it is successively reduced, quarter by quarter, until the south-facing side is left to rise upward. The staggered truncation of each triangular column creates a prismatic effect.

Many local Hong Kong Chinese see the building as a huge violation of the principles of feng shui. For example, the bank's four triangular prisms are negative symbols in the geomancer's rule book; being the opposite to circles, these triangles contradict what circles suggest – money, prosperity, perfection. The public viewing gallery on the 43rd floor (🕙 8am-6pm Mon-Fri) offers panoramic views of Hong Kong.

LEGISLATIVE COUNCIL BUILDING
Map pp400–3
8 Jackson Rd
This colonnaded and domed neoclassical building on the east side of Statue Square is the Old Supreme Court. Built in 1912, of granite quarried on Stonecutters Island, it has served as the seat of the Legislative Council (Legco) since 1985. Standing atop the pediment is a blindfolded statue of Themis, the Greek goddess of justice and natural law. During WWII it was the headquarters of the Gendarmerie, the Japanese version of the Gestapo, and many people were executed here. Across Jackson Rd to the east is **Chater Garden**, which was a cricket pitch until 1975.

EXCHANGE SQUARE Map pp400–3
8 Connaught Pl
West of Jardine House, this complex of three elevated office towers is home to the Hong Kong Stock Exchange. Access is via a network of overhead pedestrian walkways stretching west to Sheung Wan and linking to many of the buildings on the other side of Connaught Rd, including Central Market. The ground level of the 52-storey Towers I and II is given over to the Central bus and minibus terminus; Tower III is 32 levels. The stock exchange is located at the main entrance to the twin towers. Guided tours of the stock exchange are possible but are generally intended for people involved in the financial field and must be requested by fax five days in advance (☎ 2522 1122; fax 2868 4084).

Outside Towers I and II is a seating area surrounding a fountain, which is an excellent place to relax, especially in the early evening; note the Henry Moore work *Oval with Points*. The statue in front of the Forum shopping centre is of a *taijiquan* posture known as 'snake creeps down', although the sculpture is

simply called *Taiji*; it's by Taiwanese sculptor Ju Ming. The amusing **bronzes of water buffaloes** both standing and lying down in a pool of cooling water are by Dame Elisabeth Frink.

ONE & TWO INTERNATIONAL FINANCE CENTRE Map pp400–3
1 Harbour View St
These two tapering, pearl-coloured colossi sit atop the International Finance Centre (IFC) Shopping Centre and Airport Express Hong Kong station, terminus of the Airport Express and Tung Chung MTR lines. Both were partly designed by Cesar Pelli, the man responsible for Canary Wharf in London. Tower One IFC, which opened in 1999, is a 'mere' 38 levels tall. At 88 storeys, Two IFC, topped out in mid-2003, is Hong Kong's tallest (though not prettiest) building.

CENTRAL MARKET Map pp400–3
Queen's Rd Central & Queen Victoria St; 🕙 6am-8pm
It should be easy to locate Central Market, just over the pedestrian walkway from One IFC; if the wind is blowing in the right direction, you'll smell it before you see it. It's a three-storey affair and more a zoo than a market, although because the government has raised the rents of the market stalls considerably in recent years, covered markets like this one are not as well stocked or frequented as they once were in Hong Kong.

If you want to see even more exotic produce for sale, head uphill to the **Graham St Market** (p172). The squeamish should stay away; fish are cut lengthwise, but above the heart so that it continues to beat and pump blood around the body, keeping it fresher than fresh.

Central Market marks the start of the 800m-long **Central Escalator**, which transports pedestrians through Central and Soho and as far as Conduit Rd in the Mid-Levels. For details, see the boxed text 'Central Escalator' p155.

THE CENTER Map pp400–3
99 Queen's Rd Central
This 73-storey, star-shaped building, which most travellers will end up visiting at some stage (the main branch of the HKTB is on the ground floor), has quickly become a landmark in the western part of Central. The steel-and-glass tower rises from a landscaped plaza that allows pedestrian flow. Even if you don't make it here, you'll see the Center from afar – it does some amazing chameleon-like colour changes by night.

LI YUEN STREET EAST & WEST
Map pp400–3

These two narrow and crowded alleyways linking Des Voeux Rd Central with Queen's Rd Central are simply called 'the lanes' by Hong Kong residents and were traditionally the place to go for fabric and piece goods. Most vendors have now moved to Western Market in Sheung Wan (see p259), and today you'll find the usual mishmash of cheap clothes, handbags and backpacks and tacky costume jewellery.

LAN KWAI FONG & SOHO Map pp404–5

South of Queen's Rd Central and up hilly D'Aguilar St or Wyndham St is Lan Kwai Fong, a narrow, L-shaped pedestrian way that is Hong Kong Island's chief party neighbourhood and popular with both expats and Hong Kong Chinese. The bars are generally nothing to get excited about – standing out for their similarity more then anything else – but it's a fun place to do a little pub-crawling, especially at happy hour. Lan Kwai Fong has more pubs and bars than restaurants; for the latter head west to Soho (from 'South Of HOllywood Rd). At lunch time on weekdays, **Wing Wah Lane**, the northern extension of Lan Kwai Fong, becomes a 'black mountain' (what the Chinese call a crowd) of office workers trying to squeeze a decent meal into a short break. Have a look at the little Taoist **Ting Tao shrine** at the end of Wo On Lane.

ST JOHN'S CATHEDRAL Map pp400–3

☎ 2523 4157; 4-8 Garden Rd (enter from Battery Path); admission free; ☽ 7.15am-6.30pm Mon-Tue & Fri-Sat, 9.30am-5.15pm Wed, 8.30am-1.15pm Thu, 8am-6.30pm Sun

Built in 1847, this Anglican cathedral is one of the very few colonial structures extant in Central. Criticised for blighting the colony's landscape when it was first erected, St John's is now lost in the forest of skyscrapers that make up Central. The tower was added in 1850 and the chancel was expanded in 1873.

Services have been held here continuously since the church opened, except in 1944, when the Japanese Imperial Army used it as a social club. The cathedral suffered heavy damage during WWII and after the war the front doors were remade using timber salvaged from HMS *Tamar*, a British warship that used to guard the entrance to Victoria Harbour, and the beautiful stained-glass East Window was replaced. You walk on sacred ground in more ways than one at St John's: it is the only piece of freehold land in Hong Kong.

FORMER FRENCH MISSION BUILDING Map pp400–3
1 Battery Path

The **Court of Final Appeal**, the highest judicial body in Hong Kong, is now housed in the neoclassical former French Mission building, a charming structure built for the Russian consul in Hong Kong in the 1860s but extensively rebuilt in 1917. It served as the headquarters of the provisional colonial government after WWII. Tree-lined Battery Path links Ice House St with Garden Rd. Just before the mission building is pretty **Cheung Kong Garden**, which developers were required to lay out when they built the 70-storey Cheung Kong Centre to the south.

HONG KONG ZOOLOGICAL & BOTANICAL GARDENS Map pp400–3

☎ 2530 0154; Albany Rd; admission free; ☽ terrace gardens 6am-10pm, zoo & aviaries 6am-7pm, greenhouses 9am-4.30pm

Established in 1864, these 5.4-hectare gardens are a pleasant collection of fountains, sculptures, greenhouses, a playground, a zoo and some fabulous aviaries. Along with exotic trees, plants and shrubs, some 160 species of birds are in residence here – including non-native sulphur-crested cockatoos, which are attractive but damage the local vegetation. The zoo is surprisingly comprehensive and is

Maroon-breasted Crown Pigeon, Edward Youde Aviary, Hong Kong Park (p90)

also one of the world's leading centres for the captive breeding of endangered species.

The gardens are divided by Albany Rd, with the plants and aviaries in the area to the east close to Garden Rd, and most of the animals to the west. The animal displays are mostly primates (lemurs, gibbons, macaques, orangutans etc); other residents include a jaguar and radiated tortoises. The tropical greenhouses are divided into five sections: bromeliads and orchids, ferns, climbers, carnivorous plants and scented plants.

The Zoological & Botanical Gardens are at the top (ie southern) end of Garden Rd. It's an easy walk from Central, but you can also take bus No 3B, 12 or 12M from the stop in front of Jardine House on Connaught Rd Central. The bus takes you along Upper Albert Rd and Caine Rd on the northern boundary of the gardens. Get off in front of Caritas House (2 Caine Rd) and follow the path across the street and up the hill to the gardens.

GOVERNMENT HOUSE Map pp400–3
☎ 2530 2003; Upper Albert Rd

Parts of the one-time official residence of the governor of Hong Kong, opposite the northern end of the Zoological & Botanical Gardens, date back to 1856 when Governor Sir John Bowring was in residence. Other features, including the dominant central tower linking the two original buildings, were added in 1942 by the Japanese, who used it as military headquarters during the occupation of Hong Kong in WWII.

The current chief executive, Tung Chee Hwa, refused to occupy Government House after assuming power, claiming the feng shui wasn't satisfactory. Oddly enough, he has no problem visiting the Bank of China Tower, a place notorious for its bad feng shui (see Bank of China Buildings p81).

Government House is open to the public three or four times a year, notably one Sunday in March, when azaleas in the mansion gardens are in full bloom.

LOWER ALBERT ROAD & ICE HOUSE STREET Maps pp400–3 & p500

Lower Albert Rd, where the massive **SAR Government Headquarters** (Map pp400–3; 18 Lower Albert Rd) is located, has a number of interesting buildings. The attractive off-white stucco and red-brick structure at the top of the road is the Dairy Farm Building, built for the Dairy Farm Ice and Cold Storage Company in 1898 and renovated in 1913.

Today it houses the **Fringe Club** (p237), the excellent **M at the Fringe** restaurant (p173) and the illustrious **Foreign Correspondents' Club of Hong Kong** (☎ 2521 1511; www.fcchk.org), where we've spent many a pleasant evening disgracing ourselves, while making some of the best friends we've ever had. Towering above the Dairy Farm Building on the opposite side of the road is the **Bishop's House** (Map pp404–5), the official residence of the Anglican Bishop of Victoria for the last 130 years.

From the Dairy Farm Building, Ice House St doglegs into Queen's Rd Central. Just before it turns north, a wide flight of stone steps leads down to **Duddell St** (Map pp400–3). The four **wrought-iron gas lamps** at the top and bottom of the steps were placed here in the 1870s and are listed monuments.

CENTRAL DISTRICT POLICE STATION
Map pp404–5
10 Hollywood Rd

Part of this compound of four-storey buildings dates back to 1864, though other blocks were added in 1910 and 1925. Unfortunately the station is not open to the public, but if you really want to get inside, we're sure that can be arranged.

SHEUNG WAN
Eating p180

West of Central, **Sheung Wan** once had something of a feel of old Shanghai about it. But much of that has disappeared under the jackhammer, and many of the old 'ladder streets' (steep inclined streets with steps) once lined with stalls and street vendors have been cleared away to make room for more buildings or the MTR. Nevertheless, traditional shops and businesses still abound and the area is worth exploring.

Hollywood Rd is an interesting street to explore. The eastern end is lined with upmarket antique and carpet shops and trendy eateries. However, once you head west of Aberdeen St, the scene changes: you'll soon be passing traditional wreath and coffin makers, as well as several funeral shops with hell money (fake money burned as an offering to the spirits of the departed) and paper votives in the shape of cars, mobile telephones and computers to help the dearly departed communicate and get around on the other side.

Orientation

The limits of Sheung Wan are difficult to define exactly, but basically the district stretches from the Sheung Wan MTR station in the east to King George V Memorial Park and Eastern St in the west. The harbour – or, rather, Connaught Rd West – is the northern border while Hollywood Rd is the southern limit.

Transport

MTR Sheung Wan station (Map pp400–3) on Central line

Bus Des Voeux Rd Central (Map pp400–3) for Nos 5, 5A and 10 and Hollywood Rd for No 26 (Map pp400–3) to Central and Admiralty

Tram Along Des Voeux Rd Central and Des Voeux Rd West (Map pp400–3)

Macau Ferry Macau ferry terminal (Map pp400–3) at Shun Tak Centre

MAN WA LANE Map pp400–3

Just one block east of the Sheung Wan MTR station, this narrow alley is a good introduction to traditional Sheung Wan. Stalls here specialise in name chops, a stone (or wood or jade) seal that has a name carved in Chinese on the base. When dipped in ink, the name chop can be used as a stamp or even a 'signature'. The merchant can create a Chinese name for you.

WESTERN MARKET Map pp400–3

☎ 2815 3586; 323 Des Voeux Rd Central & New Market St; ☺ 10am-7pm

When the textile vendors were driven out of the 'cloth lanes' linking Queen's and Des Voeux Rds in Central in the early 1990s, they were moved to this renovated old market built in 1906 with its distinctive four corner towers. There's a decent Chinese restaurant called the **Grand Stage** (p181) on the 2nd floor.

SHEUNG WAN GALA POINT

Map pp400–3

Chung Kong Rd; admission free; ☺ 6pm-2am Mon-Fri, 11am-2am Sat & Sun

What was once the 'Poor Man's Nightclub' has been resurrected and renamed Sheung Wan Gala Point. It's located just west of the Shun Tak Centre. This night 'market' divided into three zones – Shopping, Games and Dining – attracts families and young couples on a budget.

CAT STREET & POSSESSION STREET

Map pp400–3

Southwest of Sheung Wan MTR station and just north of (and parallel to) Hollywood Rd is **Upper Lascar Row**, known to Hong Kong people as Cat St. This narrow street used to be famous for its arts and crafts and 'diamonds to rust' piles of curios and junk, but many dealers have now disappeared, either going out of business or moving to the nearby **Cat Street Galleries** (Casey Bldg, 38 Lok Ku Rd; ☺ 11am-6pm Mon-Fri, 10am-6pm Sat), which is entered from Upper Lascar Row. But even these galleries now appear to have enjoyed better days, with five floors of arts and crafts, antiques and souvenirs reduced to just two.

A short distance west of Cat St, next to **Hollywood Road Park** and before Hollywood Rd meets Queen's Rd West, is **Possession St**. This is thought to be where Commodore Gordon Bremmer and a contingent of British marines planted the Union flag on 26 January 1841 and claimed Hong Kong Island for the Crown (though no plaque marks the spot). Queen's Rd runs in such a serpentine fashion as it heads eastward because it once formed the shoreline of Hong Kong Island's northern coast – and this was called Possession Point.

MAN MO TEMPLE

☎ 2540 0350; 124-126 Hollywood Rd; admission free; ☺ 8am-6pm

This busy temple, built in 1847, is one of the oldest and most famous in Hong Kong. Man Mo (literally, 'Civil and Martial'), is dedicated to two deities. The civil deity is a Chinese statesman of the 3rd century BC called Man Cheung, who is worshipped as the god of literature and is represented holding a writing brush.

The military deity is Kwan Yu (or Kwan Tai), a Han-dynasty soldier born in the 2nd century AD and now venerated as the red-cheeked god of war; he is holding a sword. Kwan Yu's popularity in Hong Kong probably has more to do with his additional status as the patron god of restaurants, pawnshops, the police force and secret societies such as the Triads (see the boxed text p116).

Building detail, Man Mo Temple (p85)

the temple grounds and warn menstruating women to keep out of the main hall. Inside the temple (use the left-side entrance) are two 19th-century sedan chairs shaped like houses, which are used to carry the two gods at festival time.

TAI PING SHAN TEMPLES Map pp400–3

Tai Ping Shan, a tiny neighbourhood in Sheung Wan and one of the first areas to be settled by Chinese after the founding of the colony, has three small temples clustered around where Tai Ping Shan St meets Pound Lane. **Kwun Yam Temple** (34 Tai Ping Shan St) honours the ever-popular goddess of mercy – the Buddhist equivalent of Tin Hau. Next door, the **Sui Tsing Pak Temple** is dedicated to the so-called 'Pacifying General', a god with great power to cure illness. A bit further northwest, the recently renovated **Pak Sing Ancestral Hall** (42 Tai Ping Shan St) was originally a storeroom for bodies awaiting burial in China. It contains the ancestral tablets of some 3000 departed souls.

Outside and to the left of the main entrance in the centre are four gilt plaques on poles that are carried at procession time. Two plaques describe the gods being worshipped here; the others request silence and respect within

WEST TO KENNEDY TOWN

Beyond Sheung Wan are the districts of Sai Ying Pun and Shek Tong Tsui, which are often lumped together as 'Western' by English speakers, and **Kennedy Town**, a working-class Chinese district at the end of the tramline.

Kennedy Town's maritime connections can still be felt the closer you get to the Praya (officially Kennedy Town New Praya) – a Portuguese word *praia* meaning 'beach' or 'coast' was commonly used in Hong Kong in the days when Portuguese merchants were a force to be reckoned with on the high seas.

The area wedged between the Mid-Levels and Sheung Wan doesn't have an official name as such but is usually called Pok Fu Lam after the main thoroughfare running through it. It's a district of middle-class housing blocks, colleges and Hong Kong's most prestigious university.

Transport

Bus Bonham Rd (Map pp400–3) for No 3B to Jardine House in Central, No 23, 40 or 40M to Admiralty, No 103 to Gloucester Rd in Causeway Bay

Green Minibus Bonham Rd (Map pp400–3) for No 8 to Star Ferry pier (Map pp400–3)

HONG KONG UNIVERSITY Map pp398–9

☎ 2859 2111; Pok Fu Lam Rd; www.hku.hk
Established in 1911, this is the oldest and most difficult to enter of Hong Kong's eight universities; to be accepted into the Faculty of Medicine here guarantees that the successful student will go far in life. What is unimaginatively called the **Main Building**, begun a year before the university opened and completed in 1912 in the Edwardian style, is a declared monument. Several other early-20th-century buildings on the campus, including the **Hung**

Hing Ying (1919) and **Tang Chi Ngong Buildings** (1929), are also protected.

The **University Museum & Art Gallery** (☎ 2241 5500; Fung Ping Shan Bldg, 94 Bonham Rd; admission free; ⏰ 9.30am-6pm Mon-Sat, 1.30pm-5.30pm Sun, closed public holidays), to the left of the university's Main Building and opposite the start of Hing Hon Rd, houses collections of ceramics and bronzes, plus a lesser number of paintings and carvings. The bronzes are in three groups: Shang and Zhou dynasty ritual vessels; decorative mirrors from the Warring States period to the Tang, Song, Ming and Qing dynasties; and almost 1000 Nestorian crosses from the Yuan dynasty, the largest such collection in the world. (The Nestorians were a heretical Christian sect that arose in Syria, and moved into China during the 13th and 14th centuries.) The ceramics collection includes Han-dynasty tomb pottery and recent works from the Chinese pottery centres of Jingdezhen and Shiwan in China. The art gallery has rotating exhibits.

MID-LEVELS

Eating p180; Sleeping p270

The **Mid-Levels**, halfway up the Peak both literally and figuratively, is solidly residential – home to Chinese middle-class families and the lion's share of expats. As such, it has relatively little to offer tourists in the way of sights, though there are a few gems – particularly houses of worship – hidden within the forest of marble-clad apartment blocks. Check out the **Roman Catholic Cathedral** (Map pp400–3; 16 Caine Rd), built in 1888 and financed largely by the Portuguese faithful from Macau; the **Jamia Mosque** (Map pp400–3; Mosque St); and the Ohel Leah Synagogue. In recent years, the dining and entertainment area of Soho, which straddles the borders of Central and the Mid-Levels, and the **Central Escalator** (see the boxed text p155) have brought new life and greater numbers to this district.

Orientation

Another district with rather elastic boundaries, the Mid-Levels stretches roughly from Hong Kong University and Pok Fu Lam in the west to Kennedy Rd in the east. Caine Rd is the northern boundary and the Peak the southern one. But the Mid-Levels are as much a state of mind as a physical area and some people regard the middle-class residential areas further east to be the Mid-Levels as well.

Transport

Bus Hollywood Rd (Map pp400–3) for No 26 to Central; Robinson Rd (Map pp400–3) for No 3B to Jardine House in Central, No 23 to Admiralty

Green Minibus Caine Rd and Ladder St (Map pp400–3) for No 8 or 22 to Star Ferry pier

Central Escalator Caine Rd exit (museum), Robinson Rd exit (synagogue)

HONG KONG MUSEUM OF MEDICAL SCIENCES Map pp400–3

☎ 2549 5123; 2 Caine Lane; adult/child or senior HK$10/5; ☉ 10am-5pm Tue-Sat, 1-5pm Sun, closed Mon & some public holidays

This small museum of medical implements and accoutrements including an old dentistry chair, an autopsy table, herbal medicine vials and chests and a rundown on how Hong Kong coped with the 1984 bubonic plague, is less interesting for its exhibits than for its architecture. It is housed in what was once the Pathological Institute, a breezy Edwardian-style brick-and-tiled structure built in 1905 and fronted by palms and bauhinia trees. The exhibits comparing Chinese and Western approaches to medicine are both unusual and instructive.

OHEL LEAH SYNAGOGUE Map pp400–3

☎ 2589 2621; 70 Robinson Rd; admission free; ☉ 10.30am-7pm Mon-Thu by appointment only

This renovated Moorish Romantic Jewish place of worship, built between 1878 and 1902 when that style of architecture was all the rage in Europe, is named after Lea Gubbay Sassoon, matriarch of a wealthy (and philanthropic) Sephardic Jewish family which can trace roots back to the beginning of the colony. Be sure to bring some sort of ID if you plan to visit the sumptuous interior.

THE PEAK

Eating p181

On your first clear day in Hong Kong, make tracks for the **Peak**, the highest point on the island. Not only is the view one of the most spectacular cityscapes in the world, it's also a good way to put Hong Kong and its layout into perspective. Repeat the trip up on a clear night, as the views of illuminated Central below and Kowloon across the harbour are superb.

The Peak has been *the* place to live in Hong Kong ever since the British arrived. The taipans (company bosses) built summer houses here to escape the heat and humidity (it's usually about 5°C cooler up here than lower down), and the Peak Hotel, 'removed high above the dust and noise of the town', offered the traveller 'those few days of quiet rest so necessary after a long sea voyage'. Or so a guidebook from 1911 called *Hongkong and Its Vicinity* maintained…

Orientation

When Hong Kong people refer to the Peak, they generally mean the plateau at an elevation of 396m with the seven-level Peak Tower, the huge titanium anvil rising above the Peak Tram terminus and containing themed entertainment venues, shops and restaurants, and the adjacent Peak Galleria, an overblown, overpriced four-floor shopping centre with some 60 shops and restaurants. They do not mean the summit itself, which is to the west.

Half the fun of going up to the Peak is riding the **Peak Tram** (p350). In 1885 everyone thought Phineas Kyrie and William Kerfoot Hughes were mad when they announced their intention to build a tramway to the top, but it opened three years later, silencing the scoffers and wiping out the sedan-chair trade in one fell swoop. Since then, what was originally called the High Level Tramway has never had an accident and suspended its services only during WWII and the violent rainstorms of 1966, which washed half the track down the hillside.

The Peak can also be reached directly by bus from Central, Admiralty, Wan Chai and Causeway Bay and by green minibus from Central.

Transport

Peak Tram Upper terminus (Map pp400–3) in Peak Tower (entrance level 4, exit level 3)

Bus No 15 to Central bus terminus below Exchange Square (Map pp400–3), No 15B to Wan Chai and Causeway Bay (Map pp406–8) via Police Museum Caine Rd and Ladder St, No 12S from Admiralty between 10am and midnight daily

Green Minibus No 1 to Edinburgh Pl (southeast of City Hall) in Central

PEAK TOWER Map pp400–3
128 Peak Rd

The Peak Tower, with all its attractions, shops and restaurants, is a good place to bring the kids. The **Peak Explorer** (☎ 2849 0668; adult/child HK$52/35; noon-10pm Mon-Fri, 9am-10pm Sat & Sun) on level 4 is a motion simulator that takes you into space. **Ripley's Believe It or Not Odditorium** (☎ 2849 0698; adult/child HK$75/50; 9am-10pm) on level 3 is similar to the branches of this chain seen around the world, with some 450 exhibits in 11 galleries of the weird and not-so-wonderful (mannequins of women weighing tonnes; stuffed five-legged calves; and skulls with crowbars embedded in them). On level 2 there's an outpost of **Madame Tussaud's** (☎ 2849 6966; adult/child HK$85/50; 11am-8pm Sun-Thu, 11am-9pm Fri & Sat), with eerie wax likenesses of international stars as well as local celebrities such as Jackie Chan, Andy Lau and Michelle Yeoh.

A number of combination tickets are available. Tickets for the Peak Explorer and Ripley's, which include return transport on the Peak Tram cost HK$118/78 per adult/child. Tickets for the Peak Explorer, Ripley's and Madame Tussaud's, including transport, cost HK$170/108. Combination tickets without transport cost HK$90/69 for the Peak Explorer and Ripley's, and HK$148/99 for the Peak Explorer, Ripley's and Madame Tussaud's.

The kid-friendly **Mövenpick Marché** restaurant (p181) is on levels 6 and 7. There is an open-air **viewing terrace** with coin-operated binoculars on level 5.

PEAK GALLERIA Map pp400–3
118 Peak Rd

Both the Peak Tower and the neighbouring Peak Galleria are designed to withstand winds of up to 270km/h, theoretically more than the

Peak Galleria

maximum velocity of a No 10 typhoon. You can reach the viewing deck, which is larger than the one in the Peak Tower, by taking the escalator to level 4. Inside the centre you'll find a number of expensive restaurants and retail shops, from art galleries to duty-free.

VICTORIA PEAK
Maps pp398–9 & pp400–3

Some 500m to the west of the Peak Tram terminus up steep Mt Austin Rd, Victoria Peak (552m) is the highest point on Hong Kong Island. The old governor's mountain lodge near the summit was burned to the ground by the Japanese during WWII, but the gardens remain and are open to the public.

You can walk around Victoria Peak without expending too much energy. Harlech Rd on the south side and Lugard Rd on the north slope form a 3.5km circular trail around the summit; the tree-shaded seating area where the two roads meet is a pleasant place to rest. The walk takes about an hour and is illuminated at night. If you feel like a longer walk, you can continue for another 2km along Peak Rd to Pok Fu Lam Reservoir Rd, which leaves Peak Rd near the car park exit. This goes past the reservoir to Pok Fu Lam Rd, where you can catch bus No 7 to Aberdeen or to Sheung Wan.

Another good walk takes you down to Hong Kong University. First walk to the west side of Victoria Peak by taking either Lugard Rd or Harlech Rd. After reaching Hatton Rd, follow it down. The descent is very steep, but the path is clear.

For information on the 50km-long **Hong Kong Trail**, which starts on the Peak, see p164.

POLICE MUSEUM Map pp398–9
☎ 2849 7019; 27 Coombe Rd; admission free;
☯ 2-5pm Tue, 9am-5pm Wed-Sun, closed Mon & public holidays

Housed in a former police station, this small museum in neighbouring Wan Chai Gap, an attractive residential area en route to the Peak, deals with the history of the Hong Kong Police Force, which was formed in 1844 and dropped its 'royal' tag in 1997. The museum houses an intriguing Triad Societies Gallery, as well as a very well-supplied Narcotics Gallery.

LOVER'S ROCK Map pp398–9
Off Bowen Rd

A kilometre or so northeast of the Police Museum is what the Chinese call *Yan Yuen Sek*, a phallus-shaped boulder on a bluff at the end of a track above Bowen Rd. This is a favourite pilgrimage site for childless women and those who think their lovers, husbands or sons could use a prayer and a joss stick or two. It's especially busy during the Maidens' Festival held on the seventh day of the seventh moon (mid-August).

ADMIRALTY & WAN CHAI
Eating p182; Sleeping p272

East of Central is **Admiralty**, a district you might not even notice were it not for the dominating **Pacific Place** (Map pp400–3) shopping centre and several modern buildings of note, including the Lippo Centre and the blindingly gold **Far East Finance Centre** (Map pp400–3; 16 Harcourt Rd), which is known locally as 'Amah's Tooth' in reference to the traditional Chinese maids' preference for gold fillings and caps. In fact, in Chinese, Admiralty is called 'Golden Centre'.

Next west from Admiralty is Hong Kong Island's most famous district: **Wan Chai** (Little Bay). If you choose to believe some of the tourist brochures, Wan Chai is still inseparably linked with the name of Suzie Wong – not bad considering that the book dates back to 1957 and the movie to 1960. Although Wan Chai had a reputation during the Vietnam War as an anything-goes red-light district, today it is mainly a centre for shopping, business and entertainment. If you want to see how far Wan Chai has come since then, check the fortress-like **Hong Kong Convention & Exhibition Centre** (p91) and two of Hong Kong's most important cultural centres, the **Academy for the Performing Arts** (p91) and the **Hong Kong Arts Centre** (p91), standing side by side to the southwest of the convention centre in what is sometimes referred to as Wan Chai North.

It's a different world south and southeast of this 'new' Wan Chai. Sandwiched between **Johnston Rd** and **Queen's Rd East** (Map pp406–8) are row after row of narrow streets harbouring all sorts of interesting traditional shops, markets and workshops where you can see traditional Hong Kong at work: watchmakers, blacksmiths, shoemakers, printers, sign-makers and so on. It's like Sheung Wan, but more workaday.

Orientation

Admiralty is a small district, bordered by Cotton Tree Dr in the west and Arsenal St in the north. Hong Kong Park effectively cuts it off from the Mid-Levels and the Peak to the south and Harcourt Rd is its barrier to the harbour in the north. Wan Chai carries on from Admiralty in the west to Canal Rd and Causeway Bay in the east; its three main thoroughfares are Jaffe, Lockhart and Hennessy Rds. The harbour is the limit to the north (the New Wing of the Hong Kong Convention & Exhibition Centre sits on a man-made island in the water) and to the south it's Queen's Rd East.

Districts & Islands – Hong Kong Island

Transport

MTR Admiralty station (Map pp400–3) on Central and Tsuen Wan lines and Wan Chai station (Map pp406–8) on Central line

Bus Admiralty bus terminus below Queensway Plaza and Admiralty MTR station (Map pp400–3) for No 6 to Stanley and Repulse Bay and No 15 to the Peak, No 12S to Peak Tram lower terminus, No 101 to Hung Hom and Kowloon City in Kowloon, No 960 to Tuen Mun in the New Territories; Wan Chai ferry pier bus terminus (Map pp406–8) for No 40M to the Mid-Levels, No 18 from Harbour Rd in Wan Chai (Map pp406–8) to Connaught Rd Central, No 307 from Gloucester Rd in Wan Chai to Tai Po in the New Territories

Tram East along Queensway, Johnston Rd and Hennessy Rd (Map pp406–8) to Causeway Bay; west to Central and Sheung Wan

Star Ferry Wan Chai ferry pier (Map pp406–8) to Hung Hom and Tsim Sha Tsui in Kowloon

HONG KONG PARK Map pp400–3

☎ 2521 5041; 19 Cotton Tree Dr, Admiralty; admission free; ☼ park 6.30am-11pm, conservatory & aviary 9am-5pm

Deliberately designed to look anything but natural, Hong Kong Park is one of the most unusual parks in the world, emphasising artificial creations such as its fountain plaza, conservatory, artificial waterfall, indoor games hall, playground, t'ai chi garden, viewing tower, museum and arts centre. For all its artifice, the 8-hectare park is beautiful in its own weird way and, with a wall of skyscrapers on one side and mountains on the other, makes for some dramatic and interesting photographs.

The best feature of the park is the **Edward Youde Aviary**, named after a much-loved governor (1982–87) and China scholar who died suddenly while in office. Home to more than 600 birds representing some 90 different species, the aviary is a huge and very natural-feeling place. Visitors walk along a wooden bridge suspended some 10m above the ground and at eye level with the tree branches, where most of the birds are to be found. The **Forsgate Conservatory** on the slope overlooking the park is the largest in Southeast Asia.

At the park's northernmost tip is the **Flagstaff House Museum of Tea Ware** (☎ 2869 0690; 10 Cotton Tree Dr; admission free; ☼ 10am-5pm Wed-Mon, closed Tue & some public holidays). Built in 1846 as the home of the commander of the British forces, it is the oldest colonial building in Hong Kong still standing in its original spot. The museum, a branch of the Hong Kong Museum of Art, houses a collection of antique Chinese tea ware: bowls, teaspoons, brewing trays, sniffing cups (used particularly for enjoying the fragrance of the finest oolong from Taiwan) and, of course, teapots made of porcelain or purple clay from Yixing.

The **KS Lo Gallery** (☎ 2869 0690; 10 Cotton Tree Dr; admission free; ☼ 10am-5pm Wed-Mon), in a small building just southeast of the museum, contains rare Chinese ceramics and stone seals collected by the gallery's eponymous benefactor.

The **Hong Kong Visual Arts Centre** (☎ 2521 3008; 7A Kennedy Rd; admission free; ☼ 10am-9pm Wed-Mon, closed Tue & some public holidays), housed in the former Victoria Barracks within Hong Kong Park at its eastern edge, supports local sculptors, printmakers and potters, and stages temporary exhibitions.

Hong Kong Park is an easy walk from either Central or Admiralty, or you can take bus No 3B, 12M, 23, 23B, 40 or 103 and alight at the first stop on Cotton Tree Dr.

HONG KONG DESIGN CENTRE

Map pp400–3

☎ 2522 8688; www.hkdesigncentre.org; 28 Kennedy Rd, Mid-Levels

The design centre, just opposite the Hong Kong Visual Arts Centre in Hong Kong Park, is housed in one of the most graceful colonial buildings in the territory. Built in 1896, it served as a bank, the offices of the Japanese Residents Association of Hong Kong before WWII and a school until it was renovated and given to the Hong Kong Federation of Designers. It did not have any exhibitions open to the public when we visited, but the exterior and public areas are worth a look.

HONG KONG CONVENTION & EXHIBITION CENTRE Map pp406–8

☎ 2582 8888; www.hkcec.com; 1 Expo Dr, Wan Chai

Due north of the Wan Chai MTR station, the Hong Kong Convention & Exhibition Centre, which was built in 1988 and extended for the handover in 1997, has been variously compared with a bird's wing, a banana leaf and a lotus petal.

CENTRAL PLAZA Map pp406–8

18 Harbour Rd, Wan Chai

At just under 374m, Central Plaza, completed in 1992, is three metres shorter than the new Two IFC. The glass skin of the tower has three different colours – gold, silver and terracotta – and the overall impression is rather garish. The Sky Lobby on the 46th floor offers a breathtaking panoramic sweep over Victoria Harbour and Kowloon.

Central Plaza functions as one of the world's biggest clocks. There's method to the madness of those four lines of light shining through the glass pyramid at the top of the building between 6pm and midnight. The bottom level indicates the hour: red is 6pm; white 7pm; purple 8pm; yellow 9pm; pink 10pm; green 11pm. When all four lights are the same colour, it's right on the hour. When the top light is different from the bottom ones, it's 15 minutes past the hour. If the top two and bottom two are different, it's half-past the hour. If the top three match, it's 45 minutes past the hour.

GOLDEN BAUHINIA Map pp406–8

Golden Bauhinia Sq, 1 Expo Dr, Wan Chai

A 6m-tall statue of Hong Kong's symbol, called the *Forever Blooming Bauhinia*, stands on the waterfront promenade just in front of the Hong Kong Convention & Exhibition Centre to mark the return of Hong Kong to Chinese sovereignty in 1997 and the establishment of the Hong Kong SAR. The flag-raising ceremony, held daily at 8am and conducted by the Hong Kong police, has become a 'must see' for visiting tourist groups from the mainland. There's a pipe band on the 1st, 11th and 21st of each month. From the Wan Chai MTR station, leave via exit A1.

ACADEMY FOR THE PERFORMING ARTS Map pp406–8

☎ 2584 8500; www.hkapa.edu; 1 Gloucester Rd, Wan Chai

With its striking triangular atrium and an exterior Meccano-like frame that is a work of art in itself, the academy building (1985) is a Wan Chai landmark and an important venue for music, dance and scholarship.

HONG KONG ARTS CENTRE

Map pp406–8

☎ 2582 0200; www.hkac.org.hk; 2 Harbour Rd, Wan Chai

Due east of the academy is the Hong Kong Arts Centre. Along with theatres, including the important Lim Por Yen Film Theatre (p236) here you'll find the **Pao Sui Loong & Pao Yue Kong Galleries** (☎ 2582 0255; admission free; 10am-8pm, closed some public holidays) on the 4th and 5th floors (take the lift to the 5th floor), with local and international exhibitions focusing on contemporary art.

WAN CHAI MARKET Map pp406–8

264 Queen's Rd East; 6am-8pm

Wan Chai's covered market was built in the geometric Bauhaus style in 1937. It has yet to be listed and may be torn down for yet another block of flats, so have a look before it's too late.

OLD WAN CHAI POST OFFICE

Map pp406–8

Cnr Queen's Rd East & Wan Chai Gap Rd, Wan Chai

A short distance to the east of the market is this important colonial-style building erected in 1913 and now serving as a resource centre operated by the **Environmental Protection Department** (☎ 2835 1918). If you follow Wan Chai Gap Rd uphill, you'll eventually reach the Peak.

HOPEWELL CENTRE Map pp406–8

183 Queen's Rd East, Wan Chai

This 64-storey cylinder, built as the headquarters of Hong Kong property and construction magnate Gordon Wu, wins no beauty contests, but it was the tallest building in Asia from 1980 until 1989. It is located on a slope so steep that the rear entrance is on the 17th floor. The centre's tacky revolving restaurant is accessed by two bubble-shaped external elevators. Though it's a short trip, the elevator ride is a great way to get an aerial view of Wan Chai.

HUNG SHING TEMPLE Map pp406–8
☎ 2527 0804; 129-131 Queen's Rd East, Wan Chai;
🕐 8am-6pm
Nestled in an alley on the southern side of Queen's Rd East, this long and narrow temple (which is also called Tai Wong Temple) was built to honour the god of fisherfolk and the south. Fortune-tellers used to do a brisk trade here but nowadays Hung Shing Temple is somewhat subdued.

CAUSEWAY BAY

Eating p188; Sleeping p274

Causeway Bay – Tung Lo Wan (Copper Gong Bay) in Cantonese – was the site of a British settlement in the 1840s and was once an area of godowns (a Hong Kong 'business' or 'pidgin English' word for warehouses) and a well-protected harbour for fisherfolk and boatpeople.

The new Causeway Bay, one of Hong Kong's top shopping and nightlife areas, was built up from swampland and the bottom of the harbour. Jardine Matheson, one of Hong Kong's largest *hongs* (major trading houses or companies), set up shop here, which explains why some of the streets in the district bear its name: Jardine's Bazaar, Jardine's Cres and Yee Wo St (the name for Jardine Matheson in Cantonese).

Causeway Bay is primarily for shopping, especially trendy clothing (see Fashion p28) and, to a lesser degree, dining out. The biggest and best shopping centre is in **Times Square** (☎ 2118 8850; 1 Matheson St), an enormous block with offices, four floors of restaurants and a dozen retail levels organised by types of goods sold.

Orientation

Causeway Bay is a relatively small but densely packed district. Canal Rd is its border to the west and Victoria Park is the eastern limit. From north to south it runs from the harbour and the typhoon shelter to Leighton Rd. Tin Hau, the site of Hong Kong Island's most famous temple erected in honour of the queen of heaven, is at the southeastern edge of Victoria Park.

Transport

MTR Causeway Bay and Tin Hau stations (Map pp406–8) on Central line

Bus Yee Wo St (Map pp406–8) for Nos 5, 5B and 26 to Central, No 112 to Hung Hom in Kowloon, No 170 to Sha Tin in the New Territories; Leighton Rd (Map pp406–8) for No 63 to Stanley and Repulse Bay; Gloucester Rd (Map pp406–8) for No 106 to Hung Hom and Wong Tai Sin in Kowloon

Tram Along Hennessy Rd and Yee Wo St (Map pp406–8) to Central and Shau Kei Wan; along Percival St (Map pp406–8) to Happy Valley

CAUSEWAY BAY TYPHOON SHELTER
Map pp406–8
Not so long ago the waterfront used to be a mass of junks and sampans huddling in the typhoon shelter for protection, but these days it's nearly all yachts. The land jutting out to the west is Kellett Island, which has been a misnomer ever since a causeway connected it to the mainland in 1956, and further land reclamation turned it into a peninsula. It is home to the **Royal Hong Kong Yacht Club** (☎ 2832 2817; Hung Hing Rd), which retains its 'Royal' moniker in English only. The Cross-Harbour Tunnel linking Causeway Bay and Hung Hom surfaces here.

NOONDAY GUN Map pp406–8
281 Gloucester Rd; 🕐 subway access 7am-midnight
Noel Coward made the so-called Noonday Gun famous with his satirical song 'Mad Dogs and Englishmen' (1924), about colonials who braved the fierce heat of the sun at midday while the local people sensibly remained indoors: 'In Hong Kong/they strike a gong/And fire off a noonday gun/To reprimand each inmate/Who's in late'. Apparently when Coward was invited to pull the lanyard, he showed up late and it didn't go off until 12.03pm.

Built in 1901, this recoil-mounted three-pounder is one of the few vestiges of the colonial past in Causeway Bay and is its best-known landmark. The original six-pounder was lost during WWII; its replacement was deemed too noisy and was exchanged for the current gun in 1961. The gun stands in a small garden opposite the Excelsior Hotel on Gloucester

Rd – the first plot of land to be sold by public auction in Hong Kong (1841) – and is fired at noon daily. Eight bells are then sounded, signalling the end of the forenoon watch. The gun also welcomes in the New Year at midnight on 31 December.

Exactly how this tradition got started remains a mystery. Some people say that Jardine Matheson fired the gun without permission to bid farewell to a departing managing director or to welcome one of their incoming ships. The authorities were so enraged by the company's insolence that, as punishment, Jardine's was ordered to fire the gun every day. A more prosaic explanation is that, like many ports around the world (including London), a gun was fired at noon daily so that ships' clocks – crucial for establishing longitude and east–west distances at sea – could be set accurately and uniformly.

The Noonday Gun is accessible via a tunnel through the basement car park in the World Trade Centre, just west of the Excelsior Hotel. From the taxi rank in front of the hotel, look west for the door marked 'Stairway No 1, Car Park Shroff (Marina Club & Noon Gun)'.

VICTORIA PARK Map pp406–8

At 17 hectares, the biggest patch of public greenery on the northern side of Hong Kong Island, Victoria Park is a popular place to escape to. The best time to stroll around is in the morning during the week, when it becomes a forest of people practising the slow-motion choreography of t'ai chi. At the weekend they are joined by Indonesian amahs, who prefer it to Central (see the boxed text p81).

Between April and November you can take a dip in the **swimming pool** (☎ 2570 8347; adult/child 3-13 or senior over 60 HK$19/9;

🕑 6.30am-10pm with 1hr closure at noon & 6pm Apr-Oct; 6.30am-noon & 1-6.30pm Nov). The park becomes a **flower market** a few days before the Chinese New Year and is the site of the **Hong Kong Flower Show** in March. It's also worth a visit during the **Mid-Autumn Festival** (p11), when people turn out en masse carrying lanterns.

CENTRAL LIBRARY Map pp406–8

☎ 3150 1234; www.hkpl.gov.hk; 66 Causeway Rd; 🕑 10am-9pm Thu-Tue, 1-9pm Wed, 10am-7pm some public holidays

This architectural monstrosity, a 12-storey neo-classical/postmodern building with Ionic columns, a Roman pediment and sandy-yellow tiles, is both a research and lending library and contains some 1.2 million volumes (see Libraries p364). It also has some 500 public-access computer terminals where you can check emails and surf the web (see Internet Access p362). Opened in 2001, the library was Hong Kong's biggest and most expensive civil project after the new airport.

TIN HAU TEMPLE Map pp406–8

☎ 2721 2326; 10 Tin Hau Temple Rd; 🕑 7am-5pm

Southeast of Victoria Park, Hong Kong Island's most famous Tin Hau temple is relatively small and dwarfed by surrounding high-rises. Before reclamation, this temple dedicated to the patroness of seafarers stood on the waterfront. It has been a place of worship for three centuries, though the current structure is only about 200 years old. The temple bell dates from 1747, and the central shrine contains an effigy of Tin Hau with a blackened face. The temple is a two-minute walk east from the Tin Hau MTR station (exit A1).

A circular pebble garden in Victoria Park where people come to massage their feet

HAPPY VALLEY

Eating p192

Happy Valley – Pau Ma Dei (Horse Running Place) in Cantonese – has been a popular residential area for expats since the early days of British settlement, although, having built their houses on what turned out to be swampland, early residents had to contend with severe bouts of malaria. There are some interesting cemeteries to the west and southwest of Wong Nai Chung Rd. They are divided into Protestant, Roman Catholic, Muslim, Parsi and Hindu sections and date back to the founding of Hong Kong as a colony. The district's most important drawcard, however, is Happy Valley Racecourse.

Orientation

Happy Valley is essentially the racetrack in the centre of circular Wong Nai Chung Rd and the residential areas to the east and the south, where the main streets are Shan Kwong Rd, Sing Woo Rd and Blue Pool Rd.

Transport

MTR Causeway Bay station (Map pp406–8; exit A) on Central line and a 15-minute walk south

Bus Wong Nai Chung Rd for No 1 to Exchange Square in Central and No 5A to Des Voeux Rd Central, No 19 to North Point

Tram Along Wong Nai Chung Rd (Map pp406–8) to Causeway Bay, Central and Kennedy Town and to Shau Kei Wan

HAPPY VALLEY RACECOURSE

Map pp406–8

☎ 2895 1523, 2966 8111; www.happyvalley racecourse.com; 2 Sports Rd

Apart from the Mark Six Lottery and the newly introduced football betting, horse racing is the only form of legalised gambling in Hong Kong, and is *very* popular. The SAR has the highest per capita betting on horse races in the world, with an annual turnover of more than US$1 billion.

The first horse races were held in 1846 at Happy Valley and became an annual event. Now meetings are held both here and at the newer and larger **Sha Tin Racecourse** (p133)

in the New Territories. For details on placing bets, see p30.

If you know nothing about horse racing but would like to attend, consider joining one of two Come Horseracing Tours available from the **HKTB** (☎ 2508 1234; info@hongkongtourismboard.com) during the racing season. The Classic Tour (HK$460) includes admission to the visitors box of the Hong Kong Jockey Club members enclosures and buffet lunch; the Race Tour (HK$190) is without lunch. Tours scheduled at night last about 5½ hours, while daytime tours are about seven hours long.

Racing buffs can wallow in the history of the place at the **Hong Kong Racing Museum** (☎ 2966 8065; 2nd fl, Happy Valley Stand, Wong Nai Chung Rd; admission free; ☺ 10am-5pm Tue-Sun, 10am-12.30pm on racing days, closed Mon & some public holidays), with eight galleries and a cinema showcasing celebrated trainers, jockeys and horseflesh, and key races over the past 150 years. The most important event in the history of the Happy Valley racetrack – individual winnings notwithstanding – was the huge fire in 1918 that killed hundreds of people. Many of the victims were buried in the cemeteries surrounding the track.

ISLAND EAST

Eating p192; Sleeping p276

Eastern is a large district that is primarily residential, with some of Hong Kong Island's largest housing estates (eg Tai Koo Shing) in Quarry Bay. As elsewhere on the island, however, office towers stand cheek by jowl with residential areas. There are not as many restaurants and nightspots in this area as there are in Central, Wan Chai and Causeway Bay to lure you onto the Central MTR line, but the shopping is good and there are a handful of top-class museums.

Orientation

The Eastern District runs from Causeway Bay to Siu Sai Wan, at the eastern end of Hong Kong Island's northern coast. Major settlements are North Point, Quarry Bay, Sai Wan Ho, Shau Kei Wan and Chai Wan. The MTR is the quickest way to reach any of these destinations, but the tram, which goes as far as Shau Kei Wan, is much more enjoyable. Count on about half an hour from Causeway Bay to the end of the line.

North Point & Quarry Bay

North Point, settled largely by Shanghainese after WWII, is a somewhat down-at-heel district with a couple of interesting markets, and the Sunbeam Theatre (p237), one of the best places to see and hear Chinese opera. Tong Chong St opposite the Quarry Bay MTR station has had a facelift in recent years and is something of a restaurant and nightlife strip.

Transport

MTR Central line with stations at North Point, Quarry Bay, Tai Koo Shing, Sai Wan Ho, Shau Kei Wan and Chai Wan (Map pp398–9); North Point and Quarry Bay also on Tseung Kwan O line

Bus North Point (Map pp398–9) for Nos 2 and 10 to Central, No 63 (Mon–Sat) or 65 (Sun) to Stanley and Repulse Bay, No 106 to Hung Hom in Kowloon, No 106 to Sha Tin; Shau Kei Wan (Map pp398–9) for No 2 to Quarry Bay, No 720 to Central

Tram Along King's Rd, Kornhill Rd and Shau Kei Wan Rd

Ferry North Point ferry pier (Map pp398–9) to Hung Hom, Kowloon City and Kwun Tong; Sai Wan Ho ferry pier (Map pp398–9) to Tung Lung Chau and Joss House Bay

CITYPLAZA SHOPPING CENTRE

Map pp398–9

☎ 2568 8665; 111 King's Rd, Quarry Bay

The main attraction in Quarry Bay is Cityplaza, which has a Wing On department store and an ice-skating rink and is directly linked up to the Tai Koo Shing MTR (use exit D2). Although not normally considered a tourist attraction, it has much to be recommended; shopping is much more pleasant in Hong Kong once you get out of the tourist zones, and prices are frequently lower.

Sai Wan Ho

HONG KONG FILM ARCHIVE

Map pp398–9

☎ 2739 2139, bookings 2734 9009; www.film archive.gov.hk; 50 Lei King Rd; admission free; ⊙ main foyer 10am–8pm; box office noon–8pm; resource centre Mon–Wed & Fri 10am–7pm, Sat 10am–5pm, Sun 1–5pm

The archive, which opened in 2001, is well worth a visit, even if you know nothing about Hong Kong films and film-making. It preserves, catalogues, studies and documents Hong Kong films – there are some 4300 in the vaults – and related material such as magazines, posters, records and scripts; there's a small exhibition hall with themed exhibits (opening hours vary), including videos with subtitles, and a 127-seat cinema (☎ 2734 9009; HK$30) that shows Hong Kong and other films here throughout the year.

To reach the film archive from the Sai Wan Ho MTR station, follow exit A, walk north on Tai On St and west on Lei King Rd.

Shau Kei Wan

HONG KONG MUSEUM OF COASTAL DEFENCE Map pp398–9

☎ 2569 1500; 175 Tung Hei Rd; adult/senior/child HK$10/7/5, admission free Wed; ⊙ 10am–5pm Fri-Wed, closed Thu & some public holidays

This museum doesn't exactly sound like a crowd pleaser but the displays it contains are as much about peace as war. Part of the fun is just to enjoy the museum's location. It has been built into the Lei Yue Mun Fort (1887), which took quite a beating during WWII, and has sweeping views down to the Lei Yue Mun Channel and southeastern Kowloon.

Exhibitions in the old redoubt, which you reach by escalator from street level, cover Hong Kong's coastal defence over six centuries: from the Ming and Qing dynasties, through the colonial years and Japanese invasion, to the resumption of Chinese sovereignty. There's a historical trail through the casemates, tunnels and observation posts almost down to the coast.

To reach the museum take the MTR to Shau Kei Wan station and follow exit B2. From here follow the museum signs on Tung Hei Rd (part of the busy Eastern Island Corridor) for about 15 minutes. Bus No 84 (exit A3) between Shau Kei Wan and Siu Sai Wan stops outside the museum.

Chai Wan

LAW UK FOLK MUSEUM Map pp398–9
☎ 2896 7006; 14 Kut Shing St; admission free;
🕑 10am-1pm & 2-6pm Mon-Wed, Fri & Sat, 1-6pm Sun, closed Thu & some public holidays

This small museum, a branch of the Hong Kong Museum of History, is housed in two restored Hakka village houses that have been standing in Chai Wan, a district of nondescript office buildings, warehouses and workers flats, for more than two centuries. The quiet courtyard and surrounding bamboo groves are peaceful and evocative, but the displays within are rather shabby.

In the main building there is an interesting collection of rod puppets and miniature theatre sets, along with a Cantonese-language video of the puppets in action. The farmhouses in the courtyard have been kitted out with simple but charming furniture, household items and farming implements.

To reach the museum from the Chai Wan MTR station, follow exit E and walk for five minutes to the west.

ISLAND SOUTH

Eating p193

Though largely residential, the Southern District, encompassing everything from Big Wave Bay and Shek O in the east to Aberdeen and Ap Lei Chau in the west, is full of attractions. At times it can feel like Hong Kong Island's backyard playground – from the beaches of Repulse Bay and Deep Water Bay and the outdoor activities available at Shek O, to Stanley Market, the shoppers' paradise, and Ocean Park, the largest amusement and theme park in the territory, near Aberdeen. For information on the 78km-long **Wilson Trail**, the southern section of which starts just north of Stanley, see Hikes (p162).

Orientation

Shek O lies halfway down a large peninsula in the southeast of Hong Kong Island; Stanley town is at the start of the next peninsula over, but you'll have to travel a bit further south

Surfers, Big Wave Bay (p97)

to reach the best beach on Stanley Peninsula. Further west along the southern coast is Repulse Bay, with its ever-heaving beach, Kwun Yam shrine, lucky bridge and posh shopping complex, and then Deep Water Bay, a much more serene beach and one of the best places in Hong Kong for wakeboarding (see p243). Aberdeen is at the western edge of the southern coast. From here, buses return to the northern side of the island either through the Aberdeen Tunnel or Pok Fu Lam Rd along the west coast.

Buses, and to a lesser extent green minibuses, are the way to get to and around the southern part of Hong Kong Island. Though some go via the Aberdeen Tunnel, many buses (eg the No 6 to Stanley and Repulse Bay) climb over the hills separating the north and south sides of the island. It's a scenic, winding ride; for the outbound trip, make sure you sit on the upper deck on the right-hand side.

Transport

Bus Shek O: No 9 (HK$6.50) to Shau Kei Wan MTR station (exit A3) or No 309 (Sun only) to Wan Chai and Central bus terminus below Exchange Square (Map pp400–3); Stanley: No 6, 6A, 6X or 260 (express via Aberdeen Tunnel) to Central, No 14 to Shau Kei Wan via Tai Tam Tuk reservoir, Nos 73 and 973 to Repulse Bay and Aberdeen; Repulse Bay: Nos 6, 6A, 6X and 260 to Central bus terminus, Nos 6, 6A, 73, 260 and 973 to Aberdeen; Deep Water Bay: No 6A or 260 to Central, Nos 73 and 973 to Aberdeen, Repulse Bay and Stanley; Aberdeen: No 70 to Central, No 37A, 37B, 70, or 70M to Admiralty, No 73 or 973 to Ocean Park, Repulse Bay and Stanley; Ocean Park: Nos 73 and 973 to Aberdeen, Repulse Bay and Stanley, Nos 6A, 6X, 70 or 260 (express via Aberdeen Tunnel) to Central, No 973 to Tsim Sha Tsui in Kowloon

Green Minibus Stanley: No 40 (24hr; HK$9-11 depending on time) to Tang Lung St and Yee Woo St (Map pp406–8) in Causeway Bay, No 16M (HK$5.50) to Chai Wan MTR station; Ocean Park: No 6 (HK$7.50; Mon-Sat) to Star Ferry pier in Central

Minibuses Repulse Bay to Edinburgh Place at Star Ferry pier in Central

Ferry Stanley: public pier to Aberdeen and Po Toi; Aberdeen: Aberdeen Promenade ferry pier to Yung Shue Wan, Pak Kok Tsuen, Sok Kwu Wan and Man Tat Wan on Lamma

Shek O

Sometimes referred to as the 'last real village on Hong Kong Island', Shek O (Map pp398–9), has one of the best beaches on the island. And because it is not as accessible as the beaches to the west, it's usually less crowded.

Shek O is small, so it's easy to get your bearings; the beach is about a five-minute walk from the bus stop. En route you'll pass a couple of good restaurants (see Shek O p193). If you take the road leading off to the left you'll enter a maze of village houses, home to local Chinese families and many dissolute Western dropouts. As you head out along the peninsula to the east of the beach, the houses gradually grow in size and luxury. This is Shek O Headlands, home to some of Hong Kong's wealthiest families.

ACTIVITIES

Shek O has all sorts of activities to keep you busy, amused and out of trouble. In the village itself, along with lovely **Shek O Beach**, there's miniature golf, and from **Dragon's Back**, the 280m-high ridge to the west of the village, there's both paragliding and abseiling. Walking is possible around Shek O Beach, though the terrain is steep and the underbrush quite thick in spots. You can also take advantage of the bicycle rental shops (HK$25 a day) in the village.

BIG WAVE BAY Map pp398–9

This fine and often deserted beach is located 2km to the north of Shek O. To get to Big Wave Bay follow the road north out of town, travel past the 18-hole **Shek O Golf & Country Club** (☎ 2809 4458; Shek O Rd), then turn east at the roundabout and keep going until the road ends.

One of eight prehistoric **rock carvings** (see Early Inhabitants p62) discovered in Hong Kong is located on the headland above Big Wave Bay.

Stanley

About 15km from Central as the crow flies, **Stanley** (Map p409) had about 2000 residents when the British took control of the territory in 1841, making it one of the largest settlements on the island at the time. A prison was built near the village in 1937 – just in time for the Japanese to intern the builders. Stanley Prison is a maximum security facility today. Hong Kong's contingent of British troops was housed in Stanley Fort at the southern end of the peninsula until 1995. It is now used by the People's Liberation Army (PLA). There's a beach to the northeast of town that never gets as crowded as the one at Repulse Bay. The most important dragon-boat races are held at Stanley during the Dragon Boat Festival (Tuen Ng) in early June (see p11).

STANLEY MARKET Map p409
Stanley Village Rd; ☺ 10am-6pm

The main attraction in Stanley village is this mostly covered market filled with bric-a-brac, cheap clothing and junk that fills the alleys and lanes southwest of Stanley Village Rd. It's best to go during the week; at the weekend the market is bursting at the seams (and hems and collars) with both tourists and locals alike.

OLD STANLEY POLICE STATION
Map p409

88 Stanley Village Rd

The most interesting building in the village itself is this two-storey structure built in 1859. After housing a bizarre restaurant for many years, it now contains a Wellcome supermarket.

MURRAY HOUSE Map p409
Stanley Bay

At the start of the Chung Hom Kok Peninsula across the bay from Stanley Main St, the waterfront promenade lined with bars and restaurants, stands phoenix-like Murray House. This three-storey colonnaded affair built in 1848 took colonial pride of place in Central, on the spot where the Bank of China Tower now stands, for almost 150 years, until 1982. It was re-erected here in 2000 after, well, a slight glitch (see the boxed text below).

TEMPLES & SHRINES Map p409

At the western end of Stanley Main St, past a tiny shrine devoted to Tai Wong and through the modern shopping complex called Stanley Plaza, is a **Tin Hau temple** (☎ 2813 0418; 119 Stanley Main St; ☺ 7am-5.30pm), built

---

Don't Know Much about History

Hong Kong does not have a stellar track record when it comes to preserving old buildings. Though things have improved over the past decade or so, traditionally if a structure sat on a 'valuable' piece of land (ie virtually every square centimetre of the built-up areas) or got in the way of progress (ie money) it was given a kiss on the derrière by the wrecker's ball and brought down, living on in old photographs and the memories of a dwindling population.

It came as no surprise when the government announced in 1982 that Murray House, Hong Kong's oldest colonial building, was going to have to make room for the new Bank of China Tower (p81); bigger and better old buildings nearby had met similar fates. But because Murray House had a Grade 1 classification, they couldn't just smash it to pieces as they had the old Hong Kong Club and the Central Post Office. Instead, the building would be dismantled and its 4000 pieces numbered and stored for 'safekeeping' and erection elsewhere. Time passed and when heritage societies demanded to know its whereabouts, the government admitted it had misplaced some of the pieces.

Scene and time change… It's the mid 1990s and – hurrah! hurrah! – the government has found the missing bits stored in crates in Tai Tam. The problem was, the pillars and blocks had been wrapped in plastic sheeting and the numbers written or etched into their sides had spontaneously erased due to moisture building up on the soft limestone. It took workers 3½ years to put this colossal puzzle back together again and, when they'd finished, they had six extra columns that they didn't know what to do with.

As you approach Murray House, which now contains a small exhibition area on the ground floor that looks at the history of the buildings and restaurants on the 1st floor, you'll see these idle columns standing rather forlornly off to the left along the waterfront promenade. Note, too, some of the numbers still visible on the building blocks to the right of the entrance.

in 1767 and said to be the oldest building in Hong Kong. It has undergone a complete renovation since then, however, and is now a concrete pile (though the interior is traditional).

Behind the Tin Hau temple is a huge residential estate, but if you follow the path that passes by the temple and continue up the hill, you'll reach the **Kwun Yam Temple** (☎ 2813 1849; ☺ 7am-6pm). Above the temple is a pavilion housing a massive statue of the Goddess of Mercy looking out to sea.

ST STEPHEN'S BEACH & MILITARY
CEMETERY Map p409
St Stephen's Beach, which has a café, showers and changing rooms, is south of the village. In summer you can hire sailboats, windsurfing boards and kayaks (see Sport & Fitness p237). To reach St Stephen's Beach, walk south along Wong Ma Kok Rd. Turn east (ie right) when you get to a small road leading down to a jetty.

At the end of the road, turn south and walk past the boathouse to the beach. Bus No 14 or 6A will take you close to the intersection with the small road.

Opposite the bus stop is a military cemetery for personnel and their families. The oldest graves date back to 1843, just two years after the British first settled in Hong Kong.

HONG CORRECTIONAL SERVICES
MUSEUM Map p409
☎ 2147 3199; 45 Tung Tau Wan Rd; admission free;
☺ 10am-5pm Tue-Sun, closed Mon & some public holidays
With Stanley Prison so close by, it's only natural that there should be a museum devoted to the subject here. The museum, about 500m southeast of Stanley Village Rd and also accessible on bus No 973, has nine galleries that trace the history of jails, prisons and other forms of incarceration in Hong Kong. The mock cells and gallows will convince most of the error of their ways.

Repulse Bay

The long beach with tawny sand at Repulse Bay – Chin Shui Wan (Shallow Water Bay) in Cantonese – is the most popular one on Hong Kong Island. Packed at the weekend and even during the week in summer, it's a good place if you like people-watching. The beach has showers and changing rooms, and shade trees at the road side, but the water is pretty murky. Lifeguards keep extended hours here: from 9am to 6pm from March to May and September to November, and from 8am to 7pm from June to August. Middle Bay and South Bay, about 10 and 30 minutes to the south respectively, have beaches that are usually much less crowded.

Repulse Bay is home to some of Hong Kong's richest residents, and the hills around the beach are strewn with luxury apartment blocks – some of them pretty hideous (including the pink-and-blue wave-like number with a giant square hole in the middle that was added at the behest of a feng shui expert).

KWUN YAM SHRINE Map pp398–9
Repulse Bay Beach
Towards the southeast end of Repulse Bay Beach is an unusual shrine to Kwun Yam. The surrounding area has an amazing assembly of deities and figures: goldfish, rams, the money god and other southern Chinese icons, as well as statues of the goddess of mercy and Tin Hau. Inside is a refreshment kiosk and the headquarters of the Hong Kong Life-Saving Society. In front of the

shrine to the left as you face the sea is Longevity Bridge; crossing it is supposed to add three days to your life.

REPULSE BAY Map pp398–9
109 Repulse Bay Rd
The Repulse Bay is a popular forum for faux-antique shops and restaurants (see Repulse Bay p194). It is a copy of the wonderful old colonial Repulse Bay Hotel, built in 1920 and bulldozed in 1982.

Deep Water Bay

A quiet little inlet with a beach flanked by shade trees, **Deep Water Bay** (Map pp398–9) is located a few kilometres northwest of Repulse Bay; lifeguards keep the same schedule as those at Repulse Bay Beach. There are a few decent places to eat and have a drink, and barbecue pits at the southern end of the beach. If you want a dip in the water, this spot is usually less crowded than Repulse Bay. Opposite the beach is the nine-hole **Deep Water Bay Golf Club** (☎ 2812 7070; 19 Island Rd). Deep Water Bay Beach is a centre for **wakeboarding**; for information ring the **Hong Kong Wakeboard Association** (☎ 2504 8168).

Aberdeen

For many years **Aberdeen** (Map p409) – Heung Gong Tsai (Little Fragrant Harbour) in Cantonese – was one of Hong Kong's top tourist attractions because of the large number of people (estimated at over 6000) who lived and worked on the junks moored in the harbour and in the Aberdeen Typhoon Shelter off Aberdeen Praya Rd to the west. Over the years the number of boats has dwindled as more and more of these boatpeople have moved into high-rises or abandoned fishing as a profession.

If you're feeling vigorous, the entrances to Aberdeen Country Park and Pok Fu Lam Country Park are about a 15-minute walk north – and uphill – along Aberdeen Reservoir Rd. From there you can walk up to Victoria Peak and catch the Peak Tram or a bus or minibus down to Central.

Districts & Islands – Hong Kong Island

SAMPAN TOURS
Aberdeen Promenade

Sampan tours can easily be arranged along Aberdeen Promenade, which runs south and parallel to Aberdeen Praya Rd. You can have your choice of private operators, which generally mill around the eastern end of the promenade, or licensed operators registered with the HKTB, such as the **Aberdeen Sampan Company** (Map p409; ☎ 2873 0310). The private sampans usually charge HK$40 per person for a 30-minute ride (about HK$80 to Sok Kwu Wan and HK$100 to Yung Shue Wan on Lamma), though you should easily be able to bargain this down if there are several of you.

AP LEI CHAU Map p409

On the southern side of the harbour is the island of Ap Lei Chau (Duck's Tongue Island). It used to be a centre for building junks, but now it's covered with housing estates, including a huge one called South Horizons. There's not much to see there, but Ap Lei Chau is famous for its factory outlets and a walk across the bridge to the island affords good views. From Aberdeen Promenade you can get a boat across to Ap Lei Chau (adult/child under 12 HK$1.80/1).

TEMPLES Map p409
Aberdeen Main Rd

If you've got time to spare, a short walk through Aberdeen will bring you to a renovated **Tin Hau temple** (☎ 2552 6036; 182 Aberdeen Main Rd; ☯ 7.30am-5pm). Built in 1851, it's a sleepy spot, but it remains an active house of worship. Close to the harbour is a **shrine to Hung Shing** (cnr Aberdeen Main Rd & Old Main St), a ramshackle collection of altars and smoking oven-like incense pots.

OCEAN PARK Map pp398–9

☎ 2552 0291; www.oceanpark.co.hk; Ocean Park Rd; adult/child 3-11 HK$180/90; ☯ 10am-6pm

Ocean Park, southeast of Aberdeen town centre, is a fully fledged amusement and educational theme park, complete with the celebrated Dragon roller coaster, Abyss Turbo Drop and other stomach-turning rides. It is also something of a marine park, with a Pacific Pier housing seals and sea lions, daily dolphin and killer-whale shows, and aquariums. The Atoll Reef is particularly impressive, with around 2600 fish representing 200 species in residence. The walk-through Shark Aquarium has hundreds of different sharks on view and scores of rays. Bird-watchers are also catered for, with aviaries and a flamingo pond.

The park is in two sections. The entrance is on the lowland side, where there are gardens and the Giant Panda Habitat, home to An An and Jia Jia. It is linked to the main section on the headland, where most of the attractions are found, by a scenic (and rather frightening for some) cable car. The headlands section affords a beautiful view of the South China Sea and at the rear entrance, where a giant escalator will bring you down to Tai Shue Wan and Shum Wan Rd, is the Middle Kingdom, a sort of Chinese cultural village with temples, pagodas and traditional street scenes.

As well as the transport options listed on p97, Ocean Park has Citybus package tickets that include transportation and admission to Ocean Park (adult/child HK$204/102) from Star Ferry pier and Admiralty (bus No 629) daily, and from Hung Hom train station (bus No 630) on Saturday and Sunday. Buses leave every 10 to 20 minutes from 9 or 9.30am to 3pm; the last buses return at 5.30pm.

KOWLOON

The name 'Kowloon' is thought to have originated when the last emperor of the Song dynasty passed through the area during his flight from the Mongols in the late 13th century (see An Imperial Outpost p63). He is said to have counted eight peaks on the peninsula and concluded that there must therefore be eight dragons there.

But the young emperor was reminded that with he himself present, there were actually nine dragons. Kowloon is thus derived from the Cantonese words *gau*, meaning 'nine', and *long*, the word for 'dragon'.

Kowloon proper, the area ceded 'in perpetuity' to Britain by the Convention of Peking (1860), extends north from the waterfront as far as Boundary St in Mong Kok. It covers just over 11 sq km, but land reclamation and encroachment into the New Territories – the so-called New Kowloon – over the past 150-odd years has quadrupled its size.

Kowloon's most important district, Tsim Sha Tsui, has none of the slickness or sophistication of Hong Kong Island's Central, except within the confines of its top-end hotels. The territory's historical and financial 'capital' lies on Hong Kong Island; Kowloon is the hinterland, a riot of commerce and tourism set against a backdrop of crumbling tenement blocks. Leave the glittering shopping centres and hotels behind and you begin to see where Hong Kong and China converge, culturally at least. East doesn't really meet West in Kowloon – it swallows it up.

In general, Kowloon is unexciting architecturally. Height restrictions for buildings, due to the proximity of the old Kai Tak International Airport in southeastern Kowloon, gave it a much lower skyline than that of northern Hong Kong Island. However, the Hong Kong Cultural Centre in Tsim Sha Tsui is a bold stab at turning Hong Kong into something more than a territory obsessed with wealth. The Peninsula Hotel is housed in one of Hong Kong's greatest colonial buildings and, at night, the promenade running east and northeast along Victoria Harbour from Star Ferry pier offers a technicolour backdrop of Central and Wan Chai. And there are some green spaces, such as Kowloon Park. What the more, Kowloon (and in particular Tsim Sha Tsui) has the lion's share of Hong Kong's most important museums.

Although Kowloon boasts the highest number of buses and MTR stations in the territory, most districts are best seen on foot. Buses and minibuses travel frequently up and down Nathan Rd, but there is no convenient tram to jump on and off.

TSIM SHA TSUI

Eating p195; Sleeping p277

Tsim Sha Tsui (pronounced 'jim sa joy' and meaning 'Sharp Sandy Point') is Hong Kong's tourist ghetto, and this is what most travellers see as they first step off the bus from the airport. Countless clothing and shoe shops, restaurants, pubs, sleazy bars, camera and electronics stores, and hotels are somehow crammed into an area not much bigger than a square kilometre. Around Ashley, Hankow and Lock Rds is a warren of cheap (and often shady) shops, restaur-ants and bars. It's a fun area to wander around, particularly in the evening.

Kowloon

Orientation

The hotel and shopping district of Tsim Sha Tsui ('Tsimsy' to locals) lies at the very tip of the Kowloon Peninsula to the south of Austin Rd. (The area between Austin Rd and Jordan Rd is usually called Jordan by Hong Kong people, but it can still be considered Tsim Sha Tsui here.) Chatham Rd South separates it from the hotels and shops of Tsim Sha Tsui East and transport hub of Hung Hom. Tsim Sha Tsui's western and southern boundaries – Victoria Harbour – are lined with top-end hotels, shopping centres and museums and other cultural venues.

Transport

MTR Tsim Sha Tsui station (Map pp412–14) on Tsuen Wan line

Bus Star Ferry pier (Map pp412–14) for Nos 2, 6 and 6A to Mong Kok and Yau Ma Tei and No 5C to Hung Hom station; Canton Rd (Map pp412–14) for No 973 to Pok Fu Lam, Aberdeen, Repulse Bay and Stanley; Nathan Rd (Map pp412–14) for No 271 to Tai Po and No 281A to Sha Tin; Nathan Rd for No 260X to Tuen Mun

Green Minibus Hankow Rd (Map pp412–14) for Nos 6 and 8 to Hung Hom; Star Ferry Pier (Map pp412–14) at western end of Salisbury Rd

Outlying Islands Ferries Star Ferry pier (Map pp412–14) to Lantau and Cheung Chau

Macau Ferries China ferry terminal (Map pp412–14) on Canton Rd

FORMER KCR CLOCK TOWER
Map pp412–14
Tsim Sha Tsui Public Pier; admission free;
⌚ 10am-6pm Sun

Immediately southeast of Star Ferry pier, this 45m-high clock tower (1921) was once part of the southern terminus of the Kowloon-Canton Railway (KCR), built in 1915. Operations moved to the modern train station at Hung Hom to the northeast in late 1975. The station was demolished in 1978, though you can see a scale model of what it looked like if you visit the Hong Kong Railway Museum in Tai Po in the New Territories (see p129). A station just east of Chatham Rd South in Tsim Sha Tsui East now allows travel to Hung Hom and the old KCR East Rail as well as the new KCR West Rail, which terminates in Tuen Mun. A maximum of 15 visitors at a time are allowed into the clock tower for 15 minutes on Sunday only.

OCEAN TERMINAL Map pp412–14
☎ 2118 8668; Salisbury Rd
To the north of the clock tower is **Star House** (3 Salisbury Rd), a frayed-looking retail and office complex. At its western end is the entrance to Ocean Terminal, the long building jutting into the harbour. It is part of the massive Harbour City shopping complex that stretches for half a kilometre north along Canton Rd and offers priceless views of Tsim Sha Tsui's western waterfront.

Ocean Terminal was built to serve passengers from the ocean liners that moor at Hong Kong's only large-scale pier. It is thus filled with top-end shops selling antiques and curios, carpets, designer clothing, jewellery and the like while the adjoining Ocean Centre has outlets largely catering to everyday shoppers. Ocean Terminal is not the place for cheap souvenir-hunting, but it's interesting for a stroll.

The stunning blue-and-white colonial structure on the hill above where Canton and Salisbury Rds meet is the former Marine Police Headquarters, built in 1884.

HONG KONG CULTURAL CENTRE
Map pp412–14
☎ 2734 2009; 10 Salisbury Rd; ⌚ 9am-11pm Mon-Sat, 1-11pm Sun & public holidays
The odd, wave-like building clad in pink ceramic tiles behind the clock tower and opposite Star House is the Hong Kong Cultural Centre, one of Hong Kong's most distinctive – if not loved – landmarks. It opened in 1989 and was compared with everything from a cheaply tiled public toilet to a road-side petrol station.

Its controversial design notwithstanding, the centre is a world-class venue, with a 2085-seat concert hall, a Grand Theatre that seats 1750, a studio theatre for up to 535, rehearsal studios and an impressive foyer. The concert hall even has a **Rieger Orgelbau pipe organ** (with 8000 pipes and 93 stops), one of the largest in the world. Upwards of 850 annual performances attract more than 700,000 people to the venue. On the centre's south side is the beginning of a viewing platform from where you can admire Victoria Harbour and the skyline of Central and gain access to the Tsim Sha Tsui East Promenade (see p105). Guided tours (HK$10/5 adult/child or senior) lasting 30 to 45 minutes depart on certain afternoons each week; telephone ahead to book.

HONG KONG MUSEUM OF ART

Map pp412–14

☎ 7221 0116; 10 Salisbury Rd; adult/child or senior HK$10/5, admission free Wed; ✆ 10am-6pm Fri-Wed, closed Thu & some public holidays

Behind the Hong Kong Cultural Centre to the southeast, the Hong Kong Museum of Art has seven galleries, spread over six floors, exhibiting Chinese antiquities, Chinese fine art, historical pictures and contemporary Hong Kong art, and hosting temporary international exhibitions.

The seventh gallery houses the Xubaizhi collection of painting and calligraphy. Visitors will find the **Historical Pictures Gallery**, with its 18th- and 19th-century Western-style paintings of Macau, Hong Kong and Guangzhou, and the **Contemporary Hong Kong Art Gallery** especially interesting. Audio guides are available for HK$10.

When your feet get tired, take a seat in the hallway and enjoy the harbour views. Or head for the **Museum Café** (☎ 2370 3860; ✆ 10am-9pm). The **Museum Bookshop** (p255) sells a wide range of books, prints and cards. Salisbury Gardens, which leads to the museum entrance, is lined with sculptures by contemporary Hong Kong sculptors. To reach the museum from the Tsim Sha Tsui MTR station, take exit E and walk south down Nathan Rd.

HONG KONG SPACE MUSEUM

Map pp412–14

☎ 2721 0226; 10 Salisbury Rd; adult/child or senior HK$10/5, admission free Wed; ✆ 1-9pm Mon, Wed-Fri & 10am-9pm Sat, Sun & public holidays

Just east of the Hong Kong Cultural Centre is the Hong Kong Space Museum, a peculiar-looking building shaped like a golf ball.

The museum is divided into three parts: the Hall of Space Science, the Hall of Astronomy and the ever-popular Space Theatre, one of the largest planetariums in the world. There are lots of videos and hands-on displays; exhibits include a lump of moon rock, models of a rocket ship and NASA's 1962 *Mercury* space capsule.

The Space Theatre screens 'sky shows' and films on a massive Omnimax screen; lasting about 40 minutes, they are mostly in Cantonese, but translations by headphones are available. The first show is at 1.30pm weekdays (12.20pm Saturday, 11.10am Sunday), the last at 8.30pm. Tickets are HK$32/16 for adults/seniors or children, and HK$24/12 in the front stalls; children under three are not allowed. Advance bookings can be made by phone up to one hour before show time.

TEDDY BEAR KINGDOM Map pp412–14

☎ 2130 2130; www.teddybearkingdom.com.hk; The Amazon, 12 Salisbury Rd; adult/child or senior HK$50/25; ✆ 10am-10pm

Children under three disappointed with being turned away at the Space Theatre may find distraction in the world's first indoor amusement park devoted to teddy bears. It's divided into several zones, full of faux tropical trees and stuffed beasties and even has a Teddy Bear Museum with some 400 stuffed cuddlies from around the world. You might not be overly impressed but the kids certainly will be.

PENINSULA HOTEL Map pp412–14

☎ 2920 2888; cnr Salisbury & Nathan Rds

More than a Hong Kong landmark, the Peninsula, in the throne-like building opposite the Hong Kong Space Museum, is one of the world's great hotels (see p279). Before WWII it was one of several prestigious hotels across Asia where everybody who was anybody stayed, lining up with the likes of the Raffles in Singapore, the Peace (then the Cathay) in Shanghai and the Strand in Rangoon (now Yangon).

Land reclamation has robbed the hotel of its top waterfront location since it first opened its doors in 1928, but the breathtaking interior is worth a visit if for no other reason than to take afternoon tea (from HK$180; ✆ 2-7pm) here. This is one of Hong Kong's greatest pastimes – dress neatly and be prepared to line up for a table.

NATHAN ROAD Map pp412–14

Kowloon's main thoroughfare was named after Sir Matthew Nathan, governor of Hong Kong from 1904 to 1907. As Kowloon was very sparsely populated at the time and such a wide road thought unnecessarily extravagant, it was dubbed 'Nathan's Folly'. There are

banyans lining the road at the northern end near Austin Rd, but the trees that once lined the rest of the street and can be seen in not-so-old photographs were removed in 1976 when the MTR's first line was being built.

The southern end of Nathan Rd is known as the Golden Mile, reflecting both the price of property in this high-rent area and the retailers' success. Though lacking any tourist sights per se, the lower end of this boulevard is a sight in itself. Ramshackle blocks stacked with seedy guesthouses awkwardly rub shoulders with top-end hotels; touts sell fake Rolex watches; tailors ply their trade on street corners; and the pavements are chock-a-block with consumers scurrying from one shop to another. Anyone who chooses to stay at Chungking Mansions, Mirador Mansion or Golden Crown Court (see Cheap Sleeps p280) will have this frenetic scene at their very doorstep.

KOWLOON MOSQUE & ISLAMIC CENTRE Map pp412–14

☎ 2724 0095; 105 Nathan Rd; ☯ 5am-10pm

North of the intersection of Nathan and Haiphong Rds, the Kowloon Mosque & Islamic Centre is the largest Islamic house of worship in Hong Kong. The present building, with its dome and carved marble, was completed in 1984 to serve the territory's 80,000 Muslims, half of whom are Chinese. It occupies the site of a mosque built in 1896 for Muslim Indian troops.

Muslims are welcome to attend services, but non-Muslims should seek permission to enter in advance. If permission is granted, make sure you are dressed modestly and have removed your shoes or sandals before you enter.

KOWLOON PARK Map pp412–14

☎ 2724 3344; Nathan & Austin Rds; ☯ 6am-midnight

Once the site of a barracks for Indian soldiers in the colonial army, Kowloon Park is an oasis of greenery and is a refreshing escape from the hustle and bustle of Tsim Sha Tsui. Pathways and walls crisscross the grass, birds hop around in cages, and towers and ancient banyan trees dot the landscape.

There's an **aviary** (☯ 6.30am-6.45pm Mar-Oct, 6.30am-5.45pm Nov-Feb); a Chinese Garden and Sculpture Walk, featuring works by local artists; and Kung Fu Corner, a display of traditional Chinese martial arts, takes place here from 2.30pm to 4.30pm on Sunday. The renovated **Kowloon Park Swimming Complex** (☎ 2724 3577; adult/child 3-13 or senior over 60 HK$19/9; ☯ 6.30am-10pm with 1hr close at noon & 6pm Apr-Oct, indoor 6.30am-9.30pm with 1hr close at noon & 6pm Nov-Mar) is complete with waterfalls. Visit on a weekday; on weekends there are so many bathers it's difficult to find the water.

HONG KONG OBSERVATORY

Map pp412–14

☎ 2926 8200; 134A Nathan Rd

What was until 1997 called the Royal Observatory is housed in a two-storey colonial structure east of Kowloon Park on the other side of Nathan Rd. It was built in 1883 and declared a historic monument exactly a century later. It continues to monitor Hong Kong's weather and sends up those frightening signals when a typhoon is heading for the territory (see the boxed text p357). The observatory is not open to the public, but group visits can be arranged.

TSIM SHA TSUI EAST & HUNG HOM

Eating p195; Sleeping p283

The large triangular chunk of land east and northeast of Tsim Sha Tsui proper, built entirely on reclaimed land, is a cluster of shopping centres, hotels, theatres, restaurants and nightclubs. There are none of the old, crumbling buildings of 'real' Tsim Sha Tsui – and like most reclaimed areas, it has that soulless, artificial feel that will take decades to remove. But two of Hong Kong's most important museums are here, and it offers an excellent vantage point from which to admire the harbour and Hong Kong Island's cityscape.

Among the features of Hung Hom, the contiguous district to the northeast, are the massive KCR station, on Wan Rd; the adjacent 12,500-seat Hong Kong Coliseum (☎ 2355 7234; 9 Cheong Wan Rd), which hosts concerts and sporting events; the Hong Kong Polytechnic University (☎ 2766 5100; Hong Chong Rd), opposite the station; and one of the strangest shopping venues in the territory, Whampoa Garden (☎ 2128 7465; 18 Tak Fung St), a full-scale concrete model of a luxury cruise liner. While presumably not very seaworthy, the 'ship' – 100m long and four decks tall – is impressive and works very well for what it was intended to be: a shopping centre with retail outlets, restaurants, a cinema and playground on the top deck.

Orientation

Tsim Sha Tsui East is defined by Chatham Rd South to the west and Salisbury Rd to the south. The limit to the east is Hong Chong Rd, backed by the Hong Kong Coliseum and Hung Hom train station. To the north it ends at Cheong Wan Rd.

Hung Hom is further to the north and northeast and divided by the Hung Hom Bypass into two parts: the station and coliseum on the west side and residential Hung Hom to the east.

TSIM SHA TSUI EAST PROMENADE

Map pp412–14

Along with the Peak, this amazing waterfront walkway offers some of the best views in Hong Kong. It's a lovely place to stroll during the day, and at night the view of Central lit up in neon is mesmerising.

Best of all, you can turn your back on the landfill of Tsim Sha Tsui East. You'll find yourself accompanied by lovers, joggers, musicians, photographers with tripods, and people fishing right off the walkway. The promenade becomes a 'black mountain' of people during the Chinese New Year fireworks displays in late January/early February and again in June during the **Dragon Boat Festival** (see p11).

The promenade officially starts at the New World Centre shopping centre and runs parallel to Salisbury Rd almost to the Hong Kong Coliseum and Hung Hom train station, but you can walk along the water all the way from Star Ferry pier in order to gain access to it.

HONG KONG SCIENCE MUSEUM

Map pp412–14

☎ 2732 3232; 2 Science Museum Rd; adult/child, senior or student HK$25/12.50, admission free Wed; ☿ 1-9pm Mon-Wed & Fri, 10am-9pm Sat, Sun & public holidays

The Hong Kong Science Museum is a four-level complex with more than 500 displays on computers, energy, physics, robotics, telecommunications, health and the like. Two-thirds of the exhibits are 'hands on'. Though some of them are beginning to look a little dated – the museum opened in 1991 – all the

Districts & Islands – Kowloon

Transport

MTR Tsim Sha Tsui East: Tsim Sha Tsui station (exit D; Map pp412–14) on the Tsuen Wan line and walk east on Mody Rd

KCR Hung Hom and Tsim Sha Tsui stations (Map pp412–14)

Bus Tsim Sha Tsui East and Hung Hom: Nos 5C & 8 to Star Ferry pier (Map pp412–14) in Tsim Sha Tsui

Green Minibus Hung Hom: Nos 6 and 8 to Hankow Rd in Tsim Sha Tsui

Ferry Tsim Sha Tsui East ferry pier (Map pp412–14) to Central

buttons to push and robot arms to operate will keep most young visitors entertained.

HONG KONG MUSEUM OF HISTORY

Map pp412–14

☎ 2724 9042; 100 Chatham Rd South; adult/senior/child HK$10/7/5, admission free Wed; ☿ 10am-6pm Mon & Wed-Sat, 10am-7pm Sun & public holidays

Hong Kong's newest museum, which opened its permanent exhibition in 2001, focuses on the territory's archaeology, natural history, ethnography and local history. It is well worth a visit not only to learn more about the subject but to understand how Hong Kong presents its history to the world.

'The Hong Kong Story' takes visitors on a fascinating walk through the territory's past via eight galleries, starting with the natural environment and prehistoric Hong Kong and ending with the territory's return to China in 1997. Along the way you'll encounter replicas of village dwellings; traditional Chinese costumes and beds; a re-creation of an entire arcaded street in Central from 1881, including an old Chinese medicine shop; a tram from 1913; and film footage of WWII, including recent interviews with Chinese and foreigners taken prisoner by the Japanese.

The large collection of 19th- and early-20th-century photographs is very atmospheric, but a favourite is the mishmash of toys and collectables from the 1960s and 1970s when 'Made in Hong Kong' meant 'Christmas stocking trash'. Free guided tours of the museum are available in English at 10.30am and 2.30pm on Saturday and Sunday.

YAU MA TEI

Eating p203; Sleeping p284

Immediately to the north of Tsim Sha Tsui is the district of Yau Ma Tei, pronounced 'yow ma day' and meaning 'Place of Sesame Plants'. Today the only plants you'll find in this heavily urban district are in the window boxes of six-storey crumbling tenements, known as *tong lau* in Cantonese, that don't have lifts and more often than not have illegal huts on the roof. Yau Ma Tei's narrow byways are good places to check out Hong Kong's more traditional urban society. There are many interesting **walks** to take along the streets running east to west between Kansu St and Jordan Rd (Map pp412-14): **Nanking St** (mahjong shops and parlours), **Ning Po St** (paper goods such as kites, and paper votives, such as houses, mobile phones and hell money, to burn for the dead) and **Saigon St** (herbalist shops, old-style tailors, pawnshops). On **Shanghai St** you'll find Chinese bridal and trousseau shops. See p158 for a self-guided walk in Mong Kok and Yau Ma Tei.

Orientation

Yau Ma Tei is practically indistinguishable from its neighbours to the north (Mong Kok) and south (Tsim Sha Tsui). Indeed, the official designation of the district they're in is Yau Tsim Mong. Yau Ma Tei starts at Jordan Rd and reaches north to somewhere between Waterloo Rd and Argyle St. King's Park and Gascoigne Rd are its borders to the east. To the west it reaches Yau Ma Tei Typhoon Shelter in Victoria Harbour and the Kowloon station of the Tung Chung MTR and Airport Express lines. The Jade Market, an active Tin Hau temple and the Temple St night market are just a short walk from the Yau Ma Tei MTR station.

Transport

MTR Jordan MTR station (Map pp412–14) on Tsuen Wan line and Yau Ma Tei MTR station (Map p415) on the Tsuen Wan and Kwun Tong line

Bus Nathan Rd (Map p415) for Nos 2, 6 and 6A to Tsim Sha Tsui; No 9 to Star Ferry pier; No 203 to Tsim Sha Tsui East; No 102 to Hung Hom, North Point and Quarry Bay; No 104 to Wan Chai and Central; No 60X to Tuen Mun; No 81 to Sha Tin

Airport Express Kowloon station (Map pp412–14)

JADE MARKET Map pp412–14
Kansu, Canton & Battery Sts; 🕑 9am-6pm

The Jade Market, near the Gascoigne Rd overpass just west of Nathan Rd and split into two parts by the loop formed by Battery St, has some 450 stalls selling all varieties and grades of jade from inside two covered markets. Unless you really know your nephrite from your jadeite – and intimately – it's probably not wise to buy any expensive pieces here.

You can reach the market easily on foot from either the Jordan or Yau Ma Tei MTR stations. Bus No 9 from the Star Ferry bus station will drop you off at the Kowloon Central Post Office (405 Nathan Rd), which is just around the corner from the market.

TIN HAU TEMPLE Map p415
☎ 2332 9240; cnr Public Square St & Nathan Rd; 🕑 8am-5pm

A couple of blocks northeast of the Jade Market, this decent-sized temple is dedicated to Tin Hau, the goddess of seafarers. The temple complex also houses an altar dedicated to Shing Wong, the god of the city, and to To Tei, the earth god. You'll find a long row of fortune-tellers through the last doorway on the right from the main entrance; signs indicate which ones speak English. An incense spiral that lasts 10 days will set you back HK$130.

The **Yau Ma Tei Police Station** (627 Canton Rd), a short distance to the east along Public Square St, was built in 1922 and is a listed building.

TEMPLE STREET NIGHT MARKET
Maps p415 & pp412–14
🕑 4pm-midnight

Temple St, which extends from Man Ming Lane in the north to Nanking St in the south and is cut in two by the Tin Hau temple complex, is the liveliest night market in Hong Kong, and is *the* place to go for cheap clothes, *dai pai dong* (open-air street stall) food, watches, pirate CDs, fake labels, footwear, cookware and everyday items. Any marked prices should be considered mere suggestions – this is definitely a place to bargain.

(Continued on page 115)

1 *Inscriptions, Po Lin Monastery (p148)* 2 *Statue of the god of wealth, Repulse Bay (p99)* 3 *Detail on Man Mo Temple (p85)* 4 *Burning incense at Po Lin Monastery (p148)*

1 Street-stall food 2 Durians (p169)
3 Fresh produce (p53)
4 Market, Sheung Wan (p84)

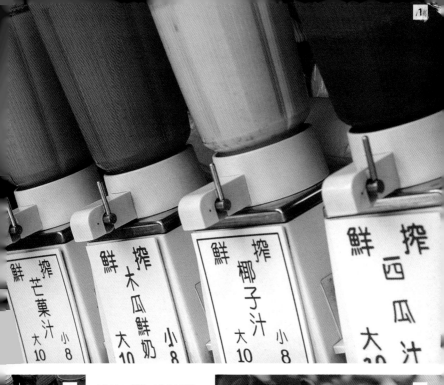

鮮搾芒菓汁 小 8 大 10

鮮搾木瓜鮮奶 小 8 大 10

鮮搾椰子汁 小 8 大 10

鮮搾西瓜汁 大

1 *Drink stall* **2** *Fresh fruit (p168)*
3 *Rice wine* **4** *Food at market stall*

1 Hong Kong Island at night, from Kowloon (p101) 2 Moon lantern 3 Neon sign 4 Nathan Rd (p103)

1 *Kubrick Bookshop Cafe (p236)*
2 *V-13 (p222)* 3 *Bar, Soho (p222)*
4 *Taxi rank (p351)*

1 Sampans (p345) 2 Advertisement for horse races (p30) 3 Longevity Bridge (p99) 4 Commuters waiting for public transport (p339)

1 *Performer, Chinese opera (p42)* 2 *Traditional Chinese dragon* 3 *Poster for California Fitness Centre (p239)* 4 *Sign for Fringe Club (p237)*

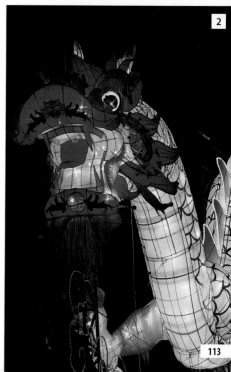

1 *Medicine jars, Eu Yan Sang (p264)* 2 *Window display, Lock Cha Tea Shop (p262)* 3 *Silk for sale (p252)* 4 *Prayers tied to oranges, Lam Tsuen Wishing Tree (p130)*

(Continued from page 106)

You'll also find a surfeit of fortune-tellers and herbalists and, occasionally, some free, open-air Cantonese opera performances.

For street food, head for Woo Sung St, running parallel to the east, or to the section of Temple St north of the temple. You can get anything from a simple bowl of noodles to a full meal. There are also a few seafood and hotpot restaurants in the area.

The market officially opens in the afternoon, but most hawkers set up at about 6pm and leave by midnight. The market is at its best from about 7pm to 10pm, when it's clogged with stalls and people. If you want to carry on, visit the colourful **wholesale fruit market** (cnr Shek Lung and Reclamation Sts; ☽ midnight-dawn).

MONG KOK

Eating p203; Sleeping p284

Mong Kok (Prosperous Point) is one of Hong Kong's most congested working-class residential areas, as well as one of its busiest shopping districts.

This is where locals come to buy everyday items such as jeans, tennis shoes, computer accessories and kitchen supplies. Take a look at Fife St, which has an amazing collection of stalls selling old records, books, ceramics, machinery and music scores. Mong Kok is also a good place to buy backpacks, hiking boots and sporting goods (see Shopping p265). Two blocks southeast of the Mong Kok MTR station (exit D3) is the **Tung Choi St market** (☽ 1-11pm), which runs from Argyle St in the north to Dundas St in the south.

The streets west of Nathan Rd reveal Hong Kong's seamier side, for this is where you'll find some of the city's seediest brothels. Mostly run by Triads, these places are often veritable prisons for young women. The Hong Kong police routinely raid these places, but a look at the rows of pastel-coloured neon strip lights on so many blocks is an indication that it's 'business as usual' despite the change in landlords. This is one of the very few places in Hong Kong that you should avoid after midnight.

Orientation

Mong Kok starts somewhere between Waterloo Rd and Argyle St to the south and ends at Boundary St in the north – strictly speaking, anything beyond that is the New Territories. The limit to the east is Waterloo Rd as it heads northward to Kowloon Tong and to the west the district of Tai Kok Tsui.

The easiest way to get to the market is to take exit C2 from the Jordan MTR station and walk along Bowring St or exit C from the Yau Ma Tei MTR station and follow Man Ming Lane.

SHANGHAI STREET ARTSPACE Map p415
☎ 2770 2157; 404 Shanghai St; admission free;
☽ 10.30am-7.30pm Thu-Tue

Funded by the Hong Kong Arts Development Council, this venue is a small space in a strange place and focuses on some cutting-edge new art by local artists. Video assemblages, photography, computer art and mixed media all get a look-in. It's almost in Mong Kok, so can be reached on foot from the Yau Ma Tei MTR (exit A1) or Mong Kok MTR (exit E1) stations.

Songbird from Yuen Po Street Bird Garden & Flower Market (p116)

Transport

MTR Mong Kok and Prince Edward MTR stations (Map p415) on Tsuen Wan and Kwun Tong lines

KCR Mong Kok station (Map p415)

Bus Nathan Rd (Map p415) for Nos 2, 6 and 6A to Tsim Sha Tsui; No 203 to Tsim Sha Tsui East; No 102 to Hung Hom, North Point and Quarry Bay; No 104 to Wan Chai and Central; No 81 to Sha Tin; Argyle St (Map p415) for No 60X to Tuen Mun

YUEN PO STREET BIRD GARDEN & FLOWER MARKET Map p415
Flower Market Rd; ☺ 7am-8pm

This market is a wonderful place to visit, if only to marvel at how the Hong Kong Chinese (especially men) fuss and fawn over their feathered friends. The Chinese have long favoured songbirds as pets; you often see local men walking around airing their birds and feeding them tasty creepy-crawlies with chopsticks. Some birds are also considered harbingers of good fortune, which is why you'll see some people carrying them to the racetrack.

There are hundreds of birds for sale from some 70 stalls here, along with elaborate cages carved from teak and bamboo. Adjacent to the bird garden is the flower market on Flower Market Rd, which keeps theoretically the same hours but only gets busy after 10am, especially on Sunday.

To get to the bird garden and flower market, from the Prince Edward MTR station, come out of exit B1 and walk east along Prince Edward Rd West for about 10 minutes.

The Triads

Hong Kong's Triads, which run the territory's drug, prostitution, gambling and loan-sharking rackets, were not always the gangster operations they are today. They were originally founded as patriotic and secret societies that opposed the corrupt and brutal Qing (Manchu) dynasty and aided the revolution that brought down that moribund dynasty in 1911. The fact that these organisations had adopted Kwan Tai (or Kwan Yu), the god of war, and the upholder of righteousness, integrity and loyalty, as their patron lent them further respectability.

Unfortunately, the Triads descended into crime and illicit activities during the civil war on the mainland, and came in droves to Hong Kong after the Communists came to power in 1949. Today they are the Chinese equivalent of the Mafia. Sporting such names as 14K, Bamboo Union, Water Room and Peace Victory Brotherhood, the Triads have been increasingly successful at recruiting disaffected teenagers in Hong Kong's high-rise housing estates. The Hong Kong police estimate that there are more than 50 Triad societies in the territory, with some 100,000 members.

The Triad armoury is a hellish array of weapons ranging from meat choppers (cleavers) and machetes to pistols and petrol bombs. If people default on a loan, Triad members encourage repayment by attacking them with large knives in the middle of the street.

Membership in a Triad is illegal in Hong Kong; indeed, it's an offence even to claim to be a member. Yet the Triads seem to be growing and have been trying to use wealth to muscle into legitimate businesses.

The Communists smashed the Triad-controlled drug racket in Shanghai after the 1949 revolution. The Triads have long memories and, before the handover, many Hong Kong-based hoods moved their operations to ethnic Chinese communities in countries like Australia, Canada and the USA. Thailand got more than its share, and even the Philippines received some of this 'overseas investment' – Triad-arranged kidnappings of wealthy Chinese families living there became something of a growth industry. However, since 1997 many Triads have moved back into Hong Kong and have even expanded their operations into the mainland, establishing links with corrupt government cadres and high-ranking soldiers in the People's Liberation Army.

It's unlikely that many foreign travellers will encounter Triad members directly during their stay in Hong Kong. The Triad-controlled brothels of Mong Kok and Sham Shui Po shun foreign clientele and you would be mad to get mixed up with drugs on the streets of Kowloon or Wan Chai. You may have the misfortune of meeting one or two of these unsavoury characters if you frequent hostess clubs (a good reason to avoid these places). Do what is expected of you; gorillas don't take 'no' for an answer.

NEW KOWLOON

Eating p204

The southernmost 31 sq km of the New Territories is officially called **New Kowloon**. Since Boundary St just above Mong Kok technically marks the division between Kowloon and the New Territories, these places – strictly speaking – belong to the latter. But they look and feel and consider themselves to be part of Kowloon and are thus considered so. 'New Kowloon' is an official designation, however, and never used by Hong Kong people.

Orientation

New Kowloon encompasses as many as 20 different neighbourhoods but only half a dozen are of much interest to travellers. From west to east they are Sham Shui Po, Kowloon Tong,

Kowloon City, Wong Tai Sin and Diamond Hill. The majority (and the places of interest described in this section) are within easy reach of an MTR station.

Transport

MTR Sham Shui Po MTR station (Map pp410–11) on Tsuen Wan line, Kowloon Tong MTR station (Map pp410–11) on Kwun Tong line, Lok Fu MTR station (Map pp410–11) on Kwun Tong line for Kowloon City, Wong Tai Sin and Diamond Hill MTR stations (Map pp410–11) on Kwun Tong line, Yau Tong MTR station (Map pp396–7) on Kwun Tong and Tseung Kwan O lines for Lei Yue Mun

KCR Kowloon Tong station (Map pp410–11)

Bus Sham Shui Po: Yen Chow St (Map pp410–11) for Nos 6 and 6A and Kweilin St for No 2 to Star Ferry pier; Kowloon Tong: Waterloo Rd (Map pp410–11) for No 182 to Admiralty and Central and No 170 to Causeway Bay; Tat Chee Ave (Map pp410–11) for Nos 2C and 203 to Tsim Sha Tsui; Kowloon City: Ma Tau Chung Rd (Map pp410–11) for Nos 5C and 26 to Tsim Sha Tsui and Nos 101 and 111 to Wan Chai, Admiralty and Central; Wong Tai Sin: Tung Tau Tsuen Rd for No 5 to Mong Kok and Tsim Sha Tsui and San Po Kong Rd for No 111 to Wan Chai, Admiralty and Central; Diamond Hill: Choi Hung Rd for No 9 to Mong Kok, Yau Ma Tei and Tsim Sha Tsui and Hollywood Plaza for No 92 to Sai King; Lei Yue Mun: Yau Tong Centre for No 14C to Kwun Tong MTR station (Map pp396–7)

Sham Shui Po

A residential area of high-rises, **Sham Shui Po** (Map pp410–11) is famous for its market and computer emporiums (see Computers p259). North of and easily accessible from the district is Lei Cheng Uk Han Tomb, an important archaeological find.

APLIU STREET MARKET Map pp410–11

Apliu St, btwn Nam Cheong & Kweilin Sts;
☾ **noon-midnight**

From the Sham Shui Po MTR station follow exit A2 and you'll soon fall right into this flea market, which features everything from clothing to antique clocks and coins but specialises in secondhand electronic goods – radios, mobile phones, stereo systems, amplifiers and spare parts. The market spills over into Pei Ho St.

DRAGON CENTRE Map pp410–11

☎ **2307 9264; 37K Yen Chow St;** ☾ **10am-midnight**

The Dragon Centre is a working-class centre with a branch of Sincere department store and a Wellcome supermarket. Take exit C1 from the Sham Shui Po MTR station if going there directly. It doesn't look like a shopping centre at first glance, but an external escalator at the end of Ki Lung St will take you from street level to the first shopping floor.

At nine levels, the Dragon Centre towers above the surrounding apartment blocks. There's a food hall on level 8 (HK$35 buys a meal of soup, egg, pork and rice). On the same level, there's the **Skyrink ice-skating rink** (p242).

The attractive **Sham Shui Po Police Station** (37A Yen Chow St), just south of the Dragon Centre and opposite Tai Nan St, was built in 1925.

LEI CHENG UK HAN TOMB MUSEUM

Map pp410–11

☎ **2386 2863; 41 Tonkin St; admission free;**
☾ **10am-1pm & 2-6pm Mon-Wed, Fri-Sat & 1-6pm Sun, closed Thu & some public holidays**

The Lei Cheng Uk Han Tomb Museum, built around an Eastern Han dynasty (AD 25–220) burial vault that was discovered in 1955 when the hillside was being levelled for an estate to house 250,000 refugees from China, is one of Hong Kong's earliest surviving historical monuments. Believe it or not, it was once on the coast.

The tomb consists of four barrel-vaulted brick chambers in the form of a cross and set around a domed central chamber; many of the bricks contained moulded patterns of fish, dragons and the like. It's encased in a concrete shell for protection and you can only peek through a plastic window; it's a bit of a journey for an anticlimactic peek through Perspex. The museum also contains some 58 pottery and bonze pieces taken from the tomb.

To reach the tomb, take bus No 2 from the Star Ferry; the bus stops in front of the museum on Tonkin St. The nearest MTR station is Cheung Sha Wan; take exit A3 and walk 10 minutes to the northeast.

Kowloon Tong

A posh residential area northeast of Mong Kok, **Kowloon Tong** (Map pp410–11) is home to colleges and universities; both the **Hong Kong Baptist University** (☎ 2339 7400), Hong Kong's most generously endowed seat of higher learning, and the **City University of Hong Kong** (☎ 2788 9191) are in the neighbourhood. You'll also find bridal shops and salons here with names like Cité du Louvre, where brides-to-be can buy their finery, have their photos done and even attend the ceremony itself.

FESTIVAL WALK SHOPPING CENTRE
Map pp410–11
☎ 2520 8025; 80-88 Tat Chee Ave;
☺ 10am-midnight

Kowloon Tong can claim Festival Walk, the territory's most luxurious shopping complex, and, in typical Hong Kong fashion, the centre boasts a fair few superlatives itself. Festival Walk has the largest cinema, bookshop and ice-skating rink in the territory (see Skating p242). From the Kowloon Tong MTR station, take exit C2.

Kowloon City

Just west of what was once Kai Tak International Airport, the rather low-rent neighbourhood of **Kowloon City** (Map pp410–11) has two drawcards: a wonderful park that was once the infamous **Kowloon Walled City**, and a string of authentic and excellent-value Thai restaurants (see New Kowloon p204). The airport, which sits on a prime chunk of land, is now abandoned and awaits development; the Southeast Kowloon Development Plan would see parkland, industrial estates, shopping complexes and housing for 250,000 people on the site.

KOWLOON WALLED CITY PARK
Map pp410–11
Carpenter, Junction, Tung Tau Tsuen & Tung Tsing Rds;
☺ 6.30am-11pm

The walls that enclose this beautiful park were once the perimeter of a notorious village that technically remained part of China throughout British rule, as it was never included in the 1898 lease of the New Territories. The enclave was known for its vice, prostitution, gambling, illegal dentists and sheer poverty. In 1984 the Hong Kong government acquired the area, rehoused the residents elsewhere and built pavilions and ponds filled with turtles and goldfish and planted exquisite trees and shrubs, including a long hedge coaxed into the form of a dragon. The park opened in 1996. Close to the Carpenter Rd entrance of the park is the renovated Yamen building, once an almshouse. It contains displays on the history of the walled city, with a scale model of the village in the mid-19th century. Further north are the remnants of the original South and East Gates.

To reach Kowloon Walled City Park, take bus No 1 from the Star Ferry bus station and alight at Tung Tau Tsuen Rd opposite the park. The closest MTR station is Lok Fu (exit B), a 20-minute walk along Junction Rd to the north.

Wong Tai Sin

The district of **Wong Tai Sin** to the north of Kowloon City is known for two things: its enormous and faceless housing estate and one of the most active temples in the territory.

SIK SIK YUEN WONG TAI SIN TEMPLE
Map pp410–11
☎ 2854 4333; Lung Cheung Rd; HK$2 donation requested; ☺ 7am-5.30pm

This large Taoist temple complex adjacent to the Wong Tai Sin housing estate, was built in 1973 and is dedicated to the god of that name, who began his life as a humble shepherd in Zhejiang province. When he was 15 an immortal taught Wong Tai Sin how to make a herbal potion that could cure all illnesses. He is thus worshipped both by the sick and those trying to avoid illness. He is also a favourite god of businesspeople. The image of the god in the main temple was brought to Hong Kong from Guangdong province in 1915 and initially installed in a temple in Wan Chai, where it remained until being moved to the present site in 1921.

Like most Chinese temples, this one is an explosion of colourful pillars, roofs, lattice work, flowers and shrubs. If you come in the early evening – Friday evening is the busiest time – you can watch hordes of business-men and secretaries praying and divining the future with *chim*, bamboo 'prediction sticks' that must be shaken out of a box on to the ground and then read by a fortune-teller (they're available free to the left of the main temple).

Behind the main temple and to the right are the **Good Wish Gardens** (HK$2 donation requested; 🕘 9am-1pm Mon, 9am-4pm Tue-Sun), replete with colourful pavilions (the hexagonal Unicorn Hall with carved doors and windows is the most beautiful), zigzag bridges, waterfalls and carp ponds.

Just below the main temple and to the left as you enter the complex is an arcade filled with dozens of booths operated by fortune-tellers, some of whom speak English.

The busiest times at the temple are around the Chinese New Year, Wong Tai Sin's birth-day (23rd day of the eighth month – usually in September) and at weekends. Getting to the temple is easy. From the Wong Tai Sin MTR station, take exit B2 and then follow the signs or crowds (or both).

Diamond Hill

Spread out below the peak of the same name, the residential district of Diamond Hill is due east of Wong Tai Sin, and contains Hong Kong's most beautiful house of worship.

CHI LIN NUNNERY Map pp410–11
☎ 2354 1604; 5 Chi Lin Dr; admission free;
🕘 nunnery 9am-4pm Thu-Tue, garden
6.30am-7pm daily
This large Buddhist complex, originally dating from the 1930s, was rebuilt completely of wood in the Tang dynasty style in 1998. It is a serene place, with lotus ponds, immaculate bonsai and silent nuns delivering offerings of fruit and rice to Buddha and his disciples. The design is intended to demonstrate the harmony of humans with nature and is pretty convincing – until you look up at the looming neighbourhood high-rises.

You enter the complex through the Sam Mun, a series of 'three gates' representing the

Buddhist precepts of compassion, wisdom and 'skilful means'. The first courtyard, which contains the delightful Lotus Pond Garden, gives way to the Hall of Celestial Kings, with a large statue of the seated Buddha surrounded by the deities of the four cardinal points. Behind that is the main hall containing a statue of the Sakyamuni Buddha flanked by two seated Bodhisattvas and two standing dis-ciples. The wooden **Pagoda of the 10,000 Buddhas** beckons from a knoll to the northeast.

To reach the nunnery from the Diamond Hill MTR station, take exit C2, walk through the Hollywood Plaza shopping centre and turn east on Fung Tak Rd. The nunnery is a five-minute walk away.

Lei Yue Mun

Southeast of the old Kai Tak International Airport is the residential neighbourhood of Kwun Tong (Map pp396–7 & Map pp398–9), and a bit further southeast is the rapidly modernis-ing fishing village of Lei Yue Mun (Map pp396–7 & Map pp398–9). *Lei yue* means 'carp' and *mun* is 'gate'; the 'carp gate' refers to the channel separating southeast Kowloon from Hong Kong Island, which is the narrowest entrance to Victoria Harbour. Across the water on the island and looming on the hillside is 19th-century Lei Yue Mun Fort, which now contains the Hong Kong Museum of Coastal Defence (p95).

SAM KA TSUEN TYPHOON SHELTER
Map pp396–7 & Map pp398–9
The 'village' of Lei Yue Mun is one of Hong Kong's prime seafood venues; there are some two dozen fish restaurants along Lei Yue Mun Praya Rd overlooking the typhoon shelter here. It's a colourful and lively place to dine by the water at night, and is always busy. To get here from the Yau Tong MTR station, use exit A2 and follow Cha Kwo Ling Rd and Shung Shun St south for 15 minutes. Bus No 14C links the Yau Tong Centre halfway down the hill with the Kwun Tong MTR station.

NEW TERRITORIES

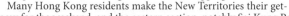

The New Territories were so named because they were leased to Britain in 1898, almost half a century after Hong Kong Island and four decades after Kowloon were ceded to the crown. For many years the area was Hong Kong's rural hinterland; however since WWII, when some 80% of the land was under cultivation, many parts of 'the NT' – as the area is known locally – have become increasingly urbanised. In the past two decades the speed at which this development has taken place has been nothing short of heart-stopping.

Many Hong Kong residents make the New Territories their get-away for the weekend, and the eastern section, notably Sai Kung Peninsula in the northeast and the area around Clearwater Bay further south, has some of Hong Kong's most beautiful scenery and hiking trails. Life in these more rural parts of Hong Kong is more redolent of times past – simpler, slower, often more friendly.

The New Territories is large, comprising just over 72% of Hong Kong's land area. Strictly speaking, everything north of Boundary St in Kowloon, up to the border with mainland China, is the New Territories. The northernmost part of the New Territories, within 1km of the Chinese frontier, is a 'closed border area' that is fenced and well marked with signs. It marks the boundary of the Hong Kong SAR with the Shenzhen Special Economic Zone (SEZ).

Some 3.37 million people, up from less than half a million in 1970, call the New Territories home – about half the total population of Hong Kong. Most of them live in 'New Towns'. Since its inception in the 1950s, the New Towns program has consumed more than half of the Hong Kong government's budget, with much of the funding spent on land reclamation, sewage, roads and other infrastructure projects. About 60% of new housing units are government-built.

In the past, the biggest impediment to growth in the New Territories was a lack of good transportation. Nowadays, getting to the New Territories has never been easier, particularly to the New Towns and areas of interest listed here. The new **KCR West Rail** (Map pp396–7) is now transporting passengers from Kowloon to the western New Territories as far as Tuen Mun. The **MTR** (Map p426) goes to Tsuen Wan (on the Tsuen Wan line) in the west and Tseung Kwan O in the east, from where you can catch buses and minibuses to explore other parts of the New Territories. Travel to the northern New Territories is simple, fast and cheap with the **KCR East Rail** (Map pp396–7), which connects Kowloon with Sha Tin, Tai Po, Sheung Shui and the Chinese border at Lo Wu. There are also a number of buses linking Hong Kong Island and Kowloon with the New Territories.

Once in the New Territories, buses – run for the most part by the **Kowloon Motor Bus Co** (KMB; ☎ 2745 4466) – and green minibuses – which run on more than 160 routes – are

Mountain silhouettes, New Territories

the main ways to get around. Catching a taxi is easy – at least to and from the New Towns; there are more than 2850 cabs cruising the streets and country roads of the New Territories. Ferries and *kaidos* (small, open-sea ferries) serve the more remote areas and a few large communities on the coast.

In the far west of the New Territories, the way to go is the **Light Rail Transit** (LRT; Map pp396–7), a modern, street-level tram system that connects Tuen Mun with Yuen Long and stops at several interesting places along the way.

The HKTB has a handy information sheet with a map detailing the major bus routes in the New Territories. For more obscure or complex routes, check the KMB's website (www.kmb.com.hk).

If you don't have the time or inclination to use public transport, consider one of the New Territories tours offered by the HKTB and some travel agencies. See Bus p78.

TSUEN WAN

Eating p206; Sleeping p286

Among the easiest destinations in the New Territories to reach, **Tsuen Wan** (Shallow Bay; Map p416) is an industrial and residential New Town northwest of Kowloon, with some 740,000 inhabitants. It's nothing special, but it does have a fine (though small) museum and some of the most colourful and active temple and monastic complexes in Hong Kong. Chung On St, south of the Tsuen Wan MTR station, is famed for its jewellery and goldsmith shops. Tak Wah Park in the centre of town has ancient trees, footbridges over ponds and ornamental stone mountains.

Orientation

The MTR station is on Sau Lau Kok Rd with the Luk Yeung Galleria shopping centre above it. The bus station is opposite the MTR on Castle Peak Rd (exit A2), but buses and green minibuses pick up and disgorge passengers throughout the New Town. The Sam Tung Uk Museum is within easy walking distance of the MTR station, though to reach the temples and monasteries in the hills to the north you should take a minibus. Tsuen Wan is the last station on the Tsuen Wan MTR line. If you're really in a hurry to get there or back, change to the new Tung Chung MTR line at Lai King, which has fewer stops.

Transport

MTR Tsuen Wan MTR station (Map p416) on Tsuen Wan line

KCR Tsuen Wan West station (Map p416)

Bus Bus station (Map p416) for No 60M (HK$6.90) to Tuen Mun town centre; No 59M (HK$7.50) to Tuen Mun ferry pier; No 68M to Yuen Long and No E33 to Tung Chung and airport; MTR station for No A31 to airport; No E31 to Tung Chung and Nos 234A and 234B to Sham Tseng (ferry to Ma Wan); Castle Peak Rd (Map p416) for No 53 (HK$8.80) to Tuen Mun; Sha Tsui Rd (Map p416) for No 930 to Admiralty and Central; Tai Ho Rd (Map p416) for bus No 43X to Sam Tung Uk Rd; Tai Ho Rd North for No 51 (HK$7.60) to Tai Mo Shan and MacLehose Trail

Green Minibus Shiu Wo St (Map p416) for No 85 to Chuk Lam Sim Monastery; No 81 to Yuen Yuen Institute and Western Monastery; Chuen Lung Rd for No 80 to Tai Mo Shan Country Park Visitor Centre and No 82 to Pineapple Dam

SAM TUNG UK MUSEUM Map p416

☎ 2411 2001; 2 Kwu Uk Lane; admission free;
🕑 9am-5pm Wed-Mon, closed Tue & some public holidays

This imaginative and well-tended museum is housed in a restored 18th-century Hakka walled village, whose former residents, the Chan clan, were only resettled in 1980. Within the complex are a dozen three-beamed houses containing traditional Hakka furnishings, kitchenware, wedding items and agricultural implements, most of which came from two 17th-century Hakka villages in Bao'an county in Guangdong province. There are also special exhibits on such topics as rice farming in the New Territories. Behind the restored assembly and ancestral halls is the old village school, with interactive displays and videos on such topics as Hakka women, traditional crafts and food.

At the Tsuen Wan MTR station, take exit B3 and walk five minutes southeast along Sai Lau Kok Rd to Kwu Uk Lane and the museum.

CHUK LAM SIM MONASTERY Map p416

☎ 2490 3392; Fu Yung Shan Rd; ☼ 8am-5pm

Chuk Lam Sim Yuen (Bamboo Forest Monastery) is one of the most impressive temple complexes in Hong Kong. The temple was completed in 1932 when an aged monk heard Tou Tei, the earth god, tell him to build it. Ascend the flight of steps to the first temple, walk to the back and enter the second. This second temple contains three of the largest golden Buddhas in the territory (though mere shadows of the big one on Lantau Island). Flanking the trio on either side is an equally impressive line-up of 12 Bodhisattvas, or deified Buddhists. The third temple contains another large image of Lord Gautama.

Chuk Lam Sim Monastery is northeast of Tsuen Wan MTR station. To reach it, take minibus No 85 (HK$3.50) from Shiu Wo St, which is two blocks due south of the MTR station (exit B1).

YUEN YUEN INSTITUTE Map p416

☎ 2492 2220; Lo Wai Rd; ☼ 8.30am-5pm

The Yuen Yuen Institute, a colourful temple complex for worshipping Taoist, Confucian and Buddhist deities in the hills northeast of Tsuen Wan, is very much on the tourist trail but well worth a visit nonetheless. The main building is a (vague) replica of the Temple of Heaven in Beijing. On the upper ground floor are three Taoist immortals seated in a quiet hall; walk down to the lower level to watch as crowds of the faithful pray and burn offerings to the 60 incarnations of Taoist saints lining the walls.

WESTERN MONASTERY Map p416

☎ 2411 5111; Lo Wai Rd; ☼ 8.30am-5.30pm

A short distance down from the Yuen Yuen Institute, the Buddhist Western Monastery feels positively comatose compared with what's going on up the hill, but it has its charms nonetheless. The focal point of the monastery is a tall pagoda, on the 1st floor of which are five Buddhas sitting on a golden lotus. Depending on what time of day you visit, you may hear monks chanting mantras from down on the ground level.

To reach both the Yuen Yuen Institute and the Western Monastery, take minibus No 81 (HK$3.60) from Shiu Wo St, two blocks due south of Tsuen Wan MTR station (exit B1). Bus No 43X (HK$6) from along Tai Ho Rd, a bit further south of the MTR station (exit D), will drop you off on Sam Tung Uk Rd. The monastery is a short distance to the northwest and the institute is a bit further up the hill.

TAI MO SHAN

Sleeping p286

Hong Kong's tallest mountain is not Victoria Peak but Tai Mo Shan (Map pp396–7), the 'big misty mountain' that, at 957m, is nearly twice as high as that relative molehill (552m) on Hong Kong Island. Climbing Tai Mo Shan is not difficult, and the views from the top are impressive when the weather is clear. There are numerous hiking trails on and around it, but you'll need to bring your own food and water, as none is available on the mountain itself. The Countryside Series *Central New Territories* map is the one you want for this area (see p364). If you don't want to go it alone, contact any of the outfits listed in the Walking Tours chapter (see Guided Hikes p166). The **Tai Mo Shan Country Park Visitor Centre** (☎ 2498 9326; ☼ 9.30am-4.30pm Wed-Mon) is at the junction of Route Twisk (the name is derived from 'Tsuen Wan into Shek Kong') and Tai Mo Shan Rd (on the MacLehose Trail).

To reach Tai Mo Shan from the Tsuen Wan MTR station, take exit A and catch bus No 51 (HK$7.60) on Tai Ho Rd North, alighting at the junction of Route Twisk and Tai Mo Shan Rd in Tsuen Kam Au. Follow Tai Mo Rd, which forms part of stage No 9 of the MacLehose Trail, east to the summit. On the right-hand side, about 45 minutes from the bus stop, a fork in the road leads south along a concrete path to the **Sze Lok Yuen Hostel** (p286). Green minibus No 80 from Chuen Lung St in Tsuen Wan goes to the visitor centre.

For information on accessing stages of the MacLehose Trail and the Wilson Trail near Tai Mo Shan, see Hikes (p162).

Transport

Bus No 51 to Tsuen Wan, No 64K to Tai Po Market

Green Minibus No 80 to Tsuen Wan; No 25K to Tai Po Market

NG TUNG CHAI WATERFALL AND KADOORIE FARM & BOTANIC GARDEN

Map pp396–7

☎ 2488 1317; www.kfbg.org.hk; Lam Kam Rd; admission free; ☼ 9.30am-5pm

The area around the Ng Tung Chai Waterfall is scenic and worth a detour. It is near the village of Ng Tung Chai, which is a few kilometres to the north of Tai Mo Shan and just south of Lam Kam Rd. There is actually a series of falls and streams here, reached by taking the path leading to Ng Tung Chai and the Lam Kam Rd from the radio station on the summit of Tai Mo Shan.

Southwest of Ng Tung Chai is the Kadoorie Farm & Botanic Garden, a conservation and teaching centre where farmers receive practical training in crop and livestock management. The gardens are especially lovely, with many indigenous birds, animals, insects and plants in residence.

You can reach Kadoorie Farm on bus No 51 by alighting where Route Twisk meets Lam Kam Rd and walking east for a couple of kilometres to the entrance, but it's easier to take bus No 64K (HK$6.90) from Tai Po Market KCR station and get off on Lam Kam Rd near the sign for Ng Tung Chai village.

If you walk from Tai Mo Shan to the village of Ng Tung Chai, you can catch the minibus No 25K (HK$4.50) to Tai Po Market KCR station. Alternatively, you can carry on up to Lam Kam Rd and catch bus No 64K to the same destination.

TUEN MUN

Eating p206

The largest and most important New Town in the western New Territories (population 510,000), Tuen Mun (Map pp396–7) has now been linked with other centres in Kowloon and the New Territories by the KCR West Rail. Tuen Mun's seemingly endless rows of high-rise housing estates can be off-putting at first, but they do hide a few interesting spots. Tuen Mun Town Hall (☎ 2450 4202; 3 Tuen Hi Rd) is one of the most active cultural venues in the New Territories. If you're travelling to Tuen Mun from Tsuen Wan or points in Kowloon or Hong Kong Island by bus, sit on the upper deck on the left side for spectacular views of the Tsing Ma Bridge linking Kowloon with Lantau Island.

Orientation

As always in New Towns, the centre of Tuen Mun is dominated by commercial developments and shopping centres, including Trend Plaza and Tuen Mun Town Plaza, which has a central courtyard with a pleasant fountain. Most buses stop at the station just west of the town hall, where you'll also find the Town Centre station of the LRT. Ferries to the airport, Tung Chung and Tai O on Lantau depart from the pier to the southwest of the town centre, which is also served by the LRT. For details, see below.

CHING SHAN MONASTERY
Map pp396–7

Tsing Shan Tsuen; ⏱ 9am-5pm

Ching Shan Monastery, which is called Castle Peak Monastery in English, is a quiet Buddhist retreat west of Tuen Mun town centre. It is one of the oldest monasteries in the territory and takes its name from Castle Peak (583m) a short distance to the south, which was proclaimed a sacred mountain by imperial edict in AD 969. Inside the main temples are three Buddhas seated on lotus blossoms covered in golden medallions.

Ching Shan is easy to reach, but it's a tough, uphill climb, especially in the warmer months. From the Town Centre LRT station in Tuen Mun, take line No 506 (or replacement bus No 506 if the line is still under construction) and alight at Tsing Shan Tsuen station. Walk north along Tsing Wun Rd for 200m, turning left on Hing Choi St just after St Peter's Church, where

Transport

KCR Tuen Mun station (Map pp396–7)

LRT Town Centre to Ferry Pier Terminus line Nos 507 and 614; to Yuen Long (Map pp396–7) line No 614

Bus Bus station for No 60M (HK$6.90) to Tsuen Wan and No 60X (HK$10.70) to Yau Ma Tei; Castle Peak Rd for No 53 (HK$8.80) to Tsuen Wan; Tuen Mun Rd for No 260X to Tsim Sha Tsui, 63X (HK$13) to Nathan Rd in Tsim Sha Tsui and No 960 (HK$18.20) to Wan Chai, Admiralty and Central; Tuen Mun ferry pier for No 59M (HK$7.50) to Tsuen Wan

Ferry Tuen Mun ferry pier for boats to airport, Tung Chung and Tai O on Lantau

you'll see a signpost for the monastery. This leads into Wan Shan Rd, which you should follow uphill for about 2km. On the way up you'll

123

be rewarded with a pavilion, shady groves of conifers and views across the Pearl River estuary as far as Shekou in the Shenzhen SEZ. Alternatively, you can catch a taxi from Tuen Mun (about HK$25), which will drop you off at the steps leading up to the monastery.

CHING CHUNG TEMPLE Map pp396–7
☎ 2462 1507; Tsing Chung Koon Rd; ☼ 6am-6pm
Ching Chung Koon (Green Pine Temple) is a huge Taoist complex northwest of Tuen Mun town centre. The main temple, **Sun Young Hall,** which is on the left at the far end of the complex past rows of bonsai trees, bamboo and ossuaries, is dedicated to Lu Sun Young, one of the eight immortals of Taoism who lived in the 8th century. Flanking a statue of him are two of his disciples and outside the entrance to the main temple are pavilions containing a bell and a drum to call the faithful to pray or to rest.

Ching Chung Temple, which can get very busy during festivals, is directly opposite the Ching Chung LRT station. To reach it from the Town Centre station in Tuen Mun, catch line No 507 and change for line No 615 at Tin King station. From the Ching Shan Monastery or Yuen Long, take line No 615.

MIU FAT MONASTERY Map pp396–7
☎ 2461 8567; 18 Castle Peak Rd; ☼ 9am-5pm
Miu Fat Monastery in Lam Tei, due north of Tuen Mun town centre, is one of the most well-kept and attractive Buddhist complexes in the territory. Guarding the entrance to the main temple are two stone lions and two stone elephants, and there are attractive gardens outside to the south. This is an active monastery that preserves more of a traditional character than many smaller temples; you'll see Buddhist nuns in droves wearing brown robes.

On the ground floor there's a golden likeness of Buddha in a glass case; on the 2nd floor are three larger statues of Lord Gautama. The 1st floor is a vegetarian restaurant serving set meals and open to all.

Miu Fat Monastery is easily reached by taking LRT line No 720 (from Town Centre) or No 610 (from Tsing Shan Tsuen or Yuen Long) to Lam Tei station. The complex is on the opposite side of Castle Peak Rd; cross over the walkway and walk north 150m. Bus No 63X (HK$13) from Nathan Rd in Tsim Sha Tsui also stops in front of the monastery.

YUEN LONG
Eating p207
There's nothing special at **Yuen Long** (Map pp396–7), which currently counts some 160,000 inhabitants, but it's the last stop on the LRT line, an important transport hub and something of a gateway to the **Mai Po Marsh** (see p126). To the west of Yuen Long is the Ping Shan Heritage Trail, one of the best spots to spend a tranquil hour or two in the western New Territories, and to the northwest the oyster-gathering and fishing village of Lau Fau Shan, a popular place for seafood by the sea (though we'd steer clear of those oysters; see the boxed text opposite).

Orientation
Yuen Long, shaped like a semicircle by a *nullah* (drainage channel), is divided neatly into two by Castle Peak Rd. The LRT runs down the centre of this road, making four stops before terminating to the northwest on the opposite side of the channel. Most important buses depart from and arrive at the station in On Tat Square off Castle Peak Rd and close to the Fung Nin Rd LRT stop. Reach it by walking north along Kik Yeung Rd.

Transport
KCR Yuen Long station (Map pp396–7)

LRT Shui Pin Wai, Fung Nin Rd, Hong Lok Rd, Tai Tong Rd and Yuen Long terminus stations

Bus Bus station for No 76K to Mai Po Marsh, Fanling and Sheung Shui and No 68M to Tsuen Wan; Castle Peak Rd for No 64K (HK$6.90) to Kam Tin and Tai Po Market KCR station; No 77K (HK$6.90) to Kam Tin, Sheung Shui and Fanling, No 54 (HK$4.70) to Kam Tin and Shek Kong, No 655 to Lau Fau Shan

Green Minibus Fung Cheung Rd for No 601 to Kam Tin

Junk, New Territories

PING SHAN HERITAGE TRAIL

The 1km Ping Shan Heritage Trail, just five LRT stops to the west of the terminus in Yuen Long, takes in half a dozen 'ancient' (by Hong Kong standards) Chinese buildings – temples, study and ancestral halls, a walled village and the territory's only surviving pagoda. Alight at Ping Shan LRT station and walk north to Ping Ha (Peaceful Building) St.

The trail begins at the 18th-century **Hung Shing Temple** and the adjacent **Kun Ting Study Hall**, where the Tangs, the first of the 'Five Clans' to settle in Hong Kong, swotted for the imperial civil service exams. Next comes the magnificent **Tang Ancestral Hall**, which dates back 700 years and has been restored, and the 16th-century **Yu Kiu Ancestral Hall**. Both are of similar design, with three halls and two internal courtyards, and retain many original features and decorative items. The trail continues past **Sheung Cheung Wai**, an inhabited walled village of narrow alleyways and miniscule houses, and ends at the **Tsui Sing Lau**, a three-storey hexagonal pagoda built in the 15th century. KCR West Rail station Tin Tsui Wai is opposite the pagoda.

Bivalves, Bye Bye

Oyster farming has been practised along the intertidal mud flats of Deep Bay in the northwest New Territories for almost two centuries. Not long ago, long plastic bags full of the briny bivalves were an irresistible treat for many an amah or housewife shopping for the family meal. But the farms at **Lau Fau Shan**, the place where salt and fresh water meet to create the perfect habitat for oysters, are now on the verge of clamming up altogether.

Lau Fau Shan oysters used to be farmed by the so-called bottom-culture method, with spat (young or immature oysters) collected by laying old shells, rocks or concrete tiles as clutch on the mud flats in May or June. In recent years, repeated failures in spat collection brought on by pollution in Deep Water Bay have had farmers turning to the fattening of young oysters from the mainland – a process that takes between six and 12 months. As a result some 80% of all oysters consumed in Hong Kong now come from over the border in Shenzhen, where production costs are lower. Annual production at Lau Fau Shan now barely reaches 60 tonnes, worth a mere HK$3 million. Overall, mariculture in Hong Kong is worth HK$136 million.

This is not the first time Lau Fau Shan has faced a very difficult future. In the 1970s oysters were regularly poached by thieves from across the border and in 1979 the oyster farms reported a 95% loss from disease. A further blow to the industry occurred when the locally grown shellfish were associated with hepatitis and high levels of cadmium. No doubt the amazing speed of growth in Shenzhen next door, with a resulting increase in levels of pollution, will also contribute to the demise of this once flourishing community of oyster farmers.

MAI PO MARSH

If you're a bird fancier, Mai Po Marsh in the northwestern New Territories is one of the best places in Hong Kong to meet up with thousands of your feathered friends (see the boxed text below).

Orientation

Mai Po Marsh comprises some 1500 hectares of wetlands. It abuts Deep Bay, south of the border with the mainland. The part open to visitors, the Mai Po Nature Reserve, is in the centre.

Transport

Bus No 76K to Yuen Long (On Tat Square station) and Fanling and Sheung Shui KCR stations

MAI PO NATURE RESERVE Map pp396–7

☎ 2526 4473; San Tin, Yuen Long; admission HK$100 (plus HK$100 deposit); ☷ 9am-6pm

The nature reserve includes the **Mai Po Visitor Centre** (☎ 2471 8272; ☷ 9am-1pm & 2-5pm Thu-Tue) at the northeastern end, where you must register; the **Mai Po Education Centre** (☎ 2471 6306) to the south, with displays on the history and ecology of the marsh and Deep Bay; **floating boardwalks** through the mangroves and mud flats; and a dozen **hides** (towers or huts from where you can watch birds up close without being observed). Disconcertingly, the cityscape of Shenzhen looms to the north.

Visitors are advised to bring binoculars (they may be available for rent at the visitor centre for HK$20) and cameras, and to wear comfortable walking shoes or boots but not bright clothing. It is best to visit at high tide, when birds in their tens of thousands – mostly ducks, gulls, cormorants and kingfishers, but many rare species as well – flock to the area. Ring the weather hotline on ☎ 187 8066 or the **Hong Kong Observatory** (☎ 2926 8200) for tidal times.

Foreign visitors (but not Hong Kong residents) can visit the nature reserve unaccompanied but numbers are limited so call in advance to book a time. Pay the HK$100 entrance fee and HK$100 deposit at the visitor centre; the latter (presumably to ensure that you get out alive) will be returned when you leave the reserve.

The **World Wide Fund for Nature Hong Kong** (WWFHK; ☎ 2526 4473, 2471 6306; www.wwf.org.hk; 1 Tramway Path), adjacent to the

A Wetland for Hong Kong

Bordering Deep Bay in the northwest New Territories, Mai Po Marsh is a protected network of mud flats, fish and shrimp ponds, reed beds and dwarf mangroves, offering a rich habitat of up to 300 species of migratory and resident birds. The area attracts birds in every season but especially winter, when some 55,000 migratory waterfowl, including endangered species such as the Dalmatian pelican, black-faced spoonbill and spotted and imperial eagles, pass through the marshes. In the centre is the 270-hectare Mai Po Nature Reserve, jointly managed by the World Wide Fund for Nature Hong Kong and the government's Agriculture, Fisheries & Conservation Department.

Despite its protected status, Mai Po's future is uncertain. The water quality in Deep Bay is among the worst in the Hong Kong coastal area. The Environmental Protection Department (EPD) has found that levels of dissolved oxygen (DO) in the water have been declining since 1988; in the summer of 1996 DO levels fell to zero on one occasion. As a result, the numbers of crabs and mudskippers, on which the birds feed in winter, have declined sharply. The pollution used to come from pig manure released into Deep Bay, but a government ordinance now requires that pig slurry be treated before being flushed away. This ordinance appears to be having an effect, but a potentially larger hazard has taken its place.

Deep Bay neighbours the city of Shenzhen in mainland China, which is pumping out a rapidly increasing amount of sewage, about half of which is untreated. The only real solution to this environmental threat is for Shenzhen to build more sewage-treatment facilities but, as the population of the city expands faster than its infrastructure, this will take time.

Meanwhile, increasingly wet summers in Hong Kong have flushed out and diluted many of the pollutants. The number of crabs and mudskippers has increased, but this could just reflect a temporary improvement in the region's ecology. If the lower links of the food chain are seriously imperilled, the 300 species of birds that depend on Mai Po as a stopping ground during migration could disappear, taking with them endangered mammals such as the leopard cat and otter.

entrance of the Peak Tram in Central, can arrange guided visits to the marsh; ring between 9am and 5pm on weekdays to book. Three-hour tours (HK$70) leave the visitor centre at 9am, 9.30am, 10am, 2pm 2.30pm and 3pm on Saturday, Sunday and public holidays, but are only conducted in English when there are a minimum of 10 visitors.

Bus No 76K, which runs between Yuen Long and the Fanling and Sheung Shui KCR stations, will drop you off at Mai Po Lo Wai, a village along the main road just east of the marsh.

The WWFHK car park is about a 20-minute walk from there. Alternatively, a taxi from Sheung Shui will cost HK$65.

KAM TIN

The area around **Kam Tin** (Brocade Field; Map pp396–7) is where the Tangs, the first of Hong Kong's mighty Five Clans, began settling in the 12th century AD and where they eventually built their walled villages.

Walled villages, which usually had moats, are a reminder that Hong Kong's early settlers were constantly menaced by marauding pirates, bandits and imperial soldiers. They remain one of the most popular destinations for visitors to the New Territories.

Orientation

Kam Tin contains two fortified villages: Kat Hing Wai and Shui Tau. Most tourists go to Kat Hing Wai, as it is just off the main thoroughfare, Kam Tin Rd, and easily accessible. Shui Tau is larger and less touristy, but don't expect to find remnants of ancient China. For details on **Ping Kong**, a seldom-visited walled village to the northeast, see **Fanling & Sheung Shui** (p128).

Transport

Bus Kam Tin Rd for No 64K (HK$6.90) to Yuen Long and Tai Po Market KCR station, No 77K (HK$6.90) to Yuen Long, Sheung Shui and Fanling, No 54 (HK$4.70) to Yuen Long and Shek Kong, No 51 (HK$7.60) to Tsuen Wan (via Route Twisk)

Green Minibus Shui Tau No 601 to Yuen Long

KAT HING WAI Map pp396–7

This tiny village is 500 years old and was walled in some time during the early Ming dynasty (1368–1644). It contains just one main street, off which a host of dark and narrow alleyways lead. There are quite a few new buildings and retiled older ones in the village. A small **temple** stands at the end of the street.

Visitors are asked to make a donation of HK$1 when they enter the village. Put the money in the coin slot by the entrance. You can take photographs of the old Hakka women in their traditional black trousers, tunics and distinctive bamboo hats with black cloth fringes, but they'll expect you to pay (about HK$10).

Kat Hing is just south of Kam Tin Rd. If travelling from Yuen Long, get off at the first bus stop, cross the road and walk east for 10 minutes.

SHUI TAU Map pp396–7

This 17th-century village, 15 minutes' walk north of Kam Tin Rd and signposted, is famous for its prow-shaped roofs decorated with dragons and fish. Tiny traditional houses huddle inside Shui Tau's walls.

The **Tang Kwok U** and, just north of it, the **Tang Ching Lok Ancestral Hall** in the middle of the village, were built in the early 19th century for ancestor worship. The ancestors' names are listed on the altar in the inner hall and on the long boards down the side. The sculpted fish, on the roof of the entrance hall, symbolise luck; in Cantonese, the word for 'fish' (yue) sounds similar to the word for 'plenty' or 'surplus'. Between these two buildings is the small **Hung Shing Temple**. South of them is Shui Tau's most impressive sight, **Yi Tai Study Hall** (☺ 9am-1pm & 2-5pm Wed, Sat & Sun), built in the first half of the 19th century and named after the gods of literature and martial arts. The large **Tin Hau temple** on the outskirts of the village to the north was built in 1722 and contains an enormous iron bell weighing 106kg.

There's been a lot of building in and around Shui Tau in recent years – massive Tsing Long Hwy and the new KCR West extension straddle it to the west – and the old sits rather uncomfortably with the new. But the further north you walk beyond the village, the calmer and more tranquil it gets.

To reach Shui Tau from Kam Tin Rd, walk north and, past Kam Tai Rd, over the *nullah* to Chi Ho Rd. Cross the small metal bridge spanning the stream, turn right and then left to enter the village from the east. There are signposts on Kam Tin Rd and Chi Ho Rd.

FANLING & SHEUNG SHUI

What were two lazy country villages just a few short years ago, Fanling and Sheung Shui now form one of the largest New Town conurbations in the New Territories, with some 240,000 inhabitants. Get a feel for what they were once like by walking around the Luen Wo Hu district at the northern end of Fanling. Major sights are thin on the ground here, but there's an important Taoist temple within easy walking distance and, a short bus ride away, a seldom-visited walled village and another heritage trail. The posh 18-hole **Fanling Golf Course** (☎ 2670 1211; Fan Kam Rd) might be a draw for some.

Orientation

Fanling and Sheung Shui are in the north-central New Territories, much closer to the mainland (5km) than they are to Tsim Sha Tsui (20km). They are linked by San Wan Rd, along which the bulk of buses and green minibuses serving the two New Towns travel. The KCR stops in both Fanling and Sheung Shui.

Districts & Islands – New Territories

Transport

KCR Fanling & Sheung Shui stations (Map pp396–7)

Bus KCR stations and Pak Wo Rd in Fanling and Choi Yun Rd in Sheung Shui for No 76K to Yuen Long and Mai Po Marsh; KCR stations and Jockey Club Rd in Fanling and Po Shek Wu Rd in Sheung Shui for No 77K (HK$6.90) to Ping Kong, Kam Tin and Yuen Long

Green Minibus Fanling KCR for No 54K to Tang Chung Ling Ancestral Hall, San Wan Rd for No 58K to Ping Kong

---

FUNG YING SIN TEMPLE Map pp396–7

☎ 2669 9186; 66 Pak Wo Rd; ☿ 9am-5pm

The main attraction in Fanling is this huge Taoist temple complex opposite the KCR station and connected by an overhead walkway. It has wonderful exterior murals of Taoist immortals and the Chinese zodiac, an orchard terrace, herbal clinic and a **vegetarian restaurant** (Bldg A7; ☿ 11am-4.30pm). Most important are the 10 ancestral halls behind the main temple, where the ashes of the departed are deposited in what might be described as miniature tombs, complete with photographs.

MARKETS Map pp396–7

Wo Mun & Luen On Sts, Fanling & Chi Cheong Rds, Sheung Shui; ☿ 6am-8pm

These two lively markets are frequented by Hakka people and are definitely worth a look, particularly early (ie before 10am) in the day.

Sheung Shui market is 250m north of the KCR station. To reach the Fanling market in the old district of Luen Wo Hui, walk north along Sha Tau Kok Rd for about 1.5km or catch bus No 77K from the Fanling KCR station. This bus also carries on to the market in Sheung Shui.

TANG CHUNG LING ANCESTRAL HALL Map pp396–7

Tsz Tong Tsuen, Lung Yuk Tau; ☿ 9am-1pm & 2-5pm Wed-Mon

Northeast of Fanling in the village of Tsz Tong Tsuen, this ancestral hall, one of the largest in the New Territories, was built in 1525 in honour of the founder of the Tang clan. It lies on the **Lung Yuk Tau Heritage Trail**, which takes in six walled villages and other historical sites within a couple of kilometres. Highlights include the entrance tower of **Mat Wat Wai**, built in the mid-18th century, and the entrance tower and enclosing walls of **Lo Wai**. You can reach the ancestral hall and the trail via green minibus No 54K from Fanling KCR station or begin the walk on foot from the end of Lok Tung St, which is about a kilometre northeast of the KCR station.

PING KONG Map pp396–7

This sleepy walled village in the hills south of Sheung Shui is seldom visited by outsiders. Like other walled villages still inhabited, it is a mix of old and new, but it's a friendly place, with a lovely little **Tin Hau temple** in the centre. You can also go exploring around the farming area behind the village compound.

To get to Ping Kong from Sheung Shui, catch green minibus No 58K (HK$3.50) from the huge minibus station south of the Landmark North shopping centre on San Wan Rd. The centre is a short distance northwest of Sheung Shui KCR station. Alternatively, bus No 77K (HK$6.90) between Yuen Long and the Sheung Shui and Fanling KCR stations travels along Fan Kam Rd. Alight at the North District Hospital stop and walk southeast along Ping Kong Rd to the village.

A taxi from the Sheung Shui KCR station to Ping Kong will cost HK$20.

TAI PO
Eating p207

Another large residential and industrial New Town that has grown astronomically in just over a generation, the small market town of **Tai Po** (Map p416) counted a total of 25,000 people in 1974; today the population tops 290,000 and Tai Po is home to many of Hong Kong's high-tech industries. It makes an excellent springboard for excursions into Plover Cove Country Park and Pat Sin Leng Country Park. Four Lanes Square, where four pedestrian streets converge in the centre of town, is a popular shopping area. The **Old Tai Po District Office** (Wan Tau Kok Lane) was built in 1907 and is one of the earliest examples of Western architecture in the New Territories.

Bicycles can be rented in season from several stalls around Tai Po Market KCR station, but try to arrive early – they often run out of bikes during the busiest times. There are a number of bicycle shops lining Kwong Fuk Rd northwest of Tai Po Market KCR station.

One route not to miss is the ride to **Plover Cove Reservoir** on the northeast side of Tolo Harbour, or to the Chinese University of Hong Kong in Ma Liu Shui on the southwest side of the harbour. Allow at least half a day for either trip. There is an inland route to the university, but the coastal route linking the university with Tai Mei Tuk has the best views. Another option is to follow Ting Kok Rd east to San Mun Tsai.

Orientation

Tai Po lies north and south of the Lam Tsuen River, at the western point of Tolo Harbour. It boasts two KCR stations – Tai Wo to the northwest and Tai Po Market to the southeast. Buses and green minibuses arrive and depart at the station on On Chee Rd, north of the Lam Tsuen River, on Heung Sze Wui St, close to the market and railway museum, and from Tai Po Market KCR station.

Transport

KCR Tai Wo and Tai Po Market KCR stations (Map p416)

Bus On Chee Rd bus and Tai Po Market KCR stations (Map p416) for No 74K (HK$3.10) to San Mun Tsai; Tai Po Market KCR for No 64K (Hk$6.90) to Lam Kam Rd, Lam Tsuen, Tai Mo Shan, Kam Tin and Yuen Long; On Chee Rd station for No 271 (HK$9.10) to Tsim Sha Tsui, No 73X (HK$6.70) to Tsuen Wan, No 74X (HK$8.40) to Kwun Tong MTR station; No 71K (HK$3) between Tai Wo and Tai Po Market KCR stations.

Green Minibus Tai Po Market KCR station and Heung Sze Wui St (Map p416) for No 20K (HK$4.70) to San Mun Tsai; Tsing Yuen St for No 25K to Ng Tung Chai (Tai Mo Shan); On Cheung Rd for overnight No 501S (HK$22.50) to Sheung Shui

HONG KONG RAILWAY MUSEUM
Map p416

☎ 2653 3455; 13 Shung Tak St; admission free;
🕑 9am-5pm Wed-Mon, closed some public holidays

The museum is housed in the former Tai Po Market train station, built in 1913 in traditional Chinese style, and spills into the outside garden. Exhibits, including a narrow-gauge steam locomotive dating back to 1911, detail the history of the development of rail transport in the territory. There is also much attention paid to the opening of the Kowloon-Canton Railway and its original terminus in Tsim Sha Tsui.

You can get to the museum most easily by alighting at Tai Wo KCR station, walking south through the Tai Wo Shopping Centre and housing estate and crossing the Lam Tsuen River via the small Tai Wo Bridge with the Chinese roof leading from Po Nga Rd. The museum is a short distance southeast.

TAI PO MARKET Map p416
Fu Shin St; 🕑 6am-8pm

Not to be confused with the KCR station of the same name, this street-long outdoor wet market is a stone's throw from the Hong Kong Railway Museum and is one of the busiest and most interesting markets in the New Territories.

Towards the northern end of the same street, the **Man Mo Temple** (🕐 8am-6pm) is a major centre of worship for the Tai Po area. It was founded in the late 19th century and, like the Man Mo Temple found in **Sheung Wan** (see p84), it is dedicated to the gods of literature and war.

LAM TSUEN WISHING TREE
Map pp396–7
Lam Kam Rd, Lam Tsuen

If you've been crossing your fingers and avoiding the cracks but still haven't got lucky, pay a visit to the wishing tree, a short bus ride away to the southwest, in the village of **Fong Ma Po** on the **Lam Tsuen River**. This large banyan is laden with wishes written on coloured streamers of paper tied to oranges. You write your wish on the paper and then throw it as high as you can up into the tree. If your fruit lodges in the branches, you're in

Prayer flags to the Sea Goddess, Lam Tsuen Wishing Tree (p130).

luck – and the higher it goes, the more chance there is of your wish coming true. Nearby is a small **Tin Hau temple**, replete with fortune-tellers to tell you what it all means.

To reach the **Lam Tsuen Wishing Tree**, take bus No 64K from the Tai Po Market KCR station and alight at Fong Ma Po.

SAN MUN TSAI

A small fishing village on a shoe-shaped peninsula in Tolo Harbour, **San Mun Tsai** (Place of Three Gates; Map pp396–7) is charming – a floating mix of homes belonging to local fishing families – and gets few visitors. The very tip of the peninsula is the Ma Shi Chau Protected Area.

Orientation
San Mun Tsai is due east of Tai Po, just off Ting Kok Rd en route to Tai Mei Tuk.

PLOVER COVE

The area around Plover Cove Reservoir is good hiking and cycling country and worth a full day. It may be worthwhile getting a copy of Universal Publications' *Tseung Kwan O, Sai Kung, Clearwater Bay* or the Countryside Series map *North-East New Territories* (see p364).

Bicycles can be rented at Tai Mei Tuk, where you'll also find a row of popular restaurants (see Tai Po & Surrounds p207) along Ting Kok Rd; a bicycle track along the coast runs from Tai Mei Tuk to Chinese University at Ma Liu Shui. The **Plover Cove Country Park Visitor Centre** (☎ 2665 3413; 🕐 9.30am-4.30pm Wed-Mon) is a short distance further east along the same road. Rowboats are available for hire on the picture-postcard bay south of the main parking lot on Tai Mei Tuk Rd, where buses and minibuses terminate.

For details on the 4km-long **Pat Sin Leng Nature Trail** to Bride's Pool (see Pat Sing Leng Nature Trail p160). For access to **Pat Sin Leng Country Park**, where you can join stage No 9 of the **Wilson Trail** see p164.

Orientation
The village of Tai Mei Tuk, the springboard for most of the activities in the Plover Cove area, is about 6km northeast of Tai Po Market KCR station and easily accessible by bus and green minibus.

Transport

Bus No 74K (HK$3.10) to On Chee Rd bus station and Tai Po Market KCR station (Map p416) in Tai Po

Green Minibus No 20K (HK$4.70) to Tai Po Market KCR station and Heung Sze Wui St (Map p416) in Tai Po

PLOVER COVER RESERVOIR

Map pp396–7

Plover Cove Reservoir was completed in 1968 and holds 230 million cubic metres of water; before then Hong Kong suffered from critical water shortages and rationing was not uncommon. Even after the reservoir opened, water sometimes had to be rationed. Taps were turned on for only eight hours a day through the dry winter of 1980/81. The reservoir was built in a very unusual way. Rather than build a dam across a river, of which Hong Kong has very few, a barrier was erected across the mouth of a great bay. The sea water was siphoned out and fresh water – mostly piped in from the mainland – was pumped in.

TAI PO KAU

South of Tai Po is the small settlement of Tai Po Kau, which most visitors wouldn't give a second thought to were it not for the wonderful nature reserve here.

Orientation

Tai Po Kau Nature Reserve lies south of Tai Po, less than a kilometre inland from Tolo Harbour. The main entrance and the information centre are at the village of Tsung Tsai Yuen in the northernmost part of the reserve along Tai Po Rd.

Transport

Bus From Po Heung St in Tai Po (Map p416) for No 70 to Yau Ma Tei, No 72 to Lai Chi Kok MTR station on Tsuen Wan Line and Olympic MTR station in Mong Kok on Tung Chung line, No 72A to Tai Wai KCR station and No 74A (HK$6.70) to Sha Tin

TAI PO KAU NATURE RESERVE

Map pp396–7 Tai Po Rd

The Tai Po Kau Nature Reserve is a thickly forested 440-hectare 'special area' and is Hong Kong's most extensive woodlands. It is home to many species of butterflies, amphibians, birds, dragonflies and trees, and is a superb place in which to enjoy a quiet walk. The reserve is crisscrossed with tracks ranging in length from 3km (red trail) to 10km (yellow trail), and a short nature trail of less than 1km. If possible, avoid the reserve on Sunday and public holidays, when the crowds descend upon the place en masse.

The reserve emphasises conservation and education rather than recreation. Opposite the reserve entrance is the **Museum of Ethnology** (☎ 2657 6657; www.taipokau.org; 2 Hung Lam Dr; adult/child or senior HK$25/16; ☻ 10.30am-6.30pm Sat & Sun) and **Interactive Nature Centre**. In the same complex is the delightful **Little Egret restaurant** (p207).

Tai Po Kau Nature Reserve is well served by buses. Alternatively, a taxi from Tai Po Market KCR station will cost about HK$25.

UNIVERSITY

The **Chinese University of Hong Kong** (Map pp396–7; ☎ 2609 6000; www.cuhk.edu.hk), established in 1963, is in Ma Liu Shui and is served by University KCR station. It is situated on a beautiful campus and its art museum is well worth a visit.

Orientation

Ma Liu Shui and the Chinese University of Hong Kong are southeast of Tai Po and Tai Po Kau, overlooking Tolo Harbour. The University KCR station is southeast of the three campuses (Chung Chi Campus, New Asia Campus and United Campus). Ferries from Ma Liu Shui ferry pier, opposite the university on the eastern side of Tolo Hwy and about 500m northeast of University station, serve the Sai Kung Peninsula (p134) and Tap Mun Chau (p137) twice daily. A taxi from the station to the pier will cost HK$12.50.

Transport

KCR University station

Bus No 74K (HK$3.10) to On Chee Rd bus and Tai Po Market KCR stations (Map p416) in Tai Po

Green Minibus No 20K (HK$4.70) to Tai Po Market KCR station and Heung Sze Wui St (Map p416) in Tai Po

Ferry To Sai Kung Peninsula, Tap Mun Chau and Ping Chau

CHINESE UNIVERSITY OF HONG KONG ART MUSEUM Map pp396–7

☎ 2609 7416; Sir Run Run Shaw Hall, Central Ave; admission free; ☺ 10am-4.45pm Mon-Sat, 12.30-5.30pm Sun, closed public holidays

The Chinese University of Hong Kong Art Museum is divided into two sections. The **East Wing Galleries** house a permanent collection of Chinese paintings, calligraphy, ceramics and other decorative arts, including 2000-year-old bronze seals and a large collection of jade flower carvings. The **West Wing Galleries** stage five to six special exhibitions each year.

A shuttle bus from University station travels through the campus to the administration building at the top of the hill; for the museum, get off at the second stop. The bus runs every 20 to 30 minutes daily and is free except on Sunday (HK$5) from September to May. From June to August, it costs HK$1 on weekdays and HK$5 at the weekend.

SHA TIN

Eating p208; Sleeping p287

Sha Tin (Sandy Field; Map p417) is an enormous New Town (population 630,000) built mostly on reclaimed land that was once a mud flat and produced some of the best rice in imperial China. Sha Tin retains some traditional Chinese houses, giving parts of it a historical feel absent in most of the other New Towns. Hong Kong Chinese flock to Sha Tin on the weekends to place their bets at the nearby racecourse or to shop at Sha Tin's New Town Plaza, one of the biggest shopping centres in the New Territories. For visitors, the drawcards are the temples and one of the best museums in Hong Kong. You can rent bicycles from a kiosk in Sha Tin Park, south of New Town Plaza shopping centre for HK$10 per hour.

Orientation

Sha Tin lies in a narrow valley on both banks of a channel of the Shing Mun River. Fo Tan, where the racecourse is located, is to the north and northeast, and Tai Wai, where you'll find the Hong Kong Heritage Museum, is to the south. Though once separate villages, they are now extensions of the Sha Tin conurbation. Sha Tin KCR station is west (and connected to) New Town Plaza in central Sha Tin. Buses arrive at and depart from the KCR station, the bus station below New Town Plaza and the one at City One Plaza on Ngan Shing St on the opposite side of the channel.

Transport

KCR Sha Tin (Map p417), Tai Wai (Map p417), Fo Tan (Map p417) and Racecourse (Map pp396–7) stations

Bus City One Plaza Sha Tin bus station (Map p417) for No 182 (HK$15.30) to Admiralty and Des Voeux Rd Central; KCR bus station (Map p417) for No 170 (HK$15.30) to Causeway Bay and Aberdeen, No 263 (HK$13) to Tuen Mun; New Town Plaza station (Map p417) for No 80K (HK$3) to Tai Wai, No 48X (HK$6.60) to Tsuen Wan, No 72 (HK$6) to Tai Po, No 299 (HK$9) to Sai Kung

10,000 BUDDHAS MONASTERY
Map p417

☎ 2691 1067; admission free; ☺ 9am-5pm

If you're big on Buddhas, head for this monastery, which sits on the top of Po Fook Hill about 500m northwest of Sha Tin KCR station. Built in the 1950s, the complex actually contains more than 10,000 Buddhas – some 12,800 miniature statues line the walls of the main temple. Dozens of life-sized golden statues of Buddha's followers flank the steep steps leading to the monastery complex. There is also a nine-storey **pagoda**.

From the main temple area, walk up some more steps to find a smaller temple housing the embalmed body of the founding monk, who died in 1965. His body was encased in gold leaf and is now on display behind glass. Put a small donation in the box next to the display case to help pay for the temple's upkeep.

To reach the 10,000 Buddhas Monastery, take exit B at Sha Tin KCR station and walk down the ramp, passing a series of traditional village houses on the left. Take the left onto Pai Tau St, but do not mistake the modern **Po Fook Hill temple complex** with the tacky pagoda and escalator, at the end of Pai Tau St, for your destination. Instead, turn right onto Sheung Wo Che St, passing some government buildings on the left. At the end of the road, a series of signs in English will direct you to the left along a concrete path and through bamboo groves to the first of some 400 steps leading up to the monastery.

CHE KUNG TEMPLE Map p417

☎ 2691 1733; Che Kung Miu Rd; admission free; ☯ 7am-6pm

This large Taoist temple complex, built in 1993, is on the opposite bank of the Shing Mun River channel in Tai Wai. It's dedicated to Che Kung, a Song-dynasty general credited with ridding Sha Tin of the plague; you'll see an enormous and quite powerful statue of the good general in the main temple to the left as you enter the complex. The main courtyard, flanked by eight statues of Taoist immortals, is a hive of activity; fortune-tellers reveal the future to the credulous in the arcade near the entrance. The temple is especially busy on the third day of the Lunar New Year, which is Che Kung's birthday and when gamblers pay homage to the general.

To reach the temple, take the KCR to Tai Wai station and follow the exit marked 'Che Kung Temple' to the left off the escalator. This will lead you south down Mei Tin Rd to the roundabout, where you will turn east onto Che Kung Miu Rd. The temple is on the right side about a kilometre along this road.

Bus No 80K from Sha Tin KCR station stops near the temple along Che Kung Miu Rd, as does No 182 from Hong Kong Island. A taxi from Sha Tin will cost about HK$20.

HONG KONG HERITAGE MUSEUM

Map p417

☎ 2180 8188, 2180 8222; 1 Man Lam Rd; adult/senior or student HK$10/ 5, admission free Wed; ☯ 10am-6pm Mon & Wed-Sat, 10am-7pm Sun, closed Tue & some public holidays

Located southwest of Sha Tin town centre, this exceptional museum is housed in a three-storey, purpose-built structure that is reminiscent of an ancestral hall. It has both rich permanent collections and innovative temporary exhibits in a dozen different galleries.

The ground floor contains a book and gift shop, the wonderful **Children's Discovery Gallery**, with eight learning and play zones (including 'Life in a Village', 'Shrimp Harvesting', 'Mai Po Marsh') for kids aged four to 10, and an **Orientation Theatre** with a 12-minute introductory video in English on the hour and in Chinese three times an hour. There's also a lovely **teahouse** (☎ 2605 6151; ☯ 10am-6pm), with

set teas from HK$35 to HK$200 and snacks from HK$10.

Along with five temporary galleries, the 1st floor contains the best of the museum's permanent collections: the **New Territories Heritage Hall**, with mock-ups of traditional shops, a Hakka fishing village and history of the New Towns; the **Cantonese Opera Heritage Hall**, where you can watch old operas on video with English subtitles, 'virtually' make yourself up as a Cantonese opera character on computer or just enjoy the costumes and sets; and the **Chao Shao-an Gallery**, devoted to the work of the eponymous water-colourist (1905–98) and founder of the important Lingnan School of painting (see p39).

The 2nd floor contains another thematic gallery and the **TT Tsui Gallery of Chinese Art**, an Aladdin's cave of fine ceramics, pottery, bronze, jade and lacquerware, stone carvings, and furniture. You might also be interested in some of the gifts various Chinese provinces presented to China for the reunification, which are on display in the hallways.

To reach the Hong Kong Heritage Museum, take the KCR to Sha Tin station and walk south along Tai Po Rd. If coming from the Che Kung Temple, walk east along Che Kung Miu Rd, go under the subway and cross the footbridge over the channel. The museum is 200m to the east.

SHA TIN RACECOURSE Map p417

☎ 2966 8111; Penfold Park; admission HK$10 (public stands), HK$50 (members enclosures) on race days

Northeast of Sha Tin town centre is Hong Kong's second racecourse, which opened in 1978 and can accommodate up to 80,000 punters. In general, races are held on Saturday afternoon, and sometimes on Sunday and public holidays, from September to June; a list of race meetings is available from the HKTB.

Bets are easily placed at one of the numerous computerised betting terminals run by the **Hong Kong Jockey Club** (☎ 1817; www.hongkongjockeyclub.com). For more information, see Horse Racing p30. The HKTB has a couple of horse-racing tours available for the interested but uninitiated. For details see Happy Valley in the Hong Kong Island section of this chapter.

In the centre of the Sha Tin racetrack is eight-hectare **Penfold Park**, with three small ponds, open to the public every day except when race meetings are scheduled, on Monday and on the day after a public holiday. It can get packed out on weekends – an indication of just how desperate New Town residents are to find a bit of open space and greenery among the concrete housing estates.

The KCR Racecourse station, just west of the track and Penfold Park, opens on race days only. Otherwise, get off at Fo Tan station and walk north along Lok King St, and its extension Lok Shun Path, for about 1.5km.

AMAH ROCK Map pp396–7

This boulder southwest of Sha Tin may look like just a rock, but it's an oddly shaped one and, like many local landmarks in Hong Kong, it carries a legend. It seems that for many years a fisherman's wife would stand on this spot in the hills above **Lion Rock Country Park**, watching for her husband to return from the sea while carrying her baby on her back. One day he didn't come

back – she waited and waited. The gods apparently took pity on her and transported her to heaven on a lightning bolt, leaving her form in stone. The name of the rock in Cantonese is **Mong Fu Shek**, or 'Gazing out for Husband Stone'. It's a popular place of pilgrimage for girls and young lovers during the Maiden's Festival on the seventh day of the seventh moon (mid-August).

As you take the KCR south from Sha Tin to Kowloon, Amah Rock is visible to the east (ie on the left-hand side) up on the hillside after Tai Wai KCR station, but before the train enters the tunnel. Stage No 5 of the **Wilson Trail** (see p164) passes near Amah Rock. If you want to clamber up to Amah Rock from Sha Tin, take the KCR to Tai Wai station, walk south along Mei Tin Rd and its extension, Hung Mui Kuk Rd, for about a kilometre. A trail up to the rock starts on the other side of Lion Rock Tunnel Rd.

SAI KUNG PENINSULA

Eating p208; Sleeping p287

The Sai Kung Peninsula is the garden spot of the New Territories. It is also one of the last areas left in Hong Kong – the Outlying Islands notwithstanding – reserved for outdoor activities, and most of the peninsula is one huge 7600-hectare country park, divided into Sai Kung East and Sai Kung West. Though strictly speaking not on the peninsula, **Ma On Shan Country Park** is contiguous with it and access is from Sai Kung Town. The hiking is excellent in Sai Kung – the **MacLehose Trail** (see p165) runs right across it – there's sailing galore and some of the best beaches in the territory are here.

Ferry port, Sai Kung Peninsula

Orientation

The Sai Kung Peninsula is in the north-eastern New Territories. It is washed by Tolo Harbour to the north, Mirs Bay to the east, and Port Shelter to the south. On the southern end of the peninsula is High Island Reservoir, once a sea channel and now Hong Kong's second-largest source of fresh water.

Sai Kung Town

Originally a fishing village, **Sai Kung Town** (Map p417) is now more of a suburb for people working in Kowloon and on Hong Kong Island, but it still has some of the feeling of a port. Fishing boats put in an occasional appearance, and down on the waterfront there's a string of seafood restaurants that draw customers from all around Hong Kong.

Transport

Bus Sai Kung Town (Map p417) for No 299 (HK$9) to Sha Tin KCR, No 92 (HK$5.50) and No 96R (HK$17; Sun and public holidays) to Wong Shek, Hebe Haven and Choi Hung and Diamond Hill MTR stations on Kwun Tong line, No 792M (HK$6.50) to Tseung Kwan O MTR station on the Tseung Kwan O line, No 94 (HK$5.90) to Wong Shek

Green Minibus Sai Kung Town (Map p417) for Nos 1A and 1M (HK$7.50) and No 1S (12.30am-6.10am) to Hebe Haven and Choi Hung MTR on the Kwun Tong line

Sai Kung Island Hopping

You can make any number of easy boat trips from Sai Kung Town, exploring the mosaic of islands that dot the harbour. It's a delightful way to spend a few hours or even an entire day. Most *kaidos* leave from the pier on the waterfront, just in front of Hoi Pong Square.

The easiest (and cheapest) way to go is to jump aboard a 'scheduled' *kaido* (ie one that goes according to demand and when full) bound for the small island of Yim Tin Tsai (HK$10, 15 minutes).

On the way, the boat weaves through a number of small islands. The first island to the east of Sai Kung Town **Yeung Chau** (Sheep Island). You'll be able to spot a horseshoe-shaped burial plot up on the slope; for reasons dictated by feng shui, the Chinese like to position graves with decent views of the sea. Southeast of Yeung Chau, **Pak Sha Chau** (White Sand Island) has a popular beach on its northern shore.

Just beyond Pak Sha Chau is the northern tip of the much larger **Kiu Tsui Chau** (Sharp Island), arguably the most popular island destination. Kiu Tsui Chau has a couple of fine, sandy beaches: Kiu Tsui on the western shore and Hap Mun on the island's southern tip. Both can be reached by *kaido* (HK$10) directly from Sai Kung Town.

Yim Tin Tsai (Little Salt Field) is so called because the original fisherfolk who lived here augmented their income by salt-panning. A few minutes' walk from the jetty up a small flight of steps to the left is St Joseph's Chapel, the focal point of the island. This is Yim Tin Tsai's only house of worship, which is most unusual in an area of Hong Kong where temples devoted to Tin Hau proliferate. Apparently the villagers, who all belong to the same clan, converted to Catholicism after St Peter appeared on the island to chase away pirates who had been harassing them in the last century. Beyond the chapel is the village of Yim Tin Tsai, where a handful of families still live.

Yim Tin Tsai is connected to the much larger island of **Kau Sai Chau** by a narrow spit of land that becomes submerged at high tide. Kau Sai Chau is the site of the 36-hole **Jockey Club Kau Sai Chau Golf Course** (☎ 2791 3388), a public link that can be reached by the course's direct ferry from Sai Kung (adult/child or senior HK$50/30 return, shuttle bus HK$10/5), which departs every 20 minutes daily from 6.40am to 9pm; the last boat back is at 10pm. Boats dock in Sai Kung Town at the long pier at the end of Fuk Man Rd. The 19th-century Hing Shing Temple at the southern tip of Kau Sai Chau won a Unesco restoration award in 2000.

Beyond Kau Sai Chau is **Leung Shuen Wan** (High Island), a long trip from Sai Kung Town, and the **High Island Reservoir**, which was built in 1978 by damming what was once a large bay with dolooses (huge cement barriers shaped like jacks). You can see one example, weighing 25 tonnes, on display on the pier in Sai Kung Town. You'll also see a large sign there warning of unexploded shells still unaccounted for on some of the islands and dating back to WWII. Areas of potential danger are clearly marked.

If you want to be out on the water for a longer period or to have greater flexibility as to where you go, you can hire your own boat. Finding a *kaido* for such a trip is no problem at all; you won't be on the pier for long before being approached by a bevy of enthusiastic *kaido* owners trawling for fares. Explain to the *kaido* owner where you want to go, how long you want to spend there and which way you wish to return. They don't speak much English, but if you point to the islands on Map pp396–7 in this book, they may get the picture. The usual price for this kind of trip is about HK$100 on weekdays, more at the weekend.

If travelling to Sai Kung from Choi Hung in Kowloon, the minibus is faster than bus No 92. Bus No 299 from Sha Tin takes you to Sai Kung via Ma On Shan and passes some lovely bays and isolated villages on the way.

ACTIVITIES

Sai Kung Town is an excellent springboard for hikes into the surrounding countryside. A *kaido* trip to one or more of the little offshore islands and their secluded beaches is also recommended (see the boxed text p135). Windsurfing equipment can be hired from the **Windsurfing Centre** (☎ 2792 5605; ☯ 11am-5pm Mon-Fri, 10am-6pm Sat & Sun) at Sha Ha, just north of Sai Kung Town. Bus No 94, heading for the pier at **Wong Shek** (Yellow Stone) and the springboard for **Tap Mun Chau**, will drop you off at Sha Ha. Or you can walk there from town in about 15 minutes.

Hebe Haven

The small bay of **Hebe Haven** (Map pp396–7) – Pak Sha Wan (White Sand Bay) in Cantonese – is home to the **Hebe Haven Yacht Club** (☎ 2719 9682, 2719 3673). You'll recognise the place easily enough; the fleet of yachts and other pleasure craft all but choke Marina Cove.

To swim at Trio Beach, opposite the marina, catch a sampan from Hebe Haven to the long, narrow peninsula called **Ma Lam Wat** across the bay; along the way you'll pass a small Tin Hau temple on a spit of land jutting out to the south. The beach is excellent and the sampan trip should only cost a few dollars. You can also walk to the peninsula from Sai Kung Town; it's about 4km.

Pak Tam Chung

The easternmost point on the Sai Kung Peninsula that you can reach by bus (No 94), **Pak Tam Chung** (Map pp396–7) is also the start of the **MacLehose Trail** (see Hikes p165).

SAI KUNG COUNTRY PARK VISITOR CENTRE Map pp396–7

☎ 2792 7365; Tai Mong Tsai Rd; ☯ 9.30am-4.30pm Wed-Mon

While you're in Pak Tam Chung, visit the Sai Kung Country Park Visitor Centre, which is to the south of the village, just by the road from Sai Kung. It has excellent maps, photographs and displays of the area's geology, fauna and flora.

HIGH ISLAND RESERVOIR Map pp396–7

Sai Kung East Country Park

From Pak Tam Chung you can walk southeast to High Island Reservoir, which used to be a sea channel. Both ends were blocked with dams, and the sea water was then siphoned out and fresh water pumped in. The reservoir opened in 1978.

SHEUNG YIU FOLK MUSEUM

☎ 2792 6365; admission free; ☯ 9am-4pm Wed-Mon, closed Tue & some public holidays

This unusual open-air museum is a leisurely 20-minute walk from Pak Tam Chung south along the **Pak Tam Chung Nature Trail**. The museum is actually a restored Hakka village typical of those found here in the 19th century. The village was founded about 150 years ago by the Wong clan, which built a kiln to make bricks. In the whitewashed dwellings, pigpens and cattle sheds, all surrounded by a high wall and watchtower to guard against raids by pirates, are farm implements, objects of daily use, furnishings and Hakka clothing.

Hoi Ha, Wong Shek, Chek Keng & Tai Long

There are several rewarding hikes at the northern end of the Sai Kung Peninsula, but the logistics can be a bit tricky. Be sure to take along a copy of the *Sai Kung & Clearwater Bay* Countryside Series map or Universal Publications' *Sai Kung, Clearwater Bay* (see p364).

HOI HA WAN MARINE PARK

Map pp396–7

☎ 2150 6875; Hoi Ha

A rewarding 6km walk in the area starts from the village of Hoi Ha (literally, 'Under the Sea'), on the coast of Hoi Ha Bay, now part of the Hoi Ha Wan Marine Park, a 260-hectare protected area blocked off by concrete booms from the Tolo Channel and closed to fishing vessels. It's one of the few places in Hong Kong waters where coral still grows in abundance and is a favourite with divers. You can visit anytime but 1½-hour tours of the marine park are available in English at 10.30am and 2.15pm at the weekend and on public holidays. Call the government's **Agriculture, Fisheries & Conservation Department** (AFCD; ☎ 2957 8757) for more details.

Getting to Hoi Ha is not easy, though minibus No 7 (HK$5.50) makes the run from Pak Tam Chung on Sunday and public holidays only. Otherwise, take a taxi from there or from Sai Kung (HK$100).

WALKS & HIKES

From Hoi Ha village, follow the trail east along the headland and then south following the coast of **Tai Tan Hoi Hap** (Long Harbour) all the way to **Wong Shek**, from where you can catch bus No 94 or a taxi (HK$85) to Sai Kung Town or take the ferry to **Ma Liu Shui**, near the Chinese University of Hong Kong and close to the University KCR station.

Alternatively, there's an interesting walk through a few of northern Sai Kung Peninsula's small villages that takes in a small beach. Starting at **Chek Keng** (Red Path), to the southeast of Wong Shek, you can follow stage No 2 of the MacLehose Trail, which will take you east to the tiny village of **Tai Long** (Big Wave), where you can buy food and drink, then south to the waterfront village of **Ham Tin** (Salty Field) with a nice beach. From Ham Tin, the MacLehose trail wends southward to **Sai Wan** and around High Island Reservoir. The return journey is about 8km.

To reach Chek Keng by bus, catch No 94 headed for Wong Shek and alight at Pak Tam Au (the fourth bus stop after the entrance to Sai Kung Country Park, near the top of a hill). Take the footpath at the side of the road heading east and walk for about half an hour to Chek Keng.

Ma On Shan

At 702m, **Ma On Shan** (Map pp396–7), northwest of Sai Kung Town, is the fourth-highest peak in Hong Kong. It is surrounded by the 2880-hectare Ma On Shan Country Park. Access to the mountain is via stage No 4 of the **MacLehose Trail** (see p165). The trail does not actually go over the summit, but it gets very close and the spur route to the peak is obvious. Be warned – it's a steep and strenuous climb. The mountain itself is not to be confused with Ma On Shan New Town, with its endless rows of high-rise housing estates and shopping centres. From the peak of Ma On Shan you can walk down to the New Town and catch bus No 299 to Sha Tin or bus No 85C (HK$7.50) to Hung Hom.

TAP MUN CHAU

Eating p209

Tap Mun Chau (Grass Island; Map pp396–7) is quite isolated and retains an old-world fishing village atmosphere. Indeed, many travellers say that Tap Mun Chau is the most interesting island in all of Hong Kong. If you have the time, it's definitely worth the trip, and you will be rewarded with a feeling that's hard to come by in Hong Kong – isolation. The sailing is particularly scenic from Wong Shek, as the boat cruises through the narrow Tai Tan Hoi Hap – more reminiscent of a fjord in Norway than a harbour in Hong Kong.

Tap Mun Chau does not have accommodation, but you may get away with pitching a tent. There's only one restaurant on the island (see Tap Mun Chau p209) but there are shops selling snacks and cold drinks. For ferry routes, schedules and fares for Tap Mun Chau, see New Territories Ferries (p340).

Orientation

Tap Mun Chau is off the northeast coast of the New Territories, where the Tolo Channel empties into Mirs Bay (Tai Pang Wan in Cantonese). Only Ping Chau further northeast in Mirs Bay is more remote.

Transport

Ferry Tap Mun ferry pier (Map pp396–7) to Wong Shek and Chek Keng on the Sai Kung Peninsula and Ma Liu Shui near University KCR station

SIGHTS & ACTIVITIES

As you approach the pier at Tap Mun village, you'll see fishing boats bobbing about in the small bay and, to the south, people working on fish-breeding rafts. Tap Mun village is noted for its **Tin Hau temple**, which was built during the reign of Emperor Kang Xi of the Qing dynasty in the late 17th or early 18th centuries and is northeast from where the boat docks. The Tin Hau birthday festival in late April/early May (see City Calendar p10)

is very big here, although most of the participants come from elsewhere in Hong Kong. Part of the temple is devoted to the god of war, Kwan Tai.

Other attractions here include an easy (and signposted) walk northward to **Mau Ping Shan** (125m), the island's highest point, a windy pebble **beach** on the southeastern shore and an odd stone formation called **Balanced Rock**, a couple of hundred metres south of the beach.

PING CHAU

A remote, crescent-shaped island, **Ping Chau** (Map pp396–7) is part of **Plover Cove Country Park** (☎ 2665 3413). In 2001 the waters around the island, which teem with sea life (especially corals), were declared Hong Kong's fourth marine reserve.

Ping Chau is very close to the mainland and used to be one of the most popular destinations for people emigrating illegally from China by braving the sharks and the patrol boats and taking to the water, more often than not with inflated pigs' bladders for flotation. In Cantonese the island is called Tung Ping Chau (East Peace Island), to distinguish it from Peng Chau (same pronunciation in Cantonese) near Lantau, and you will occasionally see this name transliterated in English as well.

At one time the island supported a population of 3000, but now it is virtually deserted, its people either driven off the island by pirates operating from the south coast of the mainland or, more recently, lured away by the promise of wealth in the urban areas. There are a couple of tiny settlements on the northeastern side, including Sha Tau and Tai Tong. Both of them have noodle shops.

Ping Chau is just 12km from the mainland's Daya Bay nuclear power station and has Hong Kong's only radiation shelter, at Tai Tong just north of the pier.

See Ping Chau (p341) for ferry routes, schedules and fares for Ping Chau.

Orientation

Ping Chau, sitting in splendid isolation in Mirs Bay in the far northeast of the New Territories, is as remote as it gets in Hong Kong. The distance to Ma Liu Shui, from where the ferry serving the island departs, is 25km to the southwest.

Transport

Ferry Ping Chau ferry pier (Map pp396–7) to Wong Shek and Chek Keng on the Sai Kung Peninsula and Ma Liu Shui near University KCR station

SIGHTS & ACTIVITIES

Ping Chau's highest point is only about 40m, but it has unusual rock layers in its cliffs, which glitter after the rain. The island has some sandy beaches on its east coast that are good for

swimming. The longest one is **Cheung Sha Wan** to the northeast. There is a small **Tin Hau temple** on the southern coast of the island, and some small **caves** dotting the cliffs. A good 6km **walking trail** encircles the entire island.

CLEARWATER BAY PENINSULA

Clearwater Bay Peninsula is a wonderfully untamed and rough-contoured backdrop to urban Hong Kong – at least on the eastern shore. It is wedged in by Junk Bay (Tseung Kwan O) to the west and Clearwater Bay (Tsing Sui Wan) to the east; Joss House Bay (Tai Miu Wan) nestles to the south. Junk Bay is now the site of Tseung Kwan O, a New Town built on reclaimed land with a growing population of 265,000 and a new MTR line, but the eastern coastline remains mostly unscarred and offers some exceptional walks, fine beaches and one of the many temples dedicated to Tin Hau on the coast of southern China.

Orientation

Clearwater Bay Peninsula is on the southeastern edge of the New Territories. The country park is divided into two parts: a long and narrow finger-shaped section stretching from Joss House Bay in the south almost to Port Shelter and a half-moon-shaped section to the east between Lung Ha Wan and Clearwater Bay.

Transport

Bus No 91 to Diamond Hill and Choi Hung MTR stations on Kwun Tong line

Green Minibus No 10sM to Tseung Kwan O and Nos 16 and 103 to Hang Hau on Tseung Kwan O MTR line

CLEARWATER BAY COUNTRY PARK
Map pp396–7

The heart of the country park is **Tai Au Mun**, from where trails head off in various directions, though the **Clearwater Bay Country Park Visitor Centre** (☎ 2719 0032, 2264 0595; ☺ 9.30am-4.30pm Wed-Mon) is to the southeast in Tai Hang Tun. You can take the small road (Lung Ha Wan Rd) north from Tai Au Mun to the beach at **Lung Ha Wan** (Lobster Bay) and return via the 2.3km **Lung Ha Wan Country Trail** via **Tai Leng Tung** (291m).

TAI MIU (TIN HAU TEMPLE) Map pp396–7
☎ 2519 9155; ☺ 8am-5pm

Further south along Tai Au Mun Rd is an ancient temple dedicated to Tin Hau. It is said to have been first built in the 13th century by two brothers from Fujian in gratitude to the goddess for having spared their lives during a storm at sea. It is particularly busy during the Tin Hau birthday festival in late April/early May (see City Calendar p10) and has recently been renovated.

Just behind the temple is a **Song-dynasty rock carving** dating from 1274 and recording both the visit of a superintendent of the Salt Administration and the history of two temples in Joss House Bay. It is the oldest inscription extant in Hong Kong.

From Tai Miu, hikers can follow the **High Junk Peak Country Trail** up to **Tin Ha Shan** (273m) and then continue on to **High Junk Peak** (Tiu Yu Yung; 344m) before heading eastward back to Tai Au Mun.

BEACHES Map pp396–7

Bus No 91 passes **Silverstrand Beach** (Ngan Sin Wan) north of Hang Hau before reaching Tai Au Mun; if you wish you can get off at Silverstrand and go for a dip. If you're heading for Lung Ha Wan, get off the bus at Tai Au Mun village and start walking. From Sai Kung, take bus No 92 to where Hiram's Hwy and Clearwater Bay Rd meet and change there to bus No 91.

From Tai Au Mun, Tai Au Mun Rd leads south to two fine, sandy beaches: **Clearwater Bay First Beach** and, a bit further southwest, **Clearwater Bay Second Beach**. In summer, try to go during the week, as both beaches can get very crowded on the weekend.

OUTLYING ISLANDS

In addition to Hong Kong Island, the territory of Hong Kong consists of another 234 islands. Together these 'Outlying Islands', as they are called here, make up about 16% of the territory's total land area, but they can claim only about 2% of its population.

Hong Kong's Outlying Islands vary greatly in size, appearance and character. While many are little more than uninhabited rocks poking out of the South China Sea, Lantau is almost twice the size of Hong Kong Island.

Because they are so sparsely populated, the Outlying Islands are the territory's escape routes and its playgrounds. Among the magnets that attract local day-trippers and foreign visitors alike are country parks with hundreds of kilometres of hiking trails, fresher air and some of the last remnants of traditional village life in Hong Kong.

From the tranquil lanes of Cheung Chau and Peng Chau to the monasteries of Lantau and the waterfront seafood restaurants of Lamma, Hong Kong's islands offer a world of peace and quiet along with a host of sights and activities. The islands are a colourful encyclopaedia of animal and plant life – a boon for nature lovers. What's more, some of Hong Kong's best beaches punctuate the rocky coasts.

The islands listed here are all easily accessible from Hong Kong Island, and Cheung Chau and Lantau can be reached from Kowloon at the weekend. See Outlying Islands Ferries (p341) for details on routes, schedule and fares. Because the tiny islands of Tap Mun Chau and Ping Chau are best reached from the New Territories, they are both covered in that section (p340).

LAMMA

Eating p209; Sleeping p288

At 13.5 sq km, the territory's third-largest island after Lantau and Hong Kong, **Lamma** (Map p418) is home to fishers, farmers and commuters, and the hills above the main village, Yung Shue Wan, are strewn with small homes and apartment blocks. Known mainly for the seafood restaurants at Sok Kwu Wan, the island's 'second' village, Lamma also has some good beaches, excellent hiking and lively pubs.

The most interesting way to see Lamma is to walk between Yung Shue Wan and Sok Kwu Wan (roughly 4km), which takes a little over an hour, and return to Central from there. Those with extra time should carry on to Tung O Wan, an idyllic bay some 30 minutes further south at the bottom of a steep hill, and perhaps return to Sok Kwu Wan via Mo Tat Wan. Another excellent excursion is to arrive by ferry at Pak Kok Tsuen and follow the circular path around the northern headland before heading south for Yung Shue Wan.

Orientation

Lamma is the closest inhabited island to Hong Kong Island; its northernmost tip is a mere 3km across the East Lamma Channel from Ap Lei Chau in Aberdeen. There are two main settlements on the island: Yung Shue Wan to the northwest and Sok Kwu Wan on the east coast in the middle of the island.

Information

There's a **HSBC branch** (☎ 2982 0787) at 19 Main St in Yung Shue Wan. The post office is at No 3 of the same street. Bicycles are available for rent for HK$15/50 per hour/day from **Hoi Nam Bicycle Shop** (☎ 2982 0128, 2982 2500; 37 Sha Po Old Village; ☯ 11am-7pm). The shop is a short distance southeast of Yung Shue Wan on the main path to Sok Kwu Wan.

Lamma

Transport

Ferry From Yung Shue Wan pier (Map p418) to pier 4 of Outlying Islands ferry terminal in Central, Pak Kok Tsuen (Lamma) and Aberdeen; from Sok Kwu Wan pier (Map p418) to pier 4 of Outlying Islands ferry terminal in Central, Man Tat Wan (Lamma) and Aberdeen

YUNG SHUE WAN Map p418

Though it's the larger of the island's two main villages, Yung Shue Wan (Banyan Tree Bay) remains a small place, with little more than a main street following the curve of the bay. Plastic was the big industry here at one time, but now restaurants, bars and other tourism-related businesses are the main employers. There is a small **Tin Hau temple** at the southern end of Yung Shue Wan dating from the late 19th century.

HUNG SHING YEH BEACH Map p418

About a 25-minute walk southeast from the Yung Shue Wan ferry pier, Hung Shing Yeh Beach is the most popular beach on Lamma. But arrive early in the morning or on a week-day and you'll probably find it deserted. The beach is protected by a shark net and has toi-lets, showers and changing rooms. There are a few restaurants and drinks stands nearby – the latter open at the weekend only, except in summer – as well as the **Concerto Inn** (p288), a hotel that also serves hot and cold drinks, and some mediocre Western food. The view of the power station across the bay takes some get-ting used to.

LO SO SHING BEACH Map p418

If you continue south from Hung Shing Yeh Beach, the path climbs steeply until it reaches a **Chinese-style pavilion** near the top of the hill. From this vantage point, it becomes obvious that the island is mostly hilly grassland and large boulders with relatively few trees, though more and more are being planted. You'll pass a second pavilion offering splendid views out to sea; from here a path leads from the main Yung Shue Wan–Sok Kwu Wan path down to Lo So Shing Beach, the most beautiful on Lamma. Count on about a one-hour walk from Yung Shue Wan and 20 to 25 minutes from Sok Kwu Wan. The beach is not very big, but it has a nice cover of shade trees at the back. During the swimming season, when lifeguards are on duty (ie April to October), a small snack stand opens.

SOK KWU WAN Map p418

If you continue on the main Yung Shue Wan–Sok Kwu Wan track you'll encounter another pavilion on a ridge, this time looking down onto Sok Kwu Wan (Picnic Bay), with its many fine restaurants, and fishing boats and rafts bobbing in the bay. Although still a small settlement, Sok Kwu Wan supports at least a dozen waterfront seafood restaurants that are popular with boat-ers. The small harbour at Sok Kwu Wan is filled with rafts from which cages are suspended and fish farmed. If entering Sok Kwu Wan from the south (ie from the main path linking it with Yung Shue Wan), you'll pass three **kamikaze caves** built by the occupying Japanese forces to house motorboats wired with explosives to disrupt Allied shipping during WWII. They were never used. Further on and near the entrance to Sok Kwu Wan is a **Tin Hau temple** from the 1820s.

MO TAT WAN Map p418

The clean and relatively uncrowded beach at Mo Tat Wan is a mere 20-minute walk east of Sok Kwu Wan along a coastal path. Mo Tat Wan is OK for swimming but has no lifeguards. You can also reach here by *kaido* from Aberdeen, which continues on to Sok Kwu Wan.

TUNG O WAN Map p418

A detour to this small and secluded bay, with a long stretch of sandy beach, while walking to Sok Kwu Wan from Yung Shue Wan or from Sok Kwu Wan itself is highly recommended. Just before the Tin Hau temple at the entrance to Sok Kwu Wan, follow the signposted path to the right southward, up and over the hill to the tiny village of **Tung O**. The walk takes about 30 minutes, over a rugged landscape, and the first half is a fairly strenuous climb up steps and along a path. Don't do this walk at night unless it's a full moon, as there are only a few street lights at the start in Sok Kwu Wan.

If coming from Mo Tat Wan, take the trail immediately to the west of the pavilion above the beach and follow the signposted path up the hill and through bamboo groves and fields. It takes about 25 minutes to reach the sleepy village of **Yung Shue Ha** (Under the Banyan Tree) on the fringes of the bay. All of the Chinese who live there are from the same clan and have the surname of Chow. A member of this clan, Chow Yun Fat, the bulletproof star of many John Woo films, was born and raised in Tung O, the village at the southern end of the bay.

The beach at Tung O Wan is a secluded and unspoiled stretch of sand, punctuated by chunks of driftwood and other flotsam. Travellers who fall under the bay's spell and find it difficult to leave can stay at **Tung O Bay Homestay** (p288).

SHAM WAN Map p418

Sham Wan (Deep Bay) is another beautiful bay to the southwest that can be reached from Tung O Wan by clambering over the hills. A trail on the left about 200m up the hill from Tung O leads south to a small and sandy beach. Don't come here from June to October, when Hong Kong's endangered green turtles nest.

Green Turtles & Eggs

Sham Wan has traditionally been the one beach in the whole of Hong Kong where endangered green turtles *(Chelonia mydas)*, one of three species of sea turtles found in Hong Kong waters, still struggle onto the sand to lay their eggs from early June to the end of August.

Female green turtles, which can grow to a metre in length and weigh 140kg, take between 30 and 40 years to reach sexual maturity and always head back to the same beach where they were born to lay their eggs, which occurs about every three years. Fearing that Sham Wan would catch the eye of housing-estate developers and that the turtles would swim away forever, the area was declared a Site of Special Scientific Interest and closed, and is patrolled by the Agriculture, Fisheries & Conservation Department (AFCD) from June to October. In September 2001 some 80 baby turtles were released at the nesting site.

As well as developers, a major hurdle faced by the long-suffering turtles is the appetite of Lamma locals for their eggs. In 1994 three turtles laid about 200 eggs, which were promptly harvested and consumed by villagers. Several years later villagers sold eggs to Japanese tourists for HK$100 each. There is now a HK$50,000 fine levied on anyone caught on the beach during the nesting season. Anyone taking, possessing or attempting to sell one of the eggs faces a fine of HK$100,000 and one year in prison.

Kwai taan, or 'turtle egg', by the way, is one of the rudest things you can call a Cantonese-speaking person.

CHEUNG CHAU

Eating p212; Sleeping p288

A one-time refuge for pirates, Cheung Chau (Long Island; Map p420) now supports a population of some 30,000 people on less than 2.5 sq km of territory. Many residents are commuters, but relatively few foreigners live here nowadays.

Archaeological evidence, including a 3000-year-old rock carving uncovered just below the Warwick Hotel (see p142) suggests that Cheung Chau, like Lamma and Lantau, was inhabited at least as early as the Neolithic period. The island had a thriving fishing community at the time, and the early inhabitants – Cantonese and Hakka settlers – supplemented their income with smuggling and piracy.

When Canton (present-day Guangzhou) and Macau opened up to the West in the 16th century, Cheung Chau was a perfect spot from which to prey on passing ships. The infamous and powerful 18th-century pirate Cheung Po Tsai is said to have had his base here; you can still visit the cave where he supposedly stashed his booty at the southwestern tip of the island.

Fishing and aquaculture are important industries for a large number of the island's inhabitants, some of whom still live on junks and sampans anchored in the harbour. Bring your camera for some of the best shots of traditional maritime life on the south China coast.

Cheung Chau boasts several interesting temples, the most important being Pak Tai Temple, which hosts the annual Bun Festival, *the* red-letter day on Cheung Chau (see the boxed text opposite). The island has a few worthwhile beaches, and there are some relatively easy walks, including the one described later in this section, which will take you through lush vegetation and past missionary schools, churches, retreats and cemeteries. Most can be easily done in half a day.

Orientation

Cheung Chau is a bone-shaped island lying 10km southwest of Hong Kong Island and just off the Chi Ma Wan Peninsula on southeastern Lantau. Cheung Chau village, where the ferry docks, is the only real settlement on the island.

Information

HSBC (☎ 2981 1127; 1116 Praya St) has a branch southeast of the cargo pier, and an ATM (19A Pak She Praya Rd) north of the ferry pier. The post office is in the market complex on Tai Hing Tai St. There is no transport on Cheung Chau, but you can rent bicycles from a kiosk (☎ 2986 9907) at the northern end of Praya St for HK$10/30 per hour/day and two-seat pedal bikes for HK$20/60.

CHEUNG CHAU VILLAGE Map p420

No longer really a village but a small town, the island's main settlement lies along the narrow strip of land connecting the headlands to the north and the south. The waterfront is a bustling place and the maze of streets and alleyways that make up the village are filled with tumble-down shops selling everything from plastic buckets to hell money, and old Chinese-style houses. The streets close to the waterfront are pungent with the smell of incense and fish hung out to dry in the sun.

CHEUNG CHAU TYPHOON SHELTER

Map p420

Only the typhoon shelter at Aberdeen (see p100) is larger than this one. Chartering a sampan for half an hour costs between HK$50 and HK$80, depending on the day, the season and the demand. Most sampans congregate around the cargo pier, but virtually any small boat you see in the harbour can be hired as a water taxi. Just wave and two or

Transport

Ferry From Cheung Chau ferry pier (Map p420) to pier 5 of Outlying Islands ferry terminal in Central, to Lantau (Chi Ma Wan and Mui Wo) and Peng Chau, to Tsim Sha Tsui Star Ferry pier (weekend only)

three will come forward. Be sure to agree on the fare first.

PAK TAI TEMPLE Map p420

☎ 2981 0663; Pak She Fourth Lane; ☿ 9am-5pm

This colourful temple is the oldest house of worship on the island and is the focus of the annual Cheung Chau Bun Festival in May. It is dedicated to the Taoist deity Pak Tai, the 'Supreme Emperor of the Dark Heaven', military protector of the state, guardian of peace and order and protector of fisherfolk. Legend tells that early settlers from Guangdong province brought an image of Pak Tai with them to Cheung Chau. In 1777 the statue was carried

Districts & Islands – Outlying Islands

Going for the Buns

The annual Cheung Chau Bun Festival (Tai Chiu in Cantonese), which honours the god Pak Tai and is unique to the island, takes place over eight days in late April or early May, traditionally starting on the sixth day of the fourth moon. It is a Taoist festival, and there are four days of religious observances.

The festival is renowned for its bun towers, bamboo scaffolding up to 20m high that are covered with sacred rolls. If you visit Cheung Chau a week or so before the festival, you'll see the towers being built in the courtyard of Pak Tai Temple.

In the past, hundreds of people would scramble up the towers at midnight on the designated day to grab one of the buns for good luck. The higher the bun, the greater the luck, so everyone tried to reach the top. In 1978 a tower collapsed under the weight of the climbers, injuring two dozen people. Now everyone must remain on terra firma and the buns are handed out.

Sunday, the third day of the festival, features a procession of floats, stilt walkers and people dressed as characters from Chinese legends. Most interesting are the colourfully dressed 'floating children', who are carried through the streets on long poles, cleverly wired to metal supports hidden under their clothing. The supports include footrests and a padded seat.

During the celebrations several other deities are also worshipped, including Tin Hau and Hung Shing, the god of the south and of fisherfolk, both of whom are sacred to those who make their living from the sea. Homage is also paid to Tou Tei, the earth god, and Kwun Yam, the goddess of mercy.

Offerings are made to the spirits of all the fish and livestock killed and consumed over the previous year. A priest reads out a decree calling on the villagers to abstain from killing any animals during the four-day festival, and no meat is consumed.

Accommodation on Cheung Chau is heavily booked throughout the festival, and even the extra ferries laid on are packed to the roof.

through the village and Cheung Chau was spared a plague that had decimated the populations of nearby islands. A temple dedicated to the saviour was built six years later.

OTHER TEMPLES Map p420

Cheung Chau has four temples dedicated to Tin Hau, the empress of heaven and patroness of seafarers. **Pak She Tin Hau Temple** lies a short distance northwest of the Pak Tai Temple. **Nam Tan Wan Tin Hau temple** is just north of Morning Beach; **Tai Shek Hau Tin Hau temple** is to the west on Sai Wan Rd. **Sai Wan Tin Hau temple** is west of Sai Wan (Western Bay), on the southwestern tip of the island. You can walk there or catch a *kaido* from the cargo pier. **Hung Shing Temple**, built in 1813 and dedicated to the god of the south, is on the waterfront at the southern end of Cheung Chau village.

BEACHES Map p420

Tung Wan Beach, Cheung Chau's longest and most popular (though not its prettiest) beach lies at the end of Tung Wan Rd, due east of the ferry pier. The best part of Tung Wan is the far southern end, which is a great area for windsurfing. Just south of Tung Wan Beach, Kwun Yam Wan Beach, known to English speakers as **Afternoon Beach**, and a great spot for windsurfing.

Windsurfing has always been an extremely popular pastime on Cheung Chau. Indeed, Hong Kong's only Olympic gold medal winner to date, Lee Lai-shan, who took the top prize in windsurfing at the 1996 Olympics in Atlanta, grew up on Cheung Chau. At the northern end of Afternoon Beach, the **Cheung Chau Windsurfing Centre** (☎ 2981 8316; 1 Hak Pai Rd; ☺ daily year-round) rents sailboards for between HK$60 and HK$120 per hour, as well as single/double kayaks for HK$50/80. Jet skis and water-skiing cost HK$600 per hour, banana boats HK$180/350 per half-/full hour. There are also windsurfing courses available for HK$600. The best time for windsurfing in Hong Kong is between October and December.

At the southeastern end of Afternoon Beach a footpath leads uphill past a **Kwun Yam temple**, which is dedicated to the goddess of mercy. Continue up the footpath and look for the sign to the Fa Peng Knoll. The concrete footpath takes you past quiet, tree-shrouded villas.

From the knoll you can walk down to Don Bosco Rd (look for the sign); it leads due south to rocky **Nam Tam Wan** (also known as Morning Beach), where swimming is possible. If you ignore Don Bosco Rd and continue walking west you'll come to the intersection of Peak and Kwun Yam Wan Rds. Kwun Yam Wan Rd and its extension, School Rd, will take you back to Cheung Chau village.

Peak Rd is the main route to the island's cemetery in the southwestern part of the island; you'll pass several pavilions along the way built for coffin bearers making the hilly climb. Once at the cemetery it's worth dropping down to **Pak Tso Wan** (Italian Beach), a sandy, isolated spot that is good for swimming. At this point Peak Rd West becomes Tsan Tuen Rd, which continues north to Sai Wan.

CHEUNG PO TSAI CAVE Map p420

This cave, on the southwestern peninsula of the island, is said to have been the favourite hiding place of the notorious pirate Cheung Po Tsai, who once commanded a flotilla of 600 junks and had an 'army' of 4000 men. He surrendered to the Qing government in 1810 and became an official himself, but his treasure is said to still be hidden here. In reality, the cave's association with Cheung Po Tsai is almost certainly apocryphal, as it is very small – just narrow crevices between boulders stacked on top of one another.

It's a 2km walk from Cheung Chau village along Sai Wan Rd, or take a *kaido* (adult/child HK$3/2) from the cargo ferry pier to the pier at Sai Wan. From here the walk is less than 200m (but uphill). If you really want to see everything, make sure to take a torch (flashlight) along.

LANTAU

Eating p212; Sleeping p289

Lantau (Map p419) is a Cantonese word meaning 'broken head', but Chinese call Hong Kong's largest island Tai Yue Shan (Big Island Mountain), a name that refers both to its size and elevation. At 144 sq km, Lantau is almost twice the size of Hong Kong Island, and its highest point, Lantau Peak (Fung Wong Shan; 934m), almost double the height of Victoria Peak.

Amazingly, only about 45,000 people live on Lantau, compared with Hong Kong Island's 1.4 million. They are mainly concentrated in a couple of centres along the south coast, because the interior is so mountainous, though about 20,000 people have moved into the high-rises of Tung Chung opposite the airport at Chek Lap Kok since 1997, and Discovery Bay on the northeast coast supports a population of 12,000. Not everyone on Lantau resides here of their own accord; the island is home to three prisons.

Rock carvings discovered at Shek Pik on the southwestern coast of Lantau suggest that the island was inhabited as early as the Bronze Age 3000 years ago, before the arrival of the Han Chinese; a stone circle uncovered at Fan Lau may date from Neolithic times. The last Song-dynasty emperor passed through here in the 13th century while fleeing the Mongol invaders. He is believed to have held court in the Tung Chung Valley to the north, which takes its name from a local hero who gave up his life for the emperor. Tung Chung is still worshipped by the Hakka people of Lantau, who believe he can predict the future.

Like Cheung Chau, Lantau was once a base for pirates and smugglers, and was one of the favourite haunts of Cheung Po Tsai. The island was also an important trading post for the British long before they showed any interest in Hong Kong Island.

Lantau is an excellent island on which to escape from the city. More than half of it – 78.5 sq km, in fact – is designated country park and there are several superb mountain trails, including the 70km Lantau Trail, which passes over both Lantau Peak and Sunset Peak (869m); some interesting traditional villages such as Tai O on the west coast; several important religious retreats, including the Po Lin Monastery and the adjacent Tian Tan Buddha, the largest outdoor Buddha statue in the world; and some excellent beaches including Cheung Sha, the longest and among the cleanest in Hong Kong.

Orientation

Lantau is the last inhabited island west of Hong Kong Island; next stop is Macau and the Zhuhai SEZ. Lantau has many villages, but the main settlements dot the southern coast. From east to west they are: Mui Wo, the 'capital' and where most of the ferries dock; Pui O and Tong Fuk along South Lantau Rd; and Tai O on the west coast. The New Town of Tung Chung is on the north coast and accessible from Mui Wo by buses that climb steep Tung Chung Rd. Discovery Bay, a self-contained 'bedroom community' to the northeast, can be reached from Mui Wo by ferry.

Lantau

Until the Lantau Link, the combined road and rail transport connection between Kowloon and Lantau, opened in 1997, the island was accessible only by ferry. That's still the most popular and enjoyable way to go, but today you can reach the island from the rest of the territory by MTR, the Airport Express, a fleet of buses and even by taxi. On the island there are 19 different bus lines and some 50 taxis to get you where you want to go.

Information

The **Country & Marine Parks Authority** (Map p421; ☎ 2420 0529; ☙ 8.30am-noon Mon-Fri, 8.30am-4.30pm Sat & Sun) maintains an information kiosk to the left as you leave the main ferry pier at Mui Wo. **HSBC** (☎ 2984 8271; Mui Wo Ferry Pier Rd) has a branch in Mui Wo just south of the roundabout and before the turn up South Lantau Rd. There's an HSBC ATM in Tai O on Tai O Market St, which you'll see as you cross the footbridge from the mainland to the island. The main **post office** (Ngan Kwong Wan Rd, Mui Wo) is a short distance west of the footbridge crossing the Silver River.

Bicycles are available for hire in Mui Wo a short distance from the ferry pier: **Friendly Bicycle Shop** (☎ 2984 2278; Shop 12, Mui Wo Centre, 1 Ngan Wan Rd), opposite the Wellcome supermarket, and the nearby **Bike King** (☎ 2984 9761, 9834 4727; Silver Centre Bldg, Ground fl, Mui Wo Ferry Pier Rd) just south of the HSBC branch. They cost HK$10 per hour and HK$25/35 per day during the week/at the weekend. The overnight charge is HK$35 and an all-terrain bike (eg to cycle to the Tian Tan Buddha in Ngong Ping) is HK$50.

In the warmer months **bikes** can also be hired from a stall (☎ 2984 7500) near the Silvermine Beach Hotel in Mui Wo and from several in Pui O village.

The Lantau Explorer Pass (HK$180) includes return transportation between Central and Mui Wo and a tour of Lantau, with three stops: Cheung Sha Beach (15 minutes), Ngong Ping and Tian Tan Buddha (two hours) and Tai O village (one hour). The Lantau Explorer Bus departs Mui Wo at 11.45am and 1.45pm on weekdays, returning at 4.30pm and 6.30pm respectively. On Sunday departure/return times are noon/4.40pm and 2pm/6.40pm. Tickets are available from the **New World First Ferry Services Customer Service Centre** (☎ 2131 8181) at pier 6 of the Outlying Islands ferry terminal and any HKTB centre.

Transport

Ferry From Mui Wo pier (Map p419) to pier 6 of Outlying Islands ferry terminal in Central, to Cheung Chau (via Chi Ma Wan) and Peng Chau, to Tsim Sha Tsui Star Ferry pier (weekend only) and to Discovery Bay; from Chi Ma Wan pier to Mui Wo and Cheung Chau; from Tai O piers to Tuen Mun (via Sha Lo Wan and Tung Chung); from Tung Chung New Development pier to Tuen Mun

Bus Mui Wo bus terminal (Map p421) for No 1 and N1 (overnight) to Pui O, Cheung Sha, Tong Fuk, Shek Pik, Lung Tsai Ng Garden and Tai O, No 2 to Shek Pik and Ngong Ping, No 3M to Tung Chung, No 4 to Pui O, Cheung Sha and Tong Fuk, No 7P (Sat afternoon and Sun) to Pui O, No A35 and N35 to airport; from Tai O (Map p419) for No 11 and No 21 to Lung Tsai Ng Garden and Ngong Ping; from Tung Chung MTR station (Map p419) for No 3M to Mui Wo, No 11 to Tai O, No 23 to Ngong Ping

MTR Tung Chung station (Map p419)

Airport Airport station (Map p419) at Chek Lap Kok

MUI WO Map p421

Mui Wo (Plum Nest), Lantau's main settlement 'capital', is on Silvermine Bay, so named for the silver mines that were once worked to the northwest along the Silver River. In fact, many foreign residents refer to Mui Wo as Silvermine Bay.

About a third of Lantau's population lives in the township of Mui Wo and its surrounding hamlets. There are several decent places to stay here and though the options for eating and drinking are few, they are acceptable.

Silvermine Bay Beach, to the northwest of Mui Wo, has been cleaned up and rebuilt in recent years and is now an attractive place, with scenic views and opportunities for walking in the hills above. There's a complex with toilets, showers and changing rooms open from April to October.

If you have the time, consider hiking out to **Silvermine Waterfall**, the main feature of a picturesque garden near the old **Silvermine Cave** northwest of the town and the beach. The waterfall is quite a spectacle during the rainy season, when it swells and gushes; the cave was mined for silver in the latter half of the 19th century but has now been sealed off.

En route to the waterfall you'll pass the local **Man Mo Temple**, originally built during the reign of Emperor Shen Zong (1573–1620) of the Ming dynasty and renovated a couple of times in the last century.

You can reach the temple, cave and waterfall by walking west along Mui Wo Rural Committee Rd and then following the marked path north. The 3km walk should take about an hour.

There are several old granite watchtowers in the area, including **Luk Tei Tong Watchtower** on the Silver River and **Butterfly Hill Watchtower** further north. They were built in the late 19th century as safe houses and as coastal defences against pirates.

TRAPPIST MONASTERY Map p419
☎ 2914 2933; Tai Shui Hang

Northeast of Mui Wo and south of Discovery Bay is the Trappist Monastery – or Lady of Joy Abbey, to be more precise – at Tai Shui Hang. The monastery is known throughout Hong Kong for its cream-rich milk, sold in half-pint bottles everywhere, but, alas, the cows have been moved to the New Territories and Trappist Dairy Milk now comes from over the border in China.

The Trappists, a branch of the Cistercian order, were founded by a converted courtier at La Trappe in France in 1662 and gained a reputation as being one of the most austere religious communities in the Roman Catholic Church. The Lantau congregation was established at Beijing in the 19th century. All of the monks here now are local Chinese.

Trappist monks take a vow of absolute silence, and there are signs reminding visitors to keep radios and music players turned off and to speak in low tones.

You can reach the monastery on foot by following a well-marked coastal trail from the northern end of Tung Wan Tau Rd in Mui Wo, but it's much easier to get here by *kaido* from Peng Chau, Lantau's little island neighbour to the west. For details see Outlying Island Ferries (p341).

DISCOVERY BAY Map p419
Lying on the northeastern coast of Lantau, what locals have dubbed Disco Bay (or just 'DB') is very much a world of its own, a bedroom community for professionals who commute to Central. Discovery Bay (Yue Ging Wan in Cantonese) has a fine stretch of sandy beach ringed by high-rises and more luxurious condominiums clinging to the headland to the north – but there is no pressing need to visit except to ogle at residents in their converted golf carts that cost HK$200,000 each. There is a handful of decent restaurants in **Discovery Bay Plaza** just up from the ferry pier and the central plaza and 27-hole **Discovery Bay Golf Club** (☎ 2987 7273) perched in the hills to the southwest.

Hong Kong Disneyland, a theme park scheduled to open in 2006, is under construction at Penny's Bay northeast of Discovery Bay. Some five million visitors a year are expected to visit the 126-hectare park's four lands: Fantasyland, Adventureland, Tomorrowland and Main Street, USA.

Until recently Discovery Bay existed in splendid isolation, linked only to the outside by ferries from Central, Lantau and Peng Chau and all but inaccessible from the rest of Lantau even on foot. Now buses make the run to and from Tung Chung and the airport at Chek Lap Kok via the **Discovery Bay Tunnel** and the North Lantau Hwy. A trail leading from the golf course will take you down to Silvermine Bay and the rest of Lantau in a couple of hours.

CHI MA WAN Map p419
Chi Ma Wan, the large peninsula due south of Mui Wo that can be reached via the inter-island ferry from Mui Wo and Cheung Chau, is a relatively remote part of Lantau and an excellent area for hiking; just be sure to get a map (see p364) as the trails are not always clearly defined or marked.

The Chi Ma Wan ferry pier is on the northeast coast; the large complex just south of the pier is not a hostel but the **Chi Ma Wan Correctional Institution**. There's a decent beach to the south at **Tai Long Wan** and fringing the next bay to the southwest – Yi Long Wan – is **Sea Ranch** (☎ 2989 1788/9), a residential area accessible by ferry from Central to residents and invited guests only. You can stay at the HKYHA hostel at Mong Tung Wan on the peninsula's southwestern coast; see Lantau (p289) for details.

SOUTH LANTAU ROAD Map p419

Just under 5km southwest of Mui Wo, **Pui O** is the first of several coastal villages along South Lantau Rd. Pui O has a decent beach, but as it's the closest one to Mui Wo it can get very crowded. The village has several restaurants, holiday flats galore and, in season, stalls renting bicycles.

Cheung Sha (Long Sand), at over 3km, Hong Kong's longest beach, is divided into 'upper' and 'lower' sections; a trail over a hillock links the two. **Upper Cheung Sha**, with occasional good surf, is the prettier and longer stretch and boasts a modern complex with changing rooms, toilets, showers and a snack bar. **Lower Cheung Sha** village has a fine little guesthouse and a beachfront restaurant (see Lantau p289 and p212).

The beach at **Tong Fuk**, the next village from Cheung Sha, is not as nice, but the village has holiday flats, several shops and a popular roadside barbecue restaurant (see Lantau p212). To the northwest is the rather 'scenic' sprawl of Ma Po Ping Prison.

West of Tong Fuk, South Lantau Rd begins to climb the hills inland before crossing an enormous dam holding back the **Shek Pik Reservoir** (completed in 1963), which provides Lantau, Cheung Chau and parts of Hong Kong Island with drinking water. Just below the dam is the granddaddy of Lantau's trio of jails, **Shek Pik Prison**. Below the dam to the south but before the prison is another Bronze Age **rock carving** unusual in that it is so far from the coastline.

The trail along the water-catchment area just east of Shek Pik Reservoir, with picnic tables and barbecue pits, offers some of the easiest and most peaceful walking on Lantau. From here you can also pick up the switchback trail to Dog's Tooth Peak (539m) from where another trail heads north to Lantau Peak.

NGONG PING Map p419

Perched 500m up in the western hills of Lantau is the Ngong Ping Plateau, a major drawcard for Hong Kong day-trippers and foreign visitors alike, especially since 1993, when one of the world's largest statues of Buddha was unveiled here. Ngong Ping is accessible by bus from Mui Wo, Tung Chung and Tai O. A taxi to/from the first two will cost HK$125, to/from Tai O about K$45.

Po Lin (Precious Lotus; 🕑 6am-6pm) is a large Buddhist monastery and temple complex

that was originally built in 1924. Today it is a fairground as much as a religious retreat, attracting many visitors. Most of the buildings you'll see on arrival are new, with the older, simpler ones tucked away behind them. A 5.7km cable car is being built between Ngong Ping and Tung Chung. It is expected to be completed in 2006.

The monastery is very photogenic. The Ngong Ping plateau, covered in mist in the early morning, and Lantau Peak to the southeast, create a sublime backdrop, and the rows and rows of huge, pollen-yellow incense sticks arrayed in front of the temple fill the air with the scent of sandalwood.

On a hill above the monastery is the **Tian Tan Buddha statue** (🕑 10am-5.30pm), a seated representation of Lord Gautama some 26.4m high (or just under 34m if you include the podium). There are bigger Buddha statues elsewhere – notably the 71m-high Grand Buddha in Leshan in China – but apparently these are not seated, outdoors or made of bronze. The large bell within the Buddha is controlled by computer and rings 108 times during the day to symbolise escape from what Buddhism terms the '108 troubles of mankind'.

The podium is composed of separate chambers on three different levels. In the first level are six statues of Bodhisattvas (Buddhist 'saints'), each of which weighs around two tonnes. On the second level is a small **museum** (☎ 2985 5248; admission HK$28 without meal ticket; 🕑 10am-5.30pm) containing oil paintings and ceramic plaques of the Buddha's life and teachings. Entry is free if you eat at the monastery's vegetarian restaurant (see Lantau p214).

It's well worth climbing the 260 steps for a closer look at the statue and surrounding views. The Buddha's Birthday, a public holiday celebrated in late April or May, is a lively time to visit, when thousands make the pilgrimage. Try to avoid coming here on Sunday or public holidays, when the entire complex is awash with families with radios blaring. Visitors are requested to observe some decorum in dress and behaviour. It is forbidden to bring meat or alcohol into the grounds.

A 2.5km concrete footpath to the left of the Buddha statue leads to the **Lantau Tea Garden**, the only one in Hong Kong. The tea bushes are pretty sparse and not worth a detour, but the garden is on the way to the SG Davis Hostel (p289) and Lantau Peak.

LANTAU PEAK Map p419

Known as Fung Wong Shan (Phoenix Mountain) in Cantonese, this 934m-high peak is the second-highest in Hong Kong, after Tai Mo Shan (957m) in the New Territories.

The views from the summit are absolutely stunning; on a clear day it is possible to see Macau, and Zhuhai, some 65km to the west.

If you're hiking the length or the first several stages of the **Lantau Trail** (see p165) to Ngong Ping, you'll cross the peak. If you want to just climb up from Ngong Ping, the easiest and most comfortable way to make the climb is to spend the night at the SG Davis Hostel, get up at the crack of dawn and pick up the signposted trail at the hostel that runs southeast to the peak. Many climbers get up earlier to reach the summit for sunrise; take a torch and wear an extra layer of clothes, as it can get pretty chilly at the top in the early hours.

Another signposted trail leading east from the hostel will take you along the northern slopes of Lantau Peak to **Po Lam Monastery** at Tei Tong Tsai and then south through a valley leading to Tung Chung, from where you can catch the MTR back to Kowloon or Hong Kong or the No 3M bus to Mui Wo. This charming walk – if you ignore the airport to the north – also takes you past **Lo Hon Monastery**, which has a canteen serving vegetarian food, as well as **Tung Chung Fort** and **Tung Chung Battery** (see p150 for details).

LUNG TSAI NG GARDEN Map p419

This magical garden southwest of Ngong Ping, with a lotus pond crossed by a **zigzag bridge**, was built by a wealthy merchant in the 1930s in a small valley near where the village of Lung Tsai once stood. The site is rather derelict, but atmospheric nonetheless. You can reach here via a trail from the Tai O Rd, a continuation of South Lantau Rd just west of Keung Shan on bus No 1 from Mui Wo to Tai O or bus No 21 from Ngong Ping to Tai O; alight when you see the sign for the country park management centre.

TAI O Map p419

A century ago this village on the west coast of Lantau was an important trading and fishing port, exporting salt and fish to China. As recently as the 1980s it traded in IIs (illegal immigrants) brought from China under cover of darkness by 'snakeheads' (smugglers of illegal immigrants) in long narrow boats, sending back contraband such as refrigerators, radios and televisions.

Today Tai O is in decline, except perhaps as a tourist destination. A few of the saltpans still exist, but most have been filled in to build high-rise housing. Older people still make their living from duck farming, fishing, making the village's celebrated shrimp paste and processing salt fish, which you'll see (and smell) everywhere. It remains a popular place for locals to buy seafood – both fresh and dried.

Tai O is built partly on Lantau and partly on a tiny island about 15m from the shore. Until the mid-1990s the only way to cross was via a **rope-tow ferry** pulled by elderly Hakka women. That and the large number of sampans in the small harbour earned Tai O the nickname 'the Venice of Hong Kong'. Though a narrow iron bridge now spans the canal, the rope-tow ferry has been resurrected; drop HK$1 in the box as you disembark. There are also brief **river boat tours** departing from the ferry pier on Wing On St for HK$10.

Some of the traditional-style village houses still stand in the centre. A fire in 2000 destroyed many of Tai O's famed **stilt houses** on the waterfront, but when the government tried to raze the rest and relocate residents elsewhere, the move was strongly opposed. The few houses that escaped the fire remain. There are also a number of shanties, their corrugated iron walls held in place by rope, and houseboats that haven't set sail for years – they'd capsize immediately if they tried.

The stilt houses and the local **temple** dedicated to Kwan Tai, the god of war, are on Kat Hing St. To reach them, cross the bridge from the mainland to the island, walk up Tai O Market St and go right at the Fook Lam Moon restaurant. There are a couple of other temples here, including one erected in honour of Hung Shing, patron of fisherfolk; it's on Shek Tsai Po St, about 600m west of the Fook Lam Moon restaurant.

FAN LAU Map p419

Fan Lau (Divided Flow), a small peninsula on the southwestern tip of Lantau, has a couple of good beaches and the remains of **Fan Lau Fort**, built in 1729 to protect the channel between Lantau and the Pearl River estuary from pirates. It remained in operation until the end of the 19th century and was restored in 1985. The sea views from here are sterling.

To the southeast of the fort is an ancient **stone circle**. The origins and age of the circle are uncertain, but it probably dates from the Neolithic or early Bronze Age and may have been used in rituals.

The only way to reach Fan Lau is on foot. To get here from Tai O, walk south from the bus station for 250m and pick up stage No 7 of the coastal **Lantau Trail**, a distance of about 8km. The trail then carries on to the northeast and Shek Pik for another 12km, where you can catch the No 1 bus back to Mui Wo. Off the coast from Fan Lau you may manage to flag down a passing sampan that will take you back to Tai O for about HK$300.

TUNG CHUNG Map p419

In recent years change has come to Tung Chung on Lantau's northern coast at a pace that can only happen in Hong Kong. This previously all-but-inaccessible farming region, with the small village of Tung Chung at its centre, has seen Chek Lap Kok, the mountain across Tung Chung Bay, flattened to build Hong Kong's international airport and a New Town served by the MTR rise up.

As part of the territory's plans to solve the housing crisis, Tung Chung New Town has now become a huge, residential estate. The targeted population of Tung Chung and the neighbouring New Town of Tai Ho is an astonishing 320,000.

These developments and transportation improvements have spelled the end of Tung Chung as a peaceful and secluded spot. But efforts have been made to protect **Tung Chung Old Village**. Buildings may rise no higher than three storeys and each floor can be no larger than 70 sq metres.

Annals record a settlement at Tung Chung as early as the Ming dynasty. There are several Buddhist establishments in the upper reaches of the valley, but the main attraction here is **Tung Chung Fort** (Tung Chung Rd; admission free; ☯ 10am-5pm Wed-Mon), which dates back to 1832 when Chinese troops were garrisoned on Lantau. The Japanese briefly occupied the fort during WWII. Measuring 70m by 80m and enclosed by granite-block walls, it retains six of its muzzle-loading cannons pointing out to sea.

About 1km to the north are the ruins of **Tung Chung Battery**, which is a much smaller fort built in 1817. All that remains is an L-shaped wall facing the sea, with a gun emplacement in the corner. The ruins were only discovered in 1980, having been hidden for about a century by scrub.

Facing Tung Chung Bay to the southwest in the village of Sha Tsui Tau is double-roofed **Hau Wong Temple**, founded at the end of the Song dynasty. The temple contains a bell dating from 1765 and inscribed by the Qing dynasty emperor, Qian Long.

Districts & Islands – Outlying Islands

Seeing Pink Dolphins

Up to 165 partly misnamed Chinese white dolphins *(Sousa chinensis)* – they are actually bubble-gum pink – inhabit the coastal waters around Hong Kong, finding the brackish waters of the Pearl River estuary to be the perfect habitat. Unfortunately these glorious, ever-smiling mammals, which are also called Indo-Pacific humpback dolphins, are being threatened by environmental pollution, and their numbers are dwindling.

The threat comes in many forms, but the most prevalent – and direct – dangers are sewage, chemicals, over-fishing and boat traffic. Some 200,000 cu metres of untreated sewage are dumped into the western harbour every day, and high concentrations of chemicals such as DDT have been found in tissue samples taken from some of the dolphins. Several dead dolphins have been entangled in fishing nets and, despite the dolphins' skill at sensing and avoiding surface vessels, some have collided with boats.

The dolphins' habitat has also been diminished by the erosion of the natural coastline of Lantau Island during the construction of the new airport, which required land reclamation of 9.5 sq km of seabed and the destruction of many kilometres of natural coastline. The North Lantau Hwy also consumed about 10km of the natural coastline.

Hong Kong Dolphinwatch (☎ 2984 1414; www.whaleguide.com/directory/hongkongdolphinwatch.htm; 1528A Star House, 3 Salisbury Rd, Tsim Sha Tsui), was founded in 1995 to raise awareness of these wonderful creatures and promote responsible ecotourism. It offers 2½-hour cruises (adult/child under 12 HK$320/160) to see the pink dolphins in their natural habitat every Wednesday, Friday and Sunday from January to April, and Tuesday, Wednesday and Friday to Sunday from May to December. Touts assemble in the lobbies of the Mandarin Oriental Hotel in Central at 8.30am and the Kowloon Hotel in Tsim Sha Tsui at 9am for the bus to Tung Chung via the Tsing Ma Bridge, from where the boat departs; the tours return at 1pm or 1.30pm. About 96% of the cruises result in the sighting of at least one dolphin; if none is spotted, passengers are offered a free trip.

PENG CHAU

Eating p214

Tiny **Peng Chau** (Map p421) is fairly flat and not especially beautiful, but it has its own charms. It is perhaps the most traditionally Chinese of the Outlying Islands, with narrow alleyways, crowded housing, a good covered wet market near the ferry pier, a couple of small but interesting temples, interesting shops selling everything from Thai goods to New Age products and everywhere the sound of mahjong tiles being slapped on tables. There are also a few closet-sized restaurants whose sea views have unfortunately been stolen by a new (and massive) concrete 'wave reflector' and promenade running along the shore south of the ferry pier.

Until recently the island's economy was supported by fishing and some cottage industries, notably the manufacture of porcelain, furniture, porcelain and metal tubing. These manufacturing industries are now all but dead, having moved to mainland China, though you will find a couple of porcelain shops on Wing Hing St and Wing On St, including the most famous one, **Chiu Kee Porcelain** (☎ 2983 0917; Shop 7, Ground fl, Wing Hing St; ☯ 9.30am-6.30pm). There's an **HSBC branch** (☎ 2983 0383) at 1 Wing Hing St. The **post office** is due west near the start of the promenade.

Orientation

Looking not unlike a plumped-out horse-shoe jettisoned from Lantau's northeast coast, Peng Chau is just under a square kilometre in area. It is inhabited by around 7000 people, making it far more densely populated than its larger neighbour.

Transport

Ferry From Peng Chau pier (Map p421) to pier 6 of Outlying Islands ferry terminal in Central, to the Trappist Monastery and Discovery Bay in northeast Lantau

SIGHTS & ACTIVITIES

There are no cars on Peng Chau, and you can walk around it easily in an hour. Climbing the steps up to **Finger Hill** (95m), the island's highest point and topped with the winged Chinese-style **Fung Ping Pavilion**, offers some

Dolphin statue near Ocean Terminal (p102)

light exercise and excellent views. To get to it from the ferry pier, walk up Lo Peng St, turn right at the **Tin Hau temple**, containing a century-old whale bone blackened by incense smoke, and walk south along Wing On St. This gives way to Shing Ka Rd, and Nam Shan Rd leads from here east up to Finger Hill. The water at otherwise-pleasant **Tung Wan Beach**, a five-minute walk from the ferry pier, is too dirty for swimming.

PO TOI

Eating p215

Po Toi (Map pp396–7) is a favourite of weekend holiday-makers with their own seagoing transport. They frequent the handful of seafood restaurants beyond the jetty at **Tai Wan**, the main settlement, in the island's southwest.

Orientation

Po Toi is the largest of a group of four or five islands – one is little more than a huge rock – off the southeastern coast of Hong Kong Island. Hong Kong's territorial border lies just 2km to the south.

Transport

Ferry From Po Toi ferry pier to Aberdeen and Stanley

SIGHTS & ACTIVITIES

There's some decent walking on Po Toi, a tiny **Tin Hau temple** across the bay from the pier, and, on the southern coast, some mysterious **rock carvings** resembling stylised animals and fish. You could see everything in an hour.

Walking Tours

Walking Tours

Although much of Hong Kong is best seen on foot, walking around isn't always easy or relaxing, especially in the business districts. Watch your step and persevere though, and you will be rewarded with a world of unique sights, sounds and smells.

Rural Hong Kong is a whole different matter, with the New Territories, the Outlying Islands and even Hong Kong Island itself offering some easy but outstanding walks and more arduous hikes.

The HKTB's *Hong Kong Walks* booklet has a sampling of eight strolls and hikes in the territory, with three on Hong Kong Island, one each in Kowloon and the New Territories and three on the Outlying Islands (Cheung Chau, Lamma and Lantau).

HONG KONG ISLAND

Hong Kong Island offers walkers two contrasting worlds: the glittering skyscrapers and colonial relics of Central and the traditional Chinese neighbourhoods of Sheung Wan. If you're looking for views, try the 3.5km circuit around Victoria Peak (p89).

CENTRAL

Begin the walk at the **Star Ferry pier** 1 in Central. With your back to the 2nd-class ferry entrance, Hong Kong's last few **rickshaws** 2 in front of you and **Hong Kong City Hall** 3 (p80) to your left, follow the underground walkway to Chater Rd and **Statue Square** 4 (p80). Follow Chater Rd east, with the **Legislative Council Building** 5 (p82) on your right and the **Cenotaph** 6 on your left, to **Chater Garden** 7. Walk through the park and cross over Garden Rd to the **Bank of China Tower** 8 (p81). Head east along Queen's Rd Central, go under the Cotton Tree Dr flyover and follow the path to the **Flagstaff House Museum of Tea Ware** 9 in **Hong Kong Park** 10 (p90).

Pedestrian crossing, Central

From here elevated walkways west over Cotton Tree Dr, through Citybank Tower, over Garden Rd and through **Cheung Kong Garden 11** bring you to **St John's Cathedral 12** (p83). Follow Battery Path past the **Former French Mission Building 13** (p83) to Ice House St. Cross over Queen's Rd Central and walk east. If you're hungry, **Mix 14** (p177), in the shopping mall of the Standard Chartered Bank building, is a good spot for sandwiches, salads and juices. Next door is the **Hongkong and Shanghai Bank building 15** (p81). Walk through the ground floor plaza to the two **bronze lions 16** guarding the Des Voeux Rd Central entrance. The closest Central MTR station entrance is a short distance due north, along the pedestrian walkway between Statue Square and Prince's Building.

Walk Facts

distance 2km
duration 1 hour
start Star Ferry terminal, Central
end Central MTR Station (entrance/exit K)

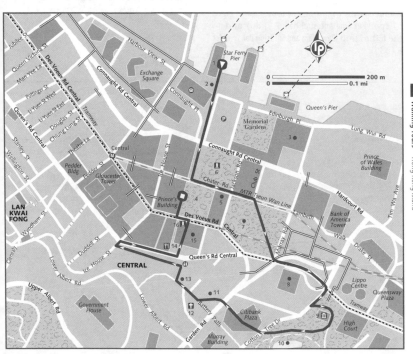

Walking Tours – Hong Kong Island

Central Escalator

One of Hong Kong's long-standing problems has been that while many middle-class residents live in the Mid-Levels, the lower portion of the Peak, they work in the skyscraper jungle down in Central. The roads are narrow and the distance is more vertical than horizontal, making the walk home a strenuous climb, especially in the humid summer months. The result has been a rush-hour nightmare of bumper-to-bumper taxis, minibuses and private cars.

Then someone came up with what is officially called the Central–Mid-Levels Escalator and Walkway System (☎ 2523 7488 for information) but known simply as the 'Central Escalator' – one of Hong Kong's more unusual forms of transport. Basically, it consists of three moving walkways and 20 elevated escalators that can be reversed; they run down in the morning from 6am to 10am and up from 10.20am till midnight every day. It's 800m long and runs from the Central Market on Des Voeux Rd, along Cochrane and Shelley Sts in Soho and up to Conduit Rd in the Mid-Levels. It is the longest escalator in the world and the complete trip takes 20 minutes.

SHEUNG WAN

Begin the tour at the Sutherland St stop of the Kennedy Town tram. Have a look at (and sniff of) Des Voeux Rd West's dried seafood and shrimp paste **shops 1** then turn left up Ko Shing St, where there are **herbal medicine wholesalers 2**. At the end of the street, walk northeast along Des Voeux Rd West and turn right onto Connaught Rd West where you'll find **Western Market 3** (p85) at the corner of Morrison St. Walk south along this street past Bonham Strand, which is lined with **ginseng root sellers 4**, and turn right on Queen's Rd West. To the right you'll pass **shops 5** selling bird's nests (for soup) and paper funeral offerings for the dead.

Cross Queen's Rd and turn left into **Possession St 6**. Climbing Pound Lane to where it meets Tai Ping Shan St, look to the right to spot **Pak Sing Ancestral Hall 7** (p86) and to the left to find **Kwun Yam and Sui Tsing Pak temples 8** (p86).

<aside>
Walk Facts

distance 1.9km
duration 1 hour
start Kennedy Town tram (Sutherland St stop)
end Sheung Wan MTR station (entrance/exit A1)
</aside>

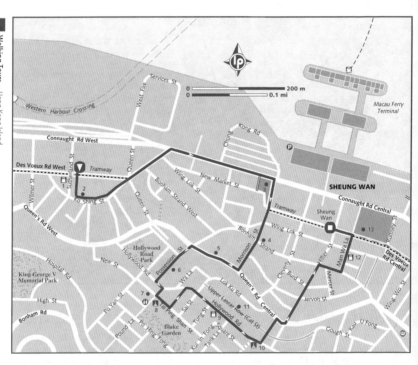

Descend Upper Station St to the start of Hollywood Rd's **antique shops 9**. Continuing east on Hollywood Rd brings you to **Man Mo Temple 10** (p85). Take a short hop down Ladder St to Upper Lascar Row, home of the **Cat St market 11**. Ladder St brings you to Queen's Rd Central. Cross the road and follow Hillier St to Bonham Strand. On Bonham Strand, head east to **Man Wa Lane 12** (p85) where you'll find traditional chops (seals) carved. Due north is Des Voeux Rd Central, where you might have some soup noodles at the **Korea Garden 13** (p181). The Sheung Wan MTR station is next door.

KOWLOON

Like Hong Kong Island, Kowloon allows urban walkers to explore two dissimilar areas: the tumultuous and highly touristed Tsim Sha Tsui and the more workaday but colourful neighbourhoods of Mong Kok and Yau Ma Tei.

TSIM SHA TSUI

Start at the **Star Ferry pier 1** in Tsim Sha Tsui. With your back to the harbour, walk east along Salisbury Rd, passing the **Former KCR Clock Tower 2** (p102), **Hong Kong Cultural Centre 3** (p102), the **Hong**

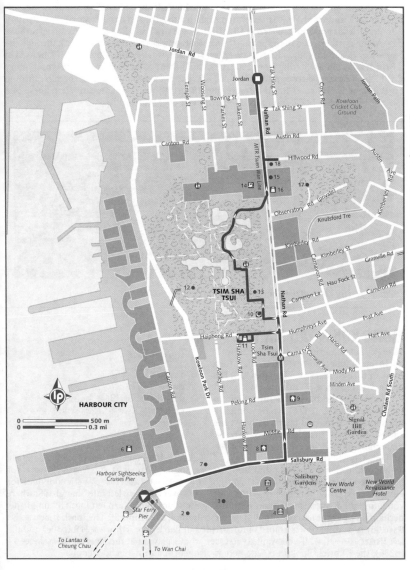

Kong Space Museum 4 (p103) and the Hong Kong Museum of Art 5 (p103) on your right; on the left, you'll walk by the entrance to the Ocean Terminal shopping mall 6 (p102), the former Marine Police Headquarters 7, built in 1884, and the venerable Peninsula Hotel 8 (p103). Turn left on Nathan Rd and continue walking north on the left-hand (west) side of the street; just opposite Peking Rd and on the other side of

Walk Facts

distance 1.6km
duration 1 hour
start Star Ferry pier, Kowloon
end Jordan MTR station (entrance/exit D)

the street are the infamous Chungking Mansions 9 (p280), a rabbit warren of hostels and guesthouses. On the corner of Haiphong Rd is the Kowloon Mosque and Islamic Centre 10 (p104), but first take a detour and have a look at what's for sale on 'Curio Alley' 11 (p253), a narrow passage linking Lock and Hankow Rds. After that, walk northward and enter Kowloon Park 12 (p104). A footpath leads north to Sculpture Walk 13 (p104), where you'll also find Kung Fu Corner on Sunday. At the northern end of the park is the Kowloon Park Swimming Complex 14 (p104); through the banyan trees 15 across Nathan Rd is the Hong Kong Antiquities and Monuments Office 16 (p37), housed in a British schoolhouse dating from 1902. On a hill behind it (and accessible via Observatory Rd) is the Hong Kong Observatory 17 (p104), which is not open to the public. The next turning on the right is Hillwood Rd; the Peace Garden 18 (p199) does some mean Vietnamese *pho* (soup). The Jordan MTR station is due north, just over Austin Rd.

Waiting on the steps of the Hong Kong Cultural Centre (p102)

MONG KOK & YAU MA TEI

Take exit A from Prince Edward MTR, walk north up Nathan Rd for 200m, then turn right onto Boundary St. The Yuen Po St Bird Garden 1 (p116) is a 10-minute walk away. Continue out the back and turn right to the Flower Market 2 (p116) where some 50 florists sell blooms and plants daily. At the end of the street, turn left onto Sai Yee St, then right onto Prince Edward Rd West.

Walk Facts

distance 4.5km
duration 2 hours
start Prince Edward MTR station (entrance/exit A)
end Jordan MTR station (entrance/exit A)

At Tung Choi St turn left: the first couple of blocks are dominated by shops 3 selling goldfish, an important element in feng shui, and bicycles. South of Argyle St, the Tung Choi St market (or Ladies' Market) 4 (p250) takes over. Turn right at Dundas St; Trendy Zone 5, with cool duds for guys and gals, is on the corner of Nathan Rd. Cross over and turn left into Shanghai St where you'll find the Shanghai Street Artspace 6 (p115). Some 400m south, turn left into Hi Lung Lane, perhaps stopping at Hing Kee 7 (p204) for a rice hotpot, to Temple St. The Temple St night market 8 (p106) runs right down to Jordan Rd, divided in two by the Tin Hau temple 9 (p106) and the Jade Market 10 (p106). If you want to rest, see what's playing at the Broadway Cinematheque 11 (p236); the Kubrick Bookshop Cafe here is also worth a browse and a cuppa.

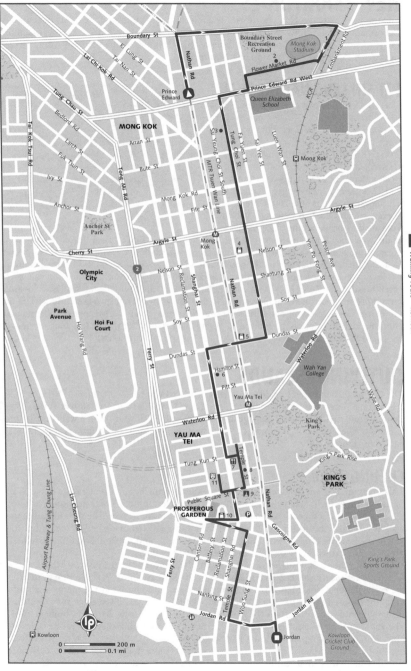

NEW TERRITORIES

For the most part the New Territories is about hiking – be it all or sections of the Mac-Lehose and Wilson trails (p164). But there are also easy nature trails to follow, including the tracks of the Tai Po Kau Nature Reserve (p131), the Ping Shan Heritage Trail (p125) near Yuen Long and the Pat Sin Leng Nature Trail.

PAT SIN LENG NATURE TRAIL

This excellent (and easy) trail (Map pp396–7) leads from the Plover Cove Country Park Visitor Centre at Tai Mei Tuk, accessible from Tai Po Market KCR station via bus No 74K (HK$4.70) or green minibus No 20K (HK$6), and heads northeast for 4km to Bride's Pool; there are signboards numbered 1 to 22 so there is little danger of getting lost. The elevation gain is only 300m, the scenery is excellent and the two waterfalls at Bride's Pool are delightful, but the place gets packed at the weekend. You can either return to Tai Mei Tuk via Bride's Pool Rd on foot or catch green minibus 20C (HK$6), which stops at Tai Mei Tuk before carrying on to Tai Po Market KCR station. On Sunday and public holidays, bus No 275R (HK$8.60) links Bride's Pool with Tai Po. If you carry on north from Bride's Pool to Luk Keng on Starling Inlet, you can catch green minibus No 56K (HK$7), which will take you to Fanling KCR station. Those looking for a more strenuous hike can join stage No 9 of the Wilson Trail (p164) at Tai Mei Tuk on the Plover Cove Reservoir and head west into the steep Pat Sin Leng range of hills (named after the 'Eight Immortals' of Taoism) to Wong Leng Shan (639m). The trail then carries on westward to Hok Tau Reservoir and Hok Tau Wai (12km, four hours).

> ### Walk Facts
>
> **distance** 4km
> **duration** 2–2½ hours
> **start** Plover Cove Country Park Visitor Centre, Tai Mei Tuk (bus No 74K, green minibus No 20K from Tai Po Market KCR station)
> **end** Bride's Pool (green minibus 20C, bus No 275R on Sun & holidays to Tai Po Market KCR station)

OUTLYING ISLANDS

The Outlying Islands were made for walking. The best way to 'do' Lamma (p140) is to walk from Yung Shue Wan ferry pier to the one at Sok Kwu Wan and Lantau boasts the 70km Lantau Trail, divided into 12 manageable sections (p165). To our mind a walk on Cheung Chau is the best choice as it combines scenic beauty with interesting glimpses at traditional southern Chinese culture.

CHEUNG CHAU

This pleasant and not particularly strenuous walk from Cheung Chau village to Sai Wan in the southwest will take you past flotillas of junks, restaurants, noisy mahjong parlours, temples, sacred trees, beaches and some wonderful vistas of the sea. The second half of the walk is especially beautiful and best undertaken in good weather towards the end of the day in the warmer months when the temperature drops and the light conditions are best. To avoid the crowds, stay away at the weekend if possible.

From the Cheung Chau ferry pier 1 turn left and head north along Praya St, where a row of mostly seafood restaurants 2 face the harbour. Praya St becomes Pak She Praya Rd after the turn-off for Kwok Man Rd, and from here you can look out at the many junks and sampans moored in the harbour. At Pak She Fourth Lane you'll see some playing fields; turn right and immediately to the east is colourful Pak Tai Temple 3 (p143), built in 1783. The Pak She Tin Hau Temple 4 is behind to the northwest. Leaving the Pak Tai Temple behind you and heading south down Pak She St, you'll pass a traditional Chinese house 5 with two stone lions on guard outside, several traditional Chinese medicine shops 6 and a bakery at No 46, which sells small Chinese cakes and buns. Further south, and on the left at the intersection of Pak She St and Kwok Man Rd, is a small Tou Tei shrine 7, dedicated to the overworked earth god. San Hing St, which leads off Pak She St after it crosses Kwok Man Rd, has **herbalist shops 8** and the shops at No 30 and No 50 sell incense and paper hell money to be burned in memory of the dead. As you turn east from San Hing St and enter Tung Wan Rd, you'll see a **sacred banyan tree 9** on the right, which is believed to be inhabited by earth spirits. Tung Wan Rd leads up to **Hometown Teahouse 10** (p212),

Walk Facts

distance 4.5km
duration 2½ hours
start Cheung Chau ferry pier (ferry from pier 5 in Central)
end Sai Wan (*kaido* to Cheung Chau ferry pier)

where you might stop for a cuppa and a snack, and Tung Wan Beach. Turn right and walk along Cheung Chau Beach Rd to the 3000-year-old **rock carving 11** of two identical geometric designs, just below the Warwick Hotel. Behind the Warwick Hotel is steep Cheung Chau Sports Rd; begin the climb and when you see a pavilion ahead, turn right onto Kwun Yam Wan Rd and past the sports ground below and on your left. A few minutes ahead and on the left is the **Kwan Kung Pavilion 12**, a temple built in 1973 and dedicated to Kwan Tai, the god of war and righteousness and a symbol of power and loyalty. As you walk down from the temple, turn left onto Peak Rd, passing the **Cheung Chau Meteorological Station 13**, which offers splendid views of the island and sea to the south. Further on is Chung

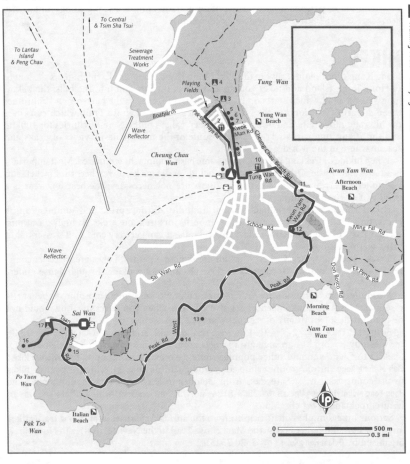

Walking Tours – Outlying Islands

161

Lok Garden and the **Yee Pavilion 14**, which is dedicated to the Chinese poet Zhang Renshi. A bit further south and through the trees to the left is Cheung Chau Cemetery, affording a quiet and solemn view out to sea. Soon you'll come to a forked road: the path to the left (signposted) leads to Italian Beach, the one to the right carries on to Sai Wan. If you take the latter, you'll soon walk through Lui Kwan Po, also known as **CARE Village 15**, a small settlement that was set up in 1968 with money from a North American charity. Further on is another sign-posted fork in the road where you can either turn left for **Cheung Po Tsai Cave 16** (p144) and the **Sai Wan Tin Hau Temple 17** or right for the *kaido* (adult/child HK$3/2) back to Cheung Chau village. Alternatively, follow Sai Wan Rd around the bay and north back to the village (20 to 30 minutes).

GUIDED WALKS

The HKTB has recorded walking tours highlighting the architecture and cultural heritage of Central on Hong Kong Island, Tsim Sha Tsui and Hung Hom in Kowloon and Tai Po and environs in the New Territories. The tours last about four hours and can be borrowed for free from HKTB visitor centres in Central (for the Hong Kong tour) and Kowloon (for the Kowloon and New Territories tours) between 8am and 1pm daily. A HK$500 deposit is required for the audio system and headset, which must be returned by 5pm the same day. For tailor-made, personal walking tours of both urban and rural Hong Kong, contact **Walk Hong Kong** (☎ 9187 8641; www.walkhongkong.com).

HIKES

Hong Kong's four main trails are the 50km-long Hong Kong Trail, which spans the length of Hong Kong Island and takes you up and out of the city and into the hills; the 78km-long Wilson Trail, which starts on Hong Kong Island, crosses the harbour and continues through part of Kowloon to the New Territories; the MacLehose Trail, which runs over the hills and mountains and down into the deep valleys of the New Territories for 100km; and the 70km-long Lantau Trail takes in some of the most majestic views of peaks and sea anywhere in the world.

When hiking or trekking in Hong Kong some basic equipment is required. Most important is a full water bottle. Other useful items include trail snacks, a weatherproof jacket, sun hat, toilet paper, maps and a compass. Boots are not necessary; the best footwear is a good pair of running shoes.

Hikers should remember that the high humidity during spring and summer can be enervating. October to March are the best months for strenuous treks. At high elevations, such as parts of the Lantau and MacLehose Trails, it can get very cold so it's essential to bring warm clothing.

Track conditions vary widely – not all are concrete paths. Snakes are rarely encountered but can be avoided by keeping to the trails and not walking through dense undergrowth.

Mosquitoes are a nuisance in spring and summer, so a good mosquito repellent is essential. Mosquito coils (incense) are also effective when you're resting, but should not be used inside a tent or any other enclosed area.

Both the **YMCA** (☎ 2771 9111; www.ymca.org.hk) and the **YWCA** (☎ 3476 1340; www.esmdywca.org.hk) arrange group hikes around such areas as Silvermine to Pui O, Shek O to Chai Wan and other popular routes. An excellent group is the **Saturday Hikers Club of Hong Kong** (http://groups.yahoo.com/group/saturdayhikers), which organises hikes in the countryside most Saturdays from October to May. Climbers should contact the **Hong Kong Mountaineering Union** (☎ 2504 8124; www.hkmu.org.hk), which offers courses in leisure, rock and sport climbing.

Serious hikers might consider joining in the annual **Trailwalker event** (www.trailwalker .org.hk), a gruelling race across the MacLehose Trail in the New Territories in November, organised by **Oxfam Hong Kong** (☎ 2520 2525).

MAPS

Good hiking maps will save you a lot of time, energy and trouble. The Map Publication Centres stocks the excellent Countryside Series of topographical maps (see p365) as well as the hiking maps produced by the Country & Marine Parks Authority for each of the four main trails (HK$30): the 1:15,000 *Hong Kong Trail*; the 1:35,000 *Wilson Trail*; the 1:25,000 *MacLehose Trail*; and the 1:20,000 *Lantau Trail*. The four trail maps are also available from the Government Publications Office (see p254) in Admiralty. For walking and nature guides, see p355.

ACCOMMODATION

The **Country & Marine Parks Authority** (☎ 2420 0529; http://parks.afcd.gov.hk) maintains 28 no-frills camp sites in the New Territories and 11 in Outlying Islands for hikers and trekkers. They are all free and are clearly labelled on the Countryside Series and four trail maps. Camping is prohibited on the 36 public beaches patrolled by lifeguards, but is generally OK on remote beaches.

You can camp at the hostels managed by the Hong Kong Youth Hostels Association (HKYHA; ☎ 2788 1638; www.yha.org.hk; info@yha.org.hk) with the exception of the Jockey Club Mount Davis hostel on Hong Kong Island and Bradbury Lodge at Tau Mei Tuk in the New Territories. The fee, which allows you to use the hostel's toilet and washroom facilities, is HK$16 for HKYHA or Hostelling International (HI) members, HK$25 for nonmembers. See the Sleeping chapter (p267) for details.

The availability of fuel is limited in camp sites so the most useful kind of stove is the type that uses disposable gas canisters, available at hardware and department stores throughout Hong Kong. A few hi-tech camp stoves can use diesel fuel, which is readily available. Kerosene is very difficult to find, as is 'white gas'. Local people use bags of charcoal for cooking during picnics and when camping.

Hiker, Hong Kong Trail (p164)

HONG KONG TRAIL

Starting from the Peak Tram upper ter-minus on the Peak, the 50km-long Hong Kong Trail (Map pp398–9) follows Lugard Rd to the west and drops down the hill to Pok Fu Lam Reservoir near Aberdeen, before turning east and zigzagging across the ridges. The trail traverses four country parks: Pok Fu Lam Country Park (2.7 sq km) south of Victoria Peak; 4.2-sq-km Aberdeen Country Park east of the Peak; 13-sq-km Tai Tam Country Park on the eastern side of the island; and Shek O Country Park, measuring just over 7 sq km, in the southeast. Tai Tam is the largest and most beautiful of the four, with its dense emerald woods and trickling streams. The Hong Kong Trail skirts the northern side of Tai Tam Reservoir, the largest body of water on the island.

It's possible to hike the entire trail – a total of eight stages from the Peak to Big Wave Bay – in one day (count on a full 15 hours), but it's quite a slog; most hikers pick a manageable section to suit, such as Section No 1 from the Peak to Pok Fu Lam Reservoir Rd (7km, two hours). There are no designated camp sites along the Hong Kong Trail.

Apart from gaining section No 1 of the trail on the Peak, you can reach section No 6 (Tai Tam) on bus Nos 6 or 61 from the Central bus terminal below Exchange Square and section No 7 (Tai Tam Bay and Shek O) on bus Nos 9 and 309 (Sunday only) from Shau Kei Wan MTR station.

WILSON TRAIL

This 78km-long Wilson Trail (Maps pp396-7 and pp398-9) – 82.5km if you include the MTR harbour crossing – is a bit unusual in that its southern section (two stages, 11.4km, 4½ hours) is on Hong Kong Island while its northern part (eight stages, 66.6km, 26½ hours) crosses on the eastern harbour to Lei Yue Mun in New Kowloon and carries on into the New Territories. The trail was named after Sir David Wilson, Hong Kong governor from 1987 to 1992.

The trail begins at Stanley Gap Rd, about 1km to the north of Stanley (Map pp398–9); bus Nos 6, 6A, 6X and 260 from Central pass the beginning of the trail about 2km short of Repulse Bay. The first steeply rising section of the trail is all concrete steps. You soon reach the summit of Stanley Mound (386m), topped by a pavilion. The summit is also known as the Twins (or Ma Kong Shan in Cantonese). On a clear day you'll have an excellent view of Stanley, Repulse Bay and as far as Lamma Island. The trail continues north over Violet Hill (Tsz Lo Lan Shan), where it intersects the Hong Kong Trail, and passes by Mt Butler, drops down into the urban chaos and terminates at the Quarry Bay MTR station. Those who wish to carry on should then take the MTR across to Yau Tong on the Tseung Kwan O line. Take the train across to Lam Tim and pick up the trail outside the station.

From the Yau Tong MTR station (Map pp396-7) the trail zigzags south to Lei Yue Mun before turning sharply north again into the hills. The trail then takes a westward turn, heading over the summit of Tate's Cairn, and passes Lion Rock and Beacon Hill. The path makes another sharp turn northward, continues through Shing Mun Country Park, returns to civilisation near Tai Po, then disappears into the hills again at Pat Sin Leng Country Park before ending at Nam Chung Reservoir on the Starling Inlet, not far from Shau Tau Kok and Hong Kong's border with Shenzhen and the mainland.

Parts of the Wilson Trail overlap with the Hong Kong Trail on Hong Kong Island and with the MacLehose Trail in the New Territories, particularly in the area east of Tai Mo Shan.

MACLEHOSE TRAIL

The 100km MacLehose Trail (Map pp396-7), the territory's longest hiking path, spans the New Territories from Tuen Mun in the west to Pak Tam Chung on the Sai Kung Peninsula in the east. The trail follows the ridge, goes over Tai Mo Shan, at 957m Hong Kong's highest peak, and passes close to Ma On Shan (702m), the territory's fourth tallest. The trail is divided into 10 stages, ranging in length from about 4.6km (1½ hours of walking) to 15.6km (five hours).

There are many areas from which you can access the MacLehose trail by public transport (see the list at the end of this section) but arguably the most convenient is reached by catching bus No 51 (HK$7.60) on Tai Ho Rd North, just north of the Tsuen Wan MTR station, and getting off where Route Twisk meets Tai Mo Shan Rd. This is the beginning (or the end) of stage No 9 of the trail. From there you have the choice of heading east towards Tai Mo Shan and Lead Mine Pass (9.7km, four hours) or west to the Tai Lam Chung Reservoir, through Tai Lam Country Park (54 sq km), and eventually all the way to Tuen Mun (22km, 7½ hours), the western end of the trail. From Tuen Mun town centre, you can catch bus No 260X (HK$8.20) or No 63X (HK$13) to Tsim Sha Tsui.

Another, perhaps more enjoyable, way to reach the trail is to take green minibus No 82 (HK$3.60) from Shiu Wo St, due south of the Tsuen Wan MTR station. This will drop you off at Pineapple Dam, adjacent to the Shing Mun Reservoir in 14-sq-km Shing Mun Country Park; the **Shing Mun Country Park Visitor Centre** (☎ 2498 1362; ☯ 9.30am-4.30pm Wed-Mon) is on the western edge of the reservoir. You can follow the Pineapple Dam Nature Trail past several picnic and barbecue areas and around the reservoir itself.

This is an area very rich in flora and fauna, and you're bound to see many colourful butterflies, birds and pesky macaque monkeys; it's unlikely, however, that you'll see the timid deer that live in the area. The signposted Shing Mun Arboretum has 70 varieties of fruit and other trees plus medicinal plants.

Running south from the Shing Mun Reservoir is stage No 6 of the MacLehose Trail, which will take you by Smugglers' Ridge and past some pretty dramatic scenery. The trail leads west and then south alongside Kowloon Reservoir to Tai Po Rd (4.6km, 1½ hours). From here stage No 5 of the trail heads east past a hill called Eagle's Nest, through woodland and up Beacon Hill, named after a lookout station positioned here under Qing-dynasty Emperor Kang Xi, which fired up a beacon when enemy ships sailed into view.

From there stage No 5 of the trail runs along a ridge to Lion Rock, from where is a path leading north to Amah Rock (see p134). The MacLehose Trail circumvents Lion Rock but you can clamber up the path leading to it. Be warned – it is quite a tough climb, though every bit worth the effort. The vista from the top is stunning, with views of sheer cliffs and rocky crags.

Coming down from Lion Rock, the MacLehose Trail leads you to Sha Tin Pass. From here you can either head south a short distance along the road and pick up green minibus No 37M (HK$2.90) at Tsz Wan Shan estate heading for Wong Tai Sin MTR in Kowloon, or walk north along a path to Sha Tin (about 2km) and jump on the KCR. If you carry on along stage No 4 of the MacLehose Trail, it will take you into the heart of Ma On Shan Country Park via Tate's Cairn (577m) and Buffalo Hill.

Other places to access the MacLehose Trail include (from east to west):

Pak Tam Chung (stage No 1) Bus No 94 (HK$5.90) from Sai Kung town, bus No 96R (HK$17; Sun & holidays) from Choi Hung or Diamond Hill MTR stations.

Pak Tam Au (stage Nos 2 & 3) Same as above.

Kei Ling Rd (stage Nos 3 & 4) Bus No 299 (HK$9) from Sha Tin or Sai Kung town.

Ma On Shan (stage No 4) Bus No 99 (HK$4.60) from Sai Kung town to Nai Chung (descend at Sai Sha Rd).

Tai Po Rd (stage No 6) Green minibus No 81 (HK$3.60) from Tsuen Wan or bus No 81C (HK$5.30-7.50) from the Hung Hom KCR station.

Tuen Mun (stage No 10) Bus Nos 53 (HK$8.80) and 60M (HK$6.90) from Tsuen Wan or bus No 63X (HK$13) from Nathan Rd in Tsim Sha Tsui.

LANTAU TRAIL

The 70km-long Lantau Trail (Map p419) follows the mountain tops from Mui Wo and then doubles back at Tai O along the coast to where it started. It takes just over 24 hours to walk in full, but the trail is divided into a dozen manageable stages ranging from 2.5km (45 minutes) to 10.5km (three hours).

A realistic approach is to do the trail's first four stages (17.5km, seven hours), which take in the highest and most scenic parts of the trail and can be accessed from Mui Wo or, conversely, from the Po Lin Monastery and SG Davis Hostel at Ngong Ping (p148). Note that the walk can be treacherous in certain steep sections. Stage No 1 (2.5km, 45 minutes) of the Lantau Trail from Mui Wo follows boring South Lantau Rd but there's an alternative, more scenic path from Mui Wo to Nam Shan, where stage No 2 begins, via Luk Tei Tong.

The western part of the trail, which follows the southwestern coast of Lantau from Tai O to Fan Lau and then up to Shek Pik, is also very scenic.

GUIDED HIKES

If you'd like to do some hiking in the countryside but would prefer to be shown the way, contact **First Step NT** (☎ 2981 3523; www.firststepnt.com) for guided nature walks in southwestern Hong Kong Island (Dragon's Back), the New Territories (Mai Po Marshes) and Lantau Island. They last between 3½ and five hours and cost from HK$275 to HK$320. **Outdoor Adventure Tours** (☎ 2486 2112, 9300 5197; www.kayak-and-hike.com) has both hiking and kayaking trips (HK$450) to Hoi Ha, Tap Mun Chau and Tai Long Wan in the New Territories. **Dragonfly** (☎ 2577 6319, 9277 6077; www.dragonfly.com.hk) has hiking and kayaking tours as well as rock climbing, caving and mountain biking trips.

Eating

Eating

Hong Kong does not live by *dim sum*, *cha siu fan* (barbecued pork with rice) and *chau min* (fried noodles) alone, but Chinese food in its various incarnations is clearly what the territory does best (see the Food chapter p46). Still, the surfeit of other cuisines available at the territory's restaurants will have you spoiled for choice and begging for more.

The HKTB distributes a useful quarterly called *Hong Kong District Food Guide* (www .hongkongfoodguide.com), with suggested restaurants throughout the territory, as well as the annual *Best of the Best Culinary Guide*. For guides with more comprehensive listings, see Guidebooks (p354).

Asian & International Food

Hong Kong's glut of Thai eateries offers the diner a lot of choice, especially in Kowloon Tong. Vietnamese and Indonesian/Malaysian are other Southeast Asian favourites; the best places to look for these cuisines are Causeway Bay and Tsim Sha Tsui.

Korean barbecue restaurants, where you cook *à table* and share up to a dozen small dishes of crisp vegetables and spicy *kimchi* (hot pickled cabbage), can be found everywhere, but especially in Sheung Wan and Causeway Bay. Japanese restaurants are usually pricey unless you go to chains like Genki Sushi, where sushi is served on a conveyor belt.

One option you shouldn't overlook is Hong Kong's subcontinental restaurants; Chungking Mansions in Tsim Sha Tsui has a vast array of Indian 'messes' (simple, usually unlicensed restaurants) serving basic but authentic Indian and Pakistani cuisine.

With Hong Kong people travelling much more frequently these days, they've been much more adventurous with Western cuisines. Nowadays you'll find everything from French and Italian to Russian and Argentinian on offer.

Vegetarian Food

Western vegetarian food is reasonably hard to come by here if you want anything more complex than a salad, but there are quite a few Chinese options (see Vegetarian Food p58).

Indian vegetarian cuisine is considerably spicier than its Chinese counterpart. Some Indian restaurants are exclusively vegetarian, but most offer a combined menu.

Fast Food

Hong Kong counts hundreds of the usual international chain food outlets, as well as several home-grown chains that serve both Western and Chinese dishes. The four biggest ones are Cafe de Coral, Maxim's, Dai Pai Dong and Fairwood.

Among the easiest places to buy sandwiches, soups, salads and baked goods are branches of the Oliver's Super Sandwiches and Délifrance chains. You'll find them everywhere – from Central to Tuen Mun.

Self-Catering

Wellcome and Park 'N' Shop, the two major supermarket chains, have branches all over Hong Kong. 7-Eleven convenience stores are ubiquitous and open 24 hours; Circle K outlets also abound.

Fruit

Along with peaches, pears and apples from North America and Europe, Hong Kong imports an enormous variety of fruits from Australia, South Africa and Southeast Asia, including some really exotic ones.

Special fruits to look out for:

Carambola This bright yellow fruit is also known as star fruit, which is exactly what it looks like when sliced.

Custard Apple This fruit is apple sized and has a bumpy green-grey skin and a sweet, custard-like taste.

Durian A large fruit shaped like a rugby ball that has tough spikes and looks impenetrable. After breaking it open with a big knife and peeling off the skin, you'll encounter the next obstacle, a powerful odour that many can't abide. The creamy fruit is actually delicious – it tastes of garlic custard with alcohol sprinkled on top – and is even used to make ice cream in Southeast Asia. The season is April to June.

Hami melon A large oval melon with the skin of a cantaloupe, this sugary fruit comes from China's Xinjiang province and is very expensive. It's sold in summer.

Jackfruit This large segmented fruit is fine stuff when ripe, but tastes a bit like American chewing gum.

Longan The name means 'dragon eyes' in Chinese. The skin is brown, and the clear fruit crunchy, but otherwise the taste similar to that of a lychee. Its season is from June to early August.

Lychee A red, pulpy fruit with white flesh. It has a single seed; the smaller the seed the better the fruit (available April to June).

Mango The variety sold in Hong Kong are the yellow-skinned fruits from the Philippines.

Mangosteen Beneath the thick purple smooth skin of this fruit is white flesh that has a delicious sour-sweet flavour.

Pomelo The pomelo is similar to a large grapefruit but sweeter and drier.

Rambutan The red and hairy skin gives rambutans the look of tiny suns. It is distantly related to the lychee and has a similar taste. Its season is from May to October.

Meal Times

Restaurants generally open from 11.30am (or noon) to 2.30pm (or 3pm) for lunch, and 6pm (or 6.30pm) to 11pm for dinner. There are exceptions of course. Some pubs' kitchens stay open until 1am, and Chinese noodle shops often run from the early morning until the wee hours.

How Much?

It's sad to say, but Hong Kong has become a pricey destination when it comes to eating out. While a bowl of noodles can cost as little as HK$10 and fried rice HK$20, a proper lunch will cost anything from HK$60. Anything under HK$50 for a meal is truly cheap eating. At dinner, anything under HK$100 is budget; expect to pay from HK$120 per person at a Chinese or other Asian restaurant and from at least HK$150 at a Western one.

The best hunting grounds for budget eateries are the little backstreets off Hollywood Rd in Central, Sheung Wan, Wan Chai, Causeway Bay and Tsim Sha Tsui. Most of these areas have the steady flow of commuters or residents needed to support a large number of noodle shops, fast-food joints and so on. They all have plenty of mid-range restaurants serving various Asian cuisines as well, and this is where Hong Kong truly comes into its own.

Tipping

Most restaurants add a 10% service charge to the bill. You need only leave a few extra coins.

HONG KONG ISLAND

Catering facilities on Hong Kong Island run the gamut from Michelin-level restaurants in five-star hotels and Asian fusion enjoyed at pavement cafés, to an embarrassment of ethnic cuisines – from Indian and Mexican to Chiu Chow and Vietnamese – served in tiny little holes in the wall upstairs, downstairs or in some obscure chamber.

CENTRAL

Though there are many exceptions to the rule, Central is not always the best place to find authentic ethnic cuisine. However, Westernised versions of the same, along with some cutting-edge international and fusion food, are available in spades, especially in Lan Kwai Fong and the top end of Wyndham St.

AL'S DINER Map pp404–5 *American, Deli*
☎ 2521 8714; Ground fl, Shop F, 27-39 D'Aguilar St; mains HK$65-158; ☽ 11am-2am Mon-Thu, 11am-4am Fri-Sat, closed Sun

A faithful copy of a 1950s chrome and glass American diner, Al's has the usual burgers fit for a giant (from HK$85 to HK$158), hot dogs with everything (HK$65 to HK$75), meatloaf (HK$76), ribs and platters of French fries.

ALIBI Map pp404–5 *International*
☎ 2167 8989; 73 Wyndham St; starters HK$95-150, pasta HK$140-160, mains HK$150-230; ☽ lunch noon-3pm, dinner 7pm-1am Mon-Sat

Lunch (don't miss the organic lunch buffet for HK$98) at this popular and stylish address is on the ground floor. At night it turns into a bar (see p220) and diners regroup in the mezzanine level restaurant for dishes like duck infused with jasmine tea and crispy salmon with green lentils. The décor is imaginative and this is the place to spot Hong Kong's most beautiful people – in every sense.

AQUA Map pp404–5 *Fusion*
☎ 2545 9889; Upper Ground fl, 49 Hollywood Rd; starters HK$65-98, mains HK$170-218; ☽ lunch noon-3.30pm, dinner 6-11pm

This ultra chichi and minimalist place boasts enormous windows facing Lyndhurst Terrace and Hollywood Rd, and 'serious fusion food'. Two-/three-course set lunches are HK$98/118.

ASSAF Map pp404–5 *Lebanese*
☎ 2851 6550; Shop B, Lyndhurst Bldg, 37 Lyndhurst Tce; starters HK$42-55, mains HK$120, set lunch HK$68, set dinner HK$140 & HK$150; ☽ lunch noon-3pm, dinner 6pm-midnight

This welcoming and cosy place specialises in meze and other tasty titbits; the set dinners are a mixture of six to eight different items. The

Assaf brothers also own the **Beyrouth Cafe** (Map pp404-5; ☎ 2854 1872; ☽ noon-11.30pm), a simple place that does takeaway, too. Salads, sandwiches, kebabs and meze here cost from HK$30 to HK$45.

BEIRUT Map pp404–5 *Lebanese*
☎ 2804 6611; Shop A, 27-39 D'Aguilar St; meze HK$45-75, mains HK$85-155; ☽ lunch noon-3pm Mon-Sat, dinner 6-11.30pm Mon-Sat, 6-11pm Sun

Beirut is an affable, slightly cramped restaurant that looks out onto the Fong and serves authentic Lebanese dishes like *kibbeh* (call it Lebanese moussaka) and *lahme bil agine* ('pizza' with minced lamb). Two-/three-course set lunches are HK$115/145.

BOMBAY DREAMS Map pp404–5 *Indian*
☎ 2971 0001; 1st fl, Carfield Commercial Bldg, 75-77 Wyndham St; dishes HK$58-178; ☽ lunch 12.30-2.30pm Mon-Sat, dinner 6.30-10.30pm daily

Taking its name from the successful musical that has taken Broadway and London's West End by storm, this place is not as all-singin', all dancin' as it first might look from the upmarket décor, but it's convenient to the pubs of Lan Kwai Fong and is still drawing in the crowds.

CAFÉ Map pp400–3 *Café*
☎ 2522 0111; Ground fl, Mandarin Oriental, 5 Connaught Rd Central; sandwiches HK$130-145, pasta HK$130-150, Asian mains HK$100-150, Western mains HK$140-185; ☽ 8am-11pm

The Café (formerly known as the Mandarin Coffee Shop) changed the face of what are called PPHR (popular-priced hotel restaurants) in the trade. The food is unswervingly excellent, the service always seamless.

CAFÉ DES ARTISTES Map pp404–5 *French*
☎ 2526 3880; Upper Ground fl, California Tower, 30-32 D'Aguilar St; starters HK$95-135, mains HK$175-195, set menu HK$165; ☽ lunch noon-2.45pm daily, dinner 6.45-10.30pm Sun-Thu, 6.45-11.30pm Fri-Sat

This place serves surprisingly good Provençale food, and the chef introduces a new menu each season. The views of Lan Kwai Fong passers-by viewing you may be mesmerising – or off-putting.

CAFE SIAM Map pp404–5 *Thai*
☎ 2851 4803; 40-42 Lyndhurst Tce; rice & noodle dishes HK$58-78, Thai salads HK$48-88, curries HK$65-82; ☽ lunch noon-2.30pm daily, dinner 6-10.30pm Sun-Thu, 6-11pm Fri-Sat

Top Five Restaurants – Central

- **Luk Yu Tea House** (p173) Dim sum with attitude in a traditional teahouse.
- **M at the Fringe** (p173) Probably the best international restaurant in town.
- **Thanying Thai Restaurant** (p175) Tom yam gung and co greet the 21st century.
- **Vong** (p175) Fusion confusion (Southeast Asian and French) with a view.
- **Yung Kee** (p175) Take a gander for the best goose in Hong Kong.

Not the best or most authentic Thai restaurant in town, Cafe Siam serves generous-sized portions of old favourites like *tom ka gai* (coconut-based chicken), green curries and *gung kaprow* (prawns cooked with basil) to a crowd *en passant* between Soho and Lan Kwai Fong.

CHINA LAN KWAI FONG Map pp404–5
Chinese, Peking

☎ 2536 0968; 17-22 Lan Kwai Fong; rice & noodle dishes HK$38-88, cold dishes HK$48-64, mains HK$82-268; ⏰ lunch 11am-3pm, dinner 6pm-midnight

This pretty restaurant – with caged songbirds, Chinese antique furnishings, excellent service and great Peking duck – is expensive, even by Lan Kwai Fong standards. But it becomes accessible to those other than brokers or solicitors at lunch, when a set menu is available for HK$138, and at Sunday brunch (HK$140), with an unlimited selection of cold dishes, dim sum, soups and main courses.

CHINA TEE CLUB

Map pp400–3   *Chinese, International*

☎ 2521 0233; Room 101-102, 1st fl, Pedder Bldg, 12 Pedder St; starters HK$60-75, vegetarian & pasta dishes HK$105-115, mains HK$110-135; ⏰ 11.30am-8pm Mon-Sat, closed Sun

This civilised tea house-cum-restaurant serving both Chinese and Western favourites is perfect for a meal or a cuppa after finishing your shopping at Shanghai Tang's below (or Blanc de Chine above, for that matter).

COCO CURRY HOUSE

Map pp404–5   *Malaysian*

☎ 2523 6911; 8 Wing Wah Lane; noodles & rice dishes HK$40-65, curries HK$50-70; ⏰ lunch 11am-3pm, dinner 6pm-12.30am

They're not exactly Penang or Malacca standard, but the curries at this no-frills and mostly open-air Malaysian place are tasty and filling. Try the nasi goreng (fried rice; HK$45) or the laksa (spicy coconut based noodle soup; HK$40).

EUROMART Map pp404–5   *Food Store*

☎ 2537 0210; Ground fl, 1B Old Bailey St (enter from Staunton St); ⏰ 10am-10.30pm Sun-Thu, 10am-11pm Fri-Sat

This is a European-style convenience store full of imported cheeses, wines, hams, coffees and packaged goods.

FRINGE CLUB Map p404–5   *Vegetarian, Buffet*

☎ 2521 7251; 2nd fl, Dairy Farm Bldg, 2 Lower Albert Rd; set lunch HK$75; ⏰ lunch noon-2pm Mon-Fri

Vegetarians weighing their options in Central at lunchtime during the week might try the vegetarian buffet available upstairs at the Fringe Club. It's located in the Volkswagen Fotogalerie.

GAIA RISTORANTE Map pp400–3   *Italian*

☎ 2167 8200; Ground fl, Grand Millennium Plaza, 181 Queen's Rd Central; meals from HK$400 per person; ⏰ lunch noon-3pm, dinner 7pm-midnight

At least one *bon vivant* friend considers this the best restaurant in Hong Kong. We're not sure about that, but we love the gold curtains, the thin-crust pizzas and the outside tables in the lush plaza.

GIGA Map pp404–5   *Seafood*

☎ 2121 8703; 14 Wo On Lane; oysters HK$22-45, starters HK$48-80, mains HK$108-180; ⏰ lunch noon-3pm daily, dinner 6pm-midnight Mon-Thu, 6pm-2am Fri-Sat, closed Sun

If you fancy oysters (and other types of seafood), head for this stylish little restaurant named after a breed of the bivalve particularly popular in France (but originally imported from Asia). The menu at Giga changes daily and three-course set lunches start at HK$68.

GRAHAM ST MARKET

Map pp400–3   *Produce Market*
Graham St; 🕐 **6am-8pm**
The stalls and shops lining Graham St south of (and up the hill from) Queen's Rd Central to Hollywood Rd are positively groaning with high-quality vegetables and fruit, as well as meat, seafood and other comestibles.

GREENLANDS INDIA CLUB

Map pp404–5   *Indian*
☎ **2522 6098; 1st fl, Yu Wing Bldg, 64-66 Wellington St; starters HK$36-62, mains HK$53-98;** 🕐 **lunch noon-3pm Mon-Sat, dinner 6-11.30pm daily**
Greenlands' low prices and high-quality food ensure that the place is always packed. The lunchtime buffet (HK$68) and dinner on Friday (HK$118) are particularly good value.

GUNGA DIN'S CLUB Map pp404–5   *Indian*
☎ **2523 1276; lower Ground fl, 57-59 Wyndham St; starters HK$25-35, curries HK$60-100, tandoori dishes HK$70-110;** 🕐 **lunch 11.30am-2.30pm Mon-Sat, dinner 6-10.30pm daily**
This popular curry house, recently given a much-needed face-lift, serves substantial if not sublime tiffin. The buffet lunch is HK$70.

HABIBI Map pp400–3   *Egyptian*
☎ **2544 6198; 112-114 Wellington St; meze HK$45-60, mains HK$110-200;** 🕐 **lunch 11am-3pm, dinner 6pm-midnight Mon-Sat, closed Sun**
Whether or not Habibi serves authentic Egyptian food is a moot point – the food is excellent. The setting is Cairo of the 1930s – all mirrors, tassels and velvet cushions. Habibi's casual and takeaway section, **Koshary Cafe** (Map pp400–3; ☎ 2544 3886; 🕐 10am-midnight daily) next door is a lot cheaper, with meze from HK$25 to HK$38, platters from HK$75 to HK$90 and mains from HK$65.

HUNAN GARDEN

Map pp400–3   *Chinese, Hunanese*
☎ **2868 2880; 3rd fl, The Forum, Exchange Square, Connaught Rd Central; meals HK$300 per person;** 🕐 **lunch 11.30am-3pm, dinner 5.30-11.30pm**
Elegant and expensive, this upmarket place specialises in spicy Hunanese food, which is often hotter that the Sichuan variety. The fried chicken with chilli is excellent and the seafood dishes (unusual in Hunan cuisine) are recommended. The views, overlooking the harbour or into the heart of Central, are a bonus.

INDOCHINE 1929 Map pp404–5   *Vietnamese*
☎ **2869 7399; 2nd fl, California Tower, 30-32 D'Aguilar St; Thai salads HK$48-88, mains HK$102-160;** 🕐 **lunch noon-2.30pm Mon-Sat, dinner 6.30-11pm Sun-Wed, 6.30-11.30pm Thu-Sat**
It's not cheap and the food quality may have dropped a notch or two over the years, but the colonial Vietnam setting will certainly bewitch you. Set lunches are HK$98 to HK$148, and set dinners HK$415.

JASMINE Map pp400–3   *Chinese, Cantonese*
☎ **2524 5098; Basement, Jardine House, Connaught Rd Central; meals HK$150-200 per person;** 🕐 **lunch 11am-3pm, dinner 6-11pm**
This cleaned-up version of the standard Hong Kong Cantonese eatery is relatively inexpensive for its location, plus the food is good and the service excellent.

JIMMY'S KITCHEN

Map pp400–3   *International*
☎ **2526 5293; Basement, South China Bldg, 1-3 Wyndham St; meals from HK$300 per person;** 🕐 **lunch 11.30am-3pm, dinner 6-11pm**
High on nostalgia and one of the oldest names in the game, Jimmy's, a Hong Kong feature for seven decades, rests on its laurels. The char-grilled king prawns (HK$215), baked onion soup (HK$50), black pepper steak (HK$235) and a whole medley of desserts (including its famous baked Alaska, HK$58) all compete for the diners' attention. There's a branch in Tsim Sha Tsui; see p198 for details.

KOH-I-NOOR Map pp404–5   *Indian*
☎ **2877 9706; 1st fl, California Entertainment Bldg, 34-36 D'Aguilar St; curries HK$46-130, kebabs from HK$68, tandoori dishes HK$70-125;** 🕐 **lunch noon-3pm, dinner 6-11pm**
This pricier sister-restaurant of the ones in Tsim Sha Tsui (p198) and Sha Tin (p208) serves equally fine northern Indian cuisine. The weekday lunch buffet is a steal at HK$48.

LA KASBAH Map pp404–5   *Maghreb*
☎ **2525 9493; Basement, 17 Hollywood Rd; starters from HK$59, couscous dishes HK$105-142, tajines HK$110-154;** 🕐 **dinner 6.30-11.30pm Mon-Sat**
La Kasbah is a Frenchified Maghreb caravanserai serving dishes from Algeria, Tunisia and Morocco, which effectively means couscous. It's good stuff but expensive for what (and where)

it is. The hookahs loaded with flavoured to-bacco are a plus.

LAN'S Map pp400–3 *Steakhouse*

☎ 2562 1212; Ground & 1st fls, 4-6 On Lan St; steak mains HK$185-298; ☽ noon-midnight

Steakhouses have hit Hong Kong with a wallop in recent times and Lan's is one of the more central. There's a four-course set dinner available for HK$288 and, during the weekend, an all-you-can-eat steak lunch for HK$228.

LIN HEUNG TEA HOUSE

Map pp400–3 *Chinese, Cantonese*

☎ 2544 4556; 160-164 Wellington St (cnr Aberdeen St); meals from HK$120; ☽ 6am-10pm Mon-Sat, closed Sun

This old-style Cantonese restaurant – packed with older men reading newspapers, ex-tended families and office groups – has OK dim sum served from trolleys, but it's particu-larly recommended for a bite late at night or a meal alone. It's a very local place, but there is an English menu.

LUK YU TEA HOUSE

Map pp404–5 *Chinese, Dim Sum*

☎ 2523 5464, 2523 1970; 24-26 Stanley St; rice & noodle dishes HK$65-130, mains HK$100-300; ☽ 7am-10pm

This old-style teahouse is a museum piece in more ways than one. Most of the staff have been here since the early Ming Dynasty and are as grumpy and ill-tempered as an emperor deposed. The booths are uncomfortable, it's not cheap, prices aren't marked in English but the dim sum served from 7am to 6pm is very tasty.

M AT THE FRINGE Map pp404–5 *International*

☎ 2877 4000; 1st fl, Fringe Club, Dairy Farm Bldg, 2 Lower Albert Rd; starters HK$78-188, mains HK$178-212, 2-/3-course set lunch HK$148/168; ☽ lunch noon-2.30pm Mon-Fri, dinner 7-10.30pm Mon-Sat, 7-10pm Sun

This palace of creative gastronomy is one of the best restaurants in Hong Kong. When Melbournian Michelle Garnaut opened M at the Fringe in 1988, she single-handedly brought Hong Kong into a new stratosphere of food and dining experience. The menu changes constantly (except for her signature lamb dish, HK$206) and everything is superbly designed, created and cooked.

MOZART STUB'N Map pp400–3 *Austrian*

☎ 2522 1763; 8 Glenealy; starters HK$48-165, mains HK$150-235; ☽ lunch 12.30-2.30pm Mon-Sat, dinner 6-10.30pm Mon-Fri, 6.30-11pm Sat

This classy, almost fastidious Austrian (do *not* say German) establishment has excellent food and wines and a delightful atmosphere.

NING PO RESIDENTS ASSOCIATION

Map pp404–5 *Chinese, Shanghainese*

☎ 2523 0648; 4th fl, Yip Fung Bldg, 2-18 D'Aguilar St; starters HK$60-90, mains HK$75-250; ☽ 10am-11pm

The Ning Po offers tasty and well-prepared Shanghainese food and is very popular with expats and locals alike. Communication might be a problem, but persevere; it will be well worth your efforts.

OLIVER'S Map pp400–3 *Supermarket, Deli*

☎ 2810 7710; Shop 233, Prince's Bldg, 10 Chater Rd; ☽ 9am-8pm

The wooden floors set the tone: this is no ordinary supermarket. Matzos or Mexican salsa? Got it. There's also a great range of international beers, the imported fruit and vegies obviously come first class and the delicatessen stocks a wide range of cheeses, sausages, pâtés and fine wines. There's also a branch of Oliver's Super Sandwiches here (see Cheap Eats p177).

PAA Map pp404–5 *Korean*

☎ 3105 1311; 1st fl, Hilltop Plaza, 49 Hollywood Rd (enter from Graham St); starters HK$78-125, rice & noodle dishes HK$90-135, barbecue HK$108-160; ☽ lunch noon-2.30pm, dinner 6-10.30pm

At Paa (apparently 'spring onion' in Kor-ean) it's hard to see what makes the food 'contemporary Korean cuisine' – a Korean barbecue is a Korean barbecue. But the presentation is Western and the setting, in a modern office building sheathed in massive windows above Hollywood Rd, comfortable and up to date.

PASTA E PIZZA Map pp404–5 *Italian*

☎ 2545 1675; Basement, 11 Lyndhurst Tce; pizza HK$65-90, pasta HK$80-90, set lunch HK$65; ☽ lunch noon-3pm Mon-Sat, dinner 6-11pm daily

This independent, simple eatery, with film posters on the wall and checked tablecloths, serves simple but excellent pasta dishes and pizzas. On Saturday it turns into **Jazz@The Basement**, a popular jazz cellar (p234).

POST 97 Map pp404–5 *International*

☎ 2186 1817; 1st fl, Cosmos Bldg, 9-11 Lan Kwai Fong; à la carte dishes HK$50-135; 🕑 9.30am-1am Mon-Thu, 9.30am-3am Fri-Sat, 9.30am-midnight Sun

This comfortable, all-day brasserie and café above the Fong serves breakfast (HK$97), buffet lunches (HK$125 or HK$150 to HK$160 with wine), two-course set lunch (HK$140) and set dinner (HK$197); à la carte dishes also are available throughout the day. At night Post 97 turns into a popular bar and gets packed very quickly.

SAN MARZANO Map pp404–5 *Italian*

☎ 2850 7898; 21 Lyndhurst Tce; pasta HK$65-95, pizza HK$75-95; 🕑 noon-midnight

This is the place for pizza and pasta if you like things, well, familiar. It's part of the UK-based Pizza Express chain and looks it and acts it. Still, it's good value and convenient to Lan Kwai Fong and Soho.

SCHNURRBART Map pp404–5 *German*

☎ 2523 4700; 29 D'Aguilar St; bar snacks & open-face sandwiches HK$33-45, starters HK$25-48, mains HK$53-98; 🕑 lunch noon-3pm, dinner 6pm-midnight

'Moustache' serves up hearty *Bierstube* fare like the best of the wurst and German meatloaf, along with lots and lots of suds. There's also a branch in Tsim Sha Tsui (p200).

SECRET GARDEN Map pp400–3 *Korean*

☎ 2801 7990; Shop 5, Ground fl, Bank of America Tower, 12 Harcourt Rd; rice & noodle dishes HK$100-140, barbecue HK$100-140, soups HK$100-220; 🕑 lunch noon-3pm, dinner 6-11pm

This authentic and central Korean eatery is highly recommended; you should book in advance (and you'll still wait for a table). Try a barbecue with all the little side dishes or the signature ginseng chicken soup (HK$130). We still haven't figured out what stewed angels (HK$350) are, though.

SHALOM GRILL

Map pp400–3 *Jewish, Kosher*

☎ 2851 6300; 2nd fl, Fortune House, 61 Connaught Rd Central; starters HK$15-60, mains HK$80-120; 🕑 lunch 12.30-3pm Sun-Fri, dinner 6.30-10pm Sun-Thu

If it's Ashkenazic and Sephardic glatt kosher food you're after, the Shalom Grill can oblige. Don't expect cordon bleu, but if you're in the mood for felafel or gefilte fish or you simply answer to a higher authority on matters culinary, this is the place. Shabbat dinner and Saturday lunch can be prearranged and paid for in advance.

SPAGHETTI HOUSE Map pp404–5 *Italian*

☎ 2523 1372; Basement, 10 Stanley St; pasta HK$48-72, small/large pizza from HK$72/102; 🕑 11am-11.30pm

You probably wouldn't want to take a date to this (or any) branch of the cheap-and-cheerful chain, but it's OK for a pizza or bowl of pasta. You'll find another outlet nearby in the **IFC Mall** (Map pp400-3; ☎ 2147 5543; Shop 2004, 2nd fl, 1 Harbour View St, Central).

STORMY WEATHER Map pp404–5 *Seafood*

☎ 2845 5533; Ground & 1st fls, 46-50 D'Aguilar St; starters HK$59-88, pasta HK$118-128, mains HK$128-228; 🕑 lunch 11.30am-3pm, dinner 6-10.30pm Sun-Thu, 6-11pm Fri-Sat

It's supposed to be an East Coast–style restaurant, so where's the Boston lobster and steamers – tiny quahog clams to the cognoscenti – with drawn butter? Still, the seafood (whatever the style) is fine, and the location prime.

SUPER STAR SEAFOOD RESTAURANT

Map pp404–5 *Chinese, Seafood*

☎ 2525 9238; Basement, Wilson House, 19-27 Wyndham St; dishes HK$68-128; 🕑 lunch noon-2.30pm, dinner 6-10.30pm

Though just one of half a dozen branches of yet another chain, the Super Star has some of the best Cantonese fish dishes in Central. Lunchtime dim sum here is legendary among Central office workers.

TAI WOO Map pp404–5 *Chinese, Cantonese*

☎ 2526 2920; 15B Wellington St; dim sum HK$20-25 per serving, rice & noodle dishes from HK$65; 🕑 7am-midnight

This steamy (in the literal sense) and very authentic Cantonese eatery may look like a 'closed shop' but persevere (with the help of the Food chapter p46) and you'll be amply rewarded. Dim sum is served from 11am to 4.30pm.

THAI LEMONGRASS Map pp404–5 *Thai*

☎ 2905 1688; 3rd fl, California Tower, 30-32 D'Aguilar St; appetisers HK$48-88, Thai salads HK$65-115, rice & noodle dishes HK$75-98, mains HK$120-215; 🕑 lunch noon-2.30pm Mon-Sat, dinner 6.30-11pm Mon-Sat, 6.30-10.30pm Sun

This quiet, discreet and very smart place serves up such treats as pomelo salad, spicy green papaya salad and mussels in red curry. There's a set lunch for HK$138.

THANYING THAI RESTAURANT

Map pp404–5   *Thai*

☎ 2522 5073; Ice House Bldg, 38 Ice House St; soups HK$68-88, Thai salads HK$78-128, curries HK$108-148; ⏰ 8am-late

This positively stunning restaurant, all cool metal surfaces, purple silk and mirrors, will serve you anything from breakfast to a late-night snack. It's super trendy and the food is done perfectly.

TOKIO JOE Map pp404–5   *Japanese*

☎ 2525 1889; 16 Lan Kwai Fong; sushi HK$25-65, cones & rolls HK$65-145; set lunches HK$120-155; ⏰ lunch noon-2.30pm Mon-Sat, dinner 6.30-11pm Sun-Thu, 6.30-11.30pm Fri-Sat

This place serves among the freshest sushi and sashimi in Hong Kong, though there is a full range of hot dishes (including *yakitori*) available as well. Joe's flashier kid brother, **Kyoto Joe** (Map pp404-5; ☎ 2804 6800; Ground fl, 21 D'Aguilar St), just down the hill, is somewhat more expensive and modern, and a venue for drinking as much as dining. There's a *robota-yaki* (barbecue) bar in back.

TW CAFE Map pp404–5   *Café*

☎ 2544 2237; Shop 2, Capitol Plaza, 2-10 Lyndhurst Tce; afternoon tea HK$34; ⏰ 8am-8pm

TW Cafe is a tiny café that has more than 20 types of coffee on offer, as well as a smattering of light snacks.

UNCLE WILLIE'S DELI Map pp404–5   *Café, Deli*

☎ 2522 7524; 36 Wyndham St; breakfast HK$55-69, soups HK$25-45, tarts HK$18-35, sandwiches HK$45-65; ⏰ 7am-11pm Mon-Sat, 9am-6pm Sun

This is a relaxing café-cum-deli that could be in the Village in New York. It serves some of the best breakfasts and sandwiches in town.

VA BENE Map pp404–5   *Italian*

☎ 2845 5577; 58-62 D'Aguilar St, Central; pasta HK$80-118, starters HK$108-138, mains HK$198-238, set lunch HK$178; ⏰ lunch noon-3pm daily, dinner 6.30-11.30pm Sun-Thu, 6.30pm-12.30am Fri-Sat

This smart restaurant bears a striking re-semblance to a neighbourhood trattoria in Venezia. It's a good choice for a special date or an extravagant celebration. Book ahead; dress smart.

VONG Map pp400–3   *Fusion*

☎ 2825 4028; 25th fl, Mandarin Oriental Hotel, 5 Connaught Rd Central; starters HK$108-175, mains

Fresh seafood for sale

HK$198-338; ⏰ lunch noon-3pm Mon-Fri, dinner 6pm-midnight daily

A jewel of a restaurant in a jewel of a hotel, Vong serves a successful blend of Vietnamese, Thai and French food amid splendid surrounds; the views alone make it all worthwhile. If you really want to see what the chef can do, try the five-course sample menu (HK$468).

YOROHACHI Map pp404–5   *Japanese*

☎ 2524 1251; 6 Lan Kwai Fong; set lunches HK$95-135, bento box lunches HK$85-180; ⏰ lunch 11am-2.30pm, dinner 6-11pm Mon-Sat, closed Sun

In the heart of Lan Kwai Fong, Yorohachi offers an excellent-value teppanyaki grill and take-away lunch boxes.

YUNG KEE Map pp404–5   *Chinese, Cantonese*

☎ 2522 1624; 32-40 Wellington St; meals HK$250 per person; ⏰ 11am-11.30pm

This long-standing institution is probably the most famous Cantonese restaurant in Central. The roast goose here has been the talk of the town since 1942 (they farm their own geese for quality control), and its dim sum (served from 11am to 5pm) is excellent.

Cheap Eats

BEPPU MENKAN Map pp404–5   *Japanese*

☎ 2536 0816; 5-11 Stanley St; starters from HK$20, noodle dishes HK$28-55, rice dishes HK$45; ⏰ lunch

11.30am-5pm Mon-Sat & noon-5pm Sun, dinner 6-11pm daily
This is a fast-food option in the middle of Central specialising in all kinds of Japanese noodles.

BON APPETIT Map pp404–5 *Vietnamese*
☎ 2525 3553; 14B Wing Wah Lane; dishes HK$20-33; 🕑 10am-midnight
Cheap but tasty dishes for those on a rock-bottom budget are available at this Vietnamese nook in Wing Wah Lane. Everything – from snacks and filled baguettes to rice and noodle dishes – costs less than HK$33.

CAFE HUE Map pp400–3 *Vietnamese*
☎ 2512 8323; Ground fl, 74 Stanley St; dishes HK$20-48; 🕑 8am-10.30pm
If you would like a *dai pai dong* experience without the fuss, head for this little Vietnamese eatery. It sets up tables for its clients at the end of Stanley St at lunch.

CUL-DE-SAC Map pp404–5 *American Fast Food*
☎ 2525 8116; 17 Wing Wah Lane; set meals with drink HK$35-45; 🕑 11am-1am Sun-Thu, 11am-4am Fri-Sat
This well-run little place does fish and chips (HK$85) and pizza slices (HK$20 to HK$25), but basically it's about burgers (HK$55), complex sandwiches (HK$38 to HK$42) and submarines (HK$58 to HK$68).

DAI PAI DONG
Map pp400–3 *Chinese, Hong Kong*
☎ 2851 6389; Ground fl, 128 Queen's Rd Central; breakfast HK$11-33, rice & noodle dishes HK$28-42, set meals HK$48; 🕑 8am-10pm Mon-Sat, 9.30am-7pm Sun
This chain of cheap Chinese eateries takes its name from the Cantonese for 'food stall', which were ubiquitous in Hong Kong until the health department – in its infinite wisdom – decided they were a threat to humanity. It's not a bad choice for something fast and inexpensive; afternoon tea is served from 2.30pm to 5.30pm. There's also a **Causeway Bay branch** (Map pp406-8; ☎ 2804 4502; Ground fl, 20 Russell St).

DÉLIFRANCE Map pp400–3 *Café*
☎ 2810 5941; 1st fl, Pacific House, 20-22 Queen's Rd Central (enter from Zetland St); soups & salads HK$12-23, sandwiches from HK$23-35, meals HK$25-35; 🕑 8am-8pm

The Délifrance chain is the place to come if you're craving croissants, doughnuts and pastries. It also serves up a selection of sandwiches, juices, coffee and tea, and hot meals at lunch and dinner.

EATING PLUS Map pp400–3 *Fusion*
☎ 2868 0599; Shop 1009, 1st fl, IFC Mall, 1 Harbour View St; side dishes HK$25-28, noodle & rice dishes HK$58-75, set meal with juice HK$98; ☎ 7.30am-10.30pm
Style comes cheap at this very vogue eatery and bar near the Outlying Islands ferry, Airport Express terminals and the territory's tallest structure. Lunch and dinner, taken at communal tables, extend to soups, noodles (a successful mix of East and West) and rice dishes, including risotto.

GOOD LUCK THAI Map pp404–5 *Thai*
☎ 2877 2971; 13 Wing Wah Lane; dishes HK$35-55; 🕑 11am-2am Mon-Sat, 4pm-midnight Sun
After sinking a few beers in Lan Kwai Fong, fight your way over to this chaotic and fun eatery for a cheap fix of Thai food. You won't be alone.

HOT DOG Map pp404–5
American Fast Food, Late Night Eats
☎ 2543 3555; Shop D, Lower Ground fl, Hollywood House, 27-29 Hollywood Rd (enter from Cochrane St); hot dogs HK$20-30; 🕑 24hr
You wouldn't cross town for the dogs sold at this miniscule outlet, but it's conveniently located just down from Soho and just up from Lan Kwai Fong.

LA BAGUETTE Map pp404–5
Sandwich Shop, Late Night Eats
☎ 2868 3716; 18 Lan Kwai Fong; sandwiches HK$35-60, small/medium/large pizza HK$48/70/90; 🕑 9.30am-1am Mon-Thu, 9.30am-4am Fri-Sat, 11am-9pm Sun
This is a great place right on the Fong if you're feeling the need for late-night sandwiches and snacks.

LA FONTAINE Map pp400–3 *Café*
☎ 2537 2938; Shop 3-5, Ground fl, The Forum, Exchange Square, Connaught Rd Central; breakfast HK$38-74, sandwiches HK$48-55, pasta HK$70-55; 🕑 8am-8pm
This little café does proper meals as well as pastries, cakes and sandwiches. You can eat in or take away.

Eating – Hong Kong Island

MAK'S NOODLE

Map pp404–5   *Chinese, Noodle Bar*
☎ 2854 3810; 77 Wellington St; dishes HK$25-50;
🕐 11am-8pm

Readers have written in praising this noodle shop; the beef brisket noodles, more of a Western taste than a Chinese one, are highly recommended. Go for lunch or eat early; it's shut tight by 8pm.

MIDNIGHT EXPRESS

Map pp404–5   *Late Night Eats*
☎ 2525 5010; 3 Lan Kwai Fong; 🕐 10am-3.30am;
meals HK$35-55

This does late-night eats – not Turkish prison food. The fare is a motley mix of Greek, Mexican and Italian.

MIX Map pp400–3   *International*

☎ 2523 7396; Shop 11, The Cascade, Standard Chartered Bank Bldg, 3 Queens Rd Central; juices HK$24, sandwiches HK$28-32, salads HK$25-28; 🕐 Mon-Sat 7am-7.30pm

This is a decent and convenient spot to grab a meal on the fly or to munch while surfing the in-house Internet. Points are deducted for meal names – *you* try ordering a 'beef injection' while keeping a straight face. There's a branch in the **IFC Mall** (Map pp400–3; ☎ 2971 0688; Shop 1015, 1 Harbour View St, Central).

OLIVER'S SUPER SANDWICHES

Map pp400–3   *Sandwich Shop*
☎ 2525 8087; Shop 10, 1st fl, The Forum, Exchange Square, Connaught Rd Central; breakfast HK$15-30, soups HK$12-16, salads HK$20, sandwiches HK$23-39; 🕐 8am-8pm

This chain offers reasonable-quality cooked breakfasts, sandwiches, salads and cakes. **Citibank Tower** (☎ 2526 2685; Shop 2, Lower Ground fl, 3 Garden Rd) and **The Landmark** (☎ 2877 6631; Shop B43-44, Basement, 1 Pedder St).

The branch in the **Prince's Building** (☎ 2523 0006; Shop 233-237, 10 Chater Rd) also has a gourmet supermarket.

PARK 'N' SHOP

Map pp400–3   *Supermarket*
77 Des Voeux Rd Central; 🕐 8am-9pm (express store 7am-11pm)

This is conveniently located branch of the supermarket chain in Central.

PEARL VIETNAMESE RESTAURANT

Map pp404–5   *Vietnamese*
☎ 2522 4223; 7 Wo On Lane; dishes HK$20-30;
🕐 11am-9pm

This tiny place is an inexpensive option for noodles or rice when frequenting the bars of the Fong. It serves cut-price dim sum (HK$12) from 2.30pm to 6pm.

TSIM CHAI KEE

Map pp404–5   *Chinese, Noodle Bar*
☎ 2850 6471; 98 Wellington St; noodles & dumplings from HK$10; 🕐 9am-9pm

This local shoebox opposite Mak's Noodle is where to head if you want a quick and cheap fix of rice or soup noodles (a major hangover cure). Choose from prawn, fish ball or sliced beef dumpling noodles. Avoid the main lunch hour (1pm to 2pm), though, unless you want to join the scrum.

XTC ON ICE Map pp404–5 *Ice-cream Parlour*

☎ 2541 0500; Shop 4B, Ground fl, Cheung Fai Bldg, 45-47 Cochrane St; 🕐 noon-midnight Sun-Thu, noon-4am Fri-Sat

The name may be a mouthful, but when ice cream (sorry, gelato) is this good, it just has to be. Choose from up to 20 exotic flavours, including ginger with cinnamon, mango paradise and guava.

SOHO

Soho is awash in restaurants; in fact there is nothing but eateries lining Elgin St. Most of them are in the middle and top-end range in terms of price.

2 SARDINES Map pp404–5   *French*

☎ 2973 6618; 43 Elgin St; starters HK$56-98, mains HK$156-210; 🕐 lunch noon-2.30pm, dinner 6-10.30pm

This small, independent French bistro deserves the crowds it draws. The namesake fish comes grilled with a yoghurt sauce; the roasted rack of lamb is worth trying, too. The wine list leans predictably to the Gallic side, but is likely to please. Set lunches at 2 Sardines are excellent value.

ARCHIE B'S DELICATESSEN

Map pp404–5 *American, Deli*

☎ 2522 1262; Lower Ground fl, 7-9 Staunton St; sandwiches & burgers HK$40-110, salads HK$50; ⏲ 10am-10pm

This little place just off the Central Escalator serves as authentic New York deli food as you'll find west of the US of A. It's pretty much an eat-and-run kind of place, but the few tables in the small alleyway just off Staunton St may have you lingering over your kosher dill pickle or Dr Brown's Cream Soda.

BLOWFISH Map pp404–5 *Japanese*

☎ 2815 7868; 20-26 Peel St; dishes from HK$55; ⏲ lunch noon-2.30pm Mon-Sat, dinner 6-11pm Mon-Thu, 6pm-midnight Fri-Sat

Blowfish, with its long sushi bar and enviable selection of saké, made quite a splash on its opening in early 2003. It's colourful, cool and costly.

Top Five Restaurants – Soho

- **Archie B's Delicatessen** (p178) Kick-ass deli so authentically American it whistles Dixie.
- **Orange Tree** (p179) Light modern Dutch food in a breezy setting.
- **Troika** (p179) Caviar, borscht and kitsch with live harp music.
- **Veda** (p421) Indian food for contemporary tastes.
- **Yi Jiang Nan** (p421) Modern Shanghainese cuisine and traditional décor.

BOCA Map pp404–5 *Fusion*

☎ 2548 1717; 65 Peel St; starters HK$32-79, paella HK$260-280, set lunch HK$88; ⏲ lunch noon-3pm Mon-Fri, brunch 11am-4pm Sat & Sun, dinner 5pm-midnight daily

This spot goes down well with expats, who sprawl on the trendy lounges and settees and over-order from the menu offering 'traditional Spanish starters' and 'not so traditional fusion' ones with an Asian twist. Sitting at the very end of Elgin St and boasting a wide frontage, Boca is a prime locale to watch the Soho parade. Weekend brunch is a favourite, with (HK$245) or without (HK$109) champers.

CARAMBA! Map pp404–5 *Mexican*

☎ 2530 9963; 26-30 Elgin St; appetisers HK$48-63, chilli HK$95, combination plates HK$110-148; ⏲ noon-midnight

Mexican is a cuisine as diametrically opposed to Chinese as you can imagine, but with a blinding selection of tequilas, this *cantina* provides a cosy and intimate venue for a fix of fajitas, enchiladas and chimichangas. Two/three-course set lunches are HK$78/98.

CUBANA Map pp404–5 *Cuban*

☎ 2869 1218; 47B Elgin St; tapas HK$59-128, mains HK$138-198; ⏲ lunch noon-2.30pm, dinner 6pm-midnight

This two-storey Cuban place has a good selection of tapas, a lot of soul, and is seriously rum-based (two for one 6pm to 9pm). Dancing starts sometime after 11pm, often to live music.

EL TACO LOCO Map pp404–5 *Mexican*

☎ 2522 1262; Lower Ground fl, 7-9 Staunton St; tacos HK$12-48, burritos HK$28-48; ⏲ noon-midnight

Next door and sister to Archie B's Delicatessen, 'The Crazy Taco' serves up authentic (as the sign informs us) tacos, burritos and tortilla chips with guacamole. And it's no idle boast; the Mexican consul is seen here noshing from time to time.

FAT ANGELO'S

Map pp404–5 *Italian, American*

☎ 2973 6808; 49A-C Elgin St; salads HK$30, pasta HK$70-145, mains HK$125-170; ⏲ noon-midnight

Fat Angelo's is one of the most successful restaurants to have opened in Soho in recent years. And the key to that success? Huge portions, free salads, unlimited bread and relatively low prices. The set lunch is only HK$68. There are three other branches in Hong Kong, including one in Tsim Sha Tsui (see p197 for details).

INDIA TODAY Map pp404–5 *Indian*

☎ 2801 5959; 1st fl, 26-30 Elgin St; tandoori dishes HK$65-97, curries HK$68-78; ⏲ lunch noon-3pm, dinner 6-11.30pm

This upstairs eatery in the thick of Soho, named after a popular Indian news weekly, serves some of the best tandoori dishes and curries in Central.

KATH+MAN+DU Map pp404–5 *Nepalese*

☎ 2869 1298; 11 Old Bailey St; curries HK$88-158, tandoori dishes HK$108-198; ⏲ lunch 11am-3pm, dinner 6-11pm

A little over the top in décor and price, this place is a great choice if you want to try 'nouvelle Nepalese' (not an oxymoron). It's akin to Indian cuisine but a little milder and sweeter. A three-course set lunch is HK$78; set dinner for two people is HK$300.

KIYOTAKI JAPANESE RESTAURANT

Map pp404–5   *Japanese*
☎ 2877 1803; 24 Staunton St; sushi/sashimi HK$150/120, tempura HK$130, set lunch HK$140; ☺ lunch noon-3pm Mon-Sat, dinner 6-11pm daily
This restaurant is one of the very few budget options for Japanese food in Soho.

LA COMIDA Map pp404–5   *Spanish*
☎ 2530 3118; 22 Staunton St; tapas HK$48-72, paella (for two) HK$178-298; ☺ lunch noon-3pm, dinner 6-11pm
This cosy place in the heart of Soho serves authentic Spanish cuisine to the denizens of Soho and Staunton St. Things at La Comida get a bit busy (and service slows down) at the weekend.

NANBANTEI Map pp404–5   *Japanese*
☎ 2810 6382; Shop A & B, 44-46 Staunton St; set lunches HK$48-98, set dinner HK$240; ☺ lunch noon-3pm, dinner 6-11pm
There's not a raw fish in sight at this friendly neighbourhood restaurant specialising in *yakitori* (meat, chicken and/or vegetables grilled on skewers).

NEPAL Map pp404–5   *Nepalese*
☎ 2869 6212; 14 Staunton St; mains HK$78-148, set lunch HK$68, set dinner HK$188; ☺ lunch noon-3pm, dinner 6-11pm
This was one of the first ethnic restaurants to find its way to Soho, and Nepalese flavours and treats remain in abundance here. Waiters rush across the road with overflowing plates to Nepal's sister-restaurant, **Sherpa** (Map pp404-5; ☎ 2973 6886; 11 Staunton St, Soho), which shares the same menu and keeps the same hours.

ORANGE TREE Map pp404–5   *Dutch*
☎ 2838 9352; 17 Shelley St; meals from HK$300 per person; ☺ lunch noon-3pm Sat & Sun, dinner 6-10.30pm daily
Modern Dutch food is served in a breezy russet setting in the higher reaches of the Central Escalator. Don't get stuck on the sausages – there are lighter dishes available, such as puff pastries. For dessert there are always *poffertjes* (Dutch pancakes) on the menu.

Traditional way of serving dim sum

SHANG-HI!

Map pp404–5   *Chinese, Shanghainese*
☎ 2810 8800; 38 Elgin St; dim sum HK$20-40, rice & noodle dishes HK$30-68, mains HK$68-138; ☺ 11am-11pm
The name is cringe-making and the décor (faux 1930s Shanghai) a bit naff, but the food aims at authenticity and comes pretty close in an area not renowned for its Chinese restaurants.

SOHO SOHO Map pp404–5   *Modern British*
☎ 2147 2618; 9 Old Bailey St; starters HK$60-105, mains HK$165-175; ☺ lunch noon-2.30pm, dinner 7-10.30pm
New British food has taken off in post-colonial Hong Kong with locals and expats alike. It's creative (crumpet with goat's cheese), comforting (herb-crusted roasted cod with new potatoes) and meaty (lamb fillets with a pepper crust). Two-/three-course set lunches are available during the week for HK$95/120, and set dinners Sunday to Wednesday for HK$170/220.

TROIKA Map pp404–5   *Russian*
☎ 2801 7839; 28 Elgin St; set lunch HK$88, set dinner HK$350; ☺ lunch noon-3pm, dinner 6-11pm
The food may not be the reason for visiting Troika, but the décor is (a tsar's wet dream is

the only possible description). Live harp music in what feels like a 19th-century drawing room in a Tolstoy novel is an added touch. Russian dishes on offer include a beluga and salmon roe starter (HK$138), sturgeon soup (HK$78) and goose liver with cherry liqueur (HK$138).

VEDA Map pp404–5 *Indian*
☎ 2868 5885; 8 Arbuthnot Rd; meals HK$350 per person; ⏰ lunch noon-3pm daily, dinner 6-11pm Mon-Sat, 6-10.30pm Sun
This stylish new restaurant is pricier than most other Indian places in Central, but is worth every rupee spent for its cool décor, excellent service and beautifully presented and innovative dishes (eg chicken in coriander and cashew nut paste, fish steamed with mint). Sunday brunch has become a tradition for many.

YI JIANG NAN
Map pp404–5 *Chinese, Shanghainese*
☎ 2111 2822; 33-35 Staunton St; meals HK$250 per person; ⏰ lunch noon-3pm, dinner 6-11pm
This place has excellent (and quite modern in preparation and presentation) Shanghainese Chinese cuisine served on blackwood tables under bird cages moonlighting as lanterns. Behind the dark wood exterior prevails a subdued, homely atmosphere, although the frescoes may be a tad too Tuscan for some.

Cheap Eats
BAGEL FACTORY
Map pp404–5 *Sandwich Shop, Bakery*
☎ 2951 0755; Shop B2, Ground fl, 41 Elgin St; filled bagels HK$15-25; ⏰ 8am-9pm
This establishment has excellent and quite innovative filled bagels, plus delicious baked goods from the adjoining **Soho Bakery**, which keeps the same hours. There's also a range of Russo-Jewish snacks, including knishes.

CHICKEN ON THE RUN
Map pp404–5 *Fast Food*
☎ 2537 8285; Shop A, Lower Ground fl, 1 Prince's Tce; dishes HK$25-60; ⏰ 11.30am-9.30pm
This brightly lit and pristine clean place is where to go if you fancy takeaway chicken.

LE RENDEZ-VOUS Map pp404–5 *Creperie*
☎ 2905 1808; 5 Staunton St; galettes & crepes HK$25-50; ⏰ 10am-11.30pm
This tiny, nautically themed crepe house primarily serves savoury filled *galettes* and sweet crepes, but also does filled baguettes and croque-monsieurs (HK$35 to HK$50) and salads (HK$38 to HK$50). The *galettes* come filled with classic combos like mushroom and cheese along with more adventurous spicy inventions.

MID-LEVELS
Restaurants in the Mid-Levels cater mostly to local residents too lazy to make the trek down to Soho or Central.

PHUKET'S SEAFOOD GRILL CLUB
Map pp400–3 *Thai*
☎ 2868 9672; Lower Ground fl, Shop D, Peace Tower, 30-32 Robinson Rd; soups & Thai salads HK$55-85, curries HK$65-78; ⏰ lunch noon-3pm, dinner 6pm-midnight
This Mid-Levels restaurant, entered from Mosque Junction, is a cosy spot, with a mural of a Thai beach to enhance the mood for an escape to Thailand's most popular island destination. The food (mainly seafood) is not all

that authentic, but it's a convenient choice if you're staying in the area.

RICO'S Map pp400–3 *Spanish*
☎ 2840 0937; 44 Robinson Rd; tapas HK$48-90, mains HK$120-185; ⏰ lunch noon-3pm, dinner 6-11pm
In the same stable and just up the road from the Thai restaurant Phuket's, Rico's serves tapas, paella (HK$160 to HK$190) and decent sangria in a candlelit Mediterranean setting. Is this really the Mid-Levels?

SHEUNG WAN
West of Central, Sheung Wan stands out for two quite disparate cuisines: Chinese (in particular, Chiu Chow) and Korean. For some reason the district has always been a 'Little Korea' and is the best place on the island to look for *bulgogi* (Korean barbecue) and *kimchi* (spicy fermented cabbage).

FUNG SHING RESTAURANT

Map pp400–3   *Chinese, Cantonese*

☎ 2815 8689; Ground fl, 7 On Tai St; meals from HK$130 per person; ☯ 7.30am-11.30pm

A cavernous place near the Western Market, the 'Phoenix City' specialises in regional Cantonese cuisine. Dim sum is served from 7.30am to 3pm.

GRAND STAGE

Map pp400–3   *Chinese, Cantonese*

☎ 2815 2311; 2nd fl, Western Market, 323 Des Voeux Rd Central & New Market St; dishes HK$58-98, meals from HK$250 per person; ☯ lunch noon-2.30pm, tea 2.30-6.15pm, dinner 7pm-12.30am

This place features ballroom music and dancing at high tea and dinner. The food's quite good – try the seafood soup with mashed pumpkin (HK$195) or the fried rice with *con-poy* (HK$98) – but come here primarily to kick your heels up.

HO CHOI SEAFOOD RESTAURANT

Map pp400–3   *Chinese, Cantonese*

☎ 2850 6722; 287-291 Des Voeux Rd Central; dim sum HK$43-80, meals from HK$150 per person; ☯ 7am-11pm

This place, entered from Cleverly St, is popular for dim sum (served 7.30am to 11.30am) and Cantonese seafood. The menu is in Chinese only, so get your pointing finger ready.

KOREA GARDEN Map pp400–3   *Korean*

☎ 2542 2339; 1st fl, Blissful Bldg, 247 Des Voeux Rd Central; meals from about HK$120 per person; ☯ 11.30am-11pm Mon-Sat, 5.30-11pm Sun

The slightly toned down Korean food here attracts young Hong Kong Chinese.

LEE FA YUEN KOREA HOUSE RESTAURANT Map pp400–3   *Korean*

☎ 2526 5293, 2544 0007; Ground fl, Honwell Commercial Centre, 119-121 Connaught Rd Central; meals about HK$150; ☯ noon-11pm

The Lee Fa Yuen Korea House, entered from Man Wa Lane, is acknowledged as having some of the most authentic Korean barbecue, *kimchi* and appetisers in Hong Kong and is always filled with Korean expats – the ultimate stamp of approval.

LEUNG HING SEAFOOD RESTAURANT

Map pp400–3   *Chinese, Chiu Chow*

☎ 2850 6666; 32 Bonham Strand West; meals from HK$150 per person; ☯ 7.30am-11pm

The staple ingredients of Chiu Chow cuisine – shellfish, goose and duck – are extensively employed and delectably prepared at this very local place.

PHOENIX Map pp400–3   *Modern British*

☎ 2546 2110; 5 U Lam Tce; meals from HK$200 per person; ☯ lunch/brunch 11am-6pm Sat & Sun, dinner 6.30-11pm daily

The territory's first gastropub sits comfortably on the border between traditional Sheung Wan and expat Mid-Levels, a perfect icon for modern Hong Kong. The food is well prepared and substantial, the old (antique?) furnishings comfortable and you can BYO without paying a corkage fee.

THE PEAK

You'd hardly venture all the way up Victoria Peak for a meal; food here falls in the queue behind the views and all the attractions of the Peak Tower. But there are a few choices.

CAFE DECO Map pp400–3   *International*

☎ 2849 5111; Levels 1 & 2, Peak Galleria, 118 Peak Rd; sushi & sashimi HK$48-128, starters HK$98-158, tandoori dishes & curries HK$104-156, pasta HK$108-136; ☯ 11.30am-midnight Mon-Thu, 11.30am-1am Fri, 9.30am-midnight Sat & Sun

With its spectacular harbour views, Art Deco furnishings and live jazz Monday to Saturday nights, this place need not have made too much effort with the menu. But the food, while an East-meets-West eclectic thing, is above average, with the bistro dishes and oyster bar scoring extra points. Breakfast and brunch are served from 9.30am to 2.30pm

Saturday and Sunday; there's a set lunch for HK$88.

MÖVENPICK MARCHÉ

Map pp400–3   *International, Asian*

☎ 2849 2000; Levels 6 & 7 (lift ex Level 4), Peak Tower, 128 Peak Rd; sushi HK$25-100, rice & noodle dishes HK$58-68, pasta HK$78-88, grills HK$48-108; ☯ 11am-11pm Mon-Fri, 9am-11pm Sat & Sun

More a Singaporean concept than a Hong Kong one, the Marché consists of a range of different stalls preparing Asian and international food from which you can order anything from noodles and teppanyaki to pasta and sausages. It has a Kids' Corner with little tables, stuffed animals and so on for the ankle-biters.

PARK 'N' SHOP Map pp400–3 *Supermarket*
Level 2, Peak Galleria, 118 Peak Rd; ☽ 8am-10.30pm
This is a convenient branch of the supermarket chain if you want to stock up on snacks and drinks before embarking on a walk.

PEAK LOOKOUT

Map pp400–3 *International, Asian*
☎ 2849 1000; 121 Peak Rd; starters HK$95-158, mains HK$168-268;

☽ 10.30am-11pm Mon-Thu, 10.30am-11.30 Fri, 8.30am-11.30pm Sat, 8.30am-11pm Sun
The erstwhile Peak Café has metamorphosed into a swish colonial-style restaurant, with seating indoors in a glassed-in veranda and on the outside terrace. As was the case with the Peak Café, the food selection here is a bit of mishmash, with everything from Indian and French to Thai and Japanese on offer. We'll stick to the oysters (HK$141 to HK$242 per half-dozen), the barbeque and the views, which are to the south of the island – not the harbour. Breakfast and brunch are available at the weekend from 8.30am to 3pm.

ADMIRALTY & WAN CHAI

Wan Chai (and to a lesser extent Admiralty) is a happy hunting ground for ethnic restaurants. Name your cuisine and MTR, bus or tram it down to the Wanch. You're certain to find it here.

369 SHANGHAI RESTAURANT

Map pp406–8 *Shanghai*
☎ 2527 8611; 30-32 O'Brien Rd, Wan Chai; cold dishes HK$34-50, soups HK$40-60; ☽ 10am-4am
This low-key eatery serves Shanghainese food that's nothing like five-star, but does the dumpling job fairly well. The place is family-run and there are some good comfy booths at the front window. It's open really late, too, so you can come here after a draining night of bopping. Try its signature hot and sour soup (HK$60) – almost a meal in itself – or the aubergine fried with garlic (HK$52).

AMERICAN RESTAURANT

Map pp406–8 *Chinese, Peking*
☎ 2527 7277, 2527 1000; 20 Lockhart Rd, Wan Chai; meals from HK$150 per person; ☽ 11.30am-11.30pm
The friendly American (which chose its name to attract Yank sailors cruising the Wanch for sustenance while on R&R during the Vietnam War) has been serving decent northern Chinese cuisine for over half a century. As you'd expect, the Peking duck (HK$275) and the beggar's chicken (HK$310; order in advance) are very good.

CARRIANA CHIU CHOW RESTAURANT

Map pp406–8 *Chinese, Chiu Chow*
☎ 2511 1282; 1st fl, 151 Gloucester Rd, Wan Chai; meals from HK$150 per person; ☽ 11.30am-11.30pm
For Chiu Chow food, the Carriana, entered from Tonnochy Rd, still rates right up there

after all these years. Try the cold dishes (sliced goose with vinegar, crab claws), pork with tofu or Chiu Chow chicken.

CHE'S CANTONESE RESTAURANT

Map pp406–8 *Chinese, Cantonese*
☎ 2528 1123; 4th fl, The Broadway, 54-62 Lockhart Rd, Wan Chai; meals from HK$300 per person;
☽ lunch 11am-3pm, dinner 6pm-midnight
This *crème de la crème* of Cantonese restaurants serves many home-style delicacies and offers a special seasonal menu with a dozen additional dishes. It's highly recommended. Though you probably won't know it, you'll be surrounded by Hong Kong celebrities and minor royalty.

Top Five Restaurants – Admiralty & Wan Chai

- **Beijing Shui Jiao Wong** (p186) Northern-style dumplings in a steamy canteen.
- **Che's Cantonese Restaurant** (p182) Hong Kong celebrities and minor royalty nosh Cantonese delights.
- **Tan Ta Wan Restaurant** (p185) Where Thai amahs go for a chilli infusion.
- **Vegetarian Court** (p186) The most upscale grazing ground for veggies – make no bones about it.
- **Victoria City** (p186) Excellent dim sum in surprisingly subdued surrounds.

CINE CITTÀ Map pp400–3 *Italian*

☎ 2529 0199; Starcrest Bldg, 9 Star St, Wan Chai; starters HK$68-158, pasta HK$118-198, mains HK$178-248; ✒ lunch noon-3pm Mon-Fri, dinner 6pm-12.30am daily

This very flash restaurant with an Italian film theme is in an area of southwest Wan Chai that is becoming something of a restaurant and nightlife district. The crowd here is more hotel bar than Lan Kwai Fong, though.

CINTA-J Map pp406–8 *Filipino, Indonesian*

☎ 2529 6622; Shop G4, Malaysia Bldg, 69 Jaffe Rd, Wan Chai; dishes HK$50-125; ✒ 11am-3.30am

This friendly restaurant and lounge has a Southeast Asian menu longer than the Bible, which covers all bases from *murtabak* to *gado-gado*, but with a strong emphasis on Pinoy dishes. It turns into a cocktail lounge in the late evening and stays open until 3.30am or so.

COYOTE BAR & GRILL

Map pp406–8 *Mexican*

☎ 2861 2221; 114-120 Lockhart Rd, Wan Chai; combination platters HK$10-121, chilli HK$98, fajitas HK$115-155; ✒ lunch noon-3pm daily, brunch noon-6pm Sat & Sun, dinner 6-10.45pm daily

With its warm, mustard-coloured décor and brassy bar, this *cantina* describes itself as 'Mexican with attitude'. And that's just what it is. Great margaritas, too.

DAN RYAN'S CHICAGO GRILL

Map pp400–3 *American*

☎ 2845 4600; Level 1, Shop 114, Pacific Place, 88 Queensway, Admiralty; starters HK$48-125, pasta HK$95-130, salads HK$98-130; ✒ 11am-midnight Mon-Sat, 9am-midnight Sun

The fare at this re-creation of a Chicago lounge restaurant always satisfies, no matter whether it's the ribs (half/full rack HK$132/198), steaks (HK$135 to HK$238) or sandwiches (HK$55 to HK$112). A big-screen video shows sports, and there's also a branch in Tsim Sha Tsui (p196).

DYNASTY

Map pp406–8 *Chinese, Cantonese*

☎ 2802 8888 ext 6971; 3rd fl, Renaissance Harbour View Hotel, 1 Harbour Rd, Wan Chai; starters HK$100-135, rice & noodle dishes HK$100-160, mains HK$95-300; ✒ lunch 11.30am-2.30pm Mon-Sat, 11am-2.30pm Sun, dinner 6.30-11pm Mon-Sat

Chicken and dumplings

Dynasty serves some of the most innovative (and Asian-Western 'fused') dim sum in town.

EAST OCEAN SEAFOOD RESTAURANT

Map pp406–8 *Chinese, Seafood*

☎ 2827 8887; 3rd fl, Harbour Centre, 25 Harbour Rd, Wan Chai; dim sum HK$28-68, meals from HK$250 per person; ✒ lunch 11am-3pm, dinner 6pm-midnight

Though the East Ocean may not be among the top 10 restaurants in the world, as the *New York Times* food critic Patricia Wells once said (opening another seven branches or other restaurants may have compromised quality just a wee bit), it still serves some of the best and inventive Cantonese seafood dishes in town. There's also a Tsim Sha Tsui East branch (Map pp412-14; ☎ 723 8128; Basement 1, East Ocean Centre, 98 Granville Rd).

GRAPPA'S RISTORANTE

Map pp400–3 *Italian*

☎ 2868 0086; Ground fl, Shop 132, Pacific Place, 88 Queensway, Admiralty; starters HK$65-198, pizza HK$98-135, pasta HK$95-160, mains HK$125-280; ✒ breakfast 9.30am-11.30am, lunch 11.30am-3pm, dinner 6pm-midnight

This is a top-notch venue for antipasto, fettuccini and other Italian dishes, though not everyone likes dining in a shopping mall. Still, of Grappa's half-dozen outlets scattered across Hong Kong Island, this is the best.

HEALTHY MESS VEGETARIAN RESTAURANT

Map pp406–8　　　　　　　　*Chinese, Vegetarian*

☎ 2527 3918; 51-53 Hennessy Rd, Wan Chai; dim sum HK$2.50-5, dishes HK$45-60, set meal for 2/4 HK$168/268; ☽ 10.30am-11pm Mon-Sat, 6-11pm Sun

This strictly Buddhist vegetarian establishment sporting the Buddhist swastika on its business card is very popular with Chinese noncarnivores. It serves tasty, filling food – lots of mock 'meat' dishes made from tofu – and is highly recommended.

HYANG CHON KOREAN RESTAURANT

Map pp406–8　　　　　　　　　　　　　*Korean*

☎ 2574 5142; 2nd fl, Workingfield Commercial Bldg, 408-412 Jaffe Rd, Wan Chai; meals from HK$250 per person; ☽ dinner 6pm-4am, closed for lunch

This somewhat expensive Korean restaurant attracts Korean expats and their friends with its authentic ginseng chicken and *bibimbab*, rice served in a sizzling pot topped with thinly sliced beef and cooked and preserved vegetables, which is then bound by a raw egg and flavoured with chilli-laced soy bean paste.

JO JO MESS CLUB Map pp406–8　　*Indian*

☎ 2527 3776; 1st fl, Block C, 86 Johnston Rd (enter from Lee Tung St), Wan Chai; dishes HK$42-50; ☽ lunch noon-3pm, dinner 6-11pm

A favourite of expats who love Indian food as Indians prepare it, Jo Jo has branched out in recent years, opening five top-class restaurants throughout the territory. But this is the original and the most authentic. There's a lunch buffet (HK$75) on Wednesday and Friday, including a half-pint of beer.

KOKAGE Map pp400–3　　　　　　*Japanese*

☎ 2529 6138; Ground fl, Starcrest Bldg, 9 Star St, Wan Chai; meals from HK$400; ☽ lunch noon-2.30pm Mon-Fri, dinner 6-11pm Sun-Thu, 6-11.30pm Fri & Sat

From the people who brought you Cine Città (and sharing the same building) is this incredibly stylish contemporary Japanese fusion restaurant and *izakaya* (a Japanese-style pub) – almost more Manhattan than Tokyo. Dress up and make sure you've got plastic with you. You might start off with a cocktail at 1/5 (p223).

LITTLE PRINCE

Map pp406–8　　　　　　　　*Mediterranean*

☎ 2528 5828; Shop A, 4-6 St Francis St, Wan Chai; starters HK$38-98, pasta & risotto HK$78-88, mains HK$128-135; ☽ lunch noon-3pm, dinner 6-10.30pm Mon-Sat, closed Sun

While this restaurant claims to have put the Star St restaurant and nightlife district on the map, it has none of the edge or style of the nearby Cine Città and Kokage. What can you expect from a place with such a cutesy name and sparkly stars hanging from the ceiling? Simple, no-risks Mediterranean fare.

LIU YUAN RESTAURANT

Map pp406–8　　　　　　　　　*Shanghainese*

☎ 2510 0483; 1st fl, CRE Bldg, 303 Hennessy Rd, Wan Chai; meals from HK$250 per person; ☽ lunch 11.30am-2.30pm, dinner 6-11pm

This stylish restaurant serves superb Shanghainese dishes, including things like crab claws cooked with duck egg, and the tiny prawns steamed with tea leaves are superb.

LOUIS' STEAK HOUSE

Map pp406–8　　　　　　　　　　*Steakhouse*

☎ 2529 8933; 1st fl, Malaysia Bldg, 50 Gloucester Rd, Wan Chai; steaks HK$170-230; ☽ lunch 11.30am-3pm, dinner 6pm-midnight

This is the sort of place that Hong Kong Chinese used to frequent when they wanted fancy Western cuisine in a Western-style restaurant (candle light, checked tablecloths etc). It's sort of 1950s, but Louis' still has its charms. And with the recent resurgence of interest in steakhouses in Hong Kong, it probably has it made, too. Happy hour in the cocktail lounge is from 5pm to 8pm.

LUNG MOON RESTAURANT

Map pp406–8　　　　　　　　*Chinese, Cantonese*

☎ 2572 9888; 130-136 Johnston Rd, Wan Chai; meals from HK$120 per person; ☽ 6am-11pm

The dining experience at this very basic Cantonese restaurant has not changed a great deal since the 1950s, and the prices, while not quite still at 1950s levels, are still reasonable.

NICHOLINI'S Map pp400–3　　　　*Italian*

☎ 2521 3838; 8th fl, Conrad International, 88 Queensway, Admiralty; meals from HK$350 per person; ☽ lunch 11.30am-3pm, dinner 6.30-11pm

This refined restaurant's approach to northern Italian cuisine has won it praise from Italian expats and even an *Insegna del Ristorante Italiano* award from the president of Italy. Simple yet superb antipasti as well as shellfish dishes are just a few firm favourites here.

ONE HARBOUR ROAD

Map pp406–8 *Chinese, Cantonese*

☎ 2588 1234; 7th & 8th fls, Grand Hyatt Hotel, 1 Harbour Rd, Wan Chai; starters HK$80-165, mains HK$140-390; ⏰ lunch noon-2.30pm, dinner 6-10.30pm

This is undoubtedly the classiest Chinese restaurant in Hong Kong. In addition to the beautiful design and fabulous harbour view, six pages of gourmet dishes await your perusal. There's a set dinner available for HK$630.

OPEN KITCHEN

Map pp406–8 *International, Asian*

☎ 2827 2923; 6th fl, Hong Kong Arts Centre, 2 Harbour Rd, Wan Chai; pies HK$25, salads HK$38-65, set lunch/dinner from HK$60/78; ⏰ 11am-10pm Sat-Thu, 11am-11pm Fri

This well-lit, smart cafeteria/canteen with great views of the harbour serves a mix of Indian, Malaysian, Japanese and Italian dishes. If you're taking in a play or a concert at the Arts Centre, Open Kitchen is a good, cheapish, arty option for meals, snacks or drinks at the bar. Bring your ticket stub from the cinema downstairs to get a free drink with your meal.

PATONG THAI RESTAURANT

Map pp400–3 *Thai*

☎ 2861 1006; 12-22 Queen's Rd East, Wan Chai; starters HK$48-70, curries HK$63-90, set menu for 2 from HK$170; ⏰ lunch 11.30am-2.30pm, dinner 5.30pm-12.30am

This rather stylish Thai restaurant is pricey but just the ticket if you feel like eating in a more salubrious setting.

PETRUS Map pp400–3 *French*

☎ 2820 8590, 2877 3838; 56th fl, Island Shangri-La Hotel, Pacific Place, 88 Queensway, Admiralty; 5-/6-course set menu HK$750/900; ⏰ lunch noon-2.30pm Mon-Sat, brunch 11.30am-2.30pm Sun, dinner 6.30pm-midnight daily

With its head (and prices) in the clouds, Petrus is one of the finest restaurants in Hong Kong. Expect traditional (not nouvelle) French cuisine, some over-the-top décor and stunning harbour views. Guys, don a jacket (required) and eschew the jeans (banned).

PORT CAFE

Map pp406–8 *International, Buffet*

☎ 2582 7731; Level 3, Phase 2, Hong Kong Convention & Exhibition Centre, 1 Expo Dr, Wan Chai; starters HK$35-65, mains HK$70-98, set lunch HK$98; ⏰ noon-6pm Mon-Sat, 11am-6pm Sun

For stunning views over Victoria Harbour and Central, fabulous décor and smooth design, try this restaurant in the colossal convention centre. Depending on what's on, the café sometimes throws on a buffet, ranging in price from HK$128 to HK$168. If you're into quantity over quality, go ahead; otherwise, choose another day. Note that it's not open for dinner.

SABAH Map pp406–8 *Malaysian*

☎ 2143 6626; Shop 4 & 5, 98-102 Jaffe Rd, Wan Chai; starters HK$38-42, rice & noodle dishes HK$45-60, mains HK$55-78; ⏰ 7.30am-midnight

This large restaurant in the heart of Wan Chai serves Malaysian food tempered for the Hong Kong palate. It's a favourite of office workers; try to avoid coming between 1pm and 2pm. A choice of five set lunches (HK$48) is available from 11am to 3pm.

SAIGON Map pp406–8 *Vietnamese*

☎ 2598 7222; Room 2A, 2nd fl, Sun Hung Kai Centre, 30 Harbour Rd, Wan Chai; set dinners HK$168-188; ⏰ lunch noon-3pm, dinner 6-10.30pm

A relatively sterilised version of a Vietnamese restaurant, Saigon has some interesting dishes (pomelo salad with dried shrimps, green papaya and beef salad with chilli) and inexpensive set lunches during the week.

SHABU SHABU Map pp406–8 *Japanese*

☎ 2893 8806; Ground fl, Kwan Chart Tower, 6 Tonnochy Rd, Wan Chai; sushi & sashimi HK$30-40, tempura HK$65-180, hotpot meals HK$70-90; ⏰ 11.30am-midnight Mon-Sat, 6pm-midnight Sun

This huge place done up in traditional Japanese décor offers a warm welcome and relatively reasonable prices.

STEAM & STEW INN

Map pp406–8 *Chinese, Cantonese*

☎ 2529 3913; 21-23 Tai Wong St East, Wan Chai; meals from HK$100 per person; ⏰ 11.30am-11pm

The Inn serves 'home-style' Cantonese food, most of which is steamed, stewed or boiled. The food is good, inexpensive and free of monosodium glutamate (MSG).

TAN TA WAN RESTAURANT

Map pp400–3 *Thai*

☎ 2865 1178; Shop 9, Ground fl, Rialto Bldg, 2 Landale St, Wan Chai; rice & noodle dishes HK$28-38, starters HK$40-78, curries HK$40-108, mains HK$50-108; ☎ 11am-11pm Mon-Fri, noon-10pm Sat & Sun

A bunch of Thai amahs can't bear the ersatz Thai food they get in Hong Kong. They open a restaurant and – presto – offer some of the most authentic Thai food in Hong Kong outside Kowloon City (see p118).

UGO Map pp406–8   *Italian*
☎ 2861 0077; Upper Ground fl, East Town Bldg, 16 Fenwick St, Wan Chai; meals from HK$250; ☺ lunch noon-3pm Mon-Sat, dinner 6pm-midnight daily

What was Rigoletto, a Hong Kong institution for decades, has been reborn as Ugo and it's pretty much of a muchness, with old-fashioned pastas and pizzas heading up the bill of fare. Ugo himself is usually at hand to greet guests and can often be heard tickling the ivories.

VEGETARIAN COURT
Map pp406–8   *Chinese, Vegetarian*
☎ 2845 1199; 2nd fl, CRE Bldg, 303 Hennessy Rd, Wan Chai; dishes from HK$50; ☺ lunch 11.30am-2.30pm, dinner 6-11pm

Not just another little vegetarian place in Wan Chai, the Vegetarian Court is Shanghainese as well, promising bigger, fuller flavours.

VICEROY Map pp406–8   *Indian*
☎ 2827 7777; Room 2B, 2nd fl, Sun Hung Kai Centre, 30 Harbour Rd, Wan Chai; starters HK$32-78, tandoori dishes HK$68-268, curries HK$82-148; ☺ lunch noon-3pm, dinner 6-11pm

The Viceroy has been an institution in Hong Kong for some two decades: an upmarket Indian restaurant with sitar music and a fun place to party later on (see Punchline Comedy Club p236).

VICTORIA CITY
Map pp406–8   *Chinese, Cantonese*
☎ 2827 9938; room 2D, 2nd fl, Sun Hung Kai Centre, 30 Harbour Rd, Wan Chai; meals from HK$250 per person; ☺ lunch 11am-2.30pm, dinner 6-10.30pm

Many in Hong Kong consider the dim sum (served 11am to 2.30pm) here to be the best in the territory.

YÈ SHANGHAI
Map pp400–3   *Chinese, Shanghainese*
☎ 2918 9833; Level 3, Shop 332, Pacific Place, 88 Queensway, Admiralty; rice & noodle dishes HK$45-88, cold dishes HK$48-60, mains HK$76-380; ☺ lunch 11.30am-3pm, dinner 6-11.30pm

This groovy place takes street-level Shanghainese cuisine and gives it a tweak here and there. The drunken pigeon (HK$100) is a wine-soaked winner and the steamed dumplings are perfectly plump, but sometimes this restaurant goes for clattery style over substance. There's live music from 9.30pm Thursday to Saturday.

Cheap Eats
BEIJING SHUI JIAO WONG
Map pp406–8   *Peking, Noodle Bar*
☎ 2527 0289; 118 Jaffe Rd, Wan Chai; dishes HK$25-40; ☺ 11am-11pm

You won't find better (or cheaper) northern-style dumplings (HK$31 to HK$35), *guo tie* (HK$31 to HK$35) or soup noodles (HK$25 to HK$32) anywhere in Hong Kong.

DÉLIFRANCE Map pp400–3   *Café*
☎ 2520 0959; Shop A1-A3, Queensway Plaza, 93 Queensway, Admiralty; soups & salads HK$12-23, sandwiches HK$23-35, meals HK$25-35; ☺ 8am-8pm

A branch of popular bakery and patisserie can be found near the Admiralty MTR station.

GENKI SUSHI Map pp400–3   *Japanese*
☎ 2865 2933; Shop C1, Ground fl, Far East Finance Centre, Admiralty; sushi HK$9-35 per pair, sushi sets HK$45-100; ☺ 11am-11pm

This cheap-and-cheerful susherie, popular with young Hong Kong Chinese, doesn't have a word of English within its four walls, but you'll recognise the logo – not a cringe-making 'smiley face' but a frowning 'meany face'.

GREAT FOOD HALL
Map pp400–3   *Deli, Food Court*
☎ 2918 9986; Lower Ground fl, Pacific Place, 88 Queensway, Admiralty; ☺ 10am-10pm Sun-Fri, 9am-10pm Sat

This food emporium has the largest stock of imported comestibles (Western and Asian, with an emphasis on Japanese and Korean) in Hong Kong, supplying a range of imported cheeses, preserved meats, breads and chocolates. A quick fix of vegetable curry with rice and a poppadom is only HK$30.

OLIVER'S SUPER SANDWICHES
Map pp400–3   *Sandwich Shop*
☎ 2522 0186; Shop 2B, 1st fl, Lippo Centre, 88 Queensway, Admiralty; breakfast HK$15-30, soups

HK$12-16, salads HK$20, sandwiches HK$23-39;
🕑 8am-8pm

This is a convenient branch of the popular sandwichery.

PEPPERONI'S PIZZA Map pp406–8 _Italian_

☎ 2865 3214; 54 Jaffe Rd, Wan Chai; pizza HK$65-75, salads HK$50-60; 🕑 7am-midnight Mon-Fri, 9am-midnight Sat & Sun

This branch of the celebrated pizzeria with branches in Stanley (p194) and Sai Kung (p209) is an inexpensive option for pizza and pasta in the Wanch.

SAIGON BEACH

Map pp406–8 _Vietnamese_

☎ 2527 3383; Ground fl, 66 Lockhart Rd, Wan Chai; noodles & rice HK$28-35, mains HK$60-70, set meals for 2 from HK$98; 🕑 lunch 11.45am-4pm, dinner 6-10.15pm

This popular little hole-in-the-wall may not impress at first sight, but the affable service and food is well worth sharing a table with strangers, which you undoubtedly will have to do.

SHAFFI'S MALIK Map pp406–8 _Indian_

☎ 2572 7474; 185 Wan Chai Rd, Wan Chai; starters HK$18-35, curries HK$44-60, kebabs HK$48-57, tandoori dishes HK$48-128; 🕑 lunch noon-3pm, dinner 6-11pm

This place boasts that it is 'probably the oldest Indian restaurant in town serving the best

Indian cuisine'. Both claims are debatable, but it's cheap, halal and here.

TIM'S KITCHEN

Map pp406–8 _Chinese, Hong Kong_

☎ 2527 2982; Shop C, Ground fl, 118 Jaffe Rd, Wan Chai; dishes HK$12-55; 🕑 7am-10pm

When as many Hong Kong Chinese queue up outside a restaurant at lunchtime as they do at Tim's every day, you can be sure that the food is both inexpensive and of good quality. It's a mix of Cantonese staples (fried rice, noodles) with some Hong Kong-style additions (fried pasta).

YOSHINOYA NOODLES

Map pp400–3 _Japanese, Noodle Bar_

☎ 2520 0953; Shop B, Ground fl, China Hong Kong Tower, 8-12 Hennessy Rd, Wan Chai; soups & noodles HK$25-40; 🕑 11am-11pm

A decent choice for a quick lunch or some blotter while trawling Wan Chai, this fast-food Japanese place near the Wesley Hotel has another 14 outlets around the territory.

ZAMBRA Map pp406–8 _Café_

☎ 2802 2226; 239 Jaffe Rd, Wan Chai; sandwiches HK$26, salads HK$35, tea sets HK$25-40; 🕑 7am-7pm

This modern Western-style café is just the ticket for a quick breakfast (the muffins are excellent) or a sandwich on the hoof. It's in quite a unique area full of noodle shops.

CAUSEWAY BAY

Causeway Bay is a strange amalgam of restaurants and cuisines but, apart from a selection of rather slick and overpriced European places on Fashion Walk (or Houston St) northeast of the Causeway MTR station, this is the place for Chinese and other Asian (particularly Southeast Asian) food. Causeway Bay also has a lot of Japanese restaurants because of all the Japanese department stores (and tourists) that used to be based here before the Land of the Rising Sun essentially went bankrupt.

ARIRANG Map pp406–8 *Korean*
☎ 2506 3298; Shop 1105, 11th fl, Food Forum, Times Square, 1 Matheson St; meals from HK$250 per person, set lunch HK$70; 🕙 lunch noon-3pm, dinner 6-11pm
A branch of the upmarket Korean restaurant chain, with an outlet in Tsim Sha Tsui (p196).

BANANA LEAF CURRY HOUSE
Map pp406–8 *Malaysian, Singaporean*
☎ 2573 8187; Ground fl, 440 Jaffe Rd; starters HK$32-78, mains HK$54-128; 🕙 lunch 11.30am-3pm, dinner 6pm-midnight Mon-Fri, 11.30-midnight Sat & Sun
This large branch of a chain dishes up Malaysian/Singaporean food served on a banana leaf; your hands are the cutlery if you choose to go authentic. There are some five other outlets, including one across the harbour in Tsim Sha Tsui (p196).

BO KUNG
Map pp406–8 *Chinese, Vegetarian*
☎ 2506 3377; Room 1203, 12th fl, Food Forum, Times Square, 1 Matheson St; soups HK$18-25, set lunches HK$48-72; 🕙 11am-11pm
If you prefer to eat your vegetables in lofty surrounds, try Bo Kung, which started operations in Vancouver BC (or is that PC?) in Canada before moving here.

CHEENA Map pp406–8 *Halal Chinese*
☎ 2127 8898; Ground fl, Catic Plaza, 8 Causeway Rd; dim sum HK$10-48, meals from HK$200 per person; 🕙 lunch 11am-3.30pm Mon-Fri, dinner 6-11pm Mon-Fri, 11am-11pm Sat, 9am-11pm Sun
Cheena, which is the Arabic word for Chinese, specialises in food eaten by Chinese Muslims, so no pork and no booze (though you can order from the Rosedale on the Park Hotel next door). It's a lovely venue, dim sum is available from 11am until 3.30pm daily and there are almost 20 vegan dishes on the menu.

CHUEN CHEUNG KUI
Map pp406–8 *Chinese, Hakka*
☎ 2577 3833; 108-120 Percival St; meals from HK$200 per person; 🕙 11am-11pm

'Gizzard soup' and 'stomach tidbit' are two of the less appealing items on the English menu here, but the pulled chicken, a Hakka classic, is the dish to insist upon.

DINING AREA Map pp406–8 *Fusion*
☎ 2915 0260; 17 Lan Fong Rd; starters HK$50-145, pasta HK$80-95, Asian dishes HK$55-145, mains HK$145-165, set menus HK$128-160; 🕙 lunch 11.30am-3pm, dinner 6-11.30pm
This place has beautifully presented Euro-Canto food. There's freaky stuff going down in the kitchen – it's the kind of place where you might get wasabi in your focaccia and artichokes with your fried noodles. Never mind – it all tastes fine. The sleek décor befits the chic clientele.

EAST LAKE
Map pp406–8 *Chinese, Cantonese*
☎ 2504 3311; 4th fl, Pearl City, 22-36 Paterson St; meals from HK$150 per person; 🕙 8am-midnight
The East Lake, one of the anchor tenants of the mammoth Pearl City building, has a Bible-like menu of Cantonese dishes that changes every three months. But its *raison d'être* is to serve appreciative diners affordable and quite good dim sum (available 8am until 5pm).

FORUM Map pp406–8 *Chinese, Cantonese*
☎ 2869 8282; 485 Lockhart Rd; meals from HK$700 per person; 🕙 lunch 11am-2.30pm, dinner 5.30-11pm

---

Top Five Restaurants – Causeway Bay

- **Forum** (p188) Abalone and other shellfish dishes fit for (cashed-up) royalty.
- **Kung Tak Lam** (p189) 100% organic Shanghai-style meatless dishes.
- **Sorabol Korean Restaurant** (p420) The Korean's Korean restaurant, with helpful staff.
- **Tai Ping Koon** (p420) Long-established East-meets-West 'soy sauce restaurant'.
- **Wasabisabi** (p191) High-fashion, models and sushi for lunch and dinner.

The Forum's abalone dishes have fans spread across the world. What restaurant owner Yeung Koon-Yat does with these marvellous molluscs has earned him praise from the late Deng Xiaoping, membership to Le Club des Chefs des Chefs and the moniker of King of Abalone. The pan-fried redfish and crunchy-skin chicken are also recommended. Dress smart, skip lunch and savour the flavour.

GLOBAL FOREVER GREEN TAIWANESE

RESTAURANT Map pp406–8 *Taiwanese*
☎ 2890 3448; 93-95 Leighton Rd (enter from Sun Wui Rd) ; meals from HK$150 per person; ☽ dinner 6pm-4am

This is Hong Kong's best Taiwanese restaurant, a cuisine that borrows heavily from Fujian cooking and is little known outside Taiwan. Try traditional specialities such as the oyster om-elette, fried tofu and *sanbeiji* (three-cup chicken). Noodle dishes are particularly good value.

GOLDEN BULL Map pp406–8 *Vietnamese*
☎ 2506 1028; 11th fl, Food Forum, Times Square, 1 Matheson St; rice & noodle dishes HK$18-58, mains HK$55-185; ☽ noon-11pm

The Bull might not be the best Vietnamese restaurant in Causeway Bay, but it's the most stylish – and highest. There's a branch in Tsim Sha Tsui (p198).

HANGZHOU RESTAURANT

Map pp406–8 *Chinese, Hangzhou*
☎ 2894 9705; 9 Lan Fong Rd; meals from HK$150 per person; ☽ lunch 11.30am-3pm, dinner 6-11.30pm

This friendly little place serves authentic Hangzhou food, a less salty and oily variant of Shanghainese cuisine.

HEICHINROU

Map pp406–8 *Chinese, Cantonese*
☎ 2506 2333; Shop 1003, 10th fl, Food Forum, Times Square, 1 Matheson St; dim sum HK$16-42, meals from HK$150 per person; ☽ 11.30am-midnight Mon-Fri, 11am-midnight Sat, 10am-midnight Sun

This stylish Cantonese restaurant is argu-ably the most elegant eateries that make up the four-level Food Forum in the Times Square shopping mall. The dim sum here is excellent.

HOI TIN ASIA HARBOUR RESTAURANT

Map pp406–80 *Chinese, Cantonese*
☎ 2891 3886; 4th fl, Elizabeth House, 250 Gloucester

Rd (enter from Percival St) ; meals from HK$200 per person; ☽ 7am-12.30am

This massive place specialises in dim sum and seafood. In winter there's hotpot – seafood, meats and vegetables cooked *à table* in vari-ous flavoured broths.

ICHIBAN Map pp406–8 *Japanese*
☎ 2591 0683; 15 Morrison Hill Rd; noodles HK$38-55, set meals HK$45-120; ☽ lunch 11.30am-3.30pm, dinner 5.30pm-midnight

For a down-to-earth atmosphere, try the 'Number One'. Ichiban has all the atmosphere of an *izakaya* (Japanese-style pub) and seems to tolerate enthusiastic bouts of saké drinking.

INDONESIAN RESTAURANT

Map pp406–8 *Indonesian*
☎ 2577 9981; 28 Leighton Rd; mains HK$58-148; ☽ 11.30am-11.30pm

This Indonesian restaurant serves pretty au-thentic *rendang, gado-gado* and the like.

KOREA RESTAURANT

Map pp406–8 *Korean*
☎ 2577 9893; Ground fl, 58 Leighton Rd; barbecue & set meals HK$75-90; ☽ 11.30am-midnight

This is a good choice for an authentic Korean barbecue, but the surrounds are a little frayed and, well, gloomy. Still, it's an inexpensive place for grills and *kimchi*.

KUNG TAK LAM

Map pp406–8 *Chinese, Vegetarian*
☎ 2890 3127; Ground fl, Lok Sing Centre, 31 Yee Wo St; meals from HK$100 per person; ☽ 11am-11pm

This long-established place, which serves Shanghai-style meatless dishes, has more of a modern-feeling than most vegetarian eateries and is usually packed out. All the vegetables are 100% organic and dishes are free of MSG.

OYSHI! Map pp406–8 *Japanese*
☎ 3162 3922; Ground fl, 4 Sun Wui Rd; meals from HK$200 per person; ☽ lunch noon-2.30pm, dinner 6pm-2.30am

What was once a wonderful restaurant serv-ing 'New Chinese' cuisine has emerged as a Japanese oyster and sushi-bar restaurant. Try the steamed oysters in black bean and chilli sauce (HK$38) or the soft-shell crab roll (HK$68).

Eating – Hong Kong Island

This long-established restaurant used to be among the best options for Sichuan food. Now that this cuisine is out of fashion, it's one of the only Sichuan choices on Hong Kong Island. The sliced pork in chilli sauce, diced chicken and Sichuan noodles are all recommended.

SORABOL KOREAN RESTAURANT

Map pp406–8 *Korean*
☎ 2881 6823; 17th fl, Lee Theatre Bldg, 99 Percival St; meals HK$150 per person; ✆ 11.30am-midnight
This is the Korean's Korean restaurant, with helpful and informative staff.

STONEGRILL Map pp406–8 *International*

☎ 2504 3333; 1 Hoi Ping Rd; steaks & grills HK$168-178, set lunches HK$68-148; ✆ lunch noon-3pm, dinner 6.30pm-midnight
Don't complain when your food arrives half-cooked – it's supposed to be that way. Steak or fish come sunny-side up and sizzling on a slab of stone; you turn it over to suit your taste. Local celebs have fallen big time for this half-baked idea: it's one of the trendiest restaurants in town at the mo'. Book ahead. An added plus: the restaurant's excellent New York–style bar.

TAI PING KOON

Map pp406–8 *International, Chinese*
☎ 2576 9161; 6 Pak Sha Rd; starters HK$40-94, mains HK$90-190; ✆ 11am-midnight
This place has been around since 1860 and offers an incredible mix of Western and Chinese flavours – what Hong Kong people called 'soy sauce restaurants' in the pre-fusion days. Try the borscht (HK$38) and the smoked pomfret (HK$148) or roast pigeon (HK$198).

TAI WOO SEAFOOD RESTAURANT

Map pp406–8 *Chinese, Cantonese*
☎ 2893 0822; 27 Percival St; meals from HK$150; ✆ 11am-3am Mon-Sat, 10am-3am Sun
Tai Woo is as well known for its vegetarian dishes (try the bean curd with vegetarian crab roe) as it is for its seafood. Better still, it's open until very late.

TOMOKAZU Map pp406–8 *Japanese*

☎ 2833 6339; Shop B, Lockhart House, 441 Lockhart Rd; sushi & sashimi HK$30-200, set meals HK$50-120; ✆ lunch noon-3pm, dinner 6pm-midnight
For its location and well-prepared Japanese food, Tomokazu is a bargain.

PERFUME RIVER

Map pp406–8 *Vietnamese*
☎ 2576 2240; 89 Percival St; set meals from HK$98; ✆ 11am-11pm
This restaurant, named after the scenic river passing through the ancient Vietnamese capital of Hué, has long been a reliable spot for such Vietnamese favourites as *pho* (HK$26 to HK$36; a hotpot of noodles, meat or shellfish and fragrant herbs) and fried spring rolls wrapped in lettuce leaves.

QUEEN'S CAFE Map pp406–8 *Russian*

☎ 2576 2658; Ground fl, Eton Tower, 8 Hysan Ave; soups HK$35-41, mains HK$72-110; ✆ noon-11.30pm
This eatery has been around since 1952 (though obviously not at the bottom of the same modern high-rise), which accounts for its subdued yet assured atmosphere. The borsch and meat set meals – White Russian dishes that filtered through China – are pretty good. Try the *zakuska* (HK$68 to HK$88), a mixture of Russian appetisers.

RED PEPPER

Map pp406–8 *Chinese, Sichuanese*
☎ 2577 3811; 7 Lan Fong Rd; rice & noodle dishes HK$80-105, mains HK$95-200; ✆ 11.30am-midnight

TOWNGAS AVENUE

Map pp406–8   *International*

☎ 2367 2710; Ground fl, 59-65 Paterson St; starters HK$48-62, mains HK$110-138, 2-/3-/4-course set lunch HK$78/98/118, 4-/5-course set dinner HK$338/398; ☽ lunch 11am-3.30pm, dinner 6-10pm

This is an odd concept for Hong Kong – a place where the cook is to be heard and not seen. Towngas, the company that supplies gas to Hong Kong, has now set up a restaurant in its Causeway Bay retail outlet where you can watch the chefs at work through a glass screen. The head chef has a Michelin five-star pedigree, you get the recipe of your dish and you may even spot the cooker or fridge of your heart's desire. Outside, contemporary sculptures on the pavement fail to block the view of a Shell petrol station.

VEGI FOOD KITCHEN

Map pp406–8   *Chinese, Vegetarian*

☎ 2890 6660; Shop B, Ground fl, Highland Mansions, 13 Cleveland St; soups HK$50-63, mains HK$50-95; ☽ 10am-11.30pm

This place is pretty serious about its vegetarianism – there's a sign here warning you not to bring meat or alcohol onto the premises. The kitchen produces some of the most memorable 'mock meat' dishes in Hong Kong.

WASABISABI Map pp406–8   *Japanese*

☎ 2506 0009; 13th fl, Times Square, 1 Matheson St; meals about HK$400 per person; ☽ lunch 11am-3pm, dinner 6-11.30pm Sun-Thu, 6-11.30pm Fri-Sat

This restaurant in the Times Square shopping mall has excellent Japanese cuisine, impeccable service... We have to cut to the chase: the interior of this new restaurant is out of this world, from the cable vines through to the rondo lounges and into the sweeping sushi bar. Eclectic magnificence; even the faux birch forest behind the bar has gumption.

W'S ENTRECÔTE

Map pp406–8   *French, Steakhouse*

☎ 2506 0133; Shop 1303, 13th fl, Food Forum, Times Square, 1 Matheson St; starters HK$48-128, steaks HK$168-210; ☽ lunch noon-2.30pm, dinner 6.30-10.30pm

This place serves steak, and steak alone, in a number of shapes and sizes but with a Gallic twist. Included in the price is a salad and as many *frites* (chips) as you can squeeze onto your plate. Starters are in the 'foie gras and snails' category.

YIN PING VIETNAMESE RESTAURANT

Map pp406–8   *Vietnamese*

☎ 2832 9038; Ground fl, 24 Cannon St; rice & noodle dishes HK$27-48, hotpot dishes HK$50-52, set lunches HK$33-46; ☽ 11am-11.30pm

This little place is the 'anchor' Vietnamese restaurant on a street with more than a few.

YUNNAN RAINBOW

Map pp406–8   *Chinese, Yunnanese*

☎ 2881 8992; 18 Shelter St; meals about HK$150 per person; ☽ lunch noon-3pm, dinner 6-11pm

Here's another corner of China to eat your way through. The food is zesty, and the spicy sauces complement meat, tofu and a forest of fungi.

Cheap Eats

DÉLIFRANCE Map pp406–8   *Café*

☎ 2506 3462; Shop B208, Basement 2, Times Square, 1 Matheson St; soups & salads HK$12-23, sandwiches HK$23-35, meals HK$25-35; ☽ 8am-8pm

While hot meals are available at Délifrance at lunch and dinner, the emphasis at this branch of the chain is croissants, pastry, soup, sandwiches and coffee.

GENROKU SUSHI Map pp406–8 *Japanese*

☎ 2889 8889; cnr Matheson St & Sharp St East; meals from HK$100 per person; ☽ 11.30am-2am

Genroku is Hong Kong's most exotic fast-food chain. The sushi is very cheap and is served on a conveyor belt. The only drawback is the potentially long wait for seats, especially during the 1pm to 2pm lunch hour.

GOGO CAFE

Map pp406–8   *Japanese, Italian*

☎ 2881 5598; 11 Caroline Hill Rd; mains HK$98-118, set lunches HK$48-50; ☽ noon-11pm Mon-Sat, closed Sun

This is where East meets West for spaghetti with *mentaiko* (fish roe) or rice with home-made bolognaise. The theme here is part Japanese teahouse, part cool café, and the light meals and easy pace make Gogo a good place to re-energise between lunch and dinner. The menu changes daily.

HTTP://WWW.IZZUE.COM CAFÉ

Map pp406–8   *Café*

☎ 2504 3084; Shop 309-311, 3rd fl, World Trade Centre, 280 Gloucester Rd; starters HK$19-45, mains HK$55-99; ☽ noon-11pm

This computer-literate café, a new venture of the fashion shop chain (p257), has both a communal dining area with benches and private seating overlooking the harbour. If fashion is fashion at http://www.izzue boutique then food is fusion at its café. Both Asian and international dishes are on the menu.

MOON GARDEN TEA HOUSE

Map pp406–8 *Chinese, Cantonese*

☎ 2882 6878; 5 Hoi Ping Rd; tea & snacks HK$120 per person; ✆ noon-midnight

The simple cuppa reaches Nirvana at the Moon Garden. Choose from many brews then lose an afternoon perusing tea books, admiring antiques (all for sale) and taking refills from the heated pot beside your table. The kitchen creates such meticulous morsels as crispy bean-curd rolls to go with your pot of tea. There is also a **Central branch** (Map pp400-3; ☎ 2541 3887; 149 Hollywood Rd).

OLIVER'S SUPER SANDWICHES

Map pp406–8 *Sandwich Shop*

☎ 2895 0218; Shop G006-010, Ground fl, World Trade Centre, 280 Gloucester Rd; breakfast HK$15-30, soups HK$12-16, salads HK$20, sandwiches HK$23-39; ✆ 8am-8pm

This convenient branch of the popular sandwich chain has comfortable seating in the WTC lobby and water service.

SAINT'S ALP TEAHOUSE

Map pp406–8 *Chinese, Hong Kong*

☎ 2147 0389; Ground fl, 470 Lockhart Rd; rice & noodle dishes HK$15-17, stir fries HK$27; ✆ 11am-12.30am Sun-Thu, 11am-1.30am Fri-Sat

This branch of the chain of cheap but clean Taiwanese-style cafés is a good pit stop for lunch or a snack while shopping in Causeway Bay. There are a couple more branches in Mong Kok; see p204.

HAPPY VALLEY

In general, the restaurants and cafés in Happy Valley tend to cater to local residents, though two places are worth making the trip out to the racecourse.

ADVENTIST VEGETARIAN CAFETERIA

Map pp398–9 *Vegetarian*

☎ 2574 6211; 7th fl, Hong Kong Adventist Hospital, 40 Stubbs Rd; soups from HK$10, mains from HK$20; ✆ breakfast 7-8am, lunch 11am-2pm, dinner 5-6pm

This is one of the greatest bargains in Hong Kong and anyone can eat here.

AMIGO Map pp406–8 *French, International*

☎ 2577 2202; Amigo Mansion, 79A Wong Nai Chung Rd; meals about HK$300 per person; ✆ lunch noon-2.30pm, dinner 6-11pm

This old-style restaurant with Gallic twists and a Spanish name is a place full of memories. The waiters still wear black tie and white gloves, there's a strolling guitarist, and women are handed roses as they leave. Swoon.

ISLAND EAST

North Point, traditionally home to a large number of people hailing from Shanghai, can (not surprisingly) boast a number of good Shanghainese eateries. Quarry Bay has largest collection of restaurants in the entire district, especially in and around Tong Chong St, a short distance southeast of the Quarry Bay MTR station.

North Point
HONG KONG OLD RESTAURANT

Map pp406–8 *Chinese, Shanghainese*

☎ 2807 2333; Basement, Newton Hotel, 218 Electric Rd; meals about HK$250 per person; ✆ lunch 11am-3pm, dinner 5-11pm

Those in the know say that this hotel restaurant, which is close to the Fortress Hill MTR station, serves some of the best Shanghainese food in Hong Kong.

JUNE Map pp406–8 *Japanese*

☎ 2234 6691; 56 Electric Rd; noodle dishes HK$50-70, sushi/sashimi plates HK$250/300, set lunches HK$60-100; ✆ lunch noon-3pm Tue-Sun, dinner 6-11.30pm Tue-Fri, 6-10.30pm Sat & Sun

By all accounts this place, at the corner of Yacht St and just north of the Tin Hau MTR station, serves the most authentic Japanese food on Hong Kong Island. It's well worth a trip.

TUNG PO SEAFOOD RESTAURANT

Map pp398–9 *Chinese, Cantonese*

☎ 2880 9399; 2nd fl, Java Rd Market, 99 Java Rd; meals from HK$150 per person; ⏱ 6am-midnight

You will have eaten seafood in more salubrious environs before, but the fish will never have been as fresh. And why stop there? There are delicious meat dishes (spareribs, sliced pork with garlic) available, too. The market is just north of the North Point MTR station.

Quarry Bay
NAPA VALLEY OYSTER BAR & GRILL

Map pp398–9 *International*

☎ 2880 0149; Ground fl, Hoi Wan Bldg, 9 Hoi Wan St; meals about HK$300 per person, set lunches HK$66-88; ⏱ lunch 11am-3pm, dinner 5-11pm

Despite its name, this modern eatery, a few steps north of Tong Chong St, serves classic pasta and meat dishes, though there's an oyster bar offering about a dozen varieties of the bivalves. Best of all there's outside seating, a rare commodity in deepest Quarry Bay.

TUNG LOK HIN

Map pp398–9 *Chinese, Fusion*

☎ 2250 5022; 2nd fl, Oxford House, Westlands Rd, Tai Koo Place; meals from HK$350 per person; ⏱ 11.30am-11.30pm Mon-Sat, 10am-10.30pm Sun

Award-winning Tung Lok Hin, due east of Tong Chong St, is one of the more successful attempts at fusing Chinese and Western dishes and cooking styles. If cream of tomato soup with shark's fin, and Yunnan ham and mushrooms wrapped in rice pasta don't sound convincing, the proof is in the tasting.

ISLAND SOUTH

The restaurants in this district are as varied and eclectic as the villages and settlements themselves. While the choice is obviously limited in smaller places such as Shek O and Repulse Bay, you'll still manage to eat decent Thai at the former, and enjoy one of the most delightful venues on any coast in the latter. Main St in Stanley offers diners and snackers an embarrassment of choices, and in Aberdeen Harbour you'll find what is – for better or worse – Hong Kong's most famous restaurant.

Shek O
BLACK SHEEP Map pp398–9 *International*

☎ 2809 2021; Ground fl, 452 Shek O Village; meals from HK$300 per person; ⏱ 7-10.30pm Mon-Fri, 1pm-10pm Sat & Sun

This extremely popular restaurant with an eclectic décor and international menu is indeed a black sheep – altogether different from anything else you'll find in these parts. The fish is good as is the Black Sheep Ale on offer.

SHEK O CHINESE & THAI SEAFOOD

Map pp398–9 *Chinese, Thai*

☎ 2809 4426; 303 Shek O Village; meals from HK$150 per person; ⏱ 11.30am-10pm

This hybrid is hardly authentic in either category, but the portions are generous, the staff convivial and the cold Tsingtao beers just keep a-flowin'.

Stanley
BAYSIDE BRASSERIE Map p409 *Fusion*

☎ 2899 0818; Ground fl, 25 Stanley Market Rd; starters HK$48-62, mains HK$78-158; ⏱ noon-11pm Mon-Fri, 11am-11pm Sat & Sun

East meets West on Hong Kong Island

This new kid on the block offers a splendid waterfront view and a menu longer than the Book of Job, including everything from oysters (HK$27 to HK$62 each) and pizzas (HK$78 to HK$108) to international and Indian main courses.

BOATHOUSE Map p409 *International*
☎ 2813 4467; 86-88 Stanley Main St; pasta HK$55-125, mains HK$119-220, set lunch/dinner HK$95/150; ☺ lunch noon-3pm, dinner 6-10.30pm
This blue pub-bistro facing the water is one of the most attractive restaurants in Stanley. A table on the roof garden is something to covet. Salads, bruschetta and Mediterranean-inspired mains make up the bulk of the Boathouse's fleet.

CHILLI N SPICE Map p409 *Asian*
☎ 2899 0147; Shop 101, 1st fl, Murray House, Stanley Plaza; rice & noodle dishes HK$42-85, mains HK$48-135; noon-11.30pm Mon-Fri, 11am-11.30pm Sat & Sun
A branch of the ever-growing chain – nine branches at last count – has found its way into Hong Kong's oldest (and now reconstructed) colonial building. Expect no surprises, but the venue and views are great.

EL CID CARAMAR Map p409 *Spanish*
☎ 2899 0858; Shop 102, 1st fl, Murray House, Stanley Plaza; tapas HK$20-55, mains HK$150-220, paella for 2 HK$220-300; ☺ noon-11pm Sun-Thu, noon-midnight Fri-Sat
This is one of four restaurants to take residence in Stanley's historical Murray House. Here they serve a good range of tapas, and with the harbour view and too many *cervezas* you'll think you're in San Sebastián.

LORD STANLEY AT THE CURRY POT
Map p409 *Indian*
☎ 2899 0811; Ground fl, 92 Stanley Main St; starters HK$30-55, mains HK$55-98, set lunches HK$75-98; ☺ lunch noon-3pm, 6-11pm Mon-Sat, noon-11pm Sun
The waterfront feels a somewhat odd place to eat Indian food, but the surrounds are terribly upmarket and the views to die for. There are some good vegetarian choices here.

LUCY'S Map p409 *International*
☎ 2813 9055; 64 Stanley Main St; starters HK$60-80, mains HK$145-190, 2-/3-course set dinner HK$190/230 (Sun-Thu only); ☺ lunch noon-3pm Mon-Sat, noon-4pm Sun, dinner 7-10pm Mon-Sat, 6.30-10pm Sun

Top Five Restaurants – Island South
- **Black Sheep** (p193) Surprisingly good chow in this Shek O find.
- **Boathouse** (p194) Salads and Mediterranean-inspired mains on Stanley Bay.
- **Jumbo Floating Restaurant** (p195) Tacky but fun and oh-so Hong Kong.
- **Lucy's** (p194) Cool grazing oasis within the hustle and bustle of Stanley market.
- **Verandah** (p194) Repulse Bay's most formal neo-colonial restaurant.

This easy-going, cool oasis within the hustle and bustle of the market doesn't overwhelm with choice but with quality food. The menu changes frequently as fresh produce and inspiration strikes, but the offerings tend to honest fusion rather than fancy flimflammery. There's a good selection of wines by the glass.

PEPPERONI'S PIZZA Map p409 *Italian*
☎ 2813 7571, 2813 8605; 18B Stanley Main St; salads HK$50-60; pizza HK$65-75; ☺ 10am-10pm
This branch of a pizzeria chain is convenient to the market. While not as famous (or frequented) as its cousins in Sai Kung (p209) and Wan Chai (p187), this place has decent pizzas, too.

STANLEY'S ITALIAN Map p409 *Italian*
☎ 2813 7313; Ground fl, 92B Stanley Main St; starters HK$45-60, pizza HK$76-105, pasta HK$80-94, mains HK$88-110; ☺ 11am-midnight Sun-Thu, 11am-1am Fri-Sat
Stanley's Italian has now combined with the watering hole Beaches (p225) to offer pizza, pasta, pints – and a ground-level view of the sea. Set lunches are HK$75 to HK$98.

CHEAP EATS
WELLCOME Map p409 *Supermarket*
88 Stanley Village; ☺ 8am-10pm
This branch of the supermarket chain is in the Old Stanley Police Station, a two-storey colonial building dating from 1859 and is convenient for beach supplies, food and drink.

Repulse Bay
VERANDAH Map pp398–9 *International*
☎ 2812 2722; 1st fl, The Repulse Bay, 109 Repulse Bay Rd; starters HK$175-225, mains HK$275-310, Sun brunch

Pomelo fruit

buffet adult/child HK$328/250; ☺ lunch noon-3pm Mon-Sat, brunch 11am-2.30pm Sun, dinner 7-10.30pm Mon-Sat, 6.30-10pm Sun

In the new-colonial bit of the wavy Repulse Bay condos, the Verandah is hushed and formal with heavy white tablecloths, demurely clinking cutlery and stunning views of Repulse Bay. The brunch is famous (book way ahead and dream about the caviar-topped eggs Benedict). Afternoon tea, the south side's best, is served from 3pm to 5.30pm.

CHEAP EATS

PALM COURT CAFE Map pp398–9 *Café*
☎ 2812 2903; Shop G110, Ground fl, The Repulse Bay, 109 Repulse Bay Rd; cakes & pastries HK$20, sandwiches HK$26-32; ☺ 11am-midnight Mon-Sat, 10am-6.30pm Sun

This little cousin of the Verandah in the courtyard below is a good place to buy the fixings for a picnic on the beach.

WELLCOME Map pp398–9 *Supermarket*
Shop G123, 1st fl, The Repulse Bay, 109 Repulse Bay Rd; ☺ 8am-10pm

This large supermarket can supply you with all your picnic needs.

Aberdeen

ABERDEEN RUBY CHINESE

RESTAURANT Map p409 *Chinese, Cantonese*
☎ 2518 8398; Shop 2, 1st fl, Aberdeen Centre, Nam Ning St (enter from 2 Chengtu St); dim sum from HK$9, meals from HK$100 per person; ☺ 6am-midnight

This restaurant is *the* place for dim sum in Aberdeen, judging from the hordes of hopefuls waiting for tables, especially at the weekend.

FLOATING RESTAURANTS

Map p409 *Chinese, Cantonese*
☎ 2553 9111, 2873 7111; Shum Wan Pier Dr, Wong Chuk Hang; meals from HK$250 per person; ☺ 11am-11.30pm Mon-Sat, 7am-11.30pm Sun

There are two floating restaurants moored in Aberdeen Harbour specialising in seafood: the **Jumbo** and the **Tai Pak**. The Jumbo is the larger of the two – with some 300 waiters serving 2300 diners at capacity – and has dim sum from 7.30am to 5.30pm on Sunday. The Tai Pak is usually reserved for groups and spillovers. The food at both generally gets bad press, and these establishments are not really recommended except as a spectacle and a fun night out. There's free transport for diners from the pier on Aberdeen Promenade; see p342 for details.

CHEAP EATS

LO YU VIETNAM RESTAURANT

Map p409 *Vietnamese*
☎ 2814 8460; Shop C, Ground fl, Kong Kai Bldg, 184-188 Aberdeen Main St; starters HK$15-40, mains HK$32-85; ☺ 11am-11pm

A lot of Vietnamese boat people who made their way to Hong Kong in the late 1970s never made it past the original 'Fragrant Harbour' (Aberdeen's name in Cantonese). Expect authentic and very cheap dishes.

Eating – Kowloon

KOWLOON

Kowloon doesn't have quite the same range of restaurants as Hong Kong Island does, but you will still find an amazing assortment of ethnic eateries in Tsim Sha Tsui. Kowloon City is renowned for its Thai eateries.

TSIM SHA TSUI & TSIM SHA TSUI EAST

Tsim Sha Tsui can claim the lion's share of ethnic restaurants in Kowloon. If you're looking for something fast and cheap, Hau Fook St (Map p412–14) is filled with food stalls (dishes about HK$25). It's a few blocks east of Nathan Rd in Tsim Sha Tsui and isn't included on many tourist maps. Walking north from the intersection of Carnarvon and Cameron Rds, it's the first lane on your right. Most of the places don't have English menus, but you can always point.

ARIRANG Map pp412–14   *Korean*

☎ 2956 3288; Shop 2306-7, 2nd fl, The Gateway, 25 Canton Rd, Tsim Sha Tsui; meals from HK$250 per person, set lunch HK$70; ⏱ lunch noon-3pm, dinner 6-11pm

This is a large, brightly lit restaurant that may not be the place for a romantic tête à tête, but is great for a party. It's mostly given over to barbecue.

AU TROU NORMAND

Map pp412–14   *French*

☎ 2366 8754; 1st fl, Taurus Building, 63 Carnarvon Rd, Tsim Sha Tsui; meals from HK$250 per person, 2-/3-course lunch HK$90/120; ⏱ lunch noon-3pm, dinner 6-11pm

Established in 1964, the 'Norman hole', which takes its name from the custom in Normandy of drinking a glass of Calvados (apple brandy) in the middle of the meal to 'dig a hole' and allow room for more courses, is a much cheaper place to try the local version of *la cuisine française*. It's a comfortable, easy-going place and highly recommended.

AVENUE Map pp412–14   *International*

☎ 2315 1118; 1st fl, Holiday Inn Golden Mile, 50 Nathan Rd, Tsim Sha Tsui; meals from HK$400 per person; ⏱ lunch noon-2.30pm, dinner 6-10.30pm Mon-Sat, closed Sun

This wonderful restaurant makes Nathan Rd its focal point and changes the menu according to the season. The vegetarian selection is particularly good.

BALI RESTAURANT

Map pp412–14   *Indonesian*

☎ 2780 2902; 10 Nanking St, Tsim Sha Tsui; meals from HK$100 per person, set lunch HK$69; ⏱ noon-11pm

The food is pretty good and the service friendly, but the best thing about the Bali is its superb tackiness: a permanent 'happy birthday' sign, vinyl booths separated by fake brick walls, and a 'resort'-style bar playing tunes from *South Pacific*. Try the nasi goreng, the vegetable curry or the pork satay. *Rijstafel*, a feast of more than a dozen little dishes, costs HK$148.

BANANA LEAF CURRY HOUSE

Map pp406–8   *Malaysian, Singaporean*

☎ 2721 4821; 3rd fl, Golden Crown Court, 68 Nathan Rd, Tsim Sha Tsui; starters HK$32-78, mains HK$54-128;

⏱ lunch 11.30am-3pm, dinner 6pm-midnight Mon-Fri, 11.30am-midnight Sat & Sun

This centrally located branch of a chain of Malaysian/Singaporean restaurants is convenient to the guesthouses on the southern end of Nathan Rd. There are five other branches, including one in Causeway Bay (see p188).

BUSAN KOREAN RESTAURANT

Map pp412–14   *Korean*

☎ 2376 3385; Ground fl, Kowloon Centre, 29 Ashley Rd, Tsim Sha Tsui; rice dishes HK$85, barbecue HK$100; ⏱ lunch 11.30am-3pm, dinner 6-11.30pm

This wonderfully authentic place in the bustling hub of touristed Tsim Sha Tsui manages to stay on, despite the nearby competition.

CHINESE RESTAURANT

Map pp412–14   *Chinese, Cantonese*

☎ 2311 1234 ext 881; 2nd fl, Hyatt Regency Hong Kong Hotel, 67 Nathan Rd, Tsim Sha Tsui; meals from HK$350 per person; ⏱ lunch 11.30am-3pm Mon-Sat, 10.30am-3pm Sun, dinner 6.30-11pm Mon-Sat

This classy place has acquired a good reputation for its original Cantonese food. The seafood is great and the high ceilings and traditional booth seating – based on Chinese teahouses of the 1920s – make for an unusual dining experience.

DAN RYAN'S CHICAGO GRILL

Map pp412–14   *American*

☎ 2735 6111; Shop 200, 2nd fl, Ocean Terminal, Zone C, Harbour City, Canton Rd, Tsim Sha Tsui; starters HK$48-125, sandwiches HK$55-112, mains HK$95-240, half/full rack ribs HK$132/198; ⏱ 11am-midnight Mon-Fri, 10am-midnight Sat & Sun

---

Top Five Restaurants – Tsim Sha Tsui

- **Felix** (p197) Excellent fusion food with Philippe Starck décor as backdrop.
- **Fook Lam Moon** (p197) One of Hong Kong's top Cantonese restaurants with a huge menu.
- **Orphée** (p199) Out-of-place minimalist but cosy *restaurant du quartier*.
- **Peace Garden** (p199) Popular Vietnamese restaurant specialising in unfaux *pho*.
- **Spring Deer** (p200) The Deer serves some of the crispiest Peking duck in town.

The theme at Dan Ryan's is 'Chicago', including a model elevated rail system overhead, and jazz and big-band music on the sound system. It is *the* place for burgers and ribs in Hong Kong. There's also a branch in Admiralty (see p183).

DONG Map pp412–14   *Chinese, Cantonese*
☎ 2315 5166; Arcade 2, Hotel Miramar, 118-130 Nathan Rd, Tsim Sha Tsui; meals from HK$200 per person; ✆ lunch 11.30am-3.30pm Mon-Sat, 10.30am-3pm Sun, dinner 6-10.30pm daily

Dong (or 'East') is the classic hotel restaurant interior right down to the cheesy music, but its menu does offer some authentically adventurous Cantonese dishes, including seafood soups and a forest of fungi. Its sister-restaurant, **Xi** ('West'; ☎ 2315 5155), just across the floor, serves international food with an Asian twist. Both have a set lunch for HK$138.

DYNASTY
Map pp412–14   *Chinese, Cantonese*
☎ 2369 4111, ext 6600; 4th fl, New World Renaissance Hotel, 22 Salisbury Rd, Tsim Sha Tsui; meals from HK$300 per person; ✆ lunch 11.30am-2.30pm Mon-Sat, 11am-2.30pm Sun, dinner 6.30-11pm daily

The traditional rosewood furniture, latticed windows and ambience (quiet elegance) of this hotel restaurant make for an unusual (if not authentic) Cantonese dining experience. Specialities include steamed sliced pork with preserved shrimp paste and fresh salmon with rice noodle strips.

EASTERN PALACE CHIU CHOW RESTAURANT
Map pp412–14   *Chinese, Chiu Chow*
☎ 2730 6011; Shop 308, 3rd fl, Marco Polo Hong Kong Hotel Shopping Arcade, Zone D, Harbour City, 3 Canton Rd, Tsim Sha Tsui; meals from HK$250 per person; ✆ lunch 11.30am-3pm, dinner 6-11pm

Chiu Chow dim sum is served at this large hotel restaurant from 11.30am to 3pm.

FAT ANGELO'S
Map pp412–14   *Italian, American*
☎ 2730 4788; 33 Ashley Rd, Tsim Sha Tsui; salads HK$30, pasta HK$70-145, mains HK$125-170; ✆ noon-midnight

This branch of the popular Italian-American restaurant is generous with its portions and seamless in its service.

There's also a branch in Soho; see p178.

FELIX Map pp412–14   *Pacific Rim*
☎ 2315 3188; 28th fl, Peninsula Hotel, Salisbury Rd, Tsim Sha Tsui; meals from HK$600; ✆ 6pm-2am

The food here is East meets West, and it's about as good as that genre gets in Hong Kong. But most people come here to gawk at the Philippe Starck décor – high ceilings, vast windows (often inexplicably shuttered), hulking copper-clad columns surrounding Art Deco–style table settings – and the view (when they finally open the blinds).

FOOK LAM MOON
Map pp412–14   *Chinese, Cantonese*
☎ 2366 0286; Shop 8, 1st fl, 53-59 Kimberley Rd, Tsim Sha Tsui; meals from HK$250 per person; ✆ lunch 11.30am-3pm, dinner 6-11pm

One of Hong Kong's top Cantonese restaurants, the Fook Lam Moon takes care of you from the minute you walk out of the lifts, with cheongsam-clad hostesses waiting to escort you to your table. The enormous menu contains a lot of unusual and expensive dishes (shark's fin, frog, abalone), but there are many old favourites as well. You might sample the pan-fried lobster balls, which are a house speciality.

GADDI'S Map pp412–14   *French*
☎ 2315 3171; Peninsula Hotel, Salisbury Rd, Tsim Sha Tsui; meals from HK$600 per person; ✆ lunch noon-3pm, dinner 7-11pm

Legendary for decades, Gaddi's still holds onto its reputation as *the* French restaurant in Hong Kong. It has boasted virtually the same menu (and some of the same staff, apparently) for more than 30 years. The atmosphere is a bit stilted, making it hard to relax, but the food will probably keep you excited. Guys must wear a jacket.

GAYLORD Map pp412–14   *Indian*
☎ 2376 1001; 1st fl, Ashley Centre, 23-25 Ashley Rd, Tsim Sha Tsui; vegetarian dishes HK$52-6, meat mains & tandoori dishes HK$78-308; ✆ lunch noon-3pm, dinner 6-11pm

The first Indian restaurant to open in Hong Kong, the Gaylord has been going strong since 1972. Dim lighting, booth seating and live Indian music set the scene for enjoying the excellent *rogan josh*, dhal and other favourite Indian dishes. There's a lunch buffet (HK$95) available Monday to Saturday.

Gogo Cafe (p191)

GOLDEN BULL Map pp412–14 *Vietnamese*
☎ 2730 4866; Shop 101, 1st fl, Ocean Centre, Zone B, Harbour City, Canton Rd, Tsim Sha Tsui; rice & noodle dishes HK$18-58, mains HK$55-185; ☼ noon-11.30pm

There's a queue outside this place almost every night. They're not coming for the atmosphere (noisy) or service (abrupt), but the excellent-quality, low-cost Vietnamese food. There's a branch in Causeway Bay (see p189 under Hong Kong Island).

GOMITORI Map pp412–14 *Japanese*
☎ 2367 8519; Shop LG5, Lower Ground fl, Energy Plaza, 92 Granville Rd, Tsim Sha Tsui East; dishes HK$150-250; ☼ dinner 7pm-1am Mon-Sat, closed Sun

This *yakitori* restaurant the size of a cupboard will grill you chicken in a variety of ways. It's always packed with Japanese expats – always a good sign.

GREAT SHANGHAI RESTAURANT
Map pp412–14 *Chinese, Shanghainese*
☎ 2366 8158; 1st fl, 26-36 Prat Ave, Tsim Sha Tsui; meals from HK$150 per person; ☼ 11am-11pm

One of Hong Kong's oldest – it opened in 1959 – and best Shanghainese restaurants, the Great Shanghai may be a bit touristy, but that makes it easier for non-Chinese speakers to negotiate. The steamed and fried dumplings and the stir-fried freshwater shrimps are specialities.

HARD ROCK CAFE
Map pp412–14 *International*
☎ 2375 1323; Ground & 1st fls, Silvercord Shopping Centre, 30 Canton Rd, Tsim Sha Tsui; set lunch HK$65, salads & sandwiches HK$78-85, burgers HK$88-90; ☼ 11am-1am Sun-Thu, 11am-3am Sat & Sun

Why you'd come here is beyond us, but here it is should you need onion rings, chicken strips and/or a 'Hard Rock Cafe Kowloon' T-shirt. It's a popular dance space on Friday and Saturday nights.

ISLAND SEAFOOD & OYSTER BAR
Map pp412–14 *Seafood*
☎ 2312 6663; Ground fl, 10 Knutsford Tce, Tsim Sha Tsui; starters HK$55-150, pasta & rice dishes HK$105-125, fish dishes HK$160; ☼ lunch noon-3pm, dinner 6pm-midnight

The oyster bar here offers some 20 different varieties, and main courses are available by the half-portion.

JADE GARDEN
Map pp412–14 *Chinese, Cantonese*
☎ 2730 6888; 4th fl, Middle Block, Star House, 3 Salisbury Rd, Tsim Sha Tsui; dim sum HK$16-38, meals HK$200 per person; ☼ 11am-11pm Mon-Sat, 10am-11pm Sun

People turn their noses up at the Maxim's chain of 'Garden' restaurants, but they're not half bad, the service is excellent and the food reliable, if somewhat predictable. This branch is just opposite the Tsim Sha Tsui Star Ferry terminal. It's particularly well known for its dim sum, served from 11am (10am on Sunday) to 3pm daily.

JIMMY'S KITCHEN
Map pp412–14 *International*
☎ 2376 0327; 1st fl, Kowloon Centre, 29-39 Ashley Rd, Tsim Sha Tsui; starters HK$65-110, mains HK$160-235; ☼ lunch 11.30am-3pm, dinner 6-11pm

This place has a lengthy and generous menu that has attracted a loyal following. It's been around since 1928 and there's also a branch in Central (see p172 for details).

KOH-I-NOOR Map pp412–14 *Indian*
☎ 2369 0783; 1st fl, Shop 3-4, 1st fl, Penin-sula Mansion, 16C Mody Rd, Tsim Sha Tsui; lunch vegetarian/meat buffet HK$48/68 Mon-Fri, set menu for 2/4 HK$188/468; ☼ lunch 11.30am-3pm, dinner 6-11.30pm

One of a chain of restaurants, this branch is cheaper and less stylish than its counterpart in Central (p172), but the food is great and the staff friendly. The speciality is North Indian food, though it 'goes south' on Monday.

KUNG TAK LAM
Map pp412–14   *Chinese, Vegetarian*
☎ 2367 7881; 1st fl, 45-47 Carnarvon Rd, Tsim Sha Tsui; meals from HK$100 per person; ⏱ 11.30am-11pm
Like its sister-restaurant in Causeway Bay (see p189), this MSG-free place serves Shanghai vegetarian cuisine and attracts a loyal clientele who wouldn't eat anywhere else. It's won awards. Dim sum is available from 11.30am to 5pm.

KYO-ZASA Map pp412–14   *Japanese*
☎ 2376 1888; 20 Ashley Rd, Tsim Sha Tsui; dishes HK$48-68; ⏱ lunch noon-2.30pm, dinner 6pm-midnight
This colourful and cosy Japanese eatery is very authentic. The food is spot-on and the prices reasonable.

KYUSHU-ICHIBAN
Map pp412–14   *Japanese*
☎ 2314 7889; Ground & 1st fls, 144 Austin Rd, Tsim Sha Tsui; sushi HK$28-48, rice & noodle dishes HK$38-88; ⏱ lunch 11.30am-3pm daily, dinner 6pm-1am Mon-Sat, 6pm-midnight Sun
This inexpensive Japanese eatery is a favourite with the local young bloods of Tsim Sha Tsui.

LA TAVERNA Map pp412–14   *Italian*
☎ 2376 1945; Ground fl, Astoria Bldg, 36-38 Ashley Rd, Tsim Sha Tsui; meals from HK$250 per person; ⏱ lunch noon-3pm Mon-Sat, dinner 6.30pm-midnight daily
This is a popular, though not especially authentic, Italianesque eatery with very attentive service and naff décor.

MABUHAY Map pp412–14   *Filipino*
☎ 2367 3762; 11 Minden Ave, Tsim Sha Tsui; mains HK$45-100; ⏱ 9.30am-11pm
This basic café serves authentic Filipino food, which is not to everyone's taste (lots of garlic, lots of tamarind and little of anything else). Still, the staff are friendly and the *singang* (HK$50 to HK$90), described as 'our own *tom yum gung*, sir', by the waiter, and the *abobong pusit* (squid with garlic and red pepper; HK$40) are good.

MARGAUX Map pp412–14   *French*
☎ 2733 8750; Mezzanine, Kowloon Shangri-La Hotel, 64 Mody Rd, Tsim Sha Tsui East; soups HK$80-90,

starters HK$135-248, mains HK$225-305, 3-course set lunch HK$250; ⏱ lunch noon-2.30pm, dinner 6.30-10.30pm Mon-Sat
Margaux is a more relaxed and less pretentious French restaurant than many of its hotel counterparts.

NADAMAN Map pp412–14   *Japanese*
☎ 2733 8751; Basement 2, Kowloon Shangri-La Hotel, 64 Mody Rd, Tsim Sha Tsui East; set meals HK$350-400; ⏱ lunch noon-2.30pm, dinner 6-10.30pm
The authentic Japanese food at this restaurant has won it a well-deserved reputation, but the décor falls short and badly. It is very expensive, though the set meals at lunchtime are excellent value.

NEW NORTH SEA FISHING VILLAGE
Map pp412–14   *Chinese, Cantonese*
☎ 2723 6843; 2nd basement, Auto Plaza, 65 Mody Square, Tsim Sha Tsui East; meals from HK$150 per person; ⏱ 10.30am-midnight
If you can ignore the cheesy nautical décor, this place is worth a visit for its inexpensive but well-prepared fish dishes. It also has good dim sum.

ORPHÉE Map pp412–14   *French*
☎ 2730 1128; 18A Austin Ave, Tsim Sha Tsui; starters HK$55-85, mains HK$168-188, 3-course set dinner HK$168; ⏱ lunch noon-2.30pm, dinner 6.45-10.15pm
Entering this minimalist but cosy '*restaurant français*' is like stumbling on a small pocket of Paris in deepest Tsim Sha Tsui. If you feel like a fill of *filet de bœuf* or some foie gras, Orphée is the choice.

OSAKA Map pp412–14   *Japanese*
☎ 2376 3323; 3rd fl, Ashley Bldg, 14 Ashley Rd, Tsim Sha Tsui; meals from HK$200 per person; ⏱ lunch noon-3pm, dinner 6-11pm
A splash of class above the hustle of Ashley Rd, this atmospheric restaurant has pinafored waitresses and a menu that extends from sushi to Japanese-style steaks. There are reasonably priced set lunches, too.

PEACE GARDEN
Map pp412–14   *Vietnamese*
☎ 2721 2582, 2721 2747; 1st fl, 4-4A Hillwood Rd, Tsim Sha Tsui; meals from HK$150 per person, set lunches HK$42-118; ⏱ noon-midnight
This immensely popular Vietnamese restaurant upstairs on a relatively quiet street off Nathan

Rd is a favourite among Hong Kong celebrities, who come here for the real *pho* and dishes like king prawns cooked in fish sauce.

PEKING RESTAURANT

Map pp412–14   *Chinese, Peking*

☎ 2730 1315; 1st fl, 227 Nathan Rd, Tsim Sha Tsui; meals from HK$120 per person; ☻ 11am-10pm

This no-frills restaurant keeps Peking duck fans merrily chomping away. If duck doesn't do it for you, try the Peking-style crab dishes and pastries.

PEP 'N' SPICES Map pp412–14   *Asian*

☎ 2376 0893; Basement, 10 Peking Rd, Tsim Sha Tsui; set lunches HK$39-45, set dinners HK$136-152; ☻ lunch noon-3pm, dinner 6-11pm Mon-Fri, noon-11pm Sat & Sun

This friendly place serves anything that happens to be hot and spicy and Asian: from satay to *tom yum gung*. Pep 'n' Spices is a fun restaurant for a group. You can also enter from 8 Ashley Rd.

ROYAL COURT

Map pp412–14   *Chinese, Cantonese*

☎ 2739 3311 ext 176; 1st fl, Guangdong Hotel, 18 Prat Ave, Tsim Sha Tsui; meals from HK$200; ☻ 7am-11pm Sun-Fri, 7am-midnight Sat

This ever-vibrant hotel restaurant serves excellent dim sum from 7am to 3pm.

ROYAL GARDEN CHINESE RESTAURANT Map pp412–14

                      Chinese, Cantonese

☎ 2721 5215; Lower Basement, Royal Garden Hotel, 69 Mody Rd, Tsim Sha Tsui East; meals from HK$200 per person; ☻ 11am-11pm

This splendid hotel restaurant is one of the best places in Tsim Sha Tsui for dim sum.

RUBY TUESDAY

Map pp412–14   *American, International*

☎ 2376 3122; Shop 283, 2nd fl, Ocean Terminal, Zone C, Harbour City, Canton Rd, Tsim Sha Tsui; salad bar HK$75, mains HK$118-208; ☻ 11.30am-11pm

This place boasts 'awesome food' a 'serious salad bar' and 'plentiful platters'; it's just, like, gotta be American. Huge portions.

SABATINI Map pp412–14   *Italian*

☎ 2721 5215, 2733 2000; 3rd fl, Royal Garden Hotel, 69 Mody Rd, Tsim Sha Tsui East; starters HK$110-190, pasta HK$150-230, mains HK$260-33; ☻ lunch noon-2.30pm, dinner 6-11pm

Sabatini is a direct copy of its namesake in Rome (as is the branch in Tokyo). The food and the ambience are equally memorable and there are set lunches of between two and four courses for HK$125 to HK$250.

SALISBURY DINING ROOM

Map pp412–14   *International, Buffet*

☎ 2268 7000; 4th fl, The Salisbury, 41 Salisbury Rd, Tsim Sha Tsui; lunch/dinner buffet HK$98/218; ☻ lunch noon-2.30pm, dinner 6.15-9.30pm Mon-Sat

Unlimited sushi and smoked salmon make the buffets at this YMCA-run hotel a pretty good bet. Book ahead if you want a table by the window and unimpeded harbour views. Guzzlers will be glad to note that the buffets include bottomless wine and draught beer.

SCHNURRBART Map pp412–14   *German*

☎ 2366 2986; 9-11 Prat Ave, Tsim Sha Tsui; bar snacks HK$65, mains HK$86-115; ☻ lunch noon-3pm, dinner 6pm-midnight

This is the Kowloon branch of the German eatery. Happy hour lasts from noon to 9pm.

SNOW GARDEN SHANGHAI RESTAURANT

Map pp412–14   *Chinese, Shanghainese*

☎ 2736 9188; 10th fl, 219 Nathan Rd, Tsim Sha Tsui; meals from HK$200 per person; ☻ lunch noon-3pm, dinner 5.30-11.30pm

This is another popular venue for Shanghainese food; come here for drunken pigeon, sautéed freshwater shrimps, crab with green beans or just try the *siu long bao* (traditional Shanghainese meat-filled steamed buns).

SPRING DEER

Map pp412–14   *Chinese, Peking*

☎ 2366 4012; 1st fl, 42 Mody Rd, Tsim Sha Tsui; meals from HK$150 per person; ☻ lunch noon-3pm, dinner 6-11pm

This is probably Hong Kong's most famous (not best, mind) Peking restaurant and serves some of the crispiest Peking duck (HK$280 for the whole bird) in town. This place is extremely popular, so book several days in advance.

SPRING MOON

Map pp412–14   *Chinese, Cantonese*

☎ 2315 3160; 1st fl, Peninsula Hotel, Salisbury Rd, Tsim Sha Tsui; meals from HK$400; ☻ lunch 11.30am-2.30pm Mon-Sat, 11am-3pm Sun, afternoon tea 3-4.30pm Mon-Sat, 3-5pm Sun, dinner 6-10.30pm daily

The décor in the hotel restaurant is Japanese minimalist with bits of Art Deco thrown in. The food is traditional Cantonese favourites, and excellent.

SWEET DYNASTY

Map pp412–14   *Chinese, Cantonese*
☎ 2199 7799; 88 Canton Rd, Tsim Sha Tsui; meals about HK$100 per person; ⏰ 10am-midnight Mon-Thu, 10am-1pm Fri, 7.30am-1am Sat, 7.30am-midnight Sun

Sweet Dynasty has it all, from fine dim sum (weekends only) to tofu soups to bowls of congee big enough to swim in. It's a riot at lunchtime, but somehow, amid all the clatter and kids, Sweet Dynasty retains a sense of style.

TAI FUNG LAU PEKING RESTAURANT

Map pp412–14   *Chinese, Peking*
☎ 2366 2494; Windsor Mansion, 29-31 Chatham Rd South, Tsim Sha Tsui; meals from HK$150 per person; ⏰ noon-11pm

If you can't get into the Spring Deer, try this place, which serves some fine northern specialities, including Peking duck (half/whole HK$130/240).

THREE-FIVE KOREAN RESTAURANT

Map pp412–14   *Korean*
☎ 2376 1545; 6 Ashley Rd, Tsim Sha Tsui; mains HK$88-130, set lunch courses HK$30-50; ⏰ lunch 11am-5pm, dinner 6-11pm

This place is small but sizzlingly popular.

TONY ROMA'S FAMOUS FOR RIBS

Map pp412–14   *American*
☎ 2736 6850; Shop 3000, 3rd fl, Miramar Shopping Centre, 132 Nathan Rd, Tsim Sha Tsui; pasta HK$118-148, mains HK$172-198; ⏰ 11.30am-midnight

The name says it all. Head to Tony's if you crave something that will stick to your, well... A fat slab of what made Eve walk starts at HK$172. There's also a **Causeway Bay branch** (Map pp406-8; ☎ 2882 3743; Shop 413-418, 4th fl, World Trade Centre, 280 Gloucester Rd).

TOUCH OF SPICE

Map pp412–14   *SouthEast Asian*
☎ 2312 1118; 1st fl, 10 Knutsford Tce, Tsim Sha Tsui; starters HK$45-70, curries HK$72-98, seafood dishes HK$80-165; ⏰ lunch noon-3pm, dinner 6-11.30pm

This is one of four restaurant/bars stacked up at the same address on trendy Knutsford Terrace. It does Thai curries, Indonesian and Vietnamese noodles, and stir-fried dishes. It's pretty reasonably priced and the set lunches (HK$52 to HK$68) are excellent value.

VALENTINO

Map pp412–14   *Italian*
☎ 2721 6449; Ground fl, Ocean View Court, 27A Chatham Rd South, Tsim Sha Tsui; starters HK$88-128, pasta HK$114-128, mains HK$178-198; ⏰ lunch noon-3pm, dinner 6-11pm

This long-established *ristorante Italiano* is an upmarket alternative to the pasta- and pizzajoints of Tsim Sha Tsui. It's a romantic Italian classic with soft lights and nuzzling music. The seasonal menu has super soups (look out for a light tomato and zucchini broth in summer) and a good range of salads, pasta and meats.

WAN LOONG COURT

Map pp412–14   *Chinese, Cantonese*
☎ 2734 3722; Lower level 2, Kowloon Hotel, 19-21 Nathan Rd, Tsim Sha Tsui; meals HK$250-300 per person; ⏰ lunch 11am-3pm Mon-Fri, 11am-5pm Sat & Sun, dinner 6-11.30pm daily

There's wonderful Cantonese food with modern touches here; the dim sum takes some beating. Standout dumplings include steamed beef with tangerine peel, and grouper (or garoupa) with lemongrass and minced squid. The house-special dessert is *tai chi* cake, a chestnut paste and poppy seed pastry.

WEINSTUBE

Map pp412–14   *Austrian, German*
☎ 2376 1800; 1st fl, Honeytex Bldg, 22 Ashley Rd, Tsim Sha Tsui; mains HK$99-115; ⏰ noon-1am Mon-Sat, closed Sun

Pfannengebratener fleischkäse (pan-fried meat-loaf), *Schweinshaxe* (Bavarian-style pork knuckle) and other hearty mains await you at this Austro-German wine bar, which has been going strong for over 20 years. Happy hour is from 3pm to 8pm Monday to Friday and from noon to 8pm Saturday.

WOODLANDS INDIAN VEGETARIAN RESTAURANT

Map pp412–14   *Indian, Vegetarian*
☎ 2369 3718; Shops 5 & 6, Ground fl, Mirror Tower, 61 Mody Rd, Tsim Sha Tsui East; meals from HK$100 per person; ⏰ lunch noon-2pm, dinner 6.30-11pm

If you can't handle the less-than-salubrious surrounds of Chungking Mansions (p202), this place offers inexpensive Indian meals in Tsim Sha Tsui East.

Eating – Kowloon

Sauce products on display

WU KONG SHANGHAI RESTAURANT

Map pp412–14   *Chinese, Shanghainese*

☎ 2366 7244; Basement, Alpha House, 27-33 Nathan Rd, Tsim Sha Tsui; dim sum HK$11-48, rice & noodle dishes HK$32-78, meat mains HK$60-110, seafood mains HK$110-280; ⏲ 11.30am-11.15pm

This place and its signature dishes, cold pigeon in wine sauce and crispy fried eels, are excellent. The beggar's chicken (HK$360) is also very good. Dim sum is served all day.

YAN TOH HEEN Map pp412–14

Chinese, Cantonese

☎ 2721 1211; Shop L059, Ground fl, Hotel Inter-Continental Hong Kong, 18 Salisbury Rd, Tsim Sha Tsui; dim sum HK$36-65, mains HK$120-160; ⏲ lunch noon-2.30pm, dinner 6-11pm

On the harbour side of the Inter-Con, the recently renamed Yan Toh Heen lives up to the standards of its predecessor. The menu changes with each lunar month, and if the selections get confusing there's always a waiter hovering nearby to act as a guide. The assorted seafood in a crispy taro basket is out of this world.

Cheap Eats
BRANTO PURE VEGETARIAN INDIAN
CLUB Map pp412–14   *Indian, Vegetarian*

☎ 2366 8171; 1st fl, 9 Lock Rd, Tsim Sha Tsui; dishes HK$29-60; ⏲ lunch 11am-3pm, dinner 6-10.30pm

This cheap and excellent place is where to go if you want to try South Indian dishes. Order a *thali*, a steel tray of *idlis* (rice cakes) and *dosas* with dipping sauces.

CHUNGKING MANSIONS

Map pp412–14   *Indian*
36-44 Nathan Rd, Tsim Sha Tsui

The greatest concentration of cheap Indian and Pakistani restaurants in Kowloon is in this rabbit warren of hostels and guesthouses. Despite the grotty appearance of the building, many of these 'messes' are quite plush, though somewhat claustrophobic. The food varies in quality, but if you follow the recommendations below you should be in for a cheap and very filling meal. A good lunch or dinner will cost from about HK$50; for HK$100 you'll get a blow-out. Only one of the places is licensed, but you are usually allowed to BYO.

Delhi Club (☎ 2368 1682; Flat C3, 3rd fl, C Block; ⏲ lunch noon-3.30pm, dinner 6-11.30pm) does very good-value Indian and Nepalese food. Try the chicken tandoori (HK$25).

Pretty flash by Chungking Mansions standards, **Everest Club** (☎ 2316 2718; Flat D6, 3rd fl, D Block; ⏲ lunch noon-3pm, dinner 6-11.30pm) boasts a cornucopia of 'Everest' cuisines.

Islamabad Club (☎ 2721 5362; Flat C4, 4th fl, C Block; ⏲ lunch noon-3.30pm, dinner 6-11pm), a spartan place, will fill you up with Indian and Pakistani halal food.

Swagat Restaurant (☎ 2722 5350; Flat C4, 1st fl, C Block; ⏲ lunch noon-3pm, dinner 6-11pm) is one of the most popular in Chungking Mansions, probably less to do with the quality of food than its liquor licence, the only one held by a mess in the building.

Taj Mahal Club (☎ 2722 5454; Flat B4, 3rd fl, B Block; ⏲ lunch 11am-3.30pm, dinner 5.30-11.30pm) is popular with those who like truly hot curries, such as the chicken Madras (HK$38).

DAI PAI DONG

Map pp412–14   *Chinese, Hong Kong*

☎ 2317 7728; Ground fl, Hanley House, 70 Canton Rd, Tsim Sha Tsui; breakfast HK$11-33, rice & noodle dishes HK$28-42, set meals HK$48; ⏲ 8am-10pm Mon-Sat, 9.30am-7pm Sun

This modern version of the outdoor food-stall (ish) serves breakfast (bacon and eggs, porridge, noodles), lunch and dinner (rice and noodles), but it's best to come for afternoon tea (2.30pm to 5.30pm) for such oddities as *yuan yang* (equal parts coffee and black tea with milk), boiled cola with lemon and ginger, and toast smeared with condensed milk.

DELICATESSEN CORNER

Map pp412–14   *German, Deli*
☎ 2315 1020; Basement 1, Holiday Inn Golden Mile, 50 Nathan Rd, Tsim Sha Tsui; 🕙 8am-9.30pm
This is an excellent place to shop for a picnic or just to pause for a pastry and coffee while thumbing through the morning papers; there's a café attached (🕙 7.30am-11.30).

DELICIOUS CHOW NOODLE RESTAURANT

Map pp412–14   *Chinese, Noodle Bar*
☎ 2367 0824; 22 Prat Ave, Tsim Sha Tsui; snacks & starters HK$19.50-29, main dishes HK$28-70; 🕙 7am-3am
This simple and very friendly restaurant is worth trying for a cheap lunch, though the décor is a bit basic.

DÉLIFRANCE Map pp412–14   *Café*
☎ 2629 1845; Shop G101, Ground fl, The Gateway, 25-27 Canton Rd, Tsim Sha Tsui; soups & salads HK$12-23, sandwiches from HK$23-35, meals HK$25-35; 🕙 8am-8pm
This is a branch of the popular bakery and patisserie chain noted for its pastries, muffins, submarine sandwiches and quiche (not to mention coffee). There's another branch (Map pp412–14; ☎ 2369 2180; Shop 04-05B, ground fl, Carnarvon Plaza, 20 Carnarvon Rd, Tsim Sha Tsui) to the east.

GENKI SUSHI Map pp412–14   *Japanese*
☎ 2722 6689; Shop G7-G9, Ground fl, East Ocean Centre, 98 Granville Rd, Tsim Sha Tsui East; sushi HK$9-35 per pair, sushi sets HK$45-100; 🕙 11.30am-11.30pm
This is a branch of the popular susherie with a 'meany face' logo.

HAPPY GARDEN NOODLE & CONGEE KITCHEN

Map pp412–14   *Chinese, Noodle Bar*
☎ 2377 2604, 2314 9513; 76 Canton Rd, Tsim Sha Tsui; snacks HK$20, rice & noodle dishes HK$22-33, congee HK$30; 🕙 7am-1am
This is a budget option, with a choice of some 200 rice, noodle and congee dishes on the menu. Try the shrimp won ton noodles (HK$22). Among the few main dishes on offer is beef in oyster sauce (HK$55).

OLIVER'S SUPER SANDWICHES

Map pp412–14   *Sandwich Shop*
☎ 2367 0881; Shop LG1-1A, Tung Ying Bldg, 100 Nathan Rd (enter from Granville Rd), Tsim Sha Tsui; breakfast HK$15-30, soups HK$12-16, salads HK$20, sandwiches HK$23-39; 🕙 8am-8pm
This is a great place for breakfast – inexpensive bacon, eggs and toast. The sandwiches are equally good. The restaurant packs out during lunch hour, but is blissfully uncrowded at other times. There's another **Tsim Sha Tsui branch** (Map pp412-14; ☎ 2376 2826; Shop 2, Upper Ground fl, China Hong Kong City, 33 Canton Rd) to the west.

WELLCOME Map pp412–14   *Supermarket*
28 Hankow Rd, Tsim Sha Tsui; 🕙 8am-10pm
This branch of the supermarket chain is much better stocked and maintained than its other **Tsim Sha Tsui branch** (Map pp412-14; 74-78 Nathan Rd), which keeps the same hours.

YAU MA TEI

Temple St, the area around the night market, is a traditional place for cheap eats and snacks. Market cuisine, served from a pushcart, includes fish balls or squid on skewers and there's a large choice on offer from the nearby stalls. Anything upmarket in this part of Kowloon will usually be had in a hotel.

PALM COURT Map p415   *Café*
☎ 2761 1711; Metropole Hotel, 75 Waterloo Rd, Yau Ma Tei; starters HK$70-75, sandwiches HK$70-85, mains HK$85-115, set lunch HK$75; 🕙 6.30am-12.30am
This California-style hotel coffee shop would probably not even merit a mention if it were in the centre of Tsim Sha Tsui. But in deepest, darkest Yau Ma Tei it's like happening upon an oasis.

SAKURADA Map p415   *Japanese*
☎ 2928 8822; 3rd fl, Royal Plaza Hotel, 193 Prince Edward Rd West, Mong Kok; teppanyaki sets HK$98-228, set lunch HK$78-188; 🕙 lunch 11am-3pm, dinner 6-11pm
This place in one of Mong Kok's flashiest hotels is good for a bite after visiting the flower or bird markets. It specialises in teppanyaki and *kaiseki* (bite-sized treats to eat with tea or saké).

Cheap Eats

HING KEE Map p415   *Chinese, Cantonese*

☎ 2384 3647; 19 Temple St (enter from Hi Lung Lane), Yau Ma Tei; meals for HK$59; 🕐 5.30am-midnight

You won't find Hing Kee if you're looking for its name in lights (there's no English signage) so keep an eye out for earthen pots filled with rice cooking out on the streets. There's only one dish served at this semi-outdoor stall – rice cooked over charcoal in an earthenware pot and topped with either beef or chicken. It's a traditional winter dish, but there are enough rice fans to keep the stall in business all year. This is just one choice in a glut of good cheap night-time dining choices at the top end of Temple St serving the night market crowd.

JOYFUL VEGETARIAN

Map p415   *Chinese, Vegetarian*

☎ 2780 2230; 530 Nathan Rd, Yau Ma Tei; meals around HK$60 per person; 🕐 open 11am-11pm

The vegetable country-style hotpot is made with a ravishing range of fungi. There's a snack stall out the front of this Buddhist establishment if you're looking for a bite on the hoof (sorry).

MIU GUTE CHEONG VEGETARIAN RESTAURANT

Map pp412–14   *Chinese, Vegetarian*

☎ 2771 6218; 31 Ning Po St, Yau Ma Tei; meals from HK$50 per person; 🕐 11am-11pm

This inexpensive place is family oriented. There's a bit of spill-over bustle from Temple St, but an unruffled serenity prevails. The tofu

is fresh and firm, the vegetables are the pick of the market and the tea flows freely.

PAK BO VEGETARIAN KITCHEN

Map p415   *Chinese Vegetarian*

☎ 2380 2681; Ground fl, Lee Tat Building, 785 Nathan Rd, Mong Kok; meals from HK$60 per person; 🕐 11am-11pm

This vegetarian restaurant up near Boundary St isn't really worth a detour, but it is here should you be dragging the streets in Mong Kok.

SAINT'S ALP TEAHOUSE

Map p415   *Chinese, Hong Kong*

☎ 2393 2928; 134 Sai Yeung Choi St, Mong Kok; rice & noodle dishes HK$15-17, stir fries HK$27; 🕐 10am-11pm Sun-Thu, 10am-midnight Fri-Sat

There are literally dozens of these clean, cheap Taiwanese-style snackeries in Hong Kong; recognise them by the footprint in front of the name (always written in Chinese). They're a great pit stop for frothy tea with tapioca drops and Chinese snacks like toast with condensed milk, shrimp balls, noodles and rice puddings. There's a second **Mong Kok branch** (☎ 2782 1438; 61A Shantung St, Mong Kok) nearby.

VERY GOOD RESTAURANT

Map p415   *Chinese, Noodle Bar*

☎ 2394 8414; 148-150 Sai Yeung Choi St South, Mong Kok; dishes HK$20-36; 🕐 24hr

This busy, all-night noodle shop with no ego problems is known for its won ton soups and shredded pork noodles with spicy bean sauce. This is an eat-and-go sort of place – don't come here if you feel like slurping slowly and lingering.

NEW KOWLOON

About the only reason you'd travel further north than Tsim Sha Tsui specifically for a meal would be to try one of the Thai restaurants in Kowloon City, but there are other options.

AMARONI'S LITTLE ITALY

Map pp410–11   *Italian American*

☎ 2265 8818; Shop LG1, Lower Ground fl, Festival Walk, 80-88 Tat Chee Ave, Kowloon Tong; meals from HK$200 per person; 🕐 11am-11.30pm Sun-Wed, 11am-midnight Thu-Sat

The first rule of American-Italian cuisine, obviously the flavour of the season in Hong Kong, is to make it big. And Amaroni's, part of the Dan Ryan's group, doesn't stray from that law, dishing up pasta, seafood and steak so large

that they make the floor staff strain. Kids get a free feed during the week. There's also a **Wan Chai branch** (Map pp406-8; ☎ 2891 8555; Shop 3-4, Wu Chung House, 213 Queen's Rd East).

CAFÉ ROUGE

Map pp410–11   *American, International*

☎ 2383 8188; 16 Nam Kok Rd, Kowloon City; starters HK$22-55, mains HK$52-120; 🕐 lunch noon-3pm, dinner 6-11.30pm Mon-Sat, noon-11.30pm Sat & Sun

This mostly American-style restaurant (buffalo

wings, baby ribs) with a French name is a welcome oasis in *very* ethnic Kowloon City.

CHONG FAT CHIU CHOW RESTAURANT

Map pp410–11   *Chinese, Chiu Chow*

☎ 2383 3114, 2383 1296; 60-62 South Wall Rd, Kowloon City; meals from HK$150 per person; ✆ 11am-11pm

While this place isn't easy to get to and communications are limited, it has some of the best and freshest Chiu Chow seafood in the territory. Don't miss the crab dishes, *sek lau gai* (chicken wrapped in little egg-white sacs) and the various goose offerings.

FEDERAL RESTAURANT

Map pp410–11   *Chinese, Cantonese*

☎ 2626 0011; 3rd fl, Hollywood Plaza, 3 Lung Poon St, Diamond Hill; meals from HK$120 per person; ✆ 7.30am-11pm

This is a bustling restaurant so big that the captains are armed with walkie-talkies to seat diners and have tables cleared. Dim sum is served until mid-afternoon and Cantonese à la carte at dinner. The dim sum menu is in Chinese only – ask your waiter to choose for you or gawp at other tables and point. Feature windows look onto a very Hong Kong vista of apartments, the Diamond MTR station is right downstairs and the Chi Lin Nunnery (p119) just around the corner.

ISLAM FOOD Map pp410–11   *Halal Chinese*

☎ 2382 2822; 1 Lung Kong Rd, Kowloon City; meals from HK$150 per person; ✆ 11am-11pm

If you fancy trying the cuisine of the *Hui* (Chinese Muslims), come here. Try the mutton with scallions on a hotplate, or minced beef with pickled cabbage stuffed into sesame rolls.

SNAKE KING Map pp410–11   *Chinese, Snake*

☎ 2383 6297; 11 Lung Kong Rd, Kowloon City; soups HK$50-210; ✆ 10am-11pm

Should you visit Hong Kong in winter and are anxious to indulge in a taste of one of these slithering 'narrow fellows', the Snake King can oblige.

ZEN Map pp410–11   *Chinese, Cantonese*

☎ 2265 7328; Shop G25, Ground fl, Festival Walk, 80-88 Tat Chee Ave, Kowloon Tong; mains HK$75-110; ✆ lunch 11.30am-3pm Mon-Fri, 11.30am-5pm Sat, 10.30am-5pm Sun, dinner 5.30-11pm daily

Zen has won praise from the public and restaurateurs alike for its dynamic approach to Chinese cuisine, which is Cantonese served in stunning Japanese surrounds. You'll enjoy mangoes with your prawns and a multitude of dim sum dishes. There's also an **Admiralty branch** (Map pp400-3; ☎ 2845 4555; shop LG1, Lower Ground fl, The Mall, Pacific Place, 88 Queensway).

Cheap Eats

KOWLOON CITY THAI RESTAURANTS

Map pp410–11   *Thai*

The district of Kowloon City, which abuts the old Kai Tak Airport to the northeast of Tsim Sha Tsui, has a high concentration of Thai residents and Thai restaurants (there are also a few Indian and Chinese, notably Chiu Chow, restaurants). You'll eat a meal for HK$60 and a feast for HK$100 at all these places, so it makes it worth the trip.

One of the most authentic Thai restaurants in the area, **Friendship Thai Food** (☎ 2382 8671; 38 Kai Tak Rd; ✆ 11am-midnight) is always full of Thai domestics. **Golden Orchid Thai**

(☎ 2383 3076; 12 Lung Kong Rd; ☺ noon-1am) is slightly more expensive than the Friendship but the food is excellent.

The standards at **Cambo Thai Restaurant** (☎ 2716 7318; 15 Nga Tsin Long Rd; ☺ 11.30am-1am) have fallen as it opens more Thai and Vietnamese outlets in the area.

Sweet Basil Thai Cuisine (☎ 2718 1088; 31-33 Kai Tak Rd; ☺ 11am-11pm) is a branch of a three-strong chain and serves decent Thai in very upmarket (for this neighbourhood) surrounds.

Thai Farm Restaurant (☎ 2382 0992; 21-23 Nam Kok Rd; ☺ lunch 11.30am-3pm, dinner 6pm-midnight Mon-Fri, 11.30am-midnight Sat & Sun), with its panelled walls and banquettes, is a cut above most of the other Thai eateries.

NEW TERRITORIES

With very few exceptions, the New Territories is not an area offering a surfeit of culinary surprises. The following recommendations are basically for sustenance along the way.

TSUEN WAN

As in most of the New Towns of the New Territories, the happiest hunting grounds for a snack or lunch in Tsuen Wan are in the shopping mall that – inevitably – tops the MTR station. But there are also often surprises further afield.

CHIANTI RISTORANTE Map p416 _Italian_

☎ 2409 3226; Panda Hotel, 4th fl, 3 Tsuen Wah St; meals from HK$200 per person, set lunch/dinner HK$98/168; ☺ lunch noon-3pm, dinner 6-11pm
You wouldn't travel all the way to Tsuen Wan for Italian food, but if you're touring around the area Chianti Ristorante does have decent pasta dishes and the service is good. The set meals include an antipasto buffet. Take exit B2 from the Tsuen Wan MTR station.

LUK YEUNG GALLERIA

Map p416 _Food Court_
Sau Lau Kok Rd; ☺ 8am-midnight
This shopping mall attached to the Tsuen Wan MTR station has a number of places to eat, including the usual fast-food outlets (eg **Fairwood**) as well as a huge **Park 'N' Shop** (2nd fl; ☺ 7am-11pm) for the makings of a picnic.

TUEN MUN

You'll find plenty of Chinese restaurants and noodle shops in Tuen Mun town centre, but it's best to travel out a way for something unusual and delicious.

Top Five Restaurants – New Territories

- **Chung Shing Thai** (p207) Tai Mei Tuk's flagship restaurant, popular for its authentic Thai dishes.
- **Miu Fat Monastery** (p206) Meatless meals at the monastery's vegetarian restaurant.
- **Nang Kee Goose Restaurant** (p206) Far-flung place worth the trip for its most famous roast goose.
- **Sauce** (p209) Stylish Sai Kung eatery with outside seating and live music at night.
- **Tung Kee Restaurant** (p209) Pick of the crop for Cantonese seafood on Sai Kung's waterfront.

MIU FAT MONASTERY

Map pp396–7 _Chinese, Vegetarian_
☎ 2461 8567; 18 Castle Peak Rd; set lunch HK$75; ☺ 11am-3pm
This restaurant, on the 1st floor of Miu Fat Monastery in Lam Tei, due north of Tuen Mun town centre, serves veggie meals at lunch only.

NANG KEE GOOSE RESTAURANT

Map pp396–7 _Chinese, Cantonese_
☎ 2491 0392; Sham Tseng Sun Tsuen, Sham Tseng; dishes from HK$50, whole roast goose HK$230; ☺ 10.30am-10.30pm
This restaurant is a bit far-flung from Tuen Mun for a casual meal, but if you are on your way to the island of Ma Wan, this is the place to come. It's the most famous roast goose restaurant in a village renowned for its tasty preparation of the bird.

YUEN LONG

Should you feel peckish while in Yuen Long, there are a number of restaurants and snack places in Yuen Long Plaza in the centre of town, just opposite the Fung Nin Rd LRT stop.

KAR SHING RESTAURANT

Map pp396–7 · *Chinese, Cantonese*
☎ 2476 3228; 3rd fl, Yuen Long Plaza, 249 Castle Peak Rd; meals from HK$100 per person;

🕑 lunch & dim sum noon-4pm, dinner 6-11pm
Excellent dim sum is served from 7am to 4pm at this cavernous Cantonese restaurant in Yuen Long Plaza.

TAI PO & SURROUNDS

Tai Po is not the gourmet centre of the New Territories, but there are a few decent eateries to choose from in the centre and to the northwest of Tai Po Market KCR station. Tai Mei Tuk, the springboard for the Plover Cover area some 6km to the northeast, boasts a number of interesting eateries along Ting Kok Rd, many of them Thai. And Tai Po Kau, to the south, has a wonderful little restaurant in the same complex as the Museum of Ethnology.

CHILI CHILI Map pp396–7 · *Asian*
☎ 2662 6767; 101 Lung Mei Village, Ting Kok Rd, Tai Mei Tuk; rice & noodle dishes HK$30-50, mains HK$52-68; 🕑 11am-11pm Mon-Fri, 7.30am-2am Sat, 7.30am-11pm Sun

The newest and flashiest of the Tai Mei Tuk eateries, Chili Chili is at the western end of the strip in the direction of Tai Po town. It's a comfortable place with outside seating and an eclectic menu (Thai curries, Cantonese noodles etc).

CHUNG SHING THAI Map pp396–7 · *Thai*
☎ 2664 5218; 69 Tai Mei Tuk Village, Ting Kok Rd, Tai Mei Tuk; mains HK$40-60; 🕑 lunch noon-3pm, dinner 6pm-midnight

This is the flagship restaurant of the restaurant strip in Tai Mei Tuk, the one that launched the fleet. It remains very popular for its authentic Thai curries, soups and fish dishes but caters to less adventurous locals with a few Chinese offerings.

COSMOPOLITAN CURRY HOUSE
Map p416 · *Indonesian, Malaysian*
☎ 2650 7056; 80 Kwong Fuk Rd, Tai Po; curries HK$61-82, set meals HK$30-60; 🕑 11.30am-midnight
The Indonesian/Malaysian curries at this Tai Po institution are excellent, but be sure to book, especially in the evening.

EMPEROR SUSHI Map p416 · *Japanese*
☎ 2638 0222; 28-32 Tai Wing Lane, Tai Po; sushi HK$10-50, sashimi HK$65-100; 🕑 11.30am-10pm

This little sushi bar, in the popular shopping area also called Four Lanes Square and opposite a garden with a fountain, is a cut above the usual and very centrally located.

LITTLE EGRET Map pp396–7 · *International*
☎ 2657 6628; 2 Hung Lam Dr, Tai Po Kau; dishes HK$60-80; 🕑 11am-11pm
In the same complex as the Interactive Nature Centre and Museum of Ethnology is this attractive little restaurant serving a mix of dishes – from seafood to pasta. No doubt you'll spot some of the eponymous creatures from the window of the restaurant.

SHALIMAR Map p416 · *Indian*
☎ 2653 7790; 127 Kwong Fuk Rd, Tai Po; mains HK$35-100, set lunches HK$30-40, set dinner for 2 HK$175; 🕑 lunch 11.30am-3pm, dinner 6-11pm
If you prefer your curries more subcontinental or you can't get into the Cosmopolitan, the Shalimar is a short distance from the latter to the southeast.

WONG'S
Map pp396–7 · *Chinese, Cantonese*
☎ 2948 2282; 69A Tai Mei Tuk Village, Ting Kok Rd, Tai Mei Tuk; rice & noodle dishes HK$30, mains HK$40-55; 🕑 11am-10pm
Not quite a *dai pai dong* but with that sort of feeling to it, Wong's is a friendly and traditional Hong Kong restaurant specialising in hotpot dishes; try the seafood, vegetable or beef brisket varieties.

Eating – New Territories

207

SHA TIN

The multi-level New Town Plaza shopping mall (Map p417) connected to the Sha Tin KCR station has more restaurants and snack bars than you can shake a chopstick at.

A-1 RESTAURANT *International*

☎ 2699 0428; Shop 140-151, 1st fl, New Town Plaza Phase I; starters HK$45-63, mains HK$68-103; ☽ 11am-11pm

The A1 fills a welcome Western void in an area rife with Chinese and ethnic offerings. It serves the usual international dishes – steaks and seafood – and is popular with families at the weekend. The attached **A1 Bakery Shop** (☎ 2697 6377) is a plus.

BANTHAI THAI CUISINE *Thai*

☎ 2609 3686; Shop A172 & A184-187, 1st fl, New Town Plaza Phase III; dishes HK$48-118; ☽ 11am-midnight

If you're in need of a quick fix of *tom yom gung*, a green curry and/or yet another golden Buddha, this is the place to come. It has a loyal following.

KAGA SUSHI RESTAURANT *Japanese*

☎ 2603 0545; Shop A191A-193A, 1st fl, New Town Plaza Phase III; sushi HK$12-35, tempura HK$70-90; ☽ lunch 11.30am-3pm Mon-Fri, dinner 6-11pm Mon-Fri, 11am-11pm Sat & Sun

Kaga is a bit sterile and the service somewhat abrupt, but the sushi (salmon, yellow tail tuna) and grilled eel make up for its shortcomings.

KOH-I-NOOR *Indian*

☎ 2601 5339; Shop A181-182, 1st fl, New Town Plaza Phase III; curries HK$62-80, tandoori dishes HK$70-125, set menu for 2 HK$188; ☽ lunch noon-3pm, dinner 6-11.30pm

This popular place, with branches in Central (p172) and Tsim Sha Tsui (p198) is a good and stylish choice for Northern Indian food.

SAI KUNG

Sai Kung town is chock-a-block with eateries. Here you'll find curry, pizzas and bangers and mash just as easily as Chinese seafood, but you'd make a special trip here only for the last category.

ALI-OLI Map p417 *Bakery, Café*

☎ 2792 2655; 11 Sha Tsui Path; meals from HK$100 per person; ☽ 7am-7pm

This bakery-cum-café has sandwiches (HK$22), pizza slices (HK$9), quiches (HK$65 whole, HK$15 slice), Cornish pasties (HK$24) and assorted loaves, cakes and pies.

CHUEN KEE SEAFOOD RESTAURANT

Map p417 *Chinese, Cantonese*

☎ 2792 9294; 87-89 Man Nin St; meals HK$150-200 per person; ☽ 11am-11pm

Chuen Kee, the granddaddy of the Sai Kung seafood restaurants, has three nearby waterfront branches so they'll always be a room for you somewhere.

DIA Map p417 *Indian*

☎ 2791 4466; 42-56 Fuk Man Rd; starters HK$35-50, curries HK$65-78, tandoori dishes HK$80-130, set lunch HK$48; ☽ 11am-11pm

This stylish new place, all blue satin and rattan, serves Northern Indian cuisine.

FIRENZE Map p417 *Italian*

☎ 2792 0898; 60 Po Tung Rd; starters HK$20-78, mains HK$88-98; ☽ noon-11pm

This perennial Italian favourite does full meals as well as excellent pizza (HK$60 to HK$115) and pasta (HK$65 to HK$75).

HUNG KEE SEAFOOD RESTAURANT

Map p417 *Chinese, Cantonese*

☎ 2792 1348; Shop 4-8, Ground & 1st fls, Siu Yat Building, Sai Kung Hoi Pong Square; meals HK$150-200 per person; ☽ 6.30pm-midnight

See that queue of plastic basins that ends at the kitchen? That's dinner. Choose your live fish or shellfish from the stall outside and tell the staff how you want it cooked; most want their catch simply steamed with ginger. Facing right out onto the water, Hung Kee has one of the largest selection of seafood in town and dim sum from 6.30am to 3.30pm.

INDIAN CURRY HUT Map p417 *Indian*

☎ 2791 2929; 64 Po Tung Rd;

starters HK$28-46, tandoori dishes HK$48-95, curries HK$52-79; 🕙 11.30am-11.30pm

If you can't stand looking at finned creatures from the deep any longer, head for the Indian Curry House. This is also the place for vegetarians, with some 15 dishes on offer (HK$46 to HK$66).

JASPA'S Map p417 *International, Fusion*
☎ 2792 6388; 13 Sha Tsui Path; starters HK$60-95, mains HK$90-100, set lunch HK$88 (Mon-Fri), set dinner for 2 HK$290; 🕙 8am-10.30pm Mon-Sat, 9am-midnight Sun

Jaspa's is an upbeat and casual place serving international and fusion food. There's also a **Soho branch** (Map pp404-5; ☎ 2869 0733; 28-30 Staunton St) on Hong Kong Island.

PEPPERONI'S PIZZA Map p417 *Italian*
☎ 2791 0394, 2791 1738; Lot 1592, Po Tung Rd; salads HK$50-60, pizzas HK$65-75; 🕙 11am-11pm

This place serves up some fine pizza and other dishes, and the atmosphere is relaxing and fun.

SAUCE Map p417 *International*
☎ 2791 2348; 9 Sha Tsui Path; starters HK$52-92, mains HK$88-135; 🕙 11am-11pm Mon-Fri, 10am-11pm Sat & Sun

This very stylish restaurant on a narrow pedestrian path in the centre of Sai Kung town has outside sitting and live music at night.

STEAMERS BAR & RESTAURANT
Map p417 *International*
☎ 2792 6991; 23 Chan Man St; breakfast HK$38-65, pies HK$28-45, mains HK$28-75; 🕙 9am-1am Mon-Thu, 9am-2am Fri-Sun

This minimalist bar-restaurant is a popular place with outside seating. It serves decent meals – bangers and mash (HK$48) and giant burgers (HK$75) – to a largely expat crowd. Happy hour is 2pm to 9pm Monday to Friday and 5pm to 8pm Sunday.

TUNG KEE RESTAURANT
Map p417 *Chinese, Cantonese*
☎ 2792 7453; 96-102 Man Nin St; meals HK$150-200; 🕙 6am-11pm

This is the pick of the crop for Cantonese seafood in Sai Kung. It's not cheap, of course, but then the food is outstanding. Try to call first – though it has a few other branches, including one on See Cheung St, where they'll seat you as an alternative. Dim sum is available from 6am to 3pm.

Cheap Eats
SAI KUNG SUPERMARKETS
Map p417 *Supermarket*
For self-catering, Sai Kung has both a **Park 'N' Shop** (18-20 Fuk Man Rd; 🕙 7.30am-10.30pm) and a **Wellcome** (Chan Man St; 🕙 7am-10pm).

TAP MUN CHAU
You won't starve to death here, but nor will you have much of a choice in the way of venues. There's only one restaurant on this far-flung island, but the food is good and the staff helpful and friendly.

NEW HON KEE
Map pp396–7 *Chinese, Cantonese*
☎ 2328 2428; 4 Hoi Pong St; meals under HK$100 per person; 🕙 11am-2pm Mon-Fri, 11am-6pm Sat & Sun

This seafood restaurant, popular with islanders and visitors alike, is a short walk northeast of the ferry pier on the way to the Tin Hau temple. The grilled prawns and squid are excellent.

OUTLYING ISLANDS
Restaurants and other eateries vary from island to island. Some, like those on Lantau and, to a large extent Cheung Chau, are just convenient refuelling stations as you head for (or return from) your destination. Others, such as the seafood restaurants in Sok Kwu Wan on Lamma or on Po Toi are destinations in their own right.

LAMMA
Lamma offers the greatest choice of restaurants and cuisines than any of the other Outlying Islands. Most people head directly to Sok Kwu Wan for a fix of Cantonese-style seafood,

but Yung Shue Wan has a vast and eclectic range, and there are a couple of other venues on the island that are worth the trip in itself.

Yung Shue Wan

Yung Shue Wan has a large choice of places to eat. Along its main (and only) street, not only will you find Chinese restaurants, but Western, vegetarian, Thai and even Indian ones.

BLUE BIRD Map p418 *Japanese*

☎ 2982 0687; 24 Main St; dishes HK$35-50; ☽ lunch noon-3pm, dinner 6-11.30pm

This relatively new addition to the Yung Shue Wan line-up offers simple but tasty Japanese dishes, from teppanyaki to tempura.

BOOKWORM CAFÉ

Map p418 *Café, Vegetarian*

☎ 2982 4838; 79 Main St; main dishes HK$40-80; ☽ 10am-7pm Mon-Fri, 9am-10pm Sat, 9am-9pm Sun

This place is everything to everyone (except carnivores): a vegetarian café/restaurant with excellent breakfasts (HK$25 to HK$60) and fruit juices, a second-hand bookshop and an Internet café (HK$0.50 per minute). A true oasis, this place.

LAMMA BISTRO Map p418 *International*

☎ 2982 4343; 44 Main St; mains HK$95-125; ☽ noon-10pm Mon-Fri, 10am-midnight Sat & Sun

A change of ownership has turned this place into a jack of all trades. Lamma Bistro serving breakfast (HK$25 to HK$65), snacks and full meals. If you're not overly hungry, go for tapas (HK$30 to HK$60) or a sandwich (HK$55 to HK$65). There's plenty of outside seating here.

Top Five Restaurants – Outlying Islands

- **Han Lok Yuen** (p211) Lamma restaurant celebrated for its roast pigeon
- **Jo Jo Indian Restaurant** (p213) Discovery Bay's more upmarket version of Jo Jo Mess in Wan Chai
- **Lamma Bistro** (p210) Jack-of-all-trades eatery with plenty of outside seating
- **Rainbow Seafood Restaurant** (p211) Multi-outlet place on Sok Kwu Wan Bay
- **Stoep Restaurant** (p214) Mediterranean-style terrace restaurant on a Lantau beach

---

LANCOMBE SEAFOOD RESTAURANT

Map p418 *Chinese, Seafood*

☎ 2982 0881; 47 Main St; meals from HK$150 per person; ☽ 10.30am-10.30pm

This popular seafood restaurant has a delightful terrace facing the sea on the 1st floor. The deep-fried squid with salt and pepper and the steamed prawns are excellent.

LUNG WAH SEAFOOD RESTAURANT

Map p418 *Chinese, Seafood*

☎ 2982 0791; 20 Main St; meals HK$180 per person; ☽ 6am-midnight

Just next to the HSBC, Lung Wah is fronted by tanks from which you can choose fish and crustaceans from the briny deep. The restaurant also does excellent dim sum from 6am to 11am (until noon at the weekend).

MAN FUNG SEAFOOD RESTAURANT

Map p418 *Chinese, Seafood*

☎ 2982 0719; 5 Main St; meals HK$200 per person; ☽ 11am-10pm

This friendly place just up from the ferry pier also has the main ingredients of its dishes on full, living display. The lobster and prawns are especially recommended here.

PIZZA MILANO Map p418 *Italian*

☎ 2982 4848; Ground & 1st fls, 2 Back St; small/medium/large pizzas from HK$50/62/98, pasta HK$58-70; ☽ 6-11pm Mon-Fri, noon-11pm Sat & Sun

If you're looking for pizza, pasta, calzone or crostini, Lamma's only Italian restaurant is the correct choice.

SAMPAN SEAFOOD RESTAURANT

Map p418 *Chinese, Seafood*

☎ 2982 2388; 16 Main St; meals HK$180-200 per person; ☽ 6am-10.30pm

Sampan remains very popular with locals (always a sure sign) both for its seafood and its pigeon dishes. It has dim sum from 6am to 11am and boasts an excellent sea view.

SPICY ISLAND Map p418 *Indian*

☎ 2982 0830; 23 Main St; starters HK$20-35, curries HK$35-80, tandoori dishes HK$45-115; ☽ noon-midnight

This place promises (and delivers, locals say) 'genuine Indian cuisine'. You can dine alfresco.

Hung Shing Yeh

This popular beach southeast of Yung Shue Wan has a convenient waterfront hotel where you can lunch on the terrace. It also boasts one of the most famous nonseafood restaurants on the outlying islands.

CONCERTO INN

Map p418   *Asian, International*
☎ 2982 1668; 28 Hung Shing Yeh Beach; dishes HK$49-58; ☺ 8am-10pm
The food is no great shakes at Lamma's only real hotel, but if you're on the beach at Hung Shing Yeh and fancy rice or noodles (HK$33 to HK$55), pasta (HK$49) or a sandwich (HK$39 to HK$53), you won't have to travel far.

HAN LOK YUEN

Map p418   *Chinese, Cantonese*
☎ 2982 0608; 16-17 Hung Shing Yeh; dishes HK$55-85; ☺ 11am-9.30pm
This restaurant is famous throughout Hong Kong for its roast pigeon, but make sure to book at the weekend. The quail (HK$62) and salted prawns (HK$85) are also exceptional.

Sok Kwu Wan

An evening meal at Sok Kwu Wan is an enjoyable way to end a trip to Lamma. The restaurants line the waterfront on either side of the ferry pier and will be chock-a-block on weekend nights with Chinese and expats who have arrived by ferry, on boats laid on by the restaurants themselves, on company junks or the ostentatious yachts known locally as 'gin palaces'. Most of the dozen or so restaurants offer the same relatively high-quality seafood at similar prices, but a few places stand out from the pack.

LAMMA HILTON SHUM KEE SEAFOOD RESTAURANT

Map p418   *Chinese, Seafood*
☎ 2982 8241; 26 First St; meals HK$150-200 per person; ☺ 10.30am-11pm
Some people consider this the best seafood restaurant in Sok Kwu Wan (and, no, it's not connected with the hotel chain).

RAINBOW SEAFOOD RESTAURANT

Map p418   *Chinese, Seafood*
☎ 2982 8100; Shops 1A-1B, 16-20 & 23-24 First St; meals HK$150-200 per person; ☺ 11am-11pm

The Rainbow, with three waterfront locations, specialises in steamed grouper, fried lobster in butter sauce and steamed abalone. What's more, book a table (in advance) and you'll be transported by small ferry from Queen's Pier in Central (up to seven sailings on weekday evenings from 5.30pm to 8.30pm, and up to 13 at weekends from 11.30am to 8.30pm) or from Aberdeen.

WAN KEE SEAFOOD RESTAURANT

Map p418   *Chinese, Seafood*
☎ 2982 8548, 2982 8279; 28 First Street; meals HK$150-200; ☺ lunch noon-2pm, dinner 6.30-11pm
This smaller place with an unfortunate name offers less frenetic, friendlier service than most of the other places in Sok Kwu Wan.

Mo Tat Wan

Surprisingly, in this relatively remote corner of Lamma there's an upmarket Western restaurant.

COCOCABANA Map p418   *Fusion*
☎ 2328 2138; 7 Mo Tat Wan; starters HK$52-88, mains HK$138-160; ☺ noon-10pm Tue-Sun, closed Mon
This is arguably the most romantic spot on Lamma. The main menu is a mix of North African and Mediterranean, but there are also a half-dozen Asian dishes (HK$55 to HK$88).

Lin Heung Tea House (p173)

CHEUNG CHAU

In Cheung Chau village, south of the cargo pier and at the start of Tai Hing Tai Rd, there are a number of food stalls with fish tanks where you can choose your favourite finned or shelled creatures at more or less market prices and then pay the stall holders to cook them the way you like.

Pak She Praya Rd, running northwest off Praya St, is loaded with seafood restaurants that face the typhoon shelter and its flotilla of junks and sampans.

EAST LAKE Map p420   *Chinese, Cantonese*
☎ 2981 3869; 85 Tung Wan Rd; mains HK$30-50, fish from HK$120; ☽ 10am-10pm
This Cantonese restaurant, away from the waterfront and close to Tung Wan Beach, is popular with locals and expats, especially in the evening when tables are set up outside.

HING LOK Map p420   *Chinese, Seafood*
☎ 2981 9773; 2A Pak She Sixth Lane; mains HK$50-80, fish from HK$120; ☽ 10am-10pm
Hing Lok is a titch further north along the waterfront than neighbours Hong Kee and New Baccarat, but it serves excellent seafood and is within casting distance of the harbour.

HOMETOWN TEAHOUSE Map p420   *Café*
☎ 2981 5038; 12 Tung Wan Rd; afternoon tea HK$20; ☽ noon-midnight
This wonderfully relaxed place run by an amiable Japanese couple serves lunch and dinner, but the afternoon tea – sushi, pancake, tea – is what you should come for. It's convenient to Tung Wan Beach.

HONG KEE Map p420   *Chinese, Seafood*
☎ 2981 9916; 11A Pak She Praya Rd; mains HK$40-80, fish from HK$140; ☽ 10.30am-10.30pm
This is one of the top spots along Pak She Praya St and should be your first choice.

LONG ISLAND RESTAURANT
Map p420   *Chinese, Seafood*
☎ 2981 1678; 51-53 San Hing St; dishes HK$38-60; ☽ 5am-2am

This Cantonese restaurant goes several steps beyond seafood. You can order a variety of dishes, including hotpot, steamed pigeons and dim sum, until mid-afternoon.

NEW BACCARAT
Map p420   *Chinese, Seafood*
☎ 2981 0606; 9A Pak She Praya Rd; meals from HK$120 per person; ☽ 11am-10.30pm
Head for this place, which has blue-checked tablecloths outside, if Hong Kee is full.

SEA DRAGON KING
Map p420   *Chinese, Seafood*
☎ 2981 1699; 16 Tai Hing Tai Rd; dishes HK$45-60, fish from HK$100; ☽ 10am-11.30pm
Sea Dragon King, at the corner of Praya St, has a wonderful choice of live seafood on display. It's away from the flasher waterfront restaurants and, as a result, is more popular with local people and cheaper.

Cheap Eats
CHEUNG CHAU SUPERMARKETS
Map p420   *Supermarket*
There is both a **Wellcome** (Praya St; ☽ 8am-11pm) and a **Park 'N' Shop** (cnr Tung Wan Rd & Tai San Back St; ☽ 8am-10.30pm) in Cheung Chau village. These two supermarkets are conveniently located near the ferry pier, so you can stock up on food and drink if you are going hiking or spending the day on the beach. **Park 'N' Shop** has a smaller branch on Praya St.

LANTAU

The lion's share of Lantau's restaurants are, naturally enough, in Mui Wo (Silvermine Bay), but you certainly won't starve in places further afield such as the villages along South Lantau Rd, on the Ngong Ping Plateau and in Tai O. Discovery Bay has its own line-up of eateries around Discovery Bay Plaza.

Mui Wo

You'll find a slew of restaurant, noodle shops and bars southwest of the ferry pier. There are also some restaurants on the way to Silvermine Bay Beach and on the beach itself. For some pub recommendations, see p227.

LA PIZZERIA Map p421 *Italian*

☎ 2984 8933; Ground fl, Grand View Mansion, 11C Mui Wo Ferry Pier Rd; pizza HK$55-80, mains HK$60-110; ⏱ 10am-11pm

Most people come here for the pizza, but there are lots of pasta choices (HK$45 to HK$60) and main courses such as fajitas (HK$78) and barbecued spareribs (HK$110) on the menu.

ROME RESTAURANT

Map p421 *Chinese, Cantonese*

☎ 2984 7982; Shop A-B, Ground fl, Grand View Mansion, 11A Mui Wo Ferry Pier Rd; meals for under HK$100 per person; ⏱ 11am-10.30pm

The food isn't the best and you may have trouble making yourself understood (unless you just point at the dim sum, available from 11am to 6pm), but Rome is close to the ferry pier.

SILVERMINE BEACH HOTEL

Map p421 *Chinese, International*

☎ 2984 8295; Tung Wan Tau Rd; set meals HK$98-158; ⏱ lunch 11.30am-3pm, dinner 6.30-10pm

The coffee shop and Chinese restaurant at this relatively flashy hotel is no great shakes, but can be recommended for its all you-can-eat buffet dinner (adult/child HK$98/78) from Sunday to Friday and its barbecue dinner buffet (HK$158/88) on Saturday.

TAK JUK KEE SEAFOOD RESTAURANT

Map p421 *Chinese, Seafood*

☎ 2984 1265; 1 Chung Hau Rd; dishes HK$50-96; ⏱ lunch noon-3pm, dinner 6-10pm

This friendly restaurant catches delightful sea breezes from Silvermine Bay and is arguably the best Chinese restaurant in Mui Wo. Try the chilli prawns (HK$80), squid with vegetables (HK$50), chicken with cashew nuts (HK$50) or crab with ginger (HK$96).

CHEAP EATS
CURRY CORNER Map p421 *Indian*

Shop 8, Ground fl, Mui Wo Centre, 3 Ngan Wan Rd; snacks HK$20, lunch boxes HK$22-25, vegetarian dishes HK$35-38, meat curries & tandoori dishes HK$40-65; ⏱ 11am-10pm

This takeaway place visible from the ferry pier does basic Indian dishes and has a decent selection of vegetarian options.

MUI WO COOKED FOOD MARKET

Map p421 *Chinese, Cantonese*

Ngan Kwong Rd; ⏱ 6am-midnight

The food isn't great at this series of covered food stalls northwest of the ferry pier, but it's cheap and convenient – especially if you're headed for the beach. Only a few of the stalls and restaurants have English menus, including **Yee Henn Seaview Restaurant** (☎ 2986 2778), the last restaurant on the western side of the market.

MUI WO MARKET Map p421 *Market*

Ngan Shek St; ⏱ 6am-8pm

Silvermine Bay's covered wet market is towards the west after you cross the footbridge over the Silver River.

MUI WO SUPERMARKETS

Map p421 *Supermarket*

You'll find both a **Park 'N' Shop** (Mui Wo Ferry Pier Rd; ⏱ 8am-9pm) and a **Wellcome** (Ngan Wan Rd; ⏱ 8am-10pm) supermarket in the centre of Mui Wo.

Discovery Bay

The restaurants in the circular plaza opposite the ferry pier at Discovery Bay (Map p419) offer a wide variety of cuisines.

BREZZA *Italian*

☎ 2914 1906; Shop G01, Block A, Discovery Bay Plaza; starters HK$35-75, pasta HK$80-110, pizza HK$75-95, mains HK$95-145; ⏱ noon-10pm

Though it does more substantial dishes, this Italian place is a good choice for pizza and pasta dishes and has pleasant outside seating.

CHILLI N SPICE *Asian*

☎ 2987 9191; Shop 102F, 1st fl, Discovery Bay Plaza; noodle dishes HK$42-85, mains HK$48-135; ⏱ lunch 11.30am-2.30pm, dinner 5.30pm-midnight Mon-Fri, 11.30am-midnight Sat & Sun

This branch of the popular – and growing – chain is a potpourri of spicy Singaporean, Thai and Indonesian flavours.

JO JO INDIAN RESTAURANT *Indian*

☎ 2987 0122; Shop 101A, Discovery Bay Plaza; dishes HK$60-70; ⏱ lunch 11am-3pm, dinner 6-11pm

This much more stylish sister-restaurant of the popular Jo Jo Mess in Wan Chai (see p184 under Hong Kong Island) has punters lining up for its lamb dishes, especially the tandoori ones.

SHOUGON
Korean

☎ 2987 9299; Shop G07, Discovery Bay Plaza; mains HK$50-80, barbecue from HK$60; ☺ lunch 11.30am-2.30pm, dinner 5.30-10.30pm Mon-Fri, 11.30am-10.30pm Sat & Sun

The Korean food at the Shougon, which has nothing to do with a Japanese shogun, might not be as authentic as what you'd find in Sheung Wan, but it's good nonetheless.

South Lantau Road

Two of the villages along Lantau's main east-west thoroughfare have decent restaurants from which to choose.

KUNG SHING
Map p419
Chinese, Cantonese

☎ 2980 2711; 35 Lower Cheung Sha Village; rice & noodle dishes HK$25-40, main dishes HK$45-60, fish dishes from HK$120; ☺ 7am-8pm

If you can't get into the Stoep, this Chinese eatery next door, which will happily place your table right on the sand, is a viable alternative.

LOWER CHEUNG SHA BEACH STOEP RESTAURANT
Map p419
Mediterranean, South African

☎ 2980 2699; 32 Lower Cheung Sha Village; mains HK$50-150; ☺ 11am-10pm Tue-Sun

This Mediterranean-style restaurant with a huge terrace right on the beach has good fish dishes (HK$50 to HK$85) and a South African *braai* (barbecue; HK$80 to HK$150). Be sure to book at the weekend.

TONG FUK GALLERY
Map p419
Middle Eastern, Barbecue

☎ 2980 2582; 26 Tong Fuk Village; meze HK$35-45, kebabs & grills HK$75-165, fish dishes HK$95-175; ☺ 6pm-late Mon-Fri, noon-late Sat & Sun

This Middle Eastern restaurant, with outdoor seating on a flower-bedecked terrace overlooking South Lantau Rd, has some international dishes and, at the weekend, a barbecue.

Ngong Ping

The car park at the Po Lin Monastery is awash with snack bars and kiosks selling vegetarian edibles but you should try to have a meatless meal inside the monastery complex itself.

PO LIN VEGETARIAN RESTAURANT
Map p419
Chinese, Cantonese

☎ 2985 5248; Ngong Ping; snacks HK$10, set vegetarian meals regular/deluxe HK$60/100; ☺ 11.30am-4.30pm

The monastery, in west-central Lantau, has a good reputation for its inexpensive but substantial vegetarian food. The simple restaurant is in the covered arcade to the left of the main monastery building. Buy your ticket there or at the ticket office below the Tian Tan Buddha statue. Sittings are every half-hour.

Tai O

Tai O, a village on the western coast, is famous for its seafood restaurants, many of which display their names in Chinese only.

FOOK LAM MOON
Map p419
Chinese, Cantonese

☎ 2985 7071; 29 Tai O Market St; meals HK$100 per person; ☺ 5.30am-9pm

This relatively upmarket (for Tai O, that is) restaurant serves tasty and not-over-refined dishes. Dim sum is available from 5.30am to 10am.

PENG CHAU

Peng Chau has a couple of popular pub-restaurants south of the ferry pier that are worth checking out. Unfortunately, the construction of a mammoth concrete 'wave reflector' and promenade has robbed them of their fine sea views, but there is still outside seating in the back in what now look like courtyards.

SEA BREEZE Map p421
International

☎ 2983 1787; 38 Wing Hing St; starters HK$28-58, mains HK$48-108; ☺ 5pm-1am Tue-Fri, noon-1am Sat & Sun, closed Mon

The Sea Breeze is known for its fine steaks (HK$68 to HK$108), and the place is so popular that Discovery Bay residents hop on a kaido to dine here.

TYPHOON SHELTER

Map p421   *Italian, Pub Grub*

☎ 2983 8033; 34 Wing Hing St; pasta & pizza HK$35-88, mains HK$48-138, set dinners HK$68-75;
🕑 10.30am-late Wed-Mon, closed Tue

The first of the pub-restaurants lining Wing Hing St, the Typhoon Shelter serves both pizza and pasta dishes, as well as steaks (HK$68 to HK$138) and pub fare like fish and chips (HK$58).

Cheap Eats

PENG CHAU MARKET Map p421   *Market*

Cnr Lo Peng & Po Peng Sts; 🕑 6am-8pm

The island's indoor wet market is housed in the same block as the Peng Chau Indoor Recreation Centre near the ferry pier. Enter from the rear.

WELLCOME Map p421   *Supermarket*

Lo Peng St; 🕑 8am-10pm

You'll find Peng Chau's only supermarket on Lo Peng St just up from the ferry pier and after the crossing with Po Peng St.

PO TOI

MING KEE SEAFOOD RESTAURANT

Map pp396-7   *Chinese, Seafood*

☎ 2849 7038; meals about HK$150 per person;
🕑 11am-11pm

This is one of three restaurants in Po Toi village (on Po Toi Island south of Hong Kong Island) and by far the most popular with day-trippers. Make sure you book ahead at the weekend.

Entertainment

Entertainment

When you want to be wowed after dark, Hong Kong is a capable entertainer. Most weeks, half a dozen local arts companies perform anything from Cantonese opera to an English-language version of a Chekhov play. Locally cultivated drama and dance is among the most enjoyable in Asia, and the schedule of foreign performances is also often impressive; recent imports have included the incomparable Philadelphia Orchestra, the Hamburg and Stuttgart Ballets and Welsh bass baritone Bryn Terfel. The Hong Kong government subsidises the cost of international acts, so ticket prices are generally very reasonable. Expect to pay around HK$50 for a seat up the back for a local performance and up to HK$300 for a top-class international act.

That is not to say Hong Kong is a cultural honey pot. Many government initiatives appear more motivated by the idea that Hong Kong *should* be an arty town than by a heartfelt commitment to artistic endeavour. Art generally plays second fiddle to commerce, sometimes with comic results. When Happy Valley residents complained about noise spillage from an upcoming Elton John concert at Hong Kong Stadium, suggested solutions included turning off the stage speakers and issuing concert-goers with headphones, and having the audience clap with gloved hands.

Bar Strips & Neighbourhoods

Hong Kong Island has it all – the lion's share of the territory's most popular pubs, bars and clubs, plus the cultural venues of Wan Chai, so classical-music concerts, theatre, opera and the like are within easy reach.

Much of **Central's** nightlife revolves around Lan Kwai Fong, a narrow alleyway that doglegs south and then west from D'Aguilar St. In the not-so-distant past it was an area of squalid tenements and rubbish, but it has since been scrubbed, face-lifted and closed to traffic. Lan Kwai Fong's clientele tends to be young, hip and cashed-up; be warned that it can be an expensive area in which to party, with a beer costing anywhere up from HK$50 except during the cheesy two- or three-hour happy hours available at most places, when the prices 'drop' to HK$30 or so.

Soho is more geared up for dining than drinking, but there are a couple of bars and clubs worth the trek – on foot or via the Central Escalator – up the hill. **Sheung Wan** boasts a couple of attractive venues, including the Phoenix (see p181).

Wan Chai has been sleaze territory ever since it was the first port of call for American sailors and GIs on R&R from the battlefields of Vietnam. Much of the western part of the district has cleaned up its act, but hostess bars still line Lockhart Rd and there's lots of zippy club action and late-night cover band venues throughout the district. **Admiralty** sticks to what it does best: upmarket hotel bars and sports bars in towering office blocks.

Compared with Wan Chai and the Lan Kwai Fong area of Central, **Causeway Bay** is relatively tame after dark. Still, there are a few pubs and bars that do a thriving business.

The districts east of Causeway Bay are not especially attractive for their entertainment venues, though you will find a clutch of pubs and bars in **Quarry Bay** (especially on and around Tong Chong St) and, in **North Point**, a theatre with Cantonese and other Chinese opera.

For the most part, **Kowloon's** entertainment scene plays second fiddle to the after-dark hot spots of Hong Kong Island. Still, the district is littered with bars and pubs – it's just a bit tackier, less imaginative and more run-down. There are three basic clusters of bars in **Tsim Sha Tsui**: along Ashley Rd; within the triangle formed by Hanoi, Prat and Chatham Rds; and up along Knutsford Terrace. **Tsim Sha Tsui East** is the domain of swanky hostess bars and nightclubs.

Aside from its hotel bars and the odd New Town beer dive, the **New Territories** doesn't offer the visitor much in the way of after-dark entertainment, though the town halls in Sha Tin, Tuen Mun and Tsuen Wan (see p235) sometimes stage classical-music concerts and other events.

The **Outlying Islands** have a large range of pubs and bars on offer, some of them destinations in their own right. They're especially busy on Saturday, Sunday and public holidays.

Bookings

Bookings for most cultural events can be made by telephoning **Urbtix** (☎ 2734 9009; www.urbtix.gov.hk; ☒ 10am-8pm). Tickets can either be reserved with a passport number and picked up within three days, or paid for in advance by credit card. There are Urbtix windows at the **Hong Kong City Hall** (☒ 10am-9.30pm) in Central, Queen Elizabeth Stadium in Wan Chai, the Hong Kong Cultural Centre in Tsim Sha Tsui and most Tom Lee Music Company outlets. The Hong Kong Arts Centre and the Fringe Theatre use **Ticketek-HK** (☎ 31 288 288; www.ticketek.com.hk).

You can book tickets for many films and concerts and a great variety of cultural events over the phone or Internet via **Cityline** (☎ 2317 6666; www.cityline.com.hk). You pay by credit card and collect the ticket at the cinema, theatre or other venue, usually by inserting your card into a ticket-dispensing machine.

What's On

To find out what's on in Hong Kong, pick up a copy of *HK Magazine*, a very comprehensive entertainment-listings magazine that also has lively articles on current trends in the city, reviews of restaurants and bars, and a classified ad pull-out section called *black + white*. It's free, appears on Friday and can be picked up at restaurants, bars, shops and hotels throughout the territory. *HK Magazine* produces an annual insert called *Nightlife Guide* similar to (but nowhere as comprehensive as) its annual *HK Magazine Restaurant Guide* (see p355).

Also worth checking out is *bc magazine* (www.bcmagazine.net), a biweekly guide to Hong Kong's entertainment and partying scene. One of the most useful features in this highly visual and glossy publication is its complete listing of bars and clubs. It is also free and can usually be found alongside copies of *HK Magazine*.

The *South China Morning Post* newspaper has a daily city section with arts and entertainment reviews and listings. The HKTB's *Hong Kong Visitor's Kit* brochure includes a foldout of each month's attraction in the pocket at the back.

The **Hong Kong Arts Centre** (www.hkac.org.hk) publishes *Artslink*, a monthly magazine with listings of performances, exhibitions and arthouse film screenings. *GayStation* (www.gaystation.com.hk) is a monthly gay-centric listings publication.

PUBS & BARS

Watering holes in Hong Kong run the gamut from relatively authentic British-style pubs with meat pies, darts and warm beer to piss-elegant, neon-lit, 'here's looking at me' minimalist lounges. Much of Hong Kong's nightlife takes place in top-end hotels, where alluring happy hours, skilled bar staff and some of the best views in town attract visitors and locals.

Depending on where you go, beers cost at least HK$35 to HK$40 a pint, which is likely to be more expensive than the shirt on your back (if you bought it in Hong Kong). Overall, Lan Kwai Fong in Central is the best – and most expensive – area for bars, though it's the stomping grounds of expat and Chinese suits and professionals. The pubs in Wan Chai are cheaper and more relaxed, and those in Tsim Sha Tsui generally more local.

Bars generally open at noon or 6pm and close anywhere between 2am and 6am.

Happy Hour

During certain hours of the day, most pubs, bars and even certain clubs give discounts on drinks (usually one-third to one-half off) or offer two for every one purchased. Happy hour is usually in the late afternoon or early evening – 4pm to 8pm, say – but the times vary widely from place to place. Depending on the season, the day of the week and the location, some pubs' happy hours run from midday until as late as 10 and some start again after midnight.

Central

ALIBI Map pp404-5
☎ 2167 8989; 73 Wyndham St; ⏲ 11am-2am
Mon-Sat; happy hour 6pm-closing
This sleek Soho bar has a few tricks up its
staircase, including a late-night brasserie (see
p170). Down at the bar it's all wine, cocktails
and a DJ to pep up the punters from Thursday
to Saturday.

APRÈS Map pp404-5
☎ 2524 7722; Upper basement, 79 Wyndham St
(enter from Pottinger St); ⏲ 7.30am-1pm Mon-Thu,
8am-3am Fri & Sat, closed Sun; happy hour 5-8pm
Mon-Sat
This watering hole, decorated in cool purple
and silver and with its front open to steep
Pottinger St, is also a relaxed bistro with a
reasonably priced French-inspired menu (set
lunch HK$95). Stick to drinking after 8pm at
the weekend though – there usually isn't
enough room to brandish a fork.

BIT POINT Map pp404-5
☎ 2523 7436; 31 D'Aguilar St; ⏲ 10am-3am
Mon-Fri, noon-4am Sat, 4pm-2am Sun; happy hour
4-9pm daily
Bit Point is essentially a German-style bar
where beer drinking is taken very seriously.
Most beers here are draught Pilsners that you
can get in a glass boot if you've got a thirst
big enough to kick. Bit Point also serves some
pretty solid Teutonic fare (starters HK$30 to
HK$75, mains HK$58 to HK$130). Set lunches
are a snip at HK$59/75 for half/full portions.

C BAR Map pp404-5
☎ 2530 3695; Shop A, Ground fl, California Tower,
30-32 D'Aguilar St; ⏲ 7.30am-1am Mon-Thu, 7.30am-
3am Fri & Sat, 2-10pm Sun; happy hour 5-9pm daily
This strategically placed phone box of a bar
is the best place to watch the Lan Kwai Fong
throng over a frozen B52.

CALEDONIA Map pp400-3
☎ 2524 1314; Ground fl, Hutchison House, 10
Harcourt Rd; ⏲ 11am-1am Mon Sat, noon-11pm Sun;
happy hour 3-8pm daily
What was once the seemingly unshakeable
(make that unmoveable) Bull and Bear has
metamorphosed into a Scottish pub and
whisky bar. There's a restaurant serving up
Hibernian favourites (including haggis, neeps
and tatties, salmon and, of course, curry). The
curry buffet (HK$108) at lunch on Wednesday
is a favourite and the business lunch (HK$158)
a bargain for the location, but drinking and
footy on big-screen TVs are the main concerns.
Try their own brew Caledonia Brown Porter – a
bit like Guinness but sweeter.

CAPTAIN'S BAR Map pp400-3
☎ 2522 0111; Ground fl, Mandarin Oriental Hotel,
5 Connaught Rd Central; ⏲ 11am-midnight
This is a clubby, suited place that serves its
ice-cold draught beer in chilled silver mugs
plus some of the best martinis in town. This
is a good place to talk business, at least until
the covers band strikes up at 9pm. It's a bit
of a pulling zone for women and men of a
certain age.

CHAPTER 3 Map pp404-5
☎ 2526 5566; Amber Lodge, Basement, 23 Hollywood
Rd (enter from Cochrane St); ⏲ 5pm-1am (later Fri &
Sat); happy hour 5-9pm
This cheerful, very red bar below the Central
Escalator defies its dungeon setting. It's stylish
but less trendy than most bars around here,
maintaining a low-key feel and a loyal crowd.
Great two-for-one cocktails.

CLUB 64 Map pp404-5
☎ 2523 2801; 12-14 Wing Wah Lane; ⏲ 2.30pm-
2am Mon-Thu, 2.30pm-3am Fri & Sat, 6pm-1am Sun;
happy hour 2.30-9pm
This bucks the trend toward pretentious bars
in the Lan Kwai Fong area. It's a laid-back sort
of place with a memory, recalling 4 June 1989,
the date of the Tiananmen Square massacre
in Beijing. It's still one of the best bars in
town for nonposeurs, journalists, artists, angry
young men and women, and those who want
simple, unfussy fun.

DRAGON-I Map pp404-5
☎ 3110 1222; Upper Ground fl, The Centrium,
60 Wyndham St; ⏲ noon-midnight Mon-Sat; happy
hour 6-9pm Mon-Sat
This fabulous new venue located just above
the music venue Edge (see p233) has both
an indoor bar and restaurant and a huge
terrace over Wyndham St filled with caged
songbirds. You'd almost think you were in
the country.

DUBLIN JACK Map pp404-5
☎ 2543 0081; Ground fl, Cheung Hing Commercial
Bldg, 37-43 Cochrane St; ⏲ 11.30am-2am; happy
hour noon-8pm

This Irish pub is almost the real thing and a very popular after-hours watering hole for expats. We like the mock-old `Oirish village' frontage but, guys, why do you make the staff wear T-shirts with `69' in Chinese characters on the back?

GECKO Map pp404-5

☎ 2537 4680; Lower Ground fl, 15-19 Hollywood Rd; ☽ 3pm-2am Tue-Thu & Sun, 3pm-4am Fri & Sat, closed Mon; happy hour 4-10pm Tue-Thu & Sun, 4-9pm Fri & Sat

Entered from Ezra's Lane, off Cochrane St or Pottinger St, Gecko is the third avatar of this location in as many years. Now it's a hide-away lounge and wine bar run by a friendly French sommelier and wine importer with a penchant for absinthe. The well-hidden DJ mixes good grooves with kooky Parisian tunes and there's sometimes live music.

GLOBE Map pp404-5

☎ 2543 1941; 39 Hollywood Rd; ☽ 7.30am-1am Mon-Fri, 10am-1am Sat & Sun; happy hour 5-7pm, 9-10pm & midnight-1am Mon-Sat, all day Sun

This tiny, unpretentious place gets packed out with expats after work.

LA DOLCE VITA Map pp404-5

☎ 2186 1888; Cosmos Bldg, 9-11 Lan Kwai Fong; ☽ 11.30am-2am Mon-Thu, 11.30am-3am Fri, 12.30pm-3am Sat, 4pm-1am Sun; happy hour 5.30-8pm daily

This is a buzzing place for post-work brews, with room to bar-prop or stand on the terrace and watch the mob crawl by and the gorgeous young things preen themselves. `The Sweet Life' gets a bit messy at the weekend.

LE JARDIN Map pp404-5

☎ 2526 2717; 1st fl, Winner Bldg, 10 Wing Wah Lane; ☽ noon-2am; happy hour noon-8pm

This cheap and cheerful pub below Wyndham St features an enclosed-veranda seating area and has loads of atmosphere. The mostly expat crowd enjoys itself without getting too boisterous.

MAD DOGS Map pp404-5

☎ 2810 1000; Basement, Century Square, 1 D'Aguilar St; ☽ 10am-2am Mon-Thu, 10am-3am Fri & Sat, closed Sun; happy hour 11am-10pm Mon-Fri, 11am-5.30pm Sat

The first authentic British pub to hit Hong Kong is still going strong two decades on, but in another location. There's a cheap lunch buffet (HK$80), hearty blotters like bangers and mash (HK$82) and fish and chips (HK$88), free vodka on Thursday and a DJ six nights a week. Pity about those waiters in kilts, though.

MES AMIS Map pp404-5

☎ 2973 6167; Ground fl, 35 Pottinger St; ☽ 4pm-2am Sun-Thu, noon-3am Fri, 4pm-3am Sat; happy hour 4-9pm & 1am-2am daily

This little wine bar with the long bar and tables on steep Pottinger street is a good place in Central for a decent and affordable glass of wine. It tends to attract a more mature crowd that's into sipping not slurping. There's a much larger **Wan Chai branch** (Map pp406-8; ☎ 2527 6689; 83 Lockhart Rd).

METRO Map pp404-5

☎ 2815 9880; Ground fl, The Workstation, 43-45 Lyndhurst Tce; ☽ 11am-2am; happy hour 4-8pm Mon-Fri

This flash lounge and brasserie boasts huge picture windows – just perfect for ogling the crowds moving between Soho and Lan Kwai Fong – and mixes some mean martinis. And food? French bistro, with mains (HK$128 to HK$168), `little plates to share' (HK$52 to HK$148) and `sandwiches and rabbit food' (HK$26 to HK$78). Ever hear of French tapas?

Globe, Hollywood Rd

Top Five Clubs & Bars – Central & Soho

- **Alibi** (p220) A beautiful space for beautiful people.
- **C Club** (p229) Fur on the walls and punters in bed.
- **Club 64** (p220) Chilled, unfussed bar for non-poseurs.
- **Dragon-I** (p220) Country-like terrace bar in the heart of Central.
- **Feather Boa** (see right) Part camp lounge, part bordello – part the curtains!

MOVIE BLUES Map pp404-5

☎ 2524 7790; Ground & Upper Ground fls, 42 D'Aguilar St; ☿ 5pm-2.30am Sun-Thu, 5pm-4am Fri & Sat; happy hour 5-8.30pm daily

If you liked all those old black and white films, you'll love Movie Blues (the second word has nothing to do with the music or pornography). It's a roomy place for the Fong, covering two floors.

OSCAR'S Map pp404-5

☎ 2804 6561; Ground fl, 2 Lan Kwai Fong; ☿ 11am-1am Sun-Thu, 11am-4am Fri & Sat; happy hour 11am-9pm daily

This high-fashion watering hole (and Aussie restaurant) is often empty since everyone takes their drink outside on the pavement to play 'spot the model'.

PETTICOAT LANE Map pp404-5

☎ 2973 0642; 2 Tun Wo Lane; ☿ 11am-1am Mon-Thu, 11am-2am Fri & Sat, 5pm-midnight Sun; happy hour 5-7.30pm Mon-Sat, all day Sun

This salon, down a narrow alley off Cochrane St, is small, subdued and much more suited to chatting than bopping. The adjoining (and camp) Louis XIV Marquee, which offers protection in inclement weather, is open from 5pm till closing daily.

WHISKEY PRIEST Map pp404-5

☎ 2869 0099; Ground & 1st fls, 13 Lan Kwai Fong; ☿ 4pm-1am Tue-Thu, 4pm-3am Fri & Sat, noon-1am Sun; happy hour 5-9pm Sun-Thu, 1-3pm & 5-9pm Fri & Sat

The first Irish – thus the `e´ in `whiskey´ – pub to hit the Fong has Guinness, Kilkenny and Harp on tap, and 60 types of whiskey.

Soho & Sheung Wan

CLUB 1911 Map pp404-5

☎ 2810 6681; 27 Staunton St, Soho; ☿ 5pm-midnight Mon-Sat, happy hour 5-9pm

This is a refined bar with fine details (stained glass, burlwood bar, ceiling fan) and some colonial nostalgia. If you get the munchies, you can order in food from some of the surrounding eateries.

FEATHER BOA Map pp404-5

☎ 2857 2586; 38 Staunton St, Soho; ☿ 7pm-late Mon-Sat

The scenario at this plush lounge hidden behind gold drapes: 'trashy princess meets debauched gentleman for a cocktail but ends up drinking bottled beer from a chunky stemmed glass'. Part camp lounge, part bordello – part those curtains! It was once an antiques shop – thus the odd furnishings. Try the mango daiquiri.

LIQUID Map pp404-5

☎ 2517 3310, 2549 8386; Basement & Ground fl, 1-5 Elgin St, Soho; ☿ 6pm-2am Tue-Fri, 8pm-late Sat & Sun, closed Mon; happy hour 6-10pm Mon-Fri

This post-work suit hang-out makes an easy transition to sceney DJ zone; the 300-sq-m venue has a lounge at street level and a club with a large dance floor in the basement. Sunday sees singers and musicians added to the mix. On Friday happy hour is reserved for gays.

STAUNTON'S WINE BAR & CAFE

Map pp404-5

☎ 2973 6611; 10-12 Staunton St, Soho; ☿ 9am-midnight; happy hour 6-9pm

Staunton's, on the corner with Shelley St, is swish, cool and on the ball with decent wines, a Central Escalator–watching scene, a lovely terrace, a set lunch for HK$98 and often live jazz in the evenings.

V-13 Map pp404-5

☎ 8208 1313; 13 Old Bailey St, Soho; ☿ 5pm-midnight Mon-Thu, 5pm-late Fri, 6pm-late Sat, closed Sun; happy hour 5-9.30pm Tue-Sat

This clinically cool vodka bar has a huge choice of Russian mouthwash, with every flavour from chocolate to chilli. The bar staff at V-13 know their mixes intimately; at times they seem to be flying higher than their customers.

Entertainment – Pubs & Bars

Admiralty & Wan Chai

Most of the best bars and pubs line the western ends of Jaffe and Lockhart roads. As in Lan Kwai Fong, on weekend nights this area is crawling with partygoers.

1/5 Map pp400-3

☎ 2520 2515; 1st fl, Starcrest Bldg, 9 Star St, Wan Chai; ☺ 6pm-1am Mon-Wed, 6pm-2am Thu, 6pm-3am Fri, 8pm-3am Sat; happy hour 6-9pm Mon-Fri

This sophisticated lounge bar, pronounced 'one-fifth', above the chichi Japanese restaurant **Kokage** (see p184) matches your Prada outfit: an undulating, polished-floorboard entrance brings you to a broad bar backed by a two-storey drinks selection. Their bar staff shake and stir some of Hong Kong's meanest designer cocktails for the moneyed, the mighty and their model friends.

BRIDGE Map pp406-8

☎ 2865 5586; Shop A-B, 1st fl, Beverly House, 93-107 Lockhart Rd, Wan Chai; ☺ 24 hr; happy hour noon-10pm

This large and airy bar, with great windows overlooking the frenzy that is Lockhart Rd, is open 24 hours, serving round-the-clocktails to the denizens and the doomed of Wan Chai.

CHAMPAGNE BAR Map pp406-8

☎ 2588 1234; Ground fl, Grand Hyatt Hotel, 1 Harbour Rd, Wan Chai; ☺ 5pm-2am daily

The recently renovated surrounds, the live blues or jazz and that vintage glass of bubbly (that could cost up to HK$480) are all sure to impress.

CYRANO'S Map pp400-3

☎ 2820 8591; 56th fl, Island Shangri-La Hotel, Supreme Court Rd, Admiralty; ☺ 5pm-1.30am

If you need to get high in order to drink, head for this hotel bar above Pacific Place for expert bartenders and live jazz (from 9pm). Change lifts at the 39th floor for a good atrium view on the way up.

DELANEY'S Map pp406-8

☎ 2804 2880; Ground & 1st fls, One Capital Place, 18 Luard Rd, Wan Chai; ☺ noon-2.30am Sun-Thu, noon-3.30am Fri-Sun; happy hour 5-9pm daily

Delaney's, an immensely popular Irish pub, has recently expanded to another floor, nearly doubling its size. Now you can choose between the pub tiled in black and white on the ground floor and a sports bar and restaurant on the 1st floor. The food is good too; the kitchen allegedly goes through 400kg of potatoes a week. There's also a **Tsim Sha Tsui branch** (p225).

DEVIL'S ADVOCATE Map pp406-8

☎ 2865 7271; 48-50 Lockhart Rd, Wan Chai; ☺ noon-late Mon-Fri, 3pm-late Sat, 1pm-late Sun; happy hour noon-9.30pm daily

This pleasant pub in the thick of things is as relaxed as they come. The bar spills on to the pavement and the Filipino staff are charming.

FENWICK THE DOCK Map pp406-8

☎ 2861 1669; Lower Ground fl, 41 Lockhart Rd, Wan Chai; ☺ 5pm-late; happy hour 5-10pm

This basement pub on the corner of Fenwick St has a decent dance floor.

GROOVY MULE Map pp406-8

☎ 2529 6888; 13 Fenwick St, Wan Chai; ☺ noon-3am daily; happy hour noon-10pm

Like a coyote bar with less lout and hee-haw, though bar antics are still the main draw here. Slammers and gyration from the Aussie bar staff (in cork hats, no less) just about keep punters on their barstools.

HORSE & GROOM Map pp406-8

☎ 2507 2517; Ground fl, 161 Lockhart Rd, Wan Chai; ☺ 11am-2am Mon-Sat, 6pm-2am Sun; happy hour 11am-9pm Mon-Sat, 6-9pm Sun

What used to be called the 'House of Doom', and a favourite watering hole of hacks and has-beens, has gone local and is as much a popular lunch venue (set lunch HK$48) as a drinking spot.

NEW LA CAFÉ Map pp400-3

☎ 2528 2923; Shop C2, Ground fl, Far East Finance Centre, 16 Harcourt Rd, Admiralty; ☺ 11am-midnight daily; happy hour 11am-midnight Mon-Fri, 2.30-8.30pm Sat & Sun

The LA Café has moved across the street from the Lippo Centre to the 'Amah's Tooth' – the ultra-gold Far East Finance Centre – and retains its loyal following that comes for big-screen sports and Cal-Mex nosh.

OLD CHINA HAND Map pp406-8

☎ 2865 4378; 104 Lockhart Rd, Wan Chai; ☺ 8am-5am; happy hour noon-10pm & midnight-2am

This place is hardly recognisable from the gloomy old dive where the desperate-to-drink (no-one we know) would find themselves unhappy but never alone at 3am. Now it's got a generous happy hour, Internet access and set lunches for HK$48. Notice the bronze 'China hand' and its much stroked elongated pinkie fingernail.

PERFECT PINT Map pp406–8
☎ 2294 0399; 68-70 Lockhart Rd, Wan Chai; ☯ 5pm-late daily; happy hour 5pm-late
Punters come here for the happy hour, which starts when the doors open and ends when they close.

SKITZ Map pp406–8
☎ 2866 3277; 1st fl, Jubilee Centre, 18 Fenwick St, Wan Chai; ☯ noon-2am Mon-Thu, noon-late Fri & Sat, noon-1am Sun; happy hour noon-9pm daily
This huge sports bar with a dance floor has taken over a comedy club and it's no laughing matter; it's fast become one of the most popular dance bars in Wan Chai.

TANGO MARTINI Map pp406–8
☎ 2528 0855; 3rd fl, Empire Land Commercial Centre, 81-85 Lockhart Rd, Wan Chai; ☯ noon-3pm & 6pm-3am Mon-Fri, 6pm-3am Sat & Sun
This groovy animal-print restaurant-cum-lounge place serves lunch and dinner (starters HK$88 to HK$110, mains HK$110 to HK$130) but is also puuurrfect for a Wan Chai late-nighter. Its sister-bar **Amazona** (☎ 2520 2049; ☯ 6pm-3am Tue-Sun; happy hour 6-9pm) on the 2nd floor of the same building continues with the jungle theme but limits it to palm trees and other verdant growth.

WHITE STAG Map pp406–8
☎ 2866 4244; Ground fl, The Broadway, 54-62 Lockhart Rd, Wan Chai; ☯ noon-3am; happy hour noon-10pm
This is a somewhat subdued (suity, not snooty) pub with open frontage and such filling dishes as bangers and mash (HK$65), cottage pie (HK$75), fish and chips (HK$85) and chilli (HK$75).

Causeway Bay

BLUE CAFE & BAR Map pp406–8
☎ 2834 5086; 21 Sharp St East; ☯ 5pm-2am
Seeping blue lights and white chairs make this bar an instant zone. Not large, but smooth and snappy with inventive drinks, slow electronica and a zipless crowd sipping cocktails and chewing on their words.

BRECHT'S CIRCLE Map pp406–8
☎ 2576 4785; 123 Leighton Rd; ☯ 11am-2am Sun-Thu, 11am-4am Fri & Sat; happy hour 4-8pm daily
Brecht's is very small and fairly unusual. It's an arty kind of place given more to intimate, cerebral conversation than serious raging. The décor is pseudo-German, and includes oversized portraits of such charmers as Mao and Hitler.

DICKENS BAR Map pp406–8
☎ 2837 6782; Basement, Excelsior Hotel, 281 Gloucester Rd; ☯ 11am-1am Sun-Wed, 11am-2am Thu-Sat; happy hour 5-8pm daily
This evergreen place has been a popular place with expats and Hong Kong Chinese for decades. There's a curry buffet lunch for HK$98 (including a half-pint of beer) and lots of big-screen sports.

EAST END BREWERY & INN SIDE OUT
Map pp406–8
☎ 2895 2900; Ground fl, Sunning Plaza, 10 Hysan Ave; ☯ 9am-2am Sun-Thu, 9am-3am Fri & Sat; happy hour 2.30-8.30pm daily
These two related pubs flank a central covered terrace where you can while away the hours on a warm evening, throwing peanut shells on the ground. East End has imported micro-brews and a **Quarry Bay branch** (p225).

Top Five Clubs & Bars – Causeway Bay

- **1 Nitestand Comedy Club** (p237) Popular comedy club plays to packed houses.
- **Blue Cafe & Bar** (see left) Snappy drinks, slow electronica and a zipless crowd.
- **Brecht's Circle** (see above) Small bar where intimate conversation rules.
- **East End Brewery & Inn Side Out** (see above) Peanut-strewn sister pubs on a covered terrace.
- **Stix** (p231) Manhattan-like dance club with live music and DJs.

RANDOM Map pp406–8
☎ 2151 9800; 17 Sharp St East; ☯ 6pm-2am Sun-Thu, 6pm-3am Fri & Sat; happy hour 6-9pm daily
This is another stylish café-bar on increasingly trendy Sharp St East.

REEF BAR & CAFE Map pp406–8

☎ 2890 3033; 13 Caroline Hill Rd; ☽ 6pm-late; happy hour 6-9pm

Set snug in a strip of motorcycle workshops, this is an oasis of cocktails, fruit juices and fresh oysters. Take a seat or plant yourself at the bar and watch Swordman the manager shuck 'em.

SHAKESPEARE PUB Map pp406–8

☎ 2833 0029; 30 Cannon St; ☽ 11am-3am Mon-Fri, 4pm-3am Sat & Sun; happy hour 11am-9pm Mon-Fri, 4-9pm Sat & Sun

Same old, same old… This is another one of those mock-Tudor pubs that smell of old fat and stale beer and attract young Hong Kong Chinese who like to play drinking games. It's a great way to meet local people; foreigners are made to feel more than welcome.

Island East

CAFÉ EINSTEIN Map pp398–9

☎ 2960 0994; 33 Tong Chong St, Quarry Bay; ☽ 11am-1am Mon-Sat, 5pm-1am Sun; happy hour 4-9pm daily

This attractive and upbeat bar-bistro, which feels more Lan Kwai Fong than Tong Chong St, has a great bar and lounge with jazz and R&B and serves food (mains HK$95 to HK$140, set lunch HK$85) all day from a short but inspired menu.

EAST END BREWERY Map pp398–9

☎ 2811 1907; 23-27 Tong Chong St, Quarry Bay; ☽ 11.30am-late; happy hour 4-8pm

This place out in Quarry Bay is a beer-lover's must-visit. You can choose from almost 30 beers and lagers from around the world, including a couple of local microbrews. There's also a Causeway Bay branch (see p224).

Island South

BEACHES Map p409

☎ 2813 7313; Ground fl, 92B Stanley Main St, Stanley; ☽ 11am-midnight Sun-Thu, 11am-1am Fri & Sat

This place, which has joined forces with Stanley's Italian restaurant (p194) to offer pizza, pasta and more substantial mains, spills out onto the pavement and has a glorious view of the bay.

SMUGGLERS' INN Map p409

☎ 2813 8852; Ground fl, 90A Main St, Stanley;

☽ 10am-1am Sun-Thu, 10am-3am Fri & Sat; happy hour 6-10pm Mon-Fri

This good-value place is arguably the most popular pub on the Stanley waterfront.

Tsim Sha Tsui & Tsim Sha Tsui East

BIERGARTEN Map pp412–14

☎ 2721 2302; 5 Hanoi Rd, Tsim Sha Tsui; ☽ 10am-3am Mon-Fri, noon-4am Sat, 4pm-2am Sun; happy hour 4-9pm daily

Head to the 'Beer Garden' for a great selection of German beers on tap as well as hearty and filling nosh such as pork knuckle and sauerkraut (HK$95). Starters are HK$30 to HK$75, other mains HK$58 to HK$130 and set lunch is HK$48.

CHEMICAL SUZY Map pp412–14

☎ 2736 0087; AWT Centre, 2A-B Austin Ave, Tsim Sha Tsui; ☽ 6pm-4am, happy hour 6-9pm

This is a cyber-groover hideout with DJs, snacks (scallops, fish fingers), a mixed crowd and enough pop culture signifiers to leave no doubt that Suzy's in the know. Thursday is Queer Night for young gays.

DELANEY'S Map pp412–14

☎ 2301 3980; Basement, Mary Bldg, 71-77 Peking Rd, Tsim Sha Tsui; ☽ 11am-2am; happy hour 5-9pm

This pub seems more authentically Irish than its Wan Chai branch (see p223), with lots of dark wood, green felt and a long bar that you can really settle into. Try Delaney's Ale or Delaney's Lager, both house brews made by the Hong Kong SAR Brewing Company.

Top Five Clubs & Bars – Tsim Sha Tsui

- Bahama Mama's Caribbean Bar (p231) Friendly, tropical-themed spot with bopping at the weekend.
- Bottoms Up (p228) No derrieres down at Hong Kong's first topless bar.
- Chemical Suzy (see above) Cyber-groover hideout with DJs, snacks and a mixed crowd.
- Ned Kelly's Last Stand (p234) Yonks-old pub with live big band jazz nightly.
- Sky Lounge (p226) Departure lounge-like bar with a drop-dead view of Hong Kong Island.

Entertainment – Pubs & Bars

FELIX MAP Map pp412–14

☎ 2315 3188; 28th fl, Peninsula Hotel, Salisbury Rd, Tsim Sha Tsui; ✆ 6pm-2am

Enjoy a brew with a view at the bar connected to Felix restaurant, one of the swankiest restaurants in Hong Kong's swankiest hotel. Guys, the design of the men's room is beyond belief.

KANGAROO PUB Map pp412–14

☎ 2376 0083; 1st & 2nd fls, Daily House, 35 Haiphong Rd, Tsim Sha Tsui; ✆ 7am-9am, noon-3pm & 5pm-1.30am Mon-Sat, 7am-10am & 11.30am-1.30am Sun; happy hour 4-7pm daily

The infamous Kangaroo is the bane of Australian expats struggling to prove that not all their countrymen are lager louts (failing miserably in most cases). But never mind... The 'Roo is open throughout the day for tucker (mains HK$72 to HK$98), but gets pretty lively at night and has some decent Australian beers (Cooper's, VB) available. This is where you come to watch Aussie Rules football and rugby on satellite TV with the lads.

KISS BAR Map pp412–14

☎ 2724 3366; Shop 1, Ground fl, Lee Wai Commercial Bldg, 1-3 Hart Ave, Tsim Sha Tsui; ✆ 6pm-5am Mon-Fri, 7pm-5am Sat, 8pm-5am Sun; happy hour 6-9pm Mon-Sat

This narrow bar with a pair of lips hanging in the window is a friendly place but we're here for the mirror ball and it's got one in spades.

LA TASCA Map pp412–14

☎ 2723 1072; 8 Hanoi Rd, Tsim Sha Tsui; ✆ 4pm-4am; happy hour 4-9pm

La Tasca is more a cantina and bar than a restaurant nowadays and has live music from 10pm on Saturday. It still does food at night though, including both tapas (HK$48 to HK$75) and more substantial main courses (HK$75 to HK$95).

MARTINI BAR Map pp412–14

☎ 2721 5215; Ground fl, The Royal Garden Hotel, 69 Mody Rd, Tsim Sha Tsui East; ✆ 4pm-1am

This very Manhattan-style bar doesn't offer much in the way of views (unless you count the passing parade along Mody Rd) but the décor (a little Art Deco 1930s, a bit camp 1960s) is decadent and the drinks divine.

ORGAN BAR Map pp412–14

☎ 2376 0389; Basement & Ground fl, Honeytex Bldg,

22 Ashley Rd, Tsim Sha Tsui; ✆ noon-4am; happy hour noon-9pm

The erstwhile Amoeba Bar is now the Organ (is that the progression we learned in Biology 101?) and has big-screen entertainment in the basement from around 9pm. It draws a mainly hip and young Cantonese-speaking crowd.

SKY LOUNGE Map pp412–14

☎ 2369 1111; 18th fl, Sheraton Hong Kong Hotel & Towers, 20 Nathan Rd, Tsim Sha Tsui; ✆ 2pm-1am Sun-Thu, 2pm-2am Fri & Sat

Before you can begin clucking your tongue about the departure-lounge feel of this big, long bar, you've already started marvelling at the view. Don't take flight: sit down in a scoop chair, sip a drink and scoff international snacks.

WATERING HOLE Map pp412–14

☎ 2312 2288; Basement, 1A Mody Rd, Tsim Sha Tsui; ✆ 4pm-1.30am Mon-Sat, 4pm-1am Sun; happy hour 4pm-9.59pm (sic) daily

This pub with the imaginative name is a grotty, salt-of-the-earth kind of place popular with both Chinese and expats.

Sai Kung (New Territories)

DUKE OF YORK PUB Map p417

☎ 2792 8435; Ground fl, 42-56 Fuk Man Rd; ✆ 11am-2am daily; happy hour 11am-9pm Wed-Mon, all day Tue

This popular pub, just up from the waterfront, has a pool table, dart board and live music at the weekend. It's also OK blotter in the way of fish 'n' chips or basic curries (HK$50 to HK$65).

POETS Map p417

☎ 2791 7993; 55 Yi Chun St; ✆ noon-1am Mon-Fri, noon-2am Sat & Sun; happy hour 2-9pm Mon-Thu, 2-11pm Fri

This new kid on the block, with literary aspirations, is a pleasant place for a pint and does some substantial pub meals, including beef stew, shepherd's pie and fish and chips (HK$48 to HK$55).

Lamma

Yung Shue Wan has several watering holes and boozers worth checking out. You may have to sign a members' book as some operate on club licences.

Entertainment – Pubs & Bars

DIESEL SPORTS BAR Map p418

☎ 2982 4116; 51 Main St, Yung Shue Wan;
🕙 6pm-late Mon-Fri, noon-late Sat & Sun;
happy hour 6-9pm daily

This place with the charismatic Dutch barman is next to the Lamma Bistro and attracts punters with its big-screen TV during sports matches.

FOUNTAINHEAD Map p418

☎ 2982 2118; 17 Main St, Yung Shue Wan;
🕙 6pm-late Mon-Fri, noon-late Sat & Sun;
happy hour 6pm-late Mon-Fri

This is the most popular bar in Yung Shue Wan, with a good mixture of Chinese and expats regularly in attendance. There's decent music, amiable bar staff, free salted peanuts and beer at affordable prices.

ISLAND BAR Map p418

☎ 2982 1376; 6 Main St, Yung Shue Wan;
🕙 6pm-late Mon-Fri, noon-late Sat & Sun;
happy hour 6-8pm daily

The Island remains the bar of choice for long-term expats living on Lamma, so if you want the low-down on what's up, head here.

Y2K Map p418

☎ 2982 2693; 68 Main St, Yung Shue Wan; 🕙 5pm-2am Mon-Fri, 2pm-late Sat & Sun; happy hour nonstop

This recently renovated pub, at the corner of the road leading to Sok Kwu Wan and other points south, is a nice open space and is forever celebrating happy hour.

Cheung Chau

MOROCCO'S Map p420

☎ 2986 9767; 117 Praya Rd;
🕙 4pm-3am daily; happy hour 4-7pm Mon-Fri

The exodus of expats from Cheung Chau over the past several years has left the island all but bereft of quality drinking venues, but there will always be Morocco's on the waterfront. It also does decent Indian food (curries HK$45, tandoori dishes HK$50 to HK$70).

PATIO CAFÉ Map p420

☎ 2981 8316, 2981 5063; Cheung Chau Windsurfing Centre, 1 Hak Pai Rd; 🕙 noon-7pm daily Apr-Nov, noon-7pm Sat & Sun Dec-Mar

This open-air, café-cum-pub attached to the windsurfing centre at Tung Wan Beach is known locally as Lai Kam's in honour of its owner and is a Cheung Chau institution. Come here for a sundowner.

Lantau

CHINA BEACH CLUB Map p421

☎ 2983 8931; 18 Tung Wan Tau Rd; 🕙 11am-11pm Sun-Thu, 11am-midnight Sat & Sun; happy hour 11am-11pm Tue-Fri

This pleasant bar has a wonderful open-air balcony overlooking Silvermine Bay Beach. The Filipina staff are friendly and helpful.

CHINA BEAR Map p421

☎ 2984 7360; Ground fl, Mui Wo Centre, Ngan Wan Rd;
🕙 noon-3am Mon-Fri, 10am-3am Sat & Sun; happy hour 2-10pm Mon-Fri, 5-8pm Sat & Sun

The China Bear is the most popular expatriate pub-restaurant in Mui Wo, with a wonderful open bar facing the water. Among the pub-grub offerings are fish and chips (HK$85), an all-day breakfast (HK$58) and 250g fillet steak (HK$75). Snacks are HK$25 to HK$65. It has both Penny's Bay Dark Ale and Budvar on tap.

HIPPO PUB Map p421

☎ 2984 9876; Shop D, Grand View Mansion, 11 Mui Wo Ferry Pier Rd; 🕙 4pm-late Mon-Fri, 11am-late Sat, 10am-late Sun; happy hour 4-10pm Mon-Fri, 11am-10pm Sat, 10am-10pm Sun

This Western-style pub-restaurant is hidden in an alley behind the Rome restaurant. There's an excellent selection of Belgian beers and live music on the first Saturday of the month.

JK'S CLUB Map p419

☎ 2984 8366; Ground fl, 31 South Lantau Rd, Lo Wai Village, Pui O; 🕙 6pm-late Mon-Fri, noon-late Sat & Sun

This place is conveniently located close to the beach at Pui O.

Top Five Clubs & Bars – Outlying Islands

- **Diesel Sports Bar** (see above) Friendly, frenetic place on Lamma with big-screen sports TV.
- **Patio Café** (see left) Cheung Chau chill-out zone ideal for a sundowner.
- **China Beach Club** (see above) Pleasant bar with an open-air balcony on Silvermine Bay Beach.
- **China Bear** (see above) Mui Wo bar facing the water and popular with expats.
- **Forest Bar** (p228) Cosy Peng Chau watering hole with six beers on tap.

Peng Chau

FOREST BAR Map p421

☎ 2983 8837; 38C Wing Hing St; ⏲ 11am-11pm

This cosy bar has six beers on tap, a large out-side seating area and a downstairs pub with snooker. The kitchen whips up fairly authentic Thai food (snacks HK$32 to HK$55, rice and noodle dishes HK$58 to HK$130) seven days a week.

CLUBS

Hong Kong has a hot and vibed-up club scene, and there are plenty of clubs in Central, Wan Chai and Tsim Sha Tsui where you can dance till you drop or the sun rises, whichever comes first. At the same time, many bars also stage dance and theme nights.

Most of the club nights take place on Friday and Saturday, but there are some mid-week venues as well. Cover charges range from HK$50 to HK$200+ when a foreign DJ with a name is mixing, or there's an internationally recognised band on stage. On some nights, you may get in free (or for a cheaper cover) if you are among the first 50 or so through the door, dressed in '70s gear (or whatever) on theme nights or (frequently) a woman.

Hong Kong's most talked about dance parties are one-off raves, held in venues as diverse as the airport hotel and the ferry pier at Kwun Tong. Raves are advertised in *bc magazine* as well as on the Internet (www.hkclubbing.com or www.hkrave.com).

Hostess Clubs

Hostess clubs come in two varieties in Hong Kong: the sleaze pits mostly found on Peking Rd in Tsim Sha Tsui and Lockhart Rd in Wan Chai, and the more 'respectable' establishments in Tsim Sha Tsui East. The difference is that the former blatantly try to cheat customers, while the latter don't need to – they're upfront about their astronomical prices. The respectable hostess clubs offer live music, featuring Filipino bands and topless dance shows. An evening out in any of these places could easily cost HK$1000 or more.

Be wary of places where an aggressive tout, often female, stands at the entrance, and tries to persuade you to go inside. It's likely that there will be signs on the front door announcing 'Drinks Only HK$40' and naughty pictures to, er, arouse your interest. Inside, a cocktail waitress, wearing nothing but her knickers, will serve you a drink. She will probably be friendly and chat for a few minutes. It will be one of the most expensive conversations of your life: the bill you're presented with will be in excess of HK$500.

When (or if) you protest, staff will undoubtedly point to the tiny sign posted on the wall behind a vase that informs you of the HK$400 service charge for talking to the waitresses. If you baulk at paying the fee or don't have the cash, don't be surprised when two gorillas suddenly appear at your elbows, ready to frog-march you to the nearest ATM.

BOTTOMS UP Map pp412–14

☎ 2721 4509; Basement, 14-16 Hankow Rd, Tsim Sha Tsui; ⏲ 5.30pm-3.30am; happy hour 5.30-8.30pm

Hong Kong's first topless bar (opened in 1971), Bottoms Up holds particular appeal for James Bond fans. Duty brought agent 007 here on one of his Asian sojourns (*The Man with the Golden Gun*, 1974), and the club is still milking it; it's naughty but nice.

CLUB BBOSS Map pp412–14

☎ 2369 2883; Lower Ground fl, New Mandarin Plaza, 14 Science Museum Rd, Tsim Sha Tsui East; ⏲ 1pm-4am

This is one of Hong Kong's biggest and most garish hostess bars. It is a ridiculous scene:

extravagant floorshows (at 9.20pm, 10.15pm and 11.10pm), babes and men drinking Cognac by the tumbler. Bring your fat wallet; entry costs from HK$450 to HK$1000 depending on what time you arrive.

CLUB DE MILLENNIUM Map pp412–14
☎ 2723 5088; 10th & 11th fls, BCC Bldg, 25-31 Carnarvon Rd (enter from Hanoi Rd), Tsim Sha Tsui; ☺ 8.30pm-4am

If you've got the dosh, this club will most likely let you in to partake of its high-class giggly sleaze, where hostesses are rented by the minute and drinks are expensive ($150 for starters). There are lavish harem-style lounges done up as Gucci, Versace and Starck showrooms.

TODAY'S TONNOCHY NIGHTCLUB
Map pp406–8
☎ 2573 8223; 1-5 Tonnochy Rd, Wan Chai; ☺ 1pm-4am

This is the classiest and trashiest of the lot of Wan Chai hostess clubs, positively dripping with Sino-baroque (Hapsburg meets Qing dynasty?) furnishings and features. There are shows (don't ask) every night from 9.30pm till midnight.

Central

As in any world-class city, the club scene in Hong Kong changes with the speed of summer lightning so it would be in your interest to flip through any of the publications under What's On at the start of this chapter or check out www.hkclubbing.com.

AREA Map pp400–3
☎ 2542 3138; Ground fl, 28 Gough St, Sheung Wan; ☺ noon-1am Mon-Thu, noon-late Fri, 6pm-late Sat, closed Sun; happy hour 6-9pm Mon-Fri

This stylish bar on the Central/Sheung Wan border has special drinks deals throughout the week and a DJ on Friday night. We like the projected visuals near the dancing area.

C CLUB Map pp404–5
☎ 2526 1139, 2867 8800; Basement, California Tower, 30-32 D'Aguilar St; ☺ 6pm-3am Mon-Fri, 9pm-late Sat, closed Sun; happy hour 6-9pm Mon-Fri

This is a fur-lined club below Lan Kwai Fong that reeks of loucheness. Quality cocktails, sexy house music, velvet cushions and a double bed in the alcove. What more do you want?

CALIFORNIA Map pp404–5
☎ 2521 1345; Ground fl, California Tower, 30-32 D'Aguilar St; ☺ noon-1am Mon-Thu, noon-4am Fri & Sat, 6pm-midnight Sun; happy hour 5-10pm Mon-Sat, 5-9pm Sun

This ultra-cool venue (parts of *Chungking Express* were filmed here) is an American-style restaurant and bar during the week. Come 11pm on Friday and Saturday, the tables are cleared away and the dance floor fills up till 4am. It's more of a men (in suits) trying to behave badly with champagne-sipping women scene than a raucous one. No shorts.

CLUB 97 Map pp404–5
☎ 2186 1897; Ground fl, Cosmos Bldg, 9-11 Lan Kwai Fong; ☺ 6pm-2am Mon-Thu, 6pm-4am Fri, 8pm-4am Sat & Sun; happy hour 6-10pm Mon-Fri, 8-10pm Sun

This shmoozery has dropped the disco and reinvented itself as a slick lounge bar. The Friday night happy hour (6pm to 10pm) is gay night and there's reggae on Sunday. Club 97 has a selectively enforced 'members only' policy to turn away the badly dressed; make an effort, lads and ladettes.

DROP Map pp404–5
☎ 2543 8856; Basement, On Lok Mansion, 39-43, Hollywood Rd; ☺ 7pm-2am Mon & Tue, 7pm-3am Wed, 7pm-4am Thu, 7pm-5am Fri, 10pm-5am Sat, closed Sun; happy hour 7-10pm Mon-Fri

Deluxe lounge action, fat tunes and potent fresh lychee cocktails are what keeps Drop strong on the scene. It's like walking into *Wallpaper* magazine, but the vibe here is unpretentiously inclusive. A members-only policy after 11pm at the weekend is (flexibly) enforced to keep the dance floor capacity at manageable `in like sardines' level.

HOME Map pp404–5
☎ 2545 0023; 2nd fl, 23 Hollywood Rd; ☺ 9pm-3am Mon-Fri, 10pm-9am Sat, closed Sun

A meet 'n' greet for the beautiful people early, this place turns into a bump 'n' grind later in the evening. It's one of the more popular after-hours venues and one of the few places that is still partying well after dawn. You don't want to know what comes and goes on the chill-out beds.

INFINITY Map pp404–5
☎ 2524 0042; Upper Ground fl, Wilson House, 19-27 Wyndham St; ☺ 11.30am-late; happy hour 2-9pm

What was once known as Hardy's II has

re-emerged as a bar by day and dancing club by night. The huge dance floor is divided into two sections and attracts an uneven crowd most nights. It's gay on Saturday night.

INSOMNIA Map pp404–5

☎ 2525 0957; Lower Ground fl, Ho Lee Commercial Bldg, 38-44 D'Aguilar St; ☽ 9am-6am Mon-Sat, 2pm-5am Sun; happy hour 5-9pm daily

This is the place to come to if (and when) you can't sleep. It's a people-watching place with a wide open frontage, and there's a live band doing covers in the back. They do food, too, such as all-day breakfast (HK$75), fish and chips (HK$80), sandwiches and burgers (HK$50 to HK$55), and snacks (HK$50 to HK$60).

QUEEN'S Map pp400–3

☎ 2522 7773; 1st fl, Queen's Theatre, Theatre Lane; ☽ Mon, Tue & Thu 5pm-2am, Wed & Fri 5pm-4am, 9pm-5am Sat, closed Sun; happy hour 5-10pm Mon-Fri

With loud music, regular DJ nights at the weekend, '80s décor and a huge round bar, this huge venue (it used to be part of the Queen's Theatre) is popular with a younger crowd. Be prepared to wait in the queue. The name of the place takes on a new meaning from 4pm to 10pm on the first Sunday of the month when it hosts Decadence, a gay tea dance.

RED ROCK Map pp404–5

☎ 2868 3884; Lower Ground fl, 57-59 Wyndham St; ☽ 11am-2pm & 5pm-2am Mon-Thu, 11am-2pm & 5pm-5am Fri & Sat, closed Sun; happy hour 5-8pm Mon-Fri

This attractive place, backing onto the walkway above Lan Kwai Fong, is a very successful chameleon: a decent Italian restaurant at lunch and dinner (set lunch HK$87, mains HK$160 to HK$175) and popular dance venue by night (and morning). Some 13 cocktails and as many shooters go for half-price at happy hour.

Admiralty & Wan Chai

Hong Kong's late-night club galaxy revolves around Wan Chai. With a well-established reputation for all-night marathon dancing with liquid and chemical assistance, this is where the late-night crowd settles in for the wee hours.

BORACAY PUB & DISCO Map pp406–8

☎ 2529 3461; 20 Luard Rd, Wan Chai; ☽ 4pm-3am Mon-Sat; happy hour 4-10pm Mon-Sat

What was once called Big Apple, frequently nominated as one of Hong Kong's raunchiest night spots, has named itself after a popular Filipino beach resort, presumably to reflect the origins of most of its clientele. It's still the hang-out of choice for a young immigrant crowd hellbent on having a good time and the place 'where music never dies'. Entry is HK$120 Monday to Thursday, and HK$150 Friday and Saturday (including one drink).

CARNEGIE'S Map pp406–8

☎ 2866 6289; Ground fl, 53-55 Lockhart Rd, Wan Chai; ☽ 11am-late Mon-Sat, 5pm-late Sun; happy hour 11am-10pm Mon-Sat, 5-10pm Sun

This place keeps a lot of rock memorabilia, which makes it all seem a bit Hard Rock Cafe-ish. From 9pm on Friday and Saturday, however, the place fills up with revellers. Bands jam (free) on Sunday, there's unlimited vodka from 10pm to 11pm on Tuesday for HK$50 and a 'Magnificent Seven' cocktails priced at HK$15 each at 'crazy hour' (6pm to 7pm daily).

CLUB ING Map pp406–8

☎ 2824 0523; 4th fl, Renaissance Harbour View Hotel, 1 Harbour Rd, Wan Chai; ☽ 5pm-4am Mon-Fri, 9.30pm-4am Sat, closed Sun; happy hour 5-9pm Mon-Fri

This popular club, which is in (but not part of) the Renaissance Harbour View Hotel, is into big parties and theme nights. Dress smartly (no sandals, sneakers or tank tops). Women get in free every night and get a drink on the house every Thursday. Men pay HK$160 (including one drink) or HK$100 before 11pm.

DUSK TILL DAWN Map pp406–8

☎ 2528 4689; Ground fl, 76-84 Jaffe Rd, Wan Chai; ☽ noon-6am Mon-Thu, noon-7am Fri & Sat, 3pm-5am Sun; happy hour 5-10pm daily

This funny place with the yellow exterior and purple shutters has live music nightly from 9.30pm with an emphasis on beats and vibes so irresistible that you'll get your booty shaking. The dance floor can be packed but the atmosphere is usually more friendly than sleazy. Food (set lunch HK$60 Monday to Friday, set dinner HK$85 nightly) sticks to easy fillers like meat pies and burgers.

JJ'S Map pp406–8

☎ 2588 1234, ext 7323; 3rd & 4th fls, Grand Hyatt Hotel, 1 Harbour Rd, Wan Chai; ☽ 6pm-2am Mon-Thu, 6pm-3am Fri, 7pm-4am Sat, closed Sunday; happy hour 5.30-8.30pm Mon-Fri

Not as suity as you might think, JJ's is an enormous multilevel dancing club with something for everyone. A house band plays nightly from 10pm, and there's DJs in between and live salsa music on Tuesday. Women get in free; men pay HK$100 after 9.30pm. Dress up – no shorts, no sandals, no jogging clothes. JJ's has a dedicated entrance just to the right before you enter the hotel.

Top Five Clubs & Bars – Admiralty & Wan Chai

- **1/5** (p223) Mean designer cocktails for the moneyed and the mighty.
- **Champagne Bar** (p223) Vintage bubbly accompanied by live blues or jazz.
- **JJ's** (p230) Multilevel dancing club with something for everyone.
- **Old China Hand** (p223) Late-night spot for that very last one.
- **Wanch** (p234) Generous happy hour and live rock and folk nightly.

JOE BANANAS Map pp406–8

☎ 2529 1811; 23 Luard Rd; ⏱ 11am-5am Mon-Thu, 11am-6am Fri & Sat, 3pm-5am Sun; happy hour 11.30am-10pm daily

Newly renovated JB's has dropped its long-standing wet-T-shirts-and-briefs nonsense and gone for more of a bamboo-bar kind of feel. The staff's khaki uniforms look more prison camp than Phuket, though. If you go with friends, you can have some un-reconstructed fun. Unaccompanied females should expect a good sampler of really bad pick-up lines. Entry is HK$100 after 11pm on Wednesday, Friday and Saturday; there are free drinks for women from 6pm to midnight on Wednesday.

NEPTUNE DISCO II Map pp406–8

☎ 2865 2238; 98-10 Jaffe Rd, Wan Chai; ⏱ 4pm-5am Mon-Thu, 2pm-5am Fri-Sun; happy hour 5-9pm Mon-Fri

Neptune II is a fun club with a mostly Filipino crowd and a rockin' covers band. If everything's closing and you can't bear to stop dancing, this is the place to come. Men/women pay HK$100/50 (including one drink) to get in. The place really hops at the Sunday afternoon tea dance starting at 2pm.

NEW MAKATI Map pp406–8

☎ 2527 8188; 1st fl, 100 Lockhart Rd; ⏱ 5pm-5am; happy hour 5-9pm

It has to be said: you can't go lower than this sleazy pick-up joint, complete with dimly lit booths and Filipino amahs who just wanna have fun. Entry (including a drink) is HK$100/30 for men/women.

Causeway Bay

In Causeway Bay you won't find anything like the club scene that you will in Wan Chai or the Lan Kwai Fong area of Central, but there are a couple of places to consider.

GENE Map pp406–8

☎ 2591 6766; 462 Lockhart Rd; ⏱ 5pm-1am Sun, 5pm-3am Mon, Tue & Thu, 5pm-6am Wed, Fri & Sat; happy hour 5-9pm daily

The Gene mixes DJ pop and house with live covers from 6pm every night. It has a big dance floor and laser shows.

STIX Map pp406–8

☎ 2839 3397; Basement, Park Lane Hotel, 310 Gloucester Rd; ⏱ 6pm-2am Sun-Thu, 6pm-3am Fri & Sat, closed Sun; happy hour 5-9pm Mon-Sat

This place is more Manhattan than Hong Kong, with two spacious bars (one over an aquarium) and a dance floor. There's live music from 9.45pm Tuesday to Saturday in the Stix Music Room. On Sunday it hosts the 1 Nitestand Comedy Club (see p237).

Tsim Sha Tsui & Tsim Sha Tsui East

Tsim Sha Tsui does not have a great deal to offer when it comes to dancing, but this small selection should satisfy even the most ardent boppers.

BAHAMA MAMA'S CARIBBEAN BAR

Map pp412–14

☎ 2368 2121; 4-5 Knutsford Tce, Tsim Sha Tsui; ⏱ 5pm-3am Mon-Thu, 5pm-4am Fri & Sat, 6pm-2am Sun; happy hour 5-9pm daily

Bahama Mama's theme is tropical, complete with palm trees and surfboards to create an 'island' feel. It's a friendly spot and stands apart from most of the other late-night watering holes in this part of town. On Friday and

Entertainment – Clubs

Saturday nights there's a DJ spinning and folks bopping on the bonsai-sized dance floor.

RICK'S CAFÉ Map pp412–14
☎ 2311 2255; 53-59 Kimberley Rd, Tsim Sha Tsui; ☽ 5pm-late Mon-Sat, closed Sun; happy hour 5-10pm Mon-Sat

Rick's, one of Tsim Sha Tsui's better-known venues, has a cheesy 'Casablanca' décor, complete with palm trees and lots of neon. The dance floor is usually a writhing knot of Western men and Filipino girls. Check out the fab `piano bar'.

Happy Valley
GREEN SPOT
☎ 2836 0009; 1st fl, 1 Wong Nai Chung Rd; 6.30pm-3am Sun-Thu, 6.30pm-4am Fri & Sat

This place attracts local celebrities and their friends as well as (presumably from the way the champers flows) big winners from the nearby racetrack. Minimalist décor, lots of VIP rooms.

PMM
☎ 2961 3350; 3rd fl, Emperor Happy Valley Hotel, 1 Wang Tak St; ☽ 9pm-3am

Wednesday night is 'model's night' at PMM, when the city's svelte drape on chairs and sip the Moët provided for their pleasure. It's a highly charged camp kind of place, with more interest in chitchatting around the room than the R&B/rap DJ. Most people know this place as Pink Mao Mao, a moniker the club can't shake and has more to do with the Pink Panther (*mao* is 'cat' in Chinese) than a gay Zedong.

GAY & LESBIAN VENUES

What a difference a decade makes... With just a couple of sleazy speakeasies just over 10 years ago, when homosexual acts between consenting adults over the age of 18 were finally decriminalised, Hong Kong can now count upwards of two dozen bars and clubs – with more than a third in Central, Soho and Tsim Sha Tsui – and just as many gay-oriented saunas scattered throughout the territory. Grab a copy of *GayStation* or visit www.gaystation.com.hk for updated nightlife, shopping and sauna-scene info.

Central & Sheung Wan

Along with the mostly gay and lesbian clubs and bars listed here, several other straight and mixed clubs (see the Clubs section from p228) have gay nights. **Club 97** and **Liquid** have a gay happy hour from 6pm to 10pm or 10.30pm (drinks half price) on Friday, **Infinity** has a gay night on Saturday and **Decadence** at **Queen's** is a gay tea dance on the first Sunday of the month.

CURVE Map pp404–5
☎ 2523 0998; Ground & Lower Ground fls, 2 Arbuthnot Rd; ☽ 8pm-late daily; happy hour 8pm-late Sun-Tue, 8-10pm Wed-Sat

At the top of the wide staircase beside the new Centrium office block on Wyndham St, Curve is a glitzy and innovative club with design-award modern décor. Beats the socks off Propaganda, but then not everyone here is OFB (out for business).

PROPAGANDA Map pp404–5
☎ 2868 1316; Ground fl, 1 Hollywood Rd; ☽ 9pm-3.30am Mon-Thu, 9pm-5am Fri & Sat, closed Sun; happy hour 9-10.30pm Mon-Sat

Hong Kong's premier gay dance club, Propaganda has attitude in size XXXL (about the only thing that big here), but it's where everyone gay ends up at some point on a weekend night. There's a large dance floor, a long un-dulating bar and plenty of mirrors to talent-spot. It's free from Monday to Thursday, but cover charges apply at the weekend (HK$80 to HK$160, depending on when you arrive). Enter from Ezra's Lane, which runs between Pottinger and Cochrane Sts.

WORKS Map pp404–5
☎ 2868 6102; 1st fl, 30-32 Wyndham St; ☽ 7pm-2am Tue-Sun; happy hour 7-9pm

Propaganda's sister club, Works is where most boyz out on the town start the evening and sees some heavy FFFR (file-for-future-reference) cruising till it's time to move on to the P.

Sheung Wan
RICE BAR Map pp400–3
☎ 2851 4800; 33 Jervois St, Sheung Wan; ☽ 6.30pm-1am Mon-Thu, 6.30pm-2am Fri, 8pm-3am Sat, 5pm-1am Sun; happy hour 6.30-9pm daily

Rice is a small, vibey gay and lesbian hangout on the corner of Mercer St, with a lounge area that sees a bit of dancing as it gets later. Onsite tarot-card and palm readers can help you out with life's important questions. If the answer is eating, there's food to be had here.

Tsim Sha Tsui & Tsim Sha Tsui East

Apart from Chemical Suzy's one-nighter on Thursday (see p225), there's not much of a gay clubbing scene on this side of the puddle. There are a couple of OK pubs, though.

NEW WALLY MATT LOUNGE

Map pp412–14

☎ 2721 2568; 5A Humphrey's Ave, Tsim Sha Tsui; ☽ 5pm-4am; happy hour 5-10pm

The name comes from the old Waltzing Matilda pub, one of the daggiest gay watering holes in creation and where a French friend swears that the escargots on his plate were plucked from the walls of that dark and dank place. But New Wally Matt is an upbeat, busy place, and more a pub than a lounge.

TONY'S BAR Map pp412–14

☎ 2723 2726; Ground fl, 7-9 Bristol Ave, Tsim Sha Tsui; ☽ 5pm-5am; happy hour 5-10pm

This low-key gay-friendly bar is a relaxed place to come for a drink with none of the 'last chance for romance' tension of some of the other gay venues.

WALLY MATT LOUNGE Map pp412–14

☎ 2367 6874; 3A Granville Circuit, Tsim Sha Tsui; ☽ 5pm-4am; happy hour 5-10pm

Behind the Ramada Hotel, Wally Matt Lounge is more 21st century than its sister boozer. Here it's Canton pop karaoke and 'It's Raining Men' remixes in a dark industrial bar with just enough seats to retreat to with a drink and watch the action.

POP, ROCK & JAZZ

Cantopop is the name for the local pop music (see p37). If you give it a chance, you'll discover some worthwhile tunes (or ones that you won't be able to get out of your head for your entire stay).

There are usually a few decent rock bands (both local and imported) playing around town, and numerous bars have house bands that play dance music. Hotel bars and clubs have Filipino bands that can play 'Hotel California' and 'Love Is a Many-Splendored Thing' in their sleep (and yours).

Judging from the closure of a couple of key venues in recent years (Jazz & Blues Club, Brown's), jazz seems to be losing some of its following in Hong Kong, but there are still several venues in Central and in Tsim Sha Tsui where you can hear it. World music is generally a staged event, with big international acts (eg the Hungarian singer Marta Sebestyén and backup band Muzsikás and Cape Verde diva Cesaria Evora) booked at the arts centre or city hall.

Central

BLUE DOOR JAZZ CLUB Map pp404-5

☎ 2850 7060; 5th fl, Cheung Hing Commercial Bldg, 37-43 Cochrane St; ☽ 10pm-late Fri & Sat

This intimate and laid-back jazz venue has live music from 10.30pm to 12.30am at the weekends only.

EDGE Map pp404-5

☎ 2523 6690; Shop 2, Ground fl, The Centrium, 60 Wyndham St; ☽ 6pm-4.30am Mon-Thu, 6pm-5am Fri & Sat; happy hour 6-10pm Mon-Sat

This spacious new venue up the hill from Lan Kwai Fong has three bars, a restaurant and a live-music room, with gigs from 10pm during the week and from 10.30pm at the weekend.

ERNESTO & JULIO GALLO GALLERY

Map pp404-5

☎ 2521 7251, 2521 7485; Ground fl, Fringe Club, 2 Lower Albert Rd; ☽ noon-midnight Mon-Thu, noon-3am Fri & Sat; happy hour 3-9pm Mon-Sat

Up on the border of the Lan Kwai Fong quadrant, this all-purpose gallery/bar at the avant-garde Fringe Club is the venue for a whole medley of live sounds – from classic rock and pop to jazz and world music – from 10.30pm on Friday and Saturday nights. It's a pub during the rest of the week. There's a 'secret' bar on the roof that is open in the warmer months.

JAZZ@THE BASEMENT Map pp404-5

☎ 2545 1675; Basement, Pasta e Pizza,
11 Lyndhurst Tce; ⏲ lunch noon-3pm Mon-Sat,
dinner 6-11pm daily

Pasta e Pizza (see p173), a simple Italian eatery between Soho and Lan Kwai Fung, turns into a popular jazz cellar from 10.30pm till late on Saturday. Food is available until closing.

MUSIC ROOM LIVE Map pp404–5

☎ 2845 8477; 2nd fl, California Entertainment Bldg,
34-36 D'Aguilar St; ⏲ 7.30pm-late,
happy hour 6-9pm

What was once the Jazz Club has now ventured further into other forms of music. The venue is divided into the Velvet Lounge and the Live Room; in the latter you might hear anything from Cuban and salsa to blues and jazz. Wednesday from 9.30pm to 11.30pm is Open-Mike Night, when anyone can have a go.

Admiralty & Wan Chai
WANCH Map pp406–8

☎ 2861 1621; 54 Jaffe Rd; ⏲ 11am-2am Sun-Thu,
11am-4am Fri & Sat; happy hour 11am-10pm daily

This place, which derives its name from what everyone calls the district, has live music (mostly rock and folk) seven nights a week from 9pm (10pm on Friday and Saturday), with the occasional solo guitarist thrown in. Jam night is at 9pm on Wednesday. `Madness hour' between 6pm and 7pm means drinks are even cheaper and women get free vodka on Tuesday. If you're not here for the music it's a dubious scene – the Wanch is basically a pick-up joint.

Tsim Sha Tsui & Tsim Sha Tsui East
48TH STREET CHICAGO BLUES

Map pp412–14

☎ 2723 7633; Shop 4, Ground fl, 2A Hart Ave, Tsim
Sha Tsui; ⏲ 5pm-2am; happy hour 5-9pm

This welcome addition to the Tsim Sha Tsui music scene has live music (mostly jazz and blues) from 10.30pm.

CHASERS Map pp412–14

☎ 2367 9487; Shop 2, Ground fl, Carlton Bldg,
2-3 Knutsford Tce, Tsim Sha Tsui; ⏲ noon-6am;
happy hour 5-8pm

This ever-so orange-and-yellow bar is a friendly, somewhat classy place with a live Fili-

pino covers band from 10.15pm every night. Before the band cranks up there's a jukebox to party along to and DJs after the band takes its bows. There's a bar menu till midnight, snacks till 4am and dancing most nights; weekends see a major sweat-fest.

HARI'S Map pp412–14

☎ 2369 3111 ext 1345; Mezzanine, Holiday Inn
Golden Mile, 50 Nathan Rd, Tsim Sha Tsui; ⏲ 5pm-
2am daily; happy hour 5-9pm Mon-Sat, 5pm-2am Sun

Tacky or classy? You decide, after you've had a couple of speciality martinis (there are over a dozen to challenge you, including wasabi and garlic ones). There's live music nightly, from 7.30pm to 12.30am Sunday to Thursday and to 1.15am at the weekend.

NED KELLY'S LAST STAND Map pp412–14

☎ 2376 0562; 11A Ashley Rd, Tsim Sha Tsui;
⏲ 11.30am-2am; happy hour 11.30am-9pm

A great tradition continues with the Ned Kelly's Big Band playing jazz nightly till 9.30pm. Food is available and there's never a cover charge.

Venues

Hong Kong has at last arrived on the big-name concert circuit, and a growing number of internationally celebrated bands and solo acts – including Moby, Oasis, Prodigy, the Cranberries, the Petshop Boys, Elton John and (almost – they cancelled during the SARS scare) the Rolling Stones – perform in Hong Kong regularly.

Big concerts are usually held either at the 12,500-seat Hong Kong Coliseum (Map pp412-14; ☎ 2355 7234; 9 Cheong Wan Rd), located behind the KCR station in Hung Hom, and Queen Elizabeth Stadium (Map pp406-8; ☎ 2591 1346; 18 Oi Kwan Rd), in Wan Chai. The sound is abysmal in the former, and you'd get better acoustics in an empty aircraft hanger than at the latter.

Two other venues are the HITEC Rotunda (Map pp410-11; ☎ 2620 2222; Trademart Dr, Kowloon Bay) and the New Wing of the Hong Kong Convention and Exhibition Centre (☎ 2582 8888; 1 Expo Dr, Wan Chai). These are not huge venues, so the ticket prices are usually quite high.

Smaller acts are sometimes booked into the Ko Shan Theatre (Map pp412-14; ☎ 2740 9222; 77 Ko Shan Rd) in Hung Hom. The sound at this venue isn't great either, but the back portion of the seating area is open-air, and most of the seats offer a good view of the stage.

CLASSICAL MUSIC

In Hong Kong there are classical music concerts performed every week by one of the local orchestras or a foreign ensemble. Many performances are held at the **Hong Kong Cultural Centre** (Map pp412-14; ☎ 2734 2009; www.hkculturalcentre.gov.hk; Salisbury Rd, Tsim Sha Tsui), just east of the Star Ferry terminal, and home to the Hong Kong Philharmonic and the Hong Kong Chinese Orchestra. It is worth stopping by there to pick up a monthly schedule.

On Hong Kong Island the most important venues are: the **Hong Kong Academy for the Performing Arts** (Map pp406-8; ☎ 2584 8500, bookings 2584 8514; www.hkapa.edu; 1 Gloucester Rd, Wan Chai); the **Hong Kong Arts Centre** (Map pp406-8; ☎ 2582 0200, bookings 2734 9009; www.hkac.org.hk; 2 Harbour Rd, Wan Chai); and **Hong Kong City Hall** (Map pp400-3; ☎ 2921 2840, bookings 2734 9009; www.lcsd.gov.hk/ce/culturalservice/cityhall/index.html; Edinburgh Place, Central), next to the Star Ferry terminal.

The New Territories also has three important cultural centres: **Sha Tin Town Hall** (Map p417; ☎ 2694 2536; 1 Yuen Wo Rd, Sha Tin); **Tuen Mun Town Hall** (☎ 2450 4202; 3 Tuen Hi Rd, Tuen Mun); and **Tsuen Wan Town Hall** (Map p416; ☎ 2414 0144; Yuen Tun Circuit, Tsuen Wan).

CINEMA

Hong Kong has just over 60 cinemas with some 186 screens. Most show local films (with English subtitles) or Hollywood blockbusters dubbed into Cantonese, but a few – Cine-Art House in Wan Chai, UA Pacific Place in Admiralty, the Broadway Cinematheque in Yau Ma Tei and the AMC Festival Walk in Kowloon Tong – screen more interesting current releases and studio films.

Cinemas usually screen five sessions (12.30pm, 2.30pm, 5.30pm, 7.30pm and 9.30pm) weekdays, with extra screenings at 4pm and 11.30pm on Saturday, Sunday and public holidays. You must select a seat when you buy a ticket, which costs between HK$40 and HK$75, depending on the location and whether you can claim a concession. Tickets are usually cheaper (eg HK$50 for adults at UA cinemas) at the last screening of the day at weekends and on holidays (usually 11.30pm).

Almost all Hong Kong films showing in Hong Kong have both Chinese and English subtitles. You can confirm that the film has English subtitles by checking its Censorship License in the cinema.

HK Magazine and the *South China Morning Post* have listings for film screenings.

Sign for Broadway Cinematheque (p236)

Admiralty & Wan Chai

Certain cultural organisations based in this area show foreign films from time to time, including the **Alliance Française** (Map pp406-8; ☎ 2527 7825; 2nd fl, 123 Hennessy Rd, Wan Chai) and the **Goethe Institut** (Map p417; ☎ 2802 0088; 14th fl, Hong Kong Arts Centre, 2 Harbour Rd, Wan Chai).

For both studio and mainstream films, Wan Chai has two of the best and most comfortable cinemas in the territory.

CINE-ART HOUSE Map pp406-8

☎ 2827 4820; Sun Hung Kai Centre, 30 Harbour Rd, Wan Chai

The Cine-Art is an alternative cinema specialising in English-language flicks.

LIM POR YEN FILM THEATRE

Map pp406-8

☎ 2582 0200; Upper Basement, Hong Kong Arts Centre, 2 Harbour Rd, Wan Chai

This is the venue for classics, revivals, alternative screenings and travelling film festivals.

UA PACIFIC PLACE Map pp400-3

☎ 2869 0322; Level 1, Pacific Place, 88 Queensway, Admiralty

This is Hong Kong Island's plushest cinema and has the best sound system.

Causeway Bay

Causeway Bay is packed with cinemas but, with few exceptions, most of them show bogus Hollywood blockbusters and Hong Kong and mainland films.

JP CINEMA Map pp406-8

☎ 2881 5005; JP Plaza, 22-36 Paterson St

Be prepared for huge crowds at the weekend at this place, which is at the corner of Great George St in the heart of Causeway Bay.

UA TIMES SQUARE Map pp406-8

☎ 2506 2822; Ground fl, Times Square, 1 Matheson St

This comfortable cineplex with half a dozen screens is just above the Causeway Bay MTR station (exit A).

Tsim Sha Tsui & Tsim Sha Tsui East

GRAND OCEAN THEATRE Map pp412-14

☎ 2377 2100; Marco Polo Hong Kong Hotel Shopping Arcade, Zone D, Harbour City, 3 Canton Rd, Tsim Sha Tsui

The Grand Ocean screens the usual blockbusters.

SILVERCORD CINEMA Map pp412-14

☎ 2736 6218; Ground fl, Silvercord Shopping Centre, 30 Canton Rd, Tsim Sha Tsui

The Silvercord is Tsim Sha Tsui's most accessible cinema. Its three theatres screen the latest Hollywood releases.

Yau Ma Tei & New Kowloon

AMC FESTIVAL WALK Map pp410-11

☎ 2265 8545; Upper Ground fl & Levels 1 & 2, Festival Walk, 80-88 Tat Chee Ave, Kowloon Tong

This 11-screen complex at Hong Kong's poshest mall is the largest cinema in the territory.

BROADWAY CINEMATHEQUE Map p415

☎ 2782 0877; Prosperous Garden, 3 Public Square St, Yau Ma Tei

This is an unlikely place for an alternative cinema, but it's worth coming up for new art-house releases and rerun screenings. There's the **Kubrick Bookshop Cafe** (☎ 2388 5879; ☼ 11.30am-10pm) next door, which serves good coffee and decent pre-flick food (sandwiches HK$26 to HK$30, pasta HK$30 to HK$35) and stocks a great range of film-related books, magazines and paraphernalia.

COMEDY

Hong Kong's two leading venues for comedy in English are on Hong Kong Island.

Admiralty & Wan Chai

PUNCHLINE COMEDY CLUB

Map pp406-8

☎ 2827 7777; Viceroy, 2nd fl, Sun Hung Kai Centre, 30 Harbour Rd, Wan Chai; ☼ 9-11pm Fri & Sat

The Viceroy restaurant, a 'hot venue' with 'cool cuisine' – which is Indian, so go figure – hosts one-off live bands, dance parties, salsa nights and, on Friday and Saturday nights, the Punchline Comedy Club, with both local and imported acts. Entry costs HK$220; buffet dinner (from 6pm to 8.45pm) is HK$120.

Causeway Bay
1 NITESTAND COMEDY CLUB
Map pp406–8

☎ 2293 8888, 6465 1691; Stix Music Room, Basement, Park Lane Hotel, 310 Gloucester Rd; ⏲ 7.30-9.30pm Sun
This popular comedy club plays to packed houses one night a week.

THEATRE

Local theatre groups mostly perform at the Shouson Theatre of the Hong Kong Arts Centre, the Academy for Performing Arts, the Hong Kong Cultural Centre or the Hong Kong City Hall (see p325). Performances are mostly in Cantonese, though summaries in English are usually available.

Central
Apart from the major venues mentioned above, English-languages plays can also be seen at the Fringe Club's two theatres.

FRINGE STUDIO & FRINGE THEATRE
Map pp404-5

☎ 2521 7251, bookings 2521 9126; Ground & 1st fls, Fringe Club, 2 Lower Albert Rd; ⏲ 7.30pm during performances (days vary)
These intimate theatres, each seating up to 100 people, host eclectic local and international performances (HK$40 to HK$250) in English and in Cantonese.

Island East
SUNBEAM THEATRE Map pp398–9

☎ 2563 2959; Kiu Fai Bldg, 423 King's Rd, North Point
Cantonese and other Chinese opera (HK$60 to HK$25) – not the easiest type of entertainment to catch in Hong Kong these days – can be enjoyed here throughout the year at this theatre. Performances generally run for about a week, and are usually held five days a week in the evening at 7.30pm, with occasional matinées at 1.30pm. The theatre is right above the North Point MTR station, on the north side of King's Rd, near the intersection with Shu Kuk St. Use exit A4.

SPORT & FITNESS

Hong Kong offers countless ways to both have fun and keep fit. From tennis and squash courts to cycling trails and public swimming pools, you'll hardly be stumped for something

Children roller skating, Victoria Park (p93)

to do during your visit here. Many of the clubs mentioned throughout this section are headquartered at Sports House in So Kon Po (see Map pp406–8).

One excellent, all-round option is the **South China Athletic Association** (SCAA; Map pp406–8; ☎ 2577 6932; www.scaa.org.hk; 5th floor, Sports Complex, 88 Caroline Hill Rd, So Kon Po), west of Happy Valley and south of Causeway Bay. The SCAA has facilities for badminton, billiards, bowling, tennis, squash, table tennis, gymnastics, fencing, yoga, judo, karate, golf and dancing. Short-term membership for visitors is only HK$50 a month. Another good place to know about is the nearby **Hong Kong Amateur Athletic Association** (Map pp406–8; ☎ 2504 8215; www.hkaaa.com; Room 2015, Sports House, 1 Stadium Path, So Kon Po).

If you've overexerted yourself and require medical attention, see p365 for a list of medical centres.

BADMINTON & TABLE TENNIS

It's widely acknowledged that the Chinese are the best table-tennis players in the world; Hong Kong Chinese are also crazy about badminton and excel at it. For information on either of these two sports, contact the **Hong Kong Table Tennis Association** (☎ 2575 5330; www.hktta.org.hk) or the **Hong Kong Badminton Association** (Map pp406–8; ☎ 2504 8318; www .hkbadmintonassn.org.hk; Room 2005, Sports House, 1 Stadium Path, So Kon Po).

BOWLING

Some of the best facilities are on the 1st floor of the Sports Complex at the **SCAA** (☎ 2890 8528; www.scaa.org.hk; 88 Caroline Hill Rd, So Kon Po). Some 60 lanes are open 10am to 12.30am Monday to Friday and 9am to 12.30am Saturday, Sunday and holidays. Games cost HK$18 to HK$30 depending on the day of the week.

In Kowloon and the New Territories, bowling alleys tend to be located in the backwaters. One of the most accessible is **Sha Tin Super Bowl** (Map p417; ☎ 2648 2815; Level 4, City One Plaza Sha Tin, Ngan Shing St, Sha Tin). Games are HK$20 to HK$41 and shoe rental HK$6 to HK$9, depending on the day and the time.

CRICKET

Hong Kong has two cricket clubs: the very exclusive **Hong Kong Cricket Club** (Map pp398-9; ☎ 2574 6266; 137 Wong Nai Chung Gap Rd), above Deep Water Bay on Hong Kong Island, and the less posh **Kowloon Cricket Club** (Map pp412-14; ☎ 2367 4141; 10 Cox's Rd, Jordan).

For information contact the **Hong Kong Cricket Association** (Map pp406–8; ☎ 2504 8102; hkca@hkabc.net; Room 1019, Sports House, 1 Stadium Path, So Kon Po).

CYCLING

There are bicycle paths in the New Territories, mostly around Tolo Harbour. The paths run from Sha Tin to Tai Po and continue up to Tai Mei Tuk. You can rent bicycles in these three places, but the paths get very crowded on the weekends. Bicycle rentals are also available at Shek O on Hong Kong Island and on Lamma, Cheung Chau and Lantau.

Although the **Hong Kong Cycling Association** (Map pp406–8; ☎ 2573 3861; www.cycling.org.hk; Room 1015, Sports House, 1 Stadium Path, So Kon Po) mainly organises races, you can call them for information. To find out about areas for mountain biking or for equipment, ask the helpful staff at the **Flying Ball Bicycle Co** (Map p415; ☎ 2381 3661; 201 Tung Choi St, Mong Kok; ☻ 10am-8pm Mon-Sat, 10.30am-7pm Sun).

FISHING

While there are almost no restrictions on deep-sea fishing, it's a different story at Hong Kong's 17 freshwater reservoirs, where the season runs from September to March and there are limits on the quantity and size of fish taken. A licence from the **Water Supplies Department**

(Map pp406-8; ☎ 2824 5000; 1st floor, Immigration Tower, 7 Gloucester Rd, Wan Chai), costs HK$24 and is valid for three years.

FOOTBALL & RUGBY

For information on venues and matches for either sport contact the **Hong Kong Football Association** (☎ 2712 9122; www.hkfa.com) or the **Hong Kong Rugby Football Union** (☎ 2504 8311; www.hkrugby.com; Room 2001, Sports House, 1 Stadium Path, So Kon Po).

GOLF

Golf is just about the fastest-growing sport in Hong Kong. Most courses are private, but do open to the public at certain times. Greens fees for visitors vary, but range from HK$450 for two rounds at the nine-hole **Deep Water Bay Golf Club** (Map pp398-9; ☎ 2812 7070; 19 Island Rd, Deep Water Bay), on Hong Kong Island, to HK$1400 at the **Fanling Golf Course** (Map pp396-7; ☎ 2670 1211; Fan Kam Rd, Fanling, New Territories), which has three 18-hole courses.

One of the most dramatic links to play in Hong Kong – for the scenery if not the par – is the 36-hole **Jockey Club Kau Sai Chau Public Golf Course** (Map pp396-7; ☎ 2791 3388) on an island of that name, which is linked by regular ferry with Sai Kung town, northeast of Kowloon (see the boxed text 'Sai Kung Island Hopping' on p135). Greens fees are from HK$110 to HK$350 on weekdays and HK$550 to HK$900 at the weekend. Be sure to bring your passport and handicap card.

In general it costs HK$100 to HK$250 to rent clubs and HK$30 to HK$55 to rent shoes. There are several other courses in Hong Kong.

CLEARWATER BAY GOLF & COUNTRY CLUB Map pp396–7
☎ 2335 3888; 139 Tau Au Mun Rd, Clearwater Bay; 27 holes; greens fees HK$1200-1400
This course lies at the tip of the Clearwater Bay Peninsula in the New Territories.

DISCOVERY BAY GOLF CLUB Map p419
☎ 2987 7273; Discovery Bay, Lantau; 27 holes; greens fees HK$1200-1400

This course is perched high on a hill, with impressive views of the Outlying Islands.

SHEK O GOLF & COUNTRY CLUB
Map pp398–9
☎ 2809 4458; Shek O Rd, Shek O; 18 holes; greens fees HK$500
You'll find this course located on the southeastern edge of Hong Kong Island.

If you're content with just teeing off (again and again) there's a driving range at the **Kau Sai Chau Public Golf Course** (Map pp396-7; ☎ 2791 3388; ☺ 7am-8pm Mon & Thu, 11am-8pm Tue, 7am-10pm Wed & Fri-Sun). There's also the **Sai Kung Ho Chung Driving Range** (Map pp396-7; ☎ 2243 6222; 88 Ho Chung Rd, Sai Kung; HK$70 to HK$100, club rental HK$20; ☺ 9am-midnight Mon-Fri, 7am-midnight Sat & Sun).

For more information contact the **Hong Kong Golf Association** (Map pp406-8; ☎ 2504 8659; www.hkga.com, www.hkgolfclub.org; Room 2003, Sports House, 1 Stadium Path, So Kon Po).

GYMS

Getting fit is big business in Hong Kong, with the largest slices of the pie shared out between a few big names. In recent years, spas and a host of other outfits offering everything from aromatherapy and foot care to yoga and homeopathy have sprouted up in Hong Kong.

CALIFORNIA FITNESS CENTRE
Map pp404-5
☎ 2522 5229; www.calfitness.com.hk; 1 Wellington St, Central;

☺ 6am-midnight Mon-Sat, 8am-midnight Sun
Asia's largest health club, California Fitness has five outlets in Hong Kong, including a **Wan Chai** branch (☎ 2877 7070; 88 Gloucester Rd).

NEW YORK FITNESS Map pp404-5

☎ 2543 2280; www.nyfhk.com; 32 Hollywood Rd (enter from Shelley St), Soho; 🕒 6.30am-10.30pm Mon-Fri, 7.30am-9pm Sat & Sun

This gym offers aerobics, personal training, physiotherapy, massage and beauty therapy (weekly membership HK$500).

RETREAT AT THE FIRM Map pp404-5

☎ 2525 6696; 15th fl, The Centrium, 60 Wyndham St, Central; 🕒 9am-6pm

You can have your hair cut or done (that's the Firm part) and then Retreat next door to pamper yourself with anything from a cold-stone facial to an aromatherapy massage (HK$600 to HK$800).

SOUTH CHINA ATHLETIC ASSOCIATION Map p406-8

☎ 2577 6932; www.scaa.org.hk; 5th fl, Sports Complex, 88 Caroline Hill Rd, So Kon Po; 🕒 7am-10pm Mon-Sat, 10am-7pm Sun

This massive (1000-sq-metre) gym has modern exercise machinery and an aerobics room, as well as a sauna, steam room and massage (monthly membership HK$250).

SRIYOGA CENTRAL Map pp404-5

☎ 2810 9768; www.sriyoga.net; 3rd fl, Winning Centre, 46-48 Wyndham St, Central; 🕒 7.15am-10.30pm Mon-Sat

Arguably Hong Kong's best yoga studio, it offers everything from stretching *shkati* and cleansing *kundalini* to power *rudra*. Classes are HK$140 per hour, HK$170 for 1½ hours and HK$1400 for 11 hours.

STREAMLINE PILATES STUDIO Map pp404-5

☎ 2537 8074; Room 1506, 15th fl, The Centrium, 60 Wyndham St, Central; 🕒 8am-8.30pm Mon-Fri, 9am-2.30pm Sat

This studio, opened by a former Hong Kong Olympic swimmer, offers 'athletic style' Pilates; both private and group instruction is available (four regular sessions HK$1100).

HORSEBACK RIDING

The Hong Kong Riding Union (Map pp396-7; ☎ 2488 6886; Lot 3040, Kam Tin Road, Shek Kong) organises rides in the New Territories, but generally for groups. On Hong Kong Island, lessons are available at the Pok Fu Lam Public Riding School (Map pp398-9; ☎ 2550 1359; 75 Pokfulam Reservoir Road) for HK$360 per hour.

KAYAKING & CANOEING

The Cheung Chau Windsurfing Centre (Map p420; ☎ 2981 8316; 1 Hak Pai Rd, Tung Wan Beach, Cheung Chau; 🕒 daily year-round) rents single/double kayaks for HK$50/80 per hour. They are also available at the St Stephen's Beach Water Sports Centre (Map p409; ☎ 2813 5407; Wong Ma Kok Path) in Stanley.

Canoeing facilities are available through the Tai Mei Tuk Water Sports Centre (☎ 2665 3591) at Tai Mei Tuk in the New Territories. You can also inquire at the Wong Shek Water Sports Centre (☎ 2328 2370; Wong Shek pier, Sai Kung) in the New Territories.

MARTIAL ARTS

The HKTB (☎ 2508 1234) offers free one-hour t'ai chi lessons at 8am on Monday and Wednesday to Friday on the waterfront promenade outside the Hong Kong Cultural Centre (Map pp412–4) in Tsim Sha Tsui. On Sunday from 2.30pm to 4.30pm a display of traditional Chinese martial arts takes place at Kung Fu Corner near Sculpture Walk in Kowloon Park (Map pp412–14).

Among the martial arts and schools listed on the following page, Yip Man charges HK$500 a month for three lessons a week lasting for two or three hours and has a six-month intensive course (six hours a day, six days a week) for HK$5000. The Hong Kong Wushu Union only has classes for children.

RUNNING

Good places to run on Hong Kong Island include Harlech and Lugard Rds on the Peak, Bowen Rd above Wan Chai, the track in Victoria Park and the racecourse at Happy Valley

Hong Kong Chinese Martial Arts Association (Map pp406-8; ☎ 2504 8164; Room 1008, Sports House, 1 Stadium Path, So Kon Po)

Hong Kong Tai Chi Association (Map p415; ☎ 2395 4884; 11th floor, Lee on Bldg, 60 Argyle St, Mong Kok)

Hong Kong Wushu Union (Map pp406-8; ☎ 2504 8226; Room 1017, Sports House, 1 Stadium Path, So Kon Po)

Kung Fu Supplies (Map pp406-8; ☎ 2891 1912; Room 6A, 188-192 Johnston Rd, Wan Chai; ☽ 10am-7pm Mon-Sat, 1-7pm Sun) Everything you need to get started in Chinese martial arts.

Wing Chun Yip Man Martial Arts Athletic Association (Map pp412-14; ☎ 2723 2306; Flat A, 4th floor, Alpha House, 27-33 Nathan Rd, Tsim Sha Tsui)

YMCA King's Park Centenary Centre (Map pp412-14; ☎ 2782 6682; 22 Gascoigne Rd, Yau Ma Tei)

(as long as there aren't any horse races on!). In Kowloon, a popular place to run is the Tsim Sha Tsui East Promenade.

For easy runs followed by beer and good company, contact any of the many Hong Kong Hash House Harrier branches, a lively organisation with members worldwide, including the **Wan Chai Hash House Harriers** (www.wanchaih3.com) and the **Ladies' Hash House Harriers** (☎ 2881 0748; www.hkladieshash.com). The inappropriately named **Ladies Road Runners Club** (☎ 2904 9247; hklrr@yahoo.com; PO Box 20613, Hennessy Rd Post Office, Wan Chai) allows men to join in the fun. Another group that organises runs is **Athletic Veterans of Hong Kong** (www.avohk.org).

Every Sunday from 8am to 10am between April and July, and 7am to 9am between August and November, the **Adventist Hospital** (Map pp398-9; ☎ 2574 6211, ext 777; Wong Nai Chung Gap Rd, Happy Valley) organises a running clinic. The cost is HK$400 for the season.

SAUNA

This is a great way to relax following any activity, whether it's been a strenuous hike through the hills or a frantic day of dodging fellow shoppers in Causeway Bay. The places below are all reputable establishments.

CRYSTAL SPA Map pp412–14
☎ 2722 6600; Basement 2, Harbour Crystal Centre, 100 Granville Rd, Tsim Sha Tsui East
Saunas for men costs HK$300 or HK$536 (HK$596 after 5pm) with a massage.

PARADISE LADIES HEALTH CLUB
Map pp406–8
☎ 2529 5252; 20th floor, 23 Thompson Rd, Wan Chai

Sauna and massage starts at HK$198 for men/ women, and there's also facials and other beauty treatments.

SUNNY PARADISE SAUNA
Map pp406–8
☎ 2831 0123; 339-347 Lockhart Rd
Sauna/massage for men and women starts at HK$230/268.

SCUBA DIVING

Hong Kong has some surprisingly worthwhile diving spots, particularly in the far northeast, and there is no shortage of courses. For diving equipment, see p265.

BUNN'S DIVERS Map pp406–8
☎ 2574 7951; Mezzanine, Chuen Fung House, 188-192 Johnston Rd, Wan Chai
Organises dives in Sai Kung on Sunday (9am to 4.30pm) for HK$380.

MANDARIN DIVERS Map p409
☎ 2554 7110; Unit 2, Ground floor,

Aberdeen Marina
Tower, 8 Shum Wan Rd, Aberdeen
Offers a whole range of diving activities and courses at all levels.

OCEAN SKY DIVERS Map pp412–14
☎ 2366 3738; 1st floor, 17-19 Lock Rd, Tsim Sha Tsui
Gives PADI courses and organises local dives.

SKATING

The **Hong Kong Federation of Roller Sports** (Map pp406-8; ☎ 2504 8203; www.rollersports.org.hk; Room 1016, Sports House, 1 Stadium Path, So Kon Po) can provide information on venues around the territory.

There are several major ice-skating rinks in Hong Kong, with the ones in Quarry Bay and in Kowloon Tong by far the best. Ice Palace and Festival Walk Glacier include three or four sessions of skating in the price.

Cityplaza Ice Palace (Map pp398-9; ☎ 2885 4697; 1st fl, Cityplaza 2, 18 Tai Koo Shing Rd, Quarry Bay; HK$40-50 Mon-Fri, HK$60 Sat & Sun; ⏰ 8.30am-1pm, 1.30-3pm, 3.30-5.30pm; 6-10pm Mon-Fri, 8.30am-3pm, 3.30-5.30pm, 6-10pm Sat, 1-3pm, 3.30-5.30pm, 6-10pm Sun)

Festival Walk Glacier (Map pp410-11; ☎ 2265 8888; Upper Ground fl, Festival Walk, 80-88 Tat Chee Ave, Kowloon Tong; HK$40-50 Mon-Fri, HK$60 Sat & Sun; ⏰ 8.30am-1pm, 1.30-3pm, 3.30-5.30pm, 6-10pm Mon-Fri, 8.30am-3pm, 3.30-5.30pm, 6-10pm Sat, 1-3pm, 3.30-5.30pm, 6-10pm Sun)

Skyrink (Map pp410-11; ☎ 2307 9365; Dragon Centre, 8th floor, 37K Yen Chow St, Sham Shui Po; HK$35-40 weekdays, HK$50 weekend; ⏰ 8.30am-10pm Mon-Fri, 9am-10pm Sat & Sun)

SQUASH

Hong Kong has upwards of 600 public squash courts. The most modern facilities are at the **Hong Kong Squash Centre** (Map pp400-3; ☎ 2521 5072; Cotton Tree Rd; HK$27 per half-hour; ⏰ 7am-11pm daily), bordering Hong Kong Park in Central; you should book in advance. There are also squash courts at **Queen Elizabeth Stadium** (Map pp406-8; ☎ 2591 1331; 18 Oi Kwan Rd, Wan Chai) and **Kowloon Tsai Park** (Map pp410-11; ☎ 2336 7878; 13 Inverness Rd, Kowloon Tong).

SWIMMING

The most accessible beaches are on the southern side of Hong Kong Island, but the best ones are on the Outlying Islands and in the New Territories. For a list of beaches deemed safe enough for swimming and their gradings, check the Environmental Protection Department's website (www.info.gov.hk/epd).

Water aerobics, Kowloon Park (p104)

From 8am to 6pm daily, April to October, (to 7pm June to August) some three dozen gazetted beaches in Hong Kong are staffed by lifeguards and the shark nets inspected. From the first day of the official swimming season until the last, expect the beaches to be chock-a-block on weekends and holidays. When the swimming season is officially declared over, the beaches become deserted – no matter how hot the weather.

At most of the beaches you will find toilets, showers, changing rooms, refreshment stalls and sometimes cafés and restaurants.

Hong Kong also has some 18 public swimming pools. There are excellent pools in Tsim Sha Tsui's Kowloon Park (see p104) and Victoria Park in Causeway Bay (see p93). Most of these are closed between November and March, but heated indoor pools, such as the **Morrison Hill Swimming Pool** (Map pp406-8; ☎ 2575 3028; 7 Oi Kwan Rd, Wan Chai) and the one in the basement of the **South China Athletic Association** (Map pp406-8; ☎ 2890 7736; 88 Caroline Hill Rd, So Kon Po; adult/child HK$22/10) are open all year.

TENNIS

The **Hong Kong Tennis Centre** (Map pp398-9; ☎ 2574 9122; Wong Nai Chung Gap Rd; HK$42/57 per hour during the day/evening) is on the spectacular pass in the hills between Happy Valley and Deep Water Bay on Hong Kong Island. It's open from 7am until 11pm daily, but it's only easy to get a court during working hours. Other courts:

Bowen Road Sports Ground (Map pp400-3; ☎ 2528 2983; Bowen Dr, Mid-Levels; 4 courts; ⊙ 6am-7pm)

King's Park Sports Ground (Map pp412-14; ☎ 2388 8154; 6 Wylie Path, Yau Ma Tei; 6 courts; ⊙ 7am-11pm)

Victoria Park (Map pp406-8; ☎ 2890 5824; Hing Fat St, Causeway Bay; 14 courts; ⊙ 7am-10pm)

WINDSURFING & WAKEBOARDING

Windsurfing is extremely popular in Hong Kong; the territory's only Olympic gold medal (Atlanta, 1996) so far was one in that sport. The best months for windsurfing are October, November and December when a steady northeast monsoonal wind blows. Windsurfing during a typhoon is not recommended! Boards and other equipment are available for rent at **St Stephen's Beach Water Sports Centre** (Map p409; ☎ 2813 5407) in Stanley on Hong Kong Island, at the **Windsurfing Centre** (Map pp396-7; ☎ 2792 5605) in Sha Ha just north of Sai Kung in the New Territories and at the **Cheung Chau Windsurfing Centre** (Map p420; ☎ 2981 8316) on Cheung Chau.

The **Windsurfing Association of Hong Kong** (Map pp406-8; ☎ 2504 8255; Room 1001, Sports House, 1 Stadium Path, So Kon Po) has courses for those under 18.

Wakeboarding has grown in popularity tremendously in recent years. Deep Water Bay is a popular spot for the sport, but for other venues contact the **Hong Kong Wakeboarding Association** (Map pp406-8; ☎ 2504 8168; www.hkwba.org.hk; Room 1025, Sports House, 1 Stadium Path, So Kon Po).

YACHTING & SAILING

Even if you're not a member, you can check with any of the following yachting clubs to see if races are being held and whether an afternoon's sail aboard one of them is possible.

Aberdeen Boat Club (Map p409; ☎ 2552 8182; 20 Shum Wan Rd, Aberdeen)

Aberdeen Marina Club (Map p409; ☎ 2555 8321; 8 Shum Wan Rd, Aberdeen)

Hebe Haven Yacht Club (☎ 2719 9682; 10-1/2 Milestone, Hiram' s Hwy, Pak Sha Wan)

Royal Hong Kong Yacht Club (Map pp406-8; ☎ 2832 2817; Hung Hing Rd, Kellett Island, Causeway Bay)

A major sailing event in Hong Kong is the Hong Kong–Manila yacht race, which takes place every two years. Phone the Royal Hong Kong Yacht Club or the **Hong Kong Yachting Association** (Map pp406-8; ☎ 2504 8158; www.sailing.org.hk; Room 1009, Sports House, 1 Stadium Path, So Kon Po) for details.

You can rent smaller sailboats at **St Stephen's Beach Water Sports Centre** (Map p409; ☎ 2813 5407) in Stanley.

If there is a group of you, you should consider hiring a junk for the day or evening. Eight hours of vessel hire, plus a captain and deckhand, are usually included in the price. **Jubilee International Tour Centre** (Map pp400-3; ☎ 2530 0530; www.jubilee.com.hk; Room 604, Far East Consortium Bldg, 121 Des Voeux Rd Central) hires out vessels for 25 to 30 people for HK$2200 on weekdays and HK$2600 at the weekend.

Shopping

Shopping

Shopping in Hong Kong is not just about buying stuff: it's a social activity, a form of recreation, and a way of life for many people, both locals and expatriates. Though it isn't the bargain basement it once was, Honkers still wins for variety and for its passionate embrace of competitive consumerism. Any international brand worth its logo has at least one outlet here, and there are a slew of local brands worth your parting with a few 'red ones' as well. Clothing, shoes, jewellery, luggage and, to a lesser degree, electronic goods are the city's strong suits – most of them can be made to order as well.

There is no sales tax so the marked price is the price you'll pay. Credit cards are widely accepted, except at markets. It's rare for traders to accept travellers cheques or foreign currency as payment. Sales assistants in department or chain stores rarely have any leeway to give discounts, but you can try bargaining in owner-operated stores and certainly at the markets.

The HKTB produces a handy little booklet called *A Guide to Quality Merchandise*, which lists shops that are HKTB members. For more information, see Rip-Offs (p247).

Opening Hours
In the Central and Western districts, shop hours are generally 10am to between 6pm and 7.30pm, and in Causeway Bay and Wan Chai they're from 10am to 9.30pm or 10pm. In Tsim Sha Tsui, Mong Kok and Yau Ma Tei they are from 10am to 9pm. Many places close for major holidays – sometimes for up to a week – especially during Chinese New Year.

Winter sales are during the first three weeks in January and the summer ones in late June and early July.

Bargaining
Bargaining is a way of life in Hong Kong, with the exception of department stores and clothing chain shops, where prices marked are prices paid. Some visitors operate on the theory that you can get the goods for half the price originally quoted. Many Hong Kong residents believe that if you can bargain something down that low, then you shouldn't buy from that particular shop anyway. If the business is that crooked – and many are, particularly in the Tsim Sha Tsui tourist ghetto – it will probably find other ways to cheat you (such as selling you electronics goods with missing components or no international warranty).

Price tags should be displayed on all goods. If you can't find a price tag you've undoubtedly entered one of those business establishments with 'flexible' (read rip-off) prices.

Duty Free
The only imported goods on which there is duty in Hong Kong are alcohol, tobacco, perfumes, cosmetics, cars and some petroleum products. In general, almost anything – from cameras and electronics to clothing and jewellery – will be cheaper when you buy it outside duty-free shops.

Warranties & Guarantees
Every guarantee should carry a complete description of the item (including the model and serial numbers), as well as the date of purchase, the name and address of the shop it was purchased from, and the shop's official stamp.

Many imported items come with a warranty registration with the words 'Guarantee only valid in Hong Kong'. If it's a well-known brand, you can often return this card to the importer in Hong Kong to get a warranty card for your home country.

A common practice is to sell grey-market equipment (ie imported by somebody other than the official local agent). Such equipment may have no guarantee at all or the guarantee might only be valid in the country of manufacture (which will probably be either China or Japan).

Refunds & Exchanges

Most shops are loath to give refunds, but they can usually be persuaded to exchange purchases that haven't been soiled or tampered with. Make sure you get a detailed receipt that enumerates the goods as well as the amount and payment method.

There is really no reason to put a deposit on anything unless it is an article of clothing being made for you or you've ordered a new pair of glasses. Some shops might ask for a deposit, if you're ordering an unusual item that's not normally stocked, but this isn't a common practice.

Rip-Offs

How you shop is important in Hong Kong. The territory is *not* a nest of thieves just waiting to rip you off, as some guidebooks seem to suggest. There are, however, a lot of pitfalls just waiting for the uninitiated to fall into, and the longer you shop in Hong Kong, the more likely it is that you'll run into a shopkeeper who is crooked.

Whatever you're in the market for, always check prices in a few shops, take your time and return to a shop several times if necessary. Don't buy anything expensive in a hurry and always get a manufacturer's guarantee or warranty that is valid worldwide. When comparing camera prices, for example, make sure you're comparing not only the same camera body but also the comparable lenses and any other accessories included.

The most common way for shopkeepers in Hong Kong to cheat tourists is to simply overcharge. In the tourist shopping district of Tsim Sha Tsui, you'll rarely find price tags on anything. Checking prices in several shops therefore becomes essential. But Hong Kong merchants weren't born yesterday; they know tourists comparison-shop. So staff will often quote a reasonable or even low price on a big-ticket item, only to get the money back by overcharging on small items or accessories.

Spotting overcharging is the easy part. Sneakier tricks involve merchants removing vital components that should have been included free (like the connecting cords for the speakers on a stereo system) and demanding more money when you return to the shop to get them. You should be especially wary if the staff want to take the goods into the back room to 'box it up'. Another tactic is to replace some of the good components with cheap or defective ones. Only later will you discover that your 'Nikon' lens turns out to be a cheap copy.

Watch out for counterfeit-brand goods. Fake labels on clothes are the most obvious example, but there are fake Rolex watches, fake Gucci leather bags, even fake electronic goods. Pirated CDs and DVDs are a positive steal (in more ways than one) for as little as HK$30, but are of poor quality and rapidly deteriorate.

Hong Kong's customs agents have cracked down on the fake electronics and cameras, and the problem has been pretty much solved. However, counterfeit brand-name watches remain very common and are constantly being flogged by the irritating touts patrolling Nathan Rd. If you discover that you've been sold a fake brand-name watch by a shopkeeper, when you thought you were buying the genuine article, call the police. This is definitely illegal.

If you have any trouble with a dodgy merchant, call the Quality Tourism Services (QTS) scheme of the **HKTB** (☎ 2806 2823; www.qtshk.com) if he or she is a member of that association (the HKTB logo will be displayed on the front door or in some other prominent place). Otherwise, contact the **Hong Kong Consumer Council** (Map pp400-3; ☎ 2929 2222; www .consumer.org.hk; Ground fl, Harbour Bldg, 38 Pier Rd, Central).

If you are determined to take legal action against a shopkeeper, the **Small Claims Tribunal** (☎ 2582 4084, 2582 4085; 4th fl, Wan Chai Tower, 12 Harbour Rd, Wan Chai; ☒ 9am-1pm, 2-5pm Mon-Fri, 9am-noon Sat) handles civil cases involving up to a maximum of HK$50,000. The **Community Advice Bureau** (☎ 2815 5444) can help you find a lawyer.

Shopping – Refunds & Exchanges

Shipping Goods

Goods can be sent home by post, and some shops will package and post the goods for you, especially if it's a large item. It's a good idea to find out whether you will have to clear the goods at the country of destination. If the goods are fragile, it is sensible to buy 'all risks' insurance. Make sure you keep all the receipts.

Smaller items can be shipped from the post office. **United Parcel Service** (UPS; ☎ 2735 3535) also offers services from Hong Kong to some 40 countries. It ships by air and accepts parcels weighing up to 30kg. **DHL** (☎ 2765 8111) is another option.

WHERE TO SHOP

The main shopping districts are Central and Causeway Bay on Hong Kong Island and Tsim Sha Tsui in Kowloon.

Central has a mix of mid-range to top-end shopping centres and street-front retail; it's popular with locals and tourists alike. This is a good place to look for cameras, books, antiques and designer threads. The Landmark shopping mall in Central, due to be redeveloped soon, has designer boutiques, shops selling crystal and so on.

Causeway Bay has perhaps the largest weekend crowds and the broadest spectrum in terms of price. It is a crush of department stores and smaller outlets selling designer and street fashion, electronics, sporting goods and household items. In this area you'll also stumble upon lively street markets. Jardine's Bazaar (actually a street) and the area behind it are home to stalls and shops peddling cheap clothing, luggage and footwear, as well as the huge Times Square shopping mall. The World Trade Centre is another place where you'll find everything under one roof.

Wan Chai is another good spot for medium- and low-priced clothing, sporting goods and footwear, but the area caters mainly for locals. The district has little glamour, but it is well worth sifting through for bargains. **Admiralty**, bordering Wan Chai to the west, has Hong Kong Island's glitziest shopping mall: Pacific Place, just opposite (and connected by elevated walkway to) the Admiralty MTR station.

For antiques and curios, head for Hollywood Rd in **Sheung Wan**, where there is a long string of shops selling Chinese and Asian items. Some of the really good spots have genuine finds, but beware of what you buy.

On the escalators in Soho

Tsim Sha Tsui is a curious mixture of the down-at-heel and the glamorous. Nathan Rd is the main tourist strip, a huge avenue with side streets full of camera, watch and electronics shops and leather and silk emporia. Although this is the part of town where you're most likely to get ripped off, Tsim Sha Tsui is also home to a large number of above-board designer and signature shops. Some of these are found in Nathan Rd, but the bulk are in Harbour City, a labyrinthine shopping complex with a mall that stretches nearly 1km from the Star Ferry terminal north along Canton Rd. Tsim Sha Tsui East has a string of mostly upmarket shopping malls, the biggest being the Tsim Sha Tsui Centre on Mody Rd. Many hotels in Tsim Sha Tsui have very upmarket boutique shopping arcades, most notably the Peninsula and the Inter-Continental.

North of Tsim Sha Tsui, **Mong Kok** north caters mostly to local shoppers, and it offers good prices on clothing, sporting goods, camping gear, footwear and daily necessities. There's nothing very exotic, but for everyday items it's a popular spot, and it's fun to see how local people shop and what they are buying.

DEPARTMENT STORES

Hong Kong's department stores stock an enormous range of goods, with everything from clothing and household items to souvenirs and groceries. In general, however, they are not cheap, so if you're looking for bargains look elsewhere. You'll find department stores primarily in Central, Admiralty and Causeway on Hong Kong Island and in Tsim Sha Tsui in Kowloon. The territory's few remaining Japanese – many now just in name only – department stores are concentrated around Causeway Bay.

Chinese emporiums, generally owned and run by mainland interests, are a different kettle of fish, concentrating on Chinese arts and crafts, ceramics, furniture, souvenirs, cheap clothing and the daily necessities.

CHINESE ARTS & CRAFTS Map pp400–3
☎ 2523 3933; Shop 230, Pacific Place, 88 Queensway, Admiralty; ◷ 10.30am-7.30pm

Mainland-owned CAC is probably the best place to buy quality bric-a-brac and other Chinese chotchkies. There's also a **Central branch** (Map pp404-5; ☎ 2901 0338; Ground fl, Asia Standard Tower, 59 Queen's Rd, Central) and a huge **Wan Chai branch** (Map pp406-8; ☎ 2827 6667; Lower Block, China Resources Bldg, 26 Harbour Rd). There are two branches in Kowloon: in **Tsim Sha Tsui** (Map pp412-14; ☎ 2735 4061; 1st fl, Star House, 3 Salisbury Rd; ◷ 10.30am-9.30pm) and in the Nathan Hotel building in **Yau Ma Tei** (Map pp412-14; ☎ 2730 0061; Ground fl, 378 Nathan Rd; ◷ 10.30am-9.30pm).

CRC DEPARTMENT STORE Map pp406–8
☎ 2577 0222; 488 Hennessy Rd, Causeway Bay; ◷ 10am-10pm

This large Chinese emporium is cheaper than Chinese Arts & Crafts and can supply you with plastic buckets, padded jackets and herbal tonics (along with Chinese souvenirs and other miscellany). There's also a **Mong Kok branch** (Map p415; ☎ 2395 3191; Argyle Centre, Tower 1, 65 Argyle St).

LANE CRAWFORD Map pp404–5
☎ 2118 3388; 70 Queen's Rd, Central; ◷ 10am-7.30pm

This posh, four-floor emporium is Hong Kong's original Western-style department store and the territory's answer to Harvey Nichols in London. It also has branches in **Admiralty** (Map pp400-3; ☎ 2118 3668; 1st & 2nd fls, Pacific Place, 88 Queensway), **Causeway Bay** (Map pp406-8; ☎ 2118 3638; Ground & 1st fls, Times Square, 1 Matheson St) and **Tsim Sha Tsui** (Map pp412-14; ☎ 2118 3428; Ground & 1st fls, Ocean Terminal, Zone C, Harbour City, Canton Rd). The Tsim Sha Tsui branch stays open till 9pm daily.

MITSUKOSHI Map pp406–8
☎ 2576 5222; 500 Hennessy Rd, Causeway Bay; ◷ 10.30am-10pm

Mitsukoshi has cheap clothing, lots of crockery and household goods, food outlets and a **Park 'N' Shop** (◷ 7.30am-11pm), which is entered from Kai Chiu & Lee Garden Rds behind it.

SEIBU Map pp400–3
☎ 2971 3888; 1st & 2nd fls, Pacific Place, 88 Queensway, Admiralty; ◷ 10am-10pm Sun-Fri, 9am-10pm Sat

This Japanese department store is a shadow of its former self, but still boasts the best food emporium on Hong Kong Island – the **Great Food Hall** (p186) – in the basement.

SINCERE Map pp400–3

☎ 2544 2688; Wing Shan Tower, 173 Des Voeux Rd, Central; ☽ 10am-7.30pm

Sincere carries everything, but is most memorable for its line of clothing, particularly menswear. There is also a **Mong Kok branch** (Map p415; ☎ 2394 8233; 73 Argyle St; ☽ 11am-10pm).

SOGO Map pp406–8

☎ 2833 8338; 555 Hennessy Rd, Causeway Bay; ☽ 10am-10pm

This erstwhile Japanese store is the hub of Causeway Bay, with 12 well-organised floors. The range is mind-boggling: over 20 brands of neckties just for a start. Eclectic departments include the 'baby train models' area and a culture centre with patchwork and oil painting displays. There's a supermarket in the basement.

WING ON Map pp400–3

☎ 2852 1888; 211 Des Voeux Rd, Central; ☽ 10am-7.30pm

'Forever Peaceful' is notable for being locally owned. It carries a range of goods but is especially well-known for electronics and household appliances. There is another branch located in **Tsim Sha Tsui** (Map pp412-14; ☎ 2710 6288; 345 Nathan Rd; ☽ 10.30am-10.30pm).

YUE HWA CHINESE PRODUCTS EMPORIUM Map pp412–14

☎ 2384 0084; 301-309 Nathan Rd, Yau Ma Tei; ☽ 10am-10pm

This enormous place, with seven floors of ceramics, furniture, souvenirs and clothing, has absolutely everything the souvenir-hunting tourist could possibly want. There are two branches in **Tsim Sha Tsui**: one northeast of the Star Ferry pier (Map pp412-14; ☎ 2317 5333; 1 Kowloon Park Dr, enter from Peking Rd) and the other on the eastern edge of Kowloon Park (Map pp412-14; ☎ 2368 9165; 54-62 Nathan Rd).

FACTORY OUTLETS

Another place to hunt down bargains is in one of Hong Kong's factory outlets. Most of these deal in ready-to-wear garments, but there are a few that also sell carpets, shoes, leather goods, jewellery and imitation antiques. Often prices aren't that much less than in retail shops, and it's important to check purchases carefully, as refunds are rarely given and many articles are factory seconds and imperfect. You'll find these along Granville Rd in Tsim Sha Tsui, in Causeway Bay, on Ap Lei Chau opposite Aberdeen and, of course, in the Shenzhen Special Economic Zone across the border in the mainland.

Factory outlets open and close with the speed of summer lightning. The most useful guide in recent years has been *The Smart Shopper in Hong Kong* by Carolyn Radin, which is still available in some bookshops but is now very much out of date. *Shop in Shenzhen: An Insider's Guide to Factory Outlets* by Ellen McNally is invaluable for shopping across the border. The HKTB's free booklet, *A Guide to Quality Merchants*, has some factory-outlet listings.

MARKETS

For budget shopping, there's no better place to start than at one of Hong Kong's busy street markets.

Hong Kong's biggest market is the night-time one held along **Temple St**, which basically runs parallel to (and west of) Nathan Rd in Yau Ma Tei. If it's cheap (and in many cases shoddy) it'll be available: clothes, fake designer goods, watches, leather goods, pens, alarm clocks, radios, knives, cheap jewellery, pirated CDs and DVDs, illegal porn and sex toys, potions, lotions and hundreds of other downmarket items. Alongside the market are numerous noodle and seafood restaurants and stalls where you can grab a bite in between purchases.

The **Tung Choi St market**, two blocks east of the Mong Kok MTR station, mainly sells cheap clothing. It is sometimes called 'Ladies Market' (or 'Women's St') to distinguish it from 'Men's St' (the market on Temple St) because the stalls in the latter once sold only menswear. Though there are still a lot of items on sale for women on Tung Choi St, vendors don't discriminate and anyone's money will do. Stall owners start setting out their goods as early as lunchtime, but it's better to arrive between 6pm and 10pm, when there's a lot more on offer.

There are other bustling markets on **Apliu St** (☉ noon-9pm) in Sham Shui Po, one block west of Sham Shui Po MTR station, and in the streets running off Four Lane Square in Tai Po in the New Territories.

If you're looking strictly for clothing, try **Jardine's Bazaar** in Causeway Bay. A bit more upmarket and fun is **Stanley market**, located in the village of Stanley on southern Hong Kong Island.

At any of these markets, it's a good idea to check out the shops on the sides of the street, which are hidden behind all the street stalls. This is often where you'll find the real bargains, if there are any, and the staff are generally less pushy.

MICRO MALLS
Crammed in buildings, above MTR stations, up escalators and in back lanes are Hong Kong's malls of micro-shops selling designer threads, a kaleidoscope of kooky accessories and an Imelda Marcos of funky footwear. The best shopping is done from 3pm to 10pm, when *all* the shops are open.

Beverley Commercial Centre (Map pp412-14; 87-105 Chatham Rd, Tsim Sha Tsui) Enter via passage north of Observatory Rd.

Fashion Island (Map pp406-8; 19 Great George St, Causeway Bay)

Goldmark (Map pp406-8; 502 Hennessy Rd, Causeway Bay)

Island Beverley (Map pp406-8; 1 Great George St, Causeway Bay)

Rise Commercial Centre (Map pp412-14; 5-11 Granville Circuit, Tsim Sha Tsui)

StreetsMart (Map pp412-14; Chevalier House, 45-51 Chatham Rd South, Tsim Sha Tsui)

Trendy Zone (Map p415; Chow Tai Fook Centre, 580A Nathan Rd, Mong Kok)

SHOPPING CENTRES
Hong Kong is a mall-rat's heaven, but don't feel compelled to visit more than a couple; the same brands turn up over and over again. The following is a brief rundown of what distinguishes one major shopping centre from the other.

CHATER HOUSE Map pp400–3
☎ 2532 7777; 11 Chater Rd, Central
Georgio Armani's 3000-sq-metre multibrand store, the company's largest, is the anchor tenant in Hong Kong's newest shopping centre and sets the tone for the rest of the shops.

CITYPLAZA Map pp398–9
☎ 2568 8665; 111 King's Rd, Tai Koo Shing, Quarry Bay
The largest shopping centre in eastern Hong Kong, it's directly linked up to the MTR. Being further from the main business district, it charges retailers lower rents, which can translate into lower prices for shoppers.

FESTIVAL WALK Map pp410–11
☎ 2520 8028; 80-88 Tat Chee Ave, Kowloon Tong
A huge and glittering shopping mall with Hong Kong's largest cinema and ice-skating rink. There's a good middle-range selection of shops, some fine restaurants and a Park 'n' Shop superstore here.

HARBOUR CITY Map pp412–14
☎ 2118 8668; Canton Rd, Tsim Sha Tsui
This is an enormous place, with 700 shops in four zones. Every major brand is represented.

IFC MALL Map pp400–3
☎ 2147 3538; 1 Harbour View St, Central
A bright new centre with high-fashion boutiques, the great **Eating Plus** café-restaurant (p176) and the Airport Express terminus downstairs. Toilets are in short supply.

LANDMARK Map pp400–3
☎ 2525 4142; 1 Pedder St, Central
Lots of high fashion and good eating in this pleasant, open space.

PACIFIC PLACE Map pp400–3
☎ 2844 3888; 88 Queensway, Admiralty
Piped jazz, free telephones and the classiest range in town can all be found at Pacific Place.

PRINCE'S BUILDING Map pp400–3
☎ 2921 2194; 10 Chater Rd, Central
You might find the layout of Prince's Building to be poky and disorienting, but it's worth a look for its speciality fashion, toy and kitchenware shops.

TIMES SQUARE Map pp406–8
☎ 2118 8850; 1 Matheson St, Causeway Bay
A dozen floors of retail organised by type. There are restaurants on the 10th to 13th floors, some monster dim-sum spots, and snack bars and cafés in the basement.

WHAT TO BUY
ANTIQUES & CURIOS
Hong Kong has a rich and colourful array of Asian antiques and curios, but serious collectors will restrict themselves to the reputable antique shops and auction houses. This is an area where the buyer can easily be fooled. Hong Kong imports many forgeries and expert reproductions from China and Southeast Asia. Just remember that most of the really good pieces are in private collections and are often sold either through Christie's or Sotheby's (see listings in this section), especially at their auctions in spring (March to May) and autumn (September to November).

Most of Hong Kong Island's antique shops are bunched along Wyndham St and Hollywood Rd in Sheung Wan. The shops at the western end of Hollywood Rd tend to be cheaper in price and carry more dubious 'antiques'. Some of them stock a range of old books and magazines, Chinese propaganda posters, badges from the Cultural Revolution and so on. It's easy to get lost in some of these dusty holes-in-the-wall, but be cautious – tread carefully through this minefield of fakes and forgeries.

When it comes to buying antiques and curios, there are relatively few places of interest in Kowloon. The Ocean Terminal (Zone C) section of the Harbour City complex in Tsim Sha Tsui has some decent shops, but getting a good price is considerably more difficult there than on Hong Kong Island because of the high rents.

For Chinese handicrafts and other goods (hand-carved wood pieces, ceramics, paintings, cloisonné, silk garments), the main places to go are the large China-run department shops scattered throughout the territory (see Department Stores p249).

ALAN CHAN CREATIONS Map pp412–14
☎ 2723 2722; Shop 5A, The Peninsula, Salisbury Rd, Tsim Sha Tsui; ⊗ 10am-7pm Mon-Sat
Alan Chan has designed everything from airport logos to soy-sauce bottles, and he now lends his name to stylish souvenirs such as clothes and ceramics. Some he has a hand in, others he simply approves of.

ARCH ANGEL ANTIQUES Map pp404–5
☎ 2851 6828; 53-55 Hollywood Rd, Central; ⊗ 9.30am-6.30pm
This place, founded on the auspicious day of 8 August 1988, or 8/8/88 (see Superstitions p13), has a good selection of affordable antiques and curios. It also operates an art gallery in Soho, **Arch Angel Fine Art** (Map pp404-5; ☎ 2854 4255; 38 Peel St, Soho; ⊗ 9.30am-6.30pm), which deals exclusively in paintings by Vietnamese artists.

Fans for sale, Upper Lascar Row (p85)

CHINE GALLERY Map pp404–5
☎ 2543 0023; 42A Hollywood Rd, Central;
🕙 10am-6pm Mon-Sat, 1pm-6pm Sun
The carefully restored furniture – the lacquered cabinets are lovely – at this shop come from all over China and hand-knotted rugs are sourced from remote regions such as Xinjiang, Ningxia, Gansu, Inner Mongolia and Tibet.

CHRISTIE'S Map pp400–3
☎ 2521 5396; Room 2203-8, 22nd fl, Alexandra House, 16-20 Chater Rd, Central
Christie's has regular sales in ceramics, jade, modern and jadeite jewellery, stamps, snuff bottles, works of art, traditional and contemporary Chinese paintings and calligraphic works. It holds its spring and autumn pre-auction previews in the JW Marriott Hotel in Admiralty.

CURIO ALLEY Map pp412–14
Lane between Lock & Hankow Rds;
🕙 10am-6pm Mon-Fri, 10am-2pm Sat
This is a fun place to shop for chops, soapstone carvings, fans and other Chinese bric-a-brac. It's found in an alleyway linking Lock and Hankow roads, just south of Haiphong Rd in Tsim Sha Tsui.

HONEYCHURCH ANTIQUES Map pp404–5
☎ 2543 2433; 29 Hollywood Rd, Central;
🕙 10am-6pm Mon-Sat
This fine shop, run by an American couple for nigh on four decades, specialises in antique Chinese furniture, jewellery and old English silver.

KARIN WEBER ANTIQUES Map pp404–5
☎ 2544 5004; 32A Staunton St, Soho;
🕙 11am-7pm Mon-Sat
Karin Weber has an enjoyable mix of Chinese country antiques and contemporary Asian artworks. Short lectures on antiques and the scene in Hong Kong are given periodically and antique-buying trips into Guangdong can be arranged in advance.

MOUNTAIN FOLKCRAFT Map pp404–5
☎ 2523 2817; 12 Wo On Lane, Central;
🕙 9.30am-6.30pm Mon-Sat
This is one of the nicest shops in Central for folk craft and is piled with bolts of batik and sarongs, clothing, wood carvings and lacquerware made by ethnic minorities in China and other Asian countries.

Top Five Shopping Experiences – Tsim Sha Tsui & Mong Kok

- **Alan Chan** (p252) Stylish souvenirs from the man who has designed almost everything in Hong Kong.
- **http://www.izzue.com** (p257) Simple and comfortable styles in this chain of super-groovy boutiques.
- **Om International** (p263) The place for pearls, with honest and helpful staff.
- **Wing Shing Photo Supplies** (p256) Reliable photo shop, with good service and competitive prices.
- **Yuet Wah Music Company** (p265) Two-stringed *yi woo* and other Chinese musical instruments on sale.

SILK ROAD Map pp412–14
3rd fl, Marco Polo Hong Kong Hotel Shopping Arcade, Zone D, Harbour City, 3 Canton Rd, Tsim Sha Tsui;
🕙 10am-6.30pm
Antique shops are concentrated along this corridor; here you'll find cloisonné, bronzes, jade, lacquer, ceramics, rosewood furniture and screens.

SOTHEBY'S Map pp400–3
☎ 2524 8121; 5th fl, Standard Chartered Bank Bldg, 4-4A Des Voeux Rd, Central
Sotheby's usually holds its auction previews in the spring and autumn at the Island Shangri-La Hotel in Admiralty. It also has regular sales in ceramics, jade, modern and jadeite jewellery, stamps, snuff bottles, works of art, traditional and contemporary Chinese paintings and calligraphic works.

STONE VILLAGE Map p415
☎ 2787 0293; 44 Flower Market Rd, Mong Kok;
🕙 9.30am-7.30pm
Stone Village, in the heart of the Flower Market, stocks creative plant pots, pottery figurines and tea sets, plus a lot of beautiful bonsai that you're unfortunately unlikely to be able to take home.

TIBETAN GALLERY Map pp404–5
☎ 2530 4863; Shop A, Yu Yuet Lai Bldg, 43-55 Wyndham St, Central; 🕙 10am-6pm
This shop has an impressive selection of Tibetan religious art and artefacts, including mini-altars. There's a showroom on the 1st floor.

WATTIS FINE ART Map pp404–5

☎ 2524 5302; 2nd fl, 20 Hollywood Rd, Central;
🕓 10am-6pm Tue-Sat, 1-5pm Sun

No place in Hong Kong has a better collection of antique maps for sale than Wattis Fine Art, which is entered from Old Bailey St.

ZITAN Map pp404–5

☎ 2523 7584; Shop G, Yu Yuet Lai Bldg,
43-55 Wyndham, Central; 🕓 10am-6pm

If you're hunting for quality items try this shop, which has a superb range of antique Chinese furniture.

BOOKS

The territory now counts more bookshops than ever before, but the lion's share are on Hong Kong Island.

BLOOMSBURY BOOKS Map pp400–3

☎ 2526 5387; 2nd fl, Club Lusitano Bldg, 16 Ice House St, Central; 🕓 9am-7pm Mon-Fri, 9am-6pm Sat

The erstwhile Professional Bookshop has changed its name and location. It still carries an excellent selection of business, legal and other professional titles but, in deference to its new name, leans on the literary side as well. You can also enter the Club Lusitano Building from Duddell St.

BOOKAZINE Map pp400–3

☎ 2521 1649; Ground fl, Pacific House, 20 Queen's Rd Central; 🕓 9am-7.30pm Mon-Sat, 10am-6.30pm Sun

Bookazine operates atmosphere-free chain stores that are dotted all around the territory. Each shop stocks a dependable range of books, titles of local interest, magazines and some stationery. There's a **Wan Chai branch** (Map pp406-8; ☎ 2527 2092; Shops 8 & 9, 3rd fl, Hopewell Centre, 183 Queen's Rd East).

COSMOS BOOKS Map pp406–8

☎ 2866 1677; Basement & 1st fl, 30 Johnston Rd, Wan Chai; 🕓 10am-8pm

This independently owned chain with a **Tsim Sha Tsui branch** (Map p412-14; ☎ 2367 8699; 96 Nathan Rd) has a good selection of Chinese-related books in the basement. Upstairs there are English-language books (nonfiction is quite strong) plus one of Hong Kong's best stationery departments. Enter the Tsimsy branch from Granville Rd.

FLOW BOOKSHOP Map pp404–5

☎ 2964 9483, 8104 0822; 1st fl, 40 Lyndhurst Tce, Central (enter from Cochrane St); 🕓 noon-7pm

This second-hand and exchange bookstore has something of a focus on spiritual and New Age literature, but it's all a bit of a jumble sale. Meditation workshops are occasionally held; for these you'll need to levitate to the 2nd floor.

GOVERNMENT PUBLICATIONS OFFICE
Map pp400–3

☎ 2537 1914; Queensway Government Offices, 66 Queensway, Admiralty; 🕓 9am-6pm Mon-Fri, 9am-1pm Sat

All publications, including hiking maps that have been produced by the Hong Kong government are available from this outlet.

HONG KONG BOOK CENTRE
Map pp400–3

☎ 2522 7064; Basement, On Lok Yuen Bldg, 25 Des Voeux Rd Central; 🕓 9am-6.30pm Mon-Fri, 9am-5.30pm Sat, 1-5pm Sun (summer only)

This basement shop has a vast selection of books and magazines, including a mammoth number of business titles.

JOINT PUBLISHING Map pp400–3

☎ 2868 6844; 9 Queen Victoria St, Central;
🕓 10.30am-7.30pm Mon-Sat, 1-6pm Sun

This primarily Chinese-language bookshop has a good range of English-language books about China, and tapes and CDs for studying the language. It's especially strong in local maps. Most English-language titles are on the mezzanine floor. There are 17 other JP outlets, many in MTR stations, including a **Wan Chai branch** (Map pp406-8; ☎ 2838 2081; cnr Hennessy & O'Brien Rds).

KELLY & WALSH Map pp400–3

☎ 2522 5743; Shop 304, Pacific Pl, 88 Queensway, Admiralty; 🕓 9.30am-8pm Mon-Sat, 11am-8pm Sun

This smart shop has a good selection of art, design and culinary books, and a handy bonus is that the staff know the stock. Books for children are shelved in a handy kids' reading lounge. There's also a **Central branch** (Map pp400-3; ☎ 2810 5128; Shop 305, Exchange Square Tower 1).

PAGE ONE Map pp410–11

☎ 2778 2808; Shop LC1 30, Lower Ground fl, Festival Walk, 80-88 Tat Chee Ave, Kowloon Tong; ☺ 11am-10pm Mon-Thu, 10.30am-10.30pm Fri, 11am-10.30pm Sat, 10.30am-10pm Sun

A chain, yes, but one with attitude. Page One has Hong Kong's best selection of art and design magazines and books; it's also strong on photography, literature, film and children's books. There's also a **Tsim Sha Tsui branch** (☎ 2730 6080; Shop 3002, 3rd fl, Ocean Centre, Zone A, Harbour City, Canton Rd).

SWINDON BOOKS Map pp412–14

☎ 2366 8001; 13-15 Lock Rd, Tsim Sha Tsui; ☺ 9am-6.30pm Mon-Thu, 9am-7.30pm Fri-Sat, 12.30-6.30pm Sun

This is one of the best bookshops in Hong Kong. There's another **Tsim Sha Tsui branch** (Map pp412-14; ☎ 2730 0183; Shops 310 & 328, 3rd fl, Ocean Centre, Zone B, Harbour City, Canton Rd).

TAI YIP Map pp404–5

☎ 2524 5963; Room 101-102, 1st fl, Capitol Plaza, 2-10 Lyndhurst Tce, Central; ☺ 10am-9pm Mon-Fri, 10am-6.30pm Sat & Sun

Tai Yip has a terrific selection of books about anything that is Chinese and artsy: calligraphy, jade, bronze, costumes, architecture, symbolism. This is a good place to look deeper if you're planning on buying art in Hong Kong; it's also an excellent place for picking up beautiful gift cards. There are two **Tsim Sha Tsui branches**: in the Hong Kong Museum of Art (Map pp412-14; ☎ 2732 2088) and the Hong Kong Museum of History (Map pp412-14 ☎ 2191 9188).

CAMERAS & VIDEO CAMERAS

When shopping for a camera or camcorder, keep in mind that you should never buy one that doesn't have a price tag. This will basically preclude 99% of the shops in Tsim Sha Tsui. One of the best spots in Hong Kong for buying photographic equipment is Stanley St in Central and competition is keen. Everything carries price tags, though some low-level bargaining might be possible. Tsim Sha Tsui has a couple of shops on Kimberley Rd dealing in used cameras and there are plenty of photo shops on Sai Yeung Choi St in Mong Kok.

In and around the Tsim Sha Tsui rip-off zone, practically every video store has a demonstration TV set up in the rear of the store. You can expect a demonstration in which only the most expensive 'digital' video camera produces a crisp image. What you won't be told is that the TV is rigged so that it will only work properly with the overpriced digital model. You also won't be told that the 'digital' model is not digital at all, but an ordinary camera for which you get to pay double.

If you want to buy a camcorder, you must decide which standard you want. Like most of Europe and Australasia, Hong Kong uses the PAL system, which is incompatible with the American and Japanese NTSC system and the French SECAM system. A wrong choice would be a costly mistake, so pay careful attention to the labels.

COLOR SIX Map pp404–5

☎ 2526 0123; 18A Stanley St, Central; ☺ 8am-7pm Mon-Fri, 8am-5pm Sat

This offers some of the best photo-processing in town. Colour slides can be professionally processed in just three hours, and many special types of film, unavailable elsewhere in Hong Kong, are on sale here. Naturally prices aren't the lowest in town – developing costs are from HK$20 per roll and printing from HK$1.20 per exposure, while processing and mounting slide film is HK$50 – but the quality and service are excellent.

DAVID CHAN Map pp412–14

☎ 2723 3886; Shop 15, Champagne Court, 16 Kimberley Rd, Tsim Sha Tsui; ☺ 10am-8pm Mon-Sat

This dealer, one of the most reliable in Hong Kong, sells both new and antique cameras.

EVERBEST PHOTO SUPPLIES Map pp404–5

☎ 2522 1985; 28B Stanley St, Central; ☺ 9am-7pm Mon-Sat

This extremely reliable shop is where many of Hong Kong's professional photographers buy their equipment.

ONESTO PHOTO COMPANY

Map pp412–14

☎ 2723 4668; Shop 2, Ground fl, Champagne Court, 16 Kimberley Rd, Tsim Sha Tsui; ☺ 10am-11pm

This retail establishment, also known as the Kimberley Camera Company, has price tags on the equipment (a rare find in Tsim Sha Tsui), but there's always some latitude for bargaining.

PHOTO SCIENTIFIC Map pp404–5

☎ 2525 0550; 6 Stanley St, Central;
☽ 9am-7pm Mon-Sat

This is the favourite of Hong Kong's resident pros. You'll almost certainly find equipment elsewhere for less, but Photo Scientific has a rock-solid reputation with labelled prices, no bargaining, no arguing and no cheating.

WING SHING PHOTO SUPPLIES

Map p415

☎ 2396 6886; 55-57 Sai Yeung Choi St, Mong Kok;
☽ 10am-10pm

We've received letters from readers praising the quality of the service and the competitive prices at Wing Shing. We like the hours; the boys in the north always try harder.

CARPETS

While carpets are not really that cheap in Hong Kong, there is a good selection of silk and wool (new and antique) ones in several areas. Imported carpets from Afghanistan, China, India, Iran, Pakistan, Tibet and Turkey are widely available. The best carpets have a larger number of knots per square inch (over 550) and are richer in detail and colour than cheaper carpets. Silk carpets are generally hung on the wall rather than used on the floor. Older carpets are dyed with natural vegetable dye. The bulk of Hong Kong's carpet and rug shops are clustered around Wyndham St in Central, although there are some large retailers located in Wan Chai as well. In Tsim Sha Tsui, a few places in Ocean Terminal stock a decent range.

AL-SHAHZADI PERSIAN CARPET
GALLERY Map pp406–8

☎ 2834 8396; 265 Queen's Rd East, Wan Chai;
☽ 10am-6pm Tue-Sun

This shop has quality carpets from Afghanistan, Iran and Russia, but nothing Chinese.

CHINESE CARPET CENTRE

Map pp412–14

☎ 2735 1030; Shop 168, 1st fl, Ocean Terminal, Zone C, Harbour City, Canton Rd, Tsim Sha Tsui;
☽ 10am-7pm

This place has a huge selection of new Chinese carpets and rugs.

MIR ORIENTAL CARPETS Map pp404–5

☎ 2521 5641; Ground fl, New India House, 52 Wyndham St, Central; ☽ 10am-7pm Mon-Sat, 11am-5pm Sun

This is the largest stockist of fine rugs in Hong Kong, with thousands of carpets from around the world flying in and out of the shop.

TAI PING CARPETS Map pp406–8

☎ 2522 7138; Shop 816, 8th fl, Times Square, 1 Matheson St, Causeway Bay; ☽ 10am-9pm

This large shop has an excellent selection of carpets and rugs, and what you don't see you can order.

CIGARS

For some people – men and women alike – cigar smoking is an unparalleled delight.

CIGAR EXPRESS CENTRAL Map pp404–5

☎ 2110 9203; Upper Ground fl,
Cheung Fai Bldg, 45-47 Cochrane St, Central;
☽ 10am-9pm

This branch of a Hong Kong chain with six outlets sells everything from a HK$10 Piedra stogie to a hand-rolled Cuban Cohiba Pyramid for HK$320 a pop.

TABAQUERIA FILIPINA Map pp400–3

☎ 2877 1541; Shop 105, 1st fl, Alexandra House, 6 Ice House St, Central; ☽ 10am-7.30pm Mon-Fri, 10am-6.30pm Sat

Sometimes you do need a fat cigar to feel like you're making it in the big city. This boxy store comes to the rescue with Cuban, Dominican and other fine chompers.

CLOTHING & FOOTWEAR

The best places to find designer fashions and top-end boutiques are in the big shopping centres (see p251), especially the Landmark, Pacific Place and Festival Walk. The best hunting grounds for warehouse sales and factory extras are generally in Tsim Sha Tsui at the eastern end of Granville Rd; check out Austin Ave and Chatham Rd South as well. On Hong Kong Island, Jardine's Bazaar in Causeway Bay has low-cost garments and there are several sample shops and places to pick up cheap jeans in Lee Garden Rd and Li Yuen St in Central, which runs between Queen's and Des Voeux Rds Central. The cheapest clothes can be found at street markets (see p250).

For mid-priced items, Causeway Bay and Tsim Sha Tsui, particularly east of Nathan Rd, are good hunting grounds. Take the time to pop into one of the dozens of Baleno, Giordano, U2 or Esprit branches. These specialise in well-made and affordable mainstream fashion items.

The eastern end of Lockhart Rd in Causeway Bay is a good place to look for footwear. Check around, though, as some places have considerably better prices than others on the same product. It's also worth taking a stroll down Johnston Rd in Wan Chai, which has lots of mid-priced and budget clothing outlets.

Although many people still frequent Hong Kong's tailors, getting a suit or dress made is no longer a great bargain. For a quality piece of work you'll probably pay close to what you would in New York or London. An exception might be some of the Indian tailors on the streets of Tsim Sha Tsui. Remember that you usually get what you pay for; the material is often good but the work may be shoddy. Remember that most tailors will require a 50% nonrefundable deposit and the more fittings you have, the better the result.

Clothing sizes

Approximate measurements only – try before you buy

Women's Clothing

Aust/UK	8	10	12	14	16	18
Europe	36	38	40	42	44	46
Japan	5	7	9	11	13	15
USA	6	8	10	12	14	16

Women's Shoes

Aust/USA	5	6	7	8	9	10
Europe	35	36	37	38	39	40
France only	35	36	38	39	40	42
Japan	22	23	24	25	26	27
UK	3½	4½	5½	6½	7½	8½

Men's Clothing

Aust	92	96	100	104	108	112
Europe	46	48	50	52	54	56
Japan	S		M	M		L
UK/USA	35	36	37	38	39	40

Men's Shirts (Collar Sizes)

Aust/Japan	38	39	40	41	42	43
Europe	38	39	40	41	42	43
UK/USA	15	15½	16	16½	17	17½

Men's Shoes

Aust/ UK	7	8	9	10	11	12
Europe	41	42	43	44½	46	47
Japan	26	27	27½	28	29	30
USA	7½	8½	9½	10½	11½	12½

BLANC DE CHINE Map pp400–3

☎ 2524 7875; Room 201, 2nd fl, Pedder Bldg, 12 Pedder St, Central; ☉ noon-7pm Mon-Sat, noon-5pm Sun
This sumptuous store specialises in traditional men's Chinese jackets, off the rack or made to measure. There's also a lovely selection of silk dresses for women.

CARPET CENTRE Map pp404–5

☎ 2850 4993; Shop A, Lower Ground fl, 29 Hollywood Rd (enter from Cochrane St), Central; ☉ 10am-9pm
No, you're not being asked to don a dhurry. What this place has is pashmina shawls, ranging in price from HK$350 to HK$900.

DADA CABARET VOLTAIRE

Map pp406–8
☎ 2890 1708; Shop F-13A, 1st fl, Fashion Island, 19 Great George St, Causeway Bay; ☉ noon-10pm
Ragged rainbow colours that are also sported by the staff. Just one of many fine shops in the Fashion Island micro mall.

ENCYCO Map pp406–8

☎ 2504 1016; Shop 331, 3rd fl, Island Beverley, 1 Great George St, Causeway Bay; ☉ 1.30-10.30pm
Independent young Hong Kong designer with an eye for wispy wear, verging on the wacky.

HTTP://WWW.IZZUE.COM Map pp412–14

☎ 2992 0631; Shop 2225, 2nd fl, Ocean Centre, Zone A, Harbour City, Canton Rd, Tsim Sha Tsui; ☉ 11am-9pm
Simple, energetic and comfortable styles in this chain of super-groovy boutiques. There are a dozen other outlets throughout the territory, including a **Central branch** (Map pp400-3; ☎ 2868 4066; Upper Ground fl, 10 Queen's Rd Central) open the same hours.

I.T Map pp412–14

☎ 2736 9152; Shop 1030, Miramar Shopping Centre, 1-23 Kimberley Rd, Tsim Sha Tsui; ☉ noon-10pm
This shop sells the cute, trendy women's gear that surrounds you on the streets all day. There

are i.t and I.T stores in all the major shopping areas (capitalisation denotes its 'grown-up' range), including a **Causeway Bay branch** (Map pp406-8; Shop 517, 5th fl, Times Square, 1 Matheson St).

JOYCE Map pp400–3

☎ 2810 1120; Ground fl, New World Tower, 16 Queen's Rd, Central; ⏰ 10.30am-7.30pm Mon-Sat, 11am-7pm Sun

This multidesigner store is a good choice if you're pressed for time: Issey Miyake, Yves Saint Laurent, Jean Paul Gaultier, Commes des Garçons, Voyage, Yohji Yamamoto and some Hong Kong fashion designers are just some whose wearable wares are on display. There's also an **Admiralty branch** (Map pp400-3; ☎ 2524 7828; Shops 226 & 334, 2nd & 3rd fls, Pacific Place, 88 Queensway), which keeps the same hours. For the same duds at half the price, visit Joyce Warehouse (☎ 2814 8313; 21st fl, Horizon Plaza, 2 Lee Wing St, Ap Lei Chau; ⏰ 10am-7pm Tue-Sat, 11am-7pm Sun) opposite Aberdeen.

LABELS FOR LESS Map pp400–3

☎ 2295 3883; Shop 3008-11, 3rd fl, IFC Mall, 1 Harbour View St, Central; ⏰ 11am-8pm

If you've already bought up at Swank (shops at Landmark and New World Centre in Central, Pacific Place in Admiralty) it could be heartbreaking to come to LfL. Often the only difference with the so-called seconds sold at this shop is the price.

LINVA Map pp404–5

☎ 2544 2456; Ground fl, 38 Cochrane St, Central; ⏰ 10am-5pm Mon-Sat

This is the place to come to have your own cheongsam (see p29) stitched up. Bring your own silk or choose from Mr Leung's selection.

MIU MIU Map pp400–3

☎ 2523 7833; Shop B24, Basement 1, The Landmark, 1 Pedder St, Central; ⏰ 10.30am-7.30pm Mon-Sat, 11am-7pm Sun

Super-cute and creative threads for neo-adults ('oh, they've put a zip *there*?!') are available here. The shoes are exceptionally stylish.

NAMU FASHION Map pp412–14

☎ 2722 1788; Shop A, 15C Austin Ave, Tsim Sha Tsui; ⏰ 1pm-11pm

Ever wonder what's trendy in Seoul these days? No? Namu does 'women's total fashion from Korea' and it's breezy, blousy and just a bit prissy.

OCEAN BOUTIQUE Map pp412–14

☎ 2366 0889; Shop 5-6, Ground fl, 1 Minden Ave, Tsim Sha Tsui; ⏰ 10am-7pm Mon-Sat

Kiddies' gear made in China and Korea, much of it with funny English misspellings. The jump suits promise rumpus while the formal dresses are both amusing and tragic.

PRO CAM-FIS Map pp412–14

☎ 2736 9866; Shop 265, 2nd fl, Ocean Centre, Zone B, Harbour City, Canton Rd, Tsim Sha Tsui; ⏰ 11am-8pm Mon-Thu, 10.30am-8.30pm Fri-Sun

Window display, Shanghai Tang (p259)

Outdoor gear, both lightweight and cold-weather, including kids' sizes. It carries a good range of Eagle Creek travel products.

RAG BROCHURE Map p415

☎ 2391 4660; Shop 4, Trendy Zone, Chow Tai Fook Centre, 580A Nathan Rd, Mong Kok; ☽ 1-10pm

One of a crush of fashion outlets in this `alt mall' selling new and vintage gear for guys and gals. This is where the cool dudes shop for clothes, cheap jewellery, watches and action figures.

SAM'S TAILOR Map pp412–14

☎ 2367 9423; Shop K, Burlington Arcade, 92-94 Nathan Rd, Tsim Sha Tsui; ☽ 10am-7.30pm Mon-Sat, 10am-midnight Sun

It's not certain that Sam's is the best tailor in Hong Kong, but it's the best known. Sam's has stitched everyone up – from royalty and rock stars to us. Expect to pay HK$250 to HK$350 for shirts and from HK$1800 for a suit.

SHANGHAI TANG Map pp400–3

☎ 2525 7333; Basement & Ground fl, Pedder Bldg, 12 Pedder St, Central; ☽ 10am-8pm Mon-Sat, 11am-7pm Sun

Started by flamboyant Hong Kong business-man David Tang, Shanghai Tang has sparked something of a fashion wave in Hong Kong with its updated versions of traditional yet al-most neon-coloured Chinese garments. It also has accessories and delightful gift items, and custom tailoring is available.

SPY Map pp406–8

☎ 2893 7799; Shop C, 11 Sharp St East, Causeway Bay; ☽ 1-11pm

Tame yet trendy everyday wear such as slacks and short-sleeved shirts. It has two other outlets, including a **Tsim Sha Tsui branch** (Map pp412-14; ☎ 2366 5866; Shop 406-407, Rise Commercial Centre, 5-11 Granville Circuit), which is open the same hours.

STITCH-UP TAILORS Map pp412–14

☎ 2314 4000; Shop 3B, Ground fl, Star House, 3 Salisbury Rd, Tsim Sha Tsui; ☽ 9am-9pm

Need a tailor? Take a walk on Nathan Rd and they'll find you, or ask your hotel concierge for advice (many top hotels have tailors on site). Otherwise, try this unfortunately named, er, outfit. The turnaround time on most items is 48 hours, including two fittings, and they're cheaper than Sam's.

TOTO Map pp400–3

☎ 2869 4668; Shop 212, 2nd fl, Prince's Bldg, 10 Chater Rd, Central; ☽ 10am-7pm

Jump suits and other togs for under-twos; everything made by this Hong Kong brand is 100% cotton.

WESTERN MARKET Map pp400–3

☎ 2815 3586; 323 Des Voeux Rd, Central & New Market St, Sheung Wan; ☽ 10am-7pm

All the old textile vendors who were driven out of the alleys linking Queen's and Des Voeux Rds Central in the early 1990s moved to this renovated old market built in 1906. You'll find Chinese knick-knacks and chotchkies on the ground floor, and piece goods on the 1st floor.

ZOOM Map p415

☎ 2781 0920; 65 Fa Yuen St, Mong Kok; ☽ 11.30am-11pm

Superfly treads rule in this long strip of sports shoe shops. All brands and breeds of sneakers get air. It's packed at the weekend.

COMPUTERS

Hong Kong is a popular place to buy personal computers and laptops. While prices are competitive, it is also important to pay careful attention to what you buy and where you buy it. Computers are prone to breakdowns, so finding a shop with a good reputation for honesty is vital.

You may have your own ideas about what kind of computer you want to buy, but if you're just visiting Hong Kong you would be wise to choose a brand-name portable computer with an international warranty, such as Hewlett-Packard, Compac or Acer.

Be careful: you may be hit with a steep import tax when you return to your home country. Save your receipt; the older the machine, the less you're likely to pay in import duty. The rules in many countries say that the machine is tax exempt if over a year old.

Most people buy their computers in Kowloon, where there are loads of centres selling computers and related equipment, a much greater choice and prices are lower, but *caveat emptor* is the phrase to bear in mind as you browse. Hong Kong Island does have one reasonable computer arcade – the 10th to 12th floors of Windsor House in Causeway Bay, which is open 11am to 9pm daily.

COMPUTER CONSULTANTS

Map pp406–8

☎ 2576 3756; Shop 1150-1151, 11th fl, Windsor House, 311 Gloucester Rd, Causeway Bay; ⏲ 11am-8.30pm

The computer your humble author is working on at this moment was bought at this reliable shop.

GOLDEN PLAZA SHOPPING CENTRE

Map pp410–11

Basement & 1st fl, 146-152 Fuk Wa St, Sham Shui Po; ⏲ 10am-10pm

This centre has some computers and components, but has mostly switched over to software, manuals, CDs, DVDs and videos.

MONG KOK COMPUTER CENTRE

Map p415

☎ 2781 1109; 8-8A Nelson St, Mong Kok; ⏲ noon-9pm

This centre has three floors of computer shops. In general, it's geared more towards the resident Cantonese-speaking market than foreigners, but you can generally get better deals than in Tsim Sha Tsui. Check out

Winframe System (☎ 2300 1238; Shop 106-107) on the 1st floor.

NEW CAPITAL COMPUTER PLAZA

Map pp410–11

1st & 2nd fls, 85-95 Un Chau St, Sham Shui Po; ⏲ 10am-10pm

This is a decent emporium of different shops, with a good range of stock and helpful staff who can muster up enough English to close a sale.

STAR COMPUTER CITY Map pp412–14

☎ 2736 2608; 2nd fl, Star House, 3 Salisbury Rd, Tsim Sha Tsui; ⏲ 10am-7pm

This is the largest complex of retail computer outlets in Tsim Sha Tsui, with some two dozen shops. While it's not the cheapest place in Hong Kong, neither is it the most expensive (that honour goes to the rip-off shops on or near Nathan Rd). Have a look at **Reptron** (☎ 2730 2891; Shop A1, 2nd fl) for desktops, laptops and PDAs, and **Houston Crest** (☎ 2730 4382; Shop D1, 2nd fl) for accessories – modem protectors, various adaptors and the cables that could be just what you need to get roadworthy.

ELECTRONIC GOODS

Sham Shui Po in northwestern Kowloon is a good neighbourhood to search for electronic items. You can even buy and sell second-hand goods. If you take exit A2 from the MTR at Sham Shui Po station, you'll find yourself on Apliu St, one of the best places in Hong Kong to search for the numerous plug adaptors you'll need if you plan to use your purchase in Hong Kong, Macau and/or the mainland.

Mong Kok is another very good neighbourhood to look for electronic gadgetry. Starting at Argyle St and heading south, explore all the side streets running parallel to Nathan Rd, such as Canton Rd, Tung Choi St, Sai Yeung Choi St, Portland St, Shanghai St and Reclamation St.

There are also quite a few electronics shops in Causeway Bay, their windows stuffed full of video cameras, CD players and other goodies. Locals generally avoid these places – apparently many of these shops are under the same ownership, ensuring that the prices remain high throughout the area.

It's best to avoid the electronics shops in Tsim Sha Tsui, especially those along Nathan Rd or just off it, as many of which are skilled at fleecing foreign shoppers.

1010 Map pp412–14

☎ 2910 1010; 82-84 Canton Rd, Tsim Sha Tsui; ⏲ 10am-11pm

The latest, smallest, sleekest in mobile phones and palm pilots – pure binary finery. There's also a **Central branch** (Map pp404-5; ☎ 2918 1010; Ground & 4th fls, Century Square, 1-13 D'Aguilar St).

CHUNG YUEN ELECTRICAL

Map pp400–3

☎ 2524 8066; Shop 227, 2nd fl, Prince's Bldg, 10 Chater Rd, Central; ⏲ 10am-7pm

Fair-minded, fixed-price electronics store with a good selection of DVD players, sound systems, monitors and organisers. The shop is small but the gear is good.

EYEGLASSES

Both frames and lenses can be cheaper (in some case, much cheaper) in Hong Kong than what you would pay at home.

COHEN OPTICAL Map pp412–14
☎ 2369 0548; Ground fl, 45 Peking Rd, Tsim Sha Tsui; ⏰ 9am-11pm

The honest and, judging from the opening hours, hard-working staff at this large shop are always ready and willing to cut you a deal.

OCEAN OPTICAL Map pp400–3
☎ 2868 5670; Shop 5, Ground fl, The Cascade, Standard Chartered Bank Bldg, 4-4A Des Voeux Rd, Central; ⏰ 9.30am-7.30pm Mon-Sat, 10.30am-6pm Sun

We do not know of a better optician in Hong Kong.

FINE ART

Hong Kong is also an excellent place to buy fine art. For information on contemporary art in Hong Kong, see the Arts & Architecture chapter (p35).

GALERIE DU MONDE Map pp400–3
☎ 2525 0529; Shop 328, 3rd fl, Pacific Place, 88 Queensway, Admiralty; ⏰ 10am-7pm Mon-Sat, noon-5pm Sun

This long-established and very upmarket gallery shows mostly figurative work from relatively established mainland Chinese painters.

GALERIE MARTINI Map pp400–3
☎ 2526 9566; 99F Wellington St, Central; ⏰ 11am-7pm Tue-Sat

This small upstairs art nook shows international contemporary art. The exhibitions swing between introducing relatively established Western artists to Hong Kong and giving exposure to local artists on the rise.

Schoeni Art Gallery (p262)

Top Five Shopping Experiences – Central

- **Chine Gallery** (p253) Top-of-the-crop antique furniture and rugs.
- **Hanart TZ Gallery** (p261) *La crème de la crème* of fine-art galleries in Hong Kong.
- **Fook Ming Tong Tea Shop** (p262) The stylish choice for cha and cha accessories.
- **Liuligongfang** (p263) Renowned glass sculptor hawks her creations here.
- **Shanghai Tang** (p259) Retro Chinese duds in neon colours.

HANART TZ GALLERY Map pp400–3
☎ 2526 9019; Room 202, 2nd fl, Henley Bldg, 5 Queen's Rd, Central; ⏰ 10am-6.30pm Mon-Fri, 10am-6pm Sat

Hanart is *la crème de la crème* of art galleries here. It was instrumental in establishing the reputation of many of the artists discussed in the contemporary art section of the Arts & Architecture chapter (p39).

JOHN BATTEN GALLERY Map pp404–5
☎ 2854 1018; 64 Peel St, Soho; ⏰ 11am-7pm Tue-Sat, 1-5pm Sun

This small gallery is charged with the enthusiasm and vision of its director. Batten shows local and international painting, photography and video art of consistently good quality.

PLUM BLOSSOM Map pp404–5
☎ 2521 2189; Ground fl, 1 Hollywood Rd, Central; ⏰ 10am-6.30pm Mon-Sat

The shop where Rudolf Nureyev used to buy his baubles, and other celebrities continue to do so, is one of the most exquisite and well-established in Hong Kong.

SCHOENI ART GALLERY Map pp404–5
☎ 2542 3143; 27 Hollywood Rd, Central;
🕑 10.30am-6.30pm Mon-Sat
This Swiss-owned gallery, which has been a feature on Hollywood Rd for over 20 years, specialises in modern mainland Chinese art as well as Chinese antique furniture and Southeast Asian ceramics. Just up the hill there's a larger **branch gallery** (Map pp404-5; ☎ 2869 8802; 21-31 Old Bailey St, Soho) with an even bigger collection of modern fine art.

FLOWERS

Flower shops abound in Hong Kong, from tiny stalls at the bottom of Lan Kwai Fong to the flower market up in Mong Kok (see p116).

ANGLO-CHINESE FLORIST Map pp404–5
☎ 2845 4212; Ground fl, 25 D'Aguilar St, Central;
🕑 8am-10pm
If you've been invited to someone's home and you wish to bring flowers – as is *de rigueur* here – stop by Anglo-Chinese. Nobody does them better. There's a newer and much larger **branch** (Map pp404-5; ☎ 2921 2986; Shop B, Ground fl, Winway Bldg, 50 Wellington St, Central) just around the corner.

FOOD & DRINK

In a town that places so much importance on things culinary, you're bound to find some interesting food and drink shops.

AJI ICHIBAN Map pp406–8
☎ 2506 1516; Shop 1037, 10th fl, Times Square, 1 Matheson St, Causeway Bay; 🕑 10am-7pm
One of a chain of shops selling exotic dried fruit (sour plum, 10-scent olive) and the weird dried seafood (shredded squid, eel slices, fish maw) you see at the markets, but here they have English labels and bite-size tasting portions.

FOOK MING TONG TEA SHOP
Map pp400–3
☎ 2521 0337; Shop G3-4, Ground fl, The Landmark, 1 Pedder St, Central; 🕑 10am-7.30pm Mon-Sat, 11am-6pm Sun
Carefully chosen teas and tea-making accoutrements are on sale in this stylish shop. There's tea of various ages and propensities – from gunpowder (HK$8 for 37.55g) to Nanyan Ti Guan Yin Crown Grade (HK$600 for 150g) – and even a 'solitary tea' (which tastes appropriately bitter). There's another **Central branch** (Map pp400-3; ☎ 2295 0368; Shop 1016, 1st fl, IFC Mall, 1 Harbour View St) and a **Tsim Sha Tsui branch** (Map pp412-14; ☎ 2735 1077; Shop 124, 1st fl, Ocean Terminal, Zone C, Harbour City, Canton Rd).

LOCK CHA TEA SHOP Map pp400–3
☎ 2637 0027; 290A Queen's Rd, Central, Sheung Wan; 🕑 11am-7pm
This favourite shop, entered from the start of Ladder St, sells Chinese teas of infinite variety as well as tea sets, wooden tea boxes and well-presented gift packs of various cuppas. You can try before you buy.

OLYMPIA GRAECO-EGYPTIAN COFFEE Map pp404–5
☎ 2522 4653; Ground fl, 24 Old Bailey St, Soho;
🕑 10am-7pm Mon-Sat
This place has been around since, well, Soho wasn't called Soho, and it still grinds the best beans in town.

PONTI FOOD & WINE CELLAR
Map pp412–14
☎ 2721 8770; Shop 3, Ground fl, Hong Kong Pacific Centre, 28 Hankow Rd, Tsim Sha Tsui; 🕑 11am-8pm
Ponti stocks a huge range of both table and vintage wines and periodically holds attractive bin-end sales. There's also a **Central branch** (Map pp400-3; ☎ 2810 1682; Shop 110-111, 1st fl, Prince's Bldg, 10 Chater Rd).

WATSON'S WINE CELLAR Map pp404–5
☎ 2147 3641; Ground fl, Hing Wai Bldg, 36 Queen's Rd, Central; 🕑 10am-10pm
You won't get a lot of advice at this wine emporium, which you enter from the corner of D'Aguilar St and Stanley St, but the choice is enormous. There are half a dozen outlets around the territory including a **Causeway Bay branch** (Map pp406-8; ☎ 2895 6975; Basement, Windsor House, 311 Gloucester Rd).

GEMS, JEWELLERY & OBJETS D'ART

The Chinese attribute various magical qualities to jade, including the power to prevent ageing and accidents. The circular disc with a central hole worn around many necks in Hong Kong represents heaven in Chinese mythology. If you're interested in looking at and possibly purchasing jade, head for the Jade Market in Yau Ma Tei (see p106). Unless you're fairly knowledgeable about jade, though, it's probably wise to limit yourself to modest purchases. Fake jade does indeed exist; the deep green colour associated with some jade pieces can be achieved with a dye pot, as can the white, red, lavender and brown of other pieces. Green soapstone and plastic is also passed off as jade too.

Opals are said to be the best value in Hong Kong because this is where opals are cut. Hong Kong carries a great range of pearls as well. Diamonds aren't generally a good deal, because the world trade is mostly controlled by a cartel. Hong Kong does not have a diamond-cutting industry and must import from Belgium, India, Israel and the USA. Nonetheless, jewellery exporting is big business in Hong Kong, because other gemstones are imported, cut, polished, set and re-exported using cheap labour. In theory, this should make Hong Kong a cheap place to purchase jewellery. In reality, retail prices are only marginally lower than elsewhere. Your only real weapon in getting a decent price is the intense competition in Hong Kong.

A couple of reputable jewellery-shop chains, including King Fook and Tse Sui Luen, will issue a certificate that states exactly what you are buying and guarantees that the shop will buy it back at a fair market price. If you've bought something and want to know its value, you can have it appraised. There is a charge for this service, and some stones (such as diamonds) may have to be removed from their setting for testing. You can contact the **Gemmological Association of Hong Kong** (☎ 2366 6006) for the current list of approved appraisers. One company that does appraisals is **Valuation Services** (☎ 2869 4350; GPO Box 11996, Hong Kong).

The only carved-ivory products being sold here *legally* are those that were manufactured before a 1989 ban came into effect or those made of marine ivory. Ivory retailers must have all sorts of documentation proving where and when the goods were made. Many countries now ban the importation of ivory altogether, no matter how or when it was manufactured.

J'S JEWELLERY Map pp412–14

☎ 2736 8464; Shop 2522, 2nd fl, Ocean Centre, Zone C, Harbour City, Canton Rd, Tsim Sha Tsui; ☺ 10.30am-8.30pm

Hardly a typical Hong Kong jeweller, J's has affordable baubles for those who like glistering without blistering. Most pieces are silver and some feature small diamonds.

KING FOOK Map pp400–3

☎ 2822 8573; 30-32 Des Voeux Rd, Central; ☺ 9.30am-7pm Mon-Sat, 11.30am-7pm Sun

King Fook tends to be more modern than its prime competitor, Tse Sui Luen, with a large range of watches, top-end fountain pens and baubles. There's also a **Tsim Sha Tsui branch** (Map pp412-14; ☎ 2313 2788; Shop G1, Hotel Miramar Shopping Centre, 118-130 Nathan Rd; ☺ 10am-9pm Mon-Fri, 10.30am-9pm Sat, 11.30am-9pm Sun).

KING SING JEWELLERS Map pp412–14

☎ 2735 7021; Shop 14, Ground fl, Star House, 3 Salisbury Rd, Tsim Sha Tsui; ☺ 9.15am-7.30pm Mon-Sat, 9.15am-6.30pm Sun

A long-standing jeweller with a wide selection of diamonds, pearls and gold items. The sales staff are pleasant and not pushy.

LIULIGONGFANG Map pp400–3

☎ 2973 0820; Shop 20-22, Ground fl, Central Bldg, 1-3 Pedder St, Central; ☺ 10am-7.30pm Mon-Sat, 10am-7pm Sun

Exquisite coloured-glass objects, both practical (vases, candle holders, jewellery) and ornamental (figurines, crystal Buddhas, breathtaking sculptures) from a renowned Taiwanese glass sculptor are on display (and sale) here.

OM INTERNATIONAL Map pp412–14

☎ 2366 3421; 1st fl, Friend's House, 6 Carnarvon Rd, Tsim Sha Tsui; ☺ 9.30am-6pm Mon-Sat

This place has an excellent selection of saltwater and freshwater pearls. The staff are scrupulously honest, helpful and friendly.

OPAL MINE Map pp412–14

☎ 2721 9933; Shop G & H, Ground fl, Burlington Arcade, 92-94 Nathan Rd, Tsim Sha Tsui; ☺ 9.30am-7pm

This place, more of a museum than a shop, has

a truly vast selection of Australian opals that makes for fascinating viewing.

SANDY CHUNG Map pp412–14
☎ 2771 0901; Stall No 413-414, Jade Market, Kansu, Canton & Battery Sts, Yau Ma Tei; ⏰ 11am-4pm

Hong Kong's pearl queen has a stall at the Jade Market in Yau Ma Tei heaped with pearls and pearl jewellery. She does bespoke items too.

TSE SUI LUEN Map pp400–3
☎ 2921 8800; Ground fl, Commercial House, 35 Queen's Rd, Central; ⏰ 9.30am-7.30pm Mon-Sat, 10am-7pm Sun

This is the most sparkling of Tse Sui Luen's dozen or so outlets and is worth visiting for its sheer opulence or garishness – however you see it. There's also a **Tsim Sha Tsui branch** (Map pp412-14; ☎ 2926 3210; Shop A & B, Ground fl, 190 Nathan Rd; ⏰ 10am-10.30pm).

LEATHER GOODS & LUGGAGE

Most of what gets sent to the Hong Kong market from China is export quality, but check carefully because there is still a lot of rubbish on sale. All the big brand names like Gucci, Louis Vuitton and Mandarina Duck are on display in Hong Kong department stores (see p249), and you'll find some local vendors in the luggage business. If you're just looking for a casual bag or daypack, try Li Yuen St East and Li Yuen St West in Central or the Stanley market.

BEVERLEY BOUTIQUE Map pp400–3
☎ 2840 1069; Shop 2 & 4, Ground fl, The Cascade, Standard Chartered Bank Bldg, 4-4A Des Voeux Rd, Central; ⏰ 9.30am-7.30pm Mon-Sat, 10.30am-6pm Sun

This little hole-in-the-wall shop has some excellent-quality bags. You'll also find a range of wallets and briefcases in fine and exotic leathers.

MEDICINE

Eschew the McDonald's-style local chains of drugstores like Watson's and Mannings and head for an independent Western pharmacy or traditional Chinese medicine shop.

EU YAN SANG Map pp400–3
☎ 2544 3870; 152-156 Queen's Rd, Central; ⏰ 9am-7.30pm

Traditional Chinese medicine is extremely popular in Hong Kong, both as a preventative and a cure. Eu Yan is probably the most famous practice in town and the doctors speak good English. It's also an interesting place to browse as many of the healing ingredients are displayed and explained.

There's also a **Tsim Sha Tsui branch** (Map pp412-14; ☎ 2366 8321; 11-15 Chatham Rd South).

NEW WING HING DISPENSARY
Map pp400–3
☎ 2523 0980; 85 Queen's Rd, Central (enter from Queen Victoria St); ⏰ 10am-7pm Mon-Sat

New Hing Wing offers personal and informed service.

MUSIC

Hong Kong is very much on the ball when it comes to tunes. CDs sell for around HK$150 and large music stores also stock a wide range of video CDs, DVDs and music and film zines. You can also buy CDs at street markets on Temple St in Yau Ma Tei and Tung Choi St in Mong Kok, but these are usually pirated and the sound quality is poor.

Hong Kong is generally not a great place for Chinese musical instruments. There are a few shops along Wan Chai Rd between Johnston and Morrison Hill roads in Wan Chai, but what is on offer is generally not good value for money. There is one decent place, though, in Tsim Sha Tsui.

Top Five Shopping Experiences – Admiralty, Wan Chai & Causeway Bay

- **Chinese Arts & Crafts** (p249) The best place in town for quality Chinese bric-a-brac.
- **Computer Consultants** (p260) Reliable shop for hard and software.
- **Kung Fu Supplies** (p265) Kit for Bruce Lee wannabes.
- **Mountaineering Services** (p266) Climbing and hiking gear sold by people who indulge.
- **Zone-3** (p266) Extreme sports gear and apparel in designer colours.

HMV Map pp400–3

☎ 2739 0268; 1st fl, Central Bldg, 1-3 Pedder St, Central; ⏰ 9am-10pm

This Aladdin's cave not only has Hong Kong's largest choice of CDs, DVDs and cassettes, but also a great range of music-related literature. There's also a **Causeway Bay branch** (Map pp406-8; ☎ 2504 366; 1st fl, Windsor House, 311 Gloucester Rd) and **Tsim Sha Tsui branch** (Map pp412-14; ☎ 2302 0122; Sands Bldg, 12 Peking Rd; ⏰ 9am-11.45pm).

HONG KONG RECORDS Map pp400–3

☎ 2845 7088; Shop 252, 2nd fl, Pacific Place, 88 Queensway, Admiralty; ⏰ 10am-8pm Sun-Wed, 10am-9pm Thu-Sat

This local outfit has a good selection of Cantonese and international sounds, including traditional Chinese music, jazz, classical and composer music. There's also a **Kowloon Tong branch** (Map pp410-11; ☎ 2265 8299; Shop L1-02, Level 1, Festival Walk, 80-88 Tat Chee Ave).

MONITOR RECORDS Map pp412–14

☎ 2809 4603; Shop 5, Ground fl, Fortune Tce, 4-16 Tak Shing St, Tsim Sha Tsui; ⏰ noon-10pm

One of Hong Kong's only dedicated independent music stores, this is a well-presented operation that specialises in indie and imported sounds you wouldn't even bother asking for anywhere else. Check the local alternative section for a true aural souvenir.

TOM LEE MUSIC COMPANY

Map pp412–14

☎ 2723 9932; 1-9 Cameron Lane, Tsim Sha Tsui; ⏰ 10am-9pm

Tom Lee, with some 20 branches across the territory, is Mr Music in Hong Kong and the man to see if you're looking for a Western musical instruments, including guitars, flutes, recorders and mouth organs.

YUET WAH MUSIC COMPANY Map p415

☎ 2385 6880; 464 Nathan Rd, Tsim Sha Tsui; ⏰ 9.30am-7pm

Yuet Wah is one of the few shops in Hong Kong selling quality Chinese-music instruments at competitive prices – from two-stringed *yi woo* to *goo* (drums) and *bat* (brass cymbals).

SPORTING GOODS

Hong Kong is rife with sporting-goods shops. Much of the equipment on sale is manufactured over the border in the mainland.

Ahluwalia & Sons (Map pp412-14; ☎ 2368 8334; 8C Hankow Rd, Tsim Sha Tsui; ⏰ 10.30am-7.30pm) Established and recently renovated, this store is well stocked with golf gear, tennis racquets, cricket bats, shirts and balls. Haggle away.

Bunn's Divers (Map pp406-8; ☎ 2574 7951; Mezzanine, Chuen Fung House, 188-192 Johnston Rd, Wan Chai; ⏰ 10am-8pm) Masks, snorkels, fins, regulators, tanks – this is Hong Kong's most established diving shop.

Chamonix Alpine Equipment (Map p415; ☎ 2388 3626; 1st fl, On Yip Bldg, 395 Shanghai St, Mong Kok; ⏰ 11am-8pm Mon-Sat, noon-7pm Sun) This Mong Kok shop run by an avid mountaineer has a wide range of camping, hiking and climbing equipment.

Cobra International (Map pp400-3; ☎ 2544 2328; Shop 102, Vicwood Plaza, 199 Des Voeux Rd, Central; ⏰ 10am-7pm Mon-Sat, 1.30-6pm Sun) This a great little shop, with all sorts of hiking accessories and gadgets on offer.

Flying Ball Bicycle Co (Map p415; ☎ 2381 3661; 201 Tung Choi St, Mong Kok; ⏰ 10am-8pm Mon-Sat, 10.30am-7pm Sun) The No 1 choice for locals and expats alike, serious cyclists will find a great selection of bikes and accessories here.

Giga Sports (Map pp412-14; ☎ 2992 0389; Shop 033, Ground fl, Ocean Terminal, Zone C, Harbour City, Canton Rd, Tsim Sha Tsui; ⏰ 10am-8pm) This large store has a wide range of sports equipment, backpacks, clothing and footwear.

Golf Creation (Map pp412-14; ☎ 2721 8860; Shops 12 & 15, Ground fl, Hong Kong Pacific Centre, 28 Hankow Rd, Tsim Sha Tsui; ⏰ 10.30am-8.30pm Mon-Sat, 11am-6.30pm Sun) This shop keeps upwardly mobile Chinese equipped with the kit of their favourite new game.

Hong Kong Mountaineering Training Centre (Map p415; ☎ 2770 6746; Ground & 1st fls, 1K Fa Yuen St) Affiliated with Chamonix, this shop sells climbing equipment and offers classes.

Kung Fu Supplies (Map pp406-8; ☎ 2891 1912; Room 6A, 188-192 Johnston Rd, Wan Chai; ⏰ 10am-7pm Mon-Sat, 1-7pm Sun) If you need to stock up on martial arts accessories or just want to thumb through a decent collection of books, visit this place.

Ming's Sports Company (Map pp412-14; ☎ 2376 1387; Ground fl, 53 Hankow Rd, Tsim Sha Tsui; ⏰ 9.30am-8pm Mon-Sat, 11am-6pm Sun) This is an excellent place to buy gear for diving, tennis or golf.

Mountaineer Supermarket (Map p415; ☎ 2397 0585; 1st fl, 395 Portland St, Mong Kok; ☾ 11am-7pm) This is a great spot for climbing equipment and outfits.

Mountaineering Services (Map pp406-8; ☎ 2541 8876; Ground fl, 271 Gloucester Rd, Causeway Bay; ☾ 11am-7.45pm) This excellent and centrally located shop sells climbing and hiking gear.

Ocean Sky Divers (Map pp412-14; ☎ 2366 3738; 1st fl, 17-19 Lock Rd, Tsim Sha Tsui; ☾ 10.30am-9pm) This new kid on the block is giving Bunn's a run for its money with the whole range of diving and snorkelling gear in stock.

Po Kee Fishing Tackle (Map pp400-3; ☎ 2543 7541; 6 Hillier St, Central; ☾ 10am-7pm Mon-Sat) These guys have got the market cornered – hook, line and sinker – on fishing supplies.

Sunmark Camping Equipment Company (Map pp406-8; ☎ 2893 8553; 1st fl, 121 Wan Chai Rd, Wan Chai; ☾ noon-8pm Mon-Sat, 1.30-7.30pm Sun) Head here for hiking and camping gear and waterproof clothing of all sorts. Enter from Bullock Lane.

Wise Mount Sports (Map p415; ☎ 2787 3011; Ground fl, 75 Sai Yee St, Mong Kok; ☾ 10am-8pm) Specialising in outdoor equipment and clothing, this is another good choice for the enthusiast.

X Game (Map pp404-5; ☎ 2366 9293; Shop A1, Lower Ground fl, Wilson House, 19-27 Wyndham St, Central; ☾ 10am-8pm Mon-Fri, 10am-7pm Sat) This is a choice spot for windsurfing equipment and supplies as well as surfwear. There's also a **Causeway Bay branch** (Map pp406-8; ☎ 2881 8960; 1st fl, 11 Pak Sha Rd).

Zone-3 (Map pp406-8; ☎ 2723 6816; Flat E, 1st fl, Hoi To Bldg, 19 Cannon St, Causeway Bay; ☾ noon-9pm Mon-Sat) This place stocks extreme sports gear and apparel.

WATCHES

Shops selling watches are ubiquitous in Hong Kong and you can find everything from a Rolex to Russian army timepieces and diving watches. As always, you should avoid the shops that do not have price tags on the merchandise. The big department stores and City Chain are fine, but compare prices.

CITY CHAIN Map pp400–3
☎ 2815 3556; Ground fl,
General Commercial Bldg, 156 Des Voeux Rd, Central;
☾ 10am-8pm

City Chain has some two dozen outlets in Hong Kong, including a **Tsim Sha Tsui branch** (Map pp412-14; ☎ 2739 4110; Shop D, Ground fl, 16D Carnarvon Rd).

Watches for sale, Temple Street Night Market (p106)

Sleeping

Sleeping

There are three basic types of accommodation in Hong Kong: deluxe and top-end hotels, some of which count among the finest in the world; adequate but generally uninspiring mid-range hotels; and cramped hostels and guesthouses. Within each category there is a good deal of choice, and you should be able to find a comfortable place to stay.

Accommodation costs are generally higher in Hong Kong than many other Asian cities but cheaper than those in Europe and the USA. It is worth bearing in mind that in recent years many guesthouses and hotels have dropped their prices and that mid-range and even some top-end hotels are offering big discounts (especially to walk-ins during the shoulder and low seasons) on their posted rates, which are the ones listed in this chapter.

Hong Kong's two high seasons are from March to April and October to November, though things can be tight around Chinese New Year (late January or February) as well. Outside these periods, rates tend to drop and little extras can come your way: airport transport, room upgrades, late checkout, free breakfast and complimentary cocktails. If the hotel seems a bit quiet when you arrive, it can be worth asking for an upgrade.

RESERVATIONS

Making an advance reservation for accommodation is not essential, but it can save you a lot of time, hassle and, depending on the season, money. If you fly into Hong Kong without having booked anything, the **Hong Kong Hotels Association** (HKHA; ☎ 2383 8380; www.hkha.org), which deals with some 90 of the territory's hotels, has reservation centres located inside Halls A and B (level 5) of Hong Kong International Airport; look for the sign 'Hotel Reservation and Transportation' after clearing customs. They can book you into a mid-range or top-end hotel room sometimes 50% cheaper than if you were to walk in yourself.

Booking through a travel agent can also garner substantial discounts, sometimes as much as 40% off the walk-in price. If you're in Hong Kong and want to book either a mid-range or luxury hotel, call or email **Phoenix Services Agency** (☎ 2722 7378; phoenix1@netvigator.com) or **Traveller Services** (☎ 2375 2222; fax 2375 2223), both of which are in Tsim Sha Tsui (see p334). You can also try two very good hotel discount websites: www.keiotravel.com and www.planetholiday.com.

HOTELS

Hong Kong's deluxe and top-end hotels are special places, with individual qualities that propel them above the rest. Expect discreet, smooth-as-silk service, large baths, superlative climate control, extensive cable TV with Internet access, dataports, fax machines and prices from about HK$1800 per room. Of course you should be selective in this range – there are plenty of average hotels charging luxury rates too. A few hotels, such as the Peninsula, Mandarin Oriental and Island Shangri-La, offer comfort, amenities and service that compete with or surpass that of the world's finest five-star hotels. All of these hotels have an elegant range of suites for those who want both space and comfort.

Mid-range hotels tend to be generic business and/or tourist establishments with little to distinguish one from another. Rooms are spacious enough (if you don't plan on playing Twister of an evening), and usually have a bath, limited cable TV and room service. Many have business centres and Internet access as well. Sometimes there is not a great deal to distinguish mid-range from top-end hotels, except perhaps a certain ambience and sense of style.

Prices in the mid-range category start anywhere from HK$700 and reach about HK$1800 for a double room. Singles are sometimes priced a bit lower. The average price you're likely to encounter is around HK$1000. At the very least, rooms will have a separate bathroom with shower, bath and toilet, plus air-con, telephone and TV. Most mid-range hotels charge from HK$3 to HK$5 for local calls, which are actually free in Hong Kong.

The majority of Hong Kong's budget hotels – a dying breed – are in Kowloon, with many on or near Nathan Rd. Though most budget hotel rooms are very small, the places listed here are clean and cheerily shabby rather than grim and grimy. Most have telephones, TVs, air-con and private bathrooms; if not, we've said so. Anything under HK$700 should be considered budget.

Hotels in Hong Kong add 10% service and 3% government tax to your bill, something that guesthouses and hostels do not do. If using the services of hotel porters, it's customary to tip them at least HK$10.

CHEAP SLEEPS

Budget accommodation in Hong Kong amounts to guesthouses (many of which offer dormitory accommodation for those on very tight budgets) and official hostels. The **Country & Marine Parks Authority** (☎ 2420 0529; http://parks.afcd.gov.hk) of the Agriculture, Fisheries & Conservation Department maintains some 39 no-frills camp sites in the New Territories and Outlying Islands that are intended for walks and hikers (see p163 for details).

Guesthouses

Dominating the lower end of the market are guesthouses, usually a block of tiny rooms squeezed into a converted apartment or two. Often there are several guesthouses operating out of the same building. Your options are greater if there are two of you; find a double room in a clean guesthouse for HK$150 to HK$200 and your accommodation costs will fall sharply.

Some guesthouses are relatively swish, with doubles for up to HK$400. Depending on the season and location, try to negotiate a better deal as a lot of places will be eager to fill empty rooms. Most guesthouses will at least have a public pay phone if there isn't one in your room. Many offer Internet access as well.

Hostels

The **Hong Kong Youth Hostels Association** (HKYHA; ☎ 2788 1638; www.yha.org.hk; Room 225-227, Block 19, Upper Shek Kip Mei Estate, Shek Kip Mei St) maintains seven hostels affiliated with Hostelling International (HI). It sells HKYHA and HI cards (see p359) and is the place to buy hostel paraphernalia (guidebooks, patches etc). It is possible to buy membership cards at the hostels, but be sure to take along a visa-sized photo and some identification.

All HKYHA hostels have separate toilets and showers for men and women and cooking facilities, including free gas, refrigerators and utensils. They provide blankets, pillows and sheet bag, though you may prefer to take your own.

Prices for a bed in a dormitory range from HK$30 to HK$65 a night, depending on the hostel and whether you are a junior (under 18 years of age) or senior member. If you're not an HKYHA or HI member, you can still stay at the hostels, but you'll be charged HK$30 more per night. After six nights, you automatically become a member.

Only three of the hostels are open daily. Mount Davis (allows check-in from 2pm to 11pm daily; p272); Bradbury Lodge (p287) and Hongkong Bank Foundation SG Davis Hostel (p289) are open to guests from 4pm to 11pm Sunday to Friday and 2pm to 11pm on Saturday. The four other hostels open on Saturday night and the eve of public holidays only. All hostels are shut between 11pm and 7am and checkout is between 7am and noon on weekdays and 7am and 1pm at the weekend. Travellers are not normally permitted to stay more than three days, but this can be extended if the hostel has room.

If making a booking more than three days in advance, ring or email the HKYHA head office. International computerised bookings are also possible. To reserve a bed less than three days before your anticipated stay, call the hostel directly. The phone numbers of the individual hostels are listed in the relevant sections of this chapter.

Remember that theft is a problem in any dormitory-style accommodation. The problem usually comes from your fellow travellers, not the management. Most hostels have lockers available – be sure to use them.

RENTAL ACCOMMODATION

A one-bedroom apartment in the Mid-Levels will cost anywhere from HK$8000 a month. That same apartment will go for somewhat less in Tsim Sha Tsui or Wan Chai. The districts on eastern Hong Kong Island, western Hong Kong Island (eg Kennedy Town) and north-eastern or northwestern Kowloon are more affordable – you may even find a one-bedroom apartment (roughly 60 sq metres) for as little as HK$4000 a month. The most expensive place is the Peak, where rents can easily top HK$100,000 a month.

Apartments are generally rented with little or no furniture, but used furnishings can sometimes be bought from departing foreigners. Check the noticeboards at pubs or around expatriate housing areas. Also check the classified advertisements of the weekend English-language papers and *HK Magazine* or the website www.gohome.com.hk. Estate agents usually take a fee equivalent to one month's rent. Other upfront expenses include a deposit, usually equal to two months' rent, and, of course, the first month's rent in advance.

Long-term accommodation on the Outlying Islands offers far better value than the equivalent on Hong Kong Island or in Kowloon. You can still rent a three-bedroom apartment with a roof terrace on Lamma for less than HK$8000 a month or a shared flat or room for as little as HK$2000 a month. Things to weigh in the balance, however, include transportation costs and the time spent commuting. A one-way ferry trip to Lamma, for example, costs a minimum of HK$10 from Monday to Saturday (HK$14 on Sunday) and takes 20 to 30 minutes.

Those staying in Hong Kong for between one and three months may be interested in serviced apartments: relatively high-priced flats that are rented out for a short term have become more and more common, particularly in and around Central. Some of these are listed in this chapter. Many hotels (eg the Wesley and Wharney in Wan Chai, the Bishop Lei in the Mid-Levels, Caritas Lodge and YMCA International House in Yau Ma Tei, the Regal Riverside in Sha Tin) offer extraordinarily good-value long-term packages, starting as low as HK$7800 a month, depending on the season.

HONG KONG ISLAND

The lion's share of Hong Kong Island's luxury hotels are in Central and Admiralty, and cater to the business market. Wan Chai and Causeway Bay count some top-end hotels as well, but the former is better for mid-range accommodation and the latter for guesthouses, especially on or around Paterson St (though it can't compete with Tsim Sha Tsui for choice). Depending on the season, guesthouses are often struggling to fill beds and rooms; most will offer discounts to anyone staying longer than a couple of nights.

CENTRAL, SOHO & MID-LEVELS

BAUHINIA FURNISHED SUITES

Map pp400–3 *Serviced Apartments*

☎ 2156 3000; www.apartments.com.hk; 119-120 Connaught Rd Central (enter from Man Wah Lane); 1-bedroom HK$11,000-18,000, 2-bedroom HK$16,000-28,000 per month

This very central outfit has more than 100 furnished and serviced flats on offer. Prices usually depend on whether you want an open or enclosed kitchen and include daily cleaning, broadband access, all cooking utensils and crockery and laundry facilities.

BISHOP LEI INTERNATIONAL HOUSE

Map pp400–3 *Hotel*

☎ 2868 0828; fax 2868 1551; 4 Robinson Rd, Mid-Levels; s/d from HK$1080/1280, ste from HK$1880

This 203-room hotel is not sitting in the lap of luxury and is a bit away from the action, but it is a short walk to the Zoological & Botanical Gardens and has its own swimming pool and gym. The rack rates are slashed during the low season, with standard singles and doubles available by the week/month from HK$1700/9000.

GARDEN VIEW INTERNATIONAL HOUSE

Map pp400–3 *Hotel*

☎ 2877 3737; www.ywca.org.hk; gar_view@ ywca.org.hk; 1 MacDonnell Rd, Central; s & d HK$1000-

1200, ste from HK$1800, monthly packages from HK$14,000

Straddling the border of Central and the Mid-Levels, the YWCA-run Garden View (130 rooms) overlooks the Zoological & Botanical Gardens. Accommodation here is plain but comfortable enough (there's good air-con) and there's an outdoor swimming pool. Daily rates drop substantially in the low and shoulder season, typically from HK$550 to HK$925 for a single or doubles and from HK$1385 for a suite.

HANLUN HABITATS

Map pp400–3   *Serviced Apartments*

☎ 2868 0168; www.hanlunhabitats.com; 21st fl, Winway Bldg, 50 Wellington St, Central

This agency has three properties with serviced and furnished flats that are within striking distance of each other in the Mid-Levels and easily accessible via the Central Escalator to Central and Soho. **Daisy Court** (☎ 2533 7200; fax 2810 1870; 31 Shelley St, Mid-Levels) has one-bedroom flats measuring about 45 sq metres for HK$16,500 to HK$19,500 a month, depending on the floor and the view. **Peach Blossom** (☎ 2234 8200; fax 2537 7080; 15 Mosque St, Mid-Levels) has one- and two-bedroom flats of about 50 or 60 sq metres for between HK$19,500 and HK$27,500. **Lily Court** (☎ 2822 9500; fax 2521 9529; 28 Robinson Rd, Mid-Levels) has two-bedroom flats of about 65 square metres for between HK$21,000 and HK$25,500 a month.

ICE HOUSE

Map p404–5   *Serviced Apartments*

☎ 2836 7333; www.icehouse.com.hk; 38 Ice House St, Central; 350/450-sq-m studios HK$650/900 per night & HK$16,000/18,000 per month

In terms of location, this property is one of the coolest deals in Central. Situated next to the Fringe Club above the **Thanying Thai Restaurant**

(room service available; see p175) and up the hill from Lan Kwai Fong, Icehouse has 64 standard and superior open-plan `suites' spread over 13 floors that are bright, colourfully decorated and have a small kitchenette and a work desk with Internet access. It's become a favourite of visiting journalists, who water at the Foreign Correspondents' Club next door. Rates are negotiable, depending on the season.

MANDARIN ORIENTAL

Map pp400–3   *Hotel*

☎ 2522 0111; www.mandarinoriental.com; 5 Connaught Rd Central; s & d HK$2950-4200, ste from HK$5500

The Mandarin, Hong Kong Island's counterpart to the Peninsula, is not architecturally as impressive but has a healthy dose of old-world charm. Styling is subdued, and the décor in some of its 486 rooms may even be a bit outdated, but the service, food and atmosphere are stellar. If you're on business and want to give or get good face, splash out and stay here. You'll be a winner every time. Its restaurant **Vong** (p175) on the 25th floor is renowned as much for its views as for its fusion food, and **The Cafe** is the best hotel coffee shop in town.

RITZ-CARLTON HONG KONG

Map pp400–3   *Hotel*

☎ 2877 6666; ritzrchk@pacific.net.hk; 3 Connaught Rd Central; s & d HK$3200-4200, ste from HK$7800

This is a truly beautiful hotel, with 216 plush guestrooms that manage to be cosy and incredibly distinguished at the same time. Views from harbour-side rooms are – surprise, surprise – breathtaking, but the best view in the hotel might have to be the one from the outdoor pool. Lie back and soak up the skyline.

Ritz-Carlton plaque

Cheap Sleeps

JOCKEY CLUB MOUNT DAVIS HOSTEL

Map pp398–9   *Hostel*

☎ 2817 5715; www.yha.org.hk; Mt Davis Path, Kennedy Town; juniors/seniors HK$40/65, 2-/3-/4-/6-bed r HK$250/260/300/450

Hong Kong Island's only official hostel is a very clean and quiet 169-bed property on the top of Mt Davis in the northwest part of the island. It has great views of Victoria Harbour. The only problem is that it's so far away from everything. There are cooking facilities, a TV and recreation room, and secure lockers. Call ahead to make sure there's a bed before you make the trek out there, however. The hostel is open daily throughout the year; check-in time is from 2pm to 11pm daily. You can check out at noon any day of the week.

There are several ways to reach Jockey Club Mount Davis Hostel, depending on where you're coming from. The easiest way is to catch the hostel shuttle bus from below the **Shun Tak Centre** (200 Connaught Rd, Sheung Wan), from where the ferries to Macau depart, but there are only four departures a day: at 9.30am, 7pm, 9pm and 10.30pm. (They leave the hostel for the Shun Tak centre at 7.30am, 9am, 10am and 10.30pm daily.) Alternatively, you can catch bus No 5A from Admiralty or minibus No 54 from the Outlying Islands ferry terminal and alight at Felix Villas, at the junction of Victoria Rd and Mt Davis Path. From there, walk back 100m. Look for the hostel association sign and follow Mt Davis Path. There is a shortcut to the hostel, which is signposted halfway up the hill. The walk takes 30 to 35 minutes. A taxi from Central costs about HK$30.

YWCA BUILDING SERVICED APARTMENTS

Map pp400–3   *Serviced Apartments*

☎ 2915 2345; www.ywca.org.hk; ywbldg@ywca.org.hk; 38C Bonham Rd, Mid-Levels; s/d/ste from HK$380/720/1760 (min 7 nights), monthly packages HK$4900-6000

This 99-room block of serviced apartments, arguably the only budget 'hotel' on the island, is not in the most convenient of locations, but it's accessible via bus Nos 23, 40 and 40M from Admiralty and Central, open to men and women, and very cheap. There are TVs and phones with IDD in the rooms and a decent place for a light bite, **Frank's Cafe**, on the 1st floor.

ADMIRALTY & WAN CHAI

CHARTERHOUSE HOTEL

Map pp406–8   *Hotel*

☎ 2833 5566, 2591 0000; www.charterhouse.com; 209-219 Wan Chai Rd, Wan Chai; s HK$950-1600, d HK$1500-1700, ste from HK$2000

This 277-room property near the Morrison Hill sports area side of Wan Chai is a pretty good deal. You're almost getting top-end accommodation for mid-range rates. And if you feel up to it, you can always sing for your supper at the **Nightingale** karaoke bar on the 2nd floor.

CONRAD HONG KONG

Map pp400–3   *Hotel*

☎ 2521 3838; www.conrad.com.hk; Pacific Place, 88 Queensway, Admiralty; s & d HK$2850-3350, ste from HK$5700

This elegant but unstuffy 513-room hotel above Pacific Place gets enthusiastic reviews for its attention to business travellers' needs and **Nicholini's** restaurant (see p184). The foyer bar/lounge is a gossipy, corporate hang-out.

DE FENWICK

Map pp406–8   *Serviced Apartments*

☎ 2866 0862; loboinvs@i-cable.com; 42-50 Lockhart Rd, Wan Chai; 1-/2-bedroom flats from HK$9300/16,000 per month

This serviced apartment block in the heart of Wan Chai has one-bedroom flats ranging in size from 425 to 525 sq metres and two-bedroom flats from 610 to 900 sq metres. The rooms are simply but stylishly furnished and there's a full kitchen but there are a lot of extras. For a one-bedroom flat, for example, housekeeping/laundry/cable TV/utilities cost from an additional HK$450/400/328/500.

EMPIRE HOTEL HONG KONG

Map pp406–8   *Hotel*

☎ 2866 9111; fax 2861 3121; 33 Hennessy Rd (enter from Fenwick St), Wan Chai; s & d HK$1400-2000, ste from HK$2200, weekly/monthly packages from HK$4200/15,000

With its sunny staff, pleasant rooms, outdoor swimming pool and fitness centre on the 21st floor terrace – and the **Wu Kong Shanghai Restaurant**, a branch of the more established one of that name in Tsim Sha Tsui (see p202) – the 345-room Empire is a good option and an easy hop from the Hong Kong Convention and Exhibition Centre.

Sleeping – Hong Kong Island

Lockhart Road, Wan Chai

GRAND HYATT HOTEL

Map pp406–8   *Hotel*

☎ 2588 1234; www.hongkong.hyatt.com; 1 Harbour Rd, Wan Chai; s HK$3600-3900, d HK$3850-4150, ste from HK$4300

A recent revamp of the 570-room Grand Hyatt has changed it from a dated dinosaur to a sleek yet sumptuous young(ish) thing. Each room is technologically charged with cyber-concierge and Internet access. Its gourmet Chinese restaurant, **One Harbour Road** (p185) is celebrated and with good reason, and **JJ's** (p230) remains a perennially favourite club.

HARBOUR VIEW INTERNATIONAL HOUSE Map pp406–8   *Hotel*

☎ 2802 0111; www.harbour.ymca.org.hk; 4 Harbour Rd, Wan Chai; tw/d from HK$1200/1600, weekly/monthly packages from HK$2950/8000

Just next door to the Hong Kong Arts Centre and a mere stroll to the Hong Kong Convention and Exhibition Centre and Wan Chai ferry terminal, this YMCA-run, 320-room hotel is excellent value, with simply furnished but adequate rooms, most of which look out over Victoria Harbour, and exceptionally friendly and helpful staff. Twins and doubles drop to as low as HK$600 and HK$700 in the slower months.

ISLAND SHANGRI-LA HONG KONG

Map pp400–3   *Hotel*

☎ 2877 3838; www.shangri-la.com; Pacific Place, Supreme Court Rd, Admiralty; s HK$2100-3450, d HK$2300-3650, ste from HK$5800

The sterile exterior of the 56-storey Shangri-La conceals its swish sophistication; its 565 guestrooms are among the loveliest in Hong Kong. The hotel has a wonderful atrium and bubble lifts link the 39th and 56th floors. Take a quick ride up; you'll catch a glance of the hotel's signature 60m-high painting, a mountainous Chinese landscape said to be the largest in the world. Nice touches include a library where you can take afternoon tea, an outdoor spa and a 24-hour business centre. Among its fabulous outlets are the French restaurant **Petrus** (p185) and **Cyrano's** bar (p223) on the 56th floor.

JW MARRIOTT HONG KONG

Map pp400–3   *Hotel*

☎ 2810 8366; www.marriotthotels.com; Pacific Pl, 88 Queensway, Admiralty; s & d HK$1490-3000, ste from HK$6000

Though business travellers make up a large proportion of the Marriott's clientele (that would explain the almost daily fluctuations in room rates), this 602-room hotel is also popular with shopaholics who can feed their addiction in the Pacific Place shopping mall below. The cheaper city-side rooms actually have views of the hills and not just the next building's air-con infrastructure. The heated outdoor swimming pool is a verdant oasis.

LUK KWOK HOTEL Map pp406–8   *Hotel*

☎ 2866 2166; lukkwok@lukkwokhotel.com; 72 Gloucester Rd, Wan Chai; s HK$1450-1800, d HK$1600-1950, ste from HK$3600

The original Luk Kwok, which featured as the Nam Kok brothel in *The World of Suzie Wong* (see p354), has long since been demolished and it's now a 196-room hotel housed in a not-unattractive modern tower block. There aren't that many frills or outlets here, but the staff are keen and helpful and you're close to the convention centre and Wan Chai's bustle.

NOVOTEL CENTURY HONG KONG

Map pp406–8   *Hotel*

☎ 2598 8888; www.accorhotels.com/asia; 238 Jaffe Rd, Wan Chai; s HK$1600-1900, d HK$1700-2100, ste from HK$3800

The recently renovated, 512-room Century has lost all its tackiness and gained the Novotel surname. The location in Wan Chai is enviable and it has all the mod-cons you could possibly want.

RENAISSANCE HARBOUR VIEW HOTEL Map pp406–8 *Hotel*

☎ 2802 8888; www.renaissancehotels.com; 1 Harbour Rd, Wan Chai; s & d HK$2300-2700, ste from HK$3600

This spectacular, 860-room hotel adjoins the Hong Kong Convention and Exhibition Centre, ensuring steady suit-and-tie custom and marvellous harbour views from 65% of the guestrooms. Deal-cutters are catered to with a well-equipped business centre and some excellent restaurants, such as **Dynasty** (p183) on the 3rd floor. Leisure travellers will appreciate informed concierges and, perhaps, the flashy nightclub **Club Ing** (p230) on the 4th floor. The Harbour View has the largest outdoor pool of any hotel in town (naturally it looks over the harbour) and also has kiddies' pools.

SOUTH PACIFIC HOTEL HONG KONG

Map pp406–8 *Hotel*

☎ 2572 3838; www.southpacifichotel.com.hk; 23 Morrison Hill Rd, Wan Chai; s & d HK$1000-2000, ste from HK$2300

This flash, 293-room mirrored tower has a rather odd location in southern Wan Chai, but you'll be closer to the traditional back streets of the district and to the open green spaces around Queen Elizabeth Stadium, while just minutes from the Wan Chai of recreational fame.

WESLEY HONG KONG

Map pp400–3 *Hotel*

☎ 2866 6688; www.grandhotel.com.hk; 22 Hennessy Rd (enter from Anton St), Wan Chai; s & d HK$700-1800, monthly packages HK$7800-20,000

This central, 22-storey property with 251 rooms offers some of the best deals on the island, but there are very few facilities and the service is cavalier at best. Rates depend on the size of the room: a 26-sq-metre Economy costs HK$700 and a 56-sq-metre Deluxe Plus costs HK$1800. Expect generous discounts off-season.

WHARNEY HOTEL HONG KONG

Map pp406–8 *Hotel*

☎ 2861 1000, 2862 1001; www.wharney.com; 57-73 Lockhart Rd, Wan Chai; s & d HK$1000-1600, ste from

HK$2400, weekly/monthly packages from HK$3360/10,500

Noteworthy for its rooftop swimming pool and outdoor whirlpool, the 358-room Wharney is a mid-range option in the heart of Wan Chai with decent weekly and monthly packages. The so-called Departure Lounge offers a nice respite for weary departing guests awaiting late-night flights.

CAUSEWAY BAY

EXCELSIOR HONG KONG

Map pp406–8 *Hotel*

☎ 2894 8888; www.excelsiorhongkong.com; 281 Gloucester Rd; s & d HK$1900-2700, ste from HK$3800

This 863-room hotel, part of the Mandarin Oriental Group and a Causeway Bay landmark, offers some decent outlets (including the **Dickens Bar**, see p224), fabulous harbour views and convenient shopping. With all the shops in the area, however, the lobby is always a bit of a madhouse.

HONG KONG CATHAY HOTEL

Map pp406–8 *Hotel*

☎ 2577 8211; www.hkcathayhotel.com; 17 Tung Lo Wan Rd; d/tw from HK$550/650, ste from HK$1300

This cheesy but cheap 225-room hotel faces Victoria Park and is within easy walking distance of the restaurants and shopping of Causeway Bay.

METROPARK HOTEL

Map pp406–8 *Hotel*

☎ 2600 1000; www.metroparkhotel.com; 148 Tung Lo Wan Rd; s & d HK$900-1800, ste from HK$2600

This flashy new player managed by a department of China Travel Service makes the most of its easterly location, with 70% of its 243 rooms boasting sweeping city-harbour views through floor-to-ceiling windows. Open-plan rooms offer generous workspace and broadband Internet for those who like to mix business with a bit of pleasure. The 'interactive restaurant', **Cafe du Park**, where you talk Japanese-and-French fusion tastes with the chef, is a hit with guests.

PARK LANE HONG KONG

Map pp406–8 *Hotel*

☎ 2293 8888; www.parklane.com.hk; 310 Gloucester Rd; s & d HK$2000-3600, ste from HK$5000

With restful views of Victoria Park to the east and the shopper's paradise of Causeway Bay to the west, the Park Lane is the perfect hotel for those who want to be both in and out of the action. The most popular outlet at the Park Lane is **Stix** (p231), a club in the basement.

REGAL HONGKONG HOTEL

Map pp406–8   *Hotel*
☎ 2890 6633; www.regalhongkong.com; 88 Yee Wo St; s & d HK$2100-3000, ste from HK$6000

Though double glazing keeps the traffic of busy Yee Wo St at bay, this 425-room Sino-baroque palace dripping with gilt may be a bit too central and, well, shiny for some. The rooftop Roman-style pool – all mosaics and columns supporting nothing – is over the top in the nicest possible way.

ROSEDALE ON THE PARK

Map pp406–8   *Hotel*
☎ 2127 8606; www.rosedale.com.hk; 8 Shelter St; s HK$1180-1480, d HK$1280-1580, s/d ste from HK$1880/1980

This Best Western property opposite Victoria Park touts itself as 'Hong Kong's first cyber boutique hotel'. It's true that each guestroom has broadband Internet access and the rooftop Sky Zone Lounge boasts a 'cyber corner' but 274 rooms in a high rise does not a boutique hotel make. Still, the rooms are attractively appointed and some of its outlets, including **Cheena** (p188), a Chinese halal restaurant, are unusual.

Cheap Sleeps

ALISAN GUEST HOUSE

Map pp406–8   *Guesthouse*
☎ 2838 0762; http://home.hkstar.com/~alisangh; Flat A, 5th fl, Hoito Ct, 275 Gloucester Rd (enter from 23 Cannon St); s/d/tr HK$280/320/390

This excellent and spotlessly clean, family-run place has 21 rooms with air-conditioning, private showers and toilets. The multilingual owners are always willing to please and can organise visas for China.

CAUSEWAY BAY GUEST HOUSE

Map pp406–8   *Guesthouse*
☎ 2895 2013; www.cbgh.net; Flat B, 1st fl, Lai Yee Bldg, 44A-D Leighton Rd; s/d/tr HK$230/270/350

On the south side of Causeway Bay and wedged between a pub and a church, this seven-room guesthouse, entered from Leighton Lane, can get booked up quickly so phone ahead. All rooms are quite clean and have private bathrooms.

CHUNG KIU INN

Map pp406–8   *Guesthouse*
☎ 2895 3304; www.chungkiuinn.com.hk; Flat P, 15th fl, Hong Kong Mansion, 1 Yee Wo St; s/d/tr with private bath from HK$250/30/450, s/d with shared bath from HK$150/250

This hostel, with three dozen rooms spread over the 15th and 9th floors of the same building, is tidy but the rooms are quite small.

Sleeping – Hong Kong Island

Doorman, Renaissance Harbour View Hotel (p274)

It offers some attractive monthly rates: singles with private/shared bath are HK$4500/3500, and doubles with private bath HK$5000.

JETVAN TRAVELLERS' HOUSE

Map pp406–8   *Guesthouse*

☎ 2890 8133; shuikuk@ctimail3.com; Flat A, 4th fl, Fairview Mansion, 51 Paterson St; s/d HK$300/350
This rather cramped but upbeat place offers a 10% discounts for stays longer than a week.

NOBLE HOSTEL

Map pp406–8   *Guesthouse*

☎ 2576 6148; fax 2577 0847; Flat A3, 17th fl, Great George Bldg, 27 Paterson St; s/d with private bath HK$300/360, with shared bath HK$250/300
This is certainly one of the best-value guesthouses on the island. Each one of the 26 rooms is squeaky clean and is equipped with a private phone and air-conditioning.

WANG FAT HOSTEL

Map pp406–8   *Hostel, Guesthouse*

☎ 2895 1015, 9353 0514; www.wangfathostel.com .hk; Flat A2, 3rd fl, Paterson Bldg, 47 Paterson St; s/d/tr with private bath from HK$240/300/350, with shared bath from HK$200/250/300, dm HK$128
This excellent 78-room series of hostels and guesthouses, incorporating the **Hong Kong Hostel** on the same floor and the **Asia Hostel** on the 6th floor, is just about the best deal on Hong Kong Island. It's quiet and clean and most of the rooms have private phones, TVs and fridges. There's also cooking and laundry facilities and a computer room with three terminals offering free Internet access and cooking facilities. The affable owner speaks good English and Japanese, and can organise almost anything for you.

ISLAND EAST

CITY GARDEN HOTEL HONG KONG

Map pp398–9   *Hotel*

☎ 2887 2888; www.citygarden.com.hk; 9 City Garden Rd (enter from cnr Electric Rd & Power St), North Point; s & d HK$1100-2200, ste from HK$2800
Readers rave about this 613-room, exceptionally well-turned-out hotel, not only for its service and generous discounting policy (between HK$516 and HK$888 in the high-season month of November) but also for the nightly **barbecue** (HK$78; ✆ 6.30-9.30pm) in Garden Plus, the covered and leafy terrace fronting the hotel.

GRAND PLAZA APARTMENTS

Map pp398–9   *Serviced Apartments*

☎ 2886 0011; www.grandhotel.com.hk; 2 Kornhill Rd, Quarry Bay; 40/70 sq-m units without kitchenette from HK$8000/11,800, with kitchenette HK$10,800/16,800
This stylish, 248-room place is in the far-flung reaches of Quarry Bay, but is convenient located atop the Cityplaza shopping mall and the Tai Koo Shing MTR station on the Central line. You'll be in Central in 20 minutes.

NEWTON HOTEL HONG KONG

Map pp406–8   *Hotel*

☎ 2807 2333; www.newtonhk.com; 218 Electric Rd, North Point; s & d HK$900-1600, ste from HK$2600
This 363-room hotel on the corner of Oil St is a real find. Sure it's in less-than-sexy North Point, but you can easily walk to Causeway Bay through Victoria Park, and its **Hong Kong Old Restaurant** (p192) has some of the best Shanghainese food in town. The Fortress Hill MTR station on the Central line is just opposite.

KOWLOON

Kowloon is home to an incredible cross section of society, from the well-heeled residents of Kowloon Tong and Ho Man Tin to the tenement dwellers of Mong Kok and Kowloon City. Those with a sense of style and a lot of cash will also be impressed. Hong Kong's poshest hotel, the Peninsula, is here in Tsim Sha Tsui within spitting distance of the infamous Chungking Mansions, a crumbling block stacked with dirt-cheap hostels and guesthouses. Of course, a huge range of other hotels and guesthouse in Kowloon catering to all budgets can be found between these two extremes.

When you mention the words 'hotel' and 'Hong Kong', many people think of the Peninsula, which opened in 1928 and is the matriarch of the territory's luxury hotels. Across from the Pen is the Inter-Continental (formerly the Regent), with a much more modern feel to it and fabulous views. These are Kowloon's two 'face' hotels.

Tsim Sha Tsui East, an area of reclaimed land to the northeast of Tsim Sha Tsui that has yet to come of age, is weighted down with top-end hotels. It's not very convenient for public transport, but most of the hotels here run shuttle buses to Tsim Sha Tsui proper and/or to Central. You'll find many more top-end hotels lining Nathan Rd as it travels north from the harbour.

TSIM SHA TSUI

BP INTERNATIONAL HOUSE

Map pp412–14   *Hotel*

☎ 2376 1111; www.bpih.com.hk; 8 Austin Rd; s HK$990-1450, d HK$1100-1500, s/d ste from HK$2950/3100

This enormous, 535-room hotel, owned by the Scout Association of Hong Kong and named after Robert Baden-Powell, founder of the World Scout Movement, overlooks Kowloon Park from its northwest corner and is relatively convenient to most places of interest in Tsim Sha Tsui. The rooms are dowdy but comfortable; some of the more expensive ones have good harbour views. There are bunk rooms available, making this a good option if you're travelling with kids or in a group. Haggle before you book; prices are often reduced by half depending on the season and day of the week.

EMPIRE KOWLOON

Map pp412–14   *Hotel*

☎ 2685 3000; www.asiastandard.com; 62 Kimberley Rd; s & d HK$1400-2200, ste from HK$2800

This 315-room sister hotel of the Empire on Hong Kong Island (see p272) is a designer hotel boasting a central location and a truly magnificent indoor swimming pool and spa. It's an easy stroll from here to just about anywhere in Tsimsy.

GUANGDONG INTERNATIONAL HOTEL

Map pp412–14   *Hotel*

☎ 2739 3311; www.gdihml.com.hk/gdhk; 18 Prat Ave; s & d HK$850-1300, ste from HK$2200

This mainland-owned pile of grey polished granite has 245 rooms towering over the heart of Tsim Sha Tsui. The **Royal Court** Cantonese restaurant (p200) is recommended.

HOLIDAY INN GOLDEN MILE

Map pp412–14   *Hotel*

☎ 2369 3111; www.goldenmile-hk.holiday-inn.com; 50 Nathan Rd; s HK$1000-1500, d HK$1050-1600, ste from H$3500

The business-like Golden Mile isn't a bad place to base yourself. The 600 guestrooms are Holiday Inn–reliable and you've got the brilliant

Avenue (p196) restaurant on the 1st floor, the schmoozy **Hari's** (p234) bar on the mezzanine level and **Delicatessen Corner** (p203) for all your picnic needs in the basement.

HOTEL INTER-CONTINENTAL HONG KONG

Map pp412–14   *Hotel*

☎ 2721 1211; www.hongkong.intercontinental .com; 18 Salisbury Rd; s & d HK$3100-3700, ste from HK$5500

The Hotel Inter-Continental (formerly the Regent) is to rock stars what the Pen is to royalty. This 514-room hotel, which boasts the finest waterfront position in the territory, tilts at modernity while bowing to colonial traditions, such as a fleet of Rolls Royces, uniformed doormen and incessant brass polishing. The emphasis on service ensures a lot of return custom. The restaurants (eg the superb **Yan Toh Heen**; p202) are excellent and the **Lobby Lounge** bar has gorgeous white leather armchairs and the best view in Hong Kong. Even if you don't stay here, drop by for a drink.

HOTEL MIRAMAR HONG KONG

Map pp412–14   *Hotel*

☎ 2368 1111; www.miramarhk.com; 118-130 Nathan Rd; s & d HK$1200-2000, ste from HK$3800

This 525-room landmark (and very central hotel) has been renovated and reclad and looks like a new property. It has some fine outlets, including the restaurant **Dong** (p197), and the Miramar Shopping Centre is just across Kimberley Rd.

HYATT REGENCY

Map pp412–14   *Hotel*

☎ 2311 1234; www.hongkong.hyatt.com; 67 Nathan Rd (enter from Peking Rd); s HK$1300-2100, d HK$1500-2300, s/d ste from HK$1800/2000

The Hyatt, on the 'wrong' side of Nathan Rd and sitting atop a sad little shopping arcade, is lower priced than most of its neighbours in a similar category and a relaxed – almost chaotic at times – kind of hotel. Its **Chinese Restaurant** (p196) is justly revered and one of the territory's most attractive bars, **Chin Chin**, a riot of Chinese boxwood wall carvings and bird cages, is on the lobby floor.

IMPERIAL HOTEL Map pp412–14 *Hotel*

☎ 2366 2201; www.imperialhotel.com.hk; 30-34 Nathan Rd; s HK$950-1700, d HK$1100-2000

The 223 unrenovated rooms with faded pink bathrooms are prim, proper and squeaky clean. The hotel is so well located that the noise of Nathan Rd leaks right into the street-facing rooms – light sleepers should request a back room.

KIMBERLEY HOTEL Map pp412–14 *Hotel*

☎ 2723 3888; www.kimberleyhotel.com.hk; 28 Kimberley Rd; s HK$1100-1750, d HK$1200-1850, ste from HK$2150

The 546-room Kimberley Hotel isn't even slightly glam, but it's one of the better mid-range hotels in Tsim Sha Tsui. You'll find assured staff and good rooms and facilities, including golf nets and a fabulous hot and cold spa bath. The lobby, a palm- and pond-filled oasis up from the bustle, is on the 2nd floor.

KOWLOON HOTEL HONG KONG

Map pp412–14 *Hotel*

☎ 2929 2888; www.peninsula.com; 19-21 Nathan Rd; s HK$1300-2550, d HK$1400-2650, ste from HK$3600

Part of the Peninsula stable, the 736-room Kowloon Hotel has an `also ran´ feel about it, with its comically ostentatious lobby and fabulous views of the back of the Peninsula Hotel. Nevertheless, the hotel is popular for its unflappable service, decent rooms and the wonderful **Wan Loong Court** restaurant (p201) in the basement.

MARCO POLO HONG KONG HOTEL

Map pp412–14 *Hotel*

☎ 2113 0088; www.marcopolohotels.com; Harbour City, 3 Canton Rd; s HK$2300-3530, d HK$2400-3630, ste from HK$4660

The 665-room Marco Polo Hong Kong is the linchpin in the Marco Polo Hotel group's Canton Rd trio, which includes the Marco Polo Gateway and the Marco Polo Prince – both of which are in the Harbour City complex to the north. The Marco Polo Hong Kong Hotel is closest to the Star Ferry and highest priced; it has an outdoor pool and plenty of shopping in the attached mall. The 440-room **Marco Polo Gateway** (13 Canton Rd; s HK$1950-2200, d HK$2050-2300, ste from HK$3450) is a flash hotel with good business facilities, while the smaller **Marco Polo Prince** (23 Canton Rd; s HK$1950-2550, d HK$2050-2650, ste from HK$3450), at the northern end of Harbour City, is the slick little sister, with 396 smart rooms. If you stayed in one of these hotels, you could do all your shopping, eating and entertaining in Harbour City and never go outside.

NEW WORLD RENAISSANCE HOTEL

Map pp412–14 *Hotel*

☎ 2369 4111; www.renaissancehotels.com/hkgnw; 22 Salisbury Rd; s & d HK$1700-2000, ste from HK$3300

This 543-room Tsim Sha Tsui stalwart is popular with European group tours. Despite its proximity to the water, don't expect harbour views; they're only available from the **Panorama** restaurant on the 4th floor. There's an outdoor pool set in a huge tropical garden.

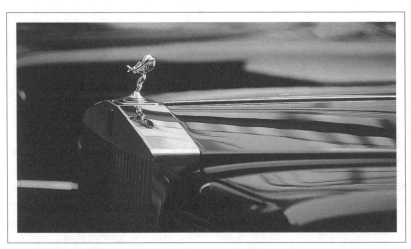

PARK HOTEL Map pp412–14 *Hotel*
☎ 2366 1371; www.parkhotel.com.hk; 61-65 Chatham Rd South; s HK$900-1500, d HK$1000-1600, ste from HK$2200

The recently renovated Park is busy and congenial with 430 rooms of good size. Family suites are available. The history and science museums are just over the road; the hustle of Granville Rd is a block away.

PENINSULA HONG KONG
Map pp412–14 *Hotel*
☎ 2920 2888; www.peninsula.com; Salisbury Rd; s & d HK$3000-4900, ste from HK$5600

Lording it over the southern tip of Kowloon, Hong Kong's finest hotel evokes colonial elegance and actually resembles a huge throne. Some 300 classic European-style rooms boast faxes, CD and DVD players, and marble bathrooms. Many rooms in the Pen's 20-storey addition offer spectacular harbour views; in the original building, you'll have to make do with interior sumptuousness. Some of the outlets, such as the French restaurant **Gaddi's** (p197), the fusion **Felix** (p197) and the Cantonese **Spring Moon** (p200) are the best eating spots of their class in the territory.

RAMADA HOTEL KOWLOON
Map pp412–14 *Hotel*
☎ 2311 1100; www.ramadahongkong.com; 73-75 Chatham Rd South; s & d HK$1300-2050, ste from HK$2800

The Ramada, with 205 rooms, has definitely seen better days (decades?), but the location, within striking distance of Kowloon's most important sights as well as all shopping, wining and dining possibilities, is excellent.

ROYAL PACIFIC HOTEL & TOWERS
Map pp412–14 *Hotel*
☎ 2736 1188; www.royalpacific.com.hk; China Hong Kong City, 33 Canton Rd; s & d HK$850-2100, ste from HK$2200

Choose between cheaper rooms in the hotel wing or flashier rooms in the harbour-facing tower – some 675 in total. The location is good: there's a walkway to Kowloon Park, leading onto Nathan Rd and the MTR station. At the back, the hotel is connected to the ferry terminal from where boats sail to Macau and China. It's also a mere skip to the shopping overkill of Harbour City. You'll find reception on the 2nd floor.

Royal Pacific Hotel

ROYAL WINDSOR HOTEL
Map pp412–14 *Hotel*
☎ 2739 5665; www.windsorhotel.com.hk; 39 Kimberley Rd; s & d HK$950-1800, ste from HK$2600

This 166-room hotel is ideally situated for anyone intending to do a lot of shopping in Tsimsy. The hotel wins an award for the inspired name of its lounge bar: **Bonkers**.

SHERATON HONG KONG HOTEL & TOWERS Map pp412–14 *Hotel*
☎ 2369 1111; www.sheraton.com/hongkong; 20 Nathan Rd; s HK$2400-3600, d HK$2600-3800, ste from HK$3600 (hotel) and HK$4600 (towers)

This very American 780-room hostelry (the ground floor is the 1st floor, escalators travel on the right) at the start of Nathan Rd is as central as you'll find in Tsim Sha Tsui. Choose between rooms in the hotel or in the towers, which offer superior harbour views (and higher prices). The **Sky Lounge** (p226) on the 18th floor is worth a visit for the stunning harbour views. Reception is on the 2nd floor.

STANFORD HILLVIEW HOTEL
Map pp412–14 *Hotel*
☎ 2722 7822, 2313 7031; www.stanfordhillview.com; 13-17 Observatory Rd (enter from Knutsford Tce); s & d HK$880-1580, ste from HK$2380

This 163-room hotel is a decent place, set back from the Nathan Rd in a quiet, leafy little corner of Tsim Sha Tsui but close to the food, fun and frolicking of Knutsford Terrace. The rooms are forgettable but fine.

Cheap Sleeps

Say 'budget accommodation' and 'Hong Kong' in one breath and everyone thinks of **Chungking Mansions** (36-44 Nathan Rd, Tsim Sha Tsui), a place like no other in the world. This huge, ramshackle high-rise dump in the heart of Tsim Sha Tsui caters for virtually all needs – from finding a bed and a curry lunch to buying a backpack and getting your hair cut.

You may be put off by the undercurrent of sleaze and the peculiar odours – a potent mixture of cooking fat, incense and shit – but don't seek sanctuary in the lifts; they're like steel coffins on cables. Perhaps the best introduction to Chungking is Wong Kar Wai's cult film *Chung-king Express* (1994), which captures all the sleaze in a haunting series of stories.

For years there had been talk about tearing down this eyesore and fire trap. A crackdown on fire-safety violations finally came at the end of 1993, and many guesthouses were forced to shut down. Others survived by upgrading and installing smoke alarms, sprinklers and walls made of fireproof material.

Much of the character of Chungking Mansions has changed. Many of the guesthouses now serve as long-term boarding houses for workers from developing countries in the subcontinent and Africa, and matchbox rooms are often occupied by two, three or even four people. Backpackers have started migrating to guesthouses in other buildings, but Chungking Mansions is still the cheapest place to stay in Hong Kong and the place to meet fellow travellers and zany characters. One thing travellers should really guard against is drugs; a few grams of hashish – and you'll be offered it frequently – in your backpack could leave you in a lot of trouble.

The entrance to Chungking Mansions is via Chungking Arcade, a parade of shops that faces Nathan Rd. You will find lifts labelled A to E with hostels in each block listed. There are only two cramped and overworked lifts for each 17-storey block, and long queues form at 'rush hour'. Otherwise there's always the less-than-salubrious stairs, which support a large amount of wildlife, including a rare species of aggressive flying cockroach. Be grateful for the stray cats as they keep the rats in check.

Despite the dilapidated appearance, most of the little guesthouses are OK – generally clean and often quite comfortable, though rooms are usually the size of cupboards. Standards do, however, vary; your best bet is to opt for the hotels that have a high percentage of foreign travellers.

Bargaining for a bed or room is always possible, though you won't get very far in the height of the season. You can often negotiate a cheaper price if you stay more than, say, a week, but never try that on the first night – stay one night and find out how you like it before handing over more rent. Once you pay, there are no refunds. Always be sure to get a receipt; paying for a room in advance so that you can have it on a certain day is not advised.

Rooms will typically come with air-conditioning and TV, although the phones are often communal and located in the lobby. Local telephone calls are free from residential phones in Hong Kong, so be suspicious if staff charge you. Many guesthouses can get you a Chinese visa quickly, and some have laundry service. Also, be prepared for varying levels of English fluency among guesthouse owners and concierges. Mobile phone numbers have been included here as many of the guesthouse owners and managers engage in all sorts of other 'beezness' and often lock their establishment during the days.

Chungking Mansions is also a cheap place to eat Indian and other subcontinental food (see p202). The ground floor is filled with shops selling everything imaginable, though the mezzanine floor has better deals. You can pick up all sorts of electrical goodies, such as alarm clocks and radios, made on the mainland and dirt cheap.

Chungking Mansions is not the only budget block in Tsim Sha Tsui. **Mirador Mansion** (Map pp412-14; 58-62 Nathan Rd, Tsim Sha Tsui), above an arcade of that name between Mody and Carnarvon Rds, is a scaled-down version of Chungking Mansions, but considerably cleaner and roomier. Much of the backpacker clientele has moved here in recent years, with the result that there can be heavy queues for the lifts during peak hours. **Golden Crown Court** (Map pp412-14; 66-70 Nathan Rd, Tsim Sha Tsui) opposite the southeast corner of Kowloon Park, has undergone a transformation in recent years and now offers a host of clean, smart guesthouses.

CHUNKING HOUSE

Map pp412–14   *Guesthouse*

☎ 2366 5362; chungkinghouse@yahoo.com.hk; 4th & 5th fls, A Block, Chungking Mansions, 36-44 Nathan Rd; s HK$200-220, d HK$300-360

This place covering two floors is pretty swish by the standards of Chungking Mansions.

COSMIC GUEST HOUSE

Map pp412–14   *Hostel, Guesthouse*

☎ 2739 4952; cosmic-gh@ctimail3.com; Flat A1-A2, F1-F4, 12th fl, Mirador Mansion, 58-62 Nathan Rd; dm HK$60, s & d HK$160-200, big d HK$220-24

This is a very clean, recently refurbished and very quiet guesthouse with big and bright rooms and a very helpful owner. The security is top-grade.

DRAGON INN

Map pp412–14   *Guesthouse*

☎ 2368 2007; fax 2724 2841; dragoninn@asiaonline .net; Flat B3 & B5, 3rd fl, B Block, Chungking Mansions, 36-44 Nathan Rd; s/d/tr HK$150/200/270

This super clean and large (21 rooms) place doubles as the Dragon International Travel Agency, with cheap air tickets and other services available in-house.

FIRST-CLASS GUEST HOUSE

Map pp412–14   *Guesthouse*

☎ 2724 0595; fax 2724 0843; Flat D1, 16th fl, Mirador Mansion, 58-62 Nathan Rd; s/d HK$120/180

While its name might be a little ambitious, the First-Class Guest House is clean and bright and the staff friendly. All rooms have attached bath.

GARDEN GUEST HOUSE

Map pp412–14   *Guesthouse*

☎ 2368 0981, 9057 5265; Flat C5, 16th fl, C Block, Chungking Mansions, 36-44 Nathan Rd; s HK$150

This is a clean place much favoured by backpackers. They have a **branch** (☎ 2366 0169; Flat C5, 7th floor) in the same block.

GARDEN HOSTEL

Map pp412–14   *Hostel, Guesthouse*

☎ 2311 1183; fax 2721 2085; Flat F4, 3rd fl, Mirador Mansion, 58-62 Nathan Rd; dm HK$60, s & d with shower HK$180, d with bath HK$300

This place, the original Garden Hostel in Mirador Mansion, is owned by the irrepressible Sam `Mr Kung Fu' Lau, who also runs a martial arts school on Nathan Rd (see p241). It's a great place for meeting other travellers and the open terrace is a delight on a warm evening. There are laundry facilities, the lockers are like Fort Knox and the staff speak excellent English.

GOLDEN CROWN GUEST HOUSE

Map pp412–14   *Hostel Guesthouse*

☎ 2369 1782; fax 2368 1740; Flats B2 & H, 5th fl, Golden Crown Court, 66-70 Nathan Rd; dm HK$80, s/d HK$250/280

This clean place is one of the better guesthouses in Golden Crown Court and has a friendly owner. The dormitory has five beds.

HUNG KIU GUEST HOUSE

Map pp412–14   *Guesthouse*

☎ 2312 1505, 9370 2325; fax 2311 4258; Flat C3, 8th fl, Mirador Mansion, 58-62 Nathan Rd; s HK$120, d HK$180-200

This is a relatively new and clean place with a friendly and helpful young Chinese manager.

KYOTO GUEST HOUSE

Map pp412–14   *Guesthouse*

☎ 2721 3574, 9077 8297; Flat A8, 15th fl, A Block, Chungking Mansions, 36-44 Nathan Rd; d & tw without/with shower from HK$100/160, s without shower HK$80

This guesthouse, run by Mrs Kam, is basic but comfortable.

Chungking Mansions (p280)

LILY GARDEN HOSTEL

Map pp412–14   *Hostel, Guesthouse*

☎ 2724 2612; lilygarden@fourseasons88.com; Flat A9, 3rd fl, Mirador Mansion, 58-62 Nathan Rd; dm HK$60, s HK$150-200, d HK$200-300, tr HK$300-350

Lily Garden has small but clean rooms. It is part of a group of guesthouses under the same management as the **New Osaka Guest House** (☎ 2724 2612; Flat F2, 5th fl) also in Mirador Mansion.

LUCKY GUESTHOUSE

Map pp412–14   *Guesthouse*

☎ 2367 3522, 9373 8779; fax 2367 3325; Flat A11, 7th fl, Mirador Mansion, 58-62 Nathan Rd; s/d/tr HK$130/180/250

This place is clean and tidy and the older owner speaks excellent English.

MAHARAJA-RANJEET GUEST HOUSE

Map pp412–14   *Guesthouse*

☎ 2368 9943; fax 3422 8501; Flats C1-C6, 4th fl, C Block, Chungking Mansions, 36-44 Nathan Rd; s with shared bath HK$80-100, d with private bath HK$150-180

This guesthouse is nicely decorated and run by an affable Indian guy.

MAN HING LUNG HOTEL

Map pp412–14   *Guesthouse*

☎ 2722 0678; http://home.hkstar.com/~mhlhotel; Flat F2, 14th fl, Mirador Mansion, 58-62 Nathan Rd; s HK$120-150, d HK$150-200, tr HK$210-240

This decent place, which likes to call itself a hotel, has clean rooms, a good atmosphere and Internet access. If you need a roommate, the very friendly manager, Mr Chan, will put you in with another traveller for HK$80.

NEW SHANGHAI GUEST HOUSE

Map pp412–14   *Guesthouse*

☎ 2311 2515; Flat D2, 16th fl, D Block, Chungking Mansions, 36-44 Nathan Rd; s/d HK$150/260

This is an old-style guesthouse run by pleasant Mrs Cheung. It's clean and there's a laundry service.

PARK GUEST HOUSE

Map pp412–14   *Guesthouse*

☎ 2368 1689; fax 2367 7889; Flat A1, 15th fl, A Block, Chungking Mansions, 36-44 Nathan Rd; s with shared/ private bath HK$120/150, d HK$150/200

This friendly guesthouse is clean and rooms have air-con.

PEKING GUEST HOUSE

Map pp412–14   *Guesthouse*

☎ 2723 8320, 9464 3684; fax 2366 6706; Flat A1-A2, 12th fl, A Block, Chungking Mansions, 36-44 Nathan Rd; s HK$120-150, d HK$160-240, tr HK$260

Peking has friendly management, the place is spotless and all rooms have a bathroom.

SALISBURY Map pp412–14   *Hostel, Hotel*

☎ 2268 7888; www.ymcahk.org.hk; 41 Salisbury Rd; dm HK$210, s from HK$630, d HK$730-930, ste from HK$1200

If you can manage to book a room at the YMCA-run Salisbury, you'll be rewarded with professional service and excellent exercise facilities, including a six-lane swimming pool, fitness centre and climbing wall. The 365 rooms and suites are comfortable but simple so keep your eyes on the harbour; that view would cost you at least five times as much at the Peninsula next door. The four-bed dormitory rooms on the 9th floor are a bonus, but there are restrictions: check-in is at 2pm and check-out at 11am; no-one can stay more than seven consecutive nights; walk-in guests aren't accepted if they've been in Hong Kong for more than 10 days.

SEALAND HOUSE

Map pp412–14   *Guesthouse*

☎ 2368 9522; www.sealandhouse.com.hk; Flat D, 8th fl, Majestic House, 80 Nathan Rd (enter from Cameron Rd); s/d HK$250/280

This seven-room place towering above Nathan Rd is small but clean and very bright. It's a good choice over the guesthouses in Mirador or Chungking Mansions.

STAR GUEST HOUSE

Map pp412–14   *Guesthouse*

☎ 2723 8951; www.starguesthouse.com; Flat B, 6th fl, 21 Cameron Rd; s without/with shower HK$180/250, d without/with shower HK$200/250, tr with shower HK$350

This excellent guesthouse and its sister property, the **Lee Garden Guest House** (☎ 2367 2284; charliechan@iname.com; 8th fl, D Block, 36 Cameron Rd), just up the road with a total of 40 rooms, are owned and run by the charismatic Charlie Chan, who can arrange most things for you, including China visas (HK$250) delivered in a day. Long-term stayers get good discounts.

TOM'S GUEST HOUSE

Map pp412–14   *Guesthouse*

☎ 2367 9258, 2722 6035, 9194 5923; fax 2366 6706;
Flat B7, 16th fl, B Block, Chungking Mansions, 36-44
Nathan Rd; s HK$130-160, d HK$150-250

Tom's, a clean, friendly and popular place, can be entered from **C Block** (Flat C1, 16th fl). There's another large branch in **A Block** (☎ 2722 4956; Flat A5, 8th fl) so you'll always find a room here.

TRAVELLERS HOSTEL

Map pp412–14   *Hostel, Guesthouse*

☎ 2368 7710; mrspau@yahoo.com.hk; Flat A1-A4,
16th fl, A Block, Chungking Mansions, 36-44 Nathan Rd;
dm HK$65, s HK$90, d without/with bath HK$120/130

This popular dormitory is a landmark in this building and cooking facilities, cable TV and student discounts are available. The Travellers Hostel is probably the best place to meet fellow travellers in Chungking Mansions.

WELCOME GUEST HOUSE

Map pp412–14   *Guesthouse*

☎ 2721 7793, 9838 8375; www.thewelcomeguest
house.net; Flat A5, 7th fl, A Block, Chungking Mansions,
36-44 Nathan Rd; s with shared shower HK$100, s with
shower HK$120-150, d with shower HK$180-200

This place is a cut above the rest in Chungking Mansions and its name says it all. Owner John Wah is exceptionally friendly, speaks excellent English and runs a small souvenir shop and gem showroom on site. What's more, Welcome has a laundry service.

YAN YAN GUEST HOUSE

Map pp412–14   *Guesthouse*

☎ 2366 8930, 9489 3891; fax 2721 0840; Flat E1,
8th fl, E Block, Chungking Mansions, 36-44 Nathan Rd;
s/d HK$130/150

This is one of the last Chinese-owned guesthouses in the overwhelmingly Subcontinental E Block of Chungking Mansions. The very swish **New Yan Yan Guesthouse** (☎ 2723 5671; Flat E5, 12th fl) in the same block is under the same management.

TSIM SHA TSUI EAST & HUNG HOM

GRAND STANFORD INTER-CONTINENTAL Map pp412–14 *Hotel*

☎ 2721 5161; www.hongkong.intercontinental.com;
70 Mody Rd, Tsim Sha Tsui East; s HK$2200-3100,
d HK$2400-3300, ste from HK$4100

This 579-room palace offers excellent discounts, depending on the season and the day of the week. Part of its harbour view is marred by the unsightly Hung Hom Bypass.

HARBOUR PLAZA

                                     Hotel

☎ 2621 3188; www.harbour-plaza.com; 20 Tak Fung
St, Hung Hom; s HK$2200-2600, d HK$2350-2750,
ste from HK$4200

This massive 411-room hotel on the waterfront in less-than-desirable Hung Hom is owned by property magnate Li Ka-shing and is where mainland honchos, like former Premier Jiang Zemin, stay when they visit Hong Kong. It's surrounded by shopping malls.

HOTEL NIKKO HONGKONG

Map pp412–14   *Hotel*

☎ 2739 1111; www.hotelnikko.com.hk; 72 Mody
Rd, Tsim Sha Tsui East; s & d HK$2100-3400, ste from
HK$5500

Another almost faceless Tsim Sha Tsui East hotel, this time with 444 guestrooms and loads of Japanese tourists. It's not a very efficiently run place, but the harbour views are stunning.

KOWLOON SHANGRI-LA

Map pp412–14   *Hotel*

☎ 2721 2111; www.shangri-la.com; 64 Mody Rd,
Tsim Sha Tsui East; s HK$2450-3600, d HK$2650-3800,
ste from HK$4300

This 725-room extravaganza is not nearly as swish as its sister hotel in 'new' Wan Chai, but the views and its eight restaurants, including the superb French **Margaux** (p99) and the Japanese **Nadaman** (p199), are stunning. We love the enormous murals of imperial Chinese scenes in the lobby.

LANGHAM HOTEL HONG KONG

Map pp412–14   *Hotel*

☎ 2375 1133; www.gehotel.com; 8 Peking Rd; s & d
HK$2100-2600, ste from HK$4000

What was called the Great Eagle Hotel for the first two years after its grand opening in 2001 is now the 487-room Langham, Hong Kong's newest five-star hotel. It has some stunning outlets of its own and is just round the corner from the restaurants and bars of Ashley and Peking Rds.

REGAL KOWLOON HOTEL

Map pp412–14   *Hotel*

☎ 2722 1818; www.regalhotel.com; 71 Mody Rd,

Tsim Sha Tsui East; s & d HK$1100-2700, ste from HK$4000

This 600-room hotel in a block rising up for 15 storeys is a bargain by Tsim Sha Tsui East standards, but the blush-pink décor that seems to sneak into every room and outlet may grate.

ROYAL GARDEN Map pp412–14 *Hotel*

☎ 2721 5215; www.rghk.com.hk; 69 Mody Rd, Tsim Sha Tsui East; s HK$2100-2600, d HK$2250-2750, s/d ste from HK$3700/3850

The 442-room Royal Garden, often overlooked, gets our vote for being the best-equipped hotel in Tsim Sha Tsui East and one of the territory's most attractive options. From the chic blonde-wood-and-chrome lobby to the rooftop sports complex (25m pool, putting green and tennis court with million dollar views), the Royal Garden kicks goals. **Sabatini** (p200) on the 3rd floor is one of the best Italian restaurants in Hong Kong, and the **Martini Bar** (p226) is a sublime place for something shaken or stirred.

YAU MA TEI & MONG KOK

DORSETT SEAVIEW HOTEL

Map p415 *Hotel*

☎ 2782 0882; www.dorsettseaview.com.hk; 268 Shanghai St, Yau Ma Tei; s HK$880-1280, d HK$1280-1580, ste from HK$2400

This hotel does a big trade in group tours from China. The 257 guestrooms in this tall, thin building are fine, and the Temple St and Jade Markets and Nathan Rd retail area are all within easy reach. The Tin Hau temple is practically outside the front door.

EATON HOTEL Map pp412–14 *Hotel*

☎ 2782 1818; www.eaton-hotel.com; 380 Nathan Rd (enter from Pak Hoi St), Yau Ma Tei; s & d HK$1000-1600, ste from HK$2000

This 468-room hotel in the huge New Astor Plaza complex has a grand lobby and a number of fine outlets, including the glass-fronted **Planter's Bar** (☎ 2710 1866; ☯ 5pm-1am Mon-Thu, 5pm-2am Fri-Sat; happy hour 5-9pm) on the 4th floor (where you'll also find reception).

HOTEL CONCOURSE HONG KONG

Map p415 *Hotel*

☎ 2397 6683; www.hotelconcourse.com.hk; 22 Lai Chi Kok Rd, Mong Kok; s & d HK$800-1480, ste HK$2380

This 430-room hotel is run by China Travel Service. It's popular with tourists from mainland China, so don't expect service with a smile. The place scrambles at the edge of stylishness, but ends up excelling at adequacy. The neighbourhood is loud but you're very close to the Prince Edward MTR if you need an escape hatch. The rates are negotiable.

MAJESTIC HOTEL Map pp412–14 *Hotel*

☎ 2781 1333; www.majestichotel.com.hk; 348 Nathan Rd (enter from Saigon St), Yau Ma Tei; s & d HK$950-1850, ste from HK$3000

This 387-room hotel housed in a 15-storey glass tower is just north of the Jordan MTR station. Reception is on the 1st floor. We've had complaints about the loud dance club here.

METROPOLE HOTEL Map p410–11 *Hotel*

☎ 2761 1711; www.metropole.com.hk; 75 Waterloo Rd, Yau Ma Tei; s & d HK$900-1700, ste from HK$3500

This 487-room baroque palace managed by a China Travel Service department is a bit out of the way, but has some excellent facilities and outlets, including a huge outdoor swimming pool and the **Palm Court** coffee shop (see p203). Check the 50m-wide mural *Magnificent China* rising above the podium.

NATHAN HOTEL Map pp412–14 *Hotel*

☎ 2388 5141; nathanhk@hkstar.com; 378 Nathan Rd (enter from Pak Hoi St), Yau Ma Tei; s HK$500-950, d HK$600-1300, tr HK$780-1450, ste from HK$1200

The Nathan Hotel is surprisingly quiet and pleasant; even the cheapest of its 185 rooms are spacious, clean and serene. It's in a good location, right near the Jordan MTR station and Temple St, and we like the moustachioed and turbaned doorman.

NEWTON HOTEL KOWLOON

Map p415 *Hotel*

☎ 2787 2338; www.newtonkln.com; 66 Boundary St, Mong Kok; s & d HK$550-800

If you don't mind being in a noisy neighbourhood, the Prince Edward MTR is an easy five-minute walk from this 175-room hotel and you're close to the Mong Kok market, clothes stalls and noodle shops. The hotel itself is reasonable for the price – no surprises – but is not quite of the same standard as the **Newton Hotel Hong Kong** in North Point (see p276).

PRUTON PRUDENTIAL HOTEL

Map pp412–14   *Hotel*

☎ 2311 8222; www.prutonhotel.com; 222 Nathan Rd, Yau Ma Tei; s & d HK$1000-2000, ste from HK$2700

This 437-room, 17-storey glass-tower hotel is very much in the centre of the action and counts some 100 boutiques in the massive shopping mall below it. You may never have to leave the building. Reception is on the 2nd floor.

ROYAL PLAZA HOTEL Map p415   *Hotel*

☎ 2928 8822; www.royalplaza.com.hk; 193 Prince Edward Rd West, Mong Kok; s & d HK$1000-1680, ste from HK$2800

The plushness is a bit overdone, but the 469-room Plaza is comfortable and central; the bird and flower markets are on the other side of Prince Edward Rd. The heated no-steam bathroom mirrors are a stroke of genius and the large outdoor pool is a lounge lizard's nirvana. The Mong Kok KCR station is accessible through the adjoining Grand Century Place shopping centre, making this a handy spot if you've business in the New Territories or China. Its Japanese restaurant, **Sakurada** (p203), is excellent.

SHAMROCK HOTEL

Map pp412–14   *Hotel*

☎ 2735 2271; www.shamrockhotel.com.hk; 223 Nathan Rd, Yau Ma Tei; s HK$550-1250, d HK$750-1450, ste from HK$1500

The Shamrock offers fantastic value for its category and location. The beds can be a bit spongy but the 158 guestrooms are well sized, clean and airy, and there are excellent kitsch lounges outside the lifts. Jordan MTR is right outside the door and there's a cheap, decent restaurant on site.

STANFORD HOTEL Map p415   *Hotel*

☎ 2781 1881; www.stanfordhongkong.com; 118 Soy St, Mong Kok; s HK$780-1480, d HK$830-1480

This 184-room hotel is equidistant from the Mong Kok MTR and KCR stations and a hop, skip and a jump to the bird and flower markets.

YMCA INTERNATIONAL HOUSE

Map p415   *Hostel Guesthouse*

☎ 2771 9111; www.bookings.org/ymca.hk.en.html; 23 Waterloo Rd, Yau Ma Tei; dm HK$220, s & d HK$780-12809, ste from HK$1800; weekly/monthly packages from HK$2730/11,700

Though a bit out of the way, this 427-room hotel with all the mod-cons is a steal for what

it offers, so book well in advance. This place is open to men and women.

Cheap Sleeps

New Lucky House (Map pp412-14; 300 Nathan Rd, Yau Ma Tei), which is entered from Jordan Rd, is a block with lots of hostels and guesthouses in a slightly better neighbourhood than the places further south in Tsim Sha Tsui. It includes the Hakka's, Ocean and Overseas guesthouses (see p286).

ANNE BLACK YWCA GUEST HOUSE

Map pp410–11   *Guesthouse*

☎ 2713 9211; www.ywca.org.hk; annblack@ywca.org.hk; 5 Man Fuk Rd, Yau Ma Tei; s with shared/private bath HK$350/550, d with shared bath HK$470, d with private bath HK$660-720

This 169-room, YWCA-run guesthouse, which welcomes both women and men, is located near Pui Ching and Waterloo Rds in Mong Kok, behind and uphill from a petrol station. There's a decent restaurant and laundry facilities here and 73 of the rooms are singles.

BOOTH LODGE Map p415   *Guesthouse*

☎ 2771 9266; http://boothlodge.salvation.org.hk; 11 Wing Sing Lane, Yau Ma Tei; standard s & d HK$420-680, deluxe r HK$840-1200

Run by the Salvation Army, 54-room Booth Lodge is appropriately spartan and clean but comfortable as well. There is efficient air-con (you can't open the windows), a pleasant café and disabled access. Room rates include breakfast. Note that reception is on the 7th floor.

CARITAS BIANCHI LODGE

Map p415   *Guesthouse*

☎ 2388 1111; cblresv@bianchi-lodge.com; 4 Cliff Rd, Yau Ma Tei; s HK$360, d & tw HK$410-600, tr HK$510

This 90-room hotel-cum-guesthouse is run by a Catholic social-welfare organisation. Though it's just off Nathan Rd (and a goalie's throw from Yau Ma Tei MTR station) the rear rooms are very quiet and some have views onto King's Park. All rooms have private bath.

CARITAS LODGE

Map pp410–11   *Guesthouse*

☎ 2339 3777; reservation@caritas-lodge.com; 134 Boundary St, Mong Kok; s/d/tw HK$300/350/450, s weekly/monthly packages HK$1960/5940, d HK$2310/7140

With just 36 rooms, this place is a lot smaller and just as nice as its sister-guesthouse, Caritas

Bianchi Lodge, but it's a bit further afield. Still, you couldn't get much closer to the bird market, and the New Territories is (officially) just across the road.

HAKKA'S GUEST HOUSE
Map pp412–14   *Guesthouse*
☎ 2771 3656; fax 2770 1470; Flat L, 3rd fl, New Lucky House, 300 Nathan Rd, Yau Ma Tei; s/d/tr HK$200/250/300

This is the nicest guesthouse in New Lucky House and each of the nine ultra-clean guestrooms have phone, TV, air-con and shower. The affable and helpful owner, Kevin Koo, is a keen hiker and often invites guests out along with him for country walks on Sunday.

NEW KINGS HOTEL Map p415   *Hotel*
☎ 2780 1281; newkings@netvigator.com; 473 Nathan Rd, Yau Ma Tei; s HK$450, d HK$495
The New Kings may look off the track, but it's hard by the Yau Ma Tei MTR station. It's a small-ish (72 rooms) long-established place and the Temple St market is nearby.

OCEAN GUEST HOUSE
Map pp412–14   *Guesthouse*
☎ 2385 0125; fax 2771 4083; Flat G, 11th fl, New

Lucky House, 300 Nathan Rd, Yau Ma Tei; s/d HK$200/250
All eight rooms in this rather comfy place have TVs, telephone, air-con and private shower.

OVERSEAS HOUSE
Map pp412–14   *Guesthouse*
☎ 2384 5079; fax 2780 9831; Flat G, 9th fl, New Lucky House, 300 Nathan Rd, Yau Ma Tei; s/d HK$180/200, quad HK$250
This place is clean and friendly and the Overseas Travel Service on site is handy for air tickets and China visas.

RENT-A-ROOM HONG KONG
Map pp412–14   *Guesthouse*
☎ 2366 3011, 9023 8022; www.rentaroomhk.com; Flat A, 2nd fl, Knight Garden, 7-8 Tak Hing St, Yau Ma Tei; s HK$300, d HK$350-400, tr HK$510
This fabulous place is run by Thomas Tang and has changed the change the face of budget accommodation in Hong Kong. He's got some 40 positively immaculate rooms in a block opposite the Pruton Prudential Hotel and around the corner from the Jordan MTR station. Each room has shower, TV, telephone (no charge for local calls), Internet access and a fridge. There's also free use of the washing machine.

NEW TERRITORIES
The New Territories does not offer travellers a tremendous choice in terms of accommodation, but there are some five official and independent hostels, usually to be found in the more remote parts of the region. Remember, too, that walkers and hikers can pitch a tent at any one of 28 NT camp sites managed by the Country & Marine Parks Authority (see p163).

TSUEN WAN
PANDA HOTEL Map p416   *Hotel*
☎ 2409 1111; www.pandahotel.com.hk; 3 Tsuen Wah St (enter from Kwan Mun Hau St); s HK$820-1150, d HK$970-1300, s/d ste from HK$1500/1600, weekly/monthly packages from HK$2999/6999

This 1025-room hotel, the largest in the New Territories by far, has some decent outlets, including the **Chianti Ristorante** (p206). The Panda is less than 1km southeast of the Tsuen Wan MTR station. To reach it, take exit B2 from the MTR station, head south down Tai Ho Rd then turn left on Tsuen Wan Market St, which leads into Kwan Mun Hau St. Reception is on the 3rd floor.

TAI MO SHAN
SZE LOK YUEN HOSTEL
Map pp396–7   *Hostel*
☎ 2488 8188; www.yha.org.hk; beds for juniors/seniors HK$30/45, camping for members/nonmembers HK$16/25
This 88-bed hostel, a few kilometres north of Tsuen Wan, is usually only open Saturday and on the eve of public holidays (telephone the HKYHA in advance on ☎ 2788 1638). It's in the shadow of Hong Kong's highest peak and at this elevation it can get pretty chilly at night so come prepared. There are cooking facilities, but you should buy food supplies while in Tsuen Wan as none are available at the hostel. Check-in is usually from 2pm to 11pm.

TAI MEI TUK

BRADBURY LODGE

Map pp396–7   *Hostel*

☎ 2662 5123; www.yha.org.hk; 66 Ting Kok Rd; dm juniors/seniors HK$35/55, d/quads HK$150/240

Bradbury Lodge (not to be confused with Bradbury Hall in Sai Kung) is the HKYHA's flagship hostel in the New Territories. It has 96 beds and is open seven days a week year-round. Check-in is from 4pm (2pm on Saturday) to 11pm. Bradbury Lodge is next to the northern tip of the Plover Cove Reservoir dam wall, a few hundred metres south of Tai Mei Tuk. Camping is not permitted here.

SHA TIN

ASCENSION HOUSE Map p417   *Hostel*

☎ 2691 4196; www.achouse.com; 33 Tao Fong Shan Rd; dm HK$125

This 11-bed place staffed by Scandinavians and affiliated with the Lutheran Church is one of the best deals in Hong Kong, since the price of a bed gets you not only free laundry service but three meals a day as well! To get there, take the KCR to Sha Tin station, leave via exit B and walk down the ramp, passing a series of traditional village houses on the left. Between them is a set of steps. Go up these steps, follow the path and when you come to a roundabout, go along the uphill road, Pak Lok Path, to your right. After about 150m you'll come to a small staircase and a sign pointing the way to Ascension House on the right. When you reach the fork in the path and the Tao Fong Shan Christian Centre, bear to the right and you'll soon come to more steps leading up to Ascension House. The walk should take between 15 and 20 minutes. A taxi from the station in Sha Tin will cost around HK$20.

REGAL RIVERSIDE HOTEL

Map p417   *Hotel*

☎ 2649 7878; www.regalhotel.com; 34-36 Tai Chung Kiu Rd; s & d HK$780-1580, ste from HK$2800, monthly packages from HK$7800

This 830-room hotel overlooks the Shing Mun River northeast of Sha Tin town centre. It has quite a spacious health club and a large outdoor swimming pool set in a garden.

ROYAL PARK HOTEL Map p417   *Hotel*

☎ 2601 2111; www.royalpark.com.hk; 8 Pak Hok Ting St; s & d HK$780-1380, ste from HK$2600

The 448-room Royal Park is next to the New Town Plaza shopping mall. Its **Royal Park Chinese Restaurant** (☎ 2601 2111, ext 3939; ◯ lunch 11am-3pm Mon-Sat, 9am-3pm Sun, dinner 6-11pm daily) on the 2nd floor is considered to be one of the best in Sha Tin. It has dim sum on Sunday.

SAI KUNG PENINSULA

BRADBURY HALL Map pp396–7   *Hostel*

☎ 2328 2458; www.yha.org.hk; Chek Keng; dm juniors/seniors HK$30/45, camping members/ nonmembers HK$16/25

This 90-bed HKYHA hostel is right on the harbour facing Chek Keng pier. In the past it's been open at the weekend and on the eve of public holidays only, so telephone the **HKYHA** (☎ 2788 1638) in advance to check. To reach Chek Keng by bus from Sai Kung town, catch No 94 headed for Wong Shek and alight at Pak Tam Au (it's the fourth bus stop after the entrance to Sai Kung Country Park near the top of a hill). Take the footpath at the side of the road heading east and walk for about half an hour to Chek Keng. Bradbury Hall is another 10 minutes to the northeast.

PAK SHA O HOSTEL

Map pp396–7   *Hostel*

☎ 2328 2327; www.yha.org.hk; Hoi Ha Rd, Hoi Ha; beds for juniors/seniors HK$30/45, camping HK$16/25 members/nonmembers

This large HKYHA hostel with 112 beds is southwest of Hoi Ha Bay and the marine park. Like Bradbury Hall, it too is not open every day. Call the **HKYHA** (☎ 2788 1638) for details. To reach the hostel, take bus No 94 from Sai Kung town and get off at Ko Tong village. Walk about 100m along Pak Tam Rd and turn left onto Hoi Ha Rd. A sign about 30m ahead shows the way to Pak Sha O. Count on walking 30 to 40 minutes. A taxi from Sai Kung will cost HK$95.

OUTLYING ISLANDS

There are not many hotels per se on the Outlying Islands, though you'll find one each on Lamma and Cheung Chau and several on Lantau. There are guesthouses on these three as well.

Sleeping – Outlying Islands

During the warmer months and at the weekends throughout most of the year estate agencies set up booking kiosks for rental apartments and holiday villas near the ferry piers on Cheung Chau and at Mui Wo (Silvermine Bay) on Lantau.

The HKYHA has two hostels on Lantau, and the Country & Marine Parks Authority (see p163) maintains some 10 basic camp sites for hikers along the Lantau Trail and a single one on Tung Lung Chau.

LAMMA

CONCERTO INN Map p418 *Hotel*
☎ 2982 1668, 2836 3388; www.concertoinn.com.hk;
28 Hung Shing Yeh Beach, Hung Shing Yeh;
s & d HK$460-680, tr & quads HK$730 Sun-Fri,
HK$780-930 & HK$1060 Sat & public holidays
This beachfront hotel southeast of Yung Shue Wan is quite some distance from the action, so you should stay here only if you really want to get away from it all. There's also a restaurant here (see p211).

JACKSON PROPERTY AGENCY
Map p418
☎ 2982 0606; fax 2982 0636; 15 Main St, Yung Shue Wan
This property agency has studios and apartments that you can rent on Lamma. All of them have TV, private bathroom, microwave and fridge; some also offer fine sea views. The cost starts at HK$250 per night for two people from Sunday to Friday and goes up to between HK$450 and HK$500 on Saturday.

LAMMA VACATION HOUSE
Map p418 *Guesthouse*
☎ 2982 0427; 29 Main St, Yung Shue Wan; r Mon-Fri from HK$200, Sat & Sun HK$400
In the thick of the action, amid all the bars and restaurants of Main St, is this 20-room guesthouse. It's the cheapest place to stay on Lamma, so don't expect the Ritz.

MAN LAI WAH HOTEL Map p418 *Hotel*
☎ 2982 0220; hotel@my.netvigator.com; 2 Po Wah Garden, Yung Shue Wan; r Mon-Fri HK$350, Sat & Sun HK$600
This eight-room hotel (or, rather, guesthouse) faces you as you get off the ferry and begin to walk up Main St. All rooms have air-con and private shower.

TUNG O BAY HOMESTAY
Map p418 *Hostel, Guesthouse*
☎ 2982 8461; Tung O Wan; tr/quads from HK$200/300
Intrepid travellers really looking to escape will head for this secluded and very basic guesthouse on the beach on Lamma's southeast coast. The owner can throw together dinner if you give advance notice.

CHEUNG CHAU

Cheung Chau is not particularly well set up for overnighters. Depending on the day of the week and the season, some four different booths just opposite the ferry pier and another couple north along Praya St rent out studios and apartments. There is also the Warwick Hotel on Tung Wan Beach.

RENTAL AGENCIES
Map p420
Cheung Chau Ferry Pier
Agents with booking kiosks on the Cheung Chau *praya* include **Bela Vista** (☎ 2981 7299), **Island Resorts** (☎ 2981 3201) and **Cheung Chau Holidays** (☎ 2981 6623), but unless you have a smattering of Cantonese or a Chinese friend in tow, you might have difficulty getting what you want at a fair price. Expect to pay from HK$200 a night for a studio accommodating two people from Sunday to Friday, and from HK$400 on Saturday.

WARWICK HOTEL Map p420 *Hotel*
☎ 2981 0081; fax 2981 9174; Cheung Chau Sports Rd, Tung Wan Beach; d with mountain view/sea view HK$990/1190, ste from HK$2190, weekly/monthly packages from HK$4850/14,850
This six-storey, 71-room carbuncle on the butt of Tung Wan Beach is the only game in town, but it does offer wonderful views across the sea to Lamma and Hong Kong Islands. Ignore the rack rates; they discount heavily here. For example, low-season packages of one/two/ three nights for two, including breakfast and dinner, are HK$495/988/1388.

LANTAU

As on Lamma and Cheung Chau during the summer, and at weekends the rest of the year, rent holiday rooms and apartments from kiosks set up at the Mui Wo ferry pier.

The HKYHA has two hostels on Lantau, one a stone's throw from the Tian Tan Buddha in Ngong Ping and the other in a remote area of the Chi Ma Wan Peninsula. The hostels are open to HKYHA/HI card-holders only, but membership is available if you pay the nonmember rate for a total of six nights.

There are three decent accommodation options along Silvermine Bay Beach.

BABYLON VILLA Map p419 — Guesthouse

☎ 2980 3145, 2984 2741; jaqueline@53545.com; 29 Lower Cheung Sha Village; s & d weekdays/weekend HK$600/700

Along Lower Cheung Sha Beach you'll find the self-proclaimed 'smallest hotel in Hong Kong'. It's a cute retreat with three nonsmoking rooms (pink, blue and yellow) right on the water and next to the **Stoep Restaurant** (p214). To reach Babylon Villa, take bus No 4 from Mui Wo or bus No 3, 3M or A35 from Tung Chung.

HONGKONG BANK FOUNDATION SG DAVIS HOSTEL Map p419 — Hostel

☎ 2985 5610; www.yha.org.hk; Ngong Ping; dm junior/senior members HK$30/45, camping members/nonmembers HK$16/25

This 46-bed hostel, open seven days a week year-round, is a 10-minute walk from the bus stop in Ngong Ping and is the ideal place to stay if you want to catch the sunrise at nearby Lantau Peak. Check-in is from 4pm (2pm on Saturday) to 11pm. From the bus stop, take the paved path to your left as you face the Tian Tan Buddha, pass the public toilets on your right and the Lantau Tea Garden on your left and follow the signs to the maze-like steps going up to the hostel. If you visit in winter be sure to bring warm clothing for the evenings and early mornings.

JOCKEY CLUB MONG TUNG WAN HOSTEL Map p419 — Hostel

☎ 2984 1389; www.yha.org.hk; Mong Tung Wan; dm junior/senior members HK$30/45, camping members/nonmembers HK$16/25

This tranquil 88-bed, waterfront property on the southeastern side of the Chi Ma Wan Peninsula is jointly operated by the HKYHA and the Jockey Club. In the past it's been open at the weekend and on the eve of public holidays only, so telephone the **HKYHA** (☎ 2788 1638) in advance. From Mui Wo, take bus No 1, 4 or 7P (or bus A35 from Hong Kong International Airport) and alight at Pui O. Follow the footpath across the fields from the bus stop and continue along Chi Ma Wan Rd until it leaves the sea edge. At a sharp bend in the road at Ham Tin, turn right onto the footpath by the sea and follow it to the hostel – about 45 minutes. Alternatively, you can take a ferry to Cheung Chau and hire a sampan (from about HK$50, more in the evening) to the jetty at Mong Tung Wan.

MUI WO ACCOMMODATION KIOSKS

Map p421 — Rental Agencies
Mui Wo Ferry Pier

Kiosks like **Brilliant Holiday** (☎ 2984 2662) and others let out rooms and apartments on Lantau and have photos of them on display. Expect to pay HK$120/200 weekdays/weekend for a double room and from HK$200 for a studio. Be warned that not all the places are in Mui Wo – many are along Cheung Sha Beach and in Pui O village.

MUI WO INN Map p421 — Hotel

☎ 2984 7225; fax 2984 1916; Tung Wan Tau Rd, Silvermine Bay Beach; s & d Sun-Fri HK$280-350, tw HK$400, s & d Sat HK$450-550, tw HK$650

This is the last hotel on the beach and can be identified by the ring of faux-classical statues in front. It's a bit ragged around the edges but it's a friendly place to stay.

REGAL AIRPORT HOTEL

Map p419 — Hotel
☎ 2286 8888; www.regalhotel.com; 9 Cheong Tat Rd, Chek Lap Kok Airport; s & d HK$1700-2950, ste from HK$6800

An easy undercover shuffle from the airport terminal, this is a stylish hotel with more than 1000 sleek and comfy rooms, many with futuristic runway views. There's a splashy indoor/outdoor pool complex, half a dozen restaurants and fun games rooms (one for adults, one for kids). Soundproofing ensures the only noise is that of your own making.

SEAVIEW HOLIDAY RESORT

Map p421   *Hotel*

☎ 2984 8877; fax 2984 8787; 11 Tung Wan Tau Rd,
Silvermine Bay Beach; d Sun-Fri HK$250, Sat HK$450

The Seaview is by far the cheapest place to stay along the beach, but it is not as nice as the other two hotels.

SILVERMINE BEACH HOTEL

Map p421   *Hotel*

☎ 2984 8295; www.resort.com.hk; Tung Wan Tau Rd, Silvermine Bay Beach; s & d HK$880-1380, monthly packages from HK$4288

This 128-room hotel (the 'Savoy' of Mui Wo) has rooms that look out to the hills, sideways to the bay and directly onto the bay.

There's a god-value barbecue buffet in the coffee shop and Chinese restaurant in the evening.

TRAPPIST MONASTERY

Map p419   *Hostel*

☎ 2914 2933; Tai Shui Hang

You can stay at this Roman Catholic monastery, whose official name is Lady of Joy Abbey, where the monks have taken a vow of silence, but applications must be made in writing or by telephone. Write to the Grand Master, Trappist Monastery, PO Box 5, Lantau, Hong Kong. Men and women sleep in separate dorms. For directions on how to reach the monastery see p147.

Macau

Macau

INTRODUCING MACAU

Lying just 65km west of Hong Kong but predating that territory's colonisation by almost 300 years, Macau was the first European enclave in Asia. When China resumed sovereignty over what is now called the Special Administrative Region of Macau in 1999, it was by far the oldest.

Macau is a fascinating mix of cultures – a fusion of Mediterranean and Asian architecture, food, lifestyles and temperaments. It is a city of cobbled backstreets, baroque churches, ancient stone fortresses and exotic street names etched on *azulejos*, the distinctive Portuguese blue enamel tiles. There are many interesting Chinese temples and restored colonial villas, and the cemeteries of Macau are the final resting places of many European and American missionaries, painters, soldiers and sailors who died here. You will also find many good hotels, excellent restaurants and lively casinos here.

Compared to how it was 10 years ago, Macau is hard to recognise today. Hong Kong Chinese had always looked down upon Macau as a sleepy, dirty, impoverished backwater, with nothing to recommend it except legalised gambling and cheap dim sum. Before the Portuguese colonial government departed in 1999, it had spent some MOP$70 million on renovating and refurbishing civil buildings, churches, gardens and public squares; the place is now a colourful palette of pastels and ordered greenery. At the same time, the post-handover government has spent a fortune on ambitious infrastructural projects and tourist facilities (see Handover & Post-1999 Macau p298) in a bid to claim the title 'recreational centre of the Pearl River delta'.

> ### Macau's Top Five
> - A visit to the ruins of the Church of St Paul (p304) and an escalator ride up to Monte Fort and the Macau Museum (p305)
> - A stroll along Praia Grande and a visit to the A-Ma Temple (p308)
> - A visit to the Taipa House Museum (p310)
> - A bowl of *caldo verde* and a plate of *bacalhau* at a Portuguese restaurant in Taipa village (p318)
> - A day of swimming and basking on the 'black sand' of Hác Sá Beach on Coloane (p312) and a meal at the incomparable Fernando's (p319)

Getting to Macau from Hong Kong has never been easier, with high-speed ferries now running between the two territories virtually every 15 minutes. Go to Macau and stay a night or even two, and you'll discover something pretty, old, curious or tasty around every corner.

Macau's climate is similar to Hong Kong's (see Climate p357), with one major difference: there is a delightfully cool sea breeze on warm summer evenings. For information on festivals and events specific to Macau, see below. For information on festivals and events celebrated in both Macau and Hong Kong, see p9.

MACAU CALENDAR

No matter when you visit, you're likely to find a festival or event taking place in Macau. Chinese New Year (p362) is chaotic in Macau and hotel rooms are a prized commodity at this time. Still, it's a colourful time to visit, as the city literally explodes with bangers and fireworks, which are legal here, and the streets have a carnival atmosphere. The Macau Formula 3 Grand Prix (p301) is also a peak time for visitors. For more information on events in Macau, check out the website of the Macau Government Tourist Office (MGTO; www.macautourism.gov.mo). For dates of public holidays, see Holidays p362.

February
PROCESSION OF THE PASSION OF OUR LORD
A 400-year-old tradition in which a colourful procession bears a statue of Jesus Christ from Macau's St Augustine Church to Macau Cathedral, where it spends the night and is returned the following day.

March
MACAU ARTS FESTIVAL
Macau's red-letter arts event kicks off the cultural year with music, drama and dance from both Asia and the West.

April
BIRTHDAY OF TIN HAU
Known in Macau as the A-Ma Festival, this festival honours Tin Hau, the patroness of fisherfolk and one of the territory's most popular goddesses.

May
BIRTHDAY OF LORD BUDDHA
A public holiday during which Buddha's statue is taken from monasteries and temples and ceremoniously bathed in scented water; it is also

One-Day Itinerary
If you only have a day in Macau, start by following the **walking tour** on p313 to get a feel for the lie of the land and Macau's living history. Spend an hour or so in the **Macau Museum** (p305), hop on a bus for **Coloane** (p311) and have lunch at **Fernando's** (p319). All that *vinho verde* (green wine) may demand a rest on adjacent **Hác Sá Beach** (p312); after that catch a bus to **Taipa** (p310) and stroll though the village to **Avenida da Praia** (p310) and the three-part **Taipa House Museum** (p310). In the evening you should also walk along peninsular Macau's more dramatic Avenida da Praia Grande, stopping for a while at the **Lisboa Casino** (p303). Have dinner at **Pousada de São Tiago** (p323) before catching the ferry back to Hong Kong.

the Feast of the Drunken Dragon, with dancing dragons in the streets of the Inner Harbour.

PROCESSION OF OUR LADY OF FATIMA
A procession from Macau Cathedral to the Chapel of Our Lady of Penha that commemorates a supposed series of appearances by the Virgin Mary to three peasant children at Fatima in Portugal in 1917.

Central Macau

June

DRAGON BOAT FESTIVAL

Also known as Tuen Ng (Double Fifth) as it falls on the fifth day of the fifth moon. This festival commemorates the death of Qu Yuan, a poet-statesman of the 3rd century BC who hurled himself into the Mi Lo River in Hunan province to protest against a corrupt government; traditional rice dumplings are eaten in memory of the event, and dragon-boat races are held.

LUSO FESTIVAL

Commemorates Portugal's national poet, Luís de Camões (1524–80), and is celebrated by Portuguese communities around the world.

October

MACAU OPEN GOLF TOURNAMENT

Part of the Asian PGA Tour, this event is held at the Macau Golf & Country Club on Coloane and attracts the region's best golfers.

MACAU INTERNATIONAL MUSIC FESTIVAL

This two-week festival is a heady mix of opera, musicals, visiting orchestras and other musical events.

November

MACAU INTERNATIONAL FIREWORKS DISPLAY CONTEST

This event, the largest of its kind in the world, adds a splash of colour to the Macau night sky in autumn.

MACAU FORMULA 3 GRAND PRIX

Some 30 national championship drivers compete to take the chequered flag in Macau's premier sporting event.

December

MACAU INTERNATIONAL MARATHON

Like its Hong Kong equivalent, this running event also includes a half-marathon.

CULTURE

Traditional culture among the Chinese of Macau is by and large indistinguishable from that of Hong Kong (see Traditional Culture p13). However, the Portuguese minority has a vastly different culture – one that has evolved under a number of different influences, including the Roman, Moorish, French, Spanish, Flemish and Italian cultures. Colonial Portuguese architecture survives throughout Macau, and Portuguese food is to be found in abundance.

Macanese culture is different again, with a unique cuisine, set of festivals and traditions, and even its own dialect or patois, called *patuá*. The *do* (traditional woman's outfit) has long disappeared, though you may catch a glimpse of it at certain festivals.

Portuguese and Chinese – with Cantonese the more widely spoken dialect – are both official languages of Macau. For key phrases and words in Cantonese and Portuguese, see Language p375.

For the vast majority – more than 90% – of Macau Chinese people, Taoism and Buddhism are the dominant religions (see Religion p17). Four-and-a-half centuries of Portuguese Christian rule left its mark, however, and the Roman Catholic Church is very strong in Macau, with an estimated 30,000 (6.5% of the population) adherents. Macau consists of a single diocese, directly responsible to Rome.

HISTORY

As with Hong Kong, the history of the Macau Special Administrative Region (SAR) dates back only a few years – to December 1999, when sovereignty of the territory returned to China. Not only did the handover put an end to more than three years of Triad-backed lawlessness that earned the territory the nickname 'The Wild East', but it closed the chapter on almost 4½ centuries of Portuguese rule.

Early Settlement

Archaeological finds from digs around Hác Sá and Ká Hó Bays on Coloane Island suggest that Macau has been inhabited since Neolithic times (from 4000 BC). Before the arrival of the Portuguese, Macau had a relatively small number of inhabitants, mainly Cantonese-speaking farmers and fisherfolk from Fujian.

Arrival of the Portuguese

In 1510–11 the Portuguese routed Arab fleets at Goa on the west coast of India and Malacca on the Malay Peninsula. At Malacca they encountered several junks with Chinese captains and crews. Realising that the so-called Chins, about whom Portuguese mariners and explorers had heard reports a century earlier, were not a mythical people at all but natives of 'Cathay', the land that Marco Polo had visited and written about 2½ centuries earlier, a small party sailed northward to try to open up trade with the Chinese.

The first Portuguese contingent, led by Jorge Álvares, set foot on Chinese soil in 1513 at the mouth of the Pearl River at a place they called Tamaõ, today known as Shangchuan Island, about 80km southwest of the mouth of the Pearl River.

What's in a Name?

The name 'Macau' is derived from the name of the goddess A-Ma, better known as Tin Hau. At the southwestern tip of Macau Peninsula, and facing the Inner Harbour, stands the A-Ma Temple, which dates back to the early 16th century. Many people believe that when the Portuguese first arrived and asked the name of the place, 'A-Ma Gau' – Bay of A-Ma – was what they were told

According to legend, A-Ma, a poor girl looking for passage to Guangzhou, was turned away by wealthy junk owners. Instead, a poor fisherman took her on board; shortly afterwards a storm blew up, wrecking all the junks but leaving the fishing boat unscathed. When it returned to the Inner Harbour, A-Ma walked to the top of nearby Barra Hill and, in a glowing aura of light, ascended to heaven. The fisherman built a temple on the spot where they had landed.

In modern Cantonese, 'Macau' is Ou Mun (Aomen in Mandarin), meaning 'Gateway of the Bay'.

Portugal's initial contacts with China were not successful and, despite the establishment of several small trading posts along the southern Chinese coast, a permanent base seemed beyond its grasp. However, in 1553 an official basis for trading was set up between the two countries, and the Portuguese were allowed to settle on Shangchuan. The exposed anchorage there forced the Portuguese traders to abandon the island that same year, however, and they moved to Lampacau, an island closer to the Pearl River estuary.

To the northeast of Lampacau was a small peninsula where the Portuguese had frequently dropped anchor. Known variously as Amagau, Aomen and Macau (see 'What's in a Name?' above), the peninsula had two natural harbours – an inner one on the Qianshan waterway facing the mainland and an outer one in a bay on the Pearl River – and two sheltered islands to the south. In 1557 officials at Guangzhou allowed the Portuguese to build temporary shelters on the peninsula in exchange for customs dues and rent, as well as an agreement to rid the area of the pirates endemic at the time.

A Trading Powerhouse

Macau grew rapidly as a trading centre, largely due to the fact that Chinese merchants were forbidden to leave the country by imperial decree. Acting as agents for Chinese merchants, Portuguese traders took Chinese goods (including porcelain and silks) to Goa on the west coast of India and exchanged them for cotton and textiles. The cloth was then taken to Malacca, where it was traded for spices and sandalwood. The Portuguese would then carry on to Nagasaki in Japan, where the cargo from Malacca was exchanged for Japanese silver, swords, lacquerware and fans that would be traded in Macau for more Chinese goods.

During the late 16th century the Portuguese in Macau were at the forefront of all international commerce between China and Japan. But the territory was not just gaining in economic strength. Such was Macau's growing status and importance that when the Holy See established the bishopric of Macau in 1576, it included both China and Japan. By 1586 Macau was large enough and important enough for the Crown to confer upon it the status of a city: Cidade de Nome de Deus (City of the Name of God).

Macau's Golden Years

By the beginning of the 17th century Macau supported several thousand permanent residents, including about 900 Portuguese, including nobles. The rest were Christian converts from Malacca and Japan and a large number of slaves from Portuguese outposts in Africa, India and the Malay Peninsula. Large numbers of Chinese had moved into Macau from across the border, and they worked there as traders, craftspeople, hawkers, labourers and coolies; by the close of the century, their numbers had reached 40,000.

Trade was the most important activity in the new town, but Macau had also become a centre of Christianity in Asia. Priests and missionaries accompanied Portuguese ships, although the interests of traders and missionaries frequently conflicted.

Among the earliest missionaries was Francis Xavier (later canonised) of the Jesuit order, who spent two years (1549–51) in Japan attempting to convert the local population before turning his attention to

Largo do Senado (Senate Square)

China. He was stalled by the Portuguese, who feared the consequences of his meddling in Chinese affairs, but made it as far as Shangchuan Island, where he developed a fever and died in December 1552. Subsequently it was Jesuit missionaries, not traders, who were able to penetrate China. In 1602 the Jesuits built the Church of Madre de Deus (later Church of St Paul), hailed at the time as the greatest monument to Christianity in Asia.

Portuguese Decline

Portugal's decline as an imperial power came as quickly as its rise. In 1580 Spanish armies occupied Portugal and for more than 60 years three Spanish kings were to rule over the country and its empire. In the early years of the 17th century the Dutch, embroiled in the Thirty Years' War with Spain, moved to seize the rich Portuguese enclaves of Macau, Nagasaki and Malacca. In June 1622 some 13 Dutch warships carrying 1300 men attacked Macau but retreated when a shell fired by a Jesuit priest from one of the cannons on Monte Fort hit a stock of gunpowder and blew the Hollanders out of the water.

The Japanese soon became suspicious of Portuguese and Spanish intentions and closed its doors to foreign trade in 1639. Two years later, Dutch harassment of Portuguese commerce and trading interests ended with the capture of Malacca. The Portuguese would no longer be able to provide the Chinese with the Japanese silver needed for their silk and porcelain or with spices from the Malay Peninsula.

A Change of Status

The overthrow of the moribund Ming dynasty in 1644 saw a flood of refugees unleashed on Macau. In 1684 the most corrupt of the new Manchu rulers, the *hoppo* (*hoi poi* in Cantonese) – the customs superintendent who held the monopoly on trade with foreigners – set up an office in the Inner Harbour.

In the mid-18th century Chinese authorities created the *cohong*, a mercantile monopoly based in Guangzhou for dealing with foreign trade. Numerous restrictions were placed on Western traders, including limitations on the amount of time they could reside in Guangzhou. Macau in effect became an outpost for all European traders in China, a position it held until the British took possession of Hong Kong in 1841.

Until the mid-19th century the history of Macau was a long series of incidents involving the Portuguese, Chinese and British as the Portuguese attempted to maintain a hold on the territory. But as time progressed and the troublesome British wrestled concession after concession out of China, the Portuguese grew bolder.

The Treaty of Nanking, signed in 1842, had ceded the island of Hong Kong in perpetuity to the British; the Treaty of Tientsin (1860) gave them Kowloon on the same terms. The Portuguese felt that they too should take advantage of China's weakness and push for sovereignty over the territory they had occupied for three centuries. Negotiation began in 1862, although it was not until 1887 that a treaty was signed in which China effectively recognised Portuguese sovereignty over Macau forever.

With the advent of the steamship and then other motorised vessels, there were fewer transhipments from Chinese ports through Macau and more direct transactions between the mainland and Hong Kong. By the close of the 19th century the ascent of the British colony and the decline of the Portuguese territory had become irreversible.

20th-Century Macau

By the turn of the 20th century Macau was little more than an impoverished backwater, its glory days a distant memory. It did, however, continue to serve as a haven for Chinese refugees fleeing war, famine and political oppression. Among them was Sun Yat Sen, founder of the republic of China, who lived in Macau before the 1911 Revolution. Even the birth of the Portuguese republic in 1910 had little effect.

In the mid-1920s large numbers of Chinese immigrants doubled the number of Macau residents to 160,000. A steady stream of refugees from the Sino-Japanese War meant that by 1939 the population had reached 245,000. During WWII many people from Hong Kong and China, as well as Asian-based Europeans, took refuge in Macau, as the Japanese respected Portugal's neutrality; by 1943 the population stood at 500,000. There was another influx of Chinese refugees in 1949 when the Communists took power in China, and from 1978 until about 1981 Macau was a haven for Vietnamese boat people. Macau was made an overseas province of Portugal in 1951.

Macau's last great upset occurred in 1966–67, when China's Cultural Revolution spilled over into the territory. Macau was stormed by Red Guards, and violent riots resulted in some of them being shot and killed by Portuguese troops. The government proposed that Portugal abandon Macau forever but, fearing the loss of foreign trade through Macau, the Chinese refused.

In 1974 a revolution restored democracy in Portugal and the new left-wing government began to divest Portugal of the last remnants of its empire, including Mozambique and Angola in Africa and East Timor in the Indonesian archipelago. Power brokers in Lisbon tried to return Macau to China as well, but the word from Beijing was that China wished Macau to remain as it was – at least for the time being.

End of Portuguese Rule

Once the Joint Declaration over Hong Kong had been signed by Britain and China in 1984, the latter turned its attentions to the future of Macau. Talks began in 1986 and an agreement was signed the following April.

Under the so-called Sino-Portuguese Pact, Macau would become a 'Special Administrative Region' (SAR) of China. The date set was 20 December 1999, ending 442 years of Portuguese rule. Like Hong Kong, the Macau SAR would enjoy a 'high degree of autonomy' for 50 years in all matters except defence and foreign affairs – under the slogan 'one country, two systems'.

The basic law for Macau differed from its Hong Kong equivalent in that holders of foreign passports were not excluded from holding high-level posts in the post-handover administration (apart from the position of chief executive). There was also no stipulation that China would station troops of the People's Liberation Army (PLA) in Macau after the return of the territory to China, though it did just that and today they are more evident here than they are in Hong Kong.

Macau had directly elected some of the members of its Legislative Assembly since the assembly's founding in 1976, but unlike Hong Kong it did not rush through proposals to widen the franchise or speed up democratisation at the last minute. The existing legislature continued to serve throughout the handover, unlike that in the British territory.

But not everything went smoothly. Macau residents were pleased when Portugal gave everyone born in Macau a Portuguese passport, which would allow them the right to live anywhere in the European Union – something the UK had refused Hong Kong Chinese people. However, not everyone in Macau benefited by Portugal's move. Until 1975, any Chinese refugee reaching Macau could obtain residency (after that anyone caught sneaking into the territory was considered an illegal immigrant and sent back). Thus, as much as 70% of the population had not actually been born in Macau and therefore didn't qualify for Portuguese citizenship.

Up to and during the transition, Portugal dragged its heels on sweeping the upper echelons of the bureaucracy of non-Chinese. As the eve of the handover approached, civil servants were bought out or retired, and a flood of Portuguese left the territory, leaving behind a population made up of Chinese and mixed-blood Macanese.

In the mid-1990s overenthusiastic speculation in housing and property left a huge glut of unoccupied buildings and offices. Property prices tumbled and as the handover approached there were 30,000 vacant apartments in Macau (one for every 15 residents). The economy, largely dependent on tourism and gambling, was faltering across the board, due not only to the regional economic downturn but also to a staggering increase in violent crime.

The years 1996 to 1998 were a grim showdown for Macau and its all-important tourism industry, with an escalating number of gangland killings. Some 40 people were killed as senior Triad leaders jostled for control of the lucrative gambling rackets, and one international hotel was raked with AK-47 gunfire. On 8 May 1998 alone, 14 cars and motorcycles and a couple of shops were engulfed in flames when Triad members, protesting the arrest of their boss, Wan Kwok 'Broken Tooth' Koi, let off a string of firebombs. Needless to say, the violence scared tourists off in a big way; arrivals fell by some 36% in August 1997.

As the handover approached, China put pressure on Portugal to clean up its act. The government issued a new anti-Triad law calling for a lengthy prison term for anyone found to be a senior leader. Koi was arrested and sentenced to 15 years, and many other Triad members, including post-1997 imports from Hong Kong, fled overseas.

Handover & Post-1999 Macau

The handover ceremony on 20 December 1999 was as stage-managed as the one held 2½ years earlier in Hong Kong. The following day 500 PLA soldiers drove down from Zhuhai. There are now an estimated 10,000 troops stationed here, though they have no responsibility for internal security.

In the past decade Macau has launched a series of enormous public works projects. The completion of Macau's US$11.8 billion airport in 1995 was one of the most ambitious, as was the construction of a deep-water port on the northeastern side of Coloane Island.

Land-reclamation projects have been equally ambitious. The one along the Praia Grande, Macau's historic waterfront, buffeted by the NAPE reclaimed area, has created two large freshwater lakes. The causeway linking Taipa and Coloane, once a narrow two-lane raised road, is now a sizable reclaimed area called Cotai with a six-lane highway.

Heading west from Cotai is the US$25 million Lotus Bridge, which opened in 2000, linking Macau with Hengqing Island in the Zhuhai Special Economic Zone (SEZ). To handle the anticipated increase in motor-vehicle traffic brought on by the airport and the Taipa City high-rise housing development on Taipa, a second bridge was built between the island and peninsular Macau in 1994 and a third bridge, a typhoon-proof covered span linking the peninsula's southwest corner with western Taipa, is under construction.

Other ongoing grand projects include the Ponte 16 and Fisherman's Wharf theme parks on the Inner and Outer Harbours respectively and the new Macau Dome on Coloane, set to open for the East Asian Games in 2005. But the most ambitious project by far is the proposed 29km-long, US$1.92 billion cross-delta bridge linking Macau and Zhuhai with Hong Kong via Tai O on Lantau Island.

ART

The most important Western artist to have lived in Macau was George Chinnery. Other influential European painters who spent time in Macau include the Scottish physician Thomas Watson (1815–60), who was a student of Chinnery and lived in Macau from 1845 to 1856; Frenchman Auguste Borget (1808–77), who spent 1836 painting Macau's waterfront and churches; and watercolourist Marciano António Baptists (1856–1930), who was born in Macau.

Guan Qiaochang (1830–50), another pupil of Chinnery, was a Chinese artist who painted in the Western style and worked under the name Lamqua. His oil portraits of mandarins and other Chinese worthies are particularly fine.

The works of these artists are on display in the Gallery of Historical Pictures of the Macau Museum of Art (see p307).

ARCHITECTURE

Portuguese architectural styles reflect a variety of forms from Romanesque and Gothic through baroque to neoclassical, and these are best seen in Macau's churches. Two of the best examples are the Chapel of St Joseph Seminary (p306), completed in 1758, and the Church of St Dominic (p304), a 17th-century replacement of a chapel built in the 1590s.

George Chinnery: Chronicler of Macau

Though George Chinnery may enjoy little more than footnote status in the history of world art, as a chronicler of his own world – colonial Macau – and his times (the early 19th century) he is without peer. In the absence of photography, taipans ('big bosses' of large companies) and mandarins turned to trade art (commissioned portraiture), and Chinnery was the master of the genre. Today he is known less for his formal portraits and paintings of factory buildings and clipper ships than his landscapes and sometimes fragmentary sketches of everyday life.

Chinnery was born in Ireland in 1774 and studied at the Royal Academy of Arts before turning his hand to portrait painting in Dublin. He sailed for India in 1802 and spent the next 23 years working and painting in Madras and Calcutta. He fled to Macau in 1825 to escape Calcutta's 'cranky formality' and his wife (who he described as 'the ugliest woman I ever saw in my life'), and took up residence at 8 Rua de Ignácio Baptista, just south of the Church of St Lawrence; he lived at this address until his death in 1852.

Although Chinnery is sometimes 'claimed' by Hong Kong (the Mandarin Oriental hotel even has a bar named after him), he visited the Crown colony only once, during the hot summer of 1846. Although he was unwell and did not like it very much, he managed to execute some vivid sketches of the place.

Civic buildings worth close inspection are the Leal Senado (p304), erected in 1784 but rebuilt after it was damaged by a typhoon a century later; the Dom Pedro V Theatre (p306), built in 1860; Government House (Map pp422-3; cnr Avenida da Praia Grande & Travessa do Padré Narciso), dating from 1849; and the exquisite villas that now form the Taipa House Museum (p310).

Macau counts some 40 skyscrapers, but only a few are memorable. Macau Tower (p308), a 338m-tall copy of the Sky Tower in Auckland, New Zealand, is Asia's 10th-tallest building. The landmark Bank of China (Map p422-3; Avenida do Doutor Mario Soares) is an attractive, 38-floor structure clad in pinkish granite.

ECONOMY

Tourism and the spin of the roulette wheel still drive Macau's economy and gambling remains Macau's major cash cow.

In 2002 the Macau government awarded gambling concessions to two American companies, thereby ending the 40-year gambling monopoly held by Sociedade de Turismo e Diversões de Macau (STDM), Stanley Ho's 'Macau Tourism and Amusement Company'. Gambling concessions contribute more than 50% of government revenue through betting tax.

Tourism usually generates more than 40% of GDP, and almost a third of the labour force works in some aspect of it. Macau welcomes some 11.5 million tourists and visitors a year, which is more than 25 times its population. Almost half are Hong Kong residents, with most of the balance coming from the mainland, Taiwan, Japan and the USA.

Macau has various light industries, such as fireworks, textile and toy production, but factories have slowed down and many companies have moved across the border. Unemployment in Macau is currently around 6.5%.

GOVERNMENT & POLITICS

The executive branch of the Macau SAR government is led by the chief executive, who is chosen by an electoral college made up of 200 local representatives. Edmund Ho, a popular Macau-born banker, has held the five-year post since 1999.

The Legislative Assembly, which sits in its own purpose-built assembly hall on reclaimed land in the Nam Van Lakes area, currently consists of 27 members, 10 of whom are directly elected in geographical constituencies, 10 chosen by interest groups and seven appointed by the chief executive.

Like Hong Kong, Macau has a Court of Final Appeal.

Population & People

Macau's population is 460,000, with an annual growth rate of 1.75%. About 95% of people live on the peninsula, making it one of the most densely populated areas on earth. Coloane Island has remained essentially rural, but Taipa Island is rapidly becoming an urban extension of peninsular Macau.

The population is about 95% Chinese. Fewer than 2% of Macau residents are Portuguese and the rest are Macanese, with mixed Portuguese, Chinese and/or African blood.

LIFESTYLE

FOOD

Eating – be it Portuguese or Macanese 'soul food', Chinese dim sum or the special treats available from street stalls and night markets (see Eating p314) – is one of the most rewarding aspects of a visit to Macau. People eat dinner relatively early here; in some restaurants the dining room is all but empty by 9pm.

The most popular alcoholic tipple in Macau is *vinho verde*, a crisp, dry, slightly effervescent 'green' wine from Portugal that goes down a treat with salty Portuguese food and spicy Macanese dishes. You might also try one of the fine wines from Dão, Douro or Alenquer.

Street stall, Macau

Portuguese & Macanese Food

Portuguese cuisine is rather heavy, meat-based and, in general, not particularly refined. It makes great use of a heavy form of olive oil, garlic and *bacalhau* (dried salted cod), which can be prepared in many different ways. It sometimes combines meat and seafood in one dish, such as *porco à Alentejana*, a tasty casserole of pork and clams. Some favourite dishes are *caldo verde*, a soup of green cabbage or kale thickened with potatoes; *pasteis de bacalhau* (codfish croquettes), *sardinhas grelhadas* (grilled sardines) and *feijoada*, a casserole of beans, pork, spicy sausages, potatoes and cabbage that is actually Brazilian in origin.

Macanese food, on the other hand, borrows a lot of its ingredients and tastes from Chinese and other Asian cuisines, as well as from those of former Portuguese colonies in Africa and India. It is redolent of coconut, tamarind, chilli, jaggery (palm sugar) and shrimp paste.

The most famous Macanese speciality is *galinha africana* (African chicken), with the bird done in coconut, garlic and chillies. As well as cod, there's plenty of other fish and seafood: shrimp, prawns, crab, squid and white fish. Sole, a tongue-shaped flat fish, is a Macanese delicacy. The contribution from the former Portuguese enclave of Goa on the west coast of India is spicy prawns.

Other Macanese favourites include *casquinha* (stuffed crab); *porco balichão* (pork cooked with tamarind and shrimp paste); *minchi* (minced beef or pork cooked with potatoes, onions and spices); and baked rice dishes made with cod, prawns or crab. Macanese desserts are *pudim*, basically crème caramel, and *serradura*, a calorie-rich 'sawdust' pudding made with crushed biscuits or cookies, cream and condensed milk. *Pastéis de nata* is a scrumptious egg-custard tartlet eaten warm.

Dining in Macau (www.dininginmacau.com) is a quarterly advertorial freebie but a good source of information about some three dozen restaurants nonetheless. You might also have a flip through the *Macau Food Guide* (www.cityguide.gov.mo/food/food_e.htm), available for free at the tourist office.

Other Cuisines

Macau is not just about Macanese and Portuguese food. Some people swear that the dim sum here is far better than anything you'll find in Hong Kong. Thai food, one of the great contributions of the Thai bar girls working here, can be excellent, especially in the area just east of St Michael's cemetery.

SPORT

Macau Stadium (Estádio de Macau; Map p425-6; ☎ 838 208; Avenida Olímpica), next to the Macau Jockey Club on Taipa Island, seats 15,000 and hosts international soccer matches and track-and-field athletics competitions. On the first Sunday in December the Macau International Marathon starts and finishes here. On Coloane is the new Macau Dome (Map p425-6), built to host the 2005 East Asian Games and the 2007 Indoor Asian Games.

Another organisation that may be worth contacting for details of forthcoming events is the **Macau Sports Institute** (Instituto do Desporto de Macau; Map pp422-3; ☎ 580 762; Avenida do Doutor Rodrigo Rodrigues) at the Macau Forum.

Grand Prix

The biggest sporting event of the year is the Macau Formula 3 Grand Prix, held in the third week of November. The 6km circuit starts near the Lisboa Hotel and follows the shoreline along Avenida da Amizade, going around the reservoir and back through the city. The Grand Prix, which celebrated its golden jubilee in 2003, attracts many international contestants as well as spectators; more than 50,000 people flock to see it and accommodation is tight.

Certain areas in Macau are designated as viewing areas for the races. Streets and alleys along the track are blocked off, so it's unlikely that you'll be able to find a decent vantage point without paying for it. Prices for seats in the Reservoir Stand are MOP$150/250 for a single day/package (which includes practice days and qualifying events before the start of the actual races) and from MOP$400 to MOP$600 at the Lisboa and Grand Stands (MOP$700 for the package). To watch just the practice days and qualifying events costs MOP$20/30 from the Grand/Lisboa Stand and is free from the Reservoir Stand. For ticket inquiries and bookings call ☎ 796 2268 or 555 555. You can also consult www.macau.grandprix.gov.mo.

GAMBLING

Casinos

At the time of writing, Macau had a dozen casinos, with at least two more on the way. All of them operate 24 hours a day.

Although the games in Macau are somewhat different from those played in Las Vegas and elsewhere (see the boxed text below), the same basic principles apply. No matter what the game, the casino enjoys a built-in mathematical advantage. In the short term, anyone

Some Fun & Games in Macau

Baccarat Also known as chemin de fer (railroad), this has become the card game of choice for the upper crust of Macau's gambling elite. Two hands are dealt simultaneously: a player hand and a bank hand. Players can bet on either (neither is actually the house hand), and the one that scores closest to nine is the winner. The casino deducts a percentage if the bank hand wins, which is how the house makes its profit. If the player understands the game properly, the house only enjoys a slightly better than 1% advantage over the player.

Blackjack Also known as 21, this card game is easy to play, although it requires some skill to play well. The dealer takes a card and gives another to the players. Face cards count as 10, aces as one or 11. Cards are dealt one at a time – the goal is to get as close as possible to 21 (blackjack) without going over. If you go over 21 you 'bust', or lose. Players are always dealt their cards before the dealer, so if they bust they will always bust before the dealer does. This is what gives the casino the edge over the player. If the dealer and player both get 21, it's a tie and the bet is cancelled. If players get 21, they get even money plus a 50% bonus. Dealers must draw until they reach 16, and stand on 17 or higher. The player is free to decide when to stand or when to draw.

Boule This is very similar to roulette, except that boule is played with a ball about the size of a billiard ball, and there are fewer numbers. Boule has 24 numbers plus a star. The payoff is 23 to one on numbers. On all bets (numbers, red or black, odd or even) the casino has a 4% advantage over players.

Dai Siu Cantonese for 'big little', this game is also known as *sik po* (dice treasure) or *cu sik* (guessing dice) and is very popular in Macau. The game is played with three dice. The dice are placed in a covered glass container, the container is then shaken and you bet on whether the toss will be from three to nine (small) or 10 to 18 (big). However, you lose on combinations where all three dice come up the same, such as 2-2-2, 3-3-3 and so on – unless you bet directly on three of a kind. For betting *dai siu* the house advantage is 2.78%. Betting on a specific three of a kind gives the house a 30% advantage.

Fan Tan This is an ancient Chinese game practically unknown in the West. The dealer takes an inverted silver cup and plunges it into a pile of porcelain buttons, then moves the cup to one side. After all bets have been placed, the buttons are counted out in groups of four. You have to bet on how many will remain after the last set of four has been taken out.

Pai Kao This is a form of Chinese dominoes similar to mahjong. One player is made banker and the others compare their hands against the banker's. The casino doesn't play, but deducts a 3% commission from the winnings for providing the gambling facilities.

Roulette The dealer spins the roulette wheel in one direction and tosses a ball the other way. Roulette wheels have 36 numbers plus a zero, so your chance of hitting any given number is one in 37. The payoff is 35 to one, which is what gives the casino its advantage. Rather than betting on a single number, it's much easier to win if you bet odd or even, or red versus black numbers, which only gives the house a 2.7% advantage. If the ball lands on zero, everyone loses to the house (unless you also bet on the zero).

can hit a winning streak and get ahead, but the longer you play, the more certain it is that the odds will catch up with you.

The legal gambling age in Macau is 18 years (21 for Macau residents). Photography is absolutely prohibited inside the casinos. Men cannot wear shorts, even relatively long ones, or a singlet (undershirt) unless they have a shirt over it. Women wearing shorts or vests are refused entry, as is anyone wearing thongs (flip-flops).

None of the casinos in Macau offers the atmosphere or level of service considered minimal in Las Vegas, though that is expected to change when the American casinos – Wynn Resorts' Wynn Macau and Sand's Venetian Casino – open in 2005 or 2006. There are no seats for slot-machine players, nor cocktail waiters offering free drinks to gamblers. A most obnoxious custom is the automatic tip: dealers and croupiers take 10% of your winnings without even asking.

Most of Macau's casinos are located within big hotels such as the **Holiday Inn Macau** (Map pp422-3; ☎ 786 424), the **Kingsway** (Map pp422-3; ☎ 701 111), the **Lisboa** (Map pp422-3; ☎ 375 111) and the **Mandarin Oriental** (Map pp422-3; ☎ 564 297) on the peninsula, and the **Hyatt Regency Macau** (Map p230; ☎ 831 536), the **New Century** (Map p230; ☎ 831 111 ext 1946) and the **Pousada Marina Infante** (Map pp425-6; ☎ 838 333), situated on Taipa.

Independent casinos include the **Macau Palace Casino** (Map pp422-3; ☎ 346 701), a 'floating casino' moored in the Outer Harbour southwest of the ferry terminal, the **Jai Alai Casino** (Map pp422-3; ☎ 726 086; Jai Alai Complex, Travessa do Reservatório), the **Kam Pek Casino** (Map pp422-3; ☎ 780 168; Rua de Foshan), close to the Lisboa Hotel, and **Pharaoh's Palace Casino** (Map pp422-3; ☎ 788 111; 3rd fl, Macau Landmark, Avenida da Amizade). The **Legend Club** (Map pp422-3; ☎ 788 822), two floors above Pharaoh's Palace, is for high-spending members only.

Horse Racing

Regular horse races are held at the **Macau Jockey Club** (Map pp425-6; ☎ 821 188, racing information hotline ☎ 820 868, Hong Kong ☎ 800-967 822; www.macauhorse.com; Estrada Governador Albano de Oliveira) racetrack on Taipa Island throughout most of the year (the summer recess is late August to early September). For more details, see the entry on p311.

Dog Racing

Macau's **Canidrome** (☎ 261 188, racing information hotline ☎ 333 399, Hong Kong ☎ 800-903 888; www.macaudog.com; Avenida do General Castelo Branco), situated on Taipa Island, is the only facility for greyhound racing in Asia. Greyhound races are held on Monday, Thursday, Saturday and Sunday at 7.45pm. There are 14 races per night, with six to eight dumb dogs chasing a mechanical rabbit around the 455m oval track. Admission to the Canidrome costs MOP$10. If you want to sit in the members stands it costs MOP$80 Monday to Thursday and MOP$120 Friday to Sunday.

DISTRICTS & ISLANDS

Macau is a tiny but ever-growing place. Nowadays it has a total land area of 26.8 sq km, which takes in the peninsula (8.5 sq km), Taipa Island (6.2 sq km), Coloane Island (7.6 sq km) and Cotai (from 'Coloane' and 'Taipa'; 4.5 sq km), the man-made isthmus linking the last two.

Macau is divided here into three main sections: the Macau Peninsula, which is attached to mainland China to the north; the middle island of Taipa, directly south of the peninsula and linked to it by the 2.5km-long Governor Nobre de Carvalho (or Macau–Taipa) Bridge, the 4.5km-long Friendship Bridge and, within the next few years, the 1.75km covered typhoon-proof bridge; and Coloane Island, south of Taipa and connected to it by the 2.2km-long Cotai causeway.

MACAU PENINSULA

Most of Macau's museums, churches, gardens, ancient cemeteries, colonial buildings and cobbled backstreets are on the peninsula. If you're after more active pursuits such as cycling, hiking and swimming, head for the islands (see Sport & Fitness p237).

Central Macau Peninsula

Avenida de Almeida Ribeiro – San Ma Lo (New St) in Cantonese – is Macau's main thoroughfare. It starts at the delightful and ends at the Inner Harbour, dividing the narrow southern peninsula from central and northern Macau. Its southern extension, Avenida do Infante Dom Henrique, runs from Avenida da Praia Grande to the Outer Harbour, just below the landmark Lisboa Hotel. Approximately in the centre of this long thoroughfare is central Largo do Senado.

LEAL SENADO Map p424
163 Avenida de Almeida Ribeiro
Facing Largo do Senado to the west is Macau's most important historical building, the 18th-century Leal Senado (Loyal Senate), which now houses the Instituto para os Assuntos Cívicos e Municipais (IACM; the Civic and Municipal Affairs Bureau) and the mayor's office. It is called the 'Loyal Senate' because the body sitting here refused to recognise Spain's sovereignty during the 60 years that Spain occupied Portugal.

In 1654, a dozen years after Portuguese sovereignty was re-established, King João IV ordered a heraldic inscription to be placed inside the senate's entrance hall, which can still be seen today. To the right of the entrance hall is the small **IACM Gallery** (☎ 387 333; admission free; ☾ 9am-9pm Tue-Sun) with rotating exhibits. On the 1st floor is the **Senate Library** (☎ 572 233; admission free; ☾ 1-7pm Mon-Sat), which has an extensive collection of books on Asia and wonderful carved wooden furnishings, panelled walls and artwork.

MUSEUM OF THE HOLY HOUSE OF MERCY Map p424
☎ 573 938; 2 Travessa da Misericordia; admission MOP$5; ☾ 10am-1pm, 3-5.30pm Mon-Sat, closed Sun
The lovely Santa Casa da Misericordia (Holy House of Mercy), on the southeastern side of Largo de Senado, was established in 1569 and is the oldest social institution in Macau. It served as a home for orphans and prostitutes in the 18th century, and its patron was the Macanese trader Martha Merop (1766–1828), heroine of Austin Coates's *City of Broken Promises* (see Books p327). Today it is a two-room

museum containing items related to the house, including religious artefacts; Chinese, Japanese and European porcelain; the skull of its founder and Macau's first bishop, Dom Belchior Carneiro; and a portrait of Merop painted in the year of her death.

MACAU CATHEDRAL Map p424
Largo da Sé; ☾ 8am-6pm
East of Largo do Senado is the Cathedral, a not particularly attractive structure built in 1850 to replace an earlier one badly damaged in a typhoon. The cathedral, which has some notable stained-glass windows, is the focus for most major Christian festivals and holy days in Macau.

CHURCH OF ST DOMINIC Map p424
Igreja de São Domingos; Largo de São Domingos; ☾ 8am-6pm
A fine example of ecclesiastical baroque architecture, this imposing church northeast of Largo do Senado is an early-17th-century replacement of a chapel built by the Dominicans in the 1590s. Today it contains the **Treasury of Sacred Art** (Tresouro de Arte Sacra; ☎ 367 706; admission free; ☾ 10am-6pm), an Aladdin's cave of ecclesiastical art and liturgical objects exhibited on three floors. Among the most interesting objects are a 17th-century portrait of St Augustine and an ivory statuette of St John the Baptist wearing a hair shirt the wrong way round.

CHINESE READING ROOM Map p424
Rua de Santa Clara; ☾ 9-10.30am, 7-10pm Tue-Sat, 9am-10pm Sun
This attractive octagonal structure, with its double stone staircase and little round tower, is a wonderful mix of Chinese and Portuguese influences that could only be found in Macau. Opposite are the lovely **St Francis Garden** (Jardim de São Francisco; Map pp422–3) and the **St Francis Barracks** (Quarteis de São Francisco; Map pp422–3) now housing PLA troops.

RUINS OF THE CHURCH OF ST PAUL Map pp422–3
Ruinas de Igreja de São Paulo; Rua de São Paulo
The façade is all that remains of this Jesuit church built in the early 17th century. But with

its wonderful statues, portals and engravings, some consider the ruins of the Church of St Paul to be the greatest monument to Christianity in Asia.

Built on one of Macau's seven hills, the church was designed by an Italian Jesuit and completed by early Japanese Christian exiles and Chinese craftsmen in 1602. The church was abandoned after the expulsion of the Jesuits in 1762 and a military battalion was stationed here. In 1835 a fire erupted in the kitchen of the barracks, destroying everything but the façade and the stone steps leading to it.

The façade has been described as a 'sermon in stone' and a *Biblia pauperum*, a 'Bible of the poor' to help the illiterate understand the Passion of Christ and the lives of the saints.

At the top is a dove, representing the Holy Spirit, surrounded by stone carvings of the sun, moon and stars. Beneath the Holy Spirit is a statue of the Infant Jesus surrounded by stone carvings of the implements of the Crucifixion (eg the whip, crown of thorns, nails, ladder and spear). In the centre of the 3rd tier stands the Virgin Mary as she is being assumed bodily into heaven along with angels and two flowers: the peony, which represents China, and the chrysanthemum, a symbol of Japan. To the right of the Virgin is a carving of the tree of life and an apocalyptic woman slaying a seven-headed hydra; the Chinese characters next to her read 'the holy mother tramples the heads of the dragon'. To the left of the central statue of Mary, a 'star' guides a ship (the Church) through a storm (sin); a carving of the devil is to the left.

The 4th tier has statues of Jesuit doctors of the church (from left to right): Blessed Francisco de Borja; St Ignatius Loyola, the founder of the order; St Francis Xavier, the apostle of the Far East; and Blessed Luís Gonzaga.

MUSEUM OF SACRED ART & CRYPT

Map pp422–3

Museu de Arte Sacra e Cripta; ☎ 387 333; Rua de São Paolo; admission free; ☼ 9am-6pm

This small museum was opened in the chancel of the Church of St Paul to the northwest of the façade in 1996 after archaeological excavations had ceased. It contains polychrome carved wooden statues, silver chalices, monstrances and oil paintings, including a copy of a 17th-century one depicting the martyrdom of 26 Japanese Christians by crucifixion at Nagasaki in 1597. The adjoining crypt contains the remains of the martyrs as well as those of Vietnamese and other Japanese Christians killed in the 17th century.

MONTE FORT Map pp422–3

Fortaleza do Monte; ☼ 6am-7pm May-Sep, 7am-6pm Oct-Apr

On a hill and accessible by escalator just east of the ruins of the Church of St Paul, Monte Fort was built by the Jesuits between 1617 and 1626 as part of the College of the Mother of God. Barracks and storehouses were designed to allow the fort to survive a two-year siege, but the cannons were fired only once: during the aborted attempt to invade Macau by the Dutch in 1622 (see Portuguese Decline p296).

MACAU MUSEUM Map pp422–3

Museu de Macau; ☎ 357 911; Praceta do Museum de Macau, Monte Fort; adult/child under 11 or senior over 60 MOP$15/8, admission free on the 15th of each month; ☼ 10am-6pm Tue-Sun

This wonderful museum within the fort tells the story of the hybrid territory of Macau with a host of CD-ROMs, videos, and other special effects.

On the 1st level, the Genesis of Macau exhibit takes you through the early history of the territory, with parallel developments in the East and the West compared and contrasted. The section devoted to the territory's religions is excellent, as is the recreated Macau street, with many different examples of architecture.

Ruins of the Church of St Paul

On the 2nd level (Popular Arts & Traditions of Macau) you'll see and hear everything from a re-created firecracker factory and the recorded cries of street vendors, to a *chá gordo* ('fat tea') of 20 dishes enjoyed on a Sunday, to the poet José dos Santos Ferreira (1919–93), known as Adé, reading from his work *patuá*, Macanese dialect forging Portuguese and Cantonese.

The top floor illustrates 'Contemporary Macau' and its contributions to literature and urban-development plans.

CEMETERY OF ST MICHAEL THE ARCHANGEL Map pp422–3
Cemitério de São Miguel Arcanjo; 2A Estrada do Cemitério; ⏰ 8am-6pm
This cemetery northeast of Monte Fort is almost exactly in the centre of the Macau Peninsula. Although a few of the tombs are plain, the vast majority are baroque ecclesiastical works of art. Near the main entrance is the **Chapel of St Michael** (Capela de São Miguel; ⏰ 10am-6pm), a doll-sized lime-green church with a tiny choir loft and lovely porticos.

KUNG TEMPLE Map p424
Cnr Rua das Estalagens & Rua de Cinco de Outubro; ⏰ 8am-6pm
This temple, in a market district west of Monte Fort, was built in 1750 and dedicated to Kwan Yu (or Kwan Tai), the god of war and other things (see the boxed text p18). His image is the one in the middle of the main altar, flanked by his son and standard-bearer. The temple gets particularly busy in May and June, when two festivals in the god's honour are celebrated.

PAWNSHOP MUSEUM Map p424
Casa de Penhores Tradicional; ☎ 921 811; 396 Avenida de Almeida Ribeiro; admission MOP$5; ⏰ 10.30am-7pm, closed 1st Mon of the month
Pawnshops can be traced back to the 17th century in Macau. They flourished during difficult times, especially the Sino-Japanese War (1938–45). This museum is housed in the former Tak Seng On (Virtue and Success) pawnshop built in 1917 and incorporates the fortress-like eight-storey granite tower with slotted windows where goods were stored on racks or in safes.

CULTURAL CLUB Map p424
Clube Cultural; ☎ 921 811; 390 Avenida de Almeida Ribeiro; admission free; ⏰ 10.30am-9pm
In the same building as the museum, the Cultural Club looks at various aspects of everyday life in Macau. There's also a library devoted to the work of martial-arts novelist Louis Cha (Ching Yung in Cantonese, Jin Yong in Mandarin), an exhibition gallery and a lovely teahouse.

CHURCH OF ST AUGUSTINE Map p424
Igreja de Santo Agostinho; Largo de São Agostinho; ⏰ 10am-6pm
Southwest of Largo do Senado via Rua Central is the Church of St Augustine. Though its foundations date from 1586, the present church was built in 1814. The high altar has a statue of Christ bearing the cross, which is carried through the streets during the Procession of the Passion of Our Lord on the first Sunday of Lent (see Macau Calendar p292).

DOM PEDRO V THEATRE Map p424
Teatro Dom Pedro V; ☎ 939 646; Calçada do Teatro
Opposite the Church of St Augustine, this colonnaded, cream-coloured theatre, built in the neoclassical style in the mid-19th century, is sometimes used for cultural performances.

CHAPEL OF ST JOSEPH SEMINARY Map p424
Capela do Seminário São José; Rua do Seminário; ⏰ 10am-5pm
To the southwest of the theatre is the Chapel of St Joseph, built in 1758 as part of a Jesuit seminary. Its 19m-high domed ceiling has exceptionally fine acoustics, and the church is used as a concert venue.

CHURCH OF ST LAWRENCE Map p424
Igreja de São Lourenço; Rua de São Lourenço (enter from Rua da Imprensa Nacional); ⏰ 10am-6pm Tue-Sun, 1-2pm Mon
Southwest along Rua de São Lourenço is Macau's most fashionable church. The original was built of wood in the 1560s but was reconstructed in stone in the early 19th century and has a magnificent painted ceiling. One of the church towers once served as an ecclesiastical prison.

Southern Macau Peninsula
Southern Macau Peninsula encompasses three areas: around the Macau Forum and Tourist Activities Centre; the rectangle of reclaimed land called NAPE to the south; and the southwest corner of the peninsula.

The Macau Forum (Forum de Macau) and the Tourist Activities Centre (Centro de Actividades Turísticas; CAT) sit side by side on Rua de Luís Gonzaga Gomes southeast of central Macau. The former is a conference and exhibition space; the latter houses two worthwhile museums.

GRAND PRIX MUSEUM Map pp422–3
Museu do Grande Prémio; ☎ 798 4130; Basement fl, CAT, 431 Rua de Luís Gonzaga Gomes; adult/child under 19 MOP$10/5, child under 11 or senior over 60 free, adult MOP$20 with Macau Wine Museum; ☽ 10am-6pm Wed-Mon

Cars from the Macau Formula 3 Grand Prix, including the bright-red Triumph TR2 driven by Eduardo de Carvalho that won the first Grand Prix in 1954, are on display here, while simulators let you test your racing skills.

MACAU WINE MUSEUM Map pp422–3
Museu do Vinho de Macau; ☎ 798 4188; Basement fl, CAT, 431 Rua de Luís Gonzaga Gomes; adult/child under 19 MOP$15/5, child under 11 or senior over 60 free, adult MOP$20 with Grand Prix Museum; ☽ 10am-6pm Wed-Mon

For the most part, this museum is a rather inert display of wine racks, barrels, presses and tools used by wine makers, as well as a rundown of Portugal's various wine regions, but some of the more recent wines on display are available for tasting, which is included in the entry fee.

NAPE
The rectangular area of reclaimed land called NAPE – pronounced 'NA-pay' and short for Novos Aterros do Porto Exterior (New Reclaimed Land of the Outer Harbour) – separates the Outer Harbour from what was once Praia Grande Bay but is now a large artificial lake. NAPE is primarily an area of warehouses, bars and restaurants, but there are a couple of important sights here as well.

MACAU CULTURAL CENTRE
Map pp422–3
Centro Cultural de Macau; ☎ 797 7215; www.ccm.gov.mo; Avenida Xian Xing Hai

This US$100-million centre is the territory's prime venue for theatre, opera and other cultural performances. The Macau Museum of Art (next) is part of the centre, and a walkway connects it with a large tower standing in the harbour. Free guided tours in English depart from the main lobby at 10.30am on Friday.

MACAU MUSEUM OF ART Map pp422–3
Museu de Arte de Macau; ☎ 791 9800, Avenida Xian Xing Hai; adult/child or student MOP$5/3; ☽ 10am-7pm Tue-Sun

Located within the Macau Cultural Centre, this museum is an enormous, five-storey complex with more than 10,000 sq metres of floor space. There's a library with art-related titles on the ground floor. On the 1st floor are ticket offices, a café and lecture halls. The 2nd floor is given over to temporary exhibits, the 3rd floor has the Gallery of Historical Pictures (mostly Western art) and the 4th floor contains Chinese painting, calligraphy and porcelain.

KUN IAM STATUE Map pp422–3
Estátua de Kun Iam; Avenida Doutor Sun Yat Sen

This bizarre 20m-high bronze monument to the goddess of mercy, emerging Venus-like from a lotus in the Outer Harbour, is actually quite restful once you've entered her 'blossom'. This is the two-level Kun Iam Ecumenical Centre (Centro Ecuménico Kun Iam; ☎ 751 516; admission free; ☽ 10am-6pm Sat-Thu), where information is available on Buddhism, Taoism and Confucianism. The statue is connected to the mainland by a 60m-long footbridge.

SOUTHWEST CORNER
The southwestern tip of the Macau Peninsula has a number of interesting sights, as it should – it was the first area of Macau to be settled.

AVENIDA DA REPÚBLICA Map pp422–3
Avenida da Praia Grande and Rua da Praia do Bom Parto form an arc that leads into Avenida da República, one of the most beautiful avenues in the territory. Towering above it is the former Bela Vista Hotel, whose rooms hold enough stories to fill several volumes. It is now the residence of the Portuguese consul-general. A short distance southwest is the Santa Sancha Palace (Palacete de Santa Sancha; Estrada de Santa Sancha), erstwhile residence of Macau's Portuguese governors.

PENHA HILL Map pp422–3
Colina da Penha

Towering above the colonial villas along Avenida da República is Penha Hill, from where you'll get an excellent view of the central area of Macau and across the Pearl River into China. The Bishop's Palace (1837) is here, as is the Chapel of Our Lady of Penha (Capela de Nostra Señora da Penha; ☽ 9am-5.30pm).

MACAU TOWER Map pp422–3
Torre de Macau; Largo da Torre de Macau;
www.macautower.com.mo; 🕑 10am-9pm

Macau Tower, at 338m the 10th-tallest free-standing structure in the world, stands on the narrow isthmus of land southeast of Avenida da República. The squat building at its base is the **Macau Convention & Entertainment Centre** (☎ 933 339).

Apart from housing observation decks on the 58th and 61st floors (adult/child 3-12 or senior over 65 MOP$70/35), and a bunch of restaurants and bars, including the revolving **360° Café** on the 60th floor and the **180° Lounge** a floor below it, the Macau Tower doesn't 'do' anything – not even relay broadcast signals. As a result, a New Zealand–based extreme-sports company called **AJ Hackett** (☎ 988 8858; Lower Ground fl, Shop 21, Macau Convention & Entertainment Centre; 🕑 10am-6pm) has been allowed to organise all kinds of adventure climbs.

The truly intrepid will go for the Mast Climb (MOP$777-1100, depending on when you do it and how many are in your group), in which you go up and down the mast's 100m of vertical ladders to 338m in two hours. Skywalk (MOP$100/120 weekdays/weekend) is a twirl around the covered walkway – attached to a lanyard – under the pod of the tower (57th floor) and 216m above ground; Skywalk II (MOP$150/180) is a rail-less walk around the *outer* rim some 233m high. The faint-hearted might try something closer to terra firma: Ironwalk (from MOP$50/60 weekdays/weekend), an 8m-high walk via rope ladder around the legs of the tower, with a Flying Fox finish; Ironwalk X (MOP$100/120), a vertical version of Ironwalk, 23m up; and Flying Fox (MOP$30/40), a 75m 'flight' on a zip line from one of the tower legs into a large net 11m below.

A-MA TEMPLE Map pp422–3
Templo de A-Ma; Rua de São Tiago da Barra;
🕑 10am-6pm

North of Barra Hill, this temple – called Ma Kok Miu in Cantonese – is dedicated to the goddess A-Ma, who is better known as Tin Hau (see 'What's in a Name?' p295). The original temple on this site was probably already standing when the Portuguese arrived, although the present one may only date back to the 17th century. At the main entrance is a large boulder with an engraved *lorcha* (traditional sailing vessel of the South China Sea). The faithful make a pilgrimage here during the A-Ma Festival (between late April and early May).

Detail on cannon, Monte Fort (p305)

MARITIME MUSEUM Map pp422–3
Museu Marítimo; ☎ 595 481; 1 Largo do Pagode da Barra; adult/child 10-17 or senior over 65 MOP$10/5;
🕑 10am-5.30pm Wed-Mon

Opposite the A-Ma Temple, this is not Macau's biggest or best museum but its collection of boats and other artefacts related to Macau's seafaring past is interesting nonetheless. Particularly good are the mock-ups of a Hakka fishing village and the displays of the long narrow boats that are raced during the Dragon Boat Festival in June (see Macau Calendar p292). There's also a small aquarium.

A motorised junk moored next to the museum offers 30-minute rides around the Inner Harbour daily. For details, see Organised Tours p327.

Northern Macau Peninsula

The northern part of the peninsula, encompassing everything northward from the Luís de Camões Garden in the west and Guia Fort in the east to the border with the mainland, was more recently developed than the southern and central areas. Nevertheless, there are quite a few important historic sites in this district and some lovely gardens.

LUÍS DE CAMÕES GARDEN & GROTTO Map pp422–3

Jardim de Luís de Camões; Praça de Luís de Camões;
🕙 6am-9pm

This lovely garden is a pleasant and shady place popular with local Chinese, who use it to 'walk' their caged songbirds, play Chinese chequers or just sit and chat. In the centre of the park is the **Camões Grotto** (Gruta de Camões), which contains a bust of the one-eyed national poet of Portugal, Luís de Camões (1524–80). He is said to have written part of his epic *Os Lusiadas* in Macau, but there is no firm evidence that he was ever in the territory.

CASA GARDEN Map pp422–3

13 Praça de Luís de Camões

This restored colonial villa east of the Luís de Camões Garden was the headquarters of the British East India Company when it was based in Macau in the early 19th century. Today the villa houses the Oriental Foundation (Fundação Oriente), an organisation founded in 1996 to promote Portuguese culture worldwide, and an **exhibition gallery** (☎ 398 1126; admission free; 🕙 10am-6pm Sat & Sun, daily during special exhibits) with both permanent and temporary exhibits of Chinese antiques, porcelain and contemporary art.

OLD PROTESTANT CEMETERY
Map pp422–3

15 Praça de Luís de Camões; 🕙 8.30am-5.30pm

To the right of the Casa Garden is the final resting place of many early non-Portuguese residents of Macau, including English, Scots, Americans and Dutch. As church law forbade the burial of non-Catholics on hallowed ground, there was nowhere to inter Protestants who died here and they were often buried clandestinely in the nearby hills. The governor finally allowed a local merchant to sell some of his land to the British East India Company, and the cemetery was established in 1821. A number of old graves were then transferred to the cemetery, which explains the earlier dates on some of the tombstones.

Among the better-known people interred in the cemetery are the Irish-born artist George Chinnery (see the boxed text p299) and Robert Morrison (1782–1834), the first Protestant missionary to China and author of the first Chinese–English dictionary.

LIN FUNG TEMPLE Map pp422–3

Templo de Lin Fung; Avenida do Almirante Lacerda;
🕙 10am-6.30pm

This complex, built in 1592 as a Taoist temple but now dedicated to Kun Iam, is where Mandarins from Guangdong province would stay when they visited Macau. The most celebrated of these visitors was Lin Zexu (see Opium & War p64), the commissioner charged with stamping out the opium trade, who stayed here in September 1839. The **Lin Zexu Memorial Hall** (☎ 550 166; adult/child under 8 or senior over 65 MOP$10/3; 🕙 9am-5pm Tue-Sun), with old photographs, a model of a Chinese war junk and opium-smoking paraphernalia, recalls his visit.

KUN IAM TEMPLE Map pp422–3

Templo de Kun Iam; Avenida do Coronel Mesquita;
🕙 10am-6pm

Dating from 1627, this is the most interesting and active Buddhist temple in Macau. Rooms adjacent to the main hall honour the goddess of mercy with a collection of pictures and scrolls. Some of the reliefs at the front were damaged by Red Guards during the Cultural Revolution.

The first treaty of trade and friendship between the USA and China was signed at a stone table in the terraced gardens at the back in 1844, and a tablet marks the spot. Also here are four ancient banyan trees with intertwined branches; lovers come here to pray before the so-called Sweetheart Tree.

LOU LIM IOC GARDEN Map pp422–3

Jardim de Lou Lim Ioc ; 10 Estrada de Adolfo de Loureiro; 🕙 6am-9pm

This cool and leafy garden contains huge shade trees, lotus ponds, bamboo groves, grottoes and a bridge with nine turns (since evil spirits can only move in straight lines). Local people use the park to practise t'ai chi or play traditional Chinese musical instruments.

The Victorian-style **Lou Lim Ioc Garden Pavilion** (Pavilhão do Jardim de Lou Lim Ioc; ☎ 988 4178; admission free; 🕙 9am-9pm Tue-Sun), which is in the centre of the pond and connected to the mainland by little bridges, is used for temporary exhibits and for recitals during the International Music Festival in late October/November (see Macau Calendar p292).

SUN YAT SEN MEMORIAL HOME
Map pp422–3

Casa Memorativa de Doutor Sun Yat Sen; ☎ 574 064; 1 Rua de Silva Mendes; admission free; 🕙 10am-5pm Wed-Mon

Around the corner from the Lou Lim Ioc Garden is a museum dedicated to Dr Sun Yat

Sen (1866–1925), the founder of the Chinese Republic. Sun practised medicine at the Kiang Wu Hospital on Rua Coelho do Amaral for a few years before turning to revolution and seeking to overthrow the Qing dynasty. The house, built in the pseudo-Moorish style, contains a collection of flags, photos and documents relating to the life and times of the 'Father of the Nation'. It replaces the original house, which blew up while being used as an explosives store. Sun's first wife, Lu Muzhen, died in the upstairs back bedroom in 1952.

GUIA FORT & LIGHTHOUSE Map pp422–3
Guia Hill

The fortress built in 1638 atop Guia Hill (Colina da Guia), the highest point on the peninsula, was originally designed to defend the border with China, but it soon came into its own

as a lookout post, and storm warnings were sounded from the bell in the **Chapel of Our Lady of Guia** (Capela de Nostra Señora da Guia; 9.30am-5.30pm), built in 1622. The walls of the little church have interesting frescoes only discovered recently, and there's a colourful choir loft above the main entrance.

The 15m-tall Guia Lighthouse (Farol da Guia; 1865) next to the chapel is the oldest lighthouse on the China coast. Guia Hill is littered with old bunkers, relics of WWII and the Cold War.

The easiest way to reach the top of Guia Hill is to hop on the little **Guia Cable Car** (Teleférico da Guia) that runs from just outside the entrance of the attractive **Flora Garden** (Rua do Túnel; 6am-7pm), off Avenida de Sidónio Pais, continuously from 8am to 6pm Tuesday to Sunday and costs MOP$3/5 one way/return for adults (MOP$3 return for children, students & seniors).

TAIPA & COLOANE ISLANDS

A visit to Macau's two islands perfectly rounds off a trip to the territory. While peninsular Macau is where the vast majority of the territory's population lives, works and makes merry, Coloane and, to a lesser extent nowadays, Taipa are oases of calm and greenery. Striking pastel-coloured colonial villas and civic buildings preside over quiet lanes and a couple of delightful beaches, there's ample opportunity for walking and cycling, and the Portuguese and Macanese restaurants of Taipa village alone are worth the trip.

Taipa Island

When the Portuguese first sighted Taipa (Tam Chai in Cantonese, Tanzai in Mandarin), it was actually two islands. Over the centuries the pair was joined together by silt pouring down from the Pearl River. Reclamation will do the same thing to Taipa and Coloane eventually.

Traditionally an island of duck farms and boat yards, with enough small fireworks factories to satisfy the insatiable demand for bangers and crackers, Taipa is rapidly becoming urbanised. The construction of Taipa City, a large high-rise housing development in the centre of the island, is a major ongoing project and the rural charm that existed here in the past is well and truly gone.

Resisting the onslaught, however, is a parade of baroque churches and buildings, Taoist and Buddhist temples, overgrown esplanades and lethargic settlements.

POU TAI UN TEMPLE Map p425–6
Temple de Pou Tai Un; 5 Estrada Lou Lim Ieok; 9am-6pm

Some 200m southwest of the Hyatt Regency Macau, this Buddhist temple is the largest temple complex on the islands. The main hall,

dedicated to the Three Precious Buddhas, contains an enormous bronze statue of Lord Gautama, and there are brightly coloured prayer pavilions and orchid greenhouses scattered around the complex. Part of the complex is being converted into a retreat centre.

If you're visiting at lunch time, the temple operates a **vegetarian restaurant** (see Taipa Island p319).

TAIPA VILLAGE Map pp425–6

This village to the south of the island and in the shadow of the Hong Kong–style 'New Town' of Taipa City has somehow managed to retain its storybook charm. It is a tidy sprawl of traditional Chinese shops and some excellent restaurants, punctuated here and there by grand colonial villas, churches and ancient temples. Down along what was once the seafront and is now an artificial lake, **Avenida da Praia** is a tree-lined esplanade with wrought-iron benches and old-world charm – it's perfect for a leisurely stroll.

TAIPA HOUSE MUSEUM Map p425–6
Casa Museum da Taipa; ☎ 825 314; Avenida da Praia; adult MOP$5, admission free child under 10 or senior over 60, admission free for all on Sun; 10am-6pm Tue-Sun

Men hanging out, Lou Lim Ioc Garden (p309)

The five lime-green villas facing the water were built in 1921 by wealthy Macanese as summer residences and three of them collectively form this unusual museum. The two houses to the east of where Avenida da Praia meets Rua do Supico are used for receptions and special exhibitions; the three to the west house permanent collections.

The first of the houses that form the museum, the **House of the Regions of Portugal**, contains costumes and examines traditional ways of life around the country. The **House of the Islands** looks at the history of Taipa and Coloane, with some interesting displays devoted to the islands' traditional industries: fishing and the manufacture of oyster sauce, shrimp paste and fireworks. The last is the **Macanese House**, a residence done up in traditional local style that looks like the *dom* and *doña* (husband and wife) residing here left just yesterday. The mix of furnishings – heavy blackwood furniture and Chinese cloisonné with statues and pictures of saints and the Sacred Heart – is fascinating and the house offers a snapshot of life in Macau in the early 20th century.

TAIPA WALK Map pp425–6
From the western end of Avenida da Praia walk up the steps to the **Church of Our Lady of Carmel**, built in 1885. The colonial **library** opposite is a recent reproduction, replacing the original that had been pulled down illegally. Surrounding it are the pretty **Carmel Gardens**.

Following Avenida de Carlos da Maia will take you past an **old police school** and into Rua da Correia Silva, which leads to a small early-19th-century **Tin Hau temple** on Largo Governador Tamagnini Barbosa. To the northeast just off Rua do Regedor is **Pak Tai Temple**, dedicated to the guardian of peace and order. The vil-

lage **market** is housed in a building at the end of the street. There's a **crafts market** in Largo de Camões on Sunday (🕒 9am-7pm).

MACAU JOCKEY CLUB
RACETRACK Map pp425–6
☎ 821 188; www.macauhorse.com; Estrada Governador Albano de Oliveira; admission free
This racetrack, also known as the Hippodrome, has been Macau's venue for horse racing since 1991. Races are held twice on Saturday or Sunday afternoon from 2pm, and at night midweek (usually Wednesday) from 5pm. Summer recess is late August to early September.

FOUR-FACED BUDDHA SHRINE
Map pp425–6
Cnr Estrada Governador Albano de Oliveira & Rua de Fat San
Northeast of the Macau Jockey Club's main entrance, this Buddhist shrine guarded by four stone elephants and festooned with gold leaf and Thai-style floral bouquets, recalls the Erawan shrine in Bangkok. Apparently it was erected shortly after the racetrack opened, when punters had a string of bad luck. It's a popular place to pray before race meetings.

Coloane Island
A haven for pirates until the beginning of the 20th century, Coloane (Lo Wan in Cantonese, Luhuan in Mandarin) fought off the last assault by buccaneers on the South China Sea in 1910, and islanders still celebrate the anniversary of the victory on 13 July. Nowadays Coloane attracts large numbers of visitors to its sleepy main village and sandy coastline.

SEAC PAI VAN PARK Map pp425–6

☎ 870 277; Estrada Seac Pai Van; admission free;
🕑 9am-6pm Tue-Sun

About a kilometre south of the causeway, this 20-hectare park built in the wooded hills on the western side of the island has well-tended gardens, with hundreds of species of plants and trees from around the world, a **Garden of Medicinal Plants**, a children's **zoo**, a **lake** with swans and other waterfowl and a decaying walk-through **aviary** (🕑 9am-5pm Tue-Sun), which contains a number of rare birds. The **Museum of Nature & Agriculture** (☎ 827 012; admission free; 🕑 10am-6pm Tue-Sun) has traditional farming equipment, dioramas of Coloane's ecosystem and displays cataloguing a wide range of the island's fauna, flora and geology.

A-MA STATUE & CULTURAL VILLAGE Map pp425–6

Estátua da Deusa A-Ma; Alto de Coloane

This colossal 20m statue of the goddess who gave Macau its name (see 'What's in a Name?' p295) atop **Alto de Coloane** (176m) was hewn from a form of white jade quarried in Fangshang near Beijing and was erected in 1998. At the time of writing, you reached it by following Estrada do Alto de Coloane southwest from Estrada Seac Pai Van or by walking along the Coloane Trail (Trilho de Coloane) from the park (see Hiking p321).

The A-Ma Cultural Village is a religious and cultural complex with the statue as the core. Eventually there will be a museum devoted to the goddess and her cult, a vegetarian restaurant, and a cable car linking the village with Hác Sá Beach to the east.

COLOANE VILLAGE Map pp425–6

The only real settlement on the island, Coloane village is still largely a fishing village in character (particularly at the northern end), although in recent years tourism has given the local economy a boost. The village is a fascinating relic of the Macau that was, and strolling along the narrow lanes, flanked by pastel-coloured shops and restaurants, is a joy.

The bus will drop you off in the village's attractive **main square**; the **market** is on the eastern side. To the west is the waterfront; China is just across the channel. From here a sign points the way north to the **Sam Seng Temple** (2 Rua dos Navegantes), which is so small it's not much more than a family altar. Just past the temple is the village pier and beyond that to the northeast about a dozen **junk-building sheds**. Junks are still built here (it takes about two months to

make one), but a fire in 1999 destroyed many of the sheds.

CHAPEL OF ST FRANCIS XAVIER Map pp425–6

Capela de São Francisco Xavier; Avenida de Cinco de Outubro; 🕑 10am-8pm

This delightful little church on the waterfront was built in 1928 to honour St Francis Xavier. He had been a missionary in Japan, and Japanese Catholics still come to Coloane to pay their respects. For many years a fragment of St Francis's arm bone was kept in the chapel but it has now been moved to St Joseph Seminary on the Macau Peninsula.

In front of the chapel is a **monument** surrounded by four cannonballs commemorating the successful – and final – routing of pirates in 1910.

TEMPLES Map pp425–6

Southeast of the chapel between Travessa de Caetano and Travessa de Pagode is a small **Kun Iam temple** – just an altar inside a little walled compound. If you walk to the southeast just a little farther, you'll find a considerably larger and more interesting **Tin Hau temple** up in Largo Tin Hau Miu.

At the southern end of Avenida de Cinco de Outubro in Largo Tam Kong Miu, the **Tam Kong Temple** is dedicated to the Taoist god of seafarers, who may be a deification of the Song-dynasty boy emperor Duan Zong (see An Imperial Outpost p63). To the right of the main altar is a long whale bone, which has been carved into a model of a ship.

CHEOC VAN BEACH Map pp425–6

Estrada de Cheoc Van

About 1.5km down Estrada de Cheoc Van, which runs east and then southeast from Coloane village, is Cheoc Van (Bamboo Bay) Beach. There are public changing rooms and toilets, and lifeguards on duty from 10am to 6pm Monday to Saturday and 9am to 6pm Sunday from May to October.

HÁC SÁ BEACH Map pp425–6

Hác Sá (Black Sand) is a much larger and more popular beach than Cheoc Van. The sand is indeed a grey to blackish colour and makes the water look somewhat dirty (especially at the tide line), but it's perfectly clean. Hác Sá Bay is beautiful, and on a clear day you can just make out the mountaintops on Hong Kong's Lantau Island. Lifeguards keep the same schedule here as on Cheoc Van Beach.

WALKING TOUR

Begin your tour of the peninsula in **Largo do Senado** 1, the beautiful 'Senate Square' in the heart of Macau. On the south side facing Avenida de Almeida Ribeiro is the **main post office** 2, built in 1931, and nearby the restored **Museum of the Holy House of Mercy** 3 (p304). Opposite the museum is the main office of the **Macau Government Tourist Office** (MGTO) 4. Walk to the northeastern end of the square. Overlooking Largo de São Domingos is the **Church of St Dominic** 5 (p304), with its distinctive cream-coloured façade and green shutters and doors. On the southern side of this square, you'll spot a narrow road called Travessa de São Domingos. Follow this up to Largo da Sé and the **Macau Cathedral** 6 (p304). Travessa da Sé leads down into Rua de São Domingos. Take a right at the bottom of the hill and follow Rua de São Domingos and its extension, Rua de Pedro Nolasco da Silva, to the corner with Calçada do Monte. Just visible across the garden to the east is the **Consulate General of Portugal** 7, housed in an exquisite colonial mansion. Begin climbing steep Calçada do Monte and once you reach Travessa do Artilheiros, turn left. A cobbled path leads up to the **Monte Fort** 8 (p305) and the **Macau Museum**

Walk Facts

distance 2.5km
duration 2½ hours
start Largo do Senado
end Maritime Museum

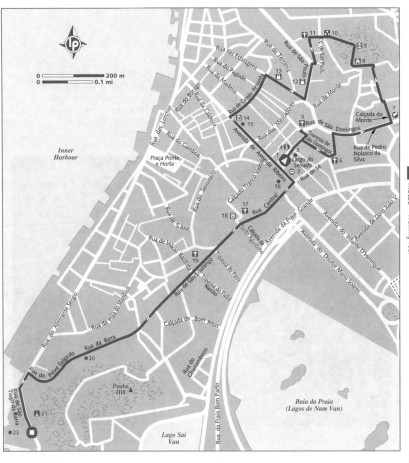

9 (p305). Take the escalator down from the museum and walk westward through the **ruins of the College of the Mother of God** 10, built by the Jesuits in the early 17th century, to the façade of the **Church of St Paul** 11 (p304); there's a platform offering stunning views over the town on the north side. Walk down the impressive stone steps in front of the façade and walk south along the Rua de São Paolo, lined with antique shops 12. Turn right onto Rua das Estalagens, full of **traditional Chinese shops** 13 and, once you reach Rua de Camilo Pessanha, turn left. At the western end of this street, turn left into Avenida de Almeida Ribeiro and immediately on your left you'll pass the **Pawnshop Museum** 14 (p306) and then the **Cultural Club** 15 (p306), where you may stop for a cup of tea and a snack at the Water Teahouse on the 2nd floor. Continue along Avenida de Almeida Ribeiro. After passing the **Leal Senado** 16 (p304), turn right onto Rua Central, which changes names several times as it heads southwest for the Inner Harbour. Towering above the western end of Rua Central is the **Church of St Augustine** 17 (p306) and opposite that the **Dom Pedro V Theatre** 18 (p306). Follow Rua Central's extensions, Rua de São Lourenço and Rua da Barra, passing the **Church of St Lawrence** 19 (p306) and the enormous **Moorish Barracks** 20, completed in 1874 and now housing the offices of the maritime police. Rua do Peixe Salgado (Street of Salted Fish) debouches into Rua do Almirante Sérgio, where you should turn left. A short distance south is the ever-active **A-Ma Temple** 21 (p308) and opposite, across Rua de São Tiago da Barra, is the **Maritime Museum** 22 (p308). From here, you can follow Avenida da República to Avenida da Praia Grande and Avenida de Almeida Ribeiro.

EATING
MACAU PENINSULA
Like Hong Kong Chinese, Macau people eat throughout the day – not just at specified meal times. Peninsular Macau's street stalls sell excellent stir-fried dishes; try any of the *dai pai dong* (open-air street stall) along Rua do Almirante Sérgio near the Inner Harbour. There are a few food stalls in Rua da Escola Commercial, a tiny lane one block west of the Lisboa Hotel and next to a sports field.

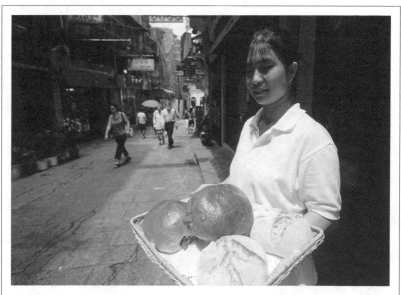

Fresh bread

Yuk gon, dried sweet strips of pork and other meats, are a Macau speciality, as are *hung yan bang*, delightful almond-flavoured biscuits or cookies sprinkled with powdery white sugar. The best places to find both are around Rua da Caldeira and Travessa do Matadouro, which are at the northern end of Avenida de Almeida Ribeiro near the Inner Harbour.

Macau has about half a dozen *mercados* (markets) selling fresh fruit, vegetables, meat and fish from 6am to 8pm daily. Two of the largest are the **Almirante Lacerda City Market** (Mercado Municipal Almirante Lacerda; Map pp422–3; 130 Avenida do Almirante Lacerda) in northern Macau and the **St Lawrence City Market** (Mercado Municipal de São Lourenço; Map p424; Rua de João Lecaros) in the south.

Top Five Restaurants – Macau

- **A Lorcha** (p315) The 'quality benchmark' of Portuguese food on the Macau mainland
- **Espaço Lisboa** (p319) Gourmet Portuguese in a renovated Coloane village house
- **Fernando's** (p319) Consistently excellent Portuguese food and fish dishes on Hác Sá beach
- **Ko Lung** (p317) Simple but super-authentic Thai eatery
- **Pinocchio** (p318) The place that launched the Taipa village restaurant phenomenon

A LORCHA

Map pp422–3   *Macanese, Portuguese*
☎ 313 193; 289A Rua do Almirante Sérgio; mains MOP$52-108; ☯ lunch 12.30-3pm, dinner 6.30-11pm
Some people refer to this place, not far from the A-Ma Temple, as the 'quality benchmark' of Portuguese food in Macau. Among the fine dishes are chicken with onion and tomato, *feijoada* and raw codfish salad.

BARRA NOVA Map pp422–3   *Macanese*
☎ 965 118; 287 Rua do Almirante Sérgio; starters MOP$25-50, mains MOP$40-128, fish dishes MOP$60-88; ☯ lunch 11.30am-3pm, dinner 5.30-10.30pm Mon-Fri, 11am-11pm Sat & Sun
This cosy restaurant, nestled in a row of excellent local eateries, serves such Macanese specialities as *porco balichão tamarino* (pork cooked with tamarind and shrimp paste), spicy *piri-piri* prawns and *galinha a cafreal* (chicken grilled with garlic and chilli).

CAFFÈ TOSCANA Map p424   *Italian*
☎ 370 354; 11 Travessa de São Domingos; pizza MOP$47-62, pasta MOP$45-60, mains MOP$50-65; ☯ 10am-10pm Wed-Mon
You can have a full meal at this Italian café, but it's especially recommended for focacce (MOP$16-35) and its excellent desserts (MOP$20).

CARLOS Map pp422–3   *Portuguese*
☎ 751 838; Ground fl, Vista Magnífica Bldg, Rua Cidade de Braga; mains MOP$55-90; ☯ lunch 11am-3pm, dinner 6-11pm
Carlos, which has some of the warmest service in town, serves decent (though not 100% authentic) Portuguese food.

CLUBE MILITAR DE MACAU

Map pp422–3   *Portuguese*
☎ 714 000; 975 Avenida da Praia Grande; starters MOP$55-80, mains MOP$95-200, set dinner MOP$90; ☯ lunch noon-3pm, dinner 6-11pm
The Portuguese and other dishes may not be the best in town, but Military Club is one of Macau's most distinguished colonial buildings.

DOM GALO

Map pp422–3   *Macanese, Portuguese*
☎ 751 383; Avenida Sir Anders Ljungstedt; mains from MOP$50; ☯ 10.30am-1am
The pleasant little 'Sir Rooster' is done up the way a child would imagine a Macanese or Portuguese town square to look. Try the clams with parsley and garlic, or the roast veal.

FOOK LAM MOON

Map pp422–3   *Chinese, Cantonese*
☎ 786 622; Kam Wah Kok Bldg, 259 Avenida da Amizade; meals from MOP$250 per person; ☯ lunch & dim sum 11am-3pm Mon-Fri, 8.30am-3pm Sat & Sun, dinner 5.30-11pm daily
This place serves some of the finest Cantonese food in Macau and is noted for its seafood dishes.

HENRI'S GALLEY

Map pp422–3   *Macanese*
☎ 556 251; 4G-H Avenida da República; mains MOP$69-97; ☯ 11am-11pm
This place, an old-timer on the Macau restaurant scene, is on the waterfront at the southern end of the Macau Peninsula. Its speciality is African chicken (MOP$85).

LITORAL

Map pp422–3 *Macanese, Portuguese*

☎ 967 878; 261A Rua do Almirante Sérgio; mains MOP$50-95; ☺ lunch 11.30am-3pm, dinner 6-11pm
This restaurant is just a short walk north of the Maritime Museum.

MEZZALUNA Map pp422–3 *Italian*

☎ 567 888, ext 3861; 2nd fl, Mandarin Oriental Hotel, 956-1110 Avenida da Amizade; starters MOP$60-105, pizzas MOP$75-125, pasta MOP$105-188, mains MOP$155-285; ☺ lunch 12.30-3pm, dinner 6.30-11pm Tue-Sun
This restaurant serves *la cucina italiana* in classy surroundings. The pasta is fresh and the pizzas piping hot from wood-fired ovens. Try either the rigatoni pasta filled with scallop mousse or the chicken risotto.

NAAM Map pp422–3 *Thai*

☎ 793 4818; Mandarin Oriental Hotel, 956-1110 Avenida da Amizade; starters MOP$40-65, salads MOP$50-65, mains MOP$50-130; ☺ lunch noon-3pm, dinner 6.30-10.30pm
If you want excellent Thai fare in sublime surrounds, head for Naam at the Mandarin. The Thai chefs obviously do not compromise for limp-tongued *farangs* (foreigners).

NEW YAOHAN SUPERMARKET

Map pp422–3 *Supermarket*

2nd fl, New Yaohan Department Store, Avenida da Amizade; ☺ 11am-10.30pm
Just opposite the ferry terminal, New Yaohan Department Store contains the largest supermarket in Macau.

OS GATOS Map pp422–3 *International*

☎ 378 111; Pousada de São Tiago, Fortaleza de São Tiago da Barra, Avenida da República; starters MPP$64-84, rice & pasta MOP$90-11, mains MOP$116-164; ☺ 7.30am-11.30pm
The flagship restaurant at the Pousada de São Tiago serves acceptable though pricey international dishes, but the outside terrace alone is worth the visit.

PARK 'N' SHOP Map pp422–3 *Supermarket*

44F Estrada da Areia Preta; ☺ 7.30am-11pm
This branch of the Hong Kong supermarket chain is in northern Macau.

PAVILIONS SUPERMERCADO

Map p424 *Supermarket*

421 Avenida da Praia Grande; ☺ 10.30am-9.30pm

Pavilions, dead in the centre of Macau, has a wide selection of imported food and drinks, including items from Portugal. The wine section is the basement is impressive.

PIZZERIA TOSCANA Map pp422–3 *Italian*

☎ 726 637; 1st fl, Apoio do Grande Premio de Macau, Avenida da Amizade; pizza MOP$47-72, pasta MOP$ 54-70; ☺ 8.30am-11pm Mon-Sat, 9.30am-11pm Sun
This pizzeria near the ferry terminal has some fine pastas and pizzas.

PLATÃO Map p424 *Portuguese*

☎ 331 818; 3 Travessa de São Domingos; starters MOP$14-40, mains MOP$70-98; ☺ noon-11pm Tue-Sun
This place is a knock-off Portuguese restaurant staffed by Filipinos, but the seafood fried rice (from MOP$54) and courtyard tables make it worth a visit.

PLAZA Map pp422–3 *Chinese, Cantonese*

☎ 706 623; 2nd fl, Xin Hua Bldg, 35 Rua da Nagasaki; soups MOP$20-100, clay pot dishes MOP$48-150, mains MOP$48-130
This positively cavernous restaurant is among the most popular Chinese restaurants in Macau. Dim sum is served from 8am to 3pm daily.

PORTO EXTERIOR

Map pp422–3 *Macanese, Portuguese*

☎ 703 276; Ground fl, Shop L, Chong Yu Bldg, 779 Avenida da Amizade; dishes MOP$65-85; ☺ noon-11pm
A new kid on the block, north of NAPE, Porto Exterior (Outer Harbour) has earned itself a loyal local following already.

PRAIA GRANDE

Map pp422–3 *Portuguese, International*

☎ 973 022; 10A Praça Lobo d'Avila; starters MOP$30-60, mains MOP$70-200; ☺ noon-11pm Mon-Fri, 11.30am-11pm Sat & Sun
This place serves a mixture of Portuguese and international favourites (pork with clams, onion soup), but the real drawing card is the outside tables along the Avenida da Praia Grande.

RITZ FINE DINING ROOM

Map pp422–3 *International*

☎ 339 955; Ground fl, Ritz Hotel, 11-13 Rua do Comendador Kou Ho Neng; starters MOP$38-148, mains MOP$118-198, set dinner MOP$338; lunch noon-3pm, dinner 6-11.30pm
For those who want to indulge, the Ritz's main restaurant is the place to go. The prices

belong more to Hong Kong than Macau, but the menu is expansive, with the stress on continental grills. The wine list is equally extensive.

SAI NAM Map p424 — Chinese, Seafood
☎ 574 072; 36 Rua da Felicidade; abalone & shark's fin plate from MOP$350; ⏰ 5.30-10.15pm
If you want to sample abalone at its freshest, try this small restaurant, which specialises in the shellfish and has quite a reputation in Macau.

SUPERMERCADO SAN MIU
Map pp422–3 — Supermarket
248 Avenida do Doutor Rodrigo Rodrigues; ⏰ 9am-4am
San Miu, one of many small supermarkets and grocery stores east of the Hotel Lisboa, is central and keeps very late hours.

TUNG YEE HEEN
Map pp422–3 — Chinese, Cantonese
☎ 793 3821; 2nd fl, Mandarin Oriental Hotel, 956-1110 Avenida da Amizade; soups MOP$35-75, mains MOP$55-160, set menus from MOP$210; ⏰ dim sum 9am-3pm, lunch noon-3pm, dinner 6-11pm
This hotel restaurant serves sophisticated Cantonese cuisine and has some interesting seafood (abalone, shark's fin, lobster) and regional (Chiu Chow, northern Chinese) specialities.

VELA LATINA Map p424 — Chinese, Cantonese
☎ 356 888; 201 Rua do Almirante Sérgio; dishes MOP$20-80; ⏰ lunch noon-3pm, dinner 6-11.30pm
This rather bizarre place serves Portuguese cuisine 'in a new way to perform' on the ground floor, and Thai on the 2nd. We'll go for the hotpot on the 1st floor.

Cheap Eats

ARUNA Map pp422–3 — Indian
☎ 701 850; Ground fl, Shop 0, Chong Yu Bldg, 779 Avenida da Amizade; curries MOP$30-38; ⏰ 11am-1am
Indian is not a cuisine easily had in Macau, but this little curry house and café serves up typical north Indian food.

CARAVELA Map p424 — Café
☎ 712 080; Ground fl, Kam Loi Bldg, 7 Rua do Comandante Mata e Oliveira; cakes MOP$10-25; ⏰ 7am-8pm
This excellent *pastelaria* (pastry shop) just north of Avenida de Dom João IV is a bit tricky to find, but the delectable pastries and snacks make it worth the effort.

CHENG CHONG
Map p424 — Chinese, Vegetarian
☎ 356 703; 12A-B Travessa de São Domingos; dishes MOP$18-58, small/large vegetarian pizza MOP$50/80; ⏰ noon-10pm
Macau doesn't offer much in the way of vegetarian restaurants, but this place, with mostly Chinese dishes but pizzas to keep the Westerners happy, is convenient to the centre.

KO LUNG Map pp422–3 — Thai
☎ 334 067; 23 Rua de Ferreira Amaral; dishes MOP$25-50; ⏰ 10am-10pm
This is one of the most authentic Thai restaurants north of Bangkok – right down to the toilet roll encased in a plastic dispenser on the table. Rua de Abreu Nunes to the west is another great street for Thai restaurants.

LONG KEI Map p424 — Chinese, Cantonese
☎ 589 508; 7B Largo do Senado; dishes from MOP$40; ⏰ lunch 11.30am-3pm, dinner 6-11.30pm
This landmark place below the neon cow on Largo do Senado is a straightforward Cantonese restaurant with more than 300 dishes on offer.

O BARRIL Map p424 — Snack Bar, Café
☎ 370 533; 14A-B Travessa de São Domingos; dishes MOP$53-90; ⏰ 8am-10pm Mon-Fri, 9am-10pm Sat & Sun
This little place is where to head if you want something fast and savoury *à portuguesa*. It shares its space with **Bolo de Arroz**, a pastry shop with a splendid and delicious range of Portuguese and Macanese pastries, cakes and aromatic coffees.

OU MUN CAFÉ Map p424 — Café
☎ 372 207; 12 Travessa de São Domingos; dishes from MOP$50; ⏰ 8am-8pm
This rather flash little café with the imaginative name of 'Macau' has good cakes and coffee and is a cut above the rest.

PAPA TUDO Map pp422–3 — Snack Bar
☎ 703 117; Ground fl, Nam Yuen Bldg, 68G-F Rua de Luís Gonzaga Gomes; snacks MOP$50; ⏰ 8am-11pm Mon-Fri, 9am-11pm Sat & Sun
This little place serves sandwiches and snacks, as well as more ambitious dishes like *naco na pedra* (beef tenderloin cooked on a hot stone; MOP$95).

SUSHI PALACE Map p424 — *Japanese*
☎ 356 336; Basement, Lung Cheong Bldg,
20-22 Rua de São Domingos; MOP$10-35, sashimi
MOP$25-120; ⏲ noon-10.30pm
This cheap and cheerful Japanese eatery is just
down from the Cathedral.

WONG CHI KEI
Map p424 — *Chinese, Cantonese*
☎ 331 313; 17 Largo do Senado; meals under
MOP$50; ⏲ 11am-12.30am

Come here if you're after a fix of late-night cheap
noodles to fill up on.

YES BRAZIL Map p424 — *Brazilian*
☎ 358 097; 6A Travessa Fortuna; mains MOP$30-78;
⏲ 11.30am-7pm Mon-Fri, 11.30am-9pm Sat, closed Sun
This tiny and very welcoming hole-in-the-wall
near the ruins of the Church of St Paul serves
an excellent *feijoada* (MOP$70) and other
Brazilian dishes and has a daily set menu for
just MOP$38.

TAIPA & COLOANE ISLANDS
The number of restaurants in Taipa, particularly in the village, has grown by leaps and
bounds in just a few short years. While much of the choice is restricted to Portuguese and
Macanese cuisine, you'll also find some excellent Cantonese eateries. Coloane is not the
treasure-trove of restaurants and other eateries that Taipa is, but there are a few decent
options offering a variety of cuisines at all price levels.

Taipa Island
A PETISQUEIRA Map pp425–6 — *Portuguese*
☎ 825 354; 15A-B Rua de São João; starters MOP$25-
35, mains MOP$75-135; ⏲ lunch 11.30am-3pm,
dinner 6.30-11pm
This excellent restaurant (in a little alley that is
easy to overlook) gets our vote for having the
best Portuguese food in Taipa. It has a decent
wine list and serves its own home-made *queijo
da cabra* (goat's cheese). Try the spicy prawns,
the *acorda de marisco* (seafood cooked with
mashed bread) or the *bife à portuguesa* (beef
cooked in a clay pot).

CHINESE RESTAURANT
Map pp425–6 — *Chinese, Cantonese*
☎ 831 234; Hyatt Regency Macau, 2 Estrada Almirante Marques Esparteiro; meals MOP$150-200 per
person; ⏲ dim sum & lunch 10.30am-3pm Mon-Fri,
8am-3pm Sat & Sun, dinner 6.30-11pm daily
The Hyatt's upmarket Chinese restaurant, just
off the main lobby and overlooking a lotus
pond, has very good Cantonese fare, including
dim sum; watch them being made by hand
and steamed in the open kitchen.

FLAMINGO
Map pp425–6 — *Macanese, Portuguese*
☎ 831 234 ext 1874; Hyatt Regency Macau, 2 Estrada
Almirante Marques Esparteiro; mains MOP$70-100;
⏲ lunch noon-3pm, dinner 7-11pm
Overlooking a duck pond and surrounded by
lush tropical growth, this restaurant serves
Portuguese seafood and classic Macanese
dishes, and is one of the most inviting hotel
restaurants in Macau.

GALO Map pp425–6 — *Macanese, Portuguese*
☎ 827 423; 45 Rua da Cunha; meals about MOP$120
per person; ⏲ lunch 11am-3pm, dinner 5.30-10.30pm
This place, on the corner with Rua dos Clérigos
and easily recognised by the picture of a red-
combed rooster above the door, is a quaint
addition to the string of eateries along Rua
da Cunha.

O CAPÍTULO Map pp425–6 — *Portuguese*
☎ 821 519; Ground fl, Nam San Bldg, Avenida de
Kwong Tung; mains MOP$62-92; ⏲ noon-10pm
This small eatery north of Macau Stadium
serves scrumptious home-made Portuguese
dishes, with specials changing daily.

O MANEL Map pp425–6 — *Portuguese*
☎ 827 571; 90 Rua de Fernão Mendes Pinto; meals
MOP$80-90 per person; ⏲ lunch noon-3.30pm,
dinner 6-10.30pm
This small but friendly place serves classic Portuguese dishes like *caldo verde* and *bacalhau*, be
it baked, grilled, stewed or boiled.

O SANTOS Map pp425–6 — *Portuguese*
☎ 827 508; 20 Rua da Cunha; mains MOP$62-75;
⏲ lunch noon-3pm, dinner 6.30-10.30pm
This tiny place is famous for its stuffed pork loin
and for its codfish dishes, especially *bacalhau à
zé do pipo* (sun-dried cod baked with mashed
potatoes; MOP$72).

PINOCCHIO Map pp425–6 — *Portuguese*
☎ 827 128; 4 Rua do Sol; starters MOP$23-50, mains
MOP$48-108; ⏲ noon-midnight

This is the place that launched the Taipa village restaurant phenomenon, and you should at least make a visit to pay your respects (provided you can get in). Recommended dishes include grilled fresh sardines and roast lamb.

CHEAP EATS
BEI FENG TONG
Map pp425–6　　　　　　*Chinese, Cantonese*
☎ 825 003; 33 Rua da Cunha; soups & hot pots from MOP$20; ☷ noon-11pm
This noodle shop, masquerading under the Portuguese name Doca de Abrigo (Harbour Dock), specialises in soups and hotpots.

POU TAI UN TEMPLE RESTAURANT
Map pp425–6　　　　　*Chinese, Vegetarian*
☎ 811 038; 5 Estrada Lou Lim Ieok; mains MOP$25-55; ☷ 11am-6pm Mon-Sat, 11am-9.30pm Sun
This restaurant in a Buddhist temple is strictly vegetarian. It's just around the corner from the Hyatt Regency Macau.

SENG CHEONG
Map pp425–6　　　　　　*Chinese, Cantonese*
☎ 825 323; 28-30 Rua da Cunha; meals under MOP$100 per person; ☷ noon-midnight
This Cantonese restaurant is celebrated for its fried fish balls and steamed eel.

Coloane Island
ESPAÇO LISBOA Map pp425–6　　*Portuguese*
☎ 882 226; 8 Rua dos Gaivotas; starters MOP$35-70, soups MOP$25-60, mains MOP$70-198; ☷ lunch noon-3pm, dinner 6-10pm Tue-Fri, noon-10.30pm Sat & Sun
This new restaurant in a renovated village house on two floors serves simply the best Portuguese food in Macau; we had no idea *bacalhau* and sardines could be prepared so innovatively. Try the swordfish stewed in a copper pan, or the curried crab. Daily specials are MOP$75–80, and the wine list is superb (indulge with a slightly effervescent white Paço de Teixeiró).

FERNANDO'S Map pp425–6　　　*Portuguese*
☎ 882 531; 9 Praia de Hác Sá; soups MOP$22-26, fish & seafood MOP$55-148, meat dishes MOP$50-128, rice dishes MOP$60-66; ☷ noon-9.30pm
This place deserves special mention for its consistently excellent Portuguese food and fish dishes. The atmosphere is pleasantly relaxed, but it can get crowded in the evening. Famed for its seafood, Fernando's has a devoted clientele and an almost legendary profile in good-dining circles.

KWUN HOI HEEN
Map pp425–6　　　　　　*Chinese, Cantonese*
☎ 871 111; 3rd fl, Westin Resort, 1918 Estrada de Hác Sá; dim sum MOP$18-48, rice & noodles MOP$23-70, mains from MOP$55; ☷ lunch 11am-3pm, dinner 6-11.30pm
The Kwun Hoi Heen stands out among the hotel restaurants on Coloane Island for its superb Cantonese cuisine, al fresco dining and sumptuous views. The weekend buffet lunch (MOP$118–158) and dinner (from MOP$198) are excellent value.

LA GONDOLA Map pp425–6　　　*Italian*
☎ 880 156; Praia de Cheoc Van; pizza MOP$45-66, pasta MOP$55-65, mains MOP$65-110; ☷ 11am-11pm
Next to the swimming pool at Cheoc Van Beach, this restaurant has some excellent pastas, pizzas cooked in a wood-fired oven and outside seating on a rather cramped terrace.

POUSADA DE COLOANE RESTAURANT
Map pp425–6　　　　*Portuguese, Macanese*
☎ 882 143; Pousada de Coloane Hotel, Estrada de Cheoc Van; starters MOP$25-60, soups MOP$20-30, mains MOP$70-90; ☷ lunch noon-3pm, dinner 7-10pm
This restaurant has decent Portuguese, Macanese and international dishes and seating on a veranda overlooking Cheoc Van Beach. The four set menus (MOP$88) and the Saturday-night barbecue and Sunday lunch buffets (both MOP$95) are particularly good value. The hotel usually offers free accommodation during the low season for people eating here (see Coloane Island p324).

CHEAP EATS
LORD STOW'S BAKERY
Map p425–6　　　　　　*Bakery, Snack Bar*
☎ 882 534; 1 Rua da Tassara; sandwiches MOP$9-15, quiche MOP$12; ☷ 7am-11pm Thu-Tue, 7am-6pm Wed
This bakery-cum-snack bar is famed for its *pastéis de nata*, a warm egg-custard tart (MOP$5.50, six for MOP$33), but it also does excellent cheesecake (MOP$12) in unsual flavours: chestnut, black sesame, green tea.

NGA TIM CAFÉ
Map p425–6　　　　　　*Chinese, Cantonese*
☎ 882 086; 8 Rua Caetano; meals about MOP$100 per person; ☷ 11.30am-1am
The food at this little place opposite the Chapel of St Francis Xavier is Sino-Portuguese, and while the restaurant is certainly no work of art, the view outside is. If it's a sunny day, take a seat in the square and savour both the scenery and the food.

ENTERTAINMENT

The **Macau Cultural Centre** (p307) is the territory's premier venue for classical music concerts, dance performances and studio film screenings. To book tickets ring ☎ 555 555 or, in Hong Kong, ☎ 7171 7171, or check the website www.macauticket.net.

PUBS & BARS

There are plenty of pubs and bars – some with live music – to keep you occupied. The main place for a pub crawl on the Macau Peninsula is the Docks – the reclaimed NAPE area; a row of attractive theme bars line the waterfront area to the southeast. But don't expect this to be like Hong Kong's Lan Kwai Fong (though that's what locals call it); at times this area can feel distinctly dead.

On Taipa Island, the area within the Nam San complex of buildings just north of the Macau Jockey Club has become something of a nightlife area in recent years, with half a dozen or so late-night pubs and bars opening their doors. They're usually open till 3am or 4am daily. Among the most popular are the **Irish Bar** (☎ 820 708; 116C Avenida de Kwong Tung), the **Bar dos Namorados** (☎ 822 451; 85E Avenida de Kwong Tung) and the **Island Pub** (☎ 822 781; 85A Avenida de Kwong Tung).

CASABLANCA CAFÉ Map pp422–3
☎ 751 281; Vista Magnífica Court Bldg, Avenida Doutor Sun Yat Sen, Macau Peninsula; 🕐 6pm-4am
This elegant watering hole has photos of Hollywood and Hong Kong film icons decorating the walls, cool jazz playing and pool tables.

EMBASSY BAR Map pp422–3
☎ 567 888; Ground fl, Mandarin Oriental Hotel, 956-1110 Avenida da Amizade, Macau Peninsula; 🕐 5pm-2am Sun-Thu, 5pm-4am Fri-Sat
This very popular bar features a live band nightly at 10.30pm and has a small dance floor. Happy hour is from 5pm to 9pm daily.

GREENHOUSE LOUNGE BAR Map pp425–6
☎ 831 234; Hyatt Regency Macau, 2 Estrada Almirante Marques Esparteiro, Taipa Island; 🕐 noon-2am
This cocktail bar just off the main lobby is where you go if you want a quiet drink. It attracts academics from the nearby University of Macau, jockeys from the racecourse and workers from the airport. Martinis here are excellent. Happy hour runs from 5pm to 7pm.

MOONWALKER BAR Map pp422–3
☎ 751 326; Vista Magnífica Court Bldg, Avenida Doutor Sun Yat Sen, Macau Peninsula; 🕐 3pm-3am Sun-Thu, 3pm-4am Fri-Sat
This place has live entertainment most nights (usually Filipina *chanteuses*).

OSKAR'S PUB Map pp422–30
☎ 783 333; Holiday Inn Macau, 82-86 Rua de Pequim, Macau Peninsula; 🕐 5pm-1.30am
This pub off the main lobby of the Holiday Inn

Macau draws a large number of local expats. Happy hour is from 5pm to 9pm.

RIO CAFÉ Map pp422–3
☎ 751 306; Vista Magnífica Court Bldg, Avenida Doutor Sun Yat Sen, Macau Peninsula; 🕐 7.30pm-2am Sun-Thu, 7.30pm-3am Sat & Sun
If you're in a former Portuguese colony, why not take your cue from another one? The orange-and-blue décor and the outside seating by the Outer Harbour *may* conjure up images of Ipanema (the Gothic windows don't).

SANSHIRO PUB Map pp422–3
☎ 751 238; Vista Magnífica Court, Avenida Doutor Sun Yat Sen, Macau Peninsula; 🕐 5pm-3am
This is a much more simple pub, and attractive for that, with beer by the pitcher, happy hour from 5pm to 8pm, and outside tables.

CLUBS

The club scene in Macau has yet to reach the level of sophistication that it has in Hong Kong, and nightlife here is largely limited to tacky nightclub floorshows and hostess clubs.

DD CLUB Map p424
☎ 711 800; cnr Avenida de Dom João IV & Avenida do Infante Dom Henrique, Macau Peninsula; 🕐 10.30pm-7am
This popular disco club opposite the landmark Escola Portuguesa de Macau has a small hall with live music, a main hall with a big dance floor, and a bar.

THEATRE

There's very little in the way of legitimate theatre in Macau, though the Lisboa offers a popular floorshow.

CRAZY PARIS SHOW Map pp422–3

☎ 377 666; Lisboa Hotel, 2-4 Avenida de Lisboa, Macau Peninsula; admission MOP$300; ⏲ shows 8pm & 9.30pm

This show, similar to the revues so popular in Las Vegas, is performed in the Lisboa's Mona Lisa Hall. Buy your tickets in the lobby of the New (or West) Wing. Under-18s are not admitted.

SPORT & FITNESS

Cycling

Bicycles (MOP$10–12 an hour) can be rented at several locations in Taipa village, including **Iao Kei Bicicleta** (Map pp425-6; ☎ 827 975; 36 Largo Governador Tamagini Barbosa). On Coloane you'll find them for MOP$20 per hour from **Viagens Pico** (Map p425-6; ☎ 832 695), next door to Fernando's restaurant on Hác Sá Beach.

You are not allowed to cross the Macau–Taipa bridge on a bicycle though they are permitted on the causeway linking Taipa and Coloane.

Go-Karting

The **Coloane Kartodrome** (Map p425-6; ☎ 881 862; Estrada de Seac Pai Van; ⏲ 10.30am-8.30pm Sun-Thu, 10.30am-10.30pm Fri-Sat), on the southern end of Cotai on Coloane's northern shore, is the region's most popular venue for go-karting. It is floodlit and there is a choice of seven different circuits. It costs MOP$100/180/200 for 10/20/25 minutes; a two-seater is MOP$150 for 10 minutes. There are all sorts of packages available (eg 25 minutes in a go-kart plus return ferry tickets from/to Hong Kong for MOP$380 or the same deal plus one night's accommodation for MOP$550/680 weekdays/weekend). Races are held here on Sunday.

Golf

The 18-hole, par-71 course at **Macau Golf & Country Club** (Map p425-6; ☎ 871 111; 1918 Estrada de Hác Sá), which is connected to the Westin Resort hotel on Coloane by walkway on the 9th floor, is open to nonguests. Green fees are MOP$700/1400 on weekdays/weekends, and you must have a handicap certificate to tee off.

Hiking

There are two trails on Guia Hill, in central Macau, which are also good for jogging. The **Walk of 33 Curves** (1.7km) circles the hill; inside this loop is the shorter Fitness Circuit Walk, with 20 exercise stations.

The **Little Taipa Trail** (Trilho de Taipa Pequena) is a 2km-long circuit around a hill (111m) of that name in the northwestern part of Taipa. The 2.2km-long **Big Taipa Trail** (Trilho de Taipa Grande) rings Taipa Grande, a 160m hill at the eastern end of the island.

Coloane's longest trail, the **Coloane Trail** (Trilho de Coloane), begins at Seac Pai Van Park and is just over 8km long. The shorter **Northeast Coloane Trail** (Trilho Nordeste de Coloane) near Ká Hó runs for about 3km. Other trails include the 1.5km-long **Altinho de Ká Hó Trail** and the 1.5km-long **Hác Sá Reservoir Circuit** (Circuito da Barragem de Hác Sá), which both loop around the reservoir northwest of Hác Sá Beach.

Water Sports

The **Hác Sá Sports & Recreation Park** (Map p425-6; ☎ 882 296, Estrada Nova de Hác Sá; ⏲ 8am-9pm Sun-Fri, 8am-11pm Sat) by the bus stop seems to have just about everything on offer, but its main draw is the **outdoor swimming pool** (adult/child MOP$15/5; ⏲ 10am-9pm Mon, 8am-9pm Tue-Fri & Sun, 8am-11pm Sat). You'll also find three **tennis courts** (MOP$30 per hour, MOP$60 after 7pm; racquet and ball hire MOP$5 each), a five-a-side **football ground** (MOP$70 per hour, MOP$100 after 7pm), a **mini-golf course** (MOP$10 per hour), **ping pong tables** (MOP$5 per hour) and **badminton courts** (MOP$10 per hour).

Cheoc Van swimming pool (Map p425-6; ☎ 870 277), which costs the same for entry and keeps the same hours as the Hác Sá Sports and Recreation Park pool, is at the southern end of the beach.

There are stands where you can rent windsurfing boards, jet skis and water scooters at either end of Hác Sá Beach. On Cheoc Van Beach, ask the **Cheoc Van Yacht Club** (Map pp225-6; ☎ 882 252; ⏲ 9am-6pm daily Apr-Oct, 9am-5pm Nov-Mar) about renting boats and windsurfing boards.

SHOPPING

The main shopping areas in peninsular Macau are along Avenida do Infante Dom Henrique and Avenida de Almeida Ribeiro. Other shopping zones can be found along Rua da Palha, Rua do Campo and Rua Pedro Nolasco da Silva.

The largest department store in Macau is the Japanese-owned **New Yaohan** (Map pp422–3) on Avenida da Amizade opposite the ferry terminal. Central Plaza (Map p424) on Avenida de Almeida Ribeiro just down from the Leal Senado has a concentration of top-end shops.

ANTIQUES & CURIOS

While exploring Macau's back lanes and streets you'll stumble across bustling markets and traditional Chinese shops. Rua de Madeira is a charming market street, with many shops selling carved Buddhas and other religious items.

Rua dos Mercadores, which leads up to Rua da Tercena, will lead you past tailors, wok sellers, tiny jewellery shops, incense and mahjong shops and other traditional businesses. At the far end of Rua da Tercena, where the road splits, is a **flea market** (Map pp422–3), where you can pick up baskets and other rattan ware, jade pieces and old Macau coins.

Great streets for antiques, ceramics and curios (eg traditional Chinese kites) are Rua de São Paulo, Rua das Estalagens and Rua de São António, and the lanes off them; most shops are open from 10.30am to 6pm, with lunch some time between 12.30pm and 2pm.

The backstreets of Coloane village, especially Rua dos Negociantes, have shops selling bric-a-brac, traditional goods and antiques. One of the best antique shops in Macau is here: **Asian Artefacts** (Map pp425-6; ☎ 881 022; 9 Rua dos Negociantes; ☷ 10am-7pm).

CLOTHING

The **St Dominic Market** (Map p424), in an alley just behind the Central Hotel and northwest of the MGTO, is a good place to pick up T-shirts and other cheap clothing. Rua das Estalagens is also good for this type of thing.

STAMPS

Macau produces some wonderful postage stamps, real collector's items that include images of everything from key colonial landmarks to roulette tables and high-speed ferries. Mint sets and first-day covers are available from next to counter No 16 at the main post office facing Largo do Senado and from Correios de Macau's **Loja de Filatelia** (Philately Shop; Map p424; ☎ 329 490; 789 Avenida da Praia Grande; ☷ 9am-6pm Mon-Fri, 9am-1pm Sat).

SLEEPING

Accommodation in Macau runs the gamut from glimmering five-star palaces to guesthouses, many of them no more than dosshouses, that go by names including *vila*, *hospedaria* or *pensão*. There are two Hostelling International–affiliated hostels on Coloane.

In general Macau's hotels are much cheaper than those in Hong Kong. On top of that, substantial discounts (30% or more) are available if you book through a travel agency, but this usually only applies to hotels of three stars and above. In Hong Kong you'll find a lot of these agents at the **Shun Tak Centre** (Map pp400-3; 200 Connaught Rd, Sheung Wan), from where the ferries to Macau depart. If you haven't booked your room before your arrival, you can do it at one of the many hotel desks in the ferry terminal pier in Macau.

Visiting Macau at the weekend, on public holidays or during the summer high season should be avoided if possible, as rooms are scarce and hotel prices can double or even treble. 'Weekend' really means just Saturday night in relation to accommodation; Friday night is usually not a problem unless it's a holiday.

Most large hotels add a 10% service charge and 5% government tax to the bill.

MACAU PENINSULA

Hotels in Macau are generally split geographically into price constituencies, with many cheap guesthouses and hotels occupying the southwestern part of the peninsula, around Rua das Lorchas and Avenida de Almeida Ribeiro, and top-end hotels generally in the east and centre of town.

FU HUA HOTEL Map pp422–3   Hotel
☎ 553 838; fax 527 575; 98-102 Rua de Francisco Xavier Pereira; s/d MOP$730/ 830, ste from MOP$1380
If for some reason you want to stay in the northern part of the Macau Peninsula, choose this modern and bright 142-room hotel a stone's throw from the Kun Iam Temple.

GUIA HOTEL Map pp422–3   Hotel
☎ 513 888; guia@macau.ctm.net; 1-5 Estrada do Engenheiro Trigo; s & d MOP$520-720, tr MOP$750, ste from MOP$850
If you want something smaller and a bit 'isolated' (if there is such a thing in Macau), choose this 90-room place at the foot of Guia Hill.

LISBOA HOTEL Map pp422–3   Hotel
☎ 377 666; www.hotellisboa.com; 2-4 Avenida de Lisboa; s & d MOP$1350-2550, ste from MOP$3800
This is Macau's most famous and unsightly (imagine a squat tin can the colour of mustard topped with a pincushion) landmark, with both an old (east) and a new (west or tower) wing and close to 1000 rooms. The Lisboa has probably the best shopping arcade in Macau, and for many its casino is the only game in town.

MANDARIN ORIENTAL
Map pp422–3   Hotel
☎ 567 888; www.mandarinoriental.com; 956-1110 Avenida da Amizade; s & d MOP$1900-2200, ste from MOP$4600
This superb five-star, 435-room hotel has a huge swimming pool, lovely gardens, three stunning restaurants and a great bar. Try to book your room through an agent to take advantage of any weekday packages on offer.

POUSADA DE MONG HÁ
Map pp422–3   Guesthouse
☎ 561 252; fax 519 058; www.ift.edu.mo; s/d MOP$400/500 Mon-Fri, MOP$500/600 Sat & Sun, ste MOP$900
This traditional-style Portuguese inn (20 rooms) with Asian touches sits atop Mong Há Hill and near the ruins of a fort built in 1849. It is run by students at the Instituto de Formação Turística (Institute for Tourism Studies). Rates include breakfast. The restaurant here is open

weekdays for lunch, on Friday night (Macanese buffet MOP$130) and for brunch on Sunday (MOP$110).

POUSADA DE SÃO TIAGO
Map pp422–3   Hotel
☎ 378 111; www.saotiago.com.mo; Fortaleza de São Tiago da Barra, Avenida da República; s & d MOP$1620-1960, ste from MOP$2300
The 'St James Inn', built into the ruins of a 17th-century Barra Fort, commands a splendid view of the harbour (as does the pool), and the interior décor, with its flagstones and wooden beams, is a delight. Even if you don't stay, it's worth stopping by for a look or a drink on the terrace. It only has 23 rooms, so book well in advance.

RITZ HOTEL Map pp422–3   Hotel
☎ 339 955; www.ritzhotel.com.mo; 11-13 Rua do Comendador Kou Ho Neng; s & d MOP$980-1380, ste from MOP$2080
This palace of a place, in a quiet street high above Avenida da República, is as close as you'll get to staying at the legendary Bela Vista across the road. It has 161 rooms and a wonderful recreation centre, with a huge heated pool.

ROYAL HOTEL Map pp422–3   Hotel
☎ 552 222; www.hotelroyal.com.mo; 2-4 Estrada da Vitória; s & d MOP$750-1100, ste from MOP$2200
This 365-room hotel is a little removed from the action, but attractive for that reason. It offers some very good-value weekday packages.

SINTRA HOTEL Map p424   Hotel
☎ 710 111; wwww.hotelsintra.com; Avenida de Dom João IV; s & d MOP$860-1260, ste from MOP$1860
This 240-room hotel south of Avenida da Praia Grande is very central and comfortable. Service here is among the best in Macau.

Cheap Sleeps
CENTRAL HOTEL Map p424   Hotel
☎ 373 888; fax 332 275; 264 Avenida de Almeida Ribeiro; s MOP$150-188 (weekend MOP$173-210), d MOP$160-198 (MOP$210-232)
The old colonial building of this hotel has had

Macau – Sleeping

a lick of pea-green paint, but it's still pretty frayed inside. Still, it's just what its name says – a short hop northwest of Largo do Senado.

EAST ASIA HOTEL Map p424 *Hotel*
☎ 922 433; fax 922 430; 1A Rua da Madeira;
s MOP$260-340, d MOP$400-500, tr MOP$500,
ste fromMOP$720
The East Asia is housed in a classic colonial-style building and, though it's been remodelled, has not lost all of its charm. The 98 rooms are spacious and have private bathrooms.

PENSÃO NAM IN Map p424 *Guesthouse*
☎ 710 024; fax 710008; 3 Travessa da Praia Grande;
s/d from MOP$150/230
This little place near the Lisboa has singles with a shared bath and pleasant doubles with a private bath.

SAN VA HOSPEDARIA
Map p424 *Guesthouse*
☎ 573 701; info@sanvahotel.com;
67 Rua de Felicidade; s/d MOP$85/150
On the 'street of happiness' that was once the hub of the red-light district, this traditional-style place has character and a homey feel to it, though the rooms are like cupboards and separated by flimsy cardboard partitions.

SUN SUN HOTEL Map p424 *Hotel*
☎ 939 393; www.hotelsunsun.com;
14-16 Praça Ponte e Horta; s & d MOP$380-580,
weekly packages from MOP$1820
This modern-looking and clean place usually offers rooms for much less than its advertised prices. The rooms on the upper floors have excellent views of the Inner Harbour.

TAIPA & COLOANE ISLANDS
Taipa has several excellent top-end hotels, one of which is more like a resort than a hotel. Coloane offers quite a diversity when it comes to accommodation – from a cosy 'inn' and the territory's most exclusive resort to two budget hostels.

Taipa Island
GRANDVIEW HOTEL Map pp425–6 *Hotel*
☎ 837 788; www.grandview.com.mo; 142 Estrada Governador Albano de Oliveira; s & d MOP$980-1280, ste from MOP$2180
This rather tasteful 406-room hotel is a short gallop northeast of the Macau Jockey Club and close to the Nam San nightlife area (see Pubs & Bars p320). If you don't want to watch the nags or bend your elbow, you can take advantage of the hotel's swimming pool, sauna and gym. This offers great discounts during the week and at the weekend during the low season.

HYATT REGENCY MACAU
Map pp425–6 *Hotel*
☎ 831 234; www.macau.hyatt.com; 2 Estrada Almirante Marques Esparteiro; s & d MOP$800-1750, ste from MOP$2800
More of a resort than a hotel, this 326-room place has four tennis courts, two squash courts, a fully equipped fitness centre and games room, spas for both men and women, a childcare centre, a huge heated swimming pool and a casino (access from 2nd floor). Restaurants in the hotel dish up Cantonese, Macanese and Portuguese fare, and there's an excellent delicatessen and bakery off the lobby if you want to make yourself a picnic.

POUSADA MARINA INFANTE
Map pp425–6 *Hotel*
☎ 838 333; www.pousadamarinainfante.com;
Marina da Taipa Sul, Cotai; s & d MOP$880-1180,
ste from MOP$1680
This hotel with the cosy-sounding name is actually a huge 312-room structure built on reclaimed land south of the Macau Jockey Club. The Pousada Marina's facilities include a popular casino; the hotel is said to possess excellent feng shui for gamblers. This place is very convenient for those crossing the nearby Lotus Bridge regularly on their way to and from Zhuhai.

Coloane Island
POUSADA DE COLOANE
Map pp425–6 *Hotel*
☎ 882 144; fax 882 251; Estrada de Cheoc Van;
s & d MOP$680-750, tr MOP$880-950
This cosy, 22-room hotel overlooking Cheoc Van Beach has a fabulous terrace above the sea and its own little swimming pool, and is known for its excellent Saturday-night barbecue and Sunday lunch buffets (see p319). If two of you spend more than MOP$600 at the hotel's restaurant, you get one night's free accommodation.

WESTIN RESORT Map pp425–6   *Hotel*
☎ 871 111; www.westin.com; 1918 Estrada de Hác Sá; s & d MOP$2100-2450, ste from MOP$5500

This five-star 'island resort' complex is on the eastern side of Hác Sá Beach. Each of the 208 rooms is the same size and has a large terrace. The overall atmosphere is that of a country club, with an attached 18-hole golf course (access from the 9th floor), eight tennis courts, two squash courts, billiard tables, two swimming pools, an outdoor spa, sauna and gymnasium on 60 hectares of land. The resort's **Café Panorama** is a delightful spot for a sundowner.

Cheap Sleeps

POUSADA DE JUVENTUDE DE CHEOC VAN Map pp425–6   *Hostel*
☎ 882 024; www.dsej.gov.mo; Rua de António Francisco; d/dm Mon-Fri MOP$70/40, Sat & Sun MOP$100/50

This very clean 34-bed hostel is on the eastern side of Cheoc Van Bay below the Pousada de Coloane. During the low season (basically winter) it's pretty easy to get in here, but during the high season (summer and holidays) competition for beds is keen. Dorm rooms have 14 and 16 beds. The hostel has a small kitchen and garden.

Pedicab, Largo do Senado

POUSADA DE JUVENTUDE DE HÁC SÁ Map pp425–6   *Hostel*
☎ 882 701; www.dsej.gov.mo; Estrada Nova de Hác Sá; d/quad/dm Mon-Fri MOP$70/50/40, Sat & Sun MOP$100/70/50

This circular, grey-tiled building at the southern end of Hác Sá Beach is more modern than the Cheoc Van hostel. It has 100 beds in 17 rooms; the three dorm rooms have 16 beds each but the rest are quads and doubles.

TRANSPORT

For details on transport by air and sea to/from Hong Kong, see Hong Kong to Macau p338. Macau levies a MOP$20 departure tax for ferries and a MOP$130 (MOP$80 children) tax for helicopters. Both are usually included in quoted fare.

MACAU PUBLIC TRANSPORTATION

Public buses and minibuses run by **TCM** (☎ 850 060) and **Transmac** (☎ 271 122) operate on 40 routes throughout the day from 6.45am till midnight. Fares – MOP$2.50 on the peninsula, MOP$3.30 to Taipa, MOP$4 to Coloane village, MOP$5 to Hác Sá Beach – are dropped into a box upon entry in using either patacas or Hong Kong dollar coins; there's no change.

Useful bus routes on the peninsula:

No 3 From the ferry terminal, past the Macau Forum and Lisboa Hotel, along Avenida Almeida Ribeiro and up to the border gate.

No 3A Follows the same route as the No 3 but goes west from Avenida Almeida Ribeiro over to the budget hotel district and terminates on Praça Ponte e Horta.

No 10 From the border gate to the ferry terminal, past the Macau Forum and the Lisboa Hotel, along part of Avenida Almeida Ribeiro and down to the A-Ma Temple (bus **No 10A** follows a similar route).

No 12 From the ferry terminal, past the Macau Forum and the Lisboa Hotel and then up to the Lou Lim Ioc Garden and Kun Iam Temple.

Useful bus routes to Taipa and Coloane:

No 21 From the A-Ma Temple and along Avenida Almeida Ribeiro to the Lisboa Hotel, over the bridge to Taipa village and on to Coloane (bus **No 21A** follows the same route but carries on to Cheoc Van and Hác Sá Beaches).

No 22 From the Kun Iam Temple, past the Lisboa Hotel to Taipa village and then the Macau Jockey Club.

No 25 From the border via Lou Lim Ioc Garden, past the Lisboa Hotel to Taipa village and the University of Macau, then on to Cheoc Van and Hác Sá Beaches on Coloane.

No 26A From Avenida Almeida Ribeiro, past the Lisboa Hotel and through Taipa to the airport and the Lotus Bridge and Cotai border crossing and then to Coloane village (and, in summer, Cheoc Van and Hác Sá beaches).

CAR & MOTORCYCLE

The streets of peninsular Macau are a gridlock of cars plastered with go-faster stripes and stickers and mopeds that will cut you off at every turn. While driving here might look like it could be fun, it's strictly for the locals. That said, a Moke (a brightly coloured Jeep-like convertible) or a motorcycle can be a convenient way to explore the islands.

Rental

Happy Rent A Car (☎ 726 868; fax 726 888), in room 1025 of the ferry terminal arrivals hall, has four-person Mokes available to rent for MOP$450/500 per day during the week/weekends and six-person vehicles for HK$500/600. Renting from just 9am to 5.30pm costs MOP$300. You can also rent Mokes for the same price from **Avis Rent A Car** (Map pp422-3; ☎ 336 789; www.avis.com.mo), which has an office at the Mandarin Oriental hotel car park. Avis also rents cheap Suzuki Swifts that cost MOP$500 a day during the week and MOP$650 at the weekend.

New Spot Tourism Bike Rental (Map pp422-3; ☎ 750 880; fax 751 852; Ground fl, Chu Kwang Bldg, Rua de Londres) in NAPE rents out motorbikes for MOP$250 a day, including petrol and insurance.

TAXI

Flag fall in a Macau taxi is MOP$10 for the first 1.5km, MOP$1 for each additional 200m. There is a MOP$5 surcharge to go to Coloane; travelling between Taipa and Coloane is MOP$2 extra. Journeys starting from the airport incur an extra charge of MOP$5. Large bags cost an extra MOP$3. Taxis can be dispatched by radio by ringing ☎ 519 519, ☎ 939 939 or ☎ 398 8800.

ORGANISED TOURS

Tours booked on the ground in Macau are generally much better value than those booked in Hong Kong, though the latter include transportation to and from Macau and sometimes a side trip across the border to Zhuhai. Tours from Hong Kong are usually one-day whirlwind tours, departing for Macau in the morning and returning to Hong Kong on the same evening. **Gray Line** (☎ 2368 7111; www.grayline.com.hk) offers such a tour for HK$630/660 weekdays/weekend (child under 10 HK$560/590).

Quality Tours organised by the MGTO and tendered to agents like **Gray Line** (☎ 3336 611) in room 1025 of the ferry terminal arrivals hall take 3½ to four hours (adult/child, including museum tickets MOP$98/78). There's an Island Highlights Tour for MOP$68/48.

The Tour Machine, run by **Avis Rent A Car** (☎ 336 789), is a replica 1920s-style English bus that seats nine people and runs on fixed routes in about two hours past some of Macau's most important sights (adult/child under 12 MOP$150/80). You're allowed to disembark, stretch your legs and take photos along the way. There are two departures a day – at 11am and 3pm – from the Macau Ferry Terminal.

A motorised junk moored at the little pier next to the **Maritime Museum** (Map pp422–3) offers 30-minute rides (MOP$10) around the Inner Harbour with taped commentary. Departures are daily at 10.30am, 11.30am, 3.30pm and 4pm; there are up to six additional sailings between 11am and 5pm when six or more tickets are sold.

MACAU TO CHINA

The Zhuhai Special Economic Zone (SEZ) in mainland China just across Macau's northern border makes for an interesting day or overnight trip. Take bus No 3, 5 or 9 to the Border Gate – known as the Portas de Cerco (Gates of Siege) in Portuguese – and simply walk across (🕒 7am-midnight). A second crossing, the Cotai Frontier Post, allows passengers to cross over the Lotus Bridge linking Macau and the Zhuhai SEZ from 9am to 5pm daily, but it is of little use to most visitors. Bus No 26 will drop you off here.

Holders of most passports will be able to purchase their visas (MOP$100) at the border, but it will ultimately save you time (if not money) to buy one in advance. These are available in Hong Kong (see Visas p334) or in Macau from **China Travel Service** (Map p422-3; 1st fl, Xin Hua Bldg, 35 Rua de Nagasaki) in one day for MOP$150 (plus photos).

If you want to travel farther afield in China, buses run by the **Kee Kwan Motor Road Co** (Map 22; ☎ 933 888) leave the small station on Rua das Lorchas, 100m southwest of the end of Avenida de Almeida Ribeiro, daily for Guangzhou (MOP$55, every 15 minutes between 7.30am and 7.30pm) and Zhongshan (MOP$15, every 20 minutes between 8am and 5.30pm).

DIRECTORY

Much of the advice given for Hong Kong applies to Macau as well. If you find any sections missing here, refer to the ones in the Hong Kong Directory chapter (p353) for more details.

BOOKS

A Macao Narrative by the late Hong Kong–based writer Austin Coates is a slim but comprehensive history of the territory until the mid-1970s. *Macau* by César Guillén-Nuñez is rather dry but can be read in one sitting. Novels set in Macau are rare but Austin Coates's *City of Broken Promises*, a fictionalised account of the life of 18th-century Macanese trader Martha Merop (see Museum of the Holy House of Mercy p304) is a classic. *Lights and Shadows of a Macao Life: The Journal of Harriett Low, Travelling Spinster* by Harriett Low Hillard is an American woman's account of Macau from 1829 to 1834. *Discover Macau* by Todd Crowell has eight historical walks: six on the peninsula and one each on the islands.

BUSINESS HOURS

Most government offices are open from 9am to 1pm and 2.30pm to 5.30pm or 5.45pm on weekdays. Banks are normally open 9am to 5pm weekdays and to 1pm on Saturday.

CUSTOMS

Customs formalities are virtually nonexistent, but Hong Kong only allows you to import small amounts of duty-free tobacco and alcohol (see Customs p328).

DISCOUNT CARDS

The Macau Museums Pass, a pass allowing you entry to half a dozen museums (Grand Prix Museum, the Wine Museum, the Maritime Museum, Lin Zexu Memorial Hall in the Lin Fung Temple, the Macau Museum of Art and the Museum of Macau) over a five-day period, is available for MOP$25/12 for adults/children under 18 and seniors over 65, from the MGTO or any participating museum.

EMERGENCIES

In the event of any emergency, phone the central SOS number (☎ 999) for the fire services, police or an ambulance. Other important numbers:

Consumer Council ☎ 307 820
Fire ☎ 572 222
Police ☎ 573 333
Tourist Assistance Unit (9am-6pm) ☎ 340 390

HOLIDAYS

In Macau half-days are allowed on the day before the start of Chinese New Year and on New Year's Eve day. For holidays celebrated in both Hong Kong and Macau, see p9.

All Souls' Day 2 November
Feast of the Immaculate Conception 8 December
Macau SAR Establishment Day 20 December
Winter Solstice 22 December

INTERNET ACCESS

You can check emails at the **UNESCO Internet Café** (Map pp422-3; ☎ 727 066; Alameda Doutor Carlos d'Assumpção; MOP$5/10 30/60 minutes; ☼ 9am-5pm Mon-Sat), in NAPE opposite the Macau Landmark, and at the more central **Team Spirit** (Map p424; ☎ 355 859; 102A Rua dos Mercadores; MOP$10 per hour; ☼ 24hr).

LEFT LUGGAGE

There are electronic lockers on both the arrivals and departure levels of the Macau ferry terminal. They cost MOP$20 or MOP$25, depending on the size, for the first two hours and MOP$25/30 for each additional 12-hour period. There is also a left-luggage office on the departures level open from 6.45am to midnight daily and charging MOP$20–40 a day, depending on the weight.

MAPS

The MGTO distributes the excellent (and free) *Macau Tourist Map*, with major tourist sights and streets labelled in Portuguese and Chinese characters, small inset maps of Taipa and Coloane, and bus routes. If you really want to know where you're going, pick up a copy of the *Atlas de Macau* (*Macau Atlas*; MOP$99), which divides the entire territory into 80 large-scale maps.

MEDICAL SERVICES

Macau has two hospitals, both of which have 24-hour emergency services: **Conde São Januário Central Hospital** (Map pp422-3; ☎ 313 731; Estrada do Visconde de São Januário) and **Kiang Wu Hospital** (Map pp422-3; ☎ 371 333; Rua Coelho do Amaral).

MONEY

Macau's currency is the pataca (MOP$), which is divided into 100 avos. Bills are issued in denominations of MOP$20, MOP$50, MOP$100, MOP$500 and MOP $1000. There are little copper coins worth 10, 20 and 50 avos and silver-coloured MOP$1 and MOP$5 coins.

The pataca is pegged to the Hong Kong dollar at the rate of MOP$103.20 to HK$100. As a result, exchange rates for the pataca are virtually the same as for the Hong Kong dollar, which is accepted everywhere in Macau (see p328 for exchange rates for the Hong Kong dollar). Usually when you spend Hong Kong dollars in big hotels, restaurants and department stores your change will be returned in that currency. You would be wise to use up all your patacas before leaving Macau.

Most ATMs, which are everywhere but especially around the Lisboa Hotel, allow you to choose between patacas and Hong Kong dollars, and credit cards are readily accepted at Macau's hotels, larger restaurants and casinos. You can also change cash and travellers cheques at the banks lining Avenida da Praia Grande and Avenida de Almeida Ribeiro, as well as at major hotels, though the latter seldom offer optimum rates.

POST

Correios de Macau, Macau's postal system, is efficient and inexpensive.

The main **post office** (Map p424; ☎ 574 491; 🕒 9am-6pm Mon-Fri, 9am-1pm Sat) is on Avenida de Almeida Ribeiro facing Largo do Senado; pick up poste restante from counter No 1 or 2. There are other post office branches in peninsular Macau (including at the ferry terminal; 🕒 10am-7pm Mon-Sat) as well as on the islands.

Speedpost (☎ 596 688) is available at the main post office. Other companies that can arrange express forwarding are **DHL** (☎ 372 828), **Federal Express** (☎ 703 333) and **UPS** (☎ 751 616).

TELEPHONE

Macau's telephone service provider is **Companhia de Telecomunicações de Macau** (CTM); inquiry hotline ☎ 1000; www.ctm.net).

Local calls are free from private or hotel telephones, while at a public payphone they cost MOP$1 for five minutes.

The international access code for every country *except* Hong Kong is ☎ 00. If you want to phone Hong Kong, dial ☎ 01 first, then the number you want; you do not need to dial Hong Kong's country code (☎ 852). To call Macau from abroad – including Hong Kong – the country code is ☎ 853.

Phonecards available from CTM come in denominations of M$50, M$100 and M$200 and most public phones accept them. Convenient CTM branches in Macau include the following:

CTM Main Office (Map pp422-3; 25 Rua Pedro Coutinho; 🕒 9am-6pm) Two blocks northeast of the Lou Lim Ioc Garden.

Tele-One Macau (Map p424; 22 Rua do Doutor Pedro José Lobo; 🕒 10am-8pm) South of Avenida da Praia Grande.

Another option is to make use of the 'country direct' service, described in the Hong

Kong Directory chapter (see International Calls & Rates p329).

Useful Numbers

The following is a list of some important telephone numbers. For numbers to call at more difficult times, see Emergencies p327.

International directory assistance	☎	101
Local directory assistance	☎	185
Macau ferry terminal	☎	790 7240
New World First Ferry	☎	726 289
Time in English	☎	140
TurboJet	☎	790 7039

TOURIST OFFICES

The Macau Government Tourist Office (MGTO; Map p424; ☎ 315 566, hotline ☎ 333 000; mgto@macautourism.gov.mo; 9 Largo do Senado), is a well-organised and helpful source of information. Open from 9am to 6pm daily, it has a large selection of free pamphlets on everything from Chinese temples and Catholic churches to fortresses, gardens and walks, and its website (www.macautourism.gov.mo) should win awards.

The MGTO has several information counters, including ones at the Guia Lighthouse (Map pp422-3; ☎ 569 808; ☉ 9am-5.30pm); the Church of St Paul (☎ 358 444; ☉ 9am-6pm); and the ferry terminal (Map pp422-3; ☎ 726 416; ☉ 9am-10pm). The MGTO runs a tourist assistance unit (☎ 340 390; ☉ 9am-6pm) to help travellers who may have run into trouble.

TRANSPORT

For details on transport between Macau and Hong Kong, see Hong Kong to Macau p338. For getting around Macau, including organised tours, see Transport p325.

VISAS

The vast majority of travellers, including citizens of the European Union (EU), Australia, New Zealand, the USA, Canada and South Africa, can enter Macau with just their passports for 30 days.

Travellers who do require them can get visas valid for 30 days on arrival in Macau. They cost M$100/50 for adults/children under 12 years of age.

You can get a one-month extension (only) from the Macau Immigration Office (Map pp422-3; ☎ 725 488; Ground fl, Travessa da Amizade; ☉ 9am-12.30pm, 2.30-5pm Mon-Fri).

WEBSITES

Useful Macau websites:

Cityguide (www.cityguide.gov.mo) Tourism, transport.

Government Statistics Department (www.dsec.gov.mo) Data.

Macau Cultural Institute (www.icm.gov.mo) Listings, events.

Macau Government Information (www.macau.gov.mo) Data.

Macau Government Tourist Office (www.macautourism.gov.mo) Tourism.

Macau Yellow Pages (www.yp.com.mo) Directory.

Transport

Transport

AIR

Information on air travel to China and Macau can be found on p335 and p338, respectively.

AIRPORT

Hong Kong International Airport (☎ 2181 0000; www.hkairport.com) at Chek Lap Kok, off the northern coast of Lantau, is the result of a HK$160 billion airport core programme that saw an island literally flattened and extended through land reclamation. The airport, which opened in July 1998, is connected to the mainland by several spans, including the 2.2km-long Tsing Ma Bridge, which is one of the world's largest suspension bridges and is capable of supporting both road and rail transport.

New motorways to and from the airport have been constructed, including the 12.5km North Lantau Hwy, and a massive harbour reclamation project made way for the six-lane Western Harbour Crossing, connecting the western part of Hong Kong Island with Kowloon for the first time. The Airport Railway Tunnel, carrying the 34km-long Airport Express high-speed train from Hong Kong Island to Chek Lap Kok via Kowloon, was laid on the seabed of Victoria Harbour to the east of the crossing.

The airport's two runways and expanded facilities have reduced the time that departing passengers spend checking in and waiting, as well as the time arriving passengers need to clear immigration and customs and claim their baggage. The airport handles up to 47 movements an hour, with some 45 million passengers a year arriving and departing.

The futuristic passenger terminal, designed by the award-winning British architect Sir Norman Foster, consists of eight levels, with check-in on level seven, departures on level six and arrivals on level five. Outlets – including three bank branches, a moneychanger and several ATMs in the arrivals hall – total 150, and there are 27 cafés, restaurants and bars, and almost 300 check-in counters.

The **Hong Kong Tourism Board** (HKTB; ☎ 2508 1234; www.discoverhongkong.com) maintains information and service centres on level five (see Tourist Offices p370). On the same level you'll also find counters run by the **Hong Kong Hotels Association** (HKHA; ☎ 2383 8380, 2769 8822; www.hkha.org; ✆ 6am-midnight); for details see Reservations (p268). The HKHA deals with mid-range and top-end hotels only and does not handle hostels, guesthouses or other budget accommodation.

If you are booked on a scheduled flight (but *not* a charter flight) and are taking the Airport Express to Chek Lap Kok, most airlines allow you to check in your bags and receive your boarding pass on the day of your flight at the in-town check-in counters at either the Hong Kong Island or Kowloon Airport Express stations. You are required, however, to check yourself in at least 90 minutes before your flight. Some airlines, including Cathay Pacific Airways, China Airlines and United Airlines, allow check-in a full day before your flight. See the airport's website for details.

If you use the porters at the airport, about HK$2 a suitcase is expected. The porters putting your bags on a push cart at Hong Kong Island or Kowloon Airport Express stations, however, do not expect a gratuity. It's all part of the service.

DEPARTURE TAX

Airport departure tax at Chek Lap Kok is currently HK$80 though it may be raised to HK$120 soon; children under 12 do not pay the tax. It (as well as an `unseen' HK$33 security tax) is always included in the price of the ticket. Travellers making the trip to Macau by helicopter (see Air p338) must also pay the same amount in departure tax.

TO/FROM THE AIRPORT

The Airport Express line of the Mass Transit Railway (MTR) is the fastest – and most expensive – way to get to and from Hong Kong International Airport. A gaggle of much cheaper buses connect the airport with Lantau, the New Territories, Kowloon and even Hong Kong Island.

Airport Express

Airport Express (AEL; ☎ 2881 8888; www.mtr
.com.hk) has trains departing from Hong
Kong station in Central every 10 minutes from
5.50am to 1.15am, calling at Kowloon station
and at Tsing Yi Island before arriving at Airport
station. The last train leaves the airport for all
three stations at 12.48am. Running at speeds
of up to 135km/h, trains make the journey
from Central/Kowloon/Tsing Yi in only 23/20/
12 minutes.

One-way adult fares from Central/ Kowloon/
Tsing Yi are HK$100/90/60, with children three
to 11 years and seniors over 65 years paying
half-fare. Adult return fares, valid for a month,
are HK$180/160/110. A same-day return is
equivalent to a one-way fare.

Airport Express has two shuttle buses on
Hong Kong Island (H1 and H2) and six in
Kowloon (K1 to K6), with free transfer for passengers between Hong Kong and Kowloon
stations and major hotels. The buses run every
30 minutes from between 6.05am and 6.25am
to 11pm. Schedules and routes are available
at Airport Express and MTR stations and on the
Airport Express website.

Boat

High-speed ferries run by **New World First Ferry
Services** (☎ 2131 8181; www.nwff.com.hk)
link Tung Chung New Development ferry pier
opposite the airport (and accessible by bus
No S56) with Tuen Mun in the New Territories.
Ferries depart from Tuen Mun every 20 to 30
minutes between 5.40am and 11pm; the first
ferry from Tung Chung pier leaves at 6am and
the last at 11.20pm (one-way adult/child &
senior HK$15/10, 18 minutes).

Bus

Most major areas of Hong Kong Island, Kowloon, the New Territories and Lantau are connected to the airport by bus, of which there
is an enormous choice. The buses are run by
different companies; for details see p345.

The most useful for travellers are the Citybus
'airbuses' A11 (HK$40) and A12 (HK$45), which
go to or near the major hotel and guesthouse
areas on Hong Kong Island, and the A21
(HK$33), which serves similar areas in Kowloon.
These buses have air-con and plenty of room
for luggage, and announcements are made in
English and Chinese notifying passengers of
hotels at each stop. But they are also the most
expensive; there are cheaper options, such as

taking 'external' bus E11 to Hong Kong Island
or 'shuttle' bus S1 to Tung Chung and then
the MTR to Kowloon or Central. There are also
quite a few night ('N') buses.

Bus drivers in Hong Kong cannot give
change, but it is available at the ground
transportation centre at the airport, as are
Octopus cards (see Travel & Tourist Passes
p339). Normal returns are double the one-
way fare, though there is a discount for those
returning on the same day. Unless stated
otherwise, children and seniors pay half-fare.

Some of the New Territories buses terminate
at MTR stations, from where you can reach
destinations in Kowloon and on Hong Kong
Island at a lower cost than the more direct
buses. You can also reach Shenzhen and
other points in southern China directly from
the airport (see Bus p335).

The following list gives the bus numbers,
service providers, routes, one-way fares and
frequencies for the airport buses most often
used by visitors.

HONG KONG ISLAND

A11 (Citybus) Sheung Wan, Central, Admiralty, Wan Chai,
Causeway Bay, North Point; HK$40; every 15 to 20 minutes
from 6.10am to midnight.

E11 (Citybus) Sheung Wan, Central, Admiralty, Wan Chai,
Causeway Bay, Tin Hau; HK$21; every 15 to 20 minutes
from 5.20am to midnight.

N11 (Citybus) Sheung Wan, Central, Admiralty, Wan Chai,
Causeway Bay; HK$31; every 20 minutes from 12.15am
to 4.45am.

A12 (Citybus) Sheung Wan, Central, Admiralty, Wan Chai,
Causeway Bay, Tin Hau, Fortress Hill, North Point, Quarry
Bay, Sai Wan Ho, Shau Kei Wan, Chai Wan, Siu Sai Wan;
HK$45; every 15 minutes from 6am to midnight.

KOWLOON

A21 (Citybus) Mong Kok, Yau Ma Tei, Jordan, Tsim Sha Tsui,
Hung Hom KCR station; HK$33; every 10 minutes from 6am
to midnight.

N21 (Citybus) Tsing Yi Rd West, Mei Foo Sun Chuen, Lai Chi
Kok, Cheung Sha Wan, Sham Shui Po, Prince Edward, Mong
Kok KCR station, Star Ferry pier; HK$23; every 20 minutes
from 12.20am to 5am.

THE NEW TERRITORIES

A31 (Long Win) Tsing Yi, Kwai Chung, Tsuen Wan MTR;
HK$17; every 15 to 20 minutes from 6am to midnight.

N31 (Long Win) Tung Chung, Tsing Yi, Tsuen Wan MTR;
HK$20; every 20 to 30 minutes from 12.20am to 5am.

Transport – Air

LANTAU

A35 (New Lantao) Tong Fuk village, Mui Wo; HK$14 (HK$23 on Sunday and public holidays); every 30 to 40 minutes from 6.30am to 12.15am.

N35 (New Lantao) Tong Fuk village, Mui Wo; HK$20 (HK$30 on Sunday and public holidays); every hour from 1.30am to 5am.

S1 (Citybus) Tung Chung MTR; HK$3.50; every six to 10 minutes from 5.30am to midnight.

S56 (Citybus) Tung Chung New Development pier (ferries to/from Tuen Mun); HK$3.50; every 30 minutes from 6am to 11.20pm.

DB02R (Discovery Bay Transportation) Discovery Bay; HK$28; every 30 minutes, 24 hours.

Taxi

Taking a taxi to or from the airport at Chek Lap Kok is an expensive affair; on top of the fare shown on the meter, passengers are required to pay a HK$30 toll for using the Lantau Link, in both directions.

Taxis to the Star Ferry pier in Tsim Sha Tsui and the Kwun Tong MTR in Kowloon cost roughly HK$270 and HK$320 respectively. For Hong Kong Island a taxi should cost around HK$335 to Central and Causeway Bay and HK$375 to Aberdeen. To Tsuen Wan and Sha Tin in the New Territories it costs about HK$235 and HK$305 respectively, though the fare is somewhat cheaper if you manage to get a New Territories taxi. A taxi to the Tung Chung MTR station should cost between HK$30 and HK$35.

There are limousine service counters in the arrivals hall and at the ground transportation centre, including **Parklane Limousine Service** (☎ 2261 0303; info@limocoach.com.hk) and **Intercontinental Hire Cars** (☎ 3193 9333; www.wingontravel.com). In a car seating four people, expect to pay from HK$450 to destinations in urban Kowloon and from around HK$550 to Hong Kong Island.

TRAVEL AGENCIES

One of the best places in Hong Kong to buy air tickets (especially round-the-world ones), arrange visas for China and seek travel advice is **Phoenix Services Agency** (Map p412-14; ☎ 2722 7378; phoenix1@netvigator.com; Room A, 7th fl, Milton Mansion, 96 Nathan Rd, Tsim Sha Tsui; ☯ 9am-6pm Mon-Fri & 9am-1pm Sat). The staff are friendly, patient and work very hard to get you the best possible price. Another dependable agency on the Kowloon side is **Traveller Services** (Map p412-14; ☎ 2375 2222; fax 2375 2223; Room 1012, Silvercord Tower 1, 30 Canton Rd, Tsim Sha Tsui; ☯ 9am-6pm Mon-Fri & 9am-1pm Sat).

On Hong Kong Island, a long-established and highly dependable outfit is **Concorde Travel** (Map p400-3; ☎ 2526 3391; info@concorde-travel.com; 1st fl, Galuxe Bldg, 8-10 On Lan St, Central; ☯ 9.30am-5.30pm Mon-Fri, 9am-1pm Sat). Two others that have loyal clienteles are **Aero International** (Map p400-3; ☎ 2543 3800; Room 603, 6th fl, Cheung's Bldg, 1 Wing Lok St, Sheung Wan; ☯ 9.15am-5.30pm Mon-Fri, 9.15am-1pm Sat), accessed from Wing Wo St, and **Natori Travel** (Map p400-3; ☎ 2810 1681; fax 2576 0311; Room 2207, Melbourne Plaza, 33 Queen's Rd Central; ☯ 9am-7pm Mon-Fri, 9am-4pm Sat).

HONG KONG TO CHINA

VISAS

Everyone except Hong Kong Chinese residents must have a visa to enter China. Holders of Canadian, American, Australian, New Zealand and most European Union passports (but *not* British ones at the moment) can get a visa on the spot for HK$100 at the Lo Wu border crossing, the last stop on the Kowloon-Canton Railway (KCR). This particular visa limits you to a maximum stay of seven days within the confines of the Shenzhen Special Economic Zone (SEZ) *only*. The queues for this visa are at most times serpentine, and the wait interminable.

Even if you plan to visit just Shenzhen, it is highly recommended that you shell out the extra money and get a proper China visa. Who knows? You might like the mainland so much that you'll want to carry on. There is a group visa valid for six days (well, 144 hours to be precise) that allows travel to 10 cities in Guangdong province, but all members of the group (three to 40 people) must enter and leave China at the same time.

If you want to arrange your visa yourself, go to the **Visa Office of the People's Republic of China** (Map p406-8; ☎ 3413 2300, 3413 2424; 7th fl, Lower Block, China Resources Centre, 26 Harbour Rd, Wan Chai; ☯ 9am-noon & 2-5pm Mon-Fri). Visas processed in one/two/three days cost HK$400/300/150. Double/multiple valid six months/multiple valid for a year entry visas are HK$220/400/600 (plus HK$150/250 if you require express/urgent service). You

Transport – Travel Agencies

must supply two photos, which can be taken at photo booths in the MTR or at the visa office for HK$35. Any photo-processing shop can oblige as well.

Visas can be arranged by **China Travel Service** (CTS; ☎ 2998 7888; www.chinatravel1.com), the mainland-affiliated agency; a good many guesthouses and hostels; and most Hong Kong travel agents, including those listed earlier on p334. For next-day delivery, agents will charge between HK$180 and HK$200 for a single-entry visa, and HK$250 for a visa allowing two entries. A visa will cost you HK$1200 at the airport.

China Travel Services Offices

Most China Travel Services (CTS) offices in Hong Kong, including the branches in Tsim Sha Tsui and Mong Kok, are open from 9am to 5pm Monday to Saturday. The Hong Kong Island and New Territories branches are also open from 9am to 5pm on Sunday.

HONG KONG ISLAND
Causeway Bay (Map p406-8; ☎ 2808 1131; Room 609, 6th fl, Hang Kung Centre, 2-20 Paterson St)

Central (Map p400-3; ☎ 2522 0450; Ground fl, China Travel Bldg, 77 Queen's Rd Central)

Central Head Office (Map p400-3; ☎ 2853 3533; Ground fl, CTS House, 78-83 Connaught Rd Central)

KOWLOON
Mong Kok (Map p415; ☎ 2789 5888; 2nd fl, Tak Po Bldg, 62-74 Sai Yee St)

Tsim Sha Tsui (Map p412-14; ☎ 2315 7188; 1st fl, Alpha House, 27-33 Nathan Rd)

NEW TERRITORIES
Sha Tin (Map p417; ☎ 2692 7773; Shop 438C, 4th fl, New Town Plaza Phase I)

AIR

There are few bargain air fares between Hong Kong and China, as the government regulates the prices. Depending on the season, seats can be difficult to book due to the enormous volume of business travellers and Asian tourists, so plan far ahead. Some one-year, normal return fares from Hong Kong include Beijing HK$4700; Chengdu HK$4600; Guangzhou HK$1020; Kunming HK$3200; and Shanghai HK$3300. One-way fares are half the return price.

You should be able to do better than that, however, both on scheduled flights and charters, especially in summer. To Beijing, **China Southern Airlines** (☎ 2973 3733; www.cs-air.com) has a fixed return ticket for as low as HK$2000. An open ticket valid for 30 days on the same airline is HK$2500, and a 90-day ticket on **Dragonair** (☎ 3193 3888; www.dragonair.com) costs HK$3900. Group (just a few friends can make up a `group') and charter flights are available to Chengdu (the gateway to Tibet) for HK$2600 and HK$3500 respectively. A direct flight to Lhasa in summer is HK$3500.

If you plan to fly to a destination in China from Hong Kong, you might save some money by heading for Shenzhen by bus (see Land following) and boarding the aircraft at Huangtian Airport there.

LAND

The only way in and out of Hong Kong by land is to cross the 30km border with mainland China. The options for surface travel to and from China have increased dramatically since the handover, with buses and trains departing throughout the day to destinations as close as Shenzhen and as far as Beijing. Travellers should be aware that, although the Hong Kong Special Administrative Region (SAR) is now an integral part of China, visas are still required to cross the border to the mainland (see Visas p334).

The border crossing at Lo Wu closes at midnight. The crossing at Lok Ma Chau is now open round the clock.

Departure Tax

A `head charge' of HK$7 to be levied on all travellers crossing the border by land into the SEZ is now being discussed.

Bus

The good news is that you can reach virtually any major destination in Guangdong province from Hong Kong by bus. The bad news is that very few of these buses call on Shenzhen proper. With KCR services so fast, efficient and cheap, just about everyone takes the train. It's a different story if you're heading for Shenzhen's Huangtian Airport, however.

Buses depart for China from eight major locations throughout the territory:

HONG KONG ISLAND

CTS Express Coach (☎ 2764 9803, 2261 2472; http://ctsbus.hkcts.com) runs buses to Dongguan (HK$100, departing 7.15am), Guangzhou (adult/child HK$100/90, between 7.30am and 4.30pm) and Foshan (HK$100/90, between 2.15pm and 3.30pm) from outside the **Southorn Centre** (Map p406-8; 138 Hennessy Rd, Wan Chai) north of the Southorn Playground.

KOWLOON

Eternal East Cross Border Coach (Map p412-14; ☎ 2723 2923; http://fasttrack.kowloon.peninsula.com/pdf/bus_schedule.pdf; Shop G11, Ground fl, Hankow Centre, 5-15 Hankow Rd, Tsim Sha Tsui; ⏱ 7am-8pm) has services to points throughout southern China, including Guangzhou (one way/return HK$100/180), Foshan (HK$100/200), Huizhou (HK$100/120); Shantou (HK$200/400); Changshan (HK$320/580) and Xiamen (HK$350/680).

Buses leave from outside the Hang Seng Bank (Hankow Rd) opposite the Eternal East office. There are some excellent packages that include two days and one night in Guangzhou (HK$450), Foshan (HK$650), Shantou (HK$560) or Xiamen (HK$1270). Prices include return bus transportation and accommodation.

Buses run by the **Motor Transport Company** (☎ 2317 7900) of Guangdong and Hong Kong to points in southern China, including Guangzhou (nine services daily between 7.05am and 5.45pm), Zhongshan (two to four services daily), Shantao (two services daily) and Xiamen via Sha Tau Kok, leave from the **Cross-Border Coach Terminus** (Map pp412-14; ☎ 2317 7900; Hong Kong Scout Centre, 8 Austin Rd, Tsim Sha Tsui; ⏱ office 6.30am-7pm, services 7am-6.30pm), just west of the BP International Hotel (enter from Scout Path).

CTS Express Coach (☎ 2764 9803; http://ctsbus.hkcts.com) has up to 11 buses a day to Guangzhou (one way/return HK$100/190, between 7.30am and 5.40pm) and other destinations in southern China in front of the **Hong Kong Coliseum** (Map pp412-14; Cheong Wan Rd) behind (ie south of) the KCR station.

CTS Express also runs buses to southern China(including one to Guangzhou at 8.30am), leaving from stops along Nelson St, opposite the **CTS Mong Kok branch** (Map p415; 62-74 Sai Yee St).

Trans-Island Limousine Service (☎ 3193 9393; www.trans-island.com.hk) has cars leaving from in front of the **Hotel Concourse Hong Kong** (Map p415; 22 Lai Chi Kok Rd) for Shenzhen (HK$50, between 7.15am and 5.30pm), Huangtian Airport (HK$110, between 7.15am and 5.30pm), Guangzhou (HK$100, between 7.45am and 2.40pm) and other destinations in southern China.

THE NEW TERRITORIES

New HK Bus (☎ 2471 0792) runs buses from the border crossing at Lok Ma Chau to Huanggang (HK$7) every 15 to 20 minutes, round the clock. You can reach Lok Ma Chau from Yee Wo St in Causeway Bay on bus No 968 or 969 and from Yuen Long on bus No 277.

LANTAU

Buses run by **CTS Express Coach** (☎ 2764 9803, 2261 2472), **Eternal East Cross Border Coach** (Map pp412-14; ☎ 2723 2923), **Gogobus** (☎ 2375 0099, 2261 0886; www.gogobus.com) and **Wing On Chinalink** (☎ 2261 2636; www.trans-island.com.hk) link Hong Kong International Airport with many points in southern China, including Guangzhou (adult/child HK$250/100), Dongguan (HK$200/100) and Foshan (HK$250/100).

Eternal East runs up to 19 buses a day (between 10.30am and 7.30pm) from the airport to major hotels in downtown Shenzhen. Tickets (adult/child HK$180/100) are available in the arrivals hall, and buses leave from the airport tour coach station.

Train

Reaching Shenzhen is a breeze. Just board the KCR train at Hung Hom (1st/2nd class HK$66/33) or at any other KCR station along the way (such as Kowloon Tong, Sha Tin, Tai Po Market) and ride it to Lo Wu; China is a couple of hundred metres away. The first train to Lo Wu leaves Hung Hom station at 5.30am, the last at 11.07pm. For more details on KCR services, see p348.

The most comfortable way to reach Guangzhou by land is via the Kowloon–Guangzhou express train (usually via Dongguan), which covers the 182km route in approximately 1¾ hours.

High-speed trains intercity leave Hung Hom station for Guangzhou East train station seven times a day (between 8.25am and 4.45pm). They leave Guangzhou East between 8.38am and 5.20pm. One-way 1st-/2nd-class tickets cost HK$230/190 for adults and HK$115/95 for children under nine. Adults/children are allowed one piece of luggage, weighing up to 20kg/10kg. Additional bags cost HK$3.90 per 5kg.

There are also direct rail links between Hung Hom and Shanghai, and Hung Hom and Beijing. Trains to Beijing West train station (via Guangzhou East, Changsha, Wuchang and Hankou) leave on alternate days, take 27 hours and one-way adult tickets cost from HK$574/934/1191 for a hard/soft/deluxe-soft sleeper. Prices for children are from HK$366/604/788.

Trains to Shanghai (via Guangzhou East and Hangzhou East) leave every other day and take 24 hours. One-way adult fares are from HK$508/825/1039 for a hard/soft/deluxe-soft sleeper; children's fares are from HK$320/527/680.

There is one daily departure to Zhaoqing (adult/child HK$235/117.50) via Guangzhou East and Foshan at 2.30pm, arriving at Zhaoqing at 6.30pm.

Immigration formalities are completed before boarding at Hung Hom; you won't get on the train without a visa. Passengers are requested to arrive at the station 45 minutes before the train departs. To get to Hung Hom station from Tsim Sha Tsui by public transport, take bus No 5C from the Star Ferry pier or the No 6 or No 8 green minibus from Hankow Rd.

Tickets can be booked up to 60 days in advance at CTS or the KCR station in Hung Hom. If tickets are booked on the phone (☎ 2947 7888), passengers must collect them at least one hour before the train departs. Tickets can also be bought at Kowloon Tong and Sha Tin KCR stations and at the Mong Kok MTR station.

If you haven't booked in advance, you could try to buy a ticket at the KCR ticket window or at the CTS counter at Hung Hom station. However, the queues are miles long at the former, and the latter block-books tickets and will probably refuse to sell you one. Instead, make your way to the counter just before the entrance to the platforms. Tickets are always available here.

A cheaper but less convenient option is to take the KCR train to Lo Wu, cross through immigration into Shenzhen and catch a local train to Guangzhou. There are around 20 trains to and from Guangzhou daily (hard/soft seat Y42/Y65, between two and 2½ hours). There is also an express train (Y80, 1½ hours).

SEA

Regularly scheduled ferries link Hong Kong with many coastal towns and cities on the Pearl River delta, with one major exception: central Shenzhen. You can, however, reach Shenzhen's Huangtian Airport and Shekou by boat, as well as Guangzhou, Zhuhai and other ports not normally of interest to travellers.

High-speed ferries run by **TurboJet** (☎ 2921 6688; www.turbojet.com.hk) leave the China ferry terminal (Map p412-14; Canton Rd, Tsim Sha Tsui) for Fuyong ferry terminal (Huangtian Airport) eight times a day between 7.30am and 6pm. There are six return sailings from Fuyong (between 9am and 7.15pm). In addition, one boat leaves the Macau ferry terminal in Central at 8am. There are three return sailings a day (4.30pm, 6.30pm and 7.45pm). Fares from Hong Kong start at HK$189, from Shenzhen HK$171.

TurboJet ferries depart from the China ferry terminal for Guangzhou at 7.30am and 2pm, with return sailings at 10.30am and 4.30pm. The economy-class fare from Kowloon is HK$198, from Guangzhou HK$189.

Some 12 Jetcats run by **Shekou Express Ferry Lines** (☎ 2858 0909) link Hong Kong with Shekou – a port about 20km west of Shenzhen town, easily accessible by bus or taxi to the centre, with a lively nightlife area in its own right – from 7.45am to 9pm daily. Eight of these leave from the China ferry terminal in Tsim Sha Tsui (between 7.45am and 7pm), while the rest go from the Macau ferry terminal in Central (between 9am and 9pm). Return sailings from Shekou are from 7.45am to 9.30pm. Ticket prices from Hong Kong start at HK$105/125 for day/night sailings (HK$90/110 from Shekou) and the trip takes one hour.

Zhuhai, the SEZ north of Macau, can be reached 14 times a day from the China ferry terminal in Tsim Sha Tsui (between 7.30am and 5.30pm) and the Macau ferry terminal in Central (between 8.40am and 9.30pm) on ferries operated by the **Chu Kong Passenger Transportation Co** (☎ 2858 3876; www.cksp.com.hk). The dozen return sailings from Zhuhai (HK$148, 70 minutes) go between 8am and 9.30pm.

Chu Kong also has ferries from the China ferry terminal to a number of ports in southern Guangdong province, including Zhongshan (HK$173, eight sailings between 8am and 8pm) and Shunde (HK$138, four sailings between 7.30am and 3.20pm).

Ferries run by **Expert Fortune** (☎ 2375 0688, 2517 3494) link the China ferry terminal with Nansha (HK$100, five sailings daily) between 8am and 3.30pm, with return sailings between 9.30am and 5.30pm.

Departure Tax

When leaving Hong Kong by sea for China, there is a departure tax of HK$19, but it's an 'invisible' tax as it's almost always included in the price of the ticket.

HONG KONG TO MACAU

The vast majority of people make their way to Macau by ferry, but if you're in a small group a flight over by helicopter is a viable alternative and becoming increasingly popular for Hong Kong residents and visitors alike.

AIR

East Asia Airlines (EAA; ☎ 2108 9898, in Macau ☎ 727 288; www.helihongkong.com), in conjunction with Heli Hong Kong, runs a twin-engine Sikorsky 12-seater helicopter shuttle service between Macau and Hong Kong (Monday to Thursday HK$1400, Friday to Sunday HK$1500, 16 minutes). There are up to 27 flights daily in each direction, from between 9.30am and 11pm from Hong Kong and 9am and 10.30pm from Macau. In Hong Kong departures are from the helipad atop the ferry pier linked to the **Shun Tak Centre** (Map p400-3; ☎ 2859 3359; 200 Connaught Rd Central, Sheung Wan). Flights arrive and depart in Macau from the roof of the ferry terminal.

SEA

Although Macau is separated from Hong Kong by 65km of water, the journey can be made in about an hour. Sometimes queues at customs and immigration can add another 30 minutes to the journey. There are frequent departures throughout the day. The schedule is somewhat reduced between midnight and 7am, but boats run virtually 24 hours.

Two ferry companies operate services to and from Macau, one from Hong Kong Island and the other from Tsim Sha Tsui.

TurboJet (information ☎ 2859 3333, bookings ☎ 2921 6688, in Macau ☎ 790 7039; www.turbojet.com.hk) runs three types of vessels from the Macau ferry pier at the **Shun Tak Centre** (Map p400-3; ☎ 2859 3359; 200 Connaught Rd Central, Sheung Wan), and

from the **Macau Ferry Terminal** (☎ 790 7240) on Macau. Jetfoils (single-hull jet-powered hydrofoils) and foil-cats (catamaran-jetfoils) take about 55 minutes to make the crossing, while turbocats (jet-powered catamarans) take 65 minutes.

You don't choose the type of vessel you take; just buy your ticket and board the vessel. Economy-/super-class tickets cost HK$130/232 on weekdays, HK$141/247 at the weekend and on public holidays, and HK$161/260 at night (ie from 5.45pm to 6.30am). They are MOP$1 more when travelling from Macau to Hong Kong.

New World First Ferry (NWFF; ☎ 2131 8181, ☎ 727 676 in Macau; www.nwff.com.hk) operates high-speed catamarans (some 435 seats on two decks) from the **China ferry terminal** (Map p412-14; Canton Rd, Tsim Sha Tsui) 25 times a day, with departures on the half-hour from 7am to between 9pm and 10pm. They depart Macau every 30 minutes from 7am to 8.30pm. The trip takes between 65 and 75 minutes and tickets cost HK$131/161 Monday to Friday during the day/night (night fares are from 6pm to 9pm or 10pm from Hong Kong and 6.30pm to 8.30pm from Macau), and HK$141/161 at weekends and on public holidays. Deluxe class is HK$232/260 during the day/night from Monday to Friday, and HK$247/260 at the weekend and on public holidays.

Tickets can be booked up to 28 days in advance and are available at the ferry terminals, all CTS branches (see p334) and many travel agents. There is a standby queue before each sailing for passengers wanting to travel before their ticketed sailing. On weekends and public holidays you'd be wise to book your return ticket in advance because the boats are often full.

You need to arrive at the pier at least 15 minutes before departure, but you should allow 30 minutes because of occasional long queues at the immigration checkpoint, especially on the Hong Kong side.

Luggage space on the jetfoils and turbocats is limited; some boats have small overhead lockers while others have storage space at the bow and stern. You are theoretically limited to 10kg of carry-on luggage in economy class (you can probably get away with more if it's not too bulky), but oversized or overweight bags can be taken on as checked luggage. There is more luggage space on the NWFF catamarans.

Departure Tax

When leaving Hong Kong for Macau by sea, there is a departure tax of HK$19, which is almost always included in the price of the ticket.

PUBLIC TRANSPORT

When it comes to public transport, nobody does it better than Hong Kong. Buses, ferries, trains and trams are plentiful, cheap, fast and efficient; you'll rarely wait more than a few minutes for the conveyance of your choice. What's more, armed with a stored-value Octopus card (see Travel & Tourist Passes p339) you need never fumble for a coin or note.

Hong Kong is a small and crowded place, and certain forms of public transport – especially the MTR – can be jam-packed during rush hour on weekdays and Saturday morning; the Outlying Islands ferries are chock-a-block with holiday-makers on Sunday. Save your sanity and try to avoid these times if you can.

TRAVEL & TOURIST PASSES

The Octopus 'smart card', originally designed for the MTR and seven other forms of transport (thus the `octopus' connection), is now valid on most forms of public transport in Hong Kong and will even allow you to make purchases at retail outlets across the territory (such as 7-Eleven and Circle K convenience stores).

All you do is touch (or, rather, 'zap') fare-deducting processors installed at stations, ferry piers, on minibuses etc with the Octopus card and the fare is deducted, indicating how much credit you have left. You don't even have to take the card out of your wallet or purse. The machines can read through them.

The Octopus card comes in three basic denominations: HK$150 for adults, HK$100 for students aged 12 to 25, and HK$70 for children aged three to 11 and seniors over 65. All cards include a refundable deposit of HK$50. If you want to add more money to your card, just go to one of the add-value machines or the ticket offices located at every station. The maximum amount you can add is HK$1000, and the card has a maximum negative value of HK$35, which is recovered the next time you reload (thus the HK$50 deposit). Octopus fares are between 5% and 10% cheaper than ordinary fares on the MTR, KCR, Light Rail Transit (LRT) systems and certain green minibuses.

You can purchase Octopus cards at ticket offices or customer service centres in MTR, KCR and LRT stations, New World First Bus customer service centres as well as Outlying Islands ferry piers on both sides. If you have any queries, call the Octopus hotline on ☎ 2266 2266 or check its website (www.octopuscards.com).

The much-advertised Airport Express Tourist Octopus card is not really worth the microchip embedded into it. The card costs HK$220 (including HK$50 deposit) and allows one single trip on the Airport Express, three days' unlimited travel on the MTR and HK$20 usable value on other forms of transport. For HK$300 you get two trips on the Airport Express and the same benefits. At the end of your trip you can claim your deposit back (plus any part of the HK$20 'usable value' still on the card) or keep the card, emblazoned with that lovely word 'tourist', as a souvenir.

BOAT

Despite Hong Kong's comprehensive road and rail public-transport system, the territory still relies very much on boats to get across the harbour and to reach the Outlying Islands.

Hong Kong's cross-harbour ferries are faster and cheaper than buses and the MTR. They're also great fun and afford stunning views. Since the advent of the Lantau Link, ferries are not the only way to reach Lantau, but for the other Outlying Islands, they remain the only game in town.

Smoking is prohibited on all ferries, and the fine is a hefty HK$5000. With the exception of Star Ferry services from Central to Hung Hom and Wan Chai to Hung Hom, the cross-harbour ferries ban the transport of bicycles. You can take bicycles on the ordinary ferries to the Outlying Islands, however.

Star Ferry

You can't say you've `done' Hong Kong until you've taken a ride on a **Star Ferry** (☎ 2367 7065; www.starferry.com.hk), that wonderful fleet of a dozen electric-diesel vessels with names like *Morning Star, Night Star, Celestial Star, Golden Star, Twinkling Star* and so on.

Try to take the trip on a clear night from Kowloon to Central. It's not half as dramatic in the opposite direction.

The Star Ferry operates on four routes, but the most popular one by far is the run between Tsim Sha Tsui and Central. The coin-operated turnstiles do not give change, but you can get

Borne on a Star

There are few modes of transport anywhere that can claim they sparked a riot, but Hong Kong's Star Ferry can. In 1966, when Communist China was in the grip of what they now call the Cultural Revolution, agitators used the ferry company's fare increase of HK$0.05 as a pretext for fomenting violent demonstrations. The disturbances continued for almost a year.

Mention of the Star Ferry service between Pedder's Wharf (now reclaimed land) and Tsim Sha Tsui first appeared in a December 1888 newspaper article. At that time, boats sailed 'every 40 minutes to one hour during all hours of the day' except on Monday and Friday, when they were seconded for coal delivery. Service has continued ever since, with the only major suspension occurring during WWII. The Star Ferry was something of a war hero; during the Japanese invasion, boats were used to evacuate refugees and Allied troops from the Kowloon Peninsula before it was suspended for more than four years.

Until the Cross-Harbour Tunnel opened in 1978 and the first line of the MTR two years later, the Star Ferry was the only way to cross the harbour. At rush hour long queues of commuters would back up as far as the General Post Office on the Hong Kong Island side and Star House in Kowloon.

this from the ticket window – unless, of course, you're carrying an Octopus card.

For details on the special four-day tourist pass valid on trams and the Star Ferry, see Trams p349.

The four Star Ferry routes:

Central (Star Ferry pier)–Tsim Sha Tsui Every four to 10 minutes from 6.30am-11.30pm; adult lower/upper deck HK$1.70/2.20, child HK$1.20/1.30, seniors free.

Central (Star Ferry pier)–Hung Hom Every 15 to 20 minutes from 7.20am-7.20pm Monday to Friday, every 20 minutes from 7am-7pm Saturday and Sunday; adult/child HK$5.30/2.70, seniors free.

Wan Chai–Tsim Sha Tsui Every eight to 20 minutes from 7.30am-11pm Monday to Saturday, every 12 to 20 minutes from 7.40am-11pm Sunday; adult/child HK$2.20/1.30, seniors free.

Wan Chai–Hung Hom Every 15 to 20 minutes from 7.08am-7.17pm Monday to Friday & 7.08am-7pm Saturday, every 20 to 22 minutes from 7.08am-7.10pm Sunday; adult/child HK$5.30/$2.70, seniors free.

Other Cross-Harbour Ferries

Three other ferry companies operate cross-harbour ferries: **Discovery Bay Transportation Service** (☎ 2987 7351; www.discoverybay.com.hk) makes trips from Central to Tsim Sha Tsui East; **New World First Ferry** (☎ 2131 8181; www.nwff.com.hk) has ferries from North Point to Hung Hom and Kowloon City; and the **Fortune Ferry Co** (☎ 2994 8155) has a service linking North Point and Kwun Tong.

Central (Queen's pier)–Tsim Sha Tsui East Every 10 to 20 minutes from 7.40am-8.20pm (from 8am on Sunday); adults HK$4.50, children & seniors HK$2.30.

North Point–Hung Hom Every 20 minutes from 7.20am-7.20pm; adults HK$4.50, children & seniors HK$2.30.

North Point–Kowloon City Every 20 minutes from 7.10am-7.30pm; adults HK$4.50, children & seniors HK$2.30.

North Point–Kwun Tong Every 30 minutes from 7.15am-7.45pm Monday to Saturday, 7am-7.30pm Sunday; adults HK$5, children & seniors HK$2.50.

New Territories Ferries
SAI KUNG PENINSULA & TAP MUN CHAU

Boats operated by the **Tsui Wah Ferry Service** (☎ 2272 2022) link the east-central New Territories near Chinese University with the Sai Kung Peninsula and Tap Mun Chau. From the pier at Ma Liu Shui, ferries cruise through Tolo Harbour to Tap Mun Chau and back, calling at various villages on the Sai Kung Peninsula both outbound and inbound.

Ferries leave Ma Liu Shui at 8.30am and 3pm daily, arriving at Tap Mun Chau at 10am and 4.20pm respectively, from where they continue on to Ko Lau Wan, Chek Keng and Wong Shek (weekdays/weekend HK$16/25). They leave for Ma Liu Shui at 11.10am and 5.30pm. On Saturday, Sunday and public holidays an extra ferry leaves Ma Liu Shui at 12.30pm, arriving and departing from Tap Mun Chau at 1.45pm.

An easier – and faster – way to reach Tap Mun Chau, with many more departures, is by *kaido* from Wong Shek pier, which is the last stop on bus No 94 from Sai Kung town. The *kaidos*, operated by Tsui Wah Ferry Service, run about once every two hours (there's a total of six sailings, with two callings at Chek Keng) from 8.30am to 6.30pm Monday to Friday (HK$8), and hourly (there are 12 sailings, with three stops at Chek Keng) between the same hours at the weekend and on public holidays (HK$12). Be aware that the last sailing back from Tap Mun Chau is at 6pm from Monday to Friday and 6.05pm at the weekend.

If you've missed the boat or can't be bothered waiting for the next, the private sampans at Wong Shek pier, which seat up to three people in addition to the driver, charge HK$60 per trip to or from the island.

PING CHAU

You can reach Ping Chau from Ma Liu Shui, near the Chinese University, by ferries operated by **Tsui Wah Ferry Service** (☎ 2272 2022), but only at the weekend and on public holidays. Ferries depart from Ma Liu Shui at 9am and 3.30pm on Saturday, returning at 5.15pm. The single ferry on Sunday and public holidays leaves Ma Liu Shui at 9am, returning from Ping Chau at 5.15pm. Only return tickets (HK$80) are available, and the trip takes 1¾ hours. The Sunday morning ferry could well be booked out, so call ahead to check availability.

Outlying Islands Ferries

The main Outlying Islands are, for the most part, linked to Hong Kong by regular ferry services. Fares are cheap and the ferries are comfortable and mostly air-conditioned. They have toilets, and a basic bar that serves drinks and snacks. The ferries can get very crowded on Saturday afternoon and Sunday, especially in summer. Depart as early as you can and return in the evening.

There are two types of ferries: the large 'ordinary ferries', which, with the exception of those to Lamma, offer ordinary and deluxe classes; and the smaller 'fast ferries', hovercraft that have one class only, and cut travel time by between 10 and 20 minutes, but cost between 50% and 100% more. 'Weekday' fares apply from Monday to Saturday; prices are higher on Sunday and public holidays. Unless stated otherwise, children aged three to 11 years, seniors over 65 years and people with disabilities pay half-fare on both types of ferries and in both classes. Return is double the single fare.

The main company serving the Outlying Islands is **New World First Ferry** (NWFF; ☎ 2131 8181; www.nwff.com.hk), which has a **customer service centre** (Map p400-3; Pier 6, Outlying

Islands ferry terminal; ☻ 10am-2pm & 3-7pm Mon & Wed-Fri, 10am-1.30pm Tue, 10.30am-3.30pm Sat & Sun). NWFF boats go to Cheung Chau, Peng Chau and Lantau, and connect all three via an interisland service. The **Hong Kong & Kowloon Ferry Co** (HKKF; ☎ 2815 6063; www.hkkf.com.hk) serves destinations on Lamma only.

Ferry timetables are subject to slight seasonal changes. They are prominently displayed at all ferry piers, but you can pick up a copy of the schedules at any Hong Kong Tourism Board (HKTB) information centre or download it from the HKTB website database (www.partnernet.hktb.com).

Tickets are available from booths at the ferry piers, but you'll avoid queuing at busy times by using an Octopus card or putting the exact change into the turnstile as you enter the pier. On some of the smaller ferries the staff run out of change, so it helps to have small coins. It's rare for ticket offices to accept bills larger than HK$100.

If your time is limited, you can go on an organised tour (see p78) or even hire your own junk (see p243).

The NWFF's Island Hopping Pass allows unlimited rides for a day on ordinary ferries to Lantau, Cheung Chau and Peng Chau. The pass costs HK$30 Monday to Saturday and HK$40 on Sunday.

LAMMA

TO/FROM CENTRAL Both Yung Shue Wan and Sok Kwu Wan are served by HKKF ferries from pier 4 at the Outlying Islands ferry terminal in Central.

Ordinary and fast ferries depart Central for Yung Shue Wan approximately every half-hour to an hour (with additional sailings around 8am and 6pm) from 6.30am to 12.30am. The last boat to Central from Yung Shue Wan leaves at 11.30pm; it is a fast ferry. The trip on the ordinary ferry takes 35 minutes, and the adult one-way fare is HK$10 (HK$14 on Sunday and public holidays). The fast ferries, which take just 20 minutes, cost HK$15 (HK$20 on Sunday and public holidays).

From Central, fast ferries reach Sok Kwu Wan in 35 minutes and cost HK$13 (HK$18 on Sunday and public holidays). Ferries leave every 1½ hours or so, with the first departing Central at 7.20am and the last at 11.30pm. The last ferry to Central from Sok Kwu Wan is at 10.40pm.

TO/FROM ABERDEEN Express ferries link the pier at Aberdeen Promenade with Yung Shue Wan (HK$11 Monday to Saturday, HK$12 on Sunday and public holidays) via Pak Kok Tsuen (HK$5.50) 10 times a day, with the first ferry leaving Aberdeen at 6.30am and the last at 8.15pm Monday to Saturday. There are up to 15 ferries on Sunday and public holidays, with the first leaving Aberdeen at 7.30am and the last at 7.30pm. The last ferry for Aberdeen leaves Yung Shue Wan at 8.45pm and Pak Kok Tsuen at 9pm Monday to Saturday. On Sunday and public holidays, the last sailing times are 8pm from Yung Shue Wan and 8.10pm from Pak Kok Tsuen.

There is also a smaller ferry – more a *kaido*, really – run by **Chuen Kee Ferry** (☎ 2375 7883, 2982 8225) between Aberdeen and Sok Kwu Wan; all but two stop at Mo Tat Wan along the way. The journey between Aberdeen and Mo Tat Wan takes 23 minutes, and it's another seven minutes from there to Sok Kwu Wan. The fare for adults/children is HK$8/4 (HK$12/6 in the evening and on Sunday and public holidays); between Mo Tat Wan and Sok Kwu Wan it costs HK$3/1.50 (HK$4/2 in the evening and on Sunday and public holidays.

There are 12 departures from Aberdeen to Sok Kwu Wan from Monday to Saturday between 6.45am and 10.40pm, leaving roughly every 1½ hours. In the other direction there are 12 departures a day from Monday to Saturday between 6.05am and 10.05pm. On Sunday and public holidays, the service increases to 18 trips in each direction. Boats depart approximately every 45 minutes; the earliest and latest boats from Aberdeen are 8am and 10.40pm. From Sok Kwu Wan, the earliest and latest trips are 6.15am and 10.05pm.

A sampan from Aberdeen to Sok Kwu Wan/Yung Shue Wan will cost about HK$80/100 during the day and double that or more in the wee hours, when drunken revellers who have missed the last ferry back from Central are trying to get home. If you should be in the same, er, boat, don't panic; there are always a number of people ready and willing to split the cost.

CHEUNG CHAU

TO/FROM CENTRAL Ordinary and fast ferries for Cheung Chau depart from pier 5 at the Outlying Islands ferry terminal in Central approximately every half-hour between 6.15am (6.30am on Sunday) and 12.30am. There are then fast ferries at 1.30am and 4.15am until

normal daytime services begin again. The last ordinary ferry back to Central from Cheung Chau leaves at 11.45pm (11.30pm on Sunday), but don't panic if you miss it; there are fast ferries at 2.20am and 5.10am seven days a week and an ordinary one at 5.50am Monday to Saturday.

The trip on the ordinary ferry takes 48 minutes, and the adult one-way fare in ordinary class is HK$10.50 (HK$15.70 on Sunday and public holidays). The fares for deluxe class, which allows you to sit on the open-air deck at the stern, are HK$16.80 and HK$25 respectively. The fast ferries, which run as frequently as the ordinary ones and take just 32 minutes, cost HK$21 (HK$31 on Sunday and public holidays).

TO/FROM TSIM SHA TSUI At the weekend and on public holidays only, fast ferries depart for Cheung Chau via Mui Wo on Lantau from the northern side of the Tsim Sha Tsui Star Ferry pier. The one-way fare is HK$31, and the voyage takes 65 minutes. Boats leave Tsim Sha Tsui between 2pm and 6pm on Saturday, and between 10am and 6pm on Sunday and public holidays. The return ferries from Cheung Chau run between 3.05pm and 7.05pm on Saturday and between 11.05am and 7.05pm on Sunday and public holidays.

INTERISLAND SERVICE An interisland ordinary ferry links Cheung Chau with Mui Wo (via Chi Ma Wan in most cases) on Lantau and Peng Chau seven days a week. The first ferry leaves Cheung Chau at 6am, and the last ferry is at 10.50pm; boats depart approximately every 1½ hours. From Cheung Chau, it takes 15 minutes to reach Chi Ma Wan, a half-hour to Mui Wo and 50 minutes to Peng Chau. The fare for all sectors is HK$8.40.

LANTAU

The main entry port for vessels serving Lantau proper is Mui Wo (Silvermine Bay). However, you can also reach other destinations on Lantau from other ports: Discovery Bay from Central, the Chi Ma Wan Peninsula from Cheung Chau, the Trappist Monastery from Peng Chau, and Tai O and Tung Chung from Tuen Mun in the New Territories.

MUI WO TO/FROM CENTRAL Both ordinary and fast ferries depart for Mui Wo about every half-hour between 6.10am (7am on Sunday and public holidays) and 12.30am from pier 6 at the Outlying Islands ferry terminal in Central. Between those times there is a 3am fast ferry to Mui Wo via Peng Chau. The last ferry from Mui Wo to Central is at 11.30pm, though there is a fast ferry at 3.40am, which calls at Peng Chau first.

The journey on the ordinary ferry takes 50 minutes, and the adult one-way fare is HK$10.50/16.80 in ordinary/deluxe class (HK$15.70/25 on Sunday and public holidays). The fast ferries, which take just 35 minutes, cost HK$21 (HK$31 on Sunday and public holidays).

MUI WO TO/FROM TSIM SHA TSUI

At the weekend and on public holidays only, ferries depart for Mui Wo from the Tsim Sha Tsui Star Ferry pier in Kowloon. Fast ferries leave Tsim Sha Tsui between 2pm and 6pm on Saturday and between 10am and 6pm on Sunday and public holidays. The return ferries from Mui Wo are between 2.40pm and 6.40pm on Saturday and between 10.40am and 6.40pm on Sunday and public holidays, calling at Cheung Chau along the way. The one-way fare is HK$31 and the trip to Mui Wo takes 40 minutes.

MUI WO & THE INTERISLAND SERVICE

The interisland ordinary ferry (HK$8.40) links Mui Wo with Cheung Chau (via Chi Ma Wan in most cases) and Peng Chau some 20 times a day. The first ferry leaves Mui Wo for Cheung Chau at 6am and for Peng Chau at 6.35am; the last ferry to Cheung Chau is at 10.20pm and to Peng Chau at 11.20pm. From Mui Wo it takes 20 to 25 minutes to reach Peng Chau, 20 minutes to Chi Ma Wan and 50 minutes to Cheung Chau.

TO/FROM THE TRAPPIST MONASTERY

For details on how to reach the Trappist Monastery on Lantau's northeast coast, see the Peng Chau section (p344).

TO/FROM DISCOVERY BAY High-speed

ferries run by the **Discovery Bay Transportation Service** (☎ 2987 7351; www.discoverybay.com.hk) leave from pier 3 at the Outlying Islands ferry terminal in Central every 10 to 30 minutes between 6.30am and 1am; after that time there are additional sailings at 1.30am (on weekends only), 2am, 2.30am (on weekends only), 3.20am and 5am until the daytime schedule resumes. Similar services run from Discovery Bay to Central. Tickets are HK$27 and the trip takes 20 to 25 minutes.

There are high-speed ferry departures Monday to Friday from Mui Wo to Discovery Bay (between 7.45am and 6.30pm), and up to eight sailings at the weekend. From Discovery Bay to Mui Wo, sailings are between 7.25am and 6.10pm Monday to Friday, and there are up to eight sailings on Saturday and Sunday. Tickets cost HK$12 and the trip takes between 12 and 15 minutes.

You can also reach Discovery Bay from Peng Chau (p344).

TO/FROM CHI MA WAN The interisland

ordinary ferry (HK$8.40) linking Cheung Chau and Mui Wo calls at the Chi Ma Wan ferry pier on the northeastern corner of the peninsula six times a day (with the first at 6.15am and the last at 8.30pm) heading for Cheung Chau, and five times a day going to Mui Wo (first at 6.55am and the last at 7.05pm) from where it carries on to Peng Chau.

Monday to Saturday, four direct ferries (and another 10 via Cheung Chau) link Queen's pier in Central with Sea Ranch on the Chi Ma Wan Peninsula. On Sunday and public holidays, five ferries go directly there and another 11 call at Cheung Chau first. You must be a resident or invited guest to visit Sea Ranch; ring ☎ 2989 1788 or ☎ 2989 1789 for details.

TO/FROM TAI O There are NWFF ferries be-

tween the Tai O pier on Wing On St and Tuen Mun in the New Territories (via Sha Lo Wan and the Tung Chung New Development pier on Lantau's north coast) daily at 9.45am, 12.15pm, 4.15pm and 7.15pm, with an additional sailing at 2.15pm on Sunday. The trip takes between one and 1½ hours and costs HK$15 (HK$25 on Sunday). On Sunday and public holidays there are three direct sailings to Tuen Mun (at 10.45am, 1.45pm and 5.45pm) departing from Tai O Shek Tsai Po pier, which is about 1.2km from the centre. The flat fare is HK$25.

TO/FROM TUNG CHUNG Another ser-

vice run by NWFF links Tung Chung New Development pier with Tuen Mun in the New Territories. Ferries depart from Tuen Mun every 20 minutes from 5.40am to 11pm, with the return boats leaving Tung Chung between 20 and 30 minutes later (from 6am to 11.20pm). The trip takes 17 minutes and costs HK$15 (HK$10 for children and seniors).

PENG CHAU

Along with Central, you can reach the Trappist Monastery and Discovery Bay from little Peng Chau.

TO/FROM CENTRAL Ordinary and fast ferries leave for Peng Chau approximately once every 45 minutes between 7am and 12.30am from pier 6 at the Outlying Islands ferry terminal in Central. There's also a 3am fast ferry to Peng Chau that carries on to Mui Wo on Lantau. The last ferry from Peng Chau to Central is at 11.30pm (11.35pm on Sunday), though there is a fast ferry at 3.25am.

The journey on the ordinary ferry takes 38 minutes, and the adult one-way fare is HK$10.50/16.80 in ordinary/deluxe class (HK$15.70/25 on Sunday and public holidays). The fast ferries, which take just 25 minutes, cost HK$21 (HK$31 on Sunday and public holidays).

INTERISLAND SERVICE An interisland ordinary ferry (HK$8.40) links Peng Chau with Mui Wo and (frequently) Chi Ma Wan on Lantau, as well as Cheung Chau, up to 11 times a day. The first ferry leaves Peng Chau at 5.40am for all three destinations; the last ferry to Mui Wo is at 11.40pm. Boats take 20 minutes to reach Mui Wo, 40 minutes to Chi Ma Wan and 70 minutes to Cheung Chau.

TO/FROM THE TRAPPIST MONASTERY Peng Chau is the main springboard for the Trappist Monastery, with up to 10 sailings a day. **Rental Kaito** (☎ 9033 8102) sails sampans to Tai Shui Hang pier from the small pier just north of the main Peng Chau ferry pier daily between 7.45am and 5pm. They return from the monastery between 8.10am and 5.10pm.

TO/FROM DISCOVERY BAY Rental Kaito (☎ 9033 8102) links Peng Chau with Discovery Bay every 30 minutes to an hour, with up to 20 sailings a day between 6.30am and 10pm, from the pier north of the main Peng Chau ferry. The last boat from Discovery Bay sails at 10.15pm.

MA WAN

Boats leave Sham Tseng, a settlement to the west of Tsuen Wan in the New Territories, for Ma Wan every half-hour between 6.15am and 11.30pm (6am to 11.15pm from Ma Wan to Sham Tseng). Monday to Friday the fare for adults/children and seniors over 65 years is HK$5/HK$2 and HK$6/3 at the weekend and on public holidays.

TUNG LUNG CHAU

At the weekend only, ferries run by **Lam Kee Kaido** (☎ 2560 9929) heading for Joss House Bay on the Clearwater Bay Peninsula from Sai Wan Ho, just east of Quarry Bay on Hong Kong Island, stop at Tung Lung Chau en route. On Saturday, boats sail from Sai Wan Ho at 9am, 10.30am, 3.30pm and 4.45pm, departing from Tung Lung Chau a half-hour later. On Sunday and public holidays there are boats from Sai Wan Ho at 8.30am, 9.45am, 11am, 2.15pm, 3.30pm and 4.45pm, with returns from Tung Lung Chau at 9am, 10.20am, 1.45pm, 3pm, 4pm and 5.30pm. The trip takes a half-hour, and the one-way fare is HK$28/14 for adults/children under 12.

To catch the ferry, take the MTR's Island line to Sai Wan Ho and then use exit A. Follow Tai On St north until you reach the quayside. The ride to Joss House Bay from Tung Lung Chau is significantly shorter than the one from Sai Wan Ho. You could go by one route and return by the other. From Joss House Bay there are buses to the Choi Hung MTR station in Kowloon.

PO TOI ISLAND

A ferry run by **Po Toi Kaido Services** (☎ 2554 4059) leaves Aberdeen for Po Toi on Tuesday, Thursday and Saturday at 9am, returning from the island at 10.30am. On Sunday a single boat leaves Aberdeen at 8am, but there are several more departures from Stanley (at 10am, 11.30am, 3.30pm and 5pm). Boats return from Po Toi at 9.15am, 10.45am, 3pm, 4.30pm and 6pm. A same-day return fare is HK$40. If you pitch a tent and return the following day, the fare is HK$70.

Other Boats

Sea and harbour transport is not limited to scheduled ferries in Hong Kong. You'll encounter several other types of boats as you travel further afield.

Kaidos (small- to medium-sized 'ferries') are able to make short runs on the open sea. Only a few *kaido* routes operate on regular schedules (eg the ones from Peng Chau to the Trappist Monastery and Discovery Bay, and from Aberdeen to Sok Kwu Wan on Lamma); most simply adjust supply to demand. *Kaidos* run most frequently at weekends and public holidays.

Sampans are motorised launches that can only accommodate a few (usually four) people. Sampans are generally too small to be considered seaworthy, but they can safely zip you around typhoon shelters like the ones at Aberdeen and Cheung Chau.

Bigger than a sampan but smaller than a *kaido*, *walla wallas* (water taxis that operate in Victoria Harbour) are a dying breed. Most of the customers are sailors stationed on ships anchored in the harbour. You can sometimes find one to transport you across the harbour after the MTR and regular ferries stop running. On Hong Kong Island look for them at Queen's pier on the east side of the Star Ferry Pier. On the Kowloon side, *walla wallas* can sometimes be found southeast of the Star Ferry pier in Tsim Sha Tsui.

BUS

Hong Kong's extensive bus system offers a bewildering number of routes that will take you just about anywhere in the territory. Most visitors use the buses to explore the southern side of Hong Kong Island and the New Territories. The northern side of Hong Kong Island and most of Kowloon are well served by the MTR.

Although buses pick up and discharge passengers at stops along the way, on Hong Kong Island the most important bus stations are the Central bus terminus below Exchange Square in Central and the one at Admiralty. From these stations you can catch buses to Aberdeen, Repulse Bay, Stanley and other destinations on the southern side of Hong Kong Island. In Kowloon, the bus terminal at the Star Ferry pier in Tsim Sha Tsui is the most important, with buses to Hung Hom station and points in eastern and western Kowloon. Almost all New Towns in the New Territories are important transport hubs, though Sha Tin is particularly so, with buses travelling as far afield as Sai Kung, Tung Chung and Tuen Mun.

Bus fares range from HK$1.20 to HK$45, depending on the destination and how many sections you cover. Fares for night buses cost from HK$12.80 to HK$23. Payment is made into a fare box upon entry so, unless you're carrying an ever-so-convenient Octopus card (see Travel & Tourist Passes p339), have plenty of coins handy, as the driver does not give change.

Hong Kong's buses are usually double-deckers. Many buses have easy-to-read LCD displays of road names and stops in Chinese and sometimes in English, and TV screens to entertain you as you roll along. Buses serving the airport and Hung Hom train station have luggage racks to the right as you board.

Hong Kong's buses are run by a half-dozen private operators, carrying some four million passengers a day (ie 39% of the total daily public-transport volume). Though it's much of a muchness as to who's driving you from A to B or even C, you may want to check the routings on their websites.

Citybus (☎ 2963 4888, hotline 2873 0818; www.citybus .com.hk)

Discovery Bay Transportation Services (☎ 2987 7351; www.discoverybay.com.hk)

KCRC Bus Service (☎ 2602 7799; www.kcrc.com)

Kowloon Motor Bus Co (KMB; ☎ 2745 4466; www.kmb .com.hk)

Long Win Bus Co (☎ 2261 2791; www.kmb.com.hk)

New Lantao Bus Company (☎ 2984 9848; www .newlantaobus.com)

New World First Bus Services (☎ 2136 8888; www .nwfb.com.hk)

Routes & Schedules

There are no good bus maps and because buses are run by so many different private operators, there is no longer a comprehensive directory for the whole territory. Your best option is Universal Publications' *Hong Kong Guidebook* or *Hong Kong Directory* (see Maps p364), which includes the *Public Transport Boarding Guide* in Chinese (mostly) and English.

The HKTB has useful leaflets on the major bus routes on Hong Kong Island, Kowloon, the New Territories and Lantau, which can be downloaded from its database (www.partner net.hktb.com). The major bus companies (see above) detail all their routings on their websites. You might also try the Yellow Pages Map Website (www.ypmap.com).

HONG KONG ISLAND, KOWLOON & THE NEW TERRITORIES

Most buses run from about 5.30am or 6am until midnight or 12.30am, but there are a handful of useful night bus services in addition to the ones linking the airport with various parts of the territory. The N121, which operates every 15 minutes between 12.45am and 5am, runs from the Macau ferry terminal on Hong Kong Island and through the Cross-Harbour

Tunnel to Chatham Rd North in Tsim Sha Tsui East before continuing on to eastern Kowloon and Ngau Tau Kok (HK$12.80).

Bus No N122, which has the same fare and schedule, runs from North Point on Hong Kong Island, through the Cross-Harbour Tunnel to Nathan Rd and on to Mei Foo Sun Chuen in the northwestern part of Kowloon. You can catch these two buses near the tunnel entrances on either side of the harbour.

Other useful night buses that cross the harbour include the N118, which runs from Siu Sai Wan in the northeastern part of Hong Kong Island to Sham Shui Po in northwest Kowloon via North Point and Causeway Bay (HK$12.80); and the N170, which runs from Wah Fu, a large estate near Aberdeen in the southwest of Hong Kong Island, through Kowloon as far as Sha Tin in the New Territories (HK$23).

LANTAU

With the opening of the Tung Chung MTR line and the two Lantau Link bridges connecting the island to the New Territories, you can travel to Lantau by MTR and by bus (No E31 from the Tsuen Wan MTR station, No E32 from the Kwai Fong MTR, or No E33 from Tuen Mun). There are also a few overnight routes that serve the airport and run through Tung Chung.

New Lantao Bus Company (☎ 2984 9848, 2984 8361; www.newlantaobus.com) runs a total of 19 lines (including three night buses) to destinations on Lantau, including Hong Kong International Airport. Buses run daily on all but two routes, with frequencies increased on Sunday and public holidays to handle the flood of visitors. There is a complicated pricing system for Lantau buses: weekday fares on ordinary/air-conditioned buses cost from HK$2.50/3.40 to HK$4.30/5.20, and Sunday fares range from HK$4.30/5.20 to HK$13/30.

Buses from Mui Wo depart from the terminal just opposite the ferry pier. For buses to the airport, see p332.

The New Lantao Bus Pass, available for HK$38 Monday to Saturday, allows unlimited travel on the New Lantao Bus Company network.

Buses to destinations around Lantau:

Bus No 1 (Monday to Saturday ordinary/air-conditioned HK$8/11.80, Sunday & at night HK$12/19) Leaves Mui Wo for Tai O every 20 to 40 minutes Monday to Saturday between 6am and 1.20am and between 6.30am and 1.10am Sunday; last bus leaves Tai O at 12.10am, though No N1 leaves for Mui Wo at 2.50am, returning from there at 3.45am.

Bus No 2 (Monday to Saturday HK$16, Sunday HK$25) Leaves Mui Wo for Ngong Ping every 20 to 50 minutes between 7.50am and 6.40pm, Monday to Saturday and between 8am and 6.20pm Sunday; last bus leaves Ngong Ping at 7.20pm.

Bus No 3M (Monday to Saturday HK$10.50, Sunday HK$17) Runs from Mui Wo to Tung Chung every 15 minutes to an hour between 6.35am and 2.05am; last bus from Mui Wo 11.15pm.

Bus No 4 (Monday to Saturday ordinary/air-conditioned HK$4/5.80, Sunday & public holidays HK$7.70/11.50) Departs from Mui Wo for Pui O, Cheung Sha Beach and Tong Fuk every 15 to 45 minutes between 7.10am and 7.25pm, and between 7.10am and 8.20pm Sunday; last No 4 bus back from Tong Fuk at 6pm (8.50pm Sunday and public holidays).

Bus No 7P (Saturday HK$2.50/3.40, Sunday & public holidays HK$4.30/5.20) Leaves Mui Wo for Pui O every 15 minutes to an hour between 2.30pm and 7.35pm on Saturday and between 7.55am and 6.20pm on Sunday and public holidays; last No 7P bus from Pui O at 6.20pm on Saturday and 6.40pm on Sunday.

Bus No 11 (Monday to Saturday HK$8/11.80, Sunday HK$13/19) Links Tai O with Tung Chung every 15 minutes to an hour between 5.20am and 12.15am; last bus from Tung Chung at 1.20pm.

Bus No 23 (Monday to Saturday HK$16, Sun HK$25) Links Ngong Ping and the centre of Tung Chung, from where you can catch the Tung Chung MTR line to Kowloon or Central, every 15 to 30 minutes between 8.10am and 6.10pm.

Public Light Bus

'Public light buses' (an official term that no-one ever uses) are vans with no more than 16 seats. They come in two varieties. Minibuses are cream-coloured with a red roof or stripe, and pick up and discharge passengers wherever they are hailed or asked to stop. Maxicabs, cream-coloured with a green roof or stripe, operate on fixed routes. Thus minibuses are more like cabs and maxicabs are more like buses. Just try not to think about it... ·

There are 4350 public light buses running in the territory, roughly divided between minibuses and maxicabs.

MINIBUS

Red minibuses can be handy for short distances, such as the trip from Central to Wan Chai or Causeway Bay, and you can be assured of a seat – by law, passengers are not allowed to stand. The destination is displayed on the front in large Chinese characters, usually with a smaller English translation below. Minibuses will stop for you almost anywhere, but not in restricted zones or at busy bus stops.

The problem for non-Chinese-speakers is not getting on but getting off. There are no buttons or bells, so you must call out your stop. Moreover, minibus drivers rarely speak English. If you call out, 'stop here, please', there is a pretty good chance the driver will do so, but otherwise try the Cantonese version yah lok (have to get down), which sounds like 'yow lok', or simply ni doh, m goi (here, please), pronounced 'lido mgoy'.

Minibus fares range from HK$2.50 to HK$20. The price to the final destination is displayed on a card propped up in the windscreen, but this is often only written in Chinese numbers. Fares are equal to or higher than those on the bus, but drivers often increase their fares on rainy days, at night and during holiday periods. You usually hand the driver the fare when you get off, and change is given. You can use your Octopus card on some minibuses.

If you're in Central, the best place to catch minibuses to Wan Chai and other points east is the Central bus terminus below Exchange Square. If heading west towards Kennedy Town, walk up to Stanley St, near Lan Kwai Fong.

There are a few minibuses that cross the harbour late at night, running between Wan Chai and Mong Kok. In Wan Chai, minibuses can be found on Hennessy and Fleming Rds. In Kowloon you may have to trudge up Nathan Rd as far as Mong Kok or over to the Hung Hom station before you'll find one. Minibuses to the New Territories can be found at the Jordan and Choi Hung MTR stations in Kowloon.

MAXICAB

More commonly known as 'green minibuses', maxicabs operate on some 325 routes, more than half of which are in the New Territories, and serve at designated stops. Fares range from HK$2.50 to HK$22.50, according to distance. You must put the exact fare in the cash box as you descend (no change is given) or, on some routes, zap your Octopus card.

In Tsim Sha Tsui the No 6 green minibus (HK$4.30) runs from Hankow Rd to Tsim Sha Tsui East and Hung Hom station every five minutes or so between 6.30am and 12.05pm. On Hong Kong Island the No 1 green minibus (HK$7.40) leaves Edinburgh Place east of Hong Kong City Hall and Star Ferry pier in Central for the Peak every five to 12 minutes from 6.30am to midnight.

MASS TRANSIT RAILWAY

The **Mass Transit Railway** (MTR; Map p426; ☎ 2881 8888; www.mtr.com.hk), Hong Kong's underground rail system and universally known as the 'MTR', is a phenomenon of modern urban public transport. Sleek, pristine and always on time, it is also rather soulless.

Though it costs a bit more than other forms of public transport, the MTR is the quickest way to get to most destinations in the urban areas. Trains run every two to four minutes from around 6am to between 12.30am and 1am.

The MTR travels on just under 88km of track and is made up of six lines, including the Airport Express (p333) and the Tseung Kwan O line, which opened in 2002. It stops at some 49 stations and carries 2.3 million passengers a day.

The Island line extends along the northern coast of Hong Kong Island from Sheung Wan in the west to Chai Wan in the east. The Tsuen Wan line runs from Central station and travels alongside the Island line as far as Admiralty, where it crosses the harbour and runs through central Kowloon, terminating at Tsuen Wan in the New Territories.

The Kwun Tong line, which begins at Yau Ma Tei, shares that and the Tsuen Wan line; at Prince Edward it branches off and heads for eastern Kowloon, crossing the KCR East line at Kowloon Tong before joining the new Tseung Kwan O line at Yau Tong and terminating at Tiu Keng Leng in the southeastern New Territories.

The new Tseung Kwan O line starts at North Point and hits Quarry Bay before crossing the eastern harbour and terminating at Po Lam in the southeastern New Territories. The Tung Chung line shares the same rail lines as the Airport Express, but stops at two additional stations in Kowloon (Kowloon and Olympic) along the way. It terminates at Tung Chung, a New Town on Lantau, which is a place of no particular interest to travellers but one that offers cheaper transport options to and from the airport.

The MTR connects with the Kowloon-Canton Railway (KCR) only at Kowloon Tong station.

For short hauls, the MTR is not great value. If you want to cross the harbour from Tsim Sha Tsui to Central, for example, at HK$9 (or HK$7.90 with an Octopus card) the MTR is more than four times the price of the Star Ferry, with none of the views, and is only marginally faster. If your destination is further away – North Point, say, or Kwun Tong – the MTR is considerably faster than a bus or minibus and about the same price. If possible, it's best to avoid the rush hours: 7.30am to 9.30am and 5pm to 7pm, including Saturday morning, when 85% of the 1050 MTR cars are in use.

Travelling by the MTR is child's play; everything, from the ticket-vending machines to the turnstiles, is automated. The system uses the stored-value Octopus card (see Travel & Tourist Passes p339), really the only way to go, and single-journey tickets with a magnetic coding strip on the back. When you pass through the turnstile, the card is encoded with the station identification and time. At the other end, the exit turnstile sucks in the ticket, reads where you came from, the time you bought the ticket and how much you paid. If everything is in order, it will let you through. If you have underpaid (by mistake or otherwise), you can make up the difference at an MTR service counter; there are no fines since no-one gets out without paying. Once you've passed through the turnstile to begin a journey you have 90 minutes to complete it before the ticket becomes invalid.

Ticket prices range from between HK$4 and HK$26 (HK$3.80 and HK$23.10 with an Octopus card); children and seniors pay between HK$3 and HK$13 (HK$2.40 and HK$11.60 with a card), depending on the destination. Ticket machines accept HK$10, HK$5, HK$2 and HK$1 and HK$0.50 coins, and they dispense change; most also take the new HK$10 note and the HK$20 note. The machines have a touch-sensitive screen with highlighted destinations. You can also buy tickets from MTR service counters and get change from the Hang Seng bank branches located in most stations.

Smoking, eating and drinking are not permitted in MTR stations or on the trains, and violators are subject to a fine of HK$5000. You are not allowed to carry large objects or bicycles aboard trains either, though backpacks and suitcases are fine.

There are no toilets in any of the MTR stations. Like the 90-minute limit on a ticket's validity, the reasoning behind this is to get bodies into stations, bums on seats (or hands on straps), and bodies out onto the street again as quickly as possible. It's a good idea, it works and few people complain.

About the only problem you may have in using the system is determining the appropriate exit for your destination. Exit signs use an alphanumerical system and there can be as many as a dozen to choose from. We give

the correct exit for sights and destinations wherever possible in the Districts & Islands chapter, but you may find yourself studying the exit table from time to time and scratching your head. There are always maps of the area at each exit.

Should you leave something behind on the MTR, you can contact the **lost property office** (☎ 2861 0020; ◷ 8am-8pm) at Admiralty MTR station.

TRAIN

The MTR underground system notwithstanding, Hong Kong has two 'real' train systems that are crucial for travellers getting around in the New Territories and/or heading for China.

Kowloon-Canton Railway

Better known as the 'KCR', the **Kowloon-Canton Railway** (Map pp396-7; ☎ 2602 7799; www.kcrc.com) is now made up of two lines. KCR East Rail, which commenced in 1910, is a single-line, 34km-long commuter railway running from southern Kowloon to the border with mainland China at Lo Wu. It serves some 13 stations and carries 800,000 passengers a day. The tracks are the same as those used by the express trains to cities in Guangdong province as well as to Shanghai and Beijing, but the trains are different and look more like MTR carriages. A KCR East Rail extension to Tsim Sha Tsui will open soon. Those to Ma On Shan on the Sai Kung Peninsula and Lok Ma Chau on the border with the mainland will be several years late.

The new **KCR West Rail** (☎ 2684 8833), a separate 30.5km-long line that opened in late 2003, links Nam Cheong station in Sham Shui Po with Tuen Mun via Yuen Long, stopping at nine new, purpose-built stations. Eventually it will be linked to the station at Hung Hom, via an extension of the KCR East Rail, with stops at Kowloon West, Canton Rd and East Tsim Sha Tsui.

The KCR is a quick way to get to the New Territories, and the ride offers some nice vistas, particularly between the Chinese University and Tai Po Market stations. The southernmost station on the line at Hung Hom can be reached most easily from Tsim Sha Tsui by taking the No 6 or No 8 green minibus (HK$4.30) from Hankow Rd. Bus K16 runs along the same route (Monday to Saturday only).

You can transfer from the MTR to the KCR East Rail only at Kowloon Tong station at the moment, and once the KCR East Rail extension opens, it will be possible to transfer at Tsim Sha Tsui as well. On the KCR West, there is interchange with the Tung Chung MTR line at Nam Cheong, with the Tsuen Wan line at Mei Foo and with the LRT at Yuen Long, Tin Shui Wan, Siu Hong and Tuen Mun.

KCR trains run every five to eight minutes, except during rush hour, when they depart every three to six minutes. The first train leaves Hung Hom at 5.30am and the last departs from Lo Wu at 12.30am, a half-hour after the border between Hong Kong and Shenzhen closes. The trip from Nam Cheong to Tuen Mun takes 30 minutes.

KCR fares are cheap, starting at HK$3.50, with a half-hour ride to Sheung Shui costing just HK$9 (1st class is double) and the 40-minute trip to Lo Wu HK$33. Children and seniors pay reduced fares of between HK$1.50 and HK$16.50.

Light Rail Transit

Known as the LRT, the **Light Rail Transit** (Map p396-7; ☎ 2468 7788; www.kcrc.com) system began operations in 1988 and has been extended several times since. It is rather like a modern, air-conditioned version of the trams in Hong Kong, but it's much faster, reaching speeds of up to 70km/h. It runs along 32km of track parallel to the road and stops at 57 designated stations. The LRT is owned and run by the KCR and carries some 320,000 passengers a day.

Until recently, only those travellers visiting the temples of the western New Territories made much use of the LRT, as it essentially was just a link between the New Towns of Tuen Mun and Yuen Long. But with the opening of the KCR West Rail, it is now an important feeder service for the KCR and, by extension, the MTR.

There are normally eight LRT lines connecting various small suburbs with Tuen Mun to the south and Yuen Long to the northeast, but a couple have been suspended for integration into the KCR West Rail feeder system. The LRT operates from 5.30am to between 11pm and 12.30am Monday to Saturday, and from 6am to midnight on Sunday and public holidays.

Trains run every six to 20 minutes, depending on the time of day. Fares on the LRT are HK$4 to HK$5.80, depending on the number of zones (from No 1 to No 5) travelled; children and seniors pay from HK$2 to HK$2.90. If you don't have an Octopus card, you can buy single-journey tickets from vending machines on the platforms.

The system of fare collection is unique in Hong Kong: there are no gates or turnstiles and customers are trusted to validate their ticket or Octopus card when they board and exit. That trust is enforced by occasional spot checks, however, and the fine is 50 times the maximum adult fare – HK$290 at present.

TRAM

Hong Kong's venerable old trams, operated by **Hongkong Tramways Ltd** (☎ 2548 7102; www .info.gov.hk/td/eng/transport/tram.html) are tall and narrow double-decker streetcars, the only all double-deck wooden-sided tram fleet in the world. They roll (and rock) along the northern coast of Hong Kong Island on 16km of track, carrying just under 280,000 passengers daily.

The electric tram line first began operating in 1904 on what was then the shoreline of Hong Kong Island. This helps to understand why roads curve and dogleg in ways that don't seem quite right. Try to get a seat at the front window on the upper deck for a first-class view while rattling through the crowded streets. Tall passengers will find it uncomfortable standing up as the ceiling is low, but there is more space at the rear of the tram on both decks.

Trams operate between 6am and 12.30pm daily and run every two to 10 minutes, but they often arrive bunched together. Be prepared to elbow your way through the crowd to alight, particularly on the lower deck.

Hong Kong's trams are not fast but they're cheap and fun; in fact, apart from the Star Ferry (p339), no form of transport is nearer and dearer to the hearts of most Hong Kong people. For a flat fare of HK$2 (children three to 11 and seniors over 65 HK$1), dropped into a box beside the driver as you descend, you can go as far as you like, whether it's one block or to the end of the line. You can also use your Octopus card on Hong Kong's trams.

A special tourist ticket that allows unlimited rides on the trams as well as the Star Ferry for four days is available for HK$30. It's obviously not much of a deal, as you'd have to take almost 15 trips over that period just to break even.

Tram routes often overlap. Some start at Kennedy Town and run to Shau Kei Wan, while others run only part of the way; one turns south and heads for Happy Valley. The longest run, and covering the entire length of the

Where Have All the Rickshaws Gone?

Rickshaws appeared in Hong Kong soon after jinriksha (literally, `person strength vehicle') were invented in mid-19th-century Japan as a more `humane' alternative to the back-breaking sedan chairs. By 1895 there were already some 700 registered and licensed in the colony; the figure jumped to an estimated 5000 by WWI. Towards the end of the war there were even 60 rickshaws registered in the name of brothels, which were used to deliver courtesans to their customers.

In the mid-1920s, despite competition from buses, trams and other forms of mechanised transport, rickshaws held tight, numbering more than 3000 and still playing a vital role in Hong Kong's transport network. Over the next 15 years, rickshaws dwindled away until there were only a few hundred left at the start of WWII. But the lack of fuel and access to other forms of transport during and after the war gave rickshaws a new lease of life; by the late 1940s there were around 8000 back trawling the streets of the colony.

It was the peak before a rapid decline; taxis and private cars swept rickshaws off the roads in the 1950s and 1960s. There was a busy trade to the bars and brothels of Wan Chai for a time during the Vietnam R&R years of the 1960s and early 1970s, but for the most part rickshaws had ceased to be a means of transport and had become a tourist attraction.

The last new rickshaw licence was issued in 1975, when there were still nearly 100 left on the streets. By the early 1980s the numbers had been halved, and the rickshaw fleet eventually contracted to the tiny group that still hang out at the Star Ferry pier on the Hong Kong Island side, waiting to take visitors on a short jaunt around the car park or to pose for photographs. By the early 1990s rickshaw numbers had fallen to less than 20 and by 2003 they were truly an endangered species. Just four were manned and three lay idle – including one for sale and one for hire (☎ 2558 9640, 9622 1858; HK$500-600 per hour; puller not included).

---

system, from Shau Kei Wan to Kennedy Town (with a change at Western Market), takes about 1½ hours. The six routes from west to east are Kennedy Town–Western Market; Kennedy Town–Happy Valley–Causeway Bay; Sai Ying Pun (Whitty St)–North Point; Sheung Wan (Western Market)–Shau Kei Wan; and Happy Valley–Shau Kei Wan.

Peak Tram

The Peak Tram is not really a tram at all, but a cable-hauled funicular railway that has been climbing, since 1888, some 396m along a steep gradient to the highest point on Hong Kong Island. It is thus the oldest form of public transport in Hong Kong.

While a few residents on the Peak and in the Mid-Levels actually use it as a form of transport – there are four intermediate stops before you reach the top – the Peak Tram is intended to transport visitors and locals to the attractions, shops and restaurants in the Peak Tower (p88) and Peak Galleria (p88).

The **Peak Tram** (☎ 2522 0922, 2849 7654; www.thepeak.com.hk/tram/location.html; one way/return adult HK$20/30, child 3-11 years HK$6/9, senior over 65 years HK$7/14; one-way intermediary stops adult/child/senior HK$18/5/6) runs every 10 to 15 minutes from 7am to midnight, making between one and four stops (Kennedy Rd, MacDonnell Rd, May Rd and Barker Rd) along the way in about seven minutes. It's such a steep ride that

the floor is angled to help standing passengers stay upright. Running for more than a century, the tram has never had an accident – a comforting thought if you start to have doubts about the strength of that cable. It carries 95,000 passengers a day.

The lower tram terminus is behind the St John's Building (Map p400-3; 33 Garden Rd). The upper tram terminus is in the Peak Tower (Map p400-3; 128 Peak Rd). Avoid going on Sunday and public holidays when there are usually long queues. Octopus cards can be used on the Peak Tram.

Between 10am and 11.45pm, open-deck (or air-conditioned) bus No 15C ferries passengers between the Star Ferry pier and the lower tram terminus. The No 12S from Admiralty goes to the same destination daily from 10am until midnight.

BICYCLE

Cycling in urbanised Kowloon or Hong Kong Island would be suicide, but in the quiet areas of the islands (including southern Hong Kong Island) or the New Territories, a bike can be a lovely way to get around. It's not really a form of transport, though – the hilly terrain will slow you down – but more recreational. Be advised that bicycle-rental shops and kiosks tend to run out of bikes early on weekends if the weather is good (see Cycling p238).

CAR & MOTORCYCLE

For a newcomer to consider driving in Hong Kong would be sheer madness. Traffic is heavy, the roads can get hopelessly clogged and the new system of highways and bridges is complicated in the extreme. And if driving the car doesn't destroy your holiday sense of spontaneity, parking the damn thing will. If you are determined to see Hong Kong under your own steam, do yourself a favour and rent a car with a driver.

DRIVING LICENCE & PERMITS

Hong Kong allows most foreigners over the age of 18 to drive for up to 12 months with their valid local licenses. It's still a good idea to carry an International Driving Permit (IDP) as well. This can be obtained from your local automobile association for a reasonable fee (eg HK$80 in Hong Kong).

Anyone driving in the territory for more than a year will need a Hong Kong licence valid for 10 years (HK$900). Apply to the **Licensing Division of the Transport Department** (Map p400-3; ☎ 2804 2600; www.info.gov.hk/td; 3rd fl, United Centre, 95 Queensway, Admiralty; ☺ 9am-4pm Mon-Fri & 9am-11.30am Sat).

RENTAL

Car-rental firms accept International Driver's Permits or driving licences from your home country. Drivers must usually be at least 25 years of age. Daily rates for small cars start at HK$580. There are weekend and weekly deals available. For example, **Avis** (Map p406-8; ☎ 2890 6988; Ground fl, Bright Star Mansion, 93 Leighton Rd, Causeway Bay; ☺ 8am-6pm Mon, 9am-6pm Tue-Fri, 9am-4pm Sat, 9am-1pm Sun) will rent you a Honda Civic or Toyota Corolla for the weekend (from 2pm on Friday to 10.30am Monday) for HK$1500; the same car for a day/week costs HK$720/3200. Rates include unlimited kilometres.

If you're looking for a car with a driver, contact **Ace Hire Car Service** (☎ 2572 7663; www.acehirecar.com.hk; 16 Min Fat St, Happy Valley), which charges between HK$160 and HK$250 per hour (minimum two to five hours, depending on the location). Avis' chauffeur-driven cars are much more expensive: HK$300 to HK$400 with a minimum of four hours on weekdays and six hours on Saturday and Sunday.

ROAD RULES

Vehicles drive on the left-hand side of the road in Hong Kong, as in the UK, Australia and Macau, but *not* in China. Seat belts must be worn by the driver and all passengers, in both the front and back seats. Police are strict and give out traffic tickets at the drop of a hat.

TAXI

Hong Kong taxis are a bargain compared with those in other world-class cities. With more than 18,000 cruising the streets, they're easy to flag down. Hong Kong is not a particularly tip-conscious place and there is no obligation to tip taxi drivers; just round the fare up.

When a taxi is available, there should be a red 'For Hire' sign illuminated on the meter that's visible through the windscreen. At night the 'Taxi' sign on the roof will be lit up as well. Taxis will not stop at bus stops or in restricted zones where a yellow line is painted next to the kerb.

The law requires that everyone in a vehicle wears a seat belt. Both driver and passenger(s) are fined if stopped by the police, and most drivers will gently remind you to buckle up before proceeding.

'Urban taxis' – those in Kowloon and on Hong Kong Island – are red with silver roofs. New Territories taxis are green with white tops, and Lantau taxis are blue.

Hong Kong Island and Kowloon taxis tend to avoid each others' turf as the drivers' street geography on the other side of the harbour can be pretty shaky. Hong Kong Island and Kowloon taxis maintain separate ranks at places like Hung Hom station and the Star Ferry pier and will sometimes refuse to take you to the 'other side'. In any case, if you're travelling from Hong Kong Island to Kowloon (or vice versa), choose the correct cab as you'll save on the tunnel toll. New Territories taxis are not permitted to pick up passengers in Kowloon or on Hong Kong Island.

The flag fall for taxis on Hong Kong Island and Kowloon is HK$15 for the first 2km and HK$1.40 for every additional 200m; waiting costs HK$1.40 per minute. In the New Territories it's HK$12.50 for the first 2km and HK$1.20 for each additional 200m; waiting costs HK$1.20 per minute. On Lantau the equivalent charges are HK$12 and HK$1.20 and HK$1.20 for per-minute waiting. There is a luggage fee of HK$5 per bag but, depending on the size, not all drivers insist on this payment. It costs an extra HK$5 to book a taxi by telephone. Try to carry smaller bills and coins; most drivers are hesitant to make change for anything over HK$100. You can tip up to 10%, but most Hong Kong people just leave the little brown coins and a dollar or two.

Lantau is one of the few places nowadays where it can be difficult to get a taxi; there are only 50 of them in operation. You'll find ranks in Mui Wo and Tong Fuk but elsewhere taxis are a rarity. You could try the call service (☎ 2984 1328), but don't hold your breath. Sample fares to Ngong Ping and the Tian Tan Buddha from Mui Wo/Tung Chung/Tai O/Hong Kong International Airport are HK$125/125/45/145.

Passengers must pay the toll if a taxi goes through any of Hong Kong's harbour or mountain tunnels or uses the Lantau Link to Tung Chung or the airport. Though the Cross-Harbour Tunnel costs only HK$10, you'll be required to pay HK$20 if, say, you take a Hong Kong taxi from Hong Kong Island to Kowloon. If you manage to find a Kowloon taxi returning 'home', you'll pay only HK$10. (It works the other way round as well, of course). If you cross the harbour via the Western Harbour Tunnel you must pay the HK$35 toll plus HK$15 for the return unless you can find a cab heading for its base. Similarly, if you use the Eastern Harbour Crossing you may have to pay the HK$15 toll twice. There's no way of

avoiding the whopping great toll of HK$30 in *both* directions when a taxi uses the Lantau Link, however.

There is no double charge for the other tunnels: Aberdeen (HK$5); Lion Rock (HK$8); Shing Mun (HK$5); Tate's Cairn (HK$10); Tai Lam (HK$22); and Tseung Kwan O (HK$3).

It's not as hard as it used to be, but you may have some trouble hailing a cab during rush hour, when it rains or during the driver shift-change period (around 4pm). Taxis are also in higher demand after midnight. There are no extra late-night charges and no extra passenger charges, though some taxis are insured to carry four passengers and some five. You can tell by glancing at the licence plate.

Some taxi drivers speak English well, others don't have a word of the language. It's never a bad idea to have your destination written down in Chinese.

Though most Hong Kong taxi drivers are scrupulously honest, if you feel you've been ripped off, take down the taxi or driver's licence number (usually displayed on the sun visor in front) and call the **taxi complaints hotline** (☎ 2889 9999), the **police report hotline** (☎ 2527 7177) or the **Transport Department hotline** (☎ 2804 2600) to lodge a complaint. Be sure to have all the relevant details: when, where and how much. Also contact the police if you leave something behind in a taxi; most drivers turn in lost property.

Directory

Directory

BOOKS

There's no shortage of books dealing with things Hong Kong, but the mark-up on them in local bookshops can be high. See what you can pick up at home before you travel.

For a selection of the best outlets, see Books (p254).

The publisher of a given book can vary from country to country. Edition numbers can also differ. Fortunately, bookshops and libraries search by title or author so they are best placed to advise you on the availability of the following titles.

Business

Generally, business books focus on China at large rather than Hong Kong specifically, though *Asia for Women on Business: Hong Kong, Taiwan, Singapore and South Korea* by Tracey and Patricia Wilen includes information and advice specific to the territory. *Living in Hong Kong* by the American Chamber of Commerce contains information on setting up a company and doing business in Hong Kong. For information on the Trade Development Council's Business InfoCentre, see p364.

For China-targeted titles, pick up a copy of *The China Business Handbook* published by the China Economic Review, *The China Investor: Getting Rich with the Next Superpower* by Cesar Bacani or *The Dragon Millennium: Chinese Business in the Coming World Economy* by Frank-Jürgen Richter.

General

Culture Shock! Hong Kong: A Guide to Customs and Etiquette by Betty Wei Pei-ti and Elizabeth Li is an excellent introduction to Hong Kong culture and modus operandi. Oxford University Press' *Images of Asia* series includes several thin volumes on topics relating to Hong Kong. Among them are *Temples of the Empress of Heaven; Chinese New Year; The Cheongsam;* and *South China Village Culture*.

Hong Kong: Somewhere Between Heaven and Earth, edited by Barbara-Sue White, is an anthology on Hong Kong, both old and new. *Hong Kong Collage* is a collection of contemporary stories and other writings edited by Martha PY Cheung.

Arguably the most famous (if hardly the best) novel set in Hong Kong is *The World of Suzie Wong* by Richard Mason. First published in 1957, it is the story of a Wan Chai prostitute with a heart of gold.

The best-known English-language novelist that Hong Kong has produced to date is the late Austin Coates. His charming *Myself a Mandarin* was based on his work as a special magistrate dealing in traditional Chinese law in the New Territories during the 1950s. *The Road* is his riveting tale of the government's attempt to build a highway across Great Island (which sounds suspiciously like Lantau), and the effect it has on the government, the builders and the islanders.

An Insular Possession by Timothy Mo is a novel set in pre-colonial Hong Kong. *Tai-Pan* by James Clavell, almost as thick as the Yellow Pages, is a rather unrealistic tale of Western traders in Hong Kong's early days, but it's an easy read. The sequel to *Tai-Pan*, also set in Hong Kong, is another epic called *Noble House*, about a fictitious *hong* (trading house). A favourite and a rollicking good read is Robert Elegant's novel *Dynasty*, which describes the life and times of a young Englishwoman who marries into a family not unlike the Ho Tungs, a powerful Eurasian family dating back to the early colonial period.

Spy-thriller writer John Le Carré's *The Honourable Schoolboy* is a story of espionage and intrigue set in the Hong Kong of the early 1970s. *Triad* by Derek Lambert is a violent fictionalised account of the Chinese underworld of the territory.

The private lives of Hong Kong Chinese families are captured in *Chinese Walls* by Sussy Chako, and *The Monkey King* by Timothy Mo. *Kowloon Tong* by Paul Theroux is an incredibly annoying novel about an expatriate family's insecurities on the eve of the handover. Equally annoying is John Lanchester's *Fragrant Harbour*, a mostly unbelievable door-stopper that manages to record 70 years of Hong Kong history from the 1930s, through the eyes of four characters whose lives intertwine.

If you'd like to learn more about the approximately 150,000 Filipino domestic workers living and working in Hong Kong, pick up a copy of *Maid to Order in Hong Kong: Stories of Filipina Workers* by Nicole Constable, based on interviews the author conducted with amahs (maidservants) in Hong Kong.

Guidebooks

Lonely Planet's *China* has a chapter dealing with the Hong Kong Special Administrative Region (SAR). *Hong Kong Condensed* is a pocket guide for those on shorter visits to the territory. The *Cantonese phrasebook* is a complete guide to *gwong dung wa*. *World Food: Hong Kong* will take you on a culinary tour of the territory.

Anyone who wants a complete assessment of the territory's best restaurants in all price categories should pick up a copy of the annual *HK Magazine Restaurant Guide*, which covers 600 eateries, including some in Macau and Shenzhen. It appears free as an insert in the *HK Magazine* in March and costs HK$50 (HK$80 overseas). To order a copy, contact the magazine's editorial office (☎ 2850 5065; fax 2543 4964; asiacity@asia-city.com.hk).

Hong Kong's Best Restaurants, containing 150 relatively tame reviews of top-end restaurants, is published annually by *Hong Kong Tatler* magazine. *The Guide: Hong Kong's Restaurant Guide* from *bc magazine* has more critical reviews of 300-plus Hong Kong restaurants in all price categories.

Arthur Hacker's *The Hong Kong Visitors Book* is an illustrated treasure-trove of trivia about the characters and personalities who have passed through or made Hong Kong their home over the centuries.

History & Politics

A History of Hong Kong by GB Endacott, first published in 1958, is a classic that covers everything you'd ever want to know about Hong Kong's past. It's pretty dull going, though. Instead, try Frank Welsh's more entertaining *History of Hong Kong*, written by a former Hong Kong banker and published just before the handover. If you like pictures with your history, *The Hong Kong Story* by Caroline Courtauld and May Holdsworth is a great choice.

One of the most readable histories of the territory is *Hong Kong: Epilogue to an Empire* by Jan Morris, which moves effortlessly between past and present as it explains what made Hong Kong so unique among the colonies of the British empire.

Maurice Collis' *Foreign Mud* tells the sordid story of the Opium Wars that Britain fought with China. *The Taipans: Hong Kong's Merchant Princes* by Colin N Crisswell deals with the European traders and 'factors' who profited from those wars.

The Last Governor by Jonathan Dimbleby is a well-written account of Chris Patten's tenure as governor of Hong Kong immediately before the 1997 handover. Stephen Vines' excellent *Hong Kong: China's New Colony* examines the territory after the change in landlords.

The government yearbook, entitled *Hong Kong 2002*, *Hong Kong 2003* etc, and published by the Hong Kong Information Services Department, is a goldmine of information about government, politics, economy, history, arts and just about any other topic relevant to Hong Kong. It usually appears in June or July of the following year.

Travel & Pictorial

Formasia's *Old Hong Kong*, a large pictorial of old photographs, comes in three volumes: Volume I covers the period from 1860 to 1900; Volume II from 1901 to 1945; and Volume III from 1950 to 1997. *Twentieth Century Impressions of Hong Kong*, edited by Arnold Wright, is a collection of old newspaper articles and illustrations of Hong Kong.

An Eye on Hong Kong is a portfolio of contemporary photographs by Keith MacGregor, though *Hong Kong: A Moment in Time* by Tim Nutt and Chris Bale is more up to date. If you like your views from on high, pick up a copy of *Over Hong Kong* by David Dodwell and Kaysan Bartlett. *The Collection: Memorabilia of a Colonial Era* by Nigel Cameron and Patrick Hase is a photographic essay on everyday objects and sights unique to Hong Kong. *Hong Kong Style* by Peter Moss is an excellent introduction to Hong Kong's approach to design and lifestyle. *Hong Kong Past & Present* by Sheung Lee is another pictorial worth flipping through.

Walking & Nature Guides

Hong Kong Hikes: The Twenty Best Walks in the Territory by Christian Wright and Tinja Tsang is the newest and most unique addition to the Hong Kong walking-guides library. It consists of a set of 20 laminated loose-leaf cards for hikes on Hong Kong Island, the Outlying Islands and the New Territories that can be unclipped and slotted into the transparent plastic folder provided, which you then hang around your neck.

Magic Walks, which comes in four volumes and is good for 50 relatively easy hikes throughout the territory, is written by Kaarlo Schepel, almost a legend among Hong Kong walkers. *Exploring Hong Kong's Countryside: A Visitor's Companion* by Edward Stokes is well written and illustrated, provides excellent background information and the maps are good.

Hong Kong Pathfinder: 23 Day-Walks in Hong Kong by Martin Williams is based on the author's 'Day Away' column in the *South China Morning Post*. The *Coastal Guides* series, published by the Friends of the Earth, include guide-maps to Sai Kung as well as Lamma, Lantau and Hong Kong Island.

Two walking guides with a twist are Patricia Lim's *Discovering Hong Kong's Cultural Heritage: The New Territories*, with a dozen walks through traditional areas of the New Territories and lots of cultural information, and *Discovering Hong Kong's Cultural Heritage: Hong Kong and Kowloon*, which has a number of interesting but more urban walks. Two lovely pictorials dealing with the countryside are *Hong Kong's Wild Places: An Environmental Exploration* by Edward Stokes, and *The MacLehose Trail* by Tim Nutt, Chris Bale and Tao Ho.

A welcome addition to Hong Kong's bookshelf is *Ruins of War: A Guide to Hong Kong's Battlefields and Wartime Sites* by Ko Tim Keung and Jason Wordie, which includes a lot of walking in the countryside.

The Birds of Hong Kong and South China by Clive Viney, Karen Phillips and Lam Chiu Ying is the definitive guide for spotting and identifying the territory's feathered creatures.

BUSINESS

Hong Kong is still very much a place to do business. For business books, see p354. Useful business contacts:

American Chamber of Commerce (Map pp400-3; ☎ 2526 0165; www.amcham.org.hk; Room 1904, 19th fl, Bank of America Tower, 12 Harcourt Rd, Central) The most active overseas chamber of commerce in Hong Kong.

Chinese General Chamber of Commerce (Map pp400-3; ☎ 2525 6385; www.cgcc.org.hk; 4th fl, Chinese General Chamber of Commerce Bldg, 24-25 Connaught Rd, Central) Authorised to issue Certificates of Hong Kong origin for trade purposes.

Chinese Manufacturers' Association of Hong Kong (Map pp400-3; ☎ 2545 6166; www.cma.org.hk; 3rd fl, CMA Bldg, 64-66 Connaught Rd, Central) Operates testing laboratories for product certification and can also issue Certificates of Hong Kong origin.

Hong Kong General Chamber of Commerce (Map pp400-3; ☎ 2386 6255, 2529 9229; www.chamber.org.hk; 22nd fl, United Centre, 95 Queensway, Admiralty) Services for foreign executives and firms, such as translation, serviced offices, secretarial help and printing.

Hong Kong Labour Department (Map pp400-3; ☎ 2717 1771; www.labour.gov.hk;16th fl, Harbour Bldg, 38 Pier Rd, Central) Contact this department for labour-relations problems and queries.

Hong Kong Trade Development Council (HKTDC; Map pp406-8; ☎ 2584 4333; www.tdctrade.com; 38th fl, Office Tower, Convention Plaza, 1 Harbour Rd, Wan Chai) Co-sponsors and participates in trade fairs, publishes a wealth of material on Hong Kong markets and runs the TDC Business InfoCentre (p364).

Hong Kong Trade & Industry Department (Map p415; ☎ 2392 2922; www.tid.gov.hk; Trade Department Tower, 700 Nathan Rd, Mong Kok) Key source for trade information, statistics, government regulations and product certification.

Support & Consultation Centre (☎ 23928 5133; Trade Department Tower, mezzanine fl, 700 Nathan Rd, Mong Kok; ☼ 9am-6pm Mon-Fri, 9am-1pm Sat) Offers information and assistance for overseas investors.

BUSINESS HOURS

Office hours in Hong Kong are from 9am to either 5.30pm or 6pm on weekdays and often (but increasingly less so) from 9am to noon or 1pm on Saturday. The lunch hour is from 1pm to 2pm. Many Hong Kong companies still run on a 5½-day working week, but this concept is beginning to fall out of favour, with staff required to work one or maybe two Saturdays a month. Banks are open from 9am to 4.30pm or 5pm weekdays and 9am to 12.30pm on Saturday.

Shops that cater to tourists keep longer hours, but almost nothing opens before 9am. For specifics, see p246.

Museums are generally open from 10am to between 5pm and 9pm and are closed on Tuesday or Thursday.

CHILDREN

Hong Kong is a great travel destination for kids, though the crowds, traffic and pollution might be off-putting to some parents. Food and sanitation is of a high standard, and the territory is jam-packed with things to entertain the young 'uns.

Lonely Planet's *Travel with Children* includes all sorts of useful advice for those travelling with their little ones.

Most public transport and museums offer half-price fares and admission fees to children under the age of 12. Hotels can recommend babysitters if you've got daytime appointments or want a night out sans child. Otherwise, call **Rent-A-Mum** (Map pp404-5; ☎ 2523 4868; rentamum@hknet.com; 12A Amber Lodge, 21-25 Hollywood Rd, Central; ☿ ring btwn 8am-8pm), which supplies qualified English-speaking sitters for between HK$120 and HK$160 per hour.

CLIMATE

Hong Kong (and Macau) has a subtropical climate characterised by hot, humid summers and cool, relatively dry winters.

October, November and most of December are the best months to visit Hong Kong – temperatures are moderate, the skies are clear and the sun shines. January and February are cloudier and colder but dry. It's a lot warmer from March to May, but the humidity is high, and the fog and drizzle can make getting around difficult. The sweltering heat and humidity from June to August can make sightseeing a sweaty proposition and it is also

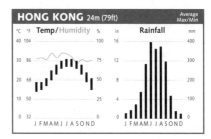

the rainy season. Still, there's a lot of sunshine and, after all, it's summer. September is a grand month if you like drama; the threat of a typhoon seems to loom every other day.

Hong Kong Observatory (☎ 2926 8200; www .hko.gov.hk; 134A Nathan Rd, Tsim Sha Tsui) issues weather reports on ☎ 187 8066 and its website (www.weather.org.hk); the hotline for cyclone warnings is ☎ 2835 1473.

CONSULATES

Hong Kong is definitely one of the world's most consulate-clogged cities. There's a complete list of consulates in the Yellow Pages.

Australia (☎ 2827 8881; 23rd fl, Harbour Centre, 25 Harbour Rd, Wan Chai)

Typhoon!

A typhoon is a violent tropical cyclone, a massive whirlpool of air currents often tens of kilometres high and hundreds of kilometres wide. Feeding off moisture, tropical cyclones can only survive over warm oceans – once typhoons hit land, they quickly die out. The 'eye' of the cyclone is generally tens of kilometres wide and basically is a column of descending air, which is much calmer than the surrounding vortex.

Cyclones can last for as long as a few weeks, but not all will mature into typhoons. Only about half the cyclones in the South China Sea ever reach typhoon ferocity. The gradation of tropical cyclones ascends as follows: tropical depression (with winds up to 62km/h); tropical storm (up to 87km/h); severe tropical storm (up to 117km/h); and typhoon (118km/h or more).

Although some two dozen typhoons develop in the South China Sea each year, and a quarter of those reach within 800km of Hong Kong, the territory is a small target, so the chances of a direct hit (when winds of typhoon intensity pass within 100km of the city) are slim.

There is a numbering system to warn of typhoons. No 1 (its visual symbol being the letter 't') means that a tropical cyclone is within 800km of the territory. No 3 (an upside-down 't') – there is no No 2 – warns that winds of up to 62km are blowing in Victoria Harbour, there is a risk of Hong Kong being hit and that people should take precautions such as securing flower pots on balconies and terraces. The system then jumps to No 8 (a triangle), which means that there are sustained winds of between 63km/h and 117km/h. People are instructed to stay indoors and to fix adhesive tape to exposed windows to reduce the damage caused by broken glass, while businesses shut down and ferries stop running. No 9 (a double triangle) warns that gale- or storm-force winds are increasing, and No 10 (a cross) is the most severe, with winds reaching upward from 118km/h and gusts exceeding 220km/h.

When a typhoon approaches the territory, warnings are broadcast continuously on the TV and radio. You can also contact Hong Kong's tropical cyclone warning hotline (☎ 2835 1473) for updates or check the websites www.weather.org.hk or www.hko.gov.hk.

Canada (☎ 2810 4321; 11th-14th fl, Tower One, Exchange Sq, 8 Connaught Pl, Central)

France (☎ 3196 6100; 26th fl, Tower II, Admiralty Centre, 18 Harcourt Rd, Admiralty)

Japan (☎ 2524 3808; 46th-47th fl, Tower One, Exchange Sq, 8 Connaught Pl, Central)

Netherlands (☎ 2522 5127; Room 5702, 57/F Cheung Kong Centre, 2 Queen's Road Central, Central)

New Zealand (☎ 2525 5044; 65th fl, Central Plaza, 18 Harbour Rd, Wan Chai)

South Africa (☎ 2577 3279; Room 2706-2710, 27/F, Great Eagle Centre, 23 Harbour Road, Wan Chai)

UK (☎ 2901 3000; 1 Supreme Court Rd, Admiralty)

USA (☎ 2523 9011; 26 Garden Rd, Central)

COURSES

The **Community Advice Bureau** (Map pp400-3; ☎ 2815 5444; www.cab.org.hk; Room 16C, Right Emperor Commercial Bldg, 122-126 Wellington St, Central; 9.30am-4.30pm Mon-Fri) is a fabulous source of information on courses of all kinds in Hong Kong. The **YMCA** (☎ 2771 9111; www.ymca.org.hk) and the **YWCA** (☎ 3476 1340; www.ywca.org.hk) both offer a broad range of cultural classes and three-month courses, from basic Cantonese and mah jong to watercolour painting and t'ai chi.

For visual arts, check with the **Hong Kong Museum of Art** (☎ 2721 0116), the **Hong Kong Visual Arts Centre** (☎ 2521 3008) or the **Hong Kong Arts Centre** (☎ 2582 0200). The **Fringe Club** (☎ 2521 7251; 2 Lower Albert Rd, Central) offers any number of courses and workshops.

The Cultural Kaleidoscope People to People programme organised by the HKTB will whet your appetite to learn more about everything from Chinese tea and blackwood furniture to geomancy and t'ai chi. It is unique in that it allows you to visit galleries, antique shops, jewellers to grade peals and jade, teahouses, even a feng shui master's studio and a t'ai chi class. It's an excellent way to learn first-hand about Hong Kong Chinese culture. Contact the **HKTB** (☎ 2508 1234) for the current schedule.

CULTURAL CENTRES

Hours for cultural centres vary according to the department (library, media centre, gallery etc) and what's on exhibit.

Alliance Française (Map pp406-8; ☎ 2527 7825; www.alliancefrancaise.com.hk; 2nd fl, 123 Hennessy Rd,

Wan Chai) This place has a library and offers a wide range of cultural activities.

British Council (Map pp400-3; ☎ 2913 5100; www.britishcouncil.org.hk; 3 Supreme Court Rd, Admiralty) Provides English-language classes, sponsors cultural programmes, has Internet access (on the 1st floor) and an **Information Services Resources Centre** (noon-8pm Mon-Fri, 11am-5pm Sat).

Goethe Institut (Map pp406-8; ☎ 2802 0088; www.goethe.de/hongkong;14th fl, Hong Kong Arts Centre, 2 Harbour Rd, Wan Chai) German classes, films, exhibitions and lectures.

CUSTOMS

Even though Hong Kong is a duty-free port, there are items on which duty is still charged. Import taxes on cigarettes and alcohol, in particular, are high: 100% on spirits, 80% on wine and 40% on beer.

The duty-free allowance for visitors coming into Hong Kong (including from Macau and mainland China) is 200 cigarettes (or 50 cigars or 250g tobacco) and 1L of alcohol (wine or spirits). Apart from these limits there are few other import taxes, so you can bring in reasonable quantities of almost anything.

Firecrackers and fireworks are banned in Hong Kong but not in Macau and mainland China, and people crossing the border are sometimes thoroughly searched for these. Customs officers are on high alert for drug smugglers. If you're arriving from Thailand or Vietnam, be prepared for a rigorous examination of your luggage.

DISABLED TRAVELLERS

People with disabilities have to cope with substantial obstacles in Hong Kong, including the stairs at many MTR and KCR stations, as well as pedestrian overpasses, narrow and crowded footpaths and steep hills. On the other hand, some buses are now accessible by wheelchair, taxis are never hard to find and most buildings have lifts (many with Braille panels). Wheelchairs can negotiate the lower decks of most of the ferries.

Hong Kong International Airport at Chek Lap Kok has been designed with facilities for passengers with disabilities and it publishes a useful brochure entitled *Hong Kong International Airport: Special Needs*, which is available from the **Hong Kong Airport Authority** (☎ 2188 7111; www.hkairport.com). For further information about facilities and services for the disabled in Hong Kong, contact the **Joint Council for the Physically and Mentally Disabled** (Map pp400-3; Room 1204, 12th fl, 31 Hennessy Rd, Wan Chai; ☎ 2864 2931; www.hkcss.org.hk; Room 1204, 12th fl, Duke of Windsor Bldg, Wan Chai).

The **Hong Kong Sports Association for the Physically Disabled** (☎ 2602 8232; www.hksap.org) can supply information to disabled travellers.

DISCOUNT CARDS
Hong Kong Museums Pass

This pass allows multiple entries to six of Hong Kong's museums: Hong Kong Museum of Coastal Defence; Hong Kong Science Museum, Hong Kong Museum of History, Hong Kong Museum of Art and Hong Kong Space Museum (excluding Space Theatre) in Kowloon; Hong Kong Heritage Museum in the New Territories. Passes valid for seven consecutive days costs HK$30; passes valid for a half-year cost HK$50/25 for adults/seniors and students; and a full-year pass is HK$100/50. Passes are available from any HKTB outlet or the participating museums.

Hostel Card

A Hostelling International (HI) card or the equivalent is of relatively limited use in Hong Kong as there are only seven HI-affiliated hostels here and most of them are pretty remote. If you arrive without a card and want to stay in one of these hostels, you can buy one from the **Hong Kong Youth Hostels Association** (HKYHA; Map pp410-11; ☎ 2788 1638; www.yha.org.hk; Room 225-227, Block 19, Shek Kip Mei Estate, Kowloon) for HK$110/50 (Hong Kong residents over/under 18) or HK$180 (nonresidents).

You are allowed to stay at any of Hong Kong's HKYHA hostels without a membership card, but you will have to buy a 'Welcome Stamp' (HK$30) for each night of your stay. Once you've stayed six nights, you are issued a card.

For information on Hong Kong's seven HI-affiliated hostels, most of which are in the New Territories, see p269.

Seniors Card

Many attractions in Hong Kong offer discounts for people over 60 or 65. Most of Hong Kong's museums are either free or half-price for those over 60 and most forms of public transport offer a 50% discount to anyone over 65. A passport or ID with a photo should be sufficient proof of age.

Student, Youth & Teacher Cards

The International Student Identity Card (ISIC), a plastic ID-style card with your photograph, provides discounts on some forms of transport and cheaper admission to museums and other sights. If you're aged under 26 but not a student, you can apply for an International Youth Travel Card (IYTC) issued by the Federation of International Youth Travel Organisations (FIYTO), which gives much the same discounts and benefits. Teachers can apply for the International Teacher Identity Card (ITIC).

Hong Kong Student Travel based at **Sincerity Travel** (Map pp412-14 ☎ 2735 6668; Room 833-834, East Block, Star House, 3 Salisbury Rd, Tsim Sha Tsui; ☼ 9am-6pm Mon-Fri & 9am-1pm Sat) can issue you any of these cards for HK$100 in a week or HK$150 in a day. Make sure you bring your student ID or other credentials along with you.

ELECTRICITY

The standard is 220V, 50 Hz AC.

Hong Kong's plug and socket system can be a bit confusing at first. The vast majority of electric outlets are designed to accommodate the British three square pins, but some take three large round prongs and others three small pins. Not surprisingly, inexpensive plug adaptors are widely available in Hong Kong, even in supermarkets.

Electrical shops in Hong Kong sell pocket-sized transformers that step down the electricity to the 110V used in the USA and Canada, but most mini-transformers are only rated for 50W. This is usually sufficient for an electric razor or laptop computer but not for those electric elements that some travellers carry to make tea and coffee.

EMERGENCIES

Hong Kong is generally very safe by both night and day but, as everywhere, things can go wrong. Although it is safe to walk around just about anywhere in the territory after dark, it's best to stick to well-lit areas. Tourist districts like Tsim Sha Tsui are heavily patrolled by the police. In the event of a real emergency, ring ☎ 999 for the fire services, police or an ambulance.

Hong Kong does have its share of local pickpockets and thieves. Carry as little cash and as few valuables as possible, and if you set a bag down, keep an eye on it. This also applies to restaurants and pubs, particularly in touristed areas such as the Star Ferry piers and the Peak Tram. If your bag doesn't accompany you to the toilet, don't expect to find it when you return.

If you are robbed, you can obtain a loss report for insurance purposes at the police station in the area in which the crime occurred. In Central, that would be the **Central Police Station** (☎ 2522 8882; 10 Hollywood Rd). For locations and contact details of police stations in Hong Kong, visit www.info.gov.hk/police/aa-home/english/services/FaxList.htm.

If you run into legal trouble, call the **Legal Aid Department** (☎ 2537 7677; ☼ 8.45am-1pm & 2-5.15pm Mon-Fri, 9am-noon Sat, 24hr hotline), which provides both residents and visitors with representation, subject to a means and merits test.

Other important numbers:

Auxiliary Medical Service (AMS) hotline	☎ 2762 2033
Bushfire Control Centre hotline	☎ 2720 0777
MediLink (Hong Kong Medical Association hotline)	☎ 90000 222 322
Police	
general inquiries	☎ 2860 2000
report hotline	☎ 2527 7177
St John's Ambulance Service	
territory-wide	☎ 2530 8032
Hong Kong Island	☎ 2576 6555
Kowloon	☎ 2713 5555
New Territories	☎ 2639 2555
Tropical Cyclone Warning	☎ 2835 1473

GAY & LESBIAN TRAVELLERS

The gay scene in Hong Kong has undergone quite a revolution a few short years. In July 1991 the enactment of the Crimes (Amendment) Ordinance removed criminal penalties for homosexual acts between consenting adults over the age of 18, and since then gay groups have been lobbying for legislation to address the issue of discrimination on the grounds of sexual orientation. Despite these changes, however, Hong Kong Chinese society remains fairly conservative, and it can still be risky for gays and lesbians to come out to family members or their employers.

Useful organisations:

Chi Heng Foundation (☎ 2517 056; www.chiheng foundation.com) Umbrella group for gay and lesbian associations and groups in Hong Kong.

Horizons (☎ 2815 9268; www.horizons.org.hk; GPO Box 6837, Central, Hong Kong; hotline ☼ 7.30-10.30pm Tue & Thu) Phone-line counselling service that can provide information and advice to local and visiting gays, lesbians and bisexuals.

Queer Sisters (☎ 2314 4348; www.qs.org.hk; GPO Box 9313, Central, Hong Kong; hotline ☼ 7.30-10pm Mon-Fri) Information and assistance organisation for lesbians.

HEALTH

The Severe Acute Respiratory Syndrome (SARS) 'epidemic' of 2003 notwithstanding, health conditions in the region are good. Travellers have a low risk of contracting infectious diseases, apart from travellers' diarrhoea, which is common throughout Asia. The health system (see Medical Services p365) is excellent.

Recommended Immunisations

Since most vaccines don't produce immunity until at least two weeks after they're given, visit a physician four to eight weeks before departure. Ask your doctor for an International Certificate of Vaccination (otherwise known as the 'yellow booklet'), which will list all of the vaccinations you've received.

If your health insurance does not cover you for medical expenses abroad, consider supplemental insurance (see www.lonelyplanet.com/subwwway for more information).

There are no required vaccinations for entry into Hong Kong or Macau, unless you have travelled from a country infected with yellow fever. In this case you will have to show your yellow-fever vaccination certificate. Recommended immunisations for Hong Kong and Macau:

Hepatitis A and B Given (Twinrix) 1ml at day 1, day 30 and six months. Minimal soreness at injection site. You are not immune until after the final shot.

Influenza shot 0.5ml is recommended if you are travelling in the winter months and especially if you are over 60 years or have a history of chronic illness. It lasts for one year. You should not have the shot if you are allergic to eggs.

Polio syrup 0.5ml orally every 10 years. There are no side effects.

Tetanus and diphtheria (DT) 0.5ml every 10 years. It will cause a sore arm and redness at the injection site.

Do not have any of these immunisations if you are pregnant or breastfeeding. Talk to your doctor about possible alternatives.

Diseases

DENGUE FEVER
This is caught from mosquito bites, and is not common in Hong Kong.

GIARDIA
This is a parasite that often jumps on board when you have diarrhoea. It then causes a more prolonged illness with intermittent diarrhoea or loose stools, bloating, fatigue and some nausea. There may be a metallic taste in the mouth. Avoiding potentially contaminated foods and always washing your hands can help to prevent giardia.

HEPATITIS A
This virus is common in Hong Kong and Macau and is transmitted through contaminated water and shellfish. It is most commonly caught at local island seafood restaurants. Immunisation and avoiding local seafood restaurants should prevent it.

HEPATITIS B
Whilst this is common in the area, it can only be transmitted by unprotected sex, sharing needles, treading on a discarded needle, or receiving contaminated blood in very remote areas of China.

INFLUENZA
Hong Kong has a bad flu season over the winter months from December to March. Symptoms include a cold (runny nose etc) with a high fever and aches and pains. You should wash your hands frequently, avoid anybody you know who has the flu, and think about getting a flu shot before you travel.

TRAVELLERS' DIARRHOEA
To prevent diarrhoea, avoid tap water unless it has been boiled, filtered, or chemically disinfected (eg with iodine tablets); only eat fresh fruits and vegetables if cooked or peeled; be wary of dairy products that might contain unpasteurised milk; and be highly selective when eating food from street vendors.

If you develop diarrhoea, be sure to drink plenty of fluids, preferably an oral rehydration solution containing lots of salt and sugar. A

Traditional Medicine
Traditional Chinese medicine is extremely popular in Hong Kong, both for prevention and cure (see the boxed text 'Herbs & Needles: Chinese Medicine Unmasked' on p15) and the main body overseeing it is the **Chinese Medicine Council of Hong Kong** (☎ 2121 1888; www.cmchk.org.hk/english). **Eu Yan Sang** (p264) in Central is probably the most famous traditional-medicine dispensary in town and the doctors speak good English. The store is also an interesting place to browse, as many of the healing ingredients are displayed and explained.

few loose stools don't require treatment but, if you start experiencing more than four or five stools a day, you should start taking an antibiotic (usually a quinolone drug) and an antidiarrhoeal agent (such as loperamide). If diarrhoea is bloody, or persists for more than 72 hours, or is accompanied by fever, shaking chills or severe abdominal pain you should seek medical attention.

Environmental Hazards

WATER
Avoid drinking the local water as it varies enormously and its quality depends on the pipes in the building you're in. Bottled water is a safer option, or you can boil tap water for three minutes.

MOSQUITOES
Mosquitoes are prevalent in Hong Kong. You should always use insect repellent and if bitten use hydrocortisone cream to reduce swelling.

SNAKES
There are many snakes in Hong Kong and some are deadly, so be careful if you go bushwalking. Go straight to a public hospital if bitten; private doctors do not stock anti-venom.

Online Resources
The World Health Organization publishes a superb book called *International Travel and Health*, which is revised annually and is available online (at no cost) at www.who.int/ith/.

SARS

The outbreak of SARS (Severe Acute Respiratory Syndrome) in March 2003 was devastating for Hong Kong. The virus, which causes a deadly type of atypical pneumonia, was brought to Hong Kong from China, and by July 2003, 1755 people were infected and almost 300 people had died.

The diagnostic criteria for SARS:

- Fever greater than 38°C
- X-ray evidence of pneumonia
- History of chills in the past two days
- Coughing or breathing difficulty
- General malaise or muscle aches
- Known history of exposure

Out of the two most aggressive outbreaks, one occurred in a lift and the other in an apartment block. With the help of international travel the virus spread quickly to other countries, especially Canada, Singapore and Taiwan. Exhaled droplets, close contact and bodily secretions spread the virus, and the first contact cases seemed to be the most contagious. Subsequently, many hospital workers were amongst those infected.

Hong Kong was brought to a standstill during this period, with schools and local activities closing. Many expatriates left, locals stayed indoors and wore facemasks when out, and business people and tourists stopped coming. Strict hygiene protocols were put into place, such as thorough cleaning in common areas and routine temperature checks, and finally the crisis came to an end.

While it was a hard economic time for Hong Kong, many people see it as a wake-up call for better hygiene practices in the region. Washing hands has increased dramatically, public areas are noticeably cleaner, and spitting has become frowned upon.

Travellers should keep track of the SARS situation in Asia through www.who.int/en/. If you suspect you might have SARS based on the above criteria, you should call your nearest public hospital to find out which of the hospitals are accepting possible SARS patients. Many hospitals and doctors' offices will not let you enter if you suspect you have SARS.

HOLIDAYS

Western and Chinese culture combine to create an interesting mix – and number – of public holidays in Hong Kong and Macau. Determining the exact date of some of them is tricky as there are traditionally two calendars in use: the Gregorian solar (or Western) calendar and the Chinese lunar calendar.

The following are public holidays in both Hong Kong and Macau. For Macau-specific holidays, see p327. For events and festivals held in both Hong Kong and Macau, see p9. For events specific to Macau see p292.

New Year's Day 1 January

Chinese New Year Late January/early February (three days)

Easter Late March/early April

Ching Ming Early April

Buddha's Birthday Late April/May

Labour Day 1 May

Dragon Boat (Tuen Ng) Festival June

Hong Kong SAR Establishment Day 1 July (not Macau)

Mid-Autumn Festival September/October

China National Day 1 & 2 October

Cheung Yeung October

Christmas Day 25 December

Boxing Day 26 December

IDENTITY CARD

Hong Kong residents are required to carry a government-issued Hong Kong Identity Card with them at all times and this rule is strictly enforced. As a visitor, you are required to carry your passport; it is the only acceptable form of identification.

Anyone over the age of 11 who stays in Hong Kong for longer than 180 days must apply for an ID card. Inquire at the Immigration Department's **ID-issuing office** (☎ 2824 6111; 8th fl, Immigration Tower, 7 Gloucester Rd, Wan Chai). Be sure to take your passport and other documents with you.

INTERNET ACCESS

Internet is extremely popular in computer-literate Hong Kong, and the territory is the first place in the world to be entirely covered by broadband. Virtually every business has a website and just about anyone you're likely to do business with can be contacted by email.

Internet Service Providers most often used in Hong Kong include **PCCW's Netvigator** (☎ 2888 1888; www.netvigator.com), **HKNet** (☎ 2110 2288; www.hknet.com) and **CPC-Net** (☎ 2331 8123; www.cpcnet-hk.com). America Online's customer service number is ☎ 2250 5678; Yahoo!'s is ☎ 2895 5769.

Most hotels and many guesthouses have Internet access. You'll also be able to log on for free at many public libraries, including the Central Library in Causeway Bay (see p93), which has more than 500 public-access terminals; at major MTR stations (eg Central and Tsim Sha Tsui); and a few big shopping malls such as Times Square in Causeway Bay, Ocean Terminal in Tsim Sha Tsui's Harbour City, and Festival Walk in Kowloon Tong (see p251).

Among some of the best (ie fast machines, good locations) private Internet cafés:

I.T. Fans (Map pp400-3; ☎ 2542 1868; www.itfans .com.hk; Units A-B, Ground fl, Man On Commercial Bldg, 12-13 Jubilee St, Central; adult/student per hour HK$16/12 Sun-Thu, HK$22/18 Fri-Sat; 🕑 24hr) This massive and very central place has 100 monitors and serves real food.

Pacific Coffee Company (Map pp404-5; ☎ 2537 1688; www.pacificcoffee.com; 23 Hollywood Rd, Central; 🕑 7am-midnight Mon-Wed, 7am-1am Thu-Sat, 9am-midnight Sunday) All it takes to log on here is the purchase of a coffee or piece of cake (HK$10 to HK$35). There's another **Central branch** (Map pp400-3; ☎ 2868 5100; Shop 1022, 1st fl, IFC Mall, 1 Harbour View St, Central; 🕑 7am-10pm Mon-Sat, 8.30am-9pm Sun).

Rainbow Online Cyber Cafe (Map p415; ☎ 2374 1723; Basement, SB Commercial Bldg, 478 Nathan Rd, Yau Ma Tei; adult/student per hour HK$12/10; 🕑 24hr) This basement café offers surfers a free drink.

Shadowman Cyber Cafe (Map pp412-14; ☎ 2366 5262; Ground fl, Karlock Bldg, 7 Lock Rd, Tsim Sha Tsui; 🕑 8am-midnight Mon-Sat, 9am-midnight Sun) A small but convivial place to surf the Web and have lunch (sandwiches HK$25 to HK$48, mains HK$25 to HK$48). The first 20 minutes are free with your purchase, then it's HK$10 every 15 minutes.

UFO Station Cyber Cafe (Map pp412-14; ☎ 2367 9128; 1st fl, 23 Lock Rd, Tsim Sha Tsui; HK$20 per hour; 🕑 10am-midnight) Two dozen terminals and cheap hot and cold drinks (HK$4 to HK$5).

For useful Hong Kong links, see Websites (p372).

LAUNDRY

Laundries are easy to find everywhere in Hong Kong – hey, this *is* China – though they're never self-service. Most hotels, guesthouses and even some hostels have a laundry service. Prices at local laundries are normally HK$28 to HK$30 for the first 3kg, and then HK$8 to HK$10 for each additional kilogram.

Drycleaners are easy to spot and some laundries also offer the service also. Dry-cleaning at the better establishments (quality varies enormously) costs from HK$50 for a dress shirt, from HK$48 for a skirt and between HK$48 and HK$60 for trousers.

Recommended laundries and dry-cleaners:

Goodwins of London (Map pp400-3; ☎ 2525 0605; Shop 27, Ground fl, Central Bldg, 1-3 Pedder St, Central; 🕑 8.30am-7pm Mon-Sat)

Martinizing (Map pp400-3; ☎ 2525 3089; Ground fl, 7 Glenealy, Central; 🕑 8.30am-7pm Mon-Sat)

New Furama Dry-Cleaning (Map pp400-3; ☎ 2537 2217; Shop 1C, Ground fl, Bank of America Tower, 12 Harcourt Rd, Central; 🕑 8am-7pm Mon-Sat)

Wei Wei Dry Cleaner & Laundry (Map pp404-5; ☎ 2522 9818; 26 Old Bailey St, Soho; 🕑 8.30am-7pm Mon-Sat)

LEFT LUGGAGE

There are left-luggage lockers in major KCR train stations, including the terminus at Hung Hom, and the Shun Tak Centre in Sheung Wan, from where the Macau ferry departs, and the China ferry pier in Tsim Sha Tsui. Luggage costs between HK$20 and HK$30 for up to two hours (depending on the locker size) and between HK$25 and HK$35 for every 12 hours after that. The Hong Kong Airport Express station has a left-luggage office open from 6am to half an hour before the last flight departs (usually 11.50pm). There's also a counter on level 5 (arrivals hall) of Hong Kong International Airport (🕑 24hr Tue-Fri & 6am-1am Sat-Mon). Storage here costs HK$35 for up to three hours, HK$50 for up to 24 hours and HK$120 for up to 48 hours.

Generally the machines do not use keys but spit out a numbered chit or ticket when you have deposited your money and closed the door. You have to punch in this number when you retrieve your bag so keep it somewhere safe or write the number down elsewhere. Some lockers have a maximum storage time of three days, so read the instructions carefully.

If you're going to visit Macau or the mainland and you'll be returning to Hong Kong, most hotels and even some guesthouses and hostels have left-luggage rooms and will let you leave your gear behind, even if you've already checked out and won't be staying on your return. There is usually a charge for this service; be sure to inquire first.

LEGAL MATTERS

Hong Kong has a serious drug problem, much of it supplied by the Triads. There are estimated to be more than 40,000 drug addicts in Hong Kong, 75% of whom are hooked on heroin, which they generally smoke (it's called `chasing the dragon') rather than inject. Some addicts finance their habit by working in the sex industry; others resort to pickpocketing, burglary and robbery.

Professional smugglers often target Westerners to carry goods into countries like Vietnam and India, where those goods are prohibited or the import taxes are high. The theory is that customs agents are less likely to stop and search foreigners. These small-time smuggling expeditions, or 'milk runs', either earn the Westerner a fee or a free air ticket to another destination. But smuggling is very, very risky.

Most foreigners who get into legal trouble in Hong Kong are involved in drugs. *All* forms of narcotics are highly illegal in Hong Kong. It makes no difference whether it's heroin, opium, 'ice', ecstasy or marijuana – the law makes no distinction. If police or customs officials find dope or even smoking equipment in your possession, you can expect to be arrested immediately. If do you run into legal trouble, contact the **Legal Aid Department** (☎ 2537 7677; ⏰ 24hr hotline).

LIBRARIES

Hong Kong has a fairly extensive public library system; you will find a list on the Internet at www.hkpl.gov.hk. The most useful for travellers is the **City Hall Public Library** (Map pp400-3; ☎ 2921 2555; ⏰ 10am-7pm Mon-Thu, 10am-9pm Fri, 10am-5pm Sat-Sun & some public holidays) spread over eight floors of the High Block of City Hall, opposite Queen's Pier in Central. With a passport and a deposit of HK$130 per item, foreign visitors can get a temporary library card, which allows them to borrow up to six books and other materials from the library.

The even larger **Central Library** in Causeway Bay (p93) has lending sections, children's and young adult libraries, some 500 terminals with Internet available to the public, and a wonderful reading room on the 5th floor with around 4000 international periodicals.

The **TDC Business InfoCentre** (☎ 1830 668; www.tdctrade.com; ☎ 9am-8pm Mon-Fri & 9am-5pm Sat), located in the New Wing of the Hong Kong Convention and Exhibition Centre (HKCEC; 1 Expo Dr, Wan Chai) and run by the Hong Kong Trade Development Council, is well stocked with relevant books, periodicals, reference materials and CD-ROMs.

MAPS

Decent tourist maps are easy to come by in Hong Kong, and they're usually free. The HKTB hands out copies of *The Hong Kong Map* at its information centres at the airport, the Star Ferry terminal in Tsim Sha Tsui and The Center in Central. It is published six times a year, covers the northern coast of Hong Kong Island from Sheung Wan to Causeway Bay and part of the Kowloon Peninsula, and has inset maps of Aberdeen, Stanley, Hung Hom, Sha Tin and Tsuen Wan.

Another free map you'll find everywhere is the *AOA Street Map*, but it's full of advertising and difficult to use. Ossimap does basic but quite useful (and free) 3D maps of Hong Kong Island and Tsim Sha Tsui.

Lonely Planet's *Hong Kong City Map* (HK$35) has five separate maps with varying scales, a street index and an inset map of Hong Kong's rail network.

Universal Publications (UP; www.up.com.hk) produces many maps of Hong Kong, including the 1:80,000 *Hong Kong Touring Map* (HK$22) and the 1:9000 *City Map of Hong Kong & Kowloon* (HK$25). It also publishes detailed street maps of Hong Kong Island and Kowloon (HK$22 each), with scales below 1:8000.

The *Hong Kong Official Guide Map* (HK$45), produced by the Survey and Mapping Office of the Lands Department, has both overall and district maps and is available from most bookshops.

If you're looking for greater detail, topographical accuracy and good colour reproduction, it's worth investing in the *Hong Kong Guidebook* (HK$62), a street atlas to the entire territory published by UP and updated annually. Compiled in both English and Chinese, it also includes useful information such as ferry timetables, hotel listings and a separate booklet called the *Public Transport Boarding Guide*, which is the only complete listing of bus and minibus routes available in Hong Kong. A larger format version of this, the *Hong Kong Directory* (HK$72; HK$90 hardback) also includes the transport guide; the pocket-size *Palm Atlas of Hong Kong* (HK$40) does not.

Along with everything from flying charts to plans of the New Towns in the New Territories, the Survey and Mapping Office produces a series of eight *Countryside Series* maps that are useful for hiking in the hills and country parks. They are available from two **Map Publication Centres** (www.info.gov.hk/landsd/mapping): the **North Point branch** (Map pp398-9; ☎ 2231 3186; 23rd fl, North Point Government Offices, 333 Java Rd; ☺ 9am-5pm Mon-Fri & 9am-noon Sat); and the **Yau Ma Tei branch** (Map pp412-14; ☎ 2780 0981; 382 Nathan Rd; ☺ 9am-5pm Mon-Fri & 9am-noon Sat).

All of the *Countryside Series* maps are 1: 25,000, with larger-scale inset maps. Two of them cover Hong Kong Island: *Hong Kong Island* (HK$45) and *Hong Kong Island & Neighbouring Islands* (HK$50). Four maps are devoted to the New Territories: *North-West New Territories* (HK$45); *Central New Territories* (HK$45), *North-East New Territories* (HK$45) and *Sai Kung & Clearwater Bay* (HK$50). For the islands, there's *Outlying Islands* (HK$50), with large-scale maps of Cheung Chau, Lamma, Peng Chau, Ma Wan, Tung Lung Chau and Po Toi, and *Lantau Island & Neighbouring Islands* (HK$50), essentially a 1:25,000-scale map of Hong Kong's largest island, with several larger-scale inset maps.

Most bookshops stock Universal Publications' 1:32,000-scale *Lantau Island, Cheung Chau & Lamma Island* (HK$25), which is laminated and contains useful transportation material, and its 1:54,000 *Tseung Kwan O, Sai Kung, Clearwater Bay* (HK$25).

If you're heading for any of Hong Kong's four major trails, you should get a copy of the trail map produced by the Country & Marine Parks Authority, which is available at map centres. See p163 for details.

MEDICAL SERVICES

The standard of medical care in Hong Kong is excellent but expensive. Always take out travel insurance before you travel. Healthcare is divided into public and private, and there is no interaction between the two. In the case of an emergency, all ambulances (☎ 999) will take you to a government-run public hospital. While the emergency care is excellent, you may wish to transfer to a private hospital once you are stable.

There are many English-speaking general practitioners, specialists and dentists in Hong Kong, who can be found through your consulate (see p357), private hospital or the Yellow Pages. If money is tight, take yourself to the nearest public hospital emergency room and be prepared to wait.

Public and private hospitals with 24-hour accident and emergency departments:

HONG KONG ISLAND

Hong Kong Central (Map pp404-5; ☎ 2523 6374, 2522 3141; 1B Lower Albert Rd, Central) Private.

Matilda International (Map pp398-9; ☎ 2849 0700, 24hr help line 2849 0111; 41 Mt Kellett Rd, The Peak) Private.

Queen Mary (Map pp398-9; ☎ 2855 3111; 102 Pok Fu Lam Rd, Pok Fu Lam) Public.

KOWLOON

Hong Kong Baptist (☎ 2339 8888; 222 Waterloo Rd, Kowloon Tong) Private.

Princess Margaret (Map pp396-7; ☎ 2990 1111, 24hr help line 2990 2000; 2-10 Princess Margaret Hospital Rd, Lai Chi Kok) Public.

Queen Elizabeth (Map pp412-14; ☎ 2958 8888; 30 Gascoigne Rd, Yau Ma Tei) Public.

NEW TERRITORIES

Prince of Wales (Map p417; ☎ 2632 2211; 30-32 Ngan Shing St, Sha Tin) Public.

There are many pharmacies in Hong Kong and Macau. They have a red and white cross outside them and there should be a registered pharmacist available. Many medications can be bought over the counter without a prescription, however you should check it is a known brand and that the expiry date is valid. Birth-control pills, pads, tampons and condoms are available over the counter in these dispensaries as well as stores such as Watsons and Mannings.

MONEY
Cash

Nothing beats cash for convenience – or risk. It's still a good idea, however, to travel with at least some of it, if only to tide you over until you get to an exchange facility.

Banks generally offer the best rates, though three of the biggest banks – HSBC, Standard

Chartered and the Hang Seng Bank – levy a HK$50 commission for each transaction on non-account holders. If you're changing the equivalent of several hundred US dollars or more, the exchange rate improves, which usually makes up for the fee. Hong Kong is littered with branches of these banks, so you should have no trouble finding one.

Changing Money

One of the main reasons why Hong Kong has become a major financial centre is because it has no currency controls; locals and foreigners can bring/send in or take out as much money as they please.

When changing money, avoid the exchange counters at the airport: they offer some of the worst rates in Hong Kong. The rates offered at hotels are only marginally better.

Licensed moneychangers such as Chequepoint are abundant in tourist areas including Tsim Sha Tsui and the Shun Tak Centre, from where ferries depart for Macau. While they are convenient (usually open on Sunday and holidays and late into the evenings) and take no commission per se, the exchange rates offered are equivalent to a 5% commission. These rates are clearly posted, though if you're changing several hundred US dollars or more you might be able to bargain for a better rate. Before the actual exchange is made, the moneychanger is required by law to give you a form to sign that clearly shows the amount due to you, the exchange rate and any service charges.

The half-dozen moneychangers operating on the ground floor of Chungking Mansions (Nathan Rd, Tsim Sha Tsui) usually offer good rates. Most will change a basket of currencies as well as travellers cheques.

No foreign currency black market exists in Hong Kong. If anyone on the street does approach you to change money, assume it's a scam.

Costs

Hong Kong is a relatively pricey destination. You survive on, say, HK$250 a day, but it will require a good deal of self-discipline. Accommodation is the biggest expense, but you can get the cost of it down to less than HK$100 a night by staying in grotty guesthouses, or even to as little as HK$35 a night if you stay in Hong Kong's far-flung hostels. Remember, though, that what you save in accommodation costs will go towards transport.

One of the easiest ways to deplete your wallet is to frequent Hong Kong's bars. Prices for beer and cocktails are on a par with those in Tokyo and are more expensive than London. A beer usually costs HK$30 to HK$50, and cocktails are slightly more. One way to avoid these prices is to drink during happy hour, which virtually every bar in the territory has between 4pm and 8pm (or even later). 'Self-caterers' will find the beer and spirits in the two largest supermarket chains, Wellcome and Park 'N' Shop, to be good value, as are the 7-Eleven stores.

Costs for some staple items:

5kg of laundry	HK$44-50
bowl of wonton noodles	HK$10-25
cup of coffee	from HK$20
litre of bottled water	HK$7.50-10
litre of petrol	HK$10.90-11.60
MTR fare	HK$9; HK$7.90 with
(Central to Tsim Sha Tsui)	Octopus card
pint of beer	from HK$35
	(happy hour from HK$25)
South China Morning Post	HK$7
souvenir T-shirt	HK$35-100
Star Ferry fare	HK$1.70/2.20 1st/
(Central to Tsim Sha Tsui)	2nd class

Credit Cards & ATMs

The most widely accepted credit cards in Hong Kong are Visa, MasterCard, American Express (Amex), Diners Club and JCB, pretty much in that order. When signing credit card receipts, make sure you always write a 'HK' in front of the dollar sign if there isn't one already printed there.

If you plan to use a credit card make sure you have a high enough credit limit to cover major expenses such as car hire or airline tickets. Alternatively, leave your card in credit when you start your travels. And don't just carry one card, go for two: an American Express or Diners Club card with a MasterCard or Visa card. Better still, combine cards and travellers cheques so you have something to fall back on if an ATM swallows your card or the bank won't accept it.

Some shops in Hong Kong may try to add a surcharge to offset the commission charged by credit companies, which can range from 2.5% to 7%. In theory, this is prohibited by the credit companies, but to get around that fact many shops will offer a 5% discount if you pay cash. It's your choice.

If a card is lost or stolen you must inform both the **police** (☎ 2527 7177) and the issuing

Directory

company as soon as possible; otherwise, you may have to pay for the purchases that the unspeakable scoundrel has made using your card. Some 24-hour numbers for cancelling cards:

American Express	☎ 2811 6888
Diners Club	☎ 2860 1888
JCB	☎ 2366 7211
MasterCard	☎ 800-966 677, 2588 8388
Visa	☎ 800-900 782

The Visa number may be able to help you (or at least point you in the right direction) should you lose your Visa card but, in general, you must deal with the issuing bank in the case of an emergency. Round-the-clock emergency bank numbers:

Chase Manhattan Bank	☎ 2890 8188
Citibank	☎ 2860 0333
HSBC	☎ 2748 8080
Standard Chartered Bank	☎ 2886 4111

Hong Kong ATMs are usually linked up to international money systems such as Cirrus, Maestro, Plus and Visa Electron.

Currency & Exchange Rates

The local currency is the Hong Kong dollar (HK$), which is divided into 100 cents. Bills are issued in denominations of HK$10 (purple and rose), HK$20 (grey), HK$50 (blue), HK$100 (red; a 'red one'), HK$500 (brown) and HK$1000 (yellow; a 'gold one'). The HK$10 note was reintroduced by the government in 2003 in a new crazy pattern based on a Dutch design when it realised the public was hoarding the discontinued green HK$10 notes and using them for New Year *laisee* packets (see 'Kung Hei Fat Choi' p10). There are little copper coins worth HK$0.10, HK$0.20 and HK$0.50, silver-coloured HK$1, HK$2 and HK$5 coins and a nickel and bronze HK$10 coin.

Except for the HK$10 notes, Hong Kong notes are issued by three banks: HSBC (formerly the Hongkong and Shanghai Bank), the Standard Chartered Bank and the Bank of China.

For exchange rates see the inside front cover, or check out the FX Converter website (www.oanda.com/convert/classic).

Personal Cheques

Personal cheques are still widely used in Hong Kong – a group of diners will often write separate cheques to pay for their share of a meal.

If you plan to stay a while in Hong Kong – or even travel around Asia and return – you might open a bank account here. There is no need to be a Hong Kong resident, and current and savings accounts can be opened in Hong Kong dollars or almost any other major currency.

Travellers Cheques

Travellers cheques offer protection from theft but are becoming less common due to the preponderance of ATMs. Most banks will cash travellers cheques, and they all charge a fee, often irrespective of whether you are an account holder or not. HSBC charges 0.375% of the total exchanged, Standard Chartered adds a flat HK$50 commission and Hang Seng charges HK$60.

If any cheques go missing, contact the issuing office or the nearest branch of the issuing agency immediately. **American Express** (☎ 800 962 403) can often arrange replacement cheques within 24 hours.

NEWSPAPERS & MAGAZINES

Some 53 daily newspapers and more than 700 periodicals are published in the well-read territory of Hong Kong. Naturally, the vast majority of the publications are in Chinese, with the two largest-selling dailies being the *Oriental Daily News* and the government's gadfly, the *Apple Daily*.

There are two major English-language newspapers. The daily broadsheet *South China Morning Post* (www.scmp.com; HK$7), which generally toes the government line and is known as the 'Pro China Morning Post', has the larger circulation and is read by more Hong Kong Chinese than expatriates. Its classified advertisement sales have placed it among the world's most profitable newspapers in the past. The tabloid *Hong Kong Standard* (www.thestandard.com.hk; HK$6), published Monday to Saturday, is generally more rigorous in its local reporting. It calls itself `Greater China's Business Newspaper', though it's hard to see how it can claim that sobriquet. The Beijing mouthpiece *China Daily* prints a Hong Kong English-language edition.

Asian editions of *USA Today,* the *International Herald Tribune* and the *Financial Times*, as well as the *Asian Wall Street Journal* are printed in Hong Kong.

Hong Kong also has its share of English-language periodicals, including the *Far Eastern Economic Review* and a slew of Asian-focused business magazines. *Time*, *Newsweek* and *The Economist* are all available in the current editions. *Hong Kong Tatler* and *Home Journal* are for those interested in local lifestyle articles.

PASSPORT

A passport is essential for visiting Hong Kong, and if yours is within six months of expiration get a new one. If you'll be staying for some time in Hong Kong, it's wise to register with your consulate. This makes the replacement process much simpler if you lose your passport or it is stolen.

Hong Kong residents are required to carry an officially issued identification card at all times (see p362). Visitors must carry their passports with them, as the immigration authorities do frequent spot checks to catch illegal workers and those who overstay their visas, and this is the only form of identification acceptable to the Hong Kong police.

PHOTOGRAPHY
Film & Equipment

Almost everything you could possibly need in the way of photographic accessories is available in Hong Kong. Stanley St on Hong Kong Island is the place to look for reputable camera stores.

Photo developing is very cheap; to develop a roll of 36 exposures and have them printed costs from HK$50 for size 3R and from HK$60 for size 4R. Any photo shop will take four passport-size photos for HK$35.

Airport Security

You will have to put your camera and film through the X-ray machine at Hong Kong International Airport. The machines are film-safe for most kinds of film. Professional photographers using ultra-sensitive film (eg ASA 1000) do need to worry about this, especially if the film is repeatedly exposed. One way to combat the problem is to put the film in a protective lead-lined bag, though it's probably safer and easier to have the film hand-inspected (if possible).

PLACES OF WORSHIP

The following places either offer services themselves, or will tell you when and where

services are held. You should also check the Yellow Pages or the HKTB's database (www .partnernet.hktb.com) for a more comprehensive list of Hong Kong churches and other places of worship.

Anglican (Church of England; ☎ 2523 4157; St John's Cathedral, 4-8 Garden Rd, Central)

Baha'í (☎ 2367 6407; Flat C-6, 11th fl, Hankow Centre, 1C Middle Rd, Tsim Sha Tsui)

Christian Scientist (☎ 2524 2701; Church of Christ, Scientist, 31 MacDonnell Rd, Central)

Hindu (☎ 2572 5284; Hindu Temple, 1B Wong Nai Chung Rd, Happy Valley)

Jewish (☎ 2801 5440; Ohel Leah Synagogue, 70 Robinson Rd, Mid-Levels)

Methodist (☎ 2575 7817; Wan Chai Methodist Church, 271 Queen's Rd East, Wan Chai)

Mormon (☎ 2559 3325; Church of Jesus Christ of the Latter-Day Saints, 7 Castle Rd, Mid-Levels)

Muslim (☎ 2724 0095; Kowloon Mosque & Islamic Centre, 105 Nathan Rd, Tsim Sha Tsui)

Quaker (☎ 9192 3477; Society of Friends, David Kwok Hall, St John's Cathedral Annexe Bldg, 3 Garden Rd, Central)

Roman Catholic (☎ 2522 8212; The Cathedral, 16 Caine Road, Mid-Levels)

Sikh (☎ 2572 4459; Khalsa Diwan Sikh Temple, 371 Queen's Rd East, Wan Chai)

POSTAL SERVICES

Hong Kong's postal system, now called **Hong Kong Post** (www.hongkongpost.com), is generally excellent; local letters are often delivered the same day they are sent and there's even a delivery on Saturday. The staff at most post offices speak English, and the lavender-coloured mail boxes with lime-green posts are clearly marked in English. Postal rates are low by North American and European standards.

Sending Mail

On Hong Kong Island, the **General Post Office** (Map pp400–3; ☎ 2921 2222) is at 2 Connaught Place, Central, just west of the Star Ferry. In Kowloon, the main post office is on the ground floor of Hermes House (10 Middle Rd, Tsim Sha Tsui). Both are open from 8am to 6pm Monday to Saturday and from 9am to 2pm on Sunday. Post office branches elsewhere keep shorter hours and usually don't open on Sunday.

SPEEDPOST

Letters and small parcels sent via Hong Kong Post's **Speedpost** (☎ 2921 2277, 2921 2288; www.hongkongpost.com/speedpost) should reach any of almost 90 destinations worldwide within four days, and are automatically registered. Speedpost rates vary enormously according to destination; every post office has a schedule of fees and a timetable.

COURIER SERVICES

Private companies offering courier delivery service include the following. All four companies have pick-up points around the territory. Many MTR stations have DHL branches, including the ones at Central (☎ 2877 2848), next to exit F, and at Admiralty (☎ 2529 5778), next to exit E.

DHL International	☎ 2710 8111, 2400 3388
Federal Express	☎ 2730 3333
TNT Express Worldwide	☎ 2331 2663
UPS	☎ 2738 5000

Receiving Mail

If a letter is addressed c/o Poste Restante, GPO Hong Kong, it will go to the GPO on Hong Kong Island. Pick it up at counter No 29. If you want your letters to go to Kowloon, have them addressed c/o Poste Restante, Hermes House, 10 Middle Rd, Tsim Sha Tsui, Kowloon. Mail is held for two months.

RADIO

The most popular English-language radio stations are RTHK Radio 3 (current affairs and talkback; 1584 kHz AM, 97.9 to 106.8 MHz FM); RTHK Radio 4 (classical music; 97.6 to 98.9 MHz FM); Commercial Radio (864 kHz AM); Metro Plus (news; 1044 kHz AM); Hit Radio (99.7 to 101.8 MHz FM); and FM Select (104 to 106.3 MHz FM). The *South China Morning Post* publishes a daily guide to radio programmes.

SENIOR TRAVELLERS

Senior travellers over 65 years of age enjoy a 50% discount on most forms of transport in Hong Kong and those over 60 get discounts at many museums and on organised tours. If you would like further information, contact **Helping Hand** (Map pp400-3; ☎ 2522 4494, 2640 8810; www.helpinghand.org.hk; 1st fl, 12 Borrett Rd, Mid-Levels).

TELEPHONE SERVICES

Local Calls & Rates

All calls made from private phones in Hong Kong are local calls and therefore free. From public pay phones calls cost HK$1 for five minutes. The pay phones accept HK$1, HK$2 and HK$5 coins. Hotels charge between HK$3 and HK$5 for local calls.

All landline numbers in the territory have eight digits (except ☎ 800 toll-free numbers), and there are no area codes.

International Calls & Rates

Hong Kong's country code is ☎ 852. To call someone outside Hong Kong, dial ☎ 001, then the country code, the local area code (you usually drop the initial zero if there is one) and the number. Country codes:

Australia	☎ 61
Canada	☎ 1
China (mainland)	☎ 86
France	☎ 33
Germany	☎ 49
Japan	☎ 81
Macau	☎ 853
Netherlands	☎ 31
New Zealand	☎ 64
South Africa	☎ 27
United Kingdom	☎ 44
United States	☎ 1

Remember that phone rates in Hong Kong are cheaper from 9pm to 8am on weekdays and throughout the weekend. If the phone you're using has the facility, dial ☎ 0060 first and then the number; rates will be cheaper at any time.

International direct dial calls to almost anywhere in the world can be made from most public telephones in Hong Kong, but you'll need a phonecard. These are available as stored-value Hello cards (HK$70 and HK$100) and as Smartcards (five denominations from HK$50 to HK$500). The latter allow you to call from any phone – public or private – on your penny, by punching in a PIN code. You can buy phonecards at any PCCW branch, 7-Eleven and Circle K convenience stores, Mannings pharmacies and Wellcome supermarkets. Other stored-value cards available are Chat Chat and Global Express for HK$50 and HK$100.

PCCW (☎ 1000; www.pccw.com), the erstwhile Hong Kong Telecom and now `Pacific

Century Cyber Works', has retail outlets called **i.Shops** (☎ 2888 0008; www.pccwshop.com) throughout the territory, where you can buy phonecards, mobile phones and accessories. The most convenient Hong Kong Island i.Shop is the **Central branch** (Ground fl, 161-163 Des Voeux Rd Central; ☺ 9am-7pm Mon-Sat, noon-6pm Sun) and the **Kowloon branch** (Shop B, Ground fl, Imperial Hotel, 32-34 Nathan Rd, Tsim Sha Tsui; ☺ 10am-7pm Mon-Sat & noon-6pm Sun).

Another option is to make use of the 'country direct' service, which connects you with a local operator in the country dialled. You can then make a reverse-charge or credit-card call with a telephone credit card valid in that country. A few places, including Hong Kong International Airport and some hotels and shopping centres, have home direct phones where you simply press a button labelled USA, UK, Canada etc to be put through to your home operator. If using a pay phone you'll need a coin or phonecard for the initial connection.

Country direct numbers:

Australia	☎ 800 0061
Canada	☎ 800 1100
New Zealand	☎ 800 0064
UK	☎ 800 0044
USA (AT&T)	☎ 800 1111
USA (MCI)	☎ 800 1121
USA (Sprint Express)	☎ 800 1877

Mobile Phones

Hong Kong has the world's highest per-capita usage of mobile telephones and pagers, and they work everywhere, including in tunnels and on the MTR. Any GSM-compatible phone can be used in Hong Kong.

PCCW i.Shops sell and hire out mobile phones, SIM chips and phone accessories. Handsets can be hired for HK$250 a week plus HK$100 deposit, rechargeable SIM chips cost HK$180/280 for 150/250 minutes, and local calls work out to about HK$1 a minute. SIM chips and phones are IDD compatible, but there's an extra charge if you need a roaming service to take to Macau or China. Top-up SIM cards (HK$99/200 for 150/250 minutes) are also available at 7-Eleven and Circle K, Wellcome supermarkets and Mannings pharmacies.

Useful Numbers

The following are some important telephone numbers and codes; for emergency numbers

see p359. Both the telephone directory and the Yellow Pages can be consulted online (see p372).

Air Temperature & Time	☎ 18501
Coastal Waters & Tidal Information	☎ 187 8970
Dial-a-Weather Service	☎ 187 8066
Local Directory Inquiries (English)	☎ 1081
International Credit Card Calls	☎ 10011
International Dialling Code	☎ 001
International Directory Inquiries	☎ 10013
International Fax Dialling Code	☎ 002
Reverse-Charge/Collect Calls	☎ 10010

Fax

Per-page fax rates at i.Shops and call centres range from HK$10 (Hong Kong) and HK$30 (rest of Asia) to HK$35 (USA) and HK$45 (Europe). You can receive faxes for about HK$10 a page. Most hotels and even some hostels allow guests to send and receive faxes. The surcharge for sending is usually 10%. You can also send faxes from some 7-Eleven stores. If dialling your own fax for an overseas transmission, use the international fax code (☎ 002).

TIME

Hong Kong does not have daylight-saving time. Hong Kong time is eight hours ahead of GMT; 13 hours ahead of New York; 16 hours ahead of San Francisco; eight hours ahead of London; the same in Singapore, Manila and Perth; and two hours behind Sydney.

TOILETS

Hong Kong has never had as many public toilets as other world-class cities but that is changing rapidly, with new ones being built and old ones reopened. They are always free to use. Almost all public toilets now have access for people with disabilities and baby-changing shelves in both men's and women's rooms. Equip yourself with tissues; public toilets in Hong Kong are often out of toilet paper.

TOURIST OFFICES

If awards were handed out for the most efficient, knowledgeable, helpful and intelligent tourist information service in the world, the enterprising **Hong Kong Tourism Board** (HKTB; ☎ 2508 1234; info@hongkongtourismboard .com) would win the top prize hands down. Staff are welcoming and have reams of information. Most of its literature is free, though they also sell a few useful publications and books, as well as postcards, T-shirts and souvenirs.

Before you depart, check the **HKTB website** (www.discoverhongkong.com), which should be able to answer any question you could possibly have. If you still can't find what you're looking for, check the HKTB's database, which can be accessed at www.partner net.hktb.com.

The **HKTB Visitor Hotline** (☎ 2508 1234; ☺ 8am-6pm) is like a multilingual, personal guide. Lost in the New Territories? Looking for a Chiu Chow restaurant in Sheung Wan? Want to know if the Tsim Sha Tsui shop where you're buying your camera is reliable and a member of the HKTB's Quality Tourism Services scheme? Just phone the hotline.

HKTB Visitor Information & Service Centres can be found on Hong Kong Island, in Kowloon and at Hong Kong International Airport on Lantau. Outside these centres and at several other places in the territory you'll find iCyberlink screens from which you can access the HKTB website and database 24 hours a day.

Hong Kong Information Services Department (☎ 2842 8777; www.info.gov.hk) Can answer specific questions or direct you to the appropriate government department, but try the HKTB Visitor Hotline first.

Hong Kong International Airport HKTB Centres (Chek Lap Kok; ☺ 7am-11pm) There are centres in Halls A and B on the arrival level and the E2 transfer area.

Hong Kong Island HKTB Centre (Map pp400-3; Ground fl, The Center, 99 Queen's Rd Central; ☺ 8am-6pm)

Kowloon HKTB Centre (Map pp412-14; Star Ferry Concourse, Tsim Sha Tsui; ☺ 8am-6pm)

New Hong Kong residents can speak to expats who volunteer at the **Community Advice Bureau** (Map pp400-3; ☎ 2815 5444; www.cab.org.hk; Room 16C, Right Emperor Commercial Bldg, 122-126 Wellington St, Central; ☺ 9.30am-4.30pm Mon-Fri).

The **Hong Kong Bird-Watching Society** (www .hkbws.org.hk; GPO Box 12460, Central, Hong Kong) can arrange organised visits to local birding venues.

TV

Hong Kong's four free terrestrial TV stations are run by two companies: Television Broadcasts (TVB) and Asia Television (ATV). Each company

operates a Cantonese-language channel and an English one (TVB Pearl and ATV World). The programme schedule is listed daily in the *South China Morning Post* and in a weekly Sunday supplement.

There are some 30 pay cable channels and a variety of satellite channels.

UNIVERSITIES

Hong Kong now has eight universities. **Hong Kong University** (Map pp398-9; ☎ 2859 2111; www.hku.hk), established in 1911, is the oldest and most difficult to get into. Its campus is on the western side of Hong Kong Island in Pok Fu Lam. The **Chinese University of Hong Kong** (Map pp396-7; ☎ 2609 6000; www.cuhk.edu.hk), established in 1963, is most applicants' second choice. It is situated on a beautiful campus at Ma Liu Shui, which is north of Sha Tin in the New Territories.

The **Hong Kong University of Science & Technology** (Map pp396-7; ☎ 2358 6000; www.ust.hk) admitted its first students in 1991, and is situated at Tai Po Tsai in Clearwater Bay in the New Territories.

The other five universities are based in Kowloon, including the **Hong Kong Polytechnic University** (Map pp412-14; ☎ 2766 5111; www.polyu.edu.hk) in Hung Hom, which was set up in 1972.

USEFUL ORGANISATIONS

Hong Kong Consumer Council (Map pp400-3; ☎ 2929 2222; www.consumer.org.hk; Ground fl, Harbour Bldg, 38 Pier Rd, Central) Can help with complaints about dishonest shopkeepers and the like.

Hong Kong Natural History Society (HKNHS; ☎ 2993 3330; nimrod@hkstar.com; GPO Box 4369, Central) Organises countryside hikes in winter and boat trips to the more remote islands in summer (membership per person/ couple HK$100/150).

Royal Asiatic Society (☎ 2813 7500; www.royalasiatic society.org.hk; GPO Box 3864, Central) Organises lectures, field trips of cultural and historical interest and puts out publications.

Royal Geographical Society (☎ 2583 9700; www.rgshk.org.hk; GPO Box 6681, Central) Organises lectures by high-profile travellers, as well as hikes and field trips.

World Wide Fund for Nature Hong Kong (WWFHK; ☎ 2526 4473, 2471 6306; www.wwf.org.hk; 1 Tramway Path, Central)

VIDEO & DVD

Like most of Europe and Australasia, Hong Kong uses the PAL system, which is incompatible with the American and Japanese NTSC system and the French SECAM system.

DVDs are divided according to regions and unless your player can be set to multiregion with a special remote control code (consult www.dvd.reviewer.co.uk/info/multiregion for information), you may have bought yourself an attractive drinks coaster. If you have a DVD drive on your desktop, you may need a copy of DVD Region-Free, available on www.dvdidle.com for US$39.95.

VISAS

The vast majority of travellers, including citizens of the European Union (EU), Australia, New Zealand, the USA, Canada and Japan, are allowed to enter the Hong Kong SAR without a visa and stay 90 days. Holders of British or EU United Kingdom passports can stay up to 180 days without a visa, but British Dependent Territories and British Overseas citizens not holding a visa only have 90 days. Holders of most African (including South African), South American and Middle Eastern passports do not require visas for a visit of 30 days or less.

If you do require a visa, you must apply beforehand at the nearest Chinese consulate or embassy (consult the website www.immd.gov.hk/ehtml/embassy.htm).

If you plan on visiting mainland China, you must have a visa; for details, see p334.

Visitors have to show that they have adequate funds for their stay (a credit card should do the trick) and that they hold an onward or return ticket. Ordinary visas cost HK$135 (or the equivalent), while transit visas are HK$70.

Visitors are not permitted to take up employment, establish any business or enrol as students. If you want to work or study, you must apply for an employment or student visa beforehand. It is very hard to change your visa status after you have arrived in Hong Kong. Anyone wishing to stay longer than the visa-free period must apply for a visa before travelling to Hong Kong. For details on applying for a work permit, see Work (p373).

Visa Extensions

In general, visa extensions (HK$135) are not readily granted unless there are special or extenuating circumstances, such as cancelled flights, illness, registration in a legitimate

course of study, legal employment, or marriage to a local.

For information contact the **Hong Kong Immigration Department** (☎ 2824 6111; www.info.gov.hk/immd; 5th fl, Immigration Tower, 7 Gloucester Rd, Wan Chai; 🕒 8.45am-4.30pm Mon-Fri & 9am-11.30am Sat).

WEBSITES

The Lonely Planet website (www.lonelyplanet.com) is a good start for many of Hong Kong's more useful links.

Other helpful sites:

Asiaxpat (www.asiaxpat.com) Lifestyle.

bc magazine (www.bcmagazine.net) Entertainment.

Business in Asia (www.business-in-asia.com) Business.

Census and Statistics Department (www.info.gov.hk/censtatd) Data.

Chinese Embassies & Consulates (www.china.org.cn/e-zhuwai) Chinese embassy and consulate listings.

Doing Business in Hong Kong (www.business.gov.hk) Business.

Gay Hong Kong (www.gayhk.com) Gay nightlife.

HK Clubbing (www.hkclubbing.com) Nightlife.

Hong Kong Information Services Department (www.info.gov.hk) Data.

Hong Kong Observatory (www.weather.gov.hk) Weather report.

Hong Kong Tourism Board (www.discoverhongkong.com) Tourism.

Hong Kong Tourism Board (www.partnernet.hktb.com) Databank.

Hong Kong Yellow Pages (www.yp.com.hk) Directory.

Jobs DB (www.jobsdb.com/hk) Employment.

South China Morning Post (www.scmp.com.hk) News and current affairs.

Weather Underground (www.weather.org.hk) Weather report.

Yellow Pages Maps (www.ypmap.com) Maps and transport.

YPExpat (www.ypexpat.com) Lifestyle.

WEIGHTS & MEASURES

Although the international metric system is in official use in Hong Kong, traditional Chinese weights and measures are still common. At local markets, meat, fish and produce are sold by the *leung*, equivalent to 37.8g, and the *gan* (catty), which is equivalent to about

600g. There are 16 *leung* to the *gan*. Gold and silver are sold by the *tael*, which is exactly the same as a *leung*.

WOMEN TRAVELLERS

Respect for women is deeply ingrained in Chinese culture. Despite the Confucian principle of the superiority of men, women in Chinese society often call the shots and wield a tremendous amount of influence at home, in business and in politics.

Hong Kong is a safe city for women, although common-sense caution should be observed, especially at night. Few women – visitors or residents – complain of bad treatment, intimidation or aggression. Having said that, some Chinese men regard Western women as 'easy' and have made passes at foreigners even in public places. If you are sexually assaulted call the **Hong Kong Rape Hotline** (☎ 2572 2733).

Other useful organisations:

Hong Kong Federation of Women (Map pp406-8; ☎ 2833 6131; hkfw.org; Ground fl, 435 Lockhart Rd, Wan Chai)

International Women's League (Map pp412-14; ☎ 2782 2207; 2nd fl, Boss Commercial Bldg, 28 Ferry St, Jordan)

WORK

Travellers on tourist visas in Hong Kong are barred from accepting employment. It is possible to obtain under-the-table work, but there are stiff penalties for employers who are caught hiring foreigners illegally. Still, to earn extra money many foreigners end up teaching English or doing some other kind of work – translating, modelling, acting in Chinese films, waiting on tables or bartending. Be warned, though, that no restaurant or bar will hire you if you don't have a Hong Kong ID card and a work permit.

For professional jobs, registering with Hong Kong personnel agencies or headhunters is important; check out the **Jobs DB** website (www.jobsdb.com/hk). **Drake International** (Map pp400-3; ☎ 2848 9288; Room 1308, 13th fl, 9 Queen's Rd Central) is a popular employment agency that often advertises work. You can always check the classified advertisements in the local English-language newspapers. The Thursday and Saturday editions of the *South China Morning Post* or the Friday edition of the *Hong Kong Standard* are particularly helpful.

Recruit (www.recruit.com.hk) and **Jiu Jik** (Job Finder; www.jiujik.com) are free job-seeker tabloids available on Tuesday and Friday in most MTR stations. *HK Magazine* also has a jobs section.

Work Permits

To work legally here you need to have a work permit. The Hong Kong authorities require proof that you have been offered employment, usually in the form of a contract. The prospective employer is obligated to show that the work you plan to do cannot be performed by a local person. If you're planning on working or studying in Hong Kong, it could be helpful to have copies of transcripts, diplomas, letters of reference and other professional qualifications in hand.

In general, visitors must leave Hong Kong (Macau and the mainland do not qualify) in order to obtain a work permit, returning only when it is ready. Exceptions are made, however, especially if the company urgently needs to fill a position. Work visas are generally granted for between one and three years. Extensions should be applied for a month before the visa expires.

From overseas, applications for work visas can be made at any Chinese embassy or consulate (see www.china.org.cn/e-zhuwai). In Hong Kong, contact the **Immigration Department** (Map p406-8; ☎ 2824 6111; www.info.gov.hk/immd; 2nd fl, Immigration Tower, 7 Gloucester Rd, Wan Chai; ⊗ 8.45am-4.30pm Mon-Fri & 9am-11.30am Sat) for information.

Language

Language

It's true – anyone can speak another language. Don't worry if you haven't studied languages before or that you studied a language at school for years and can't remember any of it. It doesn't even matter if you failed English grammar. After all, that's never affected your ability to speak English! And this is the key to picking up a language in another country. You just need to start speaking.

Learn a few key phrases before you go. Write them on pieces of paper and stick them on the fridge, by the bed or even on the computer – anywhere that you'll see them often.

You'll find that locals appreciate travellers trying their language, no matter how muddled you may think you sound. So don't just stand there, say something! If you want to learn more Cantonese than we've included here, pick up a copy of Lonely Planet's comprehensive but user-friendly *Cantonese phrasebook*.

HONG KONG

Hong Kong's two official languages are English and Cantonese. While Cantonese is used in Hong Kong in everyday life by the vast majority of the population, English remains the lingua franca of commerce, banking and international trade and it is still used in the law courts. There has been a marked decline in the level of English-speaking proficiency in the territory, however, due mainly to emigration and the switch by many secondary schools to Chinese vernacular as the language of education instead of English.

On the other hand, the ability to speak Mandarin is on the increase due to the new political realities. For a Cantonese native speaker, Mandarin is far easier to learn than English. It's not uncommon these days to hear Cantonese and Mandarin being spoken in a sort of fusion-confusion.

MACAU

Cantonese is the language of about 95% of the population, though Portuguese enjoys special status after having been spoken here for almost half a millennium. That said, most Chinese in Macau are unable to speak Portuguese – English is more commonly understood.

It's still worth familiarising yourself with a few numbers and days of the week in Portuguese, as signs will still commonly only be written in Cantonese script and Portuguese (see the boxed text on p380).

LANGUAGE COURSES

The New Asia-Yale-in-China Chinese Language Centre at the **Chinese University of Hong Kong** (☎ 2609 6227; www.cuhk.edu.hk; Fong Shu Chuen Building, Ma Liu Shui, New Territories), offers regular courses in Cantonese and Mandarin. There are four terms a year – four- and 11-week summer sessions and two regular 15-week terms in spring and autumn. The four-week summer term costs HK$8000 while the 15-week semesters are HK$23,700. Another good place to check is the School of Professional and Continuing Education at **Hong Kong University** (☎ 2559 9771; Room304, 3rd fl, TT Tsui Bldg, Pok Fu Lam Road, Pok Fu Lam).

A number of private language schools cater to individuals or companies. These schools offer more flexibility and even dispatch teachers to companies to teach the whole staff. Considering all the native Chinese speakers in town, tuition is not cheap, often running at around HK$300 plus per hour for one-on-one instruction. Language schools to consider:

Chinese Language Institute of Hong Kong
Map pp400-3 ☎ 2523 8455; 17th fl, Yue Shing Commercial Building, 15 Queen Victoria St, Central

Chinese Language Society of Hong Kong
Map pp406-8 ☎ 2529 1638; 18th fl, Kam Chung Commercial Building, 19-20 Hennessy Rd. Wan Chai

Hong Kong Institute of Languages
Map pp400-3 ☎ 2877 6160; 6th fl, Wellington Plaza, 56-58 Wellington Street, Central

CANTONESE
TONES

Chinese languages are rich in homonyms (ie words that sound alike). The Cantonese word for 'silk', for example, sounds the same as the words for 'lion', 'private', 'poem', 'corpse' and 'teacher'. What distinguishes the meaning of each are changes in a speaker's pitch or 'tone' and the context of the word within the sentence.

Cantonese has seven tones, making it a very complex system to describe. For the sake of simplicity, no tones are marked in the Romanised pronunciation guides in this book. For those wishing to learn more about the intricacies of the Cantonese tone system, Lonely Planet's *Cantonese phrasebook* has an extensive introduction on the subject, and the words and phrases throughout the book are marked for tone.

SOCIAL
Meeting People

Hello, how are you?
nei ho ma? 你好嗎?
Fine, and you?
gei ho, nei ne? 幾好,你呢?
Good morning.
jo san 早晨
Goodbye.
baai baai/joi gin 拜拜/再見
Thank you very much.
do je saai/m goi saai 多謝哂/唔該哂
Thanks. (for a gift or special favour)
do je 多謝
Thanks. (making a request or purchase)
m goi 唔該
You're welcome.
m sai haak hei 唔使客氣
Excuse me. (after bumping into someone)
dui m jue 對唔住
Excuse me. (calling someone's attention)
m goi 唔該
What's your surname? (polite)
cheng man gwai sing? 請問貴姓?
My surname is ...
siu sing ... 小姓 …
My name is ...
ngo giu ... 我叫 …
Do you speak English?
nei sik m sik gong ying man a? 你識唔識講英文呀?

Do you understand?
nei ming m ming a? 你明唔明?
I understand.
ngo ming 我明
I don't understand.
ngo m ming 我唔明
Can you repeat that please?
cheng joi gong yat chi? 請再講一次?

Going Out

What's on ...?
yau di mat ye a ...? 有啲乜嘢呀 …?
  locally
  ni do ge 呢道嘅
  this weekend
  ni go jau mut 呢個週末
  today
  gam yat 今日
  tonight
  gam maan 今晚

Where are the best ...?
bin do hei jui ho ge ...? 邊度係最好嘅 …?
  gay (clubs/bars)
  gei (wooi so/ba) 會所/基吧
  nightclubs
  ye jung wooi 夜總會
  places to eat
  sik ye ge dei fong 食嘢嘅地方
  pubs/bars
  jau ba 酒吧

Is there a gay street/district nearby?
tung ji woot dung kui? 同志活動區?
Is there a local entertainment guide?
yau mo boon dei ge yu lok ji nam? 有無本地嘅娛樂指南?

PRACTICAL
Question Words

Who?
bin go a? 邊個呀?
What?
mat ye a? 乜嘢呀?
When?
gei si a? 幾時呀?
Where?
bin do a? 邊度呀?
How?
dim yeung a? 點樣呀?

Accommodation

I'm looking for ...
ngo yiu wan ...   我要搵 …
  a guesthouse
  jiu doi so   招待所
  a hotel
  jau dim   酒店

Do you have any rooms available?
yau mo fong a?
有冇房呀?
I'd like a (single/double) room.
ngo seung yiu yat gaan (daan yan/seung yan) fong
我想要一間(單人/雙人)房?

How much is it ...?
yiu gei do chin ... a?   要幾多錢 … 呀?
  per night
  yat maan   一晚
  per person
  mui go yan   每個人

Banking

I'd like to ...
ngo seung yiu ...   我想要 …
  cash a cheque
  yung cheung ji   用張支票錢
  piu luo chin
  change money
  jau woon   找換

Where's the nearest ...?
cheng man jui kan ge ... hai bin do a?
請問最近嘅 … 喺邊度呀?
  automatic teller machine (ATM)
  ji dung tai foon gei
  自動提款機
  bank/foreign exchange office
  ngan hong/jau woon
  銀行/找換

Days

Monday
sing kei yat   星期一
Tuesday
sing kei yi   星期二
Wednesday
sing kei saam   星期三
Thursday
sing kei sei   星期四
Friday
sing kei ng   星期五

Saturday
sing kei luk   星期六
Sunday
sing kei yat   星期日

Internet

Where's the nearest internet cafe, please?
cheng man jui gan ge mong lok ga fe sut hai bin do a?
請問最近嘅網絡咖啡室喺邊度呀?
Where can I get online?
ngo ho yi hui bin do sheng mong a?
我可以去邊度上網呀?

I'd like to ...
ngo seung ...   我想 …
  check my email
  tei ngo ge din yau   睇我嘅電郵
  get Internet access
  seung mong   上網

Numbers

0	ling	零
1	yat	一
2	yi (leung)	二(兩)
3	saam	三
4	sei	四
5	ng	五
6	luk	六
7	chat	七
8	baat	八
9	gau	九
10	sap	十
11	sap yat	十一
12	sap yi	十二
20	yi sap	二十
21	yi sap yat	二十一
100	yat baak	一百
101	yat baak ling yat	一百零一
110	yat baak yat sap	一百一十
120	yat baak yi sap	一百二十
200	yi baak	二百
1000	yat chin	一千
10,000	yat maan	一萬
100,000	sap maan	十萬

Phones & Mobile Phones

I want to ring ...
ngo yiu da go din wa hui ...
我要打個電話去 …
I want to make a long-distance call to ...
ngo yiu da goh cheung to din wa hui ...
我要打個長途電話去 …

I want to buy a phone card.
ngo seung maai din wa kaat
我想買電話卡

Where can I find a/an ...?
hai bin do ho yi wan do ... a?
喺邊度可以搵到 … 呀?
I'd like a/an ...
ngo seung yiu yat go ...
我想要一個 …
  adaptor plug
  lui hang chap so
  旅行插蘇
  charger for my phone
  tung ngo go din wa chong din
  同我個電話充電
  mobile/cell phone for hire
  chut jo sou tai din wa
  出租手提電話
  prepaid mobile/cell phone
  chue jik sou tai din wa
  儲值手提電話
  SIM card for your network
  nei ge din wa mong lok SIM kaat
  你嘅電話網絡SIM卡

Post

Where's the post office, please?
cheng man yau jing guk hai bin do a?
請問郵政局喺邊度呀?

I'd like to send a ...
ngo seung ...   我想 …
  parcel
  gei go baau gwo   寄個包裹
  postcard
  gei jeung ming   寄張明信片
  sun pin

an aerogram
hong hung yau   航空郵束
gaan
an envelope
sun fung   信封
stamps
yau piu   郵票

Shopping

I want to buy ...
ngo seung maai ...
我想買 …
How much is this?
ni go gei do chin a?
呢個幾多錢呀?
Do you accept credit cards?
nei dei sau m sau sun yung kaat a?
你哋收唔收信用卡呀?

I'm just looking.
ngo sin tai yat tai
我先睇一睇

more	do di	多啲
less	siu di	少啲
bigger	daai di	大啲
smaller	sai di	細啲

Transport

Where is the ...?
... hai bin do a?   … 喺邊度呀?
  airport
  gei cheung   機場
  bus stop
  ba si jaam   巴士站
  pier
  ma tau   碼頭
  subway station
  dei tit jaam   地鐵站

I'd like to go to ...
ngo seung hui ...   我想去 …
Does this (bus, train etc) go to ...?
hui m hui ... a?   去唔去 … 呀?
How much is the fare?
gei do chin a?   幾多錢呀?
I want to get off at ...
ngo seung hai ... 我想喺 … 落車
lok ch?
Stop here please. (taxi, minibus)
m goi, ni do 唔該,呢度有落
yau lok
How far is it to walk?
haang lo yiu gei 行路要幾耐呀?
noi a?
Where is this address, please?
m goi, ni go dei ji 唔該,呢個地址
hai bin do a? 喺邊度呀?

EMERGENCIES

Help!
gau meng a!   救命呀!
Could you please help me?
ho m hoh yi cheng 可唔可以請
nei bong sau a? 你幫手呀?
Call the police!
giu ging chaat!   叫警察!
Call an ambulance!
giu gau seung che! 叫救傷車!
Call a doctor!
giu yi sang!   叫醫生!
Where's the police station?
ging chue hai bin 警署喺邊度呀?
do a?

Useful Portuguese

A few words in Portuguese will come in handy when travelling in Macau. Portuguese is still common on signs (along with Cantonese script) and where opening and closing times are written.

Monday	*segunda-feira*
Tuesday	*terça-feira*
Wednesday	*quarta-feira*
Thursday	*quinta-feira*
Friday	*sexta-feira*
Saturday	*sábado*
Sunday	*domingo*

1	*um/uma*
2	*dois/duas*
3	*três*
4	*quatro*
5	*cinco*
6	*seis*
7	*sete*
8	*oito*
9	*nove*
10	*dez*
20	*vint*
21	*vint e um*
22	*vint e dois*
30	*trinta*
40	*quarenta*
50	*cinquenta*
60	*sessenta*
70	*setenta*
80	*oitenta*
90	*noventa*
100	*cem*
1000	*mil*

Entrance	*Entrada*
Exit	*Saída*
Open	*Aberto*
Closed	*Encerrado*
No Smoking	*Não Fumadores*
Prohibited	*Proíbido*
Toilets	*Lavabos/WC*
Men	*Homens (H)*
Women	*Senhoras (S)*

FOOD

breakfast
jo chaan 早餐
dim sum
dim sam 點心
lunch
ng chaan 午餐
dinner
maan chaan 晚餐
snack
siu sik 小食

Can you recommend a ...?
ho m ho yi gai siu gaan ...?
可唔可以介紹間 …?
   bar/pub
   jau ba 酒吧
   coffee house
   ga fe teng 咖啡廳
   restaurant
   chaan teng 餐廳

For more detailed information on food and dining out, see the Eating chapter, pp167-215.

HEALTH

Where's the nearest ..., please?
cheng man jui kan ge ... hai bin do a?
請問最近嘅 … 喺邊度呀?

chemist/pharmacy (night)
yeuk fong (maan) 藥房(晚)
doctor
yi sang 醫生
dentist
nga yi sang 牙醫生
hospital
yi yuen 醫院

I'm sick.
ngo yau beng
我有病
I need a doctor (who speaks English).
ngo yiu tai (sik gong ying man ge) yi sang
我要睇(識講英文嘅)醫生

Symptoms

I have ...
ngo ... 我 …
   asthma
   yau haau chuen 有哮喘
   diarrhoea
   to ngo 肚痾
   fever
   yau faat siu 有發燒
   headache
   tau tung 頭痛
   pain
   tung 痛

Language

Glossary

Refer to the Eating chapter for a detailed glossary of food items you're likely to encounter on menus.

amah – literally, 'mummy'; a servant, traditionally a woman, who cleans houses, sometimes cooks and looks after the children

black mountain – crowds of people
Bodhisattva – Buddhist saint

chau – Cantonese for 'island'
cheongsam – a fashionable, tight-fitting Chinese dress with a slit up the side (qipao in Mandarin)
chim – bamboo sticks shaken out of a cylindrical box usually at temples, and used to divine the future
chop – see *name chop*

dai pai dong – open-air eating stalls, especially popular at night, but fast disappearing in Hong Kong
dim sum – literally, 'to touch the heart'; a Cantonese meal of various titbits eaten as breakfast, brunch or lunch and offered from wheeled steam carts in restaurants; see also *yum cha*
dragon boat – long, narrow skiff in the shape of a dragon, used in races during the Dragon Boat Festival

feng shui – Mandarin spelling for the Cantonese *fung sui* meaning 'wind-water'; the Chinese art of geomancy that manipulates or judges the environment to produce good fortune

gam bei – literally, 'dry glass'; 'cheers' or 'bottoms up'
godown – a warehouse, originally on or near the waterfront, but now anywhere
gongfu – kung fu
gwailo – literally, 'ghost person'; a derogatory word for 'foreigner', especially a Caucasian Westerner – best avoided
gwaipo – female equivalent of *gwailo*

Hakka – a Chinese ethnic group who speak a different Chinese language from the Cantonese; some Hakka people still lead traditional lives as farmers in the New Territories
hell money – fake-currency money burned as an offering to the spirits of the departed
HKTB – Hong Kong Tourism Board
Hoklo – boat dwellers who originated in the coastal regions of present-day Fujian province
hong – major trading house or company, often used to refer to Hong Kong's original trading houses, such as Jardine Matheson and Swire

II – illegal immigrant

joss – luck; fortune
joss sticks – incense
junk – originally Chinese fishing boats or war vessels with square sails; diesel-powered, wooden pleasure yachts that can be seen on Victoria Harbour

kaido – small to medium-sized ferry that makes short runs on the open sea, usually used for non-scheduled services between small islands and fishing villages; also spelled *kaito*
KCR – Kowloon-Canton Railway
KMB – Kowloon Motor Bus Company
kung fu – the basis of many Asian martial arts

LRT – Light Rail Transit

mahjong – popular Chinese game played among four persons using tiles engraved with Chinese characters
mai dan – bill (in a restaurant)
makee learnee – Anglo-Chinese pidgin for 'apprentice' or 'trainee'; rarely heard in Hong Kong today.

name chop – carved seal; the stamp it produces when dipped into pasty red ink serves as a signature
nullah – uniquely Hong Kong word referring to a gutter or drain and occasionally used in place names

oolong – high-grade, partially fermented Chinese tea

PLA – People's Liberation Army.
PRC – People's Republic of China
Punti – the first Cantonese-speaking settlers in Hong Kong

sampan – motorised launch that can only accommodate a few people and is too small to go on the open sea; mainly used for inter-harbour transport
SAR – Special Administrative Region of China; both Hong Kong and Macau are now SARs
SARS – Severe Acute Respiratory Syndrome
shroff – Anglo-Indian word meaning 'cashier'
snakehead – a smuggler of *IIs*

tai chi – slow-motion shadow boxing and form of exercise; also spelled t'ai chi
taijiquan – Mandarin for tai chi; usually shortened to *taiji*
taipan – 'big boss' of a large company
tai tai – leisured woman; businessman's wife
Tanka – Chinese ethnic group that traditionally lives on boats
Triad – Chinese secret society originally founded as patriotic associations to protect Chinese culture from the influence of usurping Manchus, but today Hong Kong's equivalent of the Mafia

walla walla – motorised launch used as a water taxi and capable of short runs on the open sea
wan – bay
wet market – local word for an outdoor market selling fruit, vegetables, fish and meat

yum cha – literally, 'drink tea'; common Cantonese term for *dim sum*

Behind the Scenes

THE LONELY PLANET STORY

The story begins with a classic travel adventure: Tony and Maureen Wheeler's 1972 journey across Europe and Asia to Australia. There was no useful information about the overland trail then, so Tony and Maureen published the first Lonely Planet guidebook to meet a growing need.

From a kitchen table, Lonely Planet has grown to become the largest independent travel publisher in the world, with offices in Melbourne (Australia), Oakland (USA), London (UK) and Paris (France).

Today Lonely Planet guidebooks cover the globe. There is an ever-growing list of books and information in a variety of media. Some things haven't changed. The main aim is still to make it possible for adventurous travellers to get out there – to explore and better understand the world.

At Lonely Planet we believe travellers can make a positive contribution to the countries they visit – if they respect their host communities and spend their money wisely.

THIS BOOK

This edition (and the previous one) was written by Steve Fallon. Dr Victoria Buntine wrote the Health section. The guide was commissioned in Lonely Planet's Melbourne office, and produced by:

Commissioning Editor Michael Day
Coordinating Editor Carolyn Boicos
Coordinating Cartographer Kusnandar
Layout Designer Patrick Marris
Editors & Proofreaders Carolyn Boicos, Peter Cruttenden, Barbara Delissen, Liz Filleul, Victoria Harrison, John Hinman, Kim Hutchins, Suzannah Shwer, Elizabeth Swan
Cartographers Kusnandar, Jody Whiteoak
Index Carolyn Boicos, Steven Cann, Pablo Gastar, Katherine Marsh, Jane Thompson
Cover Designer Brendan Dempsey
Series Designer Nic Lehman
Series Design Concept Andrew Weatherill & Nic Lehman
Managing Cartographer Corie Waddell
Mapping Development Paul Piaia
Project Manager Chris Love
Managing Editor Jane Thompson
Language Editor Quentin Frayne
Regional Publishing Manager Virginia Maxwell
Series Publishing Manager Gabrielle Green
Series Development Team Jenny Blake, Anna Bolger, Fiona Christie, Kate Cody, Erin Corrigan, Janine Eberle, Simone Egger, James Ellis, Nadine Fogale, Roz Hopkins, Dave McClymont, Leonie Mugavin, Rachel Peart, Ed Pickard, Michele Posner, Howard Ralley, Dani Valent.

Thanks to Steven Cann, Katie Cason, Hunor Csutoros, Melanie Dankel, Katharine Day, Stefanie Di Trocchio, Pablo Gastar, Kate James, Charlotte Keown, Glenn van der Knijff, Chris Lee Ack, Adriana Mammarella, Kate McDonald, Louise McGregor, Lachlan Ross, Herman So

Cover Pink fortune papers at Wong Tai Sin Temple, Lee Foster/ Lonely Planet Images (top); Chinese junk on the harbour, Getty Images (bottom); Looking up at the skyscrapers of Central in Hong Kong, Phil Weymouth/Lonely Planet Images (back).

Internal photographs by Phil Weymouth & John Hay/Lonely Planet Images except for the following: p2 (Lantau Buddha)

Adina Tovy Amsel; p296 Michael Aw; p 114 (silk merchant) Glenn Beanland; p2 (Peak Tram), p16, p24 (Peak Tower), p25 (Two IFC Building), p134 & p140 Andrew Burke; p305 & p308 Jon Davidson; p21 (rickshaw driver), p49 & p325 Richard I'Anson; p23 (Hong Kong harbour) Mark Kirby; p19 (tram) & p252 Ray Laskowitz; p19 (pedestrians) Chris Mellor; p293 Martin Moos; p281 Simon Charles Rowe; p13, p171, p179, p190, p193, p202, p206, p228, p242, p300, p311 & p314 Oliver Strewe; p22 (landscape), p108 (market), p110 (lantern), 112 (sampans), p112 (tram), p113 (Chinese opera), p120, p125 & p187 Dallas Stribley; p75 & p113 (dragon) Alison Wright.

All images are the copyright of the photographers unless otherwise indicated. Many of the images in this guide are available for licensing from Lonely Planet Images: www.lonelyplanetimages.com.

THANKS
STEVE FALLON

People who helped in the research of this book – on topics as diverse as Hong Kong politics, economy, transport, fashion, nightlife, kung fu and what's cooking in Hong Kong's best restaurants – included Diane Stormont, Rob Stewart of Bloomberg, Rocky Dang of Phoenix Services Agency, Patrick Chan of the Hong Kong Trade Development Council, Sam KS Lau of Wing Chun Yip Man Martial Arts, John Stephen and Annie W Tong of the Hong Kong Design Centre. *M goi sai* to all of you.

Thanks, too, to the inimitable Teresa Costa Gomes of the Macau Government Tourist Office for help and hospitality beyond the call of duty, as well as to the super-efficient HKTB employees at the other end of ☎ 2508 1234, the board's incomparable Visitor Hotline.

Once again, Margaret Leung and her team at Get Smart – Miko Ismail, Kaushikee `Pia' Ghose and James Lee – were extremely helpful, hospitable and excellent lunching and dining companions.

Friends who offered mirth, inspiration, sustenance and/or a pint or three along the way included Paul Bayfield, Andy Chworowsky, Robert Delfs, Nichole Garnaut, Tim Haynes, Sun Kim, Anita Lauder, Larry Lipsher and Warren Rook –

not to mention the Friday-night denizens of the Foreign Correspondents' Club. Special thanks to the gorgeous Jennifer Janin, the inspiration behind and organiser of the FCC's `Three Centuries' joint birthday party. It was wonderful catching up again with long-lost friends, including Anavel Caparros and Ken McKenzie. During production, it was a pleasure – and a great help – working with coordinating editor Carolyn Boicos.

As always, I'd like to dedicate these efforts to my partner, Michael Rothschild, who – like me – carries a part of Hong Kong in his heart wherever he goes.

OUR READERS

Many thanks to the travellers who used the last edition and wrote to us with helpful hints, useful advice and interesting anecdotes. Your names follow: Carlene Alexander, Frederik Asell, Sylvia Barnes, Tom & Deborah Beierle, Sven Berger, Alexander Berghofen, Alan Betts, Rodrigo Bibiloni, Bjorn G S Bjornsson, Geoffrey Bourke, Raphael Bousquet, Alison Boutland, Ian Boyce, Ben Brock, Marcel Brosens, Margot Brown, Margherita Buoso, Suzan Burton, Amanda Buster, Marie Butson, Elina Cabrera, Matt Carr, Phil Carter, Rene Cason, Marcella Cassiano, Tiffany Chan, Lili Chin, Chungwah Chow, Dmitry Chumakov, Ekaterina Chumakova, Cathy Chung, Simon Clark, Liesa Coates, David Colquhoun, Tim Connor, Tony Creedy, Christine & Howard Croxton, Derek Curtin, Karen Dang, Michael Dawson, Jacques de Soyres, Barry de Vent, Francesco Diodato, George Dow, June Egglestone, Meriam Espela, Choi Eunah, Edwin Evers, Jayne Fan, Irish & Jim Farley, James Fichter, Melanie Finlayson, Leonard Fitzpatrick, Daniel Forger, Jenny Frost, Bernd Gallep, Anne Geursen, Elizabeth Godfrey, Bob & Eunice Goetz, Diane B Goodpasture, Howard & Jean Groome, Karen Ha, Lance Hall, Mandy Hardie, Stuart Hardy, Claus Herting, Crispin Hill, Daniel Horn, Mike Howard, Malcolm Irwin, Lana Jamieson, Berit Johns, Riikka Jokihaara, Bonnie Jones, Judith Karena, Pius Karena, Cameron Kennedy, Thom Kenrick, Agnieszka Kula, Charles Kydd, Richard Lambourne, Winnie Lau, Marie-Therese Le Roux, Regitse Leleur, Lucas & Vanessa Leonardi, Mikelson Leong, Yurika Leong, Mun Kwong Loke, Ingrid K Lund, Jonathon Marsden, Paul Mason, Cary Math, Fred McGary, Matt McLaughlin, Piet Meijer, Laura Messenger, Yves Mestric, Mark Miller, Kjell Mittag, Kwok-Wah Mok, D Morgan, Susan Mulholland, Denise Murfitt, Eva Nagy, Moray Nairn, Angela Ngan, Kim Rene Nielsen, Vicky Palmer, Lorraine Pang, Philip Parker, Mario Pavesi, Renate Pelzl, Raymund Perez, Eduardo Peris, James Prichard, John Ransom, Brett M Reichert, Robert & Medy Rillema, Tanya Ross, Gernot Roth, Anna-Leena Saarela, Lorenza Severi, Christine & Carrie Shaw, Benjamin Shuhyta, Frauke Silberberg, Anneke Sips, Maurice Smith, Natasha Stabile, Fiona Standfield, Jianguo Tang, Hugh Tansley, Genevieve Tearle, Lucy Thomas, Fiona Thorpe, Robert Tissing, Derek Tokashiki, Joey Tse, Debra J Underwood, Peter Van Buren, Ester van Kippersluis, Renata Zupanc Varsek, Marc Vincent, Michael Vonhof, Steven Wagner, Rainer Waldmann, Colin Wallace, Dave Whyte, Chris Willcox, Ross Williams, Mark Wilson, Alan Wong, Anthony Wreford, Tony & Jean Wright, Karno Yan, Kin Yip, Tymoteusz Zera.

SEND US YOUR FEEDBACK

We love to hear from travellers – your comments keep us on our toes and help make our books better. Our well-travelled team reads every word on what you loved or loathed about this book. Although we cannot reply individually to postal submissions, we always guarantee that your feedback goes straight to the appropriate authors, in time for the next edition. Each person who sends us information is thanked in the next edition – and the most useful submissions are rewarded with a free book.

To send us your updates – and find out about LP events, newsletters and travel news – visit our award-winning website: www.lonelyplanet.com.

Note: We may edit, reproduce and incorporate your comments in Lonely Planet products such as guidebooks, websites and digital products, so let us know if you don't want your comments reproduced or your name acknowledged. For a copy of our privacy policy, email privacy@lonelyplanet.com.au.

Index

See also separate indexes for Sleeping (p392) and Eating (p392).

000 photographs
000 map pages

000 photographs
000 map pages

000 photographs
000 map pages

LEGEND

ROUTES

Tollway	Unsealed Road
Freeway	Mall/Steps
Primary Road	Tunnel
Secondary Road	Walking Tour
Tertiary Road	Walking Path
Lane	Walking Trail

TRANSPORT

Ferry	Rail
Metro	Tram

HYDROGRAPHY

River, Creek	Marine Park
Swamp	Water

BOUNDARIES

International	Regional, Suburb

AREA FEATURES

Airport	Building, Transport
Area of Interest	Cemetery, Christian
Beach	Land
Building, Featured	Mall
Building, Information	Park
Building, Other	Urban

SYMBOLS

SIGHTS/ACTIVITIES
- Beach
- Buddhist
- Castle, Fortress
- Christian
- Islamic
- Jewish
- Monument
- Museum, Gallery
- Picnic Area
- Point of Interest
- Ruin
- Shinto
- Zoo, Bird Sanctuary

DRINKING
- Drinking
- Café

EATING
- Eating

ENTERTAINMENT
- Entertainment

SHOPPING
- Shopping

SLEEPING
- Sleeping

TRANSPORT
- Airport, Airfield
- Bus Station
- Cycling, Bicycle Path
- General Transport
- Taxi Rank

INFORMATION
- Bank, ATM
- Border Crossing
- Embassy/Consulate
- Hospital, Medical
- Information
- Internet Facilities
- Parking Area
- Police Station
- Post Office, GPO
- Telephone
- Toilets

GEOGRAPHIC
- Lighthouse
- Lookout
- Mountain
- Pavilion
- Waterfall

NOTE: Not all symbols displayed above appear in this guide.

Map Section

HONG KONG SPECIAL ADMINISTRATIVE REGION (SAR)

To Huangtian Airport (15km)

CHINA

0 — 50 km

Pearl River Mouth

SHENZHEN SPECIAL ECONOMIC ZONE (SEZ)

To Guangzhou (165km)

SHENZHEN SPECIAL ECONOMIC ZONE (SEZ)

SHENZHEN
Border Crossing
Lo Wu

CHINA

Hau Hoi Wan (Deep Bay)

NEW TERRITORIES

Yuen Long
Tai Po

Tuen Mun
Sha Tin
Tsuen Wan

KOWLOON

Zhuhai

MACAU
Macau

LANTAU

HONG KONG ISLAND

SOUTH CHINA SEA

HONG KONG SPECIAL ADMINISTRATIVE REGION (SAR)

Border Crossing
Lok Ma Chau

Sheung Shui

Sheung Shui Market

San Tin
Fanling Golf Course
Mai Po Lo Wai
Ping Kong

Fanli

Mai Po Marsh

Fung Yir Sin Temp

Lam Tsuen North Country Park

Kar Shing Restaurant

Long Ping
Yuen Long

Shui Tau
Kam Tin

NEW TERRITORIES

Ng Tung Chai

Tin Shui Wan
Ping Shan Heritage Trail

Kat Hng Wai
Kam Sheung Rd

Kadoorie Farm & Botanic Garden

Miu Fat Monastery

Nim Wan
Siu Hong

KCR West

Tai Mo Shan Country Park

Ching Chung Temple

Tai Lam Country Park

Sze Lok Yuen Hostel

Tai Mo Si (957m)

Ching Shan Mun Monastery
Tuen

Shing Mun Country Pa

Castle Peak (583m)

Tuen Mun

MacLehose Trail

KCR West

Tai Lam Chung Reservoir

Tai Lam Tunnel

Tsuen Wan

Sham Tseng
Nang Kee Goose Restaurant

Tai Lam Country Park

Tsuen Wan West

MTR

Kw Chu

Macau

CHINA
0 — 6 km

Macau Peninsula

Friendship Bridge

Macau-Taipa Bridge

New Macau-Taipa Bridge

Macau International Airport

Lotus Bridge

Taipa Island

Airport Runway

CHINA (Zhuhai SEZ)

Coloane Island

SOUTH CHINA SEA

Sha Chau

Kap Shui Mun Bridge

Tsing Ma Bridge

Tsing Yi

Mei Foo

Tsing Yi

Princess Margaret Hospital

Chek Lap Kok

East Brother
West Brother

Tung Chung MTR & Airport Express

Hong Kong Disneyland Site

Ma Wan

Discovery Bay Tunnel

Reclaimed Land for Disneyland

Airport

Hong Kong International Airport

Lantau Trail

Pak Mong

Discovery Bay

Tai Pak Wan (Discovery Bay)

Siu Kau Yi Chau
Kau Yi Chau

Sha Lo Wan
Tung Chung

Tung Chung

LANTAU

Peng Chau

Lantau North Country Park

NGONG PING

Sunset Peak (869m)

Lantau South Country Park

Mui Wo

Trappist Monastery

Tai O

Lantau Trail

Lantau Peak (934m)

Cheung Sha

Pui O
Ham Tin

Silvermine Bay

Cha Kung To

Hei Ling Chau

Shek Pik Reservoir

Lower Cheung Sha Village

Chi Ma Wan Peninsula

Pak Kok Tsuen

Shek Pik
Tong Fuk
Cheung Sha Beach

Yung Shue Wan

Lamr

West Lamma Channel

Cheung Chau

Sok Kwu Wan

See Lantau Map p419

Fan Lau

To Macau (35km) (see enlargement)

Siu A Chau

Shek Kwu Chau

Lantau Channel

Ma Chau
Yuen Chau

Soko Islands

Tai A Chau

Tau Lo Chau

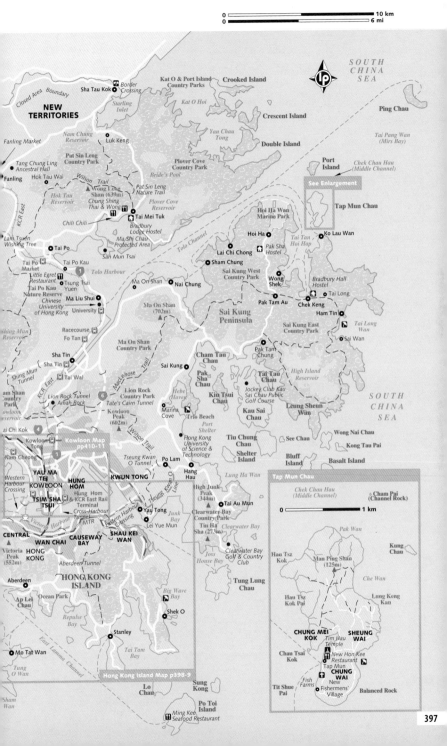

HONG KONG ISLAND

Stonecutters
Island

YAU MA
TEI

To Discovery Bay

Airport Express

Western Harbour Crossing

KCR

🚇 Kowloon

③

Cross-
Harbour
Tunnel

🚉 Hung H
KCR
Termin

MTR

KCR

②

TSIM SHA
TSUI

To Outlying Islands
& Macau

Green
Island

See Sheung Wan, Central
& Admiralty Map pp400-1

Victoria Harbour

Mt Davis
(269m)

KENNEDY
TOWN

• 8

SAI YING
PUN

Sheung
Wan

⑦

Hong Kong
Airport
Express
Station

See Wan Chai & Causeway
Bay Map pp406-7

SHEUNG
WAN

MID-LEVELS

Central

CENTRAL

CAUSEWA
BAY

Victoria Rd

✚ 24

Victoria Peak
(552m)
▲

Admiralty

🚇

WAN CHAI

Causew
Bay

SO KO
PO

ADMIRALTY

Wan Chai

✚ 28

THE PEAK

Pok Fu Lam
Country Park

Peak
Tram

13 🏛

Stubbs Rd

11 Bowen Rd

Stubbs Rd

❸

Pok Fu Lam Rd

Pok Fu Lam
Reservoir

Peak Rd

Mt
Cameron
(439m)
▲

✚ 25

Sandy Bay

West Lamma Channel

• 12

Aberdeen
Country
Park

Aberdeen
Reservoir

Aberdeen Tunnel

Mt
Nicholson
(430m)
▲

1 •

✚ 27

Wah Fu
Estate

Shek Pai

Wan Rd

See Aberdeen Map p409

ABERDEEN

①

Wong Chuk Hang Rd

SHOUSON
HILL

Magazine
Island

See Lamma Map p418

Ap Lei
Chau

WONG CHUK
HANG

Island Rd

Ocean
Park

Brick Hill
(284m)
▲

Deep Water
Bay

Pak Kok
Tsuen

Pak Kok
Shan
(138m)
▲

Luk Chau Wan

Ap Lei Pai

Aberdeen Channel

Ocean
Park

Middle
Island

East Lamma Channel

Luk Chau

Yung Shue Wan

Ngan Chau

Lamma

Ha Mei Wan

Tit Sha Long

Sok Kwu Wan
(Picnic Bay)

Sok Kwu Wan

Mo Tat Wan

❺

❻

Tung O Wan

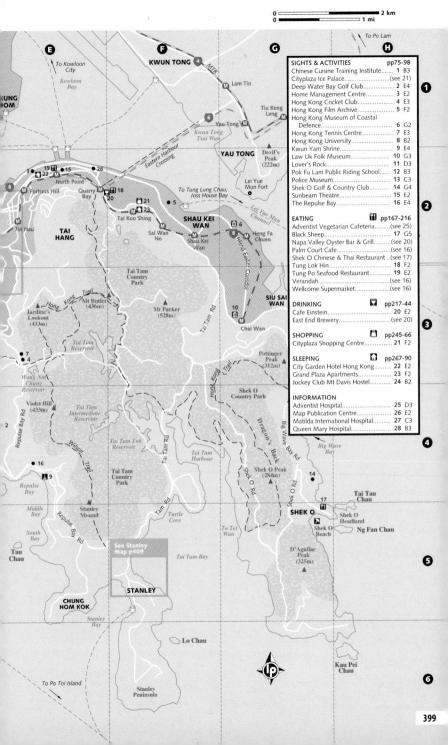

SHEUNG WAN, CENTRAL & ADMIRALTY

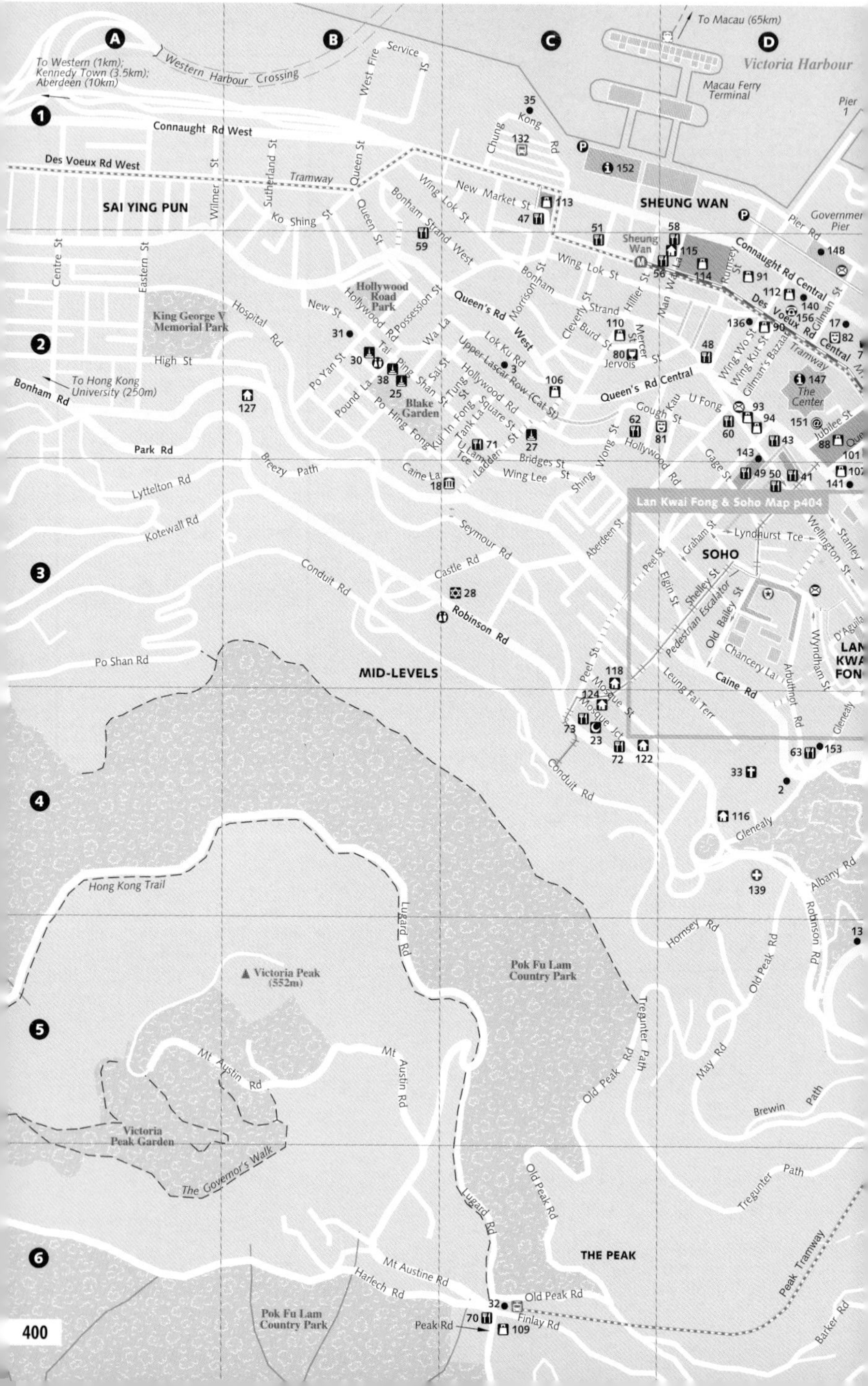

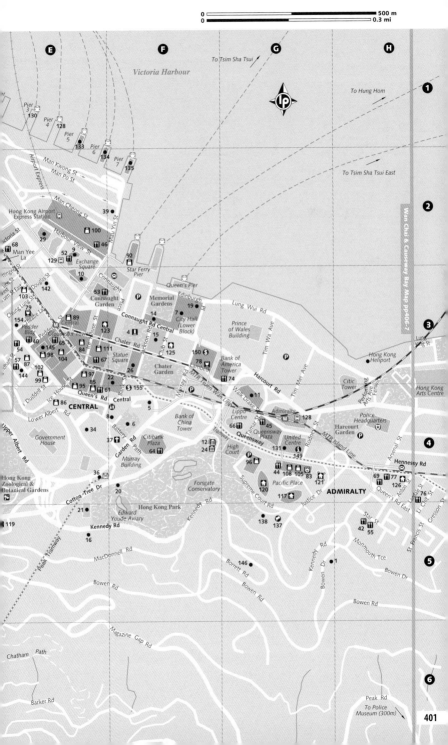

0   500 m
0   0.3 mi

E   **F**   **G**   **H**

Victoria Harbour

To Tsim Sha Tsui

To Hung Hom

To Tsim Sha Tsui East

1

Pier 3
130
Pier 4
128
Pier 5
133
Pier 6
134
Pier 7
135

Man Kwong St
Man Po St

Airport Express

Man Cheong St
39

Hong Kong Airport
Express Station

2

Victoria St
68
Man Yee La
29
Harbour View St
9
100
46
Hing St
St East
Douglas La
103
Chung Ling Rd
79
Theatre La
154
Pedder Bldg
40
54
65
145
98
104
57
87
102
99
144

Luk Yin St
100

52
129
10
Exchange Square

92
Star Ferry Pier

Queen's Pier

Lung Wui Rd

Edinburgh
19
7
City Hall (Lower Block)

Prince of Wales Building

3

Connaught Garden
53
Memorial Gardens
14
89
123
4
15
111
84
67
Statue Square
26
Chater Garden
78
Bank of America Tower
150
74

Tim Wa Ave

Hong Kong Heliport

Lung King St

Hong Kong Arts Centre

97
85
95
22
61
Queen's Rd
Central
155
5
Bank of China Tower

Citic Tower

Walk Drake

11

Harcourt Rd

Perfecting Arts Terrace

Duddell St
86
8
Battery Path
6
34
37
Garden Rd
Murray Building
20

Citibank Plaza
64

Admiralty
Lippo Centre
66
45
Queensway Plaza
131
United Centre
128
149
Harcourt Garden
Police Headquarters

Arsenal St
Hennessy Rd

4

CENTRAL

Lower Albert Rd

Upper Albert Rd

Government House

Hong Kong Zoological & Botanical Gardens

Cotton Tree Dr

36
Peak Tramway
21
16
Edward Youde Aviary
Kennedy Rd

Queensway
High Court
12
24
96
120
Pacific Place
44
108
105
83
121
117
138
137

Supreme Court Rd

Justice Dr

ADMIRALTY

Queen's Rd East
69
77
126
Li Cliff St
76
Cresson St

Star St
42
55

5

119

MacDonnell Rd

Hong Kong Park

Kennedy Rd

Forsgate Conservatory

Borrett Rd
146

Monmouth Tce

1

Bowen Dr

Bowen Rd

Bowen Rd

Bowen Rd

Chatham Path

Magazine Gap Rd

6

Barker Rd

Peak Rd
To Police Museum (300m)

401

Wan Chai & Causeway Bay Map pp400–1

SHEUNG WAN, CENTRAL & ADMIRALTY (pp400–1)

LAN KWAI FONG & SOHO

WAN CHAI & CAUSEWAY BAY

A · B · C · D

1 · 2 · 3 · 4 · 5 · 6

To Tsim Sha Tsui (1.5km)

Sheung Wan, Central & Admiralty Map pp400-1

MTR Tsuen Wan Line

Enlargement (C1–D4)

Gloucester Rd

57

109
34
100 88
146
25

62
Jaffe Rd
94
Luard Rd
92
102 67
30
78

98
81
157
110 101

96
91
90

139
93 32 68 105
103 104 35
126

140
46
Hennessy Rd
162
Wan Chai

0 — 200 m — 159

Fenwick St
Lockhart Rd
O'Brien Rd
99

3

64

Expo Dr

Hong Kong Convention & Exhibition Centre

Expo Dr East

To Hung Hom (2.3km)

161

Expo Dr Central

Atrium

165

Convention Ave
153
160

142
Flemling Rd

6
Great Eagle Centre
39
Harbour Centre
Wan Chai Sports Ground

10
Harbour Rd
Harbour Rd
Marsh Rd
War Shing St

Harbour Rd
China Resources Building
119
Causeway Centre
Sun Hung Kai Centre
69

112
115
143
Shui on Centre
169
Wan Chai Tower
Central Plaza
170
113
Jaffe Rd
164
48

5
Revenue Tower
7
Immigration Tower
8
31
71
Lockhart Rd

Lung King St
Harbour Rd
150
86
111
22

Gloucester Rd
Wan Chai Police Station
Stewart Rd
56
Hennessy Rd
MTR Island Line
Tramway

See Enlargement

117
Jaffe Rd
Jaffe Rd
Lockhart Rd
15
Heard St
Wan Chai Rd
137
49
Sharp St West
155

Arsenal St
27
Lockhart Rd
Mallory St
Marsh Rd
Bowrington Rd

12
Hennessy Rd
Wan Chai
WAN CHAI
Johnston Rd
Burrows St
Wan Chai Rd
72

Anton St
17
Thomson Rd
Southorn Playground
Thomson Rd
1
Cross La
Morrison Hill

Landale St
Tramway
130
Bullock La
Wood St
Salvation Army St
16

Li Chit St
Cresson St
Lun Fat St
129
Johnston Rd
Tai Wo St
Ruttonjee Hospital
Oi Kwan Rd

St Francis St
Queen's Rd East
55
74
51
Swatow St
Amoy St
Lee Tung St
Spring Garden La
Stone Nullah La
Cross St
Wan Chai Rd
Wan Chai Park
18

11
Hopewell Centre
61
26
Queen's Rd East
24
MORRISON HILL
13

Bowen Rd
Kennedy Rd
Chun Yuen St
Fung Wong Terr
Old Wan Chai Police Station
118
Queen's Rd East

Bowen Rd
Wan Chai Gap Rd
Stone Nullah La
Kennedy St
St Margaret's College
Stubbs Rd
Hau Tak La
Muslim Cemetery

Catholic Cemetery

Aberdeen (6km)

Hong Kong Cemetery

Aberdeen Tunnel

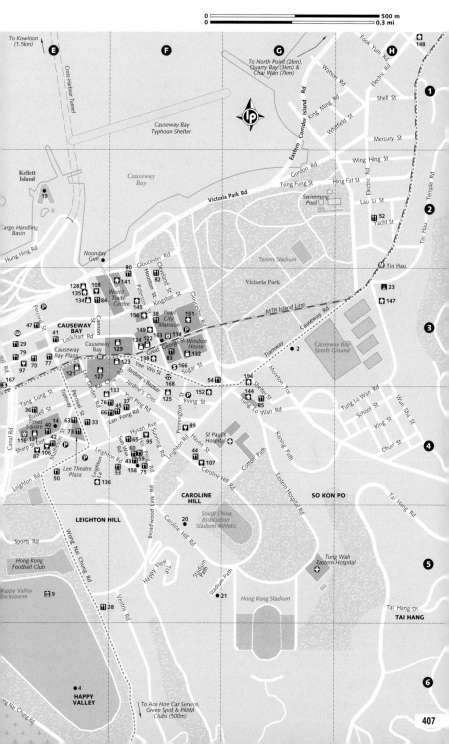

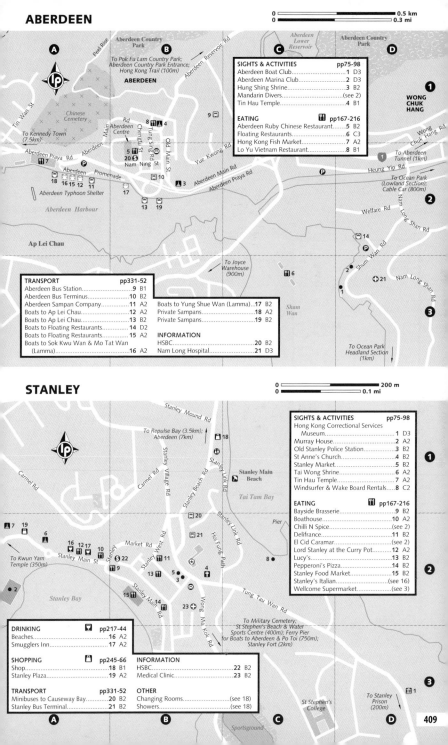

ABERDEEN

0 — 0.5 km
0 — 0.3 mi

SIGHTS & ACTIVITIES pp75-98
Aberdeen Boat Club...............................1 D3
Aberdeen Marina Club...........................2 D3
Hung Shing Shrine.................................3 B2
Mandarin Divers................................(see 2)
Tin Hau Temple....................................4 B1

EATING pp167-216
Aberdeen Ruby Chinese Restaurant........5 B2
Floating Restaurants..............................6 C3
Hong Kong Fish Market..........................7 A2
Lo Yu Vietnam Restaurant.....................8 B1

TRANSPORT pp331-52
Aberdeen Bus Station............................9 B1
Aberdeen Bus Terminus.......................10 B2
Aberdeen Sampan Company..................11 A2
Boats to Ap Lei Chau...........................12 A2
Boats to Ap Lei Chau...........................13 B2
Boats to Floating Restaurants..............14 D2
Boats to Floating Restaurants..............15 A2
Boats to Sok Kwu Wan & Mo Tat Wan
   (Lamma)...16 A2
Boats to Yung Shue Wan (Lamma)...17 B2
Private Sampans..................................18 A2
Private Sampans..................................19 A2

INFORMATION
HSBC...20 B2
Nam Long Hospital..............................21 D3

STANLEY

0 — 200 m
0 — 0.1 mi

SIGHTS & ACTIVITIES pp75-98
Hong Kong Correctional Services
   Museum..1 D3
Murray House.......................................2 A2
Old Stanley Police Station.....................3 B2
St Anne's Church..................................4 B2
Stanley Market......................................5 B2
Tai Wong Shrine...................................6 A2
Tin Hau Temple....................................7 A2
Windsurfer & Wake Board Rentals.........8 C2

EATING pp167-216
Bayside Brasserie..................................9 B2
Boathouse...10 A2
Chilli N Spice..................................(see 2)
Delifrance...11 B2
El Cid Caramar................................(see 2)
Lord Stanley at the Curry Pot............12 A2
Lucy's...13 B2
Pepperoni's Pizza................................14 B2
Stanley Food Market............................15 B2
Stanley's Italian...............................(see 16)
Wellcome Supermarket.....................(see 3)

DRINKING pp217-44
Beaches..16 A2
Smugglers Inn.....................................17 A2

SHOPPING pp245-66
Shop...18 B1
Stanley Plaza.......................................19 A2

TRANSPORT pp331-52
Minibuses to Causeway Bay................20 B2
Stanley Bus Terminal...........................21 B2

INFORMATION
HSBC...22 B2
Medical Clinic.....................................23 B2

OTHER
Changing Rooms..............................(see 18)
Showers...(see 18)

KOWLOON

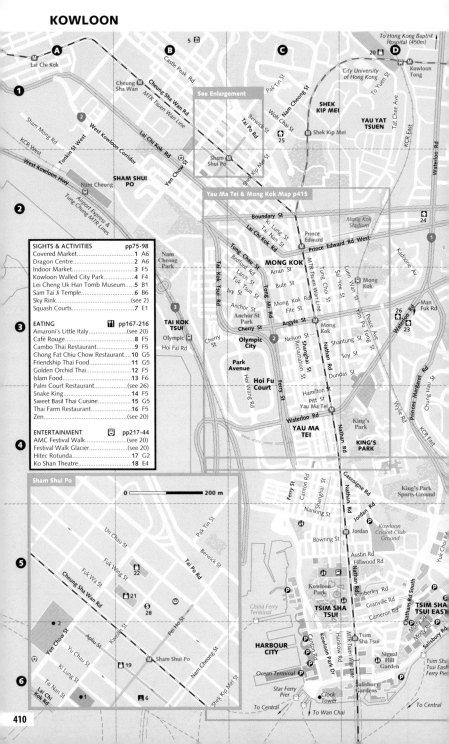

To Hong Kong Baptist Hospital (450m)

Lai Chi Kok

Castle Peak Rd

City University of Hong Kong

Kowloon Tong

Cheung Sha Wan

Cheung Sha Wan Rd

MTR Tsuen Wan Line

See Enlargement

Pak Tin St

Woh Chai St

Nam Cheong St

Tat Chee Ave

SHEK KIP MEI

YAU YAT TSUEN

Sham Mong Rd

West Kowloon Corridor

Lai Chi Kok Rd

Berwick St

Tai Po Rd

KCR West

Tonkin St West

Shek Kip Mei

KCR East

Waterloo Rd

West Kowloon Hwy

SHAM SHUI PO

Yen Chow St

Shek Kip Mei Rd

Nam Cheong

Airport Express & Tung Chung MTR Lines

Nam Cheong Park

Yau Ma Tei & Mong Kok Map p415

Boundary St

Mong Kok Stadium

Ki Lung St

Tai Nan St

Lai Chi Kok Rd

Prince Edward

Prince Edward Rd West

Kadoorie Av

SIGHTS & ACTIVITIES — pp75-98
Covered Market	1 A6
Dragon Centre	2 A6
Indoor Market	3 F5
Kowloon Walled City Park	4 F4
Lei Cheng Uk Han Tomb Museum	5 B1
Sam Tai Ji Temple	6 B6
Sky Rink	(see 2)
Squash Courts	7 E1

EATING — pp167-216
Amaroni's Little Italy	(see 20)
Café Rouge	8 F5
Cambo Thai Restaurant	9 F5
Chong Fat Chiu Chow Restaurant	10 G5
Friendship Thai Food	11 G5
Golden Orchid Thai	12 F5
Islam Food	13 F6
Palm Court Restaurant	(see 26)
Snake King	14 F5
Sweet Basil Thai Cuisine	15 G5
Thai Farm Restaurant	16 F5
Zen	(see 20)

ENTERTAINMENT — pp217-44
AMC Festival Walk	(see 20)
Festival Walk Glacier	(see 20)
Hitec Rotunda	17 G2
Ko Shan Theatre	18 E4

MONG KOK

Tung Chau St

Bedford Rd

Larch St

Ivy St

Anchor St

Anchor St Park

Argyle St

Cherry St

Arran St

Fuk Tsun St

Bute St

Mong Kok Rd

Fife St

Nelson St

Shantung St

Fa Yuen St

Sai Yee St

Tung Choi St

Nathan Rd

Reclamation St

Shanghai St

Portland St

Luen Wan St

Yim Po Fong St

Peace Ave

Mong Kok

Man Fuk Rd

Chung Hau St

Prince's Margaret Rd

TAI KOK TSUI

Olympic

Hoi Fai Rd

Cherry St

Olympic City

Park Avenue

Hoi Fu Court

Hoi Wang Rd

Soy St

Dundas St

Hamilton St

Pitt St

Yau Ma Tei

Waterloo Rd

YAU MA TEI

KING'S PARK

King's Park

KCR East

Wylie Rd

Gascoigne Rd

King's Park Sports Ground

Ferry St

Canton Rd

Shanghai St

Nathan Rd

Nanking St

Jordan Rd

Jordan

Kowloon Cricket Club Ground

Bowning St

Austin Rd

Hillwood Rd

Kowloon Park

Yuk Choi Rd

Sham Shui Po

0 ————— 200 m

Un Chau St

Pak Tin St

Fuk Wing St

Berwick St

Tai Po Rd

Fuk Wa St

Cheung Sha Wan Rd

Pei Ho St

Aplui St

Yen Chow St

Yu Chau St

Ki Lung St

Sham Shui Po

Nam Cheong St

Tai Nan St

Lai Chi Kok Rd

Kweilin St

Kimberley Rd

Granville Rd

Cameron Rd

TSIM SHA TSUI

TSIM SHA TSUI EAST

China Ferry Terminal

Chatham Rd South

Mody Rd

Signal Hill Garden

Tsim Sha Tsui East Ferry Pier

HARBOUR CITY

Kowloon Park Dr

Canton Rd

Hankow Rd

MTR Tsuen Wan Line

Tsim Sha Tsui

Salisbury Rd

Ocean Terminal

Star Ferry Pier

Clock Tower

Salisbury Gardens

To Central

To Wan Chai

To Central

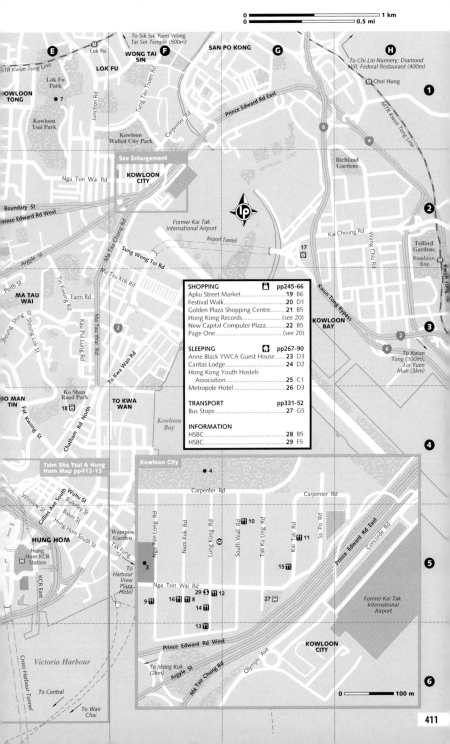

0 — 1 km
0 — 0.5 mi

To Sik Sik Yuen Wong Tai Sin Temple (500m)

E · WONG TAI SIN · F · SAN PO KONG · G · H

To Chi Lin Nunnery; Diamond Hill; Federal Restaurant (400m)

Lok Fu
MTR Kwun Tong Line
LOK FU
Choi Hung ❶
OWLOON TONG
Lok Fu Park ● 7
Kowloon Tsai Park
Junction Rd
Tung Tau Tsuen Rd
Carpenter Rd
Prince Edward Rd East
Kowloon Walled City Park
Richland Gardens ❷
See Enlargement
KOWLOON CITY
Nga Tsin Wai Rd
Kai Cheung Rd
Wang Chiu Rd
Telford Gardens
Kowloon Bay
Boundary St
Prince Edward Rd West
Former Kai Tak International Airport
Airport Tunnel
17
Perth St
Argyle St
MA TAU WAI
Tin Kwong Rd
Farm Rd
Ma Tau Chung Rd
Sung Wong Toi Rd
Ma Tau Kok Rd
Kwun Tong Bypass
KOWLOON BAY ❸
❷
To Kwun Tong (300m); Lei Yuen Mun (3km)

SHOPPING 📷 pp245-66
Apliu Street Market..................19 B6
Festival Walk.........................20 D1
Golden Plaza Shopping Centre....21 B5
Hong Kong Records...............(see 20)
New Capital Computer Plaza.....22 B5
Page One..........................(see 20)

SLEEPING 🛏 pp267-90
Anne Black YWCA Guest House....23 D3
Caritas Lodge......................24 D2
Hong Kong Youth Hostels
  Association........................25 C1
Metropole Hotel....................26 D3

TRANSPORT pp331-52
Bus Stops..........................27 G5

INFORMATION
HSBC................................28 B5
HSBC................................29 F5

Cheung Shing St
Sheung Lok St
Kau Pui Lung Rd
Ma Tau Wai Rd
To Kwa Wan Rd
❷
O MAN TIN
Fat Kwong St
Ko Shan Road Park
18
Chatham Rd North
TO KWA WAN
Kowloon Bay

Tsim Sha Tsui & Hung Hom Map pp412-13
Kowloon City
● 4
Carpenter Rd
Carpenter Rd

Winslow St
Gillies Ave South
Wuhu St
Bulkeley St
Baker St
Hung Hom South St
Hung Hom South Rd
HUNG HOM
Hung Hom KCR Station
KCR East
Wampoa Garden
Tak Fung St
To Harbour View Plaza Hotel
3
Nga Tsin Long Rd
Nam Kok Rd
Lung Kong Rd
South Wall Rd
Tak Ku Ling Rd
Kai Tak Rd
Sa Po Rd
Prince Edward Rd East
Concorde Rd
10
11
29 12
15
Nga Tsin Wai Rd
9 16 8
14
13
27
Former Kai Tak International Airport ❺
Prince Edward Rd West
To Mong Kok (2km)
Argyle St
Ma Tau Chung Rd
Olympic Ave
KOWLOON CITY

Victoria Harbour
Cross-Harbour Tunnel
To Central
To Wan Chai

0 — 100 m ❻

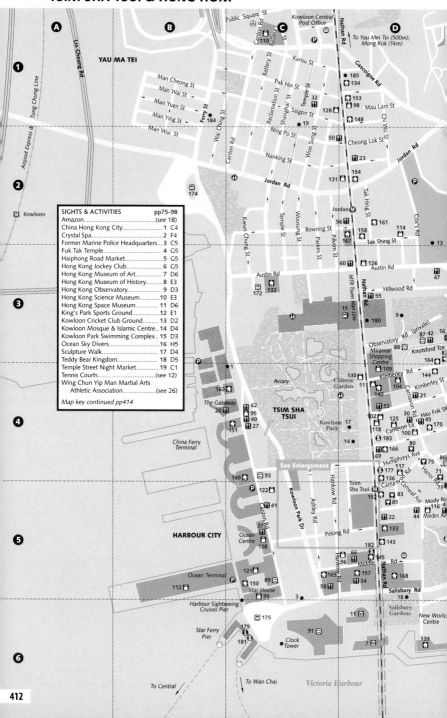

SIGHTS & ACTIVITIES pp75–98
Amazon...(see 18)
China Hong Kong City...................................1 C4
Crystal Spa...2 F4
Former Marine Police Headquarters....3 C5
Fuk Tak Temple...4 G5
Haiphong Road Market.................................5 G5
Hong Kong Jockey Club.................................6 G5
Hong Kong Museum of Art............................7 D6
Hong Kong Museum of History........................8 E3
Hong Kong Observatory.................................9 D3
Hong Kong Science Museum...........................10 E3
Hong Kong Space Museum..............................11 D6
King's Park Sports Ground.............................12 E1
Kowloon Cricket Club Ground.........................13 D2
Kowloon Mosque & Islamic Centre..14 D4
Kowloon Park Swimming Complex..15 D3
Ocean Sky Divers..16 H5
Sculpture Walk..17 D4
Teddy Bear Kingdom....................................18 D5
Temple Street Night Market............................19 C1
Tennis Courts...(see 12)
Wing Chun Yip Man Martial Arts
  Athletic Association.................................(see 26)

Map key continued pp414

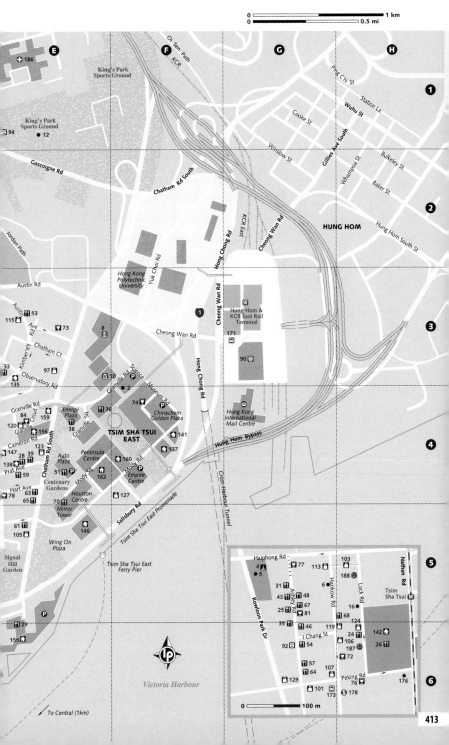

YAU MA TEI & MONG KOK

0 .... 300 m
0 .... 0.2 mi

To Sham Shui Po (800m)
To Kowloon Tong (1km)

A Boundary St **B** **C** Boundary Street Recreation Ground **D** To Caritas Lodge (400m)

19 Yu Chau St 34 Mong Kok Stadium 6 **1**

9 Nathan Rd Playing Field Rd Flower Market Rd 1 21

To Tsuen Wan (8km) Prince Edward To Kowloon Tong (2.5km)

Prince Edward Rd West 35

Queen Elizabeth School

Lai Chi Kok Rd 32 Nullah Rd **2**

16 Mong Kok

MONG KOK Bute St Mong Kok

Shanghai St Mong Kok Rd To Kowloon City (2.5km)

Mong Kok Rd Fife St Argyle St **3**

12 20 17 To Metropole Hotel; Palm Court Café; Anne Black YWCA Guesthouse (400m)

Argyle St 15 10 2 25

42 41 26 38 39 Macpherson Play Ground

Nelson St 18 28 24 11

Olympic City

Park Avenue

Shantung St 36 **4**

23 Dundas St 43 Wah Yan College

Dundas St Pitt St 37 King's Park

Hamilton St 3 14 40 8 **5**

YAU MA TEI Waterloo Rd Meteorological Station King's Park Rise

5 **KING'S PARK** **6**

Man Ming La 44 29 30

PROSPEROUS GARDEN 7 22 33 27 13 31 4 Temple St

Public Square St Market St Gascoigne Rd

SIGHTS & ACTIVITIES	pp75-98
Flower Market	1 D1
Hong Kong Tai Chi Association	2 C3
Shanghai St Artspace	3 C5
Tin Hau Temple	4 C6
Wholesale Fruit Market	5 B5
Yuen Po St Bird Garden	6 D1

EATING	pp167-216
Hing Kee	7 C6
Joyful Vegetarian	8 C5
Pak Bo Vegetarian	9 B1
Saint's Alp Teahouse	10 C3
Saint's Alp Teahouse	11 C4
Very Good	12 C3

ENTERTAINMENT	pp217-44
Broadway Cinematheque	13 C6

SHOPPING	pp245-66
Chamonix Alpine Equipment	14 B5
CRC Department Store	15 C3
Flying Ball Bicycle Co	16 C2
Hong Kong Mountaineering Training Centre	17 C3
Mong Kok Computer Centre	18 C3
Mountaineer Supermarket	19 B1
Rag Brochure	(see 23)
Sincere Department Store	20 C3
Stone Village Shop	21 D1
Temple Street Night Market	22 C6
Trendy Zone	23 C4
Tung Choi St (Ladies) Market	24 C3
Wing Shing Photo Supplies	25 C3
Wise Mount Sports	26 C3
Yuet Wah Music Company	27 C6
Zoom	28 C3

SLEEPING	pp267-90
Booth Lodge	29 C6
Caritas Bianchi Lodge	30 C6
Dorset Seaview Hotel	31 C6
Hotel Concourse Hong Kong	32 B2
New Kings Hotel	33 C6
Newton Hotel Kowloon	34 C1
Royal Plaza Hotel	35 D1
Sakurada	(see 35)
Stanford Hotel	36 D4
YMCA International House	37 C5

TRANSPORT	pp331-52
Buses to China	38 C3
Buses to China	39 C3
Buses to China	(see 35)

INFORMATION	
Bruce Lee Fans Society	40 C5
China Travel Service	(see 38)
Hong Kong Trade & Industry Department	41 C3
HSBC	42 C3
Kwong Wah Hospital	43 D4
Rainbow Online Cyber Cafe	44 C6

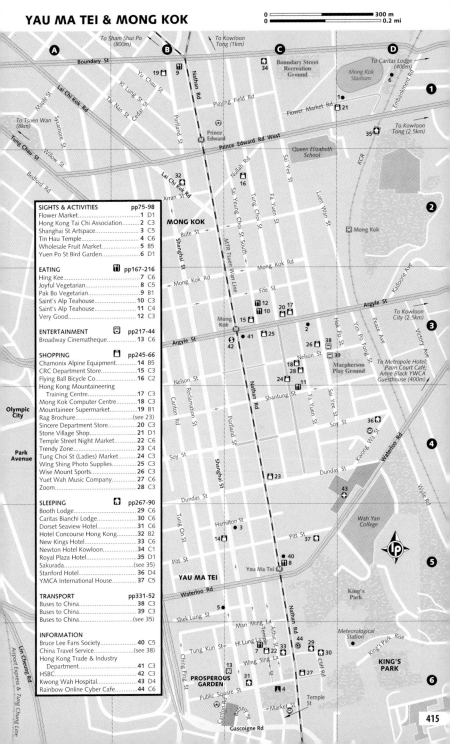

Lin Cheung Rd Airport Express & Tung Chung Line

TSUEN WAN

0 — 500 m
0 — 0.3 mi

To Tsuen Kam Au (5km)
Tai Mo Shan Country Park
To Yuen Yuen Institute (1km)
Hilltop Rd
Lo Wai Rd
To Sam Tung Uk Rd (4km)
To Tuen Mun (18km)
Tam Path
Cheung Pei Shan Rd
Ma Sim Pai Rd
Fu Yung Shan Rd
Route Twisk
Shek Wan Kok Rd
Discovery Park
Castle Peak Rd -Tsuen Wan
Tai Ho Rd North
Texaco Rd North
Wai Tsuen Rd
Tsuen Wan
Hoi Pa St
Tso Kung St
Sha Tsui Rd
Tai Chung Rd
Heung Wo St
Tai Pa St
Yuen Tun Circuit
Tai Ho Rd
Tai Ho Rd
Castle Peak Rd
Shiu Wo St
Tsuen Wan Market
Chuen Lung St
Tai Pei Square
Tai Pei Square
Che Jewellery St
Kwu Uk Ln
Sam Tung Uk Gardens
Sai Lau Kok Rd
Shing Mun Rd
Tsuen Wan Market
Tak Wah Park
Ham Tin St
Chai Wan Kok St
Kwan Mun Hau St
Tai Wo Hau
Castle Peak Rd
To Sam Pei Square

TAI PO

0 — 500 m
0 — 0.3 mi

To Lam Tsuen Wishing Tree (3km)
KCR Railway
Tai Po Tai Wo Rd
To San Mun Tsai (4.5km)
On Chee Rd
On Cheung Rd
On Pong Rd
Tai Wo
Tai Po Tai Wo Rd
To San Mun Tsai (5.5km); Tai Mei Tuk (8.5km)
Tai Wo Bridge
Po Nga Rd
Lam Tsuen River
Pak Shing St
Sui On St
Yan Hing St
Fu Shin St
Po Yick St
TAI PO HUI
Plover Cove Rd
Kwong Fuk Rd
Luk Heung La
Tsing Yuen St
Wai Yan St
Hon Ka Rd
On Fu Wai Yi St
Shung Tak St
Four Lanes Square
Tai Wing La
Kwong Tai Ming La
Kwong Fuk La
Tai Ming La
Po Heung St
Heung Sze Wui St
Wan Tau St
Wan Tau Kok La
To Bus Terminal; Uptown Plaza; Minibus/Maxicab Terminal (400m)
Park & Sports Ground

A   B   C   D

SHA TIN

0 —— 500 m
0 —— 0.3 mi

To Hong Kong Sport Institute (100m)

Rowing Centre

Sui Lek Yuen Rd

City One Plaza Sha Tin & Sha Tin Super Bowl

To Hong Kong Jockey Club, Sha Tin Racecourse (500m); Tai Po (10km)

Tai Po Rd

KCR East Rail

Fo Tan Rd

Banyan Bridge

Sha Tin Sports Centre

10,000 Buddhas Monastery

Sheung Wo Che St

Grand Central Plaza

Pai Tau St

Yuen Wo Rd

Shing Mun River

Swimming Pool

Tai Chung Kiu Rd

YUEN CHAU KOK

Ascension House

Sha Tin

Sha Tin Rural Committee Rd

Tai Po Rd

Pak Lok Path

Tung Lo Wan Hill Rd

To Fung Rd

Sha Tin Centre

New Town Plaza; Restaurants; China Travel Service & Bus Station

Sha Tin Town Hall

Bicycle Rentals

Yuen Chau Kok Rd

Regal Riverside Hotel

Sha Tin Rd

Ngan Shing St

Prince of Wales Hospital

Royal Park Hotel

Lek Yeun Bridge

Sha Tin Park

Pak Hok Ting St

Lion Rock

Sha Tin Rd

SHA TIN WAI

Sha Lek Hwy

Shing Mun Tunnel Rd

Man Lam Rd

Hong Kong Heritage Museum

Tai Chung Kiu Rd

Sha Kok St

To Amah Rock (3.5km); Kowloon (6km)

TO SHEK

TAI WAI

Shing Chuen Rd

To Tai Wai KCR Station (300m)

Tunnel Rd

To Che Kung Temple (600m)

Sha Tin Rd

Che Kung Miu Rd

SAI KUNG TOWN

0 —— 200 m
0 —— 0.1 mi

To Park (100m); Sha Ha (750m)

Tang Shiu Kin Sports Ground

Sai Kung Town Hall

Po Tung Rd

Fuk Man Rd

Sai Kung Sports Centre

Wai Man Rd

Chun Mar St

Man Nin St

Sha Tsui Path

Hoi Pong Square

Wan King Path

Yi Chun St

Nin Chuen St

Man Nin St

Old Town

See Cheung St

Sai Kung Hoi (Inner Port Shelter)

Pier

A   B   C   D   417

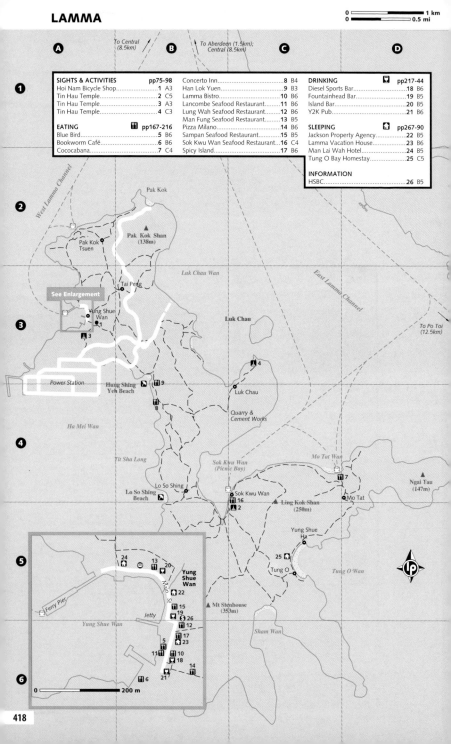

| 0 | 1 km |
| 0 | 0.5 mi |

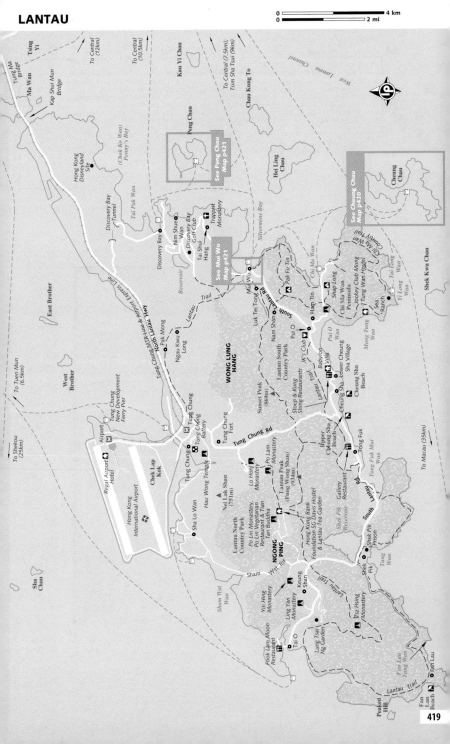

LANTAU

CHEUNG CHAU

0 ——————— 500 m
0 ——————— 0.3 mi

SIGHTS & ACTIVITIES	pp75-98
Bicycle Hire	1 C5
Bicycle Rentals	2 C6
Cheung Chau Windsurfing Centre	3 C4
Cheung Po Tsai Cave	4 A5
Helicopter Pad	5 D6
Hung Shing Temple	6 B4
Kwai Yuen Monastery	7 D4
Kwan Kung Pavilion	8 C4
Kwun Yam Temple	9 D4
Nam Tam Wan Tin Hau Temple	10 C4
Pak She Tin Hau Temple	11 B3
Pak Tai Temple	12 B3
Rock Carving	13 D6
Sacred Banyan Tree	14 C6
Sai Wan Tin Hau Temple	15 A5
Tai Shek Hau Tin Hau Temple	16 B4
Tou Tei Shrine	17 C3

EATING	pp167-216
Cheung Chau Market	18 C6
East Lake Restaurant	19 D6
Hing Lock	20 C5
Hometown Teahouse	21 C6
Hong Kee	(see 20)
Long Island Restaurant	22 C5
New Baccarat	(see 20)
Park 'N' Shop Supermarket	23 C6
Park 'N' Shop Supermarket	24 C6
Sea Dragon King	25 C6
Wellcome Supermarket	26 C5

DRINKING	pp217-44
Morocco's	27 C5
Patio Café	(see 3)

SLEEPING	pp267-290
Accommodation Booking Booths	28 C6
Warwick Hotel	29 D6

INFORMATION	
HSBC ATM	30 C5
HSBC	31 C6

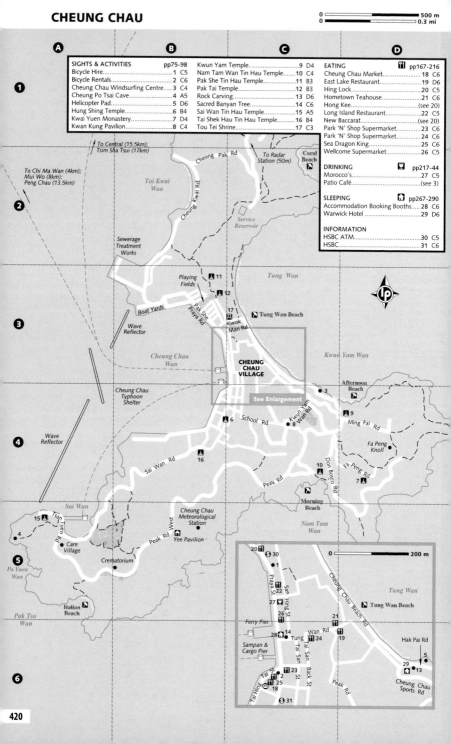

420

MUI WO

To Silvermine Cave; Waterfall & Garden (3km)

WANG TONG

To Trappist Monastery (2.5km)

Wang Tong River

Butterfly Hill (67m)

Barbeque Pits & Picnic Tables

Bay Beach Silvermine

Silvermine Bay

Mui Wo Rural Committee Rd

Silver River

Ngan Kwong Wan Rd

NGAN WAN ESTATE

To Peng Chau (5.5km)

To Tsim Sha Tsui (15km); Central (15.5km)

Ferry Pier

To Chi Ma Wan (5km); Cheung Chau (8km)

South Lantau Rd

Ngan Wan Rd

Ferry Pier Rd

PENG CHAU

To Tai Lei Island (100m)

To Transmitting Radio Station (300m)

Transmitting Radio Station

Tung Wan

Tung Wan

BBQ Area

To Trappist Monastery (1.8km); Discovery Bay (3km)

Po Peng St

Park

Lo Peng

Wing On

Tung Wan Beach

Ferry Pier

Pier

Wing Hing St

Shing Ka Rd

Graves

Finger Hill (95m)

Wave Reflector

Nam Shan Rd

To Mui Wo (5.5km); Cheung Chau (13.5km)

To Central (13km)

Ponte da Amizade Friendship Bridge

To Hong Kong

Avenida da Ponte da Amizade

Rotunda da Amizade

Rua Central da Areia Preta

Rua de Maio

Rua do Canal Novo

Avenida do Nordeste

Avenida de Maio

Estrada Marginal da Areia Preta

Rua Novo da Areia Preta

Rua dos Pescadores

Reservoir

Jetfoil Pier

Proposed Landfill

Rua Direita do Hipódromo

Avenida Leste do Hipódromo

Estrada Marginal do Hipódromo

Rua Dois

Rua Um (Bairro Iao Hon)

Estrada da Areia Preta

Estrada de Ferreira do Amaral

Montanha Russa Garden

Flora Garden

Guia Hill

Guia Tunnel

Avenida da Amizade

Avenida de Venceslau de Morais

Estrada de Ferreira do Amaral

Xavier Pereira

Mong Há Hill

Rua de Mong Há

Coronel Mesquita

Rua de Francisco Xavier Pereira

Rua de Silva Mendes

Avenida do Almirante Costa Cabral

Travessa de Sidónio Pais

Avenida de Sidónio Pais

Guia Tunnel

Rua de Entre-Campos

Vasco da Gama Garden

Rua de Malta

Rua de Luis Gonzaga Gomes

Rua de Xiamen

Rua de Nagasaki

Avenida do Dr Rodrigo Rodrigues

Terminal Marítimo

Travessa do Túnel

Avenida do Conselheiro Ferreira de Almeida

Estrada de Adolfo Loureiro

Colonial Buildings

Rua da Madre Terizina

Avenida de Horta e Costa

Estrada da Vitória

Calçada do Gaio

Rua Nova à Guia

Estrada do Visconde de São Francisco

St Francis Garden

To Portas do Cerco (Border Gate) (250m)

Avenida de Artur Tamagnini Barbosa

Avenida do Conselheiro Borja

Canidrome

Avenida do General Castelo Branco

Avenida Almirante Lacerda

Avenida de Horta e Costa

Estrada do Repouso

Rua do Campo

Rua de Abade Neves

Estrada do Cemitério

CHINA

Canal das Portas

Ilha Verde

Inner Harbour

Rua da Ribeira do Patane

Rua Entre Campos

Rua de Tomás Vieira

Rua de D. Belchior Carneiro

Rua de São Paulo

Rua de São Domingos

Rua de São Domingos

Rua de São Paulo

Rua de São Tiago

Rua de Almeida Ribeiro

Praia Grande

Avenida de Almeida Ribeiro

Rua do Tarrafeiro

Rua de Tercera

Rua das Lorchas

See Central Macau Map p424

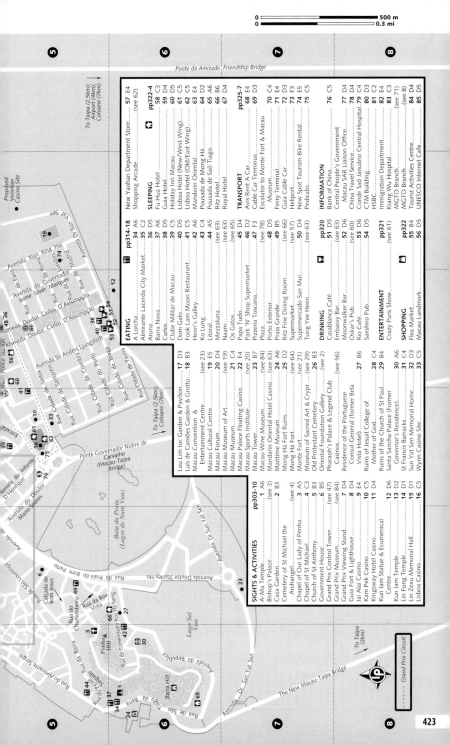

0 — 500 m
0 — 0.3 mi

Ponte da Amizade; Friendship Bridge

To Taipa (2.5km); Airport (4km); Coloane (7km)

Propdad Venetian Casino Site

Ponte Governador Nobre de Carvalho (Macau-Taipa Bridge)

To Taipa (2.5km); Coloane (7km)

Baía da Praia (Lagos de Nam Van)

Lago Sai Van

Lago Nam Van

Barra Hill

Penha Hill

To Taipa (2km)

The New Macau-Taipa Bridge

Grand Prix Circuit

423

SIGHTS & ACTIVITIES   pp303–10
A-Ma Temple	1 A6
Bishop's Palace	(see 3)
Casa Garden	2 B3
Cemetery of St Michael the Archangel	(see 4)
Chapel of Our Lady of Penha	3 A5
Chapel of St Michael	4 C3
Church of St Anthony	5 B3
Government House	6 B5
Grand Prix Control Tower	(see 47)
Grand Prix Museum	7 D4
Grand Prix Viewing Stand	(see 84)
Guia Fort & Lighthouse	8 D4
Jai Alai Casino	9 E4
Kam Pek Casino	10 C5
Kingsway Hotel Casino	11 B5
Kun Iam Statue & Ecumenical Centre	12 D6
Kun Iam Temple	13 D2
Lin Fung Temple	14 C1
Lin Zexu Memorial Hall	15 D1
Lisboa Casino	16 C5
Lou Lim Ioc Garden & Pavilion	17 D3
Luís de Camões Garden & Grotto	18 B3
Macau Convention & Entertainment Centre	(see 23)
Macau Cultural Centre	19 E5
Macau Forum	20 D4
Macau Museum of Art	21 C4
Macau Museum	22 E4
Macau Palace Floating Casino	(see 29)
Macau Sports Complex	(see 2)
Macau Tower	23 B7
Macau Wine Museum	(see 84)
Mandarin Oriental Hotel Casino	24 A4
Maritime Museum	25 D2
Mong Há Fort Ruins	(see 64)
Mong Há Fort	(see 57)
Monte Fort	26 B3
Museum of Sacred Art & Crypt	(see 29)
Old Protestant Cemetery	(see 2)
Oriental Foundation Gallery	(see 56)
Pharaoh's Palace & Legend Club Casinos	(see 84)
Residence of the Portuguese Consul-General (former Bela Vista Hotel)	27 B6
Ruins of Jesuit College of Mother of God	28 C4
Ruins of the Church of St Paul	29 B4
Santa Sancha Palace (Former Governor's Residence)	30 A6
St Francis Barracks	31 C4
Sun Yat Sen Memorial Home	32 D3
Wynn Casino Site	33 C5

EATING   pp314–18
A Lorcha	34 A6
Almirante Lacerda City Market	35 C2
Aruna	36 A6
Barra Nova	37 A6
Carlos	38 D5
Clube Militar de Macau	39 C5
Dom Galo	40 D5
Fook Lam Moon Restaurant	41 C5
Henri's Galley	42 A6
Ko Lung	43 C4
Litoral	44 A5
Mezzaluna	(see 63)
Naam	(see 63)
Os Gatos	(see 65)
Papa Tudo	45 D4
Park 'N' Shop Supermarket	46 D2
Pizzeria Toscana	47 F3
Plaza	(see 78)
Porto Exterior	48 D5
Praia Grande	49 B5
Ritz Fine Dining Room	(see 66)
Supermercado San Mui	(see 57)
Tung Yee Heen	(see 63)

DRINKING   pp320
Casablanca Café	51 D5
Embassy Bar	(see 63)
Moonwalker Bar	52 D6
Oskar's Pub	53 D6
Rio Café	54 D5
Sanshiro Pub	(see 63)

ENTERTAINMENT   pp321
Crazy Paris Show	(see 47)

SHOPPING   pp322
Flea Market	55 B4
Macau Landmark	56 D5
New Yaohan Department Store	57 E4
Shopping Arcade	(see 62)

SLEEPING   pp322–4
Fu Hua Hotel	58 C3
Guia Hotel	59 D4
Holiday Inn Macau	60 D5
Lisboa Hotel (New/West Wing)	61 C5
Lisboa Hotel (Old/East Wing)	62 C5
Mandarin Oriental	63 E4
Pousada de Mong Há	64 D2
Pousada de São Tiago	65 A6
Ritz Hotel	66 B6
Royal Hotel	67 D4

TRANSPORT   pp325–7
Avis Rent A Car	68 E4
Cable Car Terminus	69 D3
Escalator to Monte Fort & Macau Museum	70 C4
Ferry Terminal	71 E4
Guia Cable Car	72 D3
Heliport	73 F3
New Spot Tourism Bike Rental	74 E5
Pedicabs	75 C5

INFORMATION
Bank of China	76 C5
Central People's Government Macau SAR Liaison Office	77 D4
China Travel Service	78 D4
Conde São Januário Central Hospital	79 C4
CTM Building	80 D3
HSBC	81 C2
Immigration Department	82 E4
Kiang Wu Hospital	83 C3
MGTO Branch	(see 71)
MGTO Branch	84 D4
Tourist Activities Centre	85 D5
UNESCO Internet Cafe	(see 8)

CENTRAL MACAU PENINSULA

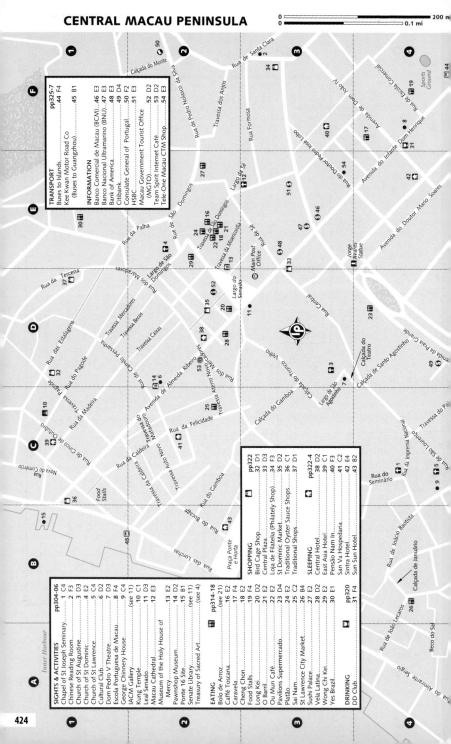

0 ——————————— 200 m
0 ——————————— 0.1 mi